THE
EVERYTHING®
BABY NAMES BOOK
3RD EDITION

Dear Reader,

Congratulations! Expecting a new baby is an exciting time. While there's a lot to prepare for, it is a journey filled with hopeful anticipation and fun. Choosing your baby's name should be a joyful process, though not always an easy one. With so many factors and options to consider, it might even seem overwhelming at times. But with this book you'll be well equipped to explore a wide world of names and on your way to narrowing down to just the right one for your new bundle of joy. With 25,000 new names added in this new edition, you'll have plenty to choose from.

Hayden, Aiden, or Braden? Hailey, Bayley, or Kaylee? What about a simple Emma or Jack? Whether trendy, one of a kind, or old-fashioned, your child's name will likely be a reflection of the times as well as your own personal tastes and values. One thing that all parents have in common is wanting the best for their child, so the best choice you can make when selecting your baby's name will be the one that, ultimately, feels right in your heart.

So grab a pad and a pen, start skimming through the book's name dictionary and sidebars, highlight your favorite choices, and, most of all, enjoy the process. Your new little star is waiting to be named!

June Rifkin

Welcome to the EVERYTHING® Series!

These handy, accessible books give you all you need to tackle a difficult project, gain a new hobby, comprehend a fascinating topic, prepare for an exam, or even brush up on something you learned back in school but have since forgotten.

You can choose to read an Everything® book from cover to cover or just pick out the information you want from our four useful boxes: e-questions, e-facts, e-alerts, and e-ssentials.

We give you everything you need to know on the subject, but throw in a lot of fun stuff along the way, too.

We now have more than 400 Everything® books in print, spanning such wide-ranging categories as weddings, pregnancy, cooking, music instruction, foreign language, crafts, pets, New Age, and so much more. When you're done reading them all, you can finally say you know Everything®!

QUESTION

Answers to
common questions

FACT

Important snippets
of information

ALERT

Urgent
warnings

ESSENTIAL

Quick
handy tips

PUBLISHER Karen Cooper

DIRECTOR OF ACQUISITIONS AND INNOVATION Paula Munier

MANAGING EDITOR, EVERYTHING® SERIES Lisa Laing

COPY CHIEF Casey Ebert

ASSISTANT PRODUCTION EDITOR Jacob Erickson

ACQUISITIONS EDITOR Kate Powers

DEVELOPMENT EDITOR Brett Palana-Shanahan

EDITORIAL ASSISTANT Ross Weisman

EVERYTHING® SERIES COVER DESIGNER Erin Alexander

LAYOUT DESIGNERS Erin Dawson, Michelle Roy Kelly, Elisabeth Lariviere, Ashley Vierra, Denise Wallace

Visit the entire Everything® series at *www.everything.com*

THE
EVERYTHING®
BABY NAMES
BOOK

3RD EDITION

From classic to contemporary, 50,000
baby names that you—and your child—will love

June Rifkin

adamsmedia
Avon, Massachusetts

Best wishes to all expectant moms and dads.
May your new baby be healthy, happy, and
live up to the fabulous name you pick!

An Everything® Series Book.
Everything® and everything.com® are registered trademarks of F+W Media, Inc.

Published by Adams Media, a division of F+W Media, Inc.
57 Littlefield Street, Avon, MA 02322 U.S.A.
www.adamsmedia.com

ISBN 10: 1-4405-2703-2
ISBN 13: 978-1-4405-2703-6
eISBN 10: 1-4405-2752-0
eISBN 13: 978-1-4405-2752-4

Printed in the United States of America.

10 9 8 7 6 5 4 3 2 1

Library of Congress Cataloging-in-Publication Data
is available from the publisher.

This publication is designed to provide accurate and authoritative information with regard to the subject matter covered. It is sold with the understanding that the publisher is not engaged in rendering legal, accounting, or other professional advice. If legal advice or other expert assistance is required, the services of a competent professional person should be sought.

—From a *Declaration of Principles* jointly adopted by a Committee of the American Bar Association and a Committee of Publishers and Associations

Many of the designations used by manufacturers and sellers to distinguish their products are claimed as trademarks. Where those designations appear in this book and Adams Media was aware of a trademark claim, the designations have been printed with initial capital letters.

This book is available at quantity discounts for bulk purchases.
For information, please call 1-800-289-0963.

Contents

Acknowledgments

Many thanks to the folks at Adams Media and to Ross Weisman, in particular, for presenting me with the opportunity of expanding and refreshing this book. Special thanks to the following for their input on the sidebar lists: Judy Frohman, Terry Anne Homan, Brenda Knight, Eve Marx, Leon Lewandowski, TVScreener.com editor Kim Potts, Randi Rifkin, and astrologer Constance Stellas. Big hugs to Stuart and Colin for always being there. And to the little light of my life, Nicholas Walker Clark, whose baby-toothed smile brightens my world every day.

The Top 10 Things to Consider when Choosing a Name for Your Baby

1. How popular is the name? You may love "Jacob" or "Isabella," but on the first day of school, your child may be one of five *other* "Jacobs" or "Isabellas."

2. Odd spellings of popular names are, well, just odd spellings. Chances are "Jakob" and "Izabellah" will have to forever correct people from misspelling their names.

3. Be mindful of nicknames. Your daughter Natalie might wind up becoming "Natty," and your son James, "Jimbo."

4. Beware of names that rhyme with something strange (for example, a pretty name like "June" rhymes with "goon" and "baboon") or that rhyme with your last name, like "Mark Clark" or "Toni Baroni."

5. Pair it up with your last name and see how it sounds. "Chantal Moreau" rolls of the tongue a lot more smoothly than "Chantal Berkowitz."

6. Avoid names that might prompt teasing from other kids. "Luna" (meaning "moon") is lovely but can sound like "Looney" to a bully.

7. Honor your heritage, but also honor your child. While you're proud of your cultural or family roots, an American-born child named Ionut Pupazon may be picked on.

8. Note those initials. Samantha Emily Xavier and Patrick Ian Granville will become S.E.X. and P.I.G. on a monogrammed sweater.

9. It's okay to ask for opinions from family and friends, but remember that the ultimate choice is the one you (and your partner) like best.

10. A name is for life. Choose well and wisely.

Introduction

YOU'RE ABOUT TO WELCOME a new baby into your life, and this bundle of joy needs a name. Seems easy to figure out, right? Think back to your teens when you scribbled down dozens of great names and kept them on file for when you had a baby. If you've found your old list and still love those names, you've got a head start. If not, the search is on.

To get started, create a list of all the important factors you want to consider in choosing a name for your baby. Ask yourself the following questions:

- Is there someone you care about or admire—living or deceased—for whom you want your baby to be named?
- Are you only considering using names that begin with a particular letter of the alphabet?
- Is there a special place that you might consider using as a name?
- Do you have a passion for something that inspires a great name?
- If you're spiritual, would your prefer a name that reflects your beliefs or religious heritage?
- Do you feel a strong enough affinity to your (or your partner's) family heritage to consider a more ethnic or culturally influenced name?
- If you have other children, would you consider getting them involved in the selection process?
- How crucial is the *meaning* of a name in making your selection?

Thinking about your priorities and making note of these criteria will help you narrow your focus considerably.

Do your tastes run traditional or trendy? Traditional names like Michael and Elizabeth remain popular among trendy choices like Jayden, Logan, and Chloe. But trendy has its place, too. Madison, Ethan, Olivia, and Aiden seem more common than ever among the tried and true. If you want to be traditional *and* trendy, creative spellings or hybrid names might be an option. Michael becomes "Mykal" and Emily becomes "Emalee"; David and Shawn merge into "Dashawn"; and Jessica and Lynn combine to form "Jessalyn."

Something else to consider is how your child might connect with his or her name. Frank Zappa, the late rock music legend, had four children, whom he named Moon Unit, Dweezil, Ahmet Emuukah Rodan, and Diva Muffin. The kids actually thrived well through the years; Moon had a hit record, and Dweezil had a cooking show on television. The quirkiness of their names helped build character. But if Dad had been a hard-working insurance broker in Cincinnati, the kids would likely have had quite a different destiny and maybe a few identity issues to boot.

Names are our identities. Even if we don't love our names, most of us learn to live with them and form our personas around them. Many of us come to truly embrace our names as we reach adulthood—and if not, we're free to choose new ones.

As you search for the right name for your baby, keep in mind how your own name may have shaped your life. Was your name popular, or were you the only one in your school? How did your name make you feel? Finally, use the name dictionary to learn the origins and meanings of different names. Check out the sidebars of name lists and tips, too. Make note of the names you like, and have your partner do the same. Better yet, do it together. Have a discussion, and narrow your choices. Then, get ready for the big birthday!

CHAPTER 1

What's in a Name?

Whether at a party, at Reception at the doctor's office, or walking into a restaurant for your dinner reservation, the first thing you're likely to say is "Hi, I'm _____." That name—your name—is the first impression you make. It distinguishes you from all the other people around you and is, in essence, your personal identity. It represents you to others and the world at large—in person, on paper, or by reputation. Your name is on your driver's license, diploma, and phone bill . . . or maybe on a hospital wing or sandwich at the Carnegie Deli. You are your name, and your name is you. No wonder the process of naming your baby can be so daunting!

A Brief History of Baby Names

While the origins are difficult to quantify, it's safe to say that throughout civilization, humans were named or acquired names in order to distinguish themselves from each other. Chances are, before written history or language, prehistoric man developed ways to identify himself among his peers, rivals, or family—though not likely by names like "Og," "Alley Oop," or "Fred and Wilma Flintstone."

A look through the history provides some clues as to the influences and trends of how people got their names. Religion played a large part, as did family and clans. In Ancient Rome, for example, children had three names: the *praenomen,* which was the first name given by the parents; the *nomen,* which was the family name; and the *cognomen,* which was the name of the family branch. Biblical names from both the Old and New Testaments were also influential with Jews and Christians, respectively, honoring their faiths through names of patriarchs and notable women (such as Abraham, Daniel, Ezra, and Esther) and saints (such as John, Paul, Mark, and Mary). As Christianity spread during the first millennium, so did the prevalence of biblical names, many of which remain popular today.

Life Imitates Art

The Renaissance (fourteenth through seventeenth centuries) and the Age of Enlightenment (eighteenth century) gave rise to great works of art, literature, philosophy, and science that became influential to society and offered new options for baby names. Michelangelo, Leonardo, Raphael, and Lorenzo reflected great artists; Antonia, Caterina, Filippa, Giovanna, Lucrezia, and Margherita were frequently chosen for girls. Characters from Shakespearean plays became popular names as did those of formidable or admirable people of the time, including Elizabeth the Queen. In England, during the sixteenth century, the top names for boys were John, Thomas, and William, and the top names for girls were Elizabeth, Joan, and Margaret— all remaining consistently popular for over 200 years to follow.

During the Victorian Era, traditional names still ruled. Along with the popularity of the names Victoria and Albert (for Queen Victoria and Prince Albert), other names on the rise in England were Emily, Lillian, Alexandra, and Arabella for girls, and Horace, Rudolph, and Spenser for boys. Influential writers of the time, like Charles Dickens and the Brontë sisters, delivered works of literature from which popular characters added a new spark to baby-name choices: Jane, Bertha, Catherine, Heathcliff, Edgar, Sydney, Lucie, Philip, Estella, Oliver, and so on. In the United States, at the end of the nineteenth century, the top baby name for a boy was John, followed by William, James, George, Charles, Joseph, Frank, Robert, Edward, and Henry; for girls, the top name was Mary, followed by Anna, Margaret, Helen, Elizabeth, Ruth, Florence, Ethel, Emma, and Marie.

The Baby Boom

In the years following World War II, the United States experienced its first "baby boom." During this time, parents moved away from many traditional and classic names. Popular culture began to have a rising influence on names as well. When John F. Kennedy became President, many baby girls were named Jacqueline after his much-admired First Lady. On the increase as well were names of favorite film and TV stars: Lucille (Ball), Sandra (Dee), Debbie (Reynolds), Marilyn (Monroe), Gary (Cooper), Elvis (Presley), Lawrence (Olivier), and Jerry (Lewis). Shortened versions of more proper names were suddenly on the rise, too: Patty (for Patricia), Liz (for Elizabeth), Jackie (for Jacqueline), and Angie (for Angela) for girls; Dave (for David), Ted (for Theodore), Bob (for Robert), Bill (for William), and Dick (for Richard) for boys.

FACT

Names Ending in "i," "ie," and "y"
In the mid-twentieth century, not only were shortened versions of names gaining in popularity, but so were names ending in "i," "ie," and "y." Many girls born during the Baby Boom were being named—not nicknamed—Cindy (Cindi, Cindie, Cindee), Lori (Laurie), Carrie, Debbie (Debi, Debbi, Debby), Shari, and Sherry (Sheri, Sheree, Sherie, Cheri, Cherie). Boys were going by shorter "ie" or "y" variations of their longer names, like Jimmy, Ricky, Tommy, Timmy, Danny, Joey, Charlie, and Larry.

By the end of the Baby Boom in the mid-'60s, parents became more experimental, partially due to the political changes occurring and the emergence of the Woodstock generation, which embraced peace and love. By the time the '70s rolled around, parents were selecting more free-spirited or earthy names like Harmony, Liberty, Sunshine, Rain, River, Sky, Eden, Rainbow, Raven, and Moon.

A Return to Tradition and Roots

During the last three decades of the twentieth century, there was a resurgence of more-traditional names, likely a way to counter the impact of the hippie-influenced names of the late '60s and early '70s. During the '80s and '90s, boys' names like Matthew, Joshua, Jason, Daniel, and Andrew moved up the list, along with Jennifer, Jessica, Melissa, Sarah, and Amanda for the girls. Parents began embracing more "old-fashioned" names, particularly for girls, to balance the trend of naming kids for popular TV characters such as Mallory, Alexis, Justin, and Dylan.

Since the late nineteenth century, America has become a true melting pot, with people of all nationalities, religions, and cultures immigrating and influencing society. The growth in acceptance of the contributions of African Americans to popular culture also led to a surge in ethnic names. The publication and subsequent TV adaptation of Alex Haley's groundbreaking book *Roots* in 1977 had everybody—not just African Americans—thinking about and wanting to pay homage to their heritage. *Roots,* the story of Kunta Kinte, a young African who is sold into slavery, and the life and times of his descendants to the present day was a bestseller, and the television miniseries was the third-highest-rated program ever to hit TV. As a result, unique hybrids of American- and African-influenced baby names began to appear more frequently in the African American community and, subsequently, blended into the culture at large. Baby boys were being named Antwon, Dashawn, Jaleel, Shaquille, and Rashawn; baby girls were being called Jaleesa, Keisha, Lateisha, Shaniqua, and Tamika.

More parents began thinking of their own backgrounds, and suddenly names from other ethnic groups and ancestral names were on the upswing.

Irish names like Megan, Erin, Ryan, and Connor gained in popularity, as did Latino names like Diego, Selena, Hector, and Paloma. French names, always desirable, especially for girls, showed a marked increase, with Nicole and Danielle climbing the rankings.

Nowadays, almost anything goes when it comes to choosing a name for a newborn. Boys' names are now girls' names and vice versa; last names are now first names; trendy names are still hot, while choices during grandma's and grandpa's generations make for nostalgic options. Each era in history, whether American or global, can be uniquely identified by the names of its citizens.

ESSENTIAL

La, De, Da . . .
The African American community in the United States cleverly spawned a creative trend in baby naming. By adding or combining "La," "D'," "Da," "De," "Ja," and "Ke" to the beginning of a classic name, the name becomes modern and unique: *Dajuan, Dewayne, Latanya, Jalinda, Keshawn.*

The Sociology of Baby Naming

In the bestselling book *Freakonomics,* authors Steven D. Levitt and Stephen J. Dubner explored how a child's name might impact its path in life. They presented the story of a Harlem father of seven who named one of his sons "Winner" and another son "Loser." Ironically, Winner grew up to be a career felon, while his brother Loser became a New York police sergeant.

While this example suggests that a name does not necessarily influence your fate in life, many psychologists and sociologists regularly examine the ways in which children live (or don't live) up to their names and how name selection is often a reflection of a parent's expectation for a child, both consciously and (often) unconsciously.

"A Boy Named Sue"

A name can impact a child's impression of himself and how others think about him. David Figlio, professor of Human Development and Social Policy at Northwestern University, has studied names. His work has shown that boys given names that were once exclusively masculine but are now popular for girls (such as Taylor or Ashley) are more likely than their peers to misbehave or be disruptive in class by the time they hit high school—especially if a female classmate shares the same name. In girls, those with more feminine-sounding names (such as those ending in "a") tended to focus their studies in humanities, whereas girls given more masculine-sounding names (like Morgan or Alex) gravitated toward science and math.

The ABCs of Success and Longevity

Researchers and statisticians have discovered a phenomenon called the "name-letter effect." The more people like the initials in their name, the greater the tendency to unconsciously gravitate to people and places or circumstances related to those initials. Dr. Brett Pelham, a psychologist and analyst at the Gallup Organization, calls this "implicit egotism" because we're subliminally attracted to things that remind us of ourselves. For example, Madison might opt to drive a Mazda over a Honda or marry a Mark rather than a Joe. This even proved true in academic performance, too. Grading by letters—A, B, C, and D—is prevalent among most educational institutions. A study conducted by Yale and the University of California, San Diego, and published in the journal *Psychological Science* examined the name-letter effect by compiling fifteen years' worth of data consisting of the grade point averages (GPAs) of business school graduates. The results: students whose names began with A or B earned higher GPAs than those whose names began with C or D. The same pattern held true with admissions to law schools: Andrew and Benjamin are more likely to attend top-tier schools (like Harvard and Stanford) than Christine and David.

At Wayne State University in Michigan, psychologists examined the lifespans of lawyers, doctors, and professional athletes born during the fifty-five-year span between 1875 and 1930. The researchers concluded that those people who had names that began with D lived shorter than those with names beginning with A, B, or C, as well as E through Z. Why? Since, culturally, the letter "D" is equated with subpar academic performance, it is reasoned that people with D names might unconsciously have lower self-esteem, which ironically, might make them more susceptible to "disease" and results in more an untimely "death."

FACT

Onomastics is the study of the history and origins of names. The American Name Society is an organization that promotes onomastics and seeks to discover what is really in a name; it investigates cultural insights, history, and linguistic characteristics revealed within.

Statistics show that since the 1950s, the number of babies whose names begin with the letter "A" have more than *doubled*. Further, "A" names now account for over 10 percent of all names given to children today. This may very well be a reflection of exactly what research has shown—that even parents are influenced by the name-letter effect.

Names and Socio-Economic Status

Think of a name like *Alexander Sumner Caldwell*. What would be your first impression? Affluent? Educated? White? Probably. In the study of baby names, some economists wondered not only how a name affects a child's life but also how a parent's life may be reflected in a child's name. Steven Levitt and economist Roland G. Fryer Jr. researched this concept in 2003; the results were featured in a paper (as well as in the book *Freakonomics*). Examining data in California through several decades, they concluded that an undereducated, unmarried, teenage mother from a low-income black community, who had a unique or distinctly black name, was likely to give her child a similarly uncommon or ethnic name, like Shanice or DeShawn, in solidarity with her community. This mother's counterpart in a white community might likely opt to name her child Kayla or Cody.

Each child's life path, in turn, becomes determined more by the parent's lot in life than by the name itself. The authors further surmise that if, as young adults, these children opt to change their names to something sounding more "affluent," the *motivation* to make this change would in itself be a greater indicator of future success.

How do parental income and education factor into name choice? Names, particularly girls' names, go in and out of vogue, and they transition through decades. The patterns also show that when a name catches on among affluent, educated parents, it moves down to middle- and lower-income families within ten years. By that time, so called "high-end" parents have embraced a whole new set of names that, in turn, will eventually be discovered and embraced by the masses and rise up the annual popularity charts. The authors of *Freakonomics* provided a sample of twenty-four male and twenty-four female names they thought were destined to mainstream. As of 2010, nine names did make the list for the Top Fifty most popular for girls and for boys: Emma (#3), Ava (#5), Ella (#13), Grace (#18), Avery (#23), Aiden (#9), Jackson (#25), Liam (#30), and Carter (#48).

According to experts, giving a child an alleged "smart" or "rich" name won't necessarily make the child smart or rich but will, for a time, give parents a sense of higher expectations for their child's destiny.

Baby-Naming Trends and Influences

When examining top baby names through the last 100 years, one of the most interesting things to note is that some popular boys' names have remarkable longevity. At the top of the list of best "staying power" is Michael (#3 in 2010). Other names that ranked high over the century, still popular in 2010, are James (#19), John (#26), Robert (#54), William (#5), David (#15), and Richard (#127).

For girls, Mary was in first place forty-five times since 1911 and ranked #109 in 2010. Of the other top girls' names—Patricia, Elizabeth, Jennifer, Linda, Barbara, and Susan—only Elizabeth, which is still one of the top twenty names, has stayed the course.

Why do boys' names remain more stable over decades? More often than not, boys are named for their fathers or grandfathers, or to keep up the tradition of a name that's always been in the family. Second, parents tend to be more sensitive to the "masculinity factor" in selecting names, and traditional names have the perception of being manlier.

That trend may change over time, however, as more cultures are honored and embraced. With an increase in single motherhood, women are free to be more creative with names for their sons. And, as all the young Braydens, Masons, Logans, Landons, and Angels enter adulthood, they will likely pave the way for new traditions to emerge.

Pop Culture Influences

Britney . . . Khloe and Kourtney . . . Elvis—whether celebrities, characters from hit films and TV shows, heroes and heroines from bestselling books, rock stars, superheroes, designers, or celebrity offspring, our popular culture has been a major influence on naming trends.

Television, in particular, has been a great source of imagination. In the early 1980s, TV characters from the hit prime-time drama *Dynasty* had a sizeable impact on many birth certificates of the time: Alexis, Krystle, Blake, Fallon, Dex, Dominique, and Amanda. In the 1990s, it was *Friends* (Rachel, Monica, Phoebe, Chandler) and *Sex and the City* (Carrie, Samantha, Miranda, Charlotte, Aidan, Trey), and in the 2000s *Glee* sang out with Finn and Quinn, while *Grey's Anatomy* showed us that the doctors were "in" with Meredith, Derek, Cristina, Preston, Izzie, Addison, Callie, Lexi, Arizona, Derek, Owen, and April.

During their heyday, soap opera characters turned up the heat in contemporary names. *All My Children* offered Erica, Bianca, Braden, Brooke, Travis, Mateo, Hayley, Kendall, and Wade; *Days of Our Lives* had Kayla, Britta, Lexie, Harper, Tanner, and Trent; and *General Hospital* brought Laura, Luke, Lucky, Colton, Trevor, Decker, Felicia, and Spencer.

And the Actors Who Play Them
For the TV show *Gossip Girls*, cast members' real-life names are just as popular as the characters they play: *Blake* Lively, *Leighton* Meester, *Penn* Badgley, *Chace* Crawford, *Taylor* Momsen, *Kelly* Rutherford, and *Kristen* Bell.

Reality TV stars rule as recent polls show Maci and Bentley, the teen mom and her son from *16 and Pregnant,* are among the hottest names rising in popularity. Will Snooki be far behind?

Though both a bestselling book and movie series, the characters from *Twilight* have recently become favorite name-chart toppers with Jacob and Isabella (Bella) taking the lead. Up and comers are Jasper, Emmet, and Cullen (a last name that's now a first name), as well as the names of some of the actors playing these roles like Kellan (Lutz) and Taylor (Lautner).

Adventures in Baby Naming

When beginning the baby-naming process, don't be overwhelmed. Try to have fun and don't be stressed. Plan a get-together with a group of friends over dinner or coffee to talk through ideas. Have a date night with your spouse, partner, or S.O. and begin an informal discussion about names you like. If you already know the sex of your baby, cut the task time in half, since you will only have to focus on either male or female names. Maybe you're even one of the lucky ones who've already had a few names picked out long before you got news that you were expecting. You may have plenty of time to make this decision, so take it at a comfortable pace and enjoy the adventure.

Tips for Choosing a Good Name

When you come up with a preliminary list of names you like, ask yourself the following questions about each name:

- Does it have a positive association for you or remind you of someone you like and respect?

- Is it compatible with your last name?
- Does it feel fresh or timeless?
- If heritage matters, does it reflect your family's culture?
- Does it have a definition that feels suitable?
- Will others respond well to the name?
- Is it easy to spell, easy to pronounce, and easy to remember?
- Do you like the initials the full name creates?
- Will it lend itself to a cute and kind nickname?
- Will the name stand the test of time and sound as good to you in thirty years as it does today?

If you can't narrow down your names to one favorite, consider turning one into a middle name. Or create a middle name from the mother's maiden name. As a final thought, once you narrow down your top few choices, take a few days to see if you are as enthusiastic about your choice tomorrow as you are today.

ESSENTIAL

Cool Tool
You can look up the historical ranking of any name over the past 100 years by going to the Social Security Administration's website at *www.ssa.gov/oact/babynames.* You'll find a box called "Popularity of a Name." Simply type in some names you like and how far back you would like to check, and hit "Go." You'll be served with a cool data list that will show you trends for any name that ever made the SSA lists.

Baby Name "Don'ts"

On the other side of the spectrum, here are a few things NOT to do when deciding on your baby's name:

- Don't choose a name that other kids are apt to pick on. Some kids can be cruel, and you want to protect your child from others' ignorance.
- Don't get too trendy. Britney is cute today, but how will "Nana Britney" sound?

- Don't pick a name that rhymes with anything bad or sounds too similar to a word that is negative, obscene, or too slangy.
- Don't go to the extreme with alternative spellings. A unique spelling makes a common name more distinctive, but you're also guaranteed that you and your child will always have to spell it out to others.
- Don't choose a name that when coupled with your last name forms the name of someone famous (like "George Clooney" or "Katy Perry"), because those comparisons will be made for a lifetime.
- Don't pick a name that sounds like it would be better suited for a pet. Fifi, Smokey, and Misty are cute for dogs and cats . . . not so cute for kids.
- Don't let choosing a name create a rift between you and your partner. The process should be unifying, not divisive.
- Don't tell too many people about the name you selected until it's on the birth certificate. Everyone has an opinion, and you're sure to hear it. Yours is the only one that counts.

Ideas for Twins or Multiple Births

What if you're having more than one baby? Even if you've settled on one name, the challenge is to come up with another one that you like equally as much, and both sound like good sibling names.

If you're having all boys or all girls, you can opt for several names that begin with the same letter (Violet and Vanessa), sound like they relate to one another (Emily and Charlotte), or if you don't get too tacky, have them slightly rhyme (Marilyn and Carolyn). Huey, Dewey, and Louie might be pushing that bar too far.

If you're having one of each gender, it's fun to think of cute couples—Ben and Jen, Will and Kate—or again, names that begin with the same letter (like Mariah Carey did with her twins, daughter Monroe and son Moroccan). On the downside, you might want to avoid couplings like Bonnie and Clyde or Eva and Adolf.

Top Names for Twins

According the Social Security Administration in 2010, these are the top names for twins:

TWIN BOYS	TWIN GIRLS	TWINS, ONE OF EACH GENDER
1. Jacob and Joshua	1. Ella and Emma	1. Madison and Mason
2. Ethan and Evan	2. Olivia and Sophia	2. Emily and Ethan
3. Jayden and Jordan	3. Gabriella and Isabella	3. Taylor and Tyler
4. Daniel and David	4. Faith and Hope	4. Madison and Michael
5. Matthew and Michael	5. Ava and Emma	5. Jayda and Jayden
6. Landon and Logan	6. Isabella and Sophia	6. Madison and Matthew
7. Elijah and Isaiah	7. Madison and Morgan	7. Sophia and Samuel
8. Jacob and Joseph	8. Ava and Ella	8. Addison and Aiden
9. Jayden and Jaylen	9. Ava and Olivia	9. Olivia and Owen
10. Isaac and Isaiah	10. Mackenzie and Madison	10. Zoe and Zachary
11. Caleb and Joshua	11. Abigail and Isabella	11. Addison and Jackson
12. Andrew and Matthew	12. Abigail and Emma	12. Ava and Aiden
13. James and John	13. Hailey and Hannah	13. Emily and Ethan
14. Alexander and Nicholas	14. Makayla and Makenzie	14. Emma and Ryan
15. Jeremiah and Josiah	15. Addison and Avery	15. Isabella and Isaac
16. Joseph and Joshua	16. Elizabeth and Emily	16. Natalie and Nathan
17. Nathan and Nicholas	17. Ava and Mia	17. Abigail and Benjamin
18. Jonathan and Joshua	18. Heaven and Nevaeh	18. Emma and Andrew
19. Logan and Lucas	19. Abigail and Emily	19. Isabella and Isaiah
20. Ethan and Nathan	20. Emma and Olivia	20. Jada and Jaden

Naming Your Adopted Child

Adoptions have been on the rise for decades, with many parents adopting from overseas. This creates a unique situation when choosing a name, especially if the child has already been given a name or comes from a different culture. Parents struggle with whether to keep the child's birth name as is or to strike a balance between maintaining the child's origins with that of her new culture. Consider the following:

- For a domestic adoption, many experts recommend keeping the child's birth name or at least part of it, such as in making the birth name the new middle name.
- The age of the child is another important factor, since by the age of two, a child will already identify with a name. Experts recommend not making the change.
- When adopting a child internationally, most parents strive to maintain a connection to the child's country of origin, so choosing a name that reflects the culture and is easy for peers and family to pronounce and embrace can work favorably. If the child is over two years old, an Americanized variation of the name may be a good compromise.

Each circumstance, and each child, is special and should be handled with forethought, respect, and sensitivity. Consulting with adoption or child development experts and networking with other adoptive parents is helpful and highly recommended.

In conclusion, the best wisdom to follow as you navigate the baby-naming process is a simple one: Go with your gut. Using a combination of your instincts and plain old common sense will go a long way.

CHAPTER 2

Boys' Names

A

AADI (Hindi) Beginning.

AAKAV (Hindi) Shape.

AAKESH (Hindi) Lord of the sky.

AAKIL (Hindi) Intelligent.

AALAM (Arabic) Great spirit.

AALOK (Hindi) Light of God.

AAMIN (Hindi) Grace of God.

AANAN (Hindi) Face.

AANDALEEB (Hindi) Bluebird.

AARON (Hebrew) Exalted. Enlightened. *Notables:* U.S. Vice President Aaron Burr; American composer Aaron Copland; singer Aaron Neville; producer Aaron Spelling. *Variations:* Aahron, Aaran, Aarao, Aaren, Aarin, Aeron, Aharon, Ahran, Ahren, Aran, Arek, Aren, Aron, Aronek, Aronne, Aronos, Arran, Arren, Arrin, Arron.

AASIM (Hindi) God's grace.

AATMADEVA (Hindi) God of the soul.

AATMIK (Hindi) Soul.

ABADDON (Hebrew) Knows God.

ABADI (Arabic) Eternal.

ABASI (African) Stern. *Variations:* Abasey, Abasy.

ABAYOMI (African) Brings happiness.

ABBA (Hebrew) Father. *Notables:* Israeli statesman Abba Eban; the Swedish music group ABBA. *Variation:* Aba.

ABBAS (Arabic) Stern. *Variation:* Abas.

ABBEY (Hebrew) A form of Abe or Abraham. *Notable:* activist Abbie Hoffman. *Variations:* Abbe, Abbie, Abby.

ABBOTT (Hebrew) Father. *Variations:* Abbitt, Abboid, Abbot, Abot, Abott.

ABDALLAH (Arabic) One who serves Allah. *Variations:* Abdala, Abdalla, Abdela, Abdulla, Abdullah.

ABDUL (Arabic) Servant of God. *Variations:* Abdal, Abdel, Abdell, Abdoul.

ABDULAZIZ (Arabic) Servant of the powerful one. *Variations:* Abdalazim, Abdalaziz, Abdul-Aziz.

ABDULLAH (Arabic) Servant of Allah. *Variations:* Abdalah, Abdalla, Abdula, Abdulah, Abdulahi, Abdulaziz, Abdulla.

ABE (Hebrew) Variation of Abraham. *Notables:* U.S. President Abe Lincoln; actor Abe Vigoda. *Variations:* Abey, Abie.

ABEEKU (African) Born on Wednesday.

ABEJIDE (African) Born in winter.

ABEL (Hebrew) Breathing spirit or breath. *Variations:* Abell, Able, Avel.

ABELARD (Old German) Highborn and steadfast. *Variations:* Ab, Abalard, Abelarde, Abelardo, Abilard.

ABERDEEN (Scottish) Place name in Scotland.

ABERLIN (German) Having ambition.

ABERNETHY (Scottish) Mouth of a river.

ABHIRAJA (Hindi) Great king.

ABI (Turkish) Elder brother.

ABIAH (Hebrew) Child of God. *Variations:* Abia, Abija, Abijah, Aviya.

ABIAS (Hebrew) One who serves the Lord.

ABID (Arabic) One who worships Allah. *Variation:* Abbud.

ABIDAN (Hebrew) Father of judgment. *Variations:* Abidin, Abidon.

ABIEL (Hebrew) God is my father. *Variations:* Abyel, Ahbiel, Aviel.

ABIODUN (African) Born during war.

ABIOLA (African) Born during the New Year.

ABIR (Hebrew) Strong.

ABISHA (Hebrew) Gift of God. *Variations:* Abisha, Abishal, Abysha.

ABISHUR (Hebrew) My father's glance.

ABNER (Hebrew) Father of light. Biblical. *Variations:* Ab, Aviner, Avner.

ABRAHAM (Hebrew) Father of many. *Notables:* Biblical patriarch Abraham; U.S. President Abraham Lincoln. *Variations:* Abe, Abrahamo, Abrahan, Abrahem, Abrahin, Abrao, Abraomas, Avraham, Ibrahim.

ABRAM (Hebrew) Form of Abraham. *Variations:* Abrama, Abramo, Abrams, Abran, Avram, Avrom, Avrum.

ABSALOM (Hebrew) Father of peace. *Variations:* Abolam, Absalaam, Absalon, Absolom.

ABU (Arabic) Father.

ACACIUS (Latin) Blameless.

ACAR (Turkish) Bright.

ACE (Latin) Unity. Nickname given to one who excels. *Notable:* Kiss lead guitarist Ace Frehley. *Variations:* Acer, Acey, Acie.

ACESTES (Greek) Mythological Trojan king.

ACHAIUS (Irish) Horseman.

ACHARON (Hebrew) Last.

ACHATES (Greek) Ancient mythological figure.

ACHAV (Hebrew) Uncle. *Variation:* Ahab.

ACHAZYA (Hebrew) God has taken. *Variations:* Achazia, Achaziah, Achazyahu, Ahaziah, Ahaziahu.

ACHBAN (Hebrew) Brother of a smart man.

ACHELOUS (Greek) God of the river.

ACHER (Hebrew) Other.

ACHERON (Greek) River of woe.

ACHIDA (Hebrew) Smart brother.

ACHILLES (Greek) Unknown meaning. *Notable:* Achilles, hero of Homer's Iliad. *Variations:* Achille, Achilleus, Achillios, Achillius, Akil, Akilles, Aquilles.

ACHIM (Hebrew) The Lord will judge. *Variation:* Acim.

ACHIMELECH (Hebrew) The king is my brother. *Variation:* Ahimelech.

ACHISAR (Hebrew) The prince is my brother.

ACHISHAR (Hebrew) My brother is a song. *Variation:* Ahishar.

ACHIYA (Hebrew) God is my brother. *Variations:* Achiyahu, Ahia, Ahiah.

ACKERLEY (Old English) Oak meadow. *Variations:* Ackerlea, Ackerlee, Ackerleigh.

ACKLEY (English) Oak-tree dweller. *Variations:* Acklea, Acklee, Ackleigh, Ackly.

ACTAEON (Greek) Ancient mythological hunter. *Variation:* Aktaion.

ACTON (English) Town in Great Britain. *Variation:* Acten.

ADAEL (Hebrew) God's ornament. *Variation:* Adiel.

ADAHY (Native American) In the oak-tree woods. *Variation:* Adahi.

ADAIAH (Hebrew) Witness of God. *Variations:* Adaia, Adaya.

ADAIR (Scottish) Of the oak tree. *Variations:* Adaire, Adare.

ADALARD (German) Brave. *Variations:* Adalarde, Adelard, Adelarde.

ADALRIC (German) Noble ruler. *Variations:* Adelric, Adelrich, Adelrick, Adelrik.

ADAM (Hebrew) Man of the red earth. *Notables:* Comedian Adam Sandler; football player Adam Vinatieri. *Variations:* Adamec, Adamek, Adamh, Adamik, Adamka, Adamko, Adamo, Adams, Adamson, Adamsson, Adan, Adao, Adas, Addam, Addams, Addamson, Addie, Addis, Addy, Adem, Adhamh, Adnet, Adnot.

ADAMNAN (Irish) Little Adam. *Variation:* Adhamhnan.

ADAMYA (Hindi) Difficult.

ADAN (Arabic) One who brings pleasure. *Variations:* Aden, Adin, Adon.

ADAPA (Greek) Ancient mythological figure.

ADAR (Syrian) Ruler or prince; (Hebrew) Noble. Fiery. *Variation:* Addar.

ADDISON (English) Son of Adam. *Variations:* Addis, Adison.

ADE (Nigerian) Royal.

ADEBEN (Ghanaian) Twelfth-born son.

ADEJOLA (African) The crown needs honor.

ADELL (German) Noble. *Variations:* Adal, Adel.

ADELPHI (Greek) Brother.

ADEN (Irish) Fiery one. Form of Aidan.

ADER (Hebrew) Flock. *Variation:* Adder.

ADESOLA (African) The crown honored us.

ADHAM (Arabic) Black.

ADHEESHA (Hindi) King.

ADHIDEVA (Hindi) Supreme god.

ADIEL (Hebrew) Ornament of the Lord. *Variation:* Addiel.

ADIKA (African) First child from second husband.

ADIL (Arabic) Fair. *Variations:* Adeel, Adeele, Adill.

ADILO (German) Noble. *Variation:* Addilo.

ADIN (Hebrew) Attractive. *Variation:* Aden.

ADIO (African) Righteous.

ADIR (Hindi) Lightning.

Top Names of 2010

BOYS:
1. Jacob
2. Ethan
3. Michael
4. Jayden
5. William
6. Alexander
7. Noah
8. Daniel
9. Aidan
10. Anthony
11. Joshua
12. Mason
13. Christopher
14. Andrew
15. David
16. Matthew
17. Logan
18. Elijah
19. James
20. Joseph

GIRLS:
1. Isabella
2. Sophia
3. Emma
4. Olivia
5. Ava
6. Emily
7. Abigail
8. Madison
9. Chloe
10. Mia
11. Addison
12. Elizabeth
13. Ella
14. Natalie
15. Samantha
16. Alexis
17. Lily
18. Grace
19. Hailey
20. Alissa

ADITSAN (Native American) Listener.

ADITYA (Hindi) The sun. *Variation:* Aaditva.

ADIV (Hebrew) Gentle. *Variation:* Adev.

ADLAI (Hebrew) My witness. *Notable:* Politician Adlai Stevenson. *Variations:* Adalia, Addlay, Adlay, Adley.

ADLER (English) Eagle. *Variations:* Addlah, Addlar, Addler, Adlar.

ADLEY (Hebrew) Righteous. *Variations:* Adlea, Adleah, Adlee, Adleigh.

ADMON (Hebrew) Red peony.

ADNAN (Arabic) Settled. *Notable:* Arms dealer Adnan Khashoggi.

ADNEY (English) Dweller at the noble one's land. *Variation:* Adny.

ADOEETE (Native American) Tree. *Variations:* Adoerte, Adooeette.

ADOFO (African) Warrior.

ADOLPH (German) Noble wolf. *Notables:* Adolph Hitler; beer-maker Adolph Coors. *Variations:* Addofo, Adolf, Adolfe, Adolfius, Adolfo, Adolfus, Adolphe, Adolphius, Adolpho, Adolphus, Dolph.

ADOM (African) God's blessing.

ADON (Hebrew) Lord. *Variation:* Adonie.

ADONIAH (Hebrew) The Lord is my God. *Variations:* Adon, Adonia, Adonijah, Adoniya, Adoniyah.

ADONIS (Greek) Handsome. *Variations:* Addonis, Adonise, Adonnis, Adonys, Adonyse.

ADRI (Hindi) Fortress. *Variation:* Adry.

ADRIAN (Latin) Dark. *Notable:* Actor Adrien Brody. *Variations:* Adrain, Adrean, Adren, Adriane, Adriano, Adrianus, Adrien, Adrin, Adrion, Adryn, Arje, Hadrian.

ADRIEL (Hebrew) God's flock. *Variations:* Adrial, Adriall, Adriell, Adryel, Adryell.

ADRIK (Latin) Of the Adriatic. *Variation:* Aidrik.

ADUNBI (African) Pleasant.

ADUSA (African) Thirteenth born.

AEACUS (Greek) Son of Zeus.

AEDUS (Irish) Fire.

AEGEUS (Greek) Goatskin shield of Zeus. *Variation:* Aegis.

AEGYPTUS (Greek) King of Egypt.

AENEAS (Greek) One who is praised. *Variations:* Aineas, Aineis, Eneas, Enneas.

AEOLUS (Greek) The changeable one. *Variations:* Aeolos, Aiolos, Aiolus.

AESON (Greek) Ancient mythological figure.

AETIOS (Greek) Eagle.

AFA (Polynesian) Hurricane.

AFI (Polynesian) Fire.

AFIFI (Arabic) Pious. *Variation:* Afif.

AFSHIN (Persian) Army commander.

AFRAM (African) Ghanaian river.

AFTON (English) From Afton, England. *Variation:* Aften.

AFU (Polynesian) Hot.

AGAMEMNON (Greek) Working slowly. *Variations:* Agamemno, Agamenon.

AGANJU (African) The son and husband of the earth-goddess Odudua.

AGAPIOS (Greek) Love.

AGASTYA (Hindi) One who moves mountains. *Variations:* Agastia, Agastiah, Agastyah.

AGATHIAS (Greek) Good.

AGNI (Hindi) Fire deity.

AGOSTINO (Italian) Respected. Form of August. *Variation:* Agostine.

AGUSTIN (Latin) Highly praised. *Variations:* Agustine, Augustine.

AHAB (Hebrew) Uncle. Father's brother.

AHANU (Native American) One who laughs.

AHARNISH (Hindi) Day and night.

AHAVA (Hebrew) Cherished one.

AHDIK (Native American) Caribou. *Variations:* Ahdic, Ahdick.

AHEARN (Irish) Horse lord. *Variations:* Ahearne, Aherin, Ahern, Aherne, Aheron, Aheryn.

AHIMELEKA (Hawaiian) Biblical priest.

AHIO (Polynesian) Whirlwind.

AHMAD (Arabic) More deserving. *Variations:* Achmad, Achmed, Ahamad, Ahmed, Amad, Amed.·

AHMED (Arabic) Praise. *Variation:* Ahmad.

AHOHAKO (Polynesian) Storm.

AHOMANA (Polynesian) Thunder.

AHRENS (German) Powerful eagle. *Variation:* Ahren.

AHSAN (Hindi) Gratitude.

AHUSAKA (Native American) Wings.

AIAKOS (Greek) The son of Zeus.

AIDAN (Irish) Fiery. *Notable:* Actor Aidan Quinn. *Variations:* Adan, Aden, Adin, Adon, Aiden, Aidin, Aidon, Aidun, Aidyn, Aydan, Ayden, Aydn.

AIKANE (Polynesian) Friendly. *Variations:* Aykan, Aykane.

AIKEN (Old English) Made of oak. *Variations:* Aicken, Aikin, Aykin.

AILBHE (Irish) Bright.

AILESH (Hindi) King of all.

AILILL (Irish) Sprite.

AILPEAN (Scottish) High mountain. *Variations:* Ailpein, Alpine.

AIMON (French) House. *Variation:* Aymon.

AIN (Scottish) Belonging to oneself. *Variation:* Ayn.

AINDREA (Irish) Courageous.

AINEAS (Greek) To praise. *Variation:* Aeneas.

AINMIRE (Irish) Great lord.

AINSLEY (Scottish) His very own meadow. *Variations:* Ainsleigh, Ainslie, Ainsly, Ansley, Aynsley, Aynslie, Aynsly.

AIOLOS (Greek) Change.

AISAKE (Polynesian) He laughs.

AISEA (Polynesian) God saves.

AIYETORO (African) Peace on earth.

AJAIA (African) Pot maker. *Variation:* Ajalah.

AJANABH (Hindi) A mountain.

AJANI (Nigerian) He fights for possession.

AJAY (Punjabi) Victorious.

AJAX (Greek) Warrior.

AKALANKA (Hindi) Pale.

AKAMU (Hawaiian) Red earth. *Variation:* Adamu.

AKANDO (Native American) Ambush.

AKANNI (African) Profitable encounter.

AKAR (Turkish) Stream. *Variation:* Akare.

AKASH (Hindi) Sky.

AKBAR (Arabic) Great.

AKE (Scandinavian) Ancestor. *Variation:* Age.

AKECHETA (Native American) Warrior. *Variation:* Akechetah.

AKEEM (Arabic) Judging thoughtfully. *Variations:* Akim, Hakeem, Hakim.

AKELA (Hawaiian) Noble. *Variation:* Asera.

AKELINA (Russian) Eagle.

AKEMI (Japanese) Beautiful dawn. *Variation:* Akeno.

AKENO (Japanese) Morning.

AKHGAR (Persian) Sign of fire.

AKHILENDRA (Hindi) Lord of the universe.

AKIHITO (Japanese) Bright.

AKIIKI (African) Friend.

AKIL (Arabic) Intelligent. *Variations:* Akile, Akyle.

AKILESH (Hindi) King of all.

AKILIANO (Hawaiian) One from the city of Adrian. *Variation:* Adiriano.

AKIM (Russian) God. *Variations:* Achim, Ackim, Ackym, Akeem.

AKINLABI (African) Boy.

AKINLANA (African) Brave.

AKINS (African) Brave. *Variations:* Akin, Akyn, Akyns.

AKIO (Japanese) Bright.

AKIRA (Japanese) Intelligent. *Notable:* Japanese film director Akira Kurosawa.

AKIVA (Hebrew) Heel. *Variations:* Akavia, Akaviah, Akavya, Akiba, Kiba, Kiva.

AKIYAMA (Japanese) Autumn. *Variations:* Akima, Akimah.

AKMAL (Arabic) Perfection.

AKOLO (Polynesian) Fence.

AKONIIA (Hawaiian) The Lord is my God. *Variation:* Adoniia.

AKONO (African) My turn.

AKSEL (German) Tiny oak tree. *Variation:* Aksell.

AKSHAN (Hindi) Eye.

AKSHAY (Hindi) Forever.

AKUA (African) Born on Thursday.

AKULE (Native American) Looks up. *Variation:* Akul.

AKWETEE (African) Second of twins.

AL (Irish) Short for Alexander or Alan. *Notables:* Reverend Al Sharpton; parody singer/songwriter "Weird Al" Yankovic.

ALA (Arabic) Superior.

ALADDIN (Arabic) Faithful. *Notable:* Aladdin is the hero of a story in the Arabian Nights and was popularized in the Walt Disney film, *Aladdin*.

ALAHMOOT (Native American) Elm branch.

ALAIR (Irish) Happy. *Variation:* Alaire.

ALAKA'I (Hawaiian) Leader.

ALAM (Arabic) Universe.

ALAN (Irish) Fair; handsome. Rock. *Notables:* Actor Alan Alda; hoopster Alan Iverson; economist Alan Greenspan. *Variations:* Ailean, Ailin, Al, Alaen, Alaene, Alain, Aland, Alano, Alao, Alen, Alin, Allan, Allayne, Allen, Alleyn, Alleyne, Allin, Allon, Allyn, Alon, Alun.

ALANSON (Irish) Son of Alan. *Variations:* Allanson, Allenson.

ALARD (German) Noble. *Variation:* Alarde.

ALARIC (German) Noble ruler. *Variations:* Alarich, Alarico, Aleric, Alleric, Alric, Alrick, Ulrich.

ALARIK (Scandinavian) Leader of all. *Variation:* Alarick.

ALASTAIR (Scottish) Protector of men. Derivative of Alexander. *Notable:* Masterpiece Theatre's Alistair Cooke. *Variations:* Alasdair, Alasdaire, Alastaire, Alastare, Alester, Alistair, Alister, Allister.

ALBAN (Latin) From Alba. *Variations:* Albain, Albany, Albean, Albein, Alben.

ALBERIC (German) Clever, wise ruler. *Variation:* Alberich.

ALBERN (German) Courageous. *Variations:* Alberne, Alburn, Alburne.

ALBERT (Old English) Bright; brilliant. *Notables:* Physicist Albert Einstein; actors Albert Finney and Albert Brooks. *Variations:* Alberto, Albie, Albin, Albrecht.

ALBIE (German; French) Bright. *Variations:* Albey, Albie, Alby.

ALBIN (Latin) Pale skinned. *Variations:* Alban, Alben, Albene, Albino, Albion, Albon.

ALBION (Latin) White mountain.

ALCANDER (Greek) Defender of humankind. A form of Alexander. *Variation:* Allcander.

ALCOTT (English) Old cottage. *Variation:* Alcot.

ALCYONEUS (Greek) Kingfisher.

ALDEN (English) Old. *Variations:* Aldan, Aldin, Aldon, Elden.

ALDER (English) Alder tree. *Variations:* Aldar, Aldare.

ALDERIDGE (English) From the alder ridge. *Variation:* Alderige.

ALDIS (French) From the old house. *Variations:* Aldiss, Aldous, Aldus.

ALDO (Italian) Old. German form of Aldous.

ALDOUS (German) Old and wealthy. *Notable:* Writer Aldous Huxley. *Variations:* Aldos, Aldus.

ALDRED (English) Advisor. *Variations:* Aldrid, Alldred, Eldred.

ALDRICH (English) An old and wise leader. *Variations:* Aldric, Aldridge, Aldrige, Eldridge, Eldrige.

ALDWIN (English) Old friend. *Variations:* Aldren, Aldryn, Aldwen, Aldwyn.

ALEC (Greek) Protector. Variation of Alex. *Notables:* Actors Alec

Guinness and Alec Baldwin. *Variations:* Aleck, Aleik, Alek, Aleko, Alic, Alik.

ALEKONA (Hawaiian) Old town. *Variation:* Aletona.

ALEM (Arabic) Wisdom. *Variations:* Alim, Alym.

ALEMANA (Hawaiian) Warrior. *Variations:* Amana, Aremana.

ALEPANA (Hawaiian) From Alba. *Variation:* Alebana.

ALEPELEKE (Hawaiian) Counselor. *Variations:* Alapai, Aleferede.

ALERIC (German) Ruler of all. *Variations:* Alerick, Alerik, Alleric.

ALERON (Latin) Wing.

ALEWINA (Hawaiian) Friend to elves. *Variation:* Alevina.

ALEX (Greek) Short for Alexander. *Notables:* Jeopardy host Alex Trebek; baseball player Alex Rodriguez. *Variations:* Aleizo, Alejo, Alexi, Alexio, Alexis, Alexx, Alexys, Alezio, Alezios, Alezius, Alix, Alixx, Allex, Allix, Allyx.

ALEXANDER (Greek) Protector. Helper and defender of mankind. *Notables:* Greek ruler Alexander the Great; U.S. President Alexander Hamilton. *Variations:* Alecsader, Alecksander, Aleckxander, Alecxander, Aleczi, Alejandro, Alejo, Aleksajender, Aleksander, Aleksandr, Aleksei, Aleksy, Alesandro, Alessander, Alessandre, Alessandri, Alessandro, Alex, Alexandre, Alexandro, Alexandros, Alexei, Alexi, Alexio, Alexius, Alezios, Alezius, Alisander, Alisandre, Alissander, Alissandre, Alisaunder, Alixsander, Alixzander, Sacha, Sascha, Sasha.

ALFIE (English) Short form of Alfred. *Variation:* Alfy.

ALFORD (English) The old river ford. *Variation:* Allford.

ALFONSO (Spanish; Italian) Noble and ready. *Variations:* Alfons, Alfonsin, Alfonsus, Alfonz, Alfonzo, Alphonso, Alphonsus, Fonzie.

ALFRED (English) Wise listener, counselor. *Notables:* Director Alfred Hitchcock; MAD Magazine's Alfred E. Neuman; Nobel Prize originator Alfred Nobel. *Variations:* Aelfric, Ailfrid, Alf, Alfeo, Alfie, Alfredas, Alfredo, Alfric, Alfrick, Alfrid, Alfried, Alfris, Alfryd, Elfric, Elfrick, Elfrid, Fred, Freddy, Fredo.

ALGERNON (Old French) Having a mustache. *Variations:* Algenon, Alger, Algie, Algin.

ALGIS (German) Spear.

ALI (Arabic) Exalted. *Variation:* Aly.

ALIIMALU (Hawaiian) Peaceful leader.

ALIM (Arabic) Wisdom. *Variations:* Alem, Alym.

ALIPATE (Polynesian) Bright.

ALISON (English) Son of the highborn. *Variations:* Allisan, Allisen, Allison, Allisyn.

ALISTAIR (Irish) Protector. *Variations:* Alister, Allistair, Allister, Allistir.

ALITZ (Hebrew) Happy. *Variation:* Aliz.

ALLAN (Irish) Handsome. Form of Alan.

ALLARD (English, French) Brave. Noble one. *Variations:* Alard, Ellard.

Top Names in Mexico

BOYS:
1. Santiago
2. Miguel Angel
3. Diego
4. Emiliano
5. Sebastian
6. Luis Angel
7. Alejandro
8. Leonardo
9. Angel Gabriel
10. Daniel

GIRLS:
1. Maria Fernanda
2. Ximena
3. Maria Jose
4. Valeria
5. Camila
6. Maria Guadalupe
7. Daniela
8. Valentina
9. Andrea
10. Regina

ALLEN (Irish) Handsome. Form of Alan.

ALLON (Hebrew) Oak tree. *Variations:* Alon, Alonn.

ALMERIC (German) Powerful ruler. *Variations:* Amauric, Amaurick, Amaurik, Americk, Amerik.

ALMO (English) Noble. *Variation:* Elmo.

ALMON (Hebrew) Widower. *Variations:* Alman, Almen, Almin, Almyn.

ALOIKI (Hawaiian) Famous war. *Variation:* Aloisi.

ALONZO (Spanish) Form of Alphonse. *Notable:* NBA's Alonzo Mourning. *Variations:* Alanzo, Allonzo, Alonso, Alonz, Alonze, Elonso, Elonzo.

ALOYSIUS (German) Warrior. Form of Louis. *Variation:* Aloisius.

ALPHA (Greek) First born. *Variations:* Alfa, Alfia, Alfya.

ALPHEUS (Greek) God of the river. *Variations:* Alfeus, Alpheous.

ALPHONSE (German) One who is ready to fight. Noble. *Notables:* U.S. Senator Alphonse D'Amato; crime czar Alphonse "Al" Capone. *Variations:* Alfons, Alfonse, Alfonso, Alfonze, Alfonzo, Alonzo, Alphonso, Alphonsus.

ALPIN (Scottish) High mountains.

ALPINOLO (Italian) Old friend.

ALRIC (German) All powerful. Form of Aleric.

ALROY (English) Red haired.

ALSTON (English) Manor; settlement. *Variations:* Allston, Alstan, Alsten, Alstin, Alstyn.

ALSWORTH (English) From the estate.

ALTAIR (Greek) Bird. Bright star. *Variations:* Altar, Altayr, Altayre, Altyr.

ALTER (German) Elder. *Variations:* Altar, Altor.

ALTMAN (German) Old man. *Variations:* Altmann, Altmen.

ALTON (English) One who lives in an old town. *Variation:* Aldon.

ALVAR (Hebrew) Justice.

ALVARO (Spanish) Cautious. *Variations:* Alvarado, Alvarro.

ALVERN (Latin) Spring. *Variation:* Alverne.

ALVIN (German) Friend. *Notables:* Choreographer Alvin Ailey; writer Alvin Toffler. *Variations:* Ailwyn, Alion, Aluin, Aluino, Alva, Alvan, Alven, Alvie, Alvino, Alvy, Alvyn, Alwin, Alwyn, Alwynn, Aylwin.

ALVIS (Scandinavian) All-wise friend. *Variation:* Elvis.

AMADEUS (Latin) Beloved of God. *Notable:* Composer Wolfgang Amadeus Mozart. *Variations:* Amadeo, Amadio, Amadis, Amado, Amedeo.

AMADO (Spanish) Loved. *Variations:* Amando, Amandus, Amato.

AMAHL (Hebrew) Hard worker. *Variations:* Amal, Amali.

AMAL (Hindi) Pure.

AMALESH (Hindi) Clean.

AMAN (Indonesian) Security. *Variation:* Amana.

AMANAKI (Polynesian) Hope.

AMAR (Arabic) Immortal. *Variations:* Amari, Amario, Amarios, Amaris, Amarjit, Ammar, Ammer.

AMARIAH (Hebrew) God has spoken. *Variations:* Amaria, Amariahu, Amarya, Amaryahu.

AMARILLO (Spanish) Yellow. *Variations:* Amarille, Amarilo.

AMASA (Hebrew) Hardship. *Variations:* Amasai, Amasia, Amasiah, Amasya, Amazu.

AMAT (Indonesian) Observation. *Variation:* Amatt.

AMATO (Spanish) Loved. *Variation:* Amat.

AMBERT (German) Shining.

AMBLER (English) Stable keeper. *Variation:* Amblar.

AMBROSE (Greek) Immortal being. *Notable:* Writer/journalist Ambrose Bierce. *Variations:* Ambroce, Ambrogio, Ambrois, Ambroise, Ambroisius, Ambros, Ambrosio, Ambrosios, Ambrossij, Ambrotos, Ambroz, Ambrozij, Ambrozio, Ambrus.

AMERIGO (Italian) Ruler. *Notable:* Explorer Amerigo Vespucci. *Variations:* America, Americo, Americus, Ameriko.

AMERY (French) Ruling worker. *Variations:* Amerie, Aymerey, Aymeric, Aymerick, Aymerie, Aymerik, Aymery.

AMES (French) Friend.

AMFRID (German) Ancestral peace. *Variations:* Amfred, Amfryd.

AMICO (Italian) Friend to all. *Variations:* Amick, Amicko, Amiko.

AMIEL (Hebrew) Lord of the people. *Variation:* Ammiel.

AMIK (Native American) Beaver. *Variation:* Amike.

AMIL (Hindi) Unattainable.

AMIN (Arabic) Trustworthy. *Variations:* Amen, Ammen, Amnon, Amon, Amyn.

AMIR (Arabic) Prince. *Variation:* Ameer.

AMIRAM (Hebrew) Powerful country.

AMIT (Hindi) Without limit. *Variations:* Amita, Amitan, Amreet, Amrit, Amrita, Amritan, Amryt, Amryta, Amrytan.

AMJAD (Arabic) More gratifying.

AMMAR (Arabic) Long life. *Variations:* Amar, Amari, Amario.

AMMIEL (Hebrew) People of God. *Variation:* Amiel.

AMMON (Egyptian) Hidden. *Variations:* Amon, Amond, Amun.

AMNON (Hebrew) Loyal. *Variation:* Amino.

AMOKA (Hawaiian) Strong one. Hawaiian version of Amos. *Variation:* Amosa.

AMON (Hebrew) Secret. *Variation:* Ammon.

AMORY (German) Leader. *Variations:* Amery, Ammorey, Ammorie, Ammory, Amoree, Amorey, Amorie.

AMOS (Hebrew) Strong one. *Notables:* Amos, the Biblical prophet; radio character Amos Jones. *Variations:* Amotz, Amoz, Amus.

AMPHION (Greek) Ancient mythological figure.

AMRAM (Hebrew) Nation of might. *Variations:* Amarien, Amran, Amren.

AMUL (Hindi) Valuable.

AMUND (Scandinavian) Guardian. *Variations:* Amond, Amondo, Amundo.

AMYCUS (Greek) Friendly.

AN (Vietnamese) Peace.

ANAD (Hindi) God. *Variation:* Anaadi.

ANAEL (Greek) Guardian for Librans.

ANAIAH (Hebrew) God answers. *Variations:* Anaia, Anaya.

ANAKALE (Hawaiian) Crown. *Variation:* Anadar.

ANAKIN (American) Warrior from Star Wars. *Variations:* Anahkin, Anahkinn, Anakinn, Annakin, Annakinn.

ANAKLETOS (Greek) To call forth. *Variations:* Anacletus, Cletus, Kletos.

ANAKONI (Hawaiian) Valuable.

ANALO (German) Ancestral.

ANAND (Hindi) Happiness. *Variations:* Ananda, Anandah, Anant, Ananth.

ANANE (African) Fourth son.

ANANTA (Hindi) Eternal.

ANANYA (Hindi) Unique.

ANASTASIO (Italian) Resurrection. *Variations:* Anas, Anastagio, Anastas, Anastasi, Anastasios, Anastasius, Anastice.

ANASTASIUS (Greek) Resurrection. *Variations:* Anastagio, Anastas, Anastase, Anastasi, Anastasij, Anastasio, Anastasios, Anastasl, Anastatius, Anastazij, Anastazy, Anastice.

ANATOLE (Greek) From the east. *Variations:* Anatol, Anatoli, Anatolia, Anatolie, Anatolio, Anatolis, Anatoly.

ANBIORN (Norse) Bear. *Variation:* Anbjorn.

ANCEL (Latin) Servant. *Variations:* Ancelin, Ancelot, Ansell, Ansellus, Ansila.

ANCHALI (Native American) Painter. *Variations:* Anchalee, Anchaley, Anchalie, Anchaly.

ANCHISES (Greek) Ancient mythological figure.

ANDERS (Swedish) Brave and manly. Form of Andrew. *Variation:* Ander.

ANDERSON (Swedish) Son of Andrew. *Variation:* Andersen.

ANDOR (Scandinavian) Combined form of eagle and Thor. (Hungarian) Manly.

ANDRÉ (French) Manly. French version of Andrew. *Notables:* Tennis champ Andre Agassi; conductor André Previn. *Variations:* Ahndray, Andrae, Andray, Aundray, Aundre, Ondre.

ANDREW (English) Brave and manly. *Notables:* U.S. Presidents Andrew Johnson and Andrew Jackson; British Prince Andrew; artists Andy Warhol and Andrew Wyeth. *Variations:* Aindrea, Aindreas, Anders, Andi, Andias, Andonis, Andor, Andras, Andre, Andrea, Andreas, Andrei, Andreian, Andrej, Andrejek, Andres, Andrey, Andros, Andrzej.

ANDROA (Greek) Brave. *Variation:* Andro.

ANDROCLES (Greek) Glory of man.

ANDWELE (African) God brings me.

ANDY (Greek) Short form of Andrew. *Notables:* Actors Andy Garcia and Andy Griffith; TV commentator Andy Rooney; tennis pro Andy Roddick. *Variations:* Andey, Andie.

ANEKELEA (Hawaiian) Manly. *Variation:* Anederea.

ANFERNY (American) Praiseworthy. Form of Anthony. *Variations:* Anfernee, Anferney, Anfernie.

ANGEL (Latin) Messenger. *Variations:* Angele, Angell.

ANGELO (Italian; Greek; Portuguese; Spanish) Angelic. *Notable:* Boxing trainer Angelo Dundee. *Variations:* Angeles, Angelito, Angello, Angelos, Angiolo, Anglico, Anjel, Anjell, Anjello, Anjelo.

ANGUS (Scottish) Only or unique choice. *Variations:* Aengus, Angos, Aonghas.

AHN (Vietnamese) Peace.

ANIKETOS (Greek) Unconquered.

ANIL (Hindi) Air, wind. *Variations:* Aneal, Aneel, Anel, Aniel, Aniello, Anielo.

ANITELU (Polynesian) Manly.

ANIWETA (African) A spirit brings it.

ANJAY (Hindi) Unconquerable.

ANKER (Scandinavian) Harvester. *Variations:* Ankor, Ankur.

ANKUR (Hindi) Blossom.

ANLUAN (Irish) Great champion. *Variations:* Anlon, Anlone.

ANNAN (Celtic) From the stream. *Variations:* Annen, Annin, Annon, Annun, Annyn.

ANNAR (Scandinavian) Second.

ANNAWON (Native American) Chief. *Variation:* Annawan.

ANNO (Hebrew) Graceful.

ANNUR (Arabic) Light.

ANOKE (Native American) Actor. *Variations:* Anokee, Anokey, Anoki, Anokie, Anoky.

ANOUSH (Persian) Everlasting.

ANSEL (French) One who follows a nobleman. *Notable:* Photographer Ansel Adams. *Variations:* Ancel, Anselino, Ansell, Anselm.

ANSELM (German) Protector. *Variations:* Anse, Anselme, Anselmi, Anselmo, Ansheim, Anzelmo.

ANSHU (Hindi) Sunbeam. *Variation:* Anshul.

ANSON (English) Son of Ann. *Notable:* Actor Anson Williams (Potsie on Happy Days). *Variations:* Annson, Ansan, Ansen, Ansin, Ansson, Ansun, Ansyn.

ANTAEUS (Greek) Enemy. *Variations:* Antaios, Anteus.

ANTARES (Greek) A star.

ANTHE (Greek) Strong and brave. *Variations:* Anthey, Anthi, Anthie, Anthy.

ANTHONY (Latin) Praiseworthy. Valuable. *Notables:* Actors Anthony Quinn, Anthony Hopkins, and Anthony Perkins. *Variations:* Andonios, Andonis, Anfonee, Anfoney, Anfoni, Anfonie, Anfony, Anntoin, Antain, Antaine, Antal, Antanas, Ante, Antek, Antholin, Anthonee, Anthoney, Anthoni, Anthonie, Antin, Anto, Antoin, Antoine, Anton, Antone, Antonello, Antoney, Antoni, Antonie, Antonij, Antonin, Antonino, Antonio, Antonius, Antons, Antony, Antos, Tony.

ANTOINE (French) Praiseworthy. Form of Anthony. *Notable:* The Little Prince writer Antoine de Saint-Exupery. *Variations:* Antione, Antjuan, Antuan, Antuwain, Antuwaine, Antuwayne, Antuwon, Antwahn, Antwain, Antwaine, Antwan, Antwaun, Antwohn, Antwoin, Antwoine, Antwon, Antwone.

ANTON (Slavic) Praiseworthy. Form of Anthony. *Notable:* Playwright Anton Chekhov.

ANTONIO (Spanish) Praiseworthy. Form of Anthony. *Notables:* Actor Antonio Banderas; composers Antonio Vivaldi and Antonio Salieri.

ANUJ (Sanskrit) Younger brother.

ANUM (African: Ghanaian) Fifth born.

ANWAR (Arabic) Shafts of light. *Notable:* Egyptian President Anwar Sadat.

ANWELL (Welsh) Dearest. *Variations:* Anwel, Anwil, Anwill, Anwyl, Anwyll.

AODH (Irish) Fire. *Variations:* Aodha, Aodhaigh, Aodhan, Aodhfin, Aodhgan, Aoidh.

APARA (African) A child who comes and goes.

APEKALOMA (Hawaiian) Peaceful father. *Variation:* Abesaloma.

APELA (Hawaiian) Breathing spirit or breath. *Variation:* Abela.

APELAHAMA (Hawaiian) Father of many. Form of Abraham. *Variation:* Aberahama.

APELAMA (Hawaiian) Many children. *Variations:* Aberama, Abiram, Apilama.

APIA (Hawaiian) God is my father. *Variation:* Abia.

APIATAN (Native American) Lance. *Variations:* Ahpeatone, Ahpiatom, Apiaton.

APIKAI (Hawaiian) Gift from God. *Variation:* Abisai.

APOLLO (Greek) Manly. Destroyer. *Variations:* Apollon, Apollos, Apolo.

APOSTOLOS (Greek) An apostle.

APPANOOSE (Native American) Child.

AQUILA (Latin) Eagle. *Variations:* Aquil, Aquill, Aquilla, Aquyl, Aquyla, Aquyll, Aquylla.

AQUILO (Greek) The north wind. *Variation:* Aquillo.

ARACH (Hebrew) Prepared.

ARAFAT (Arabic) Mountain of recognition.

ARALDO (Spanish) Ruler of the army. *Variation:* Haraldo.

ARAM (Syrian) Noble. *Variation:* Aramia.

ARAMIS (French) Clever. *Variations:* Arames, Aramith, Aramys.

ARAN (Thai) Forest. *Variation:* Arane.

ARCAS (Greek) In mythology, the son of Jupiter and Callisto.

ARCHARD (French) Archer.

ARCHER (English) Bowman; archer. *Variations:* Archar, Archard, Archor.

ARCHIBALD (German) Bold. *Notable:* Writer/poet Archibald MacLeish. *Variations:* Archaimbaud, Archambaud, Archambault, Archi, Archibaldes, Archibaldo, Archibales, Archibold, Archybald, Archybalde, Archybaldes, Archybauld, Archybaulde.

Fairest in the Land

If your child is blond, fair haired, or fair skinned, these names would be a good choice!

BOYS:	GIRLS:
Adil	Alina
Alan	Alva
Albion	Anwen
Banning	Aubrey
Bowie	Bianca
Boyd	Blanche
Dewitt	Blondelle
Dwight	Blondie
Elgin	Candace
Fairchild	Cloris
Fairfax	Eirwen
Finian	Elvira
Finlay	Fiona
Finnegan	Fulvia
Flavion	Guinevere
Kenyon	Gwendolyn
Whitman	Jennifer
	Rowena
	Xanthe

Top Names of the 1990s

BOYS:

1. Michael
2. Christopher
3. Matthew
4. Joshua
5. Jacob
6. Nicholas
7. Andrew
8. Daniel
9. Tyler
10. Joseph
11. Brandon
12. David
13. James
14. Ryan
15. John
16. Zachary
17. Justin
18. William
19. Anthony
20. Robert

GIRLS:

1. Jessica
2. Ashley
3. Emily
4. Sarah
5. Samantha
6. Amanda
7. Brittany
8. Elizabeth
9. Taylor
10. Megan
11. Hannah
12. Kayla
13. Lauren
14. Stephanie
15. Rachel
16. Jennifer
17. Nicole
18. Alexis
19. Victoria
20. Amber

ARCHIE (English) Short for Archer or Archibald. *Notables:* Comic book character Archie Andrews; TV's Archie Bunker. *Variations:* Arche, Archee, Archey, Archy.

ARCHIMEDES (Greek) To first think about. *Variations:* Archim, Archymedes.

ARDAI (Celtic) Brave warrior. *Variations:* Ardae, Ardal, Arday.

ARDAL (Irish) Valor. *Variations:* Ardall, Ardghal.

ARDELL (Latin) Eager. *Variation:* Ardel.

ARDEN (Celtic) Eager. *Variations:* Ardan, Ardent, Ardin, Ardint, Ardon.

ARDLEY (English) From the fiery meadow. *Variations:* Ardleigh, Ardli, Ardlie, Ardly.

ARDMORE (Latin) Intense desire, ardent. *Variations:* Ardmoar, Ardmoare, Ardmoor, Ardmoore, Ardmor.

ARDON (Hebrew) Bronzed. From the Bible. *Variations:* Ardan, Arden, Ardin, Ardun, Ardyn.

ARE (Scandinavian) Eagle.

AREN (Danish) Eagle.

ARENTINO (Italian) Virtuous. *Variations:* Aretin, Aretine, Artyn, Artyno.

ARES (Greek) The god of war.

ARGUS (Greek) Bright. *Variation:* Argos.

ARGYLE (Gaelic) From town in Scotland. *Variations:* Argile, Argiles, Argyles.

ARI (Hebrew) Lion. Also, short for Aristotle. *Variations:* Aree, Arey, Arie, Ary, Arye.

ARIC (English) Ruler. *Variations:* Aaric, Aarick, Aarik, Arick, Arik, Aryc, Aryck, Aryk.

ARIEL (Hebrew) Lion of God. *Notable:* Israeli Prime Minister Ariel Sharon. *Variations:* Arel, Ariell, Aryell.

ARIES (Latin) Sign of the ram in astrology. *Variations:* Arees, Ares, Aryes.

ARIF (Arabic) Knowledgeable. *Variations:* Aref, Areef, Aryf.

ARIKI (Polynesian) Chief. *Variations:* Aricki, Arikee, Arikey, Arikie, Ariky.

ARIOCH (Hebrew) Royal. *Variation:* Aryoch.

ARION (Greek) Mythological talking horse. Arian, Arien, Ariona, Arionah, Aryon, Aryona, Aryonah.

ARISTAEUS (Greek) Noble.

ARISTIDES (Greek) The best. *Variations:* Aristede, Aristedes, Aristide, Aristidis, Arisztid, Arystides, Arystydes.

ARISTOTLE (Greek) Superior. *Notables:* Greek philosopher Aristotle; shipping tycoon Aristotle Onassis. *Variations:* Ari, Aris, Aristo, Aristokles, Aristotal, Aristotel, Aristotelis. Aristotol, Aristott, Aristotyl.

ARJUN (Sanskrit) White. *Variation:* Arjuna.

ARKADY (Russian) Bold. *Variations:* Arkadee, Arkadey, Arkadi, Arkadie.

ARKELL (Norse) Eagle cauldron. *Variation:* Arkel.

ARKHIPPOS (Greek) Ruler of the horse.

ARKIN (Norwegian) Son of the eternal king. *Variations:* Aricin, Arkeen, Arkyn.

ARLEDGE (English) By the lake. *Variations:* Arlege, Arlidge, Arlledge, Arllege.

ARLEN (Irish) Pledge. *Variations:* Arlan, Arland, Arle, Arlin, Arlynd.

ARLES (Hebrew) Promise. *Variations:* Arlee, Arleigh, Arley, Arlie, Arlis, Arliss, Arly.

ARLO (Spanish) Bayberry tree. *Notable:* Singer/songwriter Arlo Guthrie. *Variation:* Arlow.

ARMAN (Hebrew) Castle. *Variations:* Armani, Armanie, Armany, Armen, Armin, Armon.

ARMAND (German) Man of the army. *Notables:* Actor Armand Assante; businessman Armand Hammer. *Variations:* Arman, Armande, Armando, Armin, Armon, Armond, Armonde, Armondo, Ormand, Ormond.

ARMOUREL (Gaelic) Dweller by the sea. *Variation:* Armourell.

ARMSTRONG (English) One who has a strong arm.

ARNAN (Hebrew) Joyful. *Variation:* Arnane.

ARNAUD (French) Ruler of eagles.

ARNBJORN (Scandinavian) Eagle bear.

ARNE (German) Eagle. A short form of Arnold.

ARNIE (German) Strong as an eagle. Short form of Arnold. *Variations:* Arne, Arney, Arni, Arny.

ARNETTE (English) Little eagle. *Variations:* Arnat, Arnatt, Arnet, Arnett, Arnot, Arnott.

ARNFINN (Norse) White. *Variations:* Arnfin, Arnfyn, Arnfynn.

ARNOLD (German) Strong as an eagle. *Notables:* Golfer Arnold Palmer; "Governator" Arnold Schwarzenegger. *Variations:* Ahnaldo, Ahnals, Ahneld, Ahneldo, Ahnold, Ahnoldo, Ahrelds, Ahrent, Arnal, Arnald, Arnalde, Arnaldo, Arnall, Arnelle, Arnaud, Arnaude, Arnaut, Arndt, Arnel, Arnele, Arnell, Arnelle, Arnes, Arness, Arnet, Arnett, Arnhold, Arnie, Arno, Arnol, Arnolde, Arnoldo, Arnoll, Arnolt, Arnot, Arnott, Arnoud, Arnst, Arnyld.

ARNON (Hebrew) Rushing stream. *Variations:* Arnan, Arnen, Arnin, Arnyn.

ARNOST (Czech) Determined.

AROD (Hebrew) Rapidly moving.

ARON (Hebrew) To sing. Form of Aaron.

AROON (Thai) Dawn. *Variation:* Aroone.

ARPAD (Hungarian) Prince.

ARRAN (Scottish) Island dweller. *Variations:* Aran, Aren, Arin, Aron, Arren, Arrin, Arron, Arryn, Aryn.

ARRIO (Spanish) Fierce; warlike. *Variations:* Ario, Arryo, Aryo.

ARSENIO (Greek) Virile; masculine. *Notable:* Comedian Arsenio Hall. *Variations:* Arcenio, Arsanio, Arsen, Arsene, Arseneo, Arsenius, Arseny, Arsenyo, Arsinio, Arsinyo, Arsonio.

ARSHA (Persian) Venerable. *Variation:* Arshah.

ARSHAD (Hindi) Devoted.

ARSHAM (Persian) Very powerful.

ART (English) Noble strength. Short form of Arthur. *Variation:* Arte.

ARTEMUS (Greek) One who follows Artemis, the Greek goddess of the hunt. *Variations:* Artamis, Artamus, Artemas, Artemis, Artimas, Artimis, Artimus.

ARTHUR (Celtic) Bear. Rock. *Notables:* King Arthur; tennis legend Arthur Ashe; mathematician/physicist/writer Arthur C. Clarke; playwright Arthur Miller. *Variations:* Artai, Artair, Artek, Arther, Arthor, Arthuro, Arthyr, Artie, Artis, Artius, Arto, Artor, Artur, Arturo, Artus, Atorus, Atur, Aurthur.

ARTIE (English) Short form of Arthur. *Variations:* Arte, Arty.

ARUN (Hindi) Reddish-brown sky.

ARUNDEL (English) Valley of the eagle. *Variations:* Arondel, Arundale, Arundell.

ARVA (Latin) From the coastal area. *Variation:* Arvah.

ARVAD (Hebrew) Exile. *Variations:* Arved, Arvid, Arvind, Arvinder.

ARVE (Scandinavian) Heir.

ARVID (Scandinavian) Eagle in a tree.

ARVIN (German) Friend of the people. *Variations:* Arv, Arvan, Arven, Arvid, Arvie, Arvon, Arvy, Arvyn.

ARVIND (Hindi) Red lotus. *Variations:* Arvinda, Aurobindo.

ARWYSTLI (Welsh) Good counsel.

ARYABHATA (Hindi) Astronomer.

ARYEH (Hebrew) Lion.

ARYO (Persian) Hero who fought against Alexander the Great.

ASA (Hebrew) Doctor. *Variations:* Ase, Aza.

ASAD (Arabic) More fortunate. *Variations:* Asid, Assad, Azad.

ASADEL (Arabic) Successful. *Variations:* Asadul, Asadyl.

ASAPH (Hebrew) Gather. *Variations:* Asaf, Asif, Asiph.

ASAREL (Hebrew) God has bound. *Variation:* Asarell.

ASARIEL (Greek) Guardian of Pisceans.

ASBRAND (Norse) Divine sword. *Variations:* Asbran, Asbrando, Asbrandt.

ASCANIUS (Greek) Ancient mythological figure.

ASCOT (English) Eastern cottage. *Variation:* Ascott.

ASEATH (Egyptian) Dedicated to God. *Variation:* Asenaf.

ASEEM (Hindi) Eternal.

ASGARD (Norse) Divine guardian. *Variation:* Asgar.

ASHBURN (English) Dweller at the ash-tree stream. *Variations:* Ashbern, Ashberne, Ashbirn, Ashbirne, Ashborn, Ashborne, Ashbourn, Ashbourne, Ashburne.

ASHBURTON (English) From the burnt-ash-tree town. *Variations:* Ashberton, Ashbirton.

ASHBY (English) Ash-tree farm. *Variations:* Ash, Ashbey, Ashbie, Ashburn.

ASHER (Hebrew) Happy. *Variations:* Asha, Ashah, Ashar, Asherman, Ashur.

ASHFORD (English) Place to cross a river near ash trees.

ASHLEY (English) Meadow of ash trees. *Variations:* Ashlea, Ashlee, Ashleigh, Ashlie, Ashlin, Ashly.

ASHLIN (English) Ash trees that encircle a pond. *Variation:* Ashlen.

ASHRAF (Arabic) More noble.

ASHTON (English) Town with ash trees. *Notable:* Actor Ashton Kutcher. *Variations:* Ashtan, Ashten, Ashtin, Ashtown, Ashtyn, Aston, Astown.

ASHRAF (Arabic) More noble.

ASHUR (Hebrew) Black. *Variations:* Asher, Ashir, Ashyr.

ASHWIN (Hindi) Star. *Variations:* Ashwan, Ashwen, Ashwon, Ashwyn.

ASIEL (Hebrew) Created by God. *Variation:* Asyel.

ASIM (Arabic) Guardian. *Variation:* Asym.

ASKER (Turkish) Warrior. *Variation:* Aske.

ASLAK (Norse) Divine sport.

ASMUNDER (Norse) Divine hand. *Variations:* Asmund, Asmundo.

ASRIEL (Hebrew) Prince of God. *Variation:* Azriel.

ASTLEY (Greek) Starlit field. *Variations:* Asterlee, Asterleigh, Asterley, Asterlie, Asterly, Astlea, Astlee, Astleigh, Astlie, Astly.

ASTON (English) Eastern town. *Variations:* Asten, Astin.

ASTRAEUS (Greek) The starry one.

ASTYANAX (Greek) King of the city.

ASVARD (Norse) Protector. *Variation:* Asvardo.

ASVOR (Norse) Discreet. *Variations:* Asvar, Asver, Asvir.

ASWAD (Arabic) Black.

ASWIN (English) Friend with a spear. *Variations:* Aswinn, Aswyn, Aswynn.

ATA (African) Twin. *Variations:* Atah, Atta.

ATAGULKALU (Native American) Pitched trees.

ATAIAH (Hebrew) God helps. *Variation:* Ataya.

ATALIK (Hungarian) Like his father. *Variation:* Atalyk.

ATARAH (Hebrew) Crown. *Variation:* Atara.

ATHELSTAN (English) High-borne rock. *Variations:* Athalstan, Athilstan, Athol, Atholstan, Athylstan.

ATHERTON (English) Town by the spring. *Variations:* Athaton, Atheton, Atholton.

ATHOL (Gaelic) From Ireland. *Variations:* Athal, Athalton, Athel, Athelton, Athil, Athilton, Atholton, Athyl.

ATIAH (Arabic) Ready.

ATID (Thai) Sun.

ATIF (Arabic) To sympathize.

ATKINS (English) Place name. *Variations:* Atkin, Atkyn, Atkyns.

ATLAS (Greek) Carry a burden.

ATLEY (English) Meadow. *Variations:* Atlea, Atlee, Atleigh, Attlee, Attleigh, Attley, Attli, Attlie, Attly.

ATMAN (Hindi) Soul.

ATREUS (Greek) Ancient mythological figure.

ATSIDI (Native American) Blacksmith.

ATSU (African) Second of twins.

ATTICUS (Latin) From Athens. *Notable:* Atticus Finch, character in To Kill a Mockingbird.

ATTILA (Old German) Little father. *Notable:* King and general Attila the

Hun. *Variations:* Atilio, Atou, Attilah, Attilio, Attyla, Attylah.

ATU (African) Born on Saturday.

ATUANYA (African) Unexpected.

ATWATER (English) By the water. *Variation:* Attwater.

ATWELL (English) At the well. *Variations:* Attwel, Atwel.

ATWOOD (English) At the woods. *Variation:* Attwood.

ATWORTH (English) At the farm. *Variation:* Attworth.

ATYAANANDA (Hindi) Joyful.

ATZEL (Hebrew) Noble. *Variation:* Azel.

AUBERON (German) King of the fairies. A form of Oberon.

AUBREY (English) Power. *Variations:* Auben, Aubery, Aubin, Aubrie, Aubry, Aubury.

AUBURN (English) Reddish brown. *Variations:* Abern, Aberne, Abirn, Abirne, Aburn, Aburne, Auban, Auben, Aubern, Aubin, Aubirn, Aubirne, Auburne.

AUDEN (English) Old friend. *Variations:* Audan, Audin, Audon, Audyn.

AUDIE (German) Strong. *Notable:* Actor and war hero Audie Murphy. *Variations:* Audi, Audley.

AUDRIC (German) Noble ruler. *Variations:* Audrick, Audrik.

AUGIE (Latin) Short for August or Augustus. *Variations:* Auggie, Augy.

AUGUST (Latin) Worthy of respect. *Notable:* Playwright August Wilson. *Variations:* Agostino, Agosto, Aguistin, Agust, Agustin, Agustino, Auguste, Augustin, Augustine,

Augustino, Augusto, Augustus, Augy, Avgust.

AUGUSTUS (Latin) Venerable. *Notable:* Roman Emperor Augustus Caesar. *Variations:* Agustas, Agustin, Agustus, Agustys, Augustinas, Augustyne.

AUKAI (Hawaiian) Sailor.

AUKAKE (Hawaiian) Wise. *Variations:* Augate, Aukukeko, Aukukino.

AULAY (Scottish) Forefather.

AULELIO (Hawaiian) Golden. *Variation:* Aurelio.

AUREK (Polish) Fair haired.

AURELIAN (Latin) Golden dawn. *Variations:* Aurel, Aurelio.

AURELIUS (Latin) Golden. *Variations:* Areliano, Aurelio, Aurelo, Auriel.

AURIEL (Hebrew) Lion of God.

AUSTIN (Latin) Form of Augustine or Augustus. *Notable:* Film spy Austin Powers. *Variations:* Astin, Austan, Austen, Auston, Austyn.

AVANINDRA (Hindi) Lord of the earth.

AVELL (Russian) Breath.

AVENALL (French) Oat pasture. *Variations:* Aveneil, Aveneill, Avenel, Avenell, Avenil, Avenill.

AVERILL (English) Fighting boar. *Notable:* U.S. diplomat Averell Harriman. *Variations:* Ave, Averel, Averell, Averil, Averyl, Averyll, Avrel, Avrell, Avrill, Avryll.

AVERY (English) Counselor. *Notable:* Philanthropist Avery Fisher.

AVI (Hebrew) My God.

School Daze: Names from Teachers (Part I)

Teachers often have the best access to up-and-coming, diverse names. This selection comes from a second grade class in Livingston, New Jersey:

Allix	Kimia
Ariella	Maanas
Bar	Mallika
Bari	Nadav
Beagy	Orentino
Cataldo	Pardis
Clement	Payton
Eeshin	Remi
Gavriel	Sahar
Giacomo	Sohan
Gianna	Tali
Hasan	Thalia
Hoihim	Yuval
Karmyn	Zain
Kashimire	Zigie

AVIAH (Hebrew) My father is Lord. *Variations:* Abia, Abiah, Abijah, Avia, Aviya.

AVIDAN (Hebrew) God is fair.

AVIDOR (Hebrew) Father of a people.

AVIKAR (Hebrew) My father is priceless.

AVINOAM (Hebrew) Pleasant father.

AVIRAM (Hebrew) My father is strong. *Variations:* Abiram, Avram, Avrom, Avrum.

AVISHAI (Hebrew) Gift from God. *Variations:* Abishai, Avisha, Avshai.

AVITAL (Hebrew) Father of dew. *Variations:* Abital, Avitul.

AVIUR (Hebrew) Father of fire.

AVIV (Hebrew) Spring.

AVLAR (German) Old army. *Variations:* Avler, Avlor.

AVNIEL (Hebrew) My God is my strength.

AWAN (Native American) Somebody. *Variations:* Awen, Awin, Awon, Awyn.

AWST (Welsh) Great.

AXEL (Scandinavian) Father of peace. Reward from God. *Notable:* Musician Axl Rose of Guns N' Roses. *Variations:* Aksel, Ax, Axe, Axell, Axelle, Axil, Axill, Axl.

AXELROD (German) Shoulder. Wheel.

AYER (French) Heir.

AYINDE (African) Given praise.

AYIZE (African) Let it come.

AYLMER (English) Noble. *Variations:* Ailmer, Elmer.

AYLWARD (English) Noble guardian. *Variation:* Ailward.

AYLWIN (Welsh) Noble friend. *Variations:* Ailwan, Ailwen, Ailwin, Ailwyn, Alwan, Alwen, Alwin, Alwon, Alwyn.

AYMAN (Arabic) Lucky.

AYMIL (Greek) Industrious. *Variations:* Aimil, Aimyl.

AYMON (French) Wise protector. *Variations:* Aiman, Aimen, Aimin, Aimon.

AYO (African) Happiness.

AZ (Hebrew) Powerful.

AZAD (Turkish) Free. *Variations:* Asad, Azzad.

AZAI (Hebrew) Strength. *Variation:* Azzai.

AZARIAH (Hebrew) God aids and blesses. *Variation:* Azaria.

AZEEM (Arabic) Defender. *Variations:* Aseem, Asim.

AZEL (Hebrew) Noble. *Variations:* Azal, Azil, Azol, Azyl.

AZI (African) Youth. *Variations:* Azee, Azie.

AZIK (Russian) Laughter.

AZIM (Arabic) Defender. *Variations:* Aseem, Asim, Azeem.

AZIZ (Arabic) Powerful.

AZRIEL (Hebrew) Help from God. *Variation:* Azrael.

AZURIAH (Hebrew) Aided by God. *Variation:* Azuria.

AZZAN (Hebrew) Great strength. *Variations:* Azza, Azzah.

BAASU (Hindi) Prosperous.

BABAR (Hindi) Lion. *Notable:* Babar the Elephant (not lion!) from children's literature. *Variation:* Baber.

BACCHUS (Latin) God of wine.

BACHIR (Hebrew) Oldest son.

BADAR (Arabic) Full moon. *Variations:* Badr, Badru.

BADEN (German) Bather. *Variations:* Baeden, Bayden.

BADRICK (English) Ax ruler. *Variations:* Badric, Badrik, Badryc, Badryck, Badryk.

BAEZ (Welsh) Boar.

BAHA (Arabic) Brilliance. Magnificent.

BAHIR (Arabic) Dazzling.

BAHJAT (Arabic) Happiness. *Variation:* Bahgat.

BAHRAM (Persian) Ancient King. *Variation:* Bairam.

BAILEY (French) Steward or bailiff. *Variations:* Bailee, Baileigh, Bailie, Bailin, Baillie, Baily, Baylee, Bayley, Bayly.

BAINBRIDGE (Irish) Pale bridge. *Variations:* Baenbridge, Bain, Baine, Baynbridge, Bayne, Baynebridge.

BAIRD (Irish) A traveling singer. *Variations:* Bard, Barde, Barr, Bayerd, Bayrd.

BAIS (Arabic) Awakens. *Variation:* Bays.

BAKARI (African) Promising. *Variations:* Bakarie, Bakary.

BAKER (English) One who bakes. *Variations:* Bax, Baxter.

BAKR (Arabic) Camel. *Variation:* Bakor.

BAL (Hindi) An infant with a full head of hair.

BALA (Hindi) Child. *Variations:* Balen, Balu, Balun.

BALABHADRA (Hindi) Lucky. *Variation:* Balu.

BALAKRISHNA (Hindi) Young Krishna.

BALDEMAR (German) Bold. *Variations:* Baldemer, Baldemero, Baldmar, Baldmare, Baldur, Baumer.

BALDER (English) Brave warrior. *Variations:* Baldur, Baudier.

BALDEV (Hindi) Strong god.

BALDRIC (German) Brave ruler. *Variations:* Baudric, Baldrick, Baldrik, Baldry, Baldryck, Baldryk.

BALDWIN (German) Brave friend. *Variations:* Bald, Baldovino, Balduin, Baldwinn, Baldwyn, Baldwynn, Balldwin, Baudoin.

BALFOUR (Gaelic) Grazing land. *Variations:* Balfor, Balfore.

BALIN (Hindi) Soldier. *Variations:* Bali, Baylin, Baylon.

BALINT (Hungarian) Healthy and strong. *Variation:* Balynt.

BALLARD (German) Mighty. *Variation:* Ballerd.

BALRAJ (Hindi) Strong king.

BALSYS (Lithuanian) War council. *Variation:* Balsis.

BALTHASAR (Greek) One of the Three Wise Men of Christmas. *Notable:* Actor Balthazar Getty.

Variations: Baldassaren, Balta, Baltasar, Baltazar, Balthazar, Belshazzar.

BANAN (Irish) White. *Variations:* Banen, Banin, Banon, Banquo, Banyn.

BANCROFT (English) Bean field.

BANDI (Hungarian) Strong and brave. *Variations:* Bandee, Bandey, Bandie, Bandy.

BANDIT (English) Outlaw. *Variation:* Banditt.

BANE (Hawaiian) Son of the farmer. A form of Bartholomew. *Variations:* Baen, Baene, Bain, Baine, Ban, Bayn, Bayne.

BANNER (English) Bearing a flag. *Variations:* Bannar, Bannor.

BANNING (Irish) Small and fair.

BAO (Chinese) Treasure.

BAOTHGHALACH (Irish) Foolish pride. *Variations:* Behellagh, Beolagh, Boetius.

BAPTIST (Greek) To baptize. *Variations:* Badezon, Baptista, Baptiste, Battista.

BAQIR (Arabic) Learned.

BARAK (Hebrew) Lightning; (African) Blessing. *Notable:* U.S. President Barack Obama. *Variations:* Barack, Barrak.

BARAM (Hebrew) Son of the people. *Variations:* Barem, Berim, Barom, Barym.

BARAN (Russian) Ram. *Variations:* Baren, Barin, Baron, Barran, Barren, Barrin, Barron, Barryn, Baryn.

BARBER (French) Hair cutter.

BARCLAY (English) Valley of the birches. *Variations:* Barcley, Barklay, Barkley, Barklie, Berkeley.

BARD (Irish) Poet. Form of Baird. *Variations:* Bairde, Barde, Bardoul, Barr.

BARDEN (English) Valley of barley. *Variations:* Bairdan, Bairden, Bairdin, Bairdon, Bairdyn, Bardan, Barden, Bardon, Bardyn.

BARDOLF (German) Wolf that wields an ax. *Variations:* Bardo, Bardolph, Bardou, Bardoul, Bardulf, Bardulph.

BARDRICK (German) Soldier with an ax. *Variations:* Bardick, Bardric, Bardrik.

BAREND (Scandinavian) Strong bear. *Variation:* Barand.

BARIS (Turkish) Peaceful.

BARKER (English) Lumberjack.

BARLOW (English) Bare hillside. *Variation:* Barlowe.

BARNABAS (Hebrew) Comfort. *Notable:* Vampire Barnabas Collins from the classic TV soap Dark Shadows. *Variations:* Barnabus, Barnebas, Barnebus, Barney, Barnibas, Barnibus.

BARNABY (English) A form of Barnabas. *Variations:* Barnabe, Barnabey, Barnabie, Burnaby.

BARNARD (French) Bold as a bear. Form of Bernard. *Variations:* Barnhard, Barnhardo, Barnhart.

BARNES (English) Barn.

BARNETT (English) Baronet. *Variation:* Barnet.

BARNEY (English) Comfort. Form of Barnabas. *Variations:* Barnie, Barny.

Contemporary Royal Names

Popular members of European royal families may add some cachet to your own family!

BOYS:
Albert
Andrea
Andrew
Carl
Charles
Edward
Henry
Phillip
Pierre
William

GIRLS:
Alexandra
Beatrice
Caroline
Charlotte
Diana
Elizabeth
Eugenie
Madeleine
Stephanie
Victoria

BARNUM (English) A baron's home. *Variation:* Barnham.

BARON (English) Nobleman. *Variations:* Baran, Baren, Barin, Baron, Baryn, Barran, Barren, Barrin, Barron, Barryn.

BARR (English) Gateway. *Variations:* Bar, Barre.

BARRA (Irish) Fair haired. *Variations:* Bara, Barah.

BARRETT (German) Strong as a bear. *Variations:* Baret, Barett, Barit, Baritt, Barret, Barrhet, Barrhett, Barrit, Barritt.

BARRIC (English) From the grain farm. *Variations:* Barrick, Barrik, Beric, Berrick, Berrik.

BARRINGTON (English) Enclosed town. *Variation:* Barington.

BARRIS (Welsh) Army son. *Variations:* Baris, Barrys, Barys.

BARRY (Irish) Marksman. *Notables:* R&B singer Barry White; baseball player Barry Bonds. *Variations:* Barrie, Barrymore.

BART (English) Short form of Bartholomew or Barton. *Notable:* Bart Simpson from the cartoon *The Simpsons*. *Variation:* Barte.

BARTHOLOMEW (Hebrew) Farmer's son. *Variations:* Baremo, Barholomee, Bart, Bartek, Bartel, Barteleleus, Bartelmes, Barteo, Barth, Barthel, Barthelemi, Barthelemy, Barthelmy, Barthlomeo, Bartholdy, Bartholomacus, Bartholome, Bartholomeus, Bartholomieu, Bartholomy, Bartoli, Bartolo, Bartolome, Bartolomeo, Bartram.

BARTLET (English) Form of Bartholomew. *Variation:* Bartlett.

BARTLEY (English) Barley meadow. *Variations:* Bartlee, Bartleigh, Bartlie, Bartly.

BARTON (English) Field of barley. *Variations:* Bartin, Bartyn.

BARTRAM (English) Raven. *Variations:* Barthram, Bertram.

BARUCH (Hebrew) Blessed.

BARUTI (African) Teacher.

BASANT (Hindi) Spring.

BASIL (Greek) Royal. *Notables:* Actor Basil Rathbone; Basil Fawlty from TV's *Fawlty Towers*. *Variations:* Basile, Basilio, Basilios, Basilius, Basino, Bazel, Bazil, Bazyl, Bazyli, Vasilis, Vassily.

BASIM (Arabic) To smile. *Variations:* Basam, Baseem, Basem, Bassam, Bassem, Bassim.

BASIR (Turkish) Intelligent. *Variation:* Bashir.

BASSETT (English) Short person. *Variations:* Baset, Basett, Basset.

BASTIAN (English) Short form of Sebastian; from Sebaste. *Variations:* Bastien, Bastion.

BAT (English) Short form of Bartholomew. Farmer.

BAUL (English) Snail.

BAURICE (African American) Variation of Maurice.

BAVOL (English; Gypsy) The wind. *Variations:* Baval, Bavel, Bavil, Beval, Bevel, Bevil.

BAXTER (English) Form of Baker.

BAY (Vietnamese) Born on Saturday. *Variation:* Baye.

BAYARD (English) Reddish-brown hair. *Variation:* Baiardo.

BEACAN (Irish) Small. *Variations:* Beag, Bec, Becan, Beagan.

BEACHER (English) Near beech trees. *Variations:* Beach, Beachy, Beecher, Beechy.

BEAGAN (Gaelic) Small child. *Variations:* Beagen, Beagin, Beegan.

BEALE (English) Handsome. *Variations:* Beal, Beall, Beals, Beil, Beill.

BEAMAN (English) Beekeeper. *Variations:* Beamen, Beeman, Beman.

BEAMER (English) Horn player. *Variation:* Beemer.

BEANON (Irish) Good. *Variations:* Beinean, Beineon, Binean.

BEARACH (Irish) Spear-like. *Variations:* Bearchan, Bercnan, Bergin.

BEASLEY (English) Pea field.

BEATTIE (Gaelic) One who brings blessings. *Variations:* Beatie, Beatty, Beetie, Beety.

BEAU (French) Handsome. *Notables:* Actor Beau Bridges; English dandy and wit Beau Brummel. *Variations:* Beaux, Bo.

BEAUFORT (French) A beautiful fort. *Variation:* Beauford.

BEAUMONT (French) Beautiful mountain. *Variations:* Beaumount, Bomont, Bomount, Bowmont.

BEAUREGARD (French) Beautiful gaze. *Variations:* Beaureguard, Boregard.

BECHER (Hebrew) First born. *Variation:* Bechor.

BECK (English) Brook. *Variation:* Bec.

BECKER (English) By the brook. *Variation:* Beckett.

BEDAWS (Welsh) Birch tree.

BEDE (English) Prayer.

BEDFORD (English) Place name.

BEDIR (Turkish) Full moon. *Variations:* Bedire, Bedyre.

BEDIVERE (Welsh) Birch tree meadow.

BEDRICH (Czech) Ruler of peace.

BEINISH (Hebrew) Son of the right hand.

BEIRCHEART (Irish) Shining army.

BELA (Czech) White. *Notable:* Actor Bela Lugosi.

BELDEN (English) Beautiful valley. *Variations:* Beldan, Beldin, Beldon, Beldyn, Bellden, Belldon.

BELEN (Greek) Arrow.

BELLAMY (French) Handsome companion. *Variations:* Belamy, Bell, Bellamey, Bellamie.

BELLO (African) Assistant. *Variation:* Belo.

BELMIRO (Portuguese) Handsome. *Variation:* Belmirow.

BELVEDERE (Italian) Handsome. *Variations:* Belveder, Belvidere.

BEM (African) Peace.

BEMIDII (Native American) River by a lake. *Variation:* Bemidi.

BEMUS (Latin) Foundation. *Variation:* Bemis.

BEN (Hebrew) Son of my right hand. Short for Benjamin. *Notables:* Ice cream entrepreneur Ben Cohen; actors Ben Affleck and Ben Stiller. *Variation:* Benn.

BENAIAH (Hebrew) God builds. *Variations:* Benaya, Benayahu, Beniah.

BEN-AMI (Hebrew) Son of the people.

BENDAL (English) Bean field. *Variations:* Bendall, Bendel.

BENEDICT (Latin) Blessed. *Notables:* Revolutionary general and traitor Benedict Arnold; Pope Benedict XVI. *Variations:* Bence, Benci, Bendek, Bendict, Bendik, Bendix, Benedek, Benedetto, Benedick, Benedictas, Benedicto, Benedictus, Benedik, Benedikt, Benedix, Benedyck, Benek.

BENITO (Italian) Blessed. Italian form of Benedict. *Notable:* Fascist dictator of Italy, Benito Mussolini. *Variations:* Benedo, Benino, Benno.

BENJAMIN (Hebrew) Son of my right hand. *Notables:* Statesman Benjamin Franklin; British Prime Minister Benjamin Disraeli; Dr. Benjamin Spock. *Variations:* Benejamen, Beniamino, Benjaman, Benjamen, Benjamino, Benjamon, Benjamyn, Benji, Benjie, Benjiman, Benjimen, Benjy, Bennie, Benny, Binyamin, Minyamin, Minyomei, Minyomi.

BENJIRO (Japanese) Peaceful.

BENNES (Czech) Blessed.

BENNETT (English) Formal version of Benedict. *Notable:* Publisher and editor Bennett Cerf. *Variations:* Benet, Benett, Bennet.

BENNY (English) Son of my right hand. Short form of Benjamin. *Notables:* British comedian Benny Hill; bandleader Benny Goodman. *Variations:* Benne, Benney, Benni, Bennie, Benno.

BENOIT (French) Blessed. Form of Benedict.

BENONI (Hebrew) Son of a sorrowful mother. *Variations:* Benonee, Benoney, Benony.

BENSON (English) Son of Benjamin. *Variations:* Bensen, Bensin, Benssen, Bensson, Bensyn.

BENTLEY (English) Meadow of coarse grass. *Variations:* Bentlea, Bentlee, Bentleigh, Bentlie, Bently.

BENTON (English) Ben's town. *Variations:* Bentan, Benten, Bentin, Bentyn.

BENZI (Hebrew) Good son. *Variations:* Benzie, Ben-Zion.

BEPPE (Italian) God will increase. *Variation:* Bepe.

BER (Hebrew) Bear.

BERACH (Irish) Looking straight at the mark. *Variations:* Berac, Berack, Berak, Birac, Birack, Birak, Burac, Burack, Burak.

BERDY (Russian) Very smart.

BERESFORD (English) Field of barley. *Variation:* Berresford.

BERG (German) Mountain. *Variations:* Borg, Burg.

BERGEN (Scandinavian) Hill dweller. *Variations:* Bergin, Birgin.

BERGER (French) Shepherd.

BERK (Turkish) Solid. *Variation:* Berke.

BERKELEY (English) Town where birches grow. *Variations:* Barclay, Barcley, Barklay, Barkley, Barklie, Barkly, Berklee, Berkley.

BERLE (German) Wine servant. *Variation:* Berl.

BERLYN (German) Son of a wine servant.

BERNAL (German) Bear-like. *Variations:* Bern, Bernald, Bernel.

BERNARD (German) Brave as a bear. *Notable:* Statesman Bernard Baruch. *Variations:* Barnard, Barnardo, Barney, Barnhard, Barnhardo, Barnie, Barny, Bearnard, Bernad, Bernadek, Bernaldim, Bernaldo, Bernardas, Bernardel, Bernardin, Bernardino, Bernardo, Bernardyn, Berneen, Berngard, Bernhard, Bernhardo, Bernhart, Bernie, Berny, Burnard.

BERNIE (German) Brave as a bear. Short form of Bernard. *Variations:* Berney, Berny, Birness, Birney, Birnie, Birny, Burney, Burnie, Burny.

BERNSTEIN (German) Amber stone. *Variation:* Bernsteen.

BERRY (English) Small fruit. *Variation:* Berrie.

BERT (English) Bright and shining. *Notables:* Actors Burt Reynolds and Burt Lancaster; composer Burt Bacharach; Sesame Street's Bert— the best friend of Ernie. *Variations:* Bertie, Berty, Burt, Burtt, Burty.

BERTHOLD (German) Bright. *Variations:* Bertold, Bertolde, Bertoldi, Bertolt, Bertuccio, Burthold, Burtholde.

BERTIE (English) Bright and shining. Short form of Bert. *Variation:* Burt.

BERTIL (Scandinavian) Bright. *Variations:* Bertel, Bertyl, Birtil, Burtil.

BERTIN (Spanish) Good friend. *Variations:* Bertan, Berten, Berton.

BERTO (Spanish) Noble. *Variation:* Burto.

BERTRAM (German) Brightly colored raven. *Variations:* Bartok, Bartram, Beltran, Bertramus, Bertran, Bertrand, Bertrando, Bertraum, Bertrem, Betram.

BERWICK (English) From the barley farm. *Variations:* Berwic, Berwik, Berwyck.

BERWIN (English) Friend at harvest time. *Variations:* Berwyn, Berwynn, Berwynne.

BETHEL (Hebrew) House of God. *Variation:* Bethell.

BETSERAI (African) Help.

BETZALEL (Hebrew) In God's shadow.

BEVAL (English) Like the wind. *Variations:* Bevel, Bevil, Bevyl.

BEVAN (Welsh) Son of Evan. *Variations:* Beavan, Beaven, Beven, Bevin, Bevon, Bevyn.

BEVERLY (English) Meadow of beavers. *Variations:* Beverlee, Beverleigh, Beverley, Beverlie.

BEVIS (French) From Beauvais, a town in France. *Variations:* Beauvais, Beavis.

BEYNON (Welsh) Reliable. *Variation:* Beinon.

BHAKATI (Hindi) Devotion.

BHANU (Hindi) The sun.

BHARAT (Hindi) Maintenance.

BHASKARA (Hindi) Provides light. *Variation:* Bhaskar.

BHASVAN (Hindi) Light. *Variation:* Bhaswar.

BHAVNISH (Hindi) King.

BHIMA (Sanskrit) Strong and mighty. *Variation:* Bhama.

BIALAS (Polish) White. *Variation:* Bialy.

BICKEL (German) Pick ax. *Variation:* Bikel.

BICKFORD (English) Ax wielding.

BIJAN (Persian) Ancient hero. *Variations:* Bihjan, Bijon, Binjhan.

BILAL (Arabic) The chosen one. *Variation:* Billal.

BILL (German) A short form of William. *Notables:* U.S. President Bill Clinton; comedians Bill Cosby, Bill Murray, and Bill Maher. *Variations:* Bil, Byl, Byll.

BILLY (German) Short form of William. *Notable:* Singer/songwriter Billy Joel. *Variations:* Billey, Billie.

BING (German) A pot-shaped hollow. Also, a type of cherry. *Notable:* Crooner Bing Crosby.

BINH (Vietnamese) Peaceful.

BIRCH (English) A birch tree. *Notable:* Senator Birch Bayh. *Variations:* Birk, Burch.

BIRGER (Scandinavian) To help. *Variations:* Birghir, Borge, Borje, Borre, Byrghir, Byrgir.

BIRKETT (English) Area with birch trees. *Variations:* Birket, Birkit, Birkitt, Burket, Burkett, Burkitt.

BIRKEY (English) Island of birch. *Variations:* Birkee, Birkie, Birky.

BIRLEY (English) Cow pasture. *Variations:* Birlie, Birly.

BIRNEY (English) Brook with an island. *Variations:* Birnie, Birny, Burney, Burnie.

BIRTLE (English) Hill with birds.

BISAHALANI (Native American) Speaker.

BISHAMON (Japanese) God of war.

BISHOP (English) Bishop. *Variation:* Bishup.

BISHVAJIT (Hindi) Victor of the world.

BIX (English) Nickname for Bixby, a last name.

BJORN (Scandinavian) Bear. Form of Bernard.

BLACKBURN (Scottish) By the dark brook. *Variations:* Blackbern, Blackberne, Blackborn, Blackborne, Blackburne.

BLADE (English) Sword. *Variations:* Bladen, Blaid, Blaide, Blayde.

BLAGDEN (English) Dark valley.

BLAGGOST (Slavic) Welcomed.

BLAINE (Irish) Thin. *Variations:* Blain, Blane, Blayne.

BLAIR (English) Flat piece of land. *Notable:* Actor Blair Underwood. *Variations:* Blaire, Blayr, Blayre.

BLAISE (Latin) Stutterer. *Variations:* Balas, Blais, Blaize, Blase, Blayse, Blayze, Blaze.

BLAKE (English) Attractive. *Notable:* Director Blake Edwards. *Variations:* Blaike, Blayke.

BLAKELY (English) Dark meadow. *Variations:* Blakelee, Blakeley, Blakelie.

BLANCO (Spanish) White.

BLANFORD (English) Ford of the gray man. *Variation:* Blandford.

BLAZEJ (Czech) Stutterer.

BLEDDYN (Welsh) Wolf hero. *Variations:* Bleddian, Bledian, Bledig, Bledin, Bledyn.

BLISS (English) Joy. *Variation:* Blyss.

BLUMENTHAL (German) From the flowery valley.

BLUNDEL (French) Blond haired. *Variations:* Blundell, Blundelle, Blunden.

Top Names of the 2000s

BOYS:	GIRLS:
1. Jacob	1. Emily
2. Michael	2. Madison
3. Joshua	3. Emma
4. Matthew	4. Olivia
5. Daniel	5. Hannah
6. Christopher	6. Abigail
7. Andrew	7. Isabella
8. Ethan	8. Samantha
9. Joseph	9. Elizabeth
10. William	10. Ashley
11. Anthony	11. Alexis
12. David	12. Sarah
13. Alexander	13. Sophia
14. Nicholas	14. Alyssa
15. Ryan	15. Grace
16. Tyler	16. Ava
17. James	17. Taylor
18. John	18. Brianna
19. Jonathan	19. Lauren
20. Noah	20. Chloe

Automobile Names

Men often name their cars after women. Today, more and more parents are inspired to name their babies after cars!

BOYS:
Acura
Amanti
Aston Martin
Audi
Bentley
Chevy
Cooper
Durango
Ferrari
Ford
Forester
Jaguar
Lancer
Lincoln
Maxima
Montero
Rio
Taurus
Yaris

GIRLS:
Acadia
Altima
Celica
Camry
Corvette
Elantra
Jetta
Kia
Lexus
Mercedes
Porsche
Maybach
Mazda
Mercedes
Savana
Sedona
Shelby
Sienna
Sierra

BLY (Native American) High. *Variations:* Bli, Bligh, Bly.

BLYTHE (English) Merry and carefree. *Variation:* Blithe.

BO (Chinese) Precious.

BOAZ (Hebrew) Quick. *Variations:* Bo, Boas, Boase.

BOB (English) Bright fame. Nickname for Robert. *Notables:* Singers Bob Dylan and Bob Marley.

BOBO (African) Born on Tuesday.

BOBBY (English) Bright fame. Short form of Robert. *Notables:* Celebrity chef Bobby Flay; baseball player/manager Bobby Cox. *Variations:* Bobbey, Bobbie, Bobby.

BODAWAY (Native American) Fire maker.

BODEN (French) Messenger of news. *Variations:* Bodin, Bowden, Bowdoin.

BODHI (Sanskrit) Enlightenment.

BODIE (Scandinavian) Shelter. *Variation:* Bodee.

BODIL (Scandinavian) Dominant. *Variation:* Bodyl.

BODNAR (Danish) Lead battle warrior. *Variations:* Bodna, Bodo.

BODUA (African) Animal tail.

BODULF (Danish) Fierce wolf leader.

BOGART (French) Strength of a bow. *Variations:* Bogar, Bogey, Bogie.

BOGDAN (Slavic) God's gift. *Variations:* Bogden, Bogdin, Bogdon, Bogdyn.

BOGO (German) Bow.

BOGUCHWAL (Polish) God's glory. *Variations:* Bogufal, Boguslaw, Bogusz, Bohusz.

BOGUMIERZ (Polish) God is great.

BOGUMIL (Polish) God's love. *Variation:* Bogomil.

BOHDAN (Czech) Gift from God. *Variations:* Bogdan, Bogdashka.

BOHUMIL (Czech) God's love.

BOHUMIR (Czech) God is great.

BOHUSLAV (Czech) God's glory.

BOJAN (Czech) War. *Variations:* Bojanek, Bojek, Bojik.

BOLDISAR (Hungarian) Member of the war council.

BOLESLAV (Czech) Great glory. *Variation:* Boleslaw.

BOLTON (English) Town in Britain.

BOMANI (African) Strong soldier. *Variation:* Bonamy.

BONAR (French) Gentle. *Variations:* Bonnar, Bonner.

BONARO (Italian) Good friend.

BONAVENTURE (Latin) Blessed adventure.

BOND (English) Man of the land. *Variations:* Bonde, Bondon, Bonds.

BON-HWA (Korean) Glorious.

BONIFACE (Latin) Fortunate. *Variations:* Bonifacio, Bonifacius.

BONO (Latin) All good. *Notable:* U2's Bono. *Variations:* Bon, Bonus.

BOOKER (English) Bible or book lover. *Notable:* Educator Booker T. Washington.

BOONE (French) Good. *Variation:* Boon.

BOOTH (English) House. *Notable:* Writer Booth Tarkington. *Variation:* Boothe.

BORAK (Arabic) Lightning flash. *Variations:* Borac, Borack.

BORDEN (English) Boar's house. *Variations:* Bordan, Bordin, Bordon, Bordyn.

BORG (Scandinavian) Castle. *Variation:* Borge.

BORIS (Slavic) Warrior. *Notables:* Actor Boris Karloff; writer Boris Pasternak; tennis player Boris Becker. *Variations:* Boriss, Borris, Borys.

BORIVOJ (Czech) Great soldier. *Variations:* Bovra, Bovrek, Bovrik.

BORKA (Russian) Warrior.

BORNANI (African) Warrior.

BORR (Scandinavian) Youth.

BORYSLAW (Polish) Glory in battle.

BOSEDA (African) Born on Sunday.

BOSLEY (English) Of or near the woods. *Variations:* Boslee, Boslie.

BOSTON (English) Named for the capital city of Massachusetts. *Variations:* Bostan, Bosten, Bostin, Bostyn.

BOSWELL (English) From the boar enclosure by the stream. *Variation:* Boswel.

BOSWORTH (English) From the boar enclosure.

BOTAN (Japanese) Long life.

BOTOLF (English) Wolf. *Variations:* Botolph, Botulf.

BOUR (African) Rock.

BOUREY (Cambodian) Country.

BOURNE (French) Boundary. *Variations:* Borne, Bourn, Bourney.

BOUTROS (Arabic; Greek) Rock. A form of Peter. *Variation:* Boutro.

BOWEN (Gaelic) Small son. *Variation:* Bow.

BOWIE (Irish) Blond. *Notable:* Former baseball commissioner Bowie Kuhn.

BOYCE (French) Forest. *Variations:* Boice, Boise.

BOYD (Gaelic) Blond. *Variations:* Boid, Boydan, Boyde, Boyden, Boydin, Boydon, Boydyn.

BOYNE (Irish) White cow. *Variations:* Boine, Boyn.

BOYNTON (Irish) From the white cow river town. *Variations:* Boyntown.

BOZIDAR (Czech) Gift from God. *Variations:* Bovza, Bovzek, Bozider, Bozydar.

BRAD (English) Short form of Bradford or Bradley. *Notables:* Actors Brad Pitt and Brad Garrett. *Variations:* Bradd, Brade.

BRADBURN (English) From the broad stream. *Variations:* Bradbern, Bradberne, Bradborn, Bradborne, Bradbourn, Bradbourne.

BRADEN (English) Broad meadow. *Variations:* Bradan, Brade, Bradie, Bradin, Bradon, Braeden, Brayden, Braydon.

BRADFORD (English) A wide stream. *Variations:* Brad, Bradburn, Braddford, Bradforde.

BRADLEY (English) A wide meadow. *Variations:* Brad, Bradlea, Bradlee, Bradleigh, Bradlie, Bradly.

BRADMAN (English) Broad man. *Variation:* Bradmen.

BRADON (English) From the broad valley. *Variations:* Bradan, Braden, Bradin, Bradon, Bradyn, Braeden, Braedin, Braedon, Braedyn.

BRADSHAW (English) Wide forest.

BRADY (English) Broad island. *Variations:* Bradey, Bradie, Braidy.

BRAEDAN (Irish) From the dark valley. *Variations:* Braeden, Braydan, Brayden.

BRAGE (Norse) Son of Odin. *Variation:* Bragg.

BRAGI (Scandinavian) Poet.

BRAHMA (Hindi) Prayer.

BRAINARD (English) Princely. *Variation:* Brainerd.

BRAM (Scottish) Bramble. *Notable:* Dracula writer Bram Stoker. *Variation:* Bramm.

BRAMWELL (English) Town in Britain. *Variations:* Brammell, Bramwel, Branwell.

BRAN (Welsh) Raven.

BRANCH (Latin) Branch from a tree.

BRAND (English) Short form of Brandon. *Variations:* Brande, Brando.

BRANDEIS (German) One who dwells in a land burned by fire. *Variation:* Brandis.

BRANDON (English) Hill afire. *Notables:* TV executives Brandon Tartikoff and Brandon Stoddard. *Variations:* Bran, Brandan, Branden, Brandin, Brandyn.

BRANNON (Irish) From the beacon hill. *Variations:* Branan, Branen, Brannan, Brannen, Brannin, Brannyn.

BRANSON (English) Son of Brandon. *Variations:* Bransan, Bransen, Bransin, Brantson.

BRANT (English) Proud. *Variations:* Brand, Brandt, Brandy.

BRANTLEY (English) Form of Brant. *Variations:* Brantly, Brentley.

BRANWELL (Celtic) Raven from the stream. *Variation:* Branwel.

BRASIL (Irish) War. *Variations:* Brazil, Breasal, Bresal, Bressal.

BRATISLAV (Czech) Glorious brother.

BRATUMIL (Polish) Brotherly love.

BRAVAC (Slavic) Wild boar. *Variations:* Bravack, Bravak, Bravoc, Bravock, Bravok.

BRAWLEY (English) Meadow on a hill. *Variations:* Brawlee, Brawleigh, Brawly.

BRAXTON (English) Brock's town. *Variations:* Brackston, Braxtan, Braxten, Braxtin, Braxtyn.

BRAYDEN (English) Form of Braden. *Variation:* Braydon.

BRECK (Irish) Freckled. *Variations:* Brecken, Breik.

BREDE (Scandinavian) Iceberg.

BRENCIS (Czech) Crown of laurel. *Variation:* Brencys.

BRENDAN (Irish) Little raven. *Notables:* Writer/preservationist Brendan Gill; actor Brendan Fraser. *Variations:* Brenden, Brendin, Brendon.

BRENNAN (Irish) Raven. *Variations:* Brenan, Brennen, Brenner, Brennon.

BRENT (English) Mountaintop. *Variations:* Brentan, Brentin, Brenton, Brentyn.

BRETISLAV (Czech) Glorious noise.

BRETT (English) From Britain. *Notables:* Writers Bret Harte and Bret Easton Ellis; Green Bay Packers quarterback Brett Favre. *Variations:* Bret, Brette, Bretton, Brit, Britt.

BREWSTER (English) Brewer. *Variations:* Brew, Brewer.

BRIAN (Irish) Strong. *Notables:* Beach Boy Brian Wilson; skater Brian Boitano; singer Bryan Ferry. *Variations:* Braiano, Briano, Briant, Brien, Brion, Bryan, Bryant, Bryon.

BRIAREUS (Greek) Mythological hundred-armed giant.

BRICE (Welch) Ambitious. Form of Bryce.

BRICK (English) Bridge. *Variations:* Bric, Bricker.

BRIDGELY (English) From the bridge. *Variations:* Bridge, Bridgeley.

BRIDGER (English) One who lives near a bridge. *Variations:* Bridgar, Bridge, Bridges, Bridgir, Bridgor.

BRIGHAM (English) Village near a bridge. *Notable:* Brigham Young, founder of Church of Jesus Christ of Latter-day Saints. *Variations:* Brigg, Briggs.

BRIGHTON (English) Bright town. *Variations:* Breighton, Bright, Bryton.

BRINLEY (English) Burnt wood. *Variations:* Brindley, Brinly, Brynley, Brynly.

BRISHEN (Gypsy) Born during a rainstorm. *Variations:* Brishan, Brishin, Brishon, Bryshan.

BRITTON (English) From Britain. *Variations:* Brit, Britain, Briton, Britt, Brittan, Britten, Brittin.

BROCK (English) Badger. *Variations:* Broc, Brockley.

BROCKTON (English) Badger town.

BRODER (Scandinavian) Brother. *Variations:* Brolle, Bror.

BRODERICK (Scottish) Brother. *Notable:* Actor Broderick Crawford. *Variations:* Brod, Broddy, Broderic, Brodric, Brodrick.

BRODNY (Slavic) From the place by the stream. *Variation:* Brodney.

BRODY (Irish) Ditch. *Variations:* Brodee, Brodey, Brodi, Brodie.

BROGAN (Irish) Work shoe.

BROMLEY (English) Meadow of brushwood. *Variations:* Bromlee, Bromleigh.

BRON (African) Origin.

BRONE (Irish) Sadness.

BRONISLAW (Polish) Glorious weapon. *Variation:* Bronislav.

BRONSON (English) Dark man's son. *Notable:* Actor Bronson Pinchot. *Variations:* Bron, Bronnson, Bronsen, Bronsin, Bronsonn, Bronsson.

BROOK (English) Stream or brook. *Variation:* Brooks.

BROUGHTON (English) Tower fortress town. *Variations:* Broughtan, Broughten.

BROWN (English) Brown. *Variation:* Browne.

BRUCE (French) Thick brush. *Notables:* Singer Bruce Springsteen; actors Bruce Willis, Bruce Lee, and Bruce Dern. *Variations:* Brucey, Brucie.

BRUNO (German) Dark skinned. *Variations:* Braun, Brunen, Brunon, Bruns.

BRUNSWICK (German) Bruno's village.

BRUTUS (Latin) Heavy.

BRYAN (Irish) Strong. Variation of Brian.

BRYANT (Irish) Strong. A form of Brian. *Notable:* Sportscaster Bryant Gumbel.

BRYCE (Celtic) Swift moving. Ambitious; go-getter. *Variations:* Brice, Bryse.

BRYCHAN (Welsh) Speckled.

BRYDEN (English) Town in Britain. *Variation:* Briden.

BRYNMOR (Welsh) Great hill. *Variations:* Brinmor, Brinmore, Bryn, Brynmore.

BRYSON (English) Nobleman's son.

BU (Vietnamese) Leader.

BUADHACH (Irish) Victory. *Variations:* Buach, Buagh.

BUBBA (German) Boy.

BUCHANAN (Gaelic) House of the clergy. *Variations:* Buchanen, Buchannan.

BUCK (English) Male deer. *Notables:* Country/Western singer Buck Owens; comedy writer Buck Henry. *Variations:* Buckey, Buckie, Bucky.

BUCKLEY (English) Meadow where deer graze. *Variations:* Buckleigh, Bucklie, Buckly.

BUCKMINSTER (English) Preacher. *Notable:* Buckminster Fuller.

BUD (English) Brother or friend. *Notable:* Comedian Bud Abbott. *Variation:* Budd.

BUDDY (English) Friend. *Notables:* Actor Buddy Ebsen; rock-and-roller Buddy Holly. *Variations:* Bud, Budd, Buddey, Buddie.

BUDINGTON (English) Area in Britain.

BUDISLAV (Czech) Glorious awakening. *Variation:* Budek.

BUDZISLAW (Polish) Awakening glory. *Variations:* Budzisz, Budzyk.

BUELL (German) Hill.

BUFORD (English) Ford near a castle. *Variation:* Burford.

BURCHARD (English) Strong castle. *Variations:* Birchard, Burckhardt, Burgard, Burgaud, Burkhart.

BURDEN (English) Birch-tree valley. *Variations:* Berdan, Berden, Berdon, Birdan, Birden, Birdin, Birdon, Burdan, Burdin, Burdon.

BURDETT (English) Little shield. *Variations:* Berdet, Berdett, Berdette, Burdet, Burdette.

BURFORD (English) From the birch-tree ford. *Variations:* Berford, Berforde, Burforde.

BURGESS (English) Citizen. *Notable:* Actor Burgess Meredith. *Variations:* Burges, Burgiss.

BURKE (French) Fortress. *Variations:* Berk, Berke, Birk, Birke, Bourke, Burk.

BURKETT (French) From the little stronghold. *Variations:* Berkette, Birket, Birkett, Burket, Burkette.

BURL (English) Knotty tree trunk. *Notable:* Folk singer Burl Ives. *Variations:* Berl, Burle, Byrle.

BURLEIGH (English) Meadow with knotted trees. *Variations:* Burley, Burlie, Byrleigh, Byrley.

BURNABY (Norse) Warrior's land. *Variation:* Burnabie.

BURNE (English) Brook. *Variations:* Bourn, Bourne, Burn, Byrn, Byrne, Byrnes.

Atlantic Hurricane Names

Tropical storms make news every year. Whenever storms arise, they are given a male or female name, alternating with each storm. A storm name might either be an interesting choice or one to avoid (note that Dennis, Katrina, Rita, Stan, and William have been retired).

2011

Arlene	Harvey	Ophelia
Bret	Irene	Philippe
Cindy	Jose	Rina
Don	Katia	Sean
Emily	Lee	Tammy
Franklin	Maria	Vince
Gert	Nate	Whitney

2012

Alberto	Helene	Oscar
Beryl	Isaac	Patty
Chris	Joyce	Rafael
Debby	Kirk	Sandy
Ernesto	Leslie	Tony
Florence	Michael	Valerie
Gordon	Nadine	William

BURNELL (French) Small child with brown hair. *Variations:* Bernal, Bernall, Bernel, Bernell, Birnel, Birnell, Burnel.

BURNETT (English) Brown haired. *Variations:* Bernet, Bernett, Birnet, Birnett, Burnet, Burnitt.

BURNEY (English) Brook. *Variations:* Burnie, Burny.

BURR (Scandinavian) Youth; (English) Bristle.

BURT (English) Fortress. Short form of Burton. *Variation:* Bert.

BURTON (English) Fort. *Variations:* Bertan, Bertin, Berton, Birton, Burten, Burtin, Burtyn.

BUSBY (Scottish) Village in the forest. *Notable:* Choreographer Busby Berkeley. *Variation:* Busbie.

BUSTER (American) To hit. *Notables:* Comedic actor Buster Keaton and actor Buster Crabbe.

BUTCH (English) Short for Butcher; (American) Manly. *Notable:* American outlaw Butch Cassidy.

BUTCHER (English) A butcher.

BUTLER (English) Chief house servant.

BUZZ (Scottish) Forest village. Short form of Busby. *Notable:* Astronaut Buzz Aldrin. *Variation:* Buzzy.

BWANA (Swahili) Gentleman.

BYFORD (English) By the river ford.

BYRAM (English) Cattle field.

BYRD (English) Like a bird. *Variation:* Bird.

BYRON (English) Barn. *Variations:* Beyren, Beyron, Biren, Biron, Byram, Byran.

CAB (American) Short for Cabot.

CABLE (English) Rope maker. *Variation:* Cabe.

CABOT (English) English family name.

CACHI (Spanish) He brings peace.

CADAL (Celtic) Warrior. *Variations:* Cadall, Kadal, Kadall.

CADAO (Vietnamese) Song.

CADBY (English) Soldier's estate. *Variations:* Cadbee, Cadbey, Cadbi, Cadbie.

CADDOCK (Welsh) Ready for war. *Variations:* Caddoc, Cadock, Cadok.

CADE (Welsh) Short form of Cadell. *Variations:* Caid, Cayd

CADELL (Welsh) Small battle. *Variations:* Caddell, Cadel, Caidel, Caidell, Caydel, Caydell, Cedell.

CADEN (Irish) Spirit of war. *Variations:* Caeden, Caidan, Caiden, Cayden, Kaden, Kadin, Kaedin, Kayden.

CADEYRN (Welsh) King of battle. *Variation:* Caderyn.

CADFAN (Welsh) High battle. *Variations:* Caedfan, Caidfan, Caydfan.

CADFER (Welsh) Lord of battle. *Variations:* Caedfer, Caidfer, Caydfer.

CADHLA (Irish) Handsome.

CADI (Arabic) Luck.

CADMAN (Welsh) Soldier.

CADMAR (Celtic) Brave warrior. *Variations:* Cadmer, Cadmir, Caedmar, Caidmar, Caydmar.

CADMUS (Greek) One who excels.

CADOC (Welsh) Warlike.

CADWALLADER (Welsh) Battle leader. *Variations:* Cadwalader, Cadwaladyr.

CADWALLON (Welsh) Battle arranger. *Variation:* Cadwallen.

CAELAN (Irish) Powerful warrior. *Variations:* Caelin, Caelon, Cailean, Calen, Caln, Caulan, Caylan, Caylen, Caylin, Caylon, Caylyn.

CAERWYN (Welsh) White fortress. *Variation:* Carwyn.

CAESAR (Latin) Hairy. *Variations:* Caezar, Ceasar, Cesar, Cesare, Cesareo, Cesario, Cesaro, Cezar, Cezary, Cezek.

CAFFAR (Irish) Helmet.

CAHILL (Celtic) Strength in battle. *Variations:* Cahal, Cahil, Cathal, Kahil.

CAHIR (Irish) Warrior. *Variation:* Cathaoir.

CAI (Welsh) Joy. *Variations:* Caio, Caius, Kai.

CAILEAN (Scottish) Triumphant in war.

CAILLUM (Welsh) Dove.

CAIN (Hebrew) Spear. *Variations:* Caen, Cainan, Caine, Cayne.

CAIRBRE (Irish) One who rides a chariot.

CAIRN (Welsh) A mound of stones. *Variations:* Cairne, Carne.

CAIRO (Arabic) Conquerer. Capital of Egypt. *Variations:* Cayro, Kairo.

CAISLAV (Slavic) Glory and honor. *Variations:* Cayslav, Kaislav, Kayslav.

CAIUS (Latin) Famous bearer.

CAL (Latin) Short form of Calvert, Calvin.

CALBHACH (Irish) Bald. *Variation:* Callough.

CALDER (English) Brook.

CALDWELL (English) Cold well. *Variation:* Caldwel.

CALE (Hebrew) Faithful. A form of Caleb. *Variations:* Cael, Kale.

CALEB (Hebrew) Brave or dog. *Variations:* Caeleb, Calab, Calib, Callob, Cayleb, Kaleb.

CALEY (Irish) Slender. *Variation:* Cailey.

CALHOUN (Irish) Small forest. *Variation:* Colhoun.

CALISTO (Greek) Most attractive. *Variations:* Callisto, Callistus.

CALLAHAN (Irish) An Irish saint. *Variation:* Callaghan.

CALLAN (Gaelic) Strong in battle. *Variations:* Calan, Calen, Calin, Callen, Callin, Callon, Callyn, Calon, Calyn, Kalan, Kalen, Kalin, Kallan, Kallen, Kallin, Kallon, Kalon.

CALLIS (Latin) Goblet. *Variations:* Calliss, Callys, Kallis.

CALLUM (Irish) Dove. *Variations:* Calam, Calem, Calim, Callam, Callem, Callim, Callym, Calum.

CALVERT (English) Calf herder. *Variation:* Calbert.

CALVIN (English) Bald. *Notables:* U.S. President Calvin Coolidge; designer Calvin Klein; baseball player Cal Ripken. *Variations:* Calvan, Calven, Calvino, Calvon, Kalvin.

CAM (Scottish) Short for Cameron. *Variation:* Cammy.

CAMDEN (English) Twisting valley. *Variations:* Camdan, Camdin, Camdon, Camdyen, Camdyn, Kamdan, Kamden, Kamdin, Kamdon, Kamdyn.

CAMERON (Scottish) Crooked nose or river. *Notable:* Writer Cameron Crowe. *Variations:* Camaron, Cameran, Camron.

CAMEY (Irish) Champion. *Variation:* Camy.

CAMILLUS (Latin) One who assists a priest. *Variation:* Camillo.

CAMLINE (Latin) Song.

CAMLO (Gypsy) Beautiful. *Variation:* Camlow.

CAMPBELL (Scottish) Crooked mouth. *Notable:* Actor Campbell Scott. *Variations:* Cam, Camp.

CAN (Vietnamese) Advice.

CANICE (Irish) Handsome. *Variation:* Coinneach.

CANNON (French) Church official. *Variations:* Canan, Canen, Canin, Cannan, Cannen, Cannin, Cannyn, Canon, Kanon.

CANTRELL (Latin) Singer. *Variation:* Cantrel.

CANUTE (Scandinavian) Knot. *Variation:* Knute.

CAOIMHIN (Irish) Noble. *Variation:* Caoimhghin.

CAOLAN (Irish) Thin.

CAPPY (English) Lucky. *Variation:* Cappi.

CAPTAIN (English) In charge.

CARADOC (Welsh) Affection. *Variations:* Caradog, Carthage.

CARDEN (Celtic) From the black fortress. *Variations:* Cardan, Cardin, Cardon, Cardyn.

CARDEW (Welsh) Black foot. *Variation:* Carew.

CAREY (Welsh) Near a castle. *Variations:* Caree, Carrey, Cary.

CARL (English) Man. Form of Charles. *Notables:* Astronomer Carl Sagan; poet Carl Sandburg; psychologist Carl Jung; Watergate journalist Carl Bernstein. *Variation:* Karl.

CARLETON (English) Farmer's land. *Variations:* Carlton, Charleton.

CARLIN (Gaelic) Little champion. *Variations:* Carlan, Carlen, Carling, Carlino.

CARLISLE (English) Fortified tower. *Variations:* Carlyle, Carlysle.

CARLO (Italian) A form of Charles. *Notable:* Director Carlo Ponti. *Variation:* Carolo.

CARLOS (Spanish) A form of Charles. *Notable:* Musician Carlos Santana. *Variations:* Carlino, Carlito.

CARMEL (Hebrew) Garden. *Variations:* Carmelo, Carmiel.

CARMICHAEL (Scottish) One who follows St. Michael.

CARMINE (Latin) Song. *Variations:* Carman, Carmen, Carmon.

CARNELL (English) Defender of the castle. *Variations:* Carnel, Karnel, Karnell.

CARNEY (Irish) Champion. *Variations:* Carny, Karney, Kearney.

CARR (Scandinavian) Marsh. *Variations:* Karr, Kerr.

CARRICK (Irish) Rock. *Variations:* Carric, Carrik, Karrick.

Top Names in Quebec, Canada (French Speaking)

BOYS:
1. William
2. Olivier
3. Thomas
4. Nathan
5. Alexis
6. Felix
7. Gabriel
8. Samuel
9. Antoine
10. Xavier

GIRLS:
1. Lea
2. Florence
3. Emma
4. Rosalie
5. Jade
6. Juliette
7. Camille
8. Gabrielle
9. Maika
10. Mia

Top Names in Canada (English Speaking)

BOYS:
1. Jacob
2. Nathan
3. Ethan
4. Alexander
5. Liam
6. Lucas
7. Benjamin
8. William
9. Matthew
10. Logan

GIRLS:
1. Emma
2. Olivia
3. Maya
4. Emily
5. Sarah
6. Isabella
7. Ava
8. Chloe
9. Alexis
10. Abigail

CARRINGTON (Welsh) Rocky town. *Variation:* Karrington.

CARROLL (English) Manly. A form of Charles. *Notable:* Actor Carroll O'Connor. *Variations:* Carol, Caroll, Carolus, Carrol, Caryl, Karol, Karoll, Karrol.

CARSON (English) Son who lives in a marsh. *Notables:* TV host Carson Daly. *Variations:* Carsen, Carsin, Carsyn, Karsen.

CARSTEN (German) Form of Christian. *Variations:* Carston, Karsten.

CARSWELL (English) Watercress. *Variations:* Carswel, Carswold, Karswel, Karswell, Karswold.

CARTER (English) Cart driver.

CARTHACH (Irish) Loving. *Variations:* Cartagh, Carthage.

CARTLAND (English) From the cart builder's land. *Variations:* Cartlan, Kartlan, Kartland.

CARTWRIGHT (English) One who builds carts. *Variation:* Cartright.

CARVELL (French) One who lives in a marsh. *Variations:* Carvel, Carvelle, Karvel, Karvell, Karvelle.

CARVER (English) Woodcarver. *Variations:* Carvar, Carvir, Carvor, Karver.

CARY (Welsh) Castle. *Notable:* Actor Cary Grant.

CASE (English) He who brings peace.

CASEY (Irish) Brave. *Notables:* Baseball player/manager Casey Stengel; DJ Casey Kasem; train engineer Casey Jones. *Variations:* Cacey, Cayce, Caycey, Caysey, Kasey.

CASH (Latin) Vain.

CASHEL (Irish) Fortified castle wall. *Variation:* Cashell.

CASHLIN (Celtic) From the little castle by the stream. *Variations:* Cashlind, Cashlyn.

CASHESEGRA (Native American) Large animal tracks. *Variation:* Koshisigre.

CASIMIR (Slavic) He brings peace. *Variations:* Casimire, Casimiro, Castimer, Castimir, Kashmir, Kazimir.

CASLAV (Slavic) Honor and glory. *Variations:* Castilav, Kaslav.

CASPAR (English) Guardian of the treasure. *Notables:* U.S. Secretary of Defense Caspar Weinberger; cartoon character Casper the Friendly Ghost. *Variations:* Casper, Caspir, Gaspar, Kaspar, Kasparas, Kaspe, Kasper, Kaspers, Kaspir.

CASSIDY (Irish) Clever. *Variation:* Cassady.

CASSIUS (Latin) Narcissistic. *Notable:* Boxing legend Cassius Clay (Muhammad Ali's real name). *Variations:* Casseus, Cassio.

CASTLE (English) Castle. *Variation:* Castel.

CASTOR (Greek) Beaver. *Variation:* Caster.

CATER (English) Caterer.

CATHAL (Irish) Ready for war. *Variation:* Cahal.

CATHBERT (English) Bright and famous. *Variations:* Cudbert, Cudbright, Cuthbrid.

CATHMOR (Irish) Great warrior. *Variations:* Cathmoor, Cathmoore, Cathmore.

CATO (Latin) Wise. *Variations:* Caton, Kato.

CAVAN (Irish) Handsome. *Variations:* Caven, Cavin.

CAVANAUGH (Irish) Handsome. *Variation:* Kavanaugh.

CAVELL (German) Bold. *Variations:* Cavel, Cavil, Caville, Kavel, Kavell.

CAW (Welsh) Joyous.

CAWLEY (Scottish) Relic. *Variations:* Cawlee, Cawleigh, Cawlie, Cawly.

CEALLACH (Irish) War. *Variations:* Ceallachan, Cillan, Cillian, Keallach.

CEARBHALL (Irish) Man.

CECIL (English) Blind. *Notables:* Director Cecil B. DeMille; jazz musician Cecil Taylor. *Variations:* Cecile, Cecilio, Cecillo, Cecillus, Celio.

CEDOMIL (Slavic) Child of love. *Variation:* Cedomilo.

CEDRIC (Welsh) Leader of war. *Notables:* Actor Sir Cedric Hardwicke; comedian Cedric the Entertainer. *Variations:* Cedrec, Cedrick, Cederic.

CELESTIN (Czech) Heavenly. *Variations:* Celestine, Celestino.

CEMAL (Arabic) Handsome.

CENON (Spanish) To receive life from Zeus. *Variations:* Xenon, Zenon.

CEPHAS (Hebrew; Aramaic) Rock.

CEPHEUS (Greek) Ancient mythological figure.

CERDIC (Welsh) Cherished. *Variations:* Ceredig, Ceretic.

CEREK (Slavic) Lord. *Variation:* Cerik.

CESAR (Latin) Form of Caesar.

CESLAV (Czech) Glorious honor. *Variation:* Cestislav.

CHACE (English) Hunter. Form of Chase. *Variations:* Chaice, Chayce.

CHAD (English) Protector. *Notable:* Actor Chad Everett. *Variations:* Ceadd, Chaad, Chadd, Chaddy.

CHADLAI (Hebrew) Stop. *Variation:* Hadlai.

CHADWICK (English) Warrior's town. *Variations:* Chadwic, Chadwik, Chadwyck.

CHAGIAH (Hebrew) Festival. *Variations:* Chagia, Chagiya, Haggiah, Hagia.

CHAGO (Spanish) Supplanter. Form of Jacob. *Variation:* Chango.

CHAIM (Hebrew) Life. *Notables:* Zionist/scientist Chaim Weizmann; writer Chaim Potok. *Variations:* Chai, Chayim, Haim, Hayim.

CHAITANYA (Hindi) Cognizance.

CHAL (Gypsy) Boy.

CHALFON (Hebrew) Change. *Variations:* Chalfan, Halfon, Halphon.

CHALIL (Hebrew) Flute. *Variations:* Halil, Hallil.

CHALMERS (Scottish) Head of the household. *Variation:* Chalmer.

CHAMPION (English) Fighter.

CHAN (Sanskrit) Shining.

CHANANIAH (Hebrew) God's sympathy. *Variations:* Chanan, Chanon.

CHANCE (English) Good fortune. *Variations:* Chancy, Chanse, Chansy.

CHANCELLOR (English) Secretary.

CHAND (Hindi) Shining moon. *Variations:* Chanda, Chandak, Chander, Chandra, Chandrabha, Chandrak, Chandrakant.

CHANDAN (Hindi) Sandalwood.

CHANDLER (French) Candle maker. *Notable:* Chandler Bing, a character on TV's *Friends*.

CHANDRARAJ (Hindi) Moon king.

CHANDRESH (Hindi) Moon leader.

CHANE (African) Plant.

CHANEY (French) Oak tree. *Variation:* Cheney.

CHANG (Chinese) Smooth.

CHANIEL (Hebrew) God's grace. *Variations:* Channiel, Haniel, Hanniel.

CHANKRISNA (Cambodian) Tree.

CHANNING (English) Church official.

CHANOCH (Hebrew) Devoted. *Variations:* Enoch, Hanoch.

CHANTI (Hispanic) Supplanter.

CHAPMAN (English) Merchant. *Variations:* Chap, Chapmann, Chapmen, Chapmin.

CHARAKA (Hindi) One who roams.

CHARAN (Thai) Feet.

CHARLES (English) Man. *Notables:* Actor Charles Bronson; evolutionist Charles Darwin; writer Charles Dickens; hoops star Charles Barkley. *Variations:* Chas, Chaz, Chick.

CHARLIE (English) Short form of Charles. *Notables:* Jazz musician Charlie Parker; comedic actors Charlie Chaplin and Charlie Sheen; cartoon character Charlie Brown. *Variation:* Charley.

CHARLTON (English) Town where Charles lives. *Notable:* Actor Charlton Heston. *Variations:* Carleton, Carlton.

CHARRO (Spanish) Horse rider. *Variation:* Charo.

CHARUDATA (Hindi) Beautiful. *Variation:* Charvaka.

CHASE (French) Hunter. *Variations:* Chace, Chaise, Chasen, Chason, Chayse.

CHASID (Hebrew) Devout. *Variation:* Chasud.

CHASIEL (Hebrew) God's refuge. *Variation:* Hasiel.

CHASIN (Hebrew) Strong. *Variations:* Chason, Hasin, Hassin.

CHASKA (Native American) First son.

CHATHAM (English) From the warrior's cottage.

CHAU (Vietnamese) Pearl.

CHAUNCEY (English) Chancellor. *Variations:* Chance, Chancey, Chaunce, Chauncy.

CHAVIV (Hebrew) Dear. *Variations:* Habib, Haviv.

CHAYIM (Hebrew) Life. *Variations:* Chaim, Chaimek, Chayyim, Chayym, Haim, Hayyim, Hayym.

CHAZAIAH (Hebrew) God sees. *Variations:* Chazaya, Chaziel, Hazaia, Hazaiah, Haziel.

CHE (Spanish) Nickname for Joseph. *Notable:* Cuban revolutionary Che Guevara.

CHEASEQUAH (Native American) Red bird.

CHEAUKA (Native American) Clay.

CHECHA (Spanish) Hairy.

CHECHE (Spanish) God will add.

CHEILEM (Hebrew) Power. *Variation:* Chelem.

CHEN (Chinese) Great.

CHENCHE (Spanish) To conquer.

CHENCHO (Spanish) Crowned with laurel.

CHENG (Chinese) Righteous.

CHENZIRA (African) Born while traveling.

CHEPE (Spanish) God will increase. *Variation:* Chepito.

CHESLAV (Russian) Camp.

CHESMU (Native American) Abrasive.

CHESTER (English) Campsite. *Variation:* Cheston.

CHET (English) Short form of Chester. *Notables:* TV news anchor Chet Huntley; Country/Western musician Chet Atkins.

CHETWIN (English) House on a winding road.

CHETZRON (Hebrew) Walled town. *Variation:* Hezron.

CHEUNG (Chinese) Luck.

CHEVALIER (French) Knight. *Variations:* Chev, Chevi, Chevrolet.

CHEVY (French) Knight. Short for Chevalier. *Notable:* Actor/comedian Chevy Chase. *Variation:* Chevey.

CHEYENNE (Native American) Red talker. *Notable:* Actor Cheyenne Jackson.

CHEYNE (Scottish) Strong as an oak.

CHI (Nigerian) Guardian angel.

CHICK (English) Short form of Charles. *Variation:* Chic.

CHICO (Spanish) Boy.

CHIK (Gypsy) Earth.

CHIKAE (African) Power of God. *Variation:* Chike.

CHILO (Spanish) Frenchman.

CHILTON (English) Farm near a well.

CHIM (Vietnamese) Bird.

CHIN-HWA (Korean) Wealthiest.

CHIN-MAE (Korean) Truth.

CHINTAK (Hindi) To think.

CHINUA (African) Blessings of God.

CHIOKE (African) Gift from God.

CHIONESU (African) Protector.

CHIP (English) Nickname for Charles. *Variation:* Chipper.

CHIRAM (Hebrew) Exalted. *Variation:* Hiram.

CHIRANJIV (Hindi) One who lives long. *Variation:* Chirayu.

CHISULO (African) Steel.

CHITTO (Native American) Brave.

CHIUMBO (African) Small child.

CHIZKIAH (Hebrew) God enriches. *Variations:* Chizkia, Chizkiya, Chizkiyahu, Hezekiah.

CHOKICHI (Japanese) Good luck.

CHONEN (Hebrew) Gracious.

CHONG DUY (Vietnamese) Eat like a bird.

CHOZAI (Hebrew) Prophet. *Variation:* Hozai.

CHRIS (Greek) Follower of Christ. Short form of Christopher. *Notables:* Comedian Chris Rock; actor Chris Noth; singer/actor Kris Kristofferson.

CHRISTIAN (Greek) Follower of Christ. *Notables:* Actors Christian Slater and Christian Bale; designer Christian Dior. *Variations:* Chresta,

Chris, Christiaan, Christianos, Chrystian, Cris, Kris, Kriss, Kristian.

CHRISTMAS (English) The holiday. Born at Christmas.

CHRISTOPHER (Greek) Christ bearer. *Notables:* Explorer Christopher Columbus; actor Christopher Plummer; comedian/actor Chris Tucker; . *Variations:* Chris, Christof, Christofer, Christoff, Christoffer, Christoforus, Christoph, Christophe, Christophoros, Christos, Cris, Cristobal, Cristoforo, Kit, Kitt, Kristof, Kristoff, Kristofer, Kristofor.

CHRYSANDER (Greek) Golden. *Variations:* Chrisander, Chrisandor, Chrisandre, Chrysandor, Chrysandre.

CHRYSANTHUS (Greek) Golden flower. *Variations:* Chrisanthias, Chrisanthius, Chrisanthus, Chrysanthias, Chrysanthus, Crisanthus, Crysanthas, Crysanthias, Crysanthus.

CHUCK (American) Nickname for Charles. *Notables:* Jazz musician Chuck Mangione; actors Chuck Connors and Chuck Norris. *Variations:* Chuckie, Chucky.

CHUIOKE (African) Talented. *Variations:* Chike, Chinelo.

CHUL (Korean) Firm.

CHUL-MOO (Korean) Iron weapon.

CHUMA (African) Bead.

CHUMIN (Spanish) Lord. *Variation:* Chuminga.

CHUMO (Spanish) Twin.

CHUNG (Chinese) Intelligent.

CHUNG-HEE (Korean) Righteous. *Variation:* Chung-Ho.

CHURCHILL (English) Church on the hill. *Variation:* Churchyll.

CIAN (Irish) Ancient; old. *Variation:* Cianan.

CIARAN (Irish) Black hair. *Variations:* Ciardha, Ciarrai, Kieran.

CIBOR (Hebrew) Strong.

CICERO (Latin) Chickpea. *Variations:* Ciceron, Cicerone.

CILOMBO (African) Camp near the road.

CINNEIDID (Irish) Helmet head. The Anglicized version of this name is Kennedy. *Variations:* Cinneide, Cinneidigh.

CIRO (Spanish) Throne.

CISCO (Spanish) Short form of Francisco.

CLANCY (Irish) Red-headed soldier. *Variation:* Clancey.

CLARENCE (English) Clear. *Notable:* U.S. Supreme Court Justice Clarence Thomas. *Variations:* Clair, Clarance, Clare, Clarey.

CLARK (English) Scholar. *Notables:* Actor Clark Gable; Superman's Clark Kent. *Variations:* Clarke, Clerc, Clerk.

CLARKSON (English) Scholar's son. *Variations:* Clarkston, Claxton.

CLAUDE (Latin) With a limp. *Notables:* Composer Claude Debussy; artist Claude Monet. *Variations:* Claud, Claudian, Claudianus, Claudio, Claudius, Klaude, Klaudio, Klaudius.

CLAUS (German) Victorious. Short form of Nicholas. *Variations:* Claas, Clause, Klaus.

CLAY (English) Maker of clay. *Notable:* Singer Clay Aiken.

Boys' Names from Popular Songs

Here's a list of popular songs that include names of boys in the titles, along with who performed the ditties:

Abraham, Martin, and John —Dion
Alejandro—Lady Gaga
Alfie—Lily Allen
Bad, Bad Leroy Brown—Jim Croce
Charlie Brown—The Coasters
Chuck E's in Love—Rickie Lee Jones
Daniel—Elton John
Eli's Coming—Three Dog Night
Fernando—ABBA
Hey Joe—Jimi Hendrix
Hey Jude—The Beatles
Jeremy—Pearl Jam
Jerome—Barenaked Ladies
Jimmy Mack—Martha & the Vandellas
Johnny Angel—Shelley Fabares
Louie, Louie—The Kingsmen
Me and Julio Down by the School-yard—Paul Simon
Mickey—Toni Basil
Oliver's Army—Elvis Costello
Stephen—Ke$ha
Sweet Baby James—James Taylor
Tom Dooley—The Kingston Trio
Uncle Albert/Admiral Halsey— Paul McCartney
Vincent—Don McLean

Top Names in the Netherlands

BOYS:
1. Sem
2. Lucas
3. Milan
4. Daan
5. Jayden
6. Tim
7. Levi
8. Thomas
9. Thijs
10. Jesse

GIRLS:
1. Sophie
2. Julia
3. Emma
4. Lotte
5. Eva
6. Lisa
7. Lieke
8. Sanne
9. Noa
10. Anna

CLAYBORNE (English) Of the clay. *Variations:* Claiborne, Claiburn, Clayburn.

CLAYTON (English) Town of clay. *Variations:* Clayten, Claytin.

CLEARY (Irish) Learned. *Variation:* Clearey.

CLEAVON (English) Cliff. *Notable:* Actor Cleavon Little. *Variations:* Cleavan, Cleaven, Cleaver, Cleavin, Clevan, Cleven, Clevin, Clevon, Clevyn.

CLEDWYN (Welsh) Rough and blessed. River in Wales. *Variation:* Cledwin.

CLEMENT (Latin) Merciful. *Variations:* Clem, Cleme, Clemen, Clemence, Clemens, Clemente, Clementius, Clemento, Clemmie, Clemmons, Clemmy.

CLEON (Greek) Famous.

CLETUS (Greek) Illustrious. *Variation:* Cleytus.

CLEVELAND (English) Land of the cliffs. *Notable:* Writer/animal rights activist Cleveland Amory. *Variation:* Cleaveland.

CLIAMAIN (Scottish) Gentle.

CLIFF (English) From the cliff. Short form of Clifford or Clifton.

CLIFFORD (English) Ford near a cliff. *Notables:* Singer Cliff Richard; writer Clifford Irving; actor Cliff Robertson; children's book character *Clifford the Big Red Dog*. *Variations:* Cliff, Clyff, Clyfford.

CLIFTON (English) Town near a cliff. *Variations:* Clift, Clyfton.

CLINT (English) Short for Clinton. *Notables:* Actor/director Clint Eastwood; singer Clint Black.

CLINTON (English) Town on a hill. *Variations:* Clindon, Clintan, Clinten, Clintin.

CLIVE (English) Cliff. *Notables:* Actor Clive Owen; music mogul Clive Davis. *Variation:* Clyve.

CLOVIS (German) Famous soldier.

CLUNY (Irish) Meadow. *Variations:* Cluney, Clunie.

CLYDE (Scottish) River in Scotland. *Variation:* Clydell.

COBB (English) Heel. *Variation:* Cob.

COBHAM (English) Homestead near a river bend.

COBY A form of Jacob. *Notables:* Soccer player Cobi Jones; basketball player Kobe Bryant. *Variations:* Cob, Cobby, Cobey, Cobi, Cobie, Kobe.

COBURN (English) Place where streams meet. *Variations:* Cobern, Coberne, Cobirn, Cobirne, Cobourn, Cobourne, Coburne, Cobyrne.

COCHISE (Native American) Wood.

CODY (English) Cushion. *Variations:* Codey, Codie, Coty, Kodey, Kodie, Kody.

COHEN (Hebrew) High position in the Jewish faith. *Variations:* Coen, Cohan.

COILEAN (Irish) Puppy. *Variation:* Cuilean.

COINNEACH (Irish) Handsome. *Variation:* Canice.

COISEAM (Scottish) Stable, steady.

COLBERT (English) Mariner. *Variations:* Colvert, Culbert.

COLBRAND (English) Black sword. *Variations:* Colbran, Colbrandt, Colbrant.

COLBY (English) Dark farm. *Variations:* Colbey, Colbie.

COLE (English) Coal miner; (Irish) Young. *Notable:* Composer Cole Porter.

COLEMAN (English) Dove. *Variations:* Clumhan, Cole, Colman.

COLIN (Irish) A young boy. *Notables:* Actors Colin Firth and Colin Farrell; comedian Colin Quinn. *Variations:* Colan, Cole, Collin, Collins, Colyn.

COLLEY (English) Dark. *Variation:* Collis.

COLLIER (English) Coal miner. *Variations:* Colier, Collyer.

COLLINGWOOD (English) Forest.

COLM (Irish) Dove. *Variations:* Colum, Columba.

COLONEL (English) Military designation.

COLSON (English) Victory. Son of Nicholas.

COLTON (English) From the coal town. *Variations:* Colt, Coltan, Colten.

COLVILLE (French) Town in France. *Variations:* Colvile, Colvill.

COLVIN (English) Coal miner.

COLWYN (Welsh) River in Wales.

COMAN (Arabic) Noble.

COMHGHALL (Irish) Hostage.

COMHGHAN (Irish) Twin. *Variation:* Comdhan.

COMPTON (English) Town in the valley.

CONAIRE (Irish) Wise. *Variations:* Conary, Connery, Conrey, Conroy, Conry.

CONALL (Irish) High and mighty. *Variations:* Conal, Conell, Connell.

CONAN (Irish) Exalted. *Notable:* TV host Conan O'Brien. *Variation:* Conant.

CONARY (Irish) Last name.

CONCETTO (Italian) Refers to the Immaculate Conception.

CONCHOBHAR (Irish) Strong dog. *Variations:* Concobhar, Conquhare.

CONG (Chinese) Smart.

CONLAN (Irish) Hero. *Variations:* Conlen, Conley, Conlin, Conlon.

CONN (Irish) Wisdom.

CONNLAODH (Irish) Pure fire. *Variations:* Connlaoi, Connlaoth.

CONNOR (Irish) Longing. *Variations:* Conner, Connie, Conor.

CONRAD (German) Courageous adviser. *Variations:* Conn, Connie, Conny, Conrade, Conrado, Konrad.

CONROY (Irish) Wise man.

CONSTANTINE (Latin) Stable, steady. *Variations:* Constant, Constantin, Constantino, Constantinos, Costa, Konstantin, Konstanz.

CONWAY (Irish) Hound of the plain. *Notable:* Conway Twitty.

COOK (English) Cook. *Variation:* Cooke.

COOPER (English) Barrel maker. *Variation:* Kooper.

CORBETT (Latin) Black haired. *Variations:* Corbitt, Corbet, Corbit.

CORBIN (Latin) Raven. *Notable:* Actor Corbin Bernsen. Corban, Corben, Corby.

CORCORAN (Irish) Ruddy.

CORDELL (English) Rope maker. *Variation:* Cordel.

CORDERO (Spanish) Little lamb.

COREY (Irish) The hollow. *Notables:* Actor Corey Feldman; singer Corey Hart. *Variations:* Corie, Corin, Corky, Correy, Corry, Cory, Korey.

CORLISS (English) Generous. *Variation:* Corley.

CORMAC (Irish) Raven's son.

CORMAG (Scottish) Raven.

CORMICK (Gaelic) Chariot driver. *Variations:* Cormac, Cormack, Cormich.

CORNELIUS (Greek) Cornell tree. *Variations:* Cornelio, Cornelis, Cornellus, Corney, Kornelius.

CORNELL (English) Town name. A college. *Variations:* Cornal, Cornall, Cornel, Corneille.

CORNWALLIS (English) From Cornwall.

CORRADO (Italian) A form of Conrad. *Variation:* Carrado.

CORRIGAN (Irish) Spearman. *Variations:* Carrigan, Corigan, Korrigan.

CORRIN (Latin) Carries a spear. *Variations:* Coren, Corin, Corion, Corren, Coryn.

CORT (German) Courageous. *Variations:* Corte, Court, Kort.

CORWIN (English) Friend of the heart. *Variations:* Corwyn, Corwynn.

CORYELL (English) One who wears a helmet. *Variations:* Coriell, Coridan.

COSGROVE (Irish) Champion. *Variation:* Cosgrave.

COSMO (Greek) Orderly. *Variations:* Cos, Cosimo, Cosme.

COSTA (Greek) Stable, steady. *Variations:* Costas, Kostas.

COTY (French) Slope. *Variations:* Cote, Cotey, Cotie, Cottey, Cottie, Cotty, Koty.

COULSON (English) Triumphant people. *Variation:* Colson.

COURTLAND (English) Court land. *Variations:* Cortland, Cortlandt, Courtlandt.

COURTNEY (English) One who lives in the court. *Variations:* Cortney, Courtenay, Courteney, Courtnay.

COVELL (English) Hill with a cave.

COVINGTON (English) Town with a cove.

COWAN (Irish) Hillside. *Variations:* Cowen, Cowyn.

COY (English) Forest.

COYLE (Irish) Battle leader. *Variation:* Coyne.

CRADDOCK (Welsh) Love. *Variations:* Caradoc, Craddoc, Craddoch.

CRAIG (Gaelic) Rock. *Notable:* Actor Craig T. Nelson. *Variations:* Craeg, Craegg, Craige, Graigg, Kraig.

CRANDALL (English) Valley of cranes. *Variations:* Crandal, Crandell.

CRANE (English) A crane bird. *Variations:* Crain, Craine, Crayn, Crayne.

CRANLEY (English) Meadow with the cranes. *Variations:* Cranleigh, Cranly.

CRANOG (Welsh) A heron.

CRANSTON (English) Community of cranes.

CRAVEN (Celtic) Stony region.

CRAWFORD (English) Ford of crows.

CREIGHTON (English) Town near a crag. *Variations:* Crayton, Crichton.

CREON (Greek) Prince.

CRESSWELL (English) River of watercress. *Variation:* Creswell.

CREVAN (Irish) Fox. *Variations:* Creven, Crevin, Crevon, Crevyn.

CRISDEAN (Scottish) Christ.

CRISPIN (Latin) Curly hair. *Notable:* Actor Crispin Glover. *Variations:* Crepin, Crispen, Crispian, Crispino, Crispo, Crispus, Krispin.

CROFTON (Irish) Town with cottages. *Variation:* Croft.

CROMWELL (English) Twisting stream.

CRONAN (Greek) Companion.

CROSBY (Scandinavian) By the cross. *Variations:* Crosbey, Crosbie.

CROSLAND (English) Land of the cross. *Variation:* Crossland.

CROSLEY (English) Meadow with a cross. *Variations:* Croslea, Crosleigh, Crossley.

CROWTHER (English) Fiddler.

CRUZ (Spanish) Cross.

CTIBOR (Czech) Honorable fight. *Variation:* Ctik.

CUINN (Irish) Wisdom.

CULLEN (Irish) Handsome. *Variations:* Cullan, Cullin.

CULVER (English) Dove. *Variation:* Colver.

CUMHAIGE (Scottish) Hound of the plain.

CUNNINGHAM (Irish) Village with a milk pail.

CURCIO (Spanish) Friendly.

CURRAN (Irish) Hero. *Variations:* Curan, Curren, Currin.

CURRO (Spanish) Frenchman.

CURT (English) Courteous. Short form of Curtis. *Variation:* Kurt.

CURTIS (French) Courteous. *Variations:* Curtiss, Kurtis.

CUTHBERT (English) Brilliant. *Variations:* Cuthberte, Cuthburt.

CUTLER (English) Maker of knives. *Variation:* Cutty.

CUYLER (Irish) Chapel. *Variation:* Cuiler.

CWRIG (Welsh) Master.

CY Short form of Cyrus. *Notables:* Songwriter Cy Coleman; baseball player/manager Denton True "Cy" Young. *Variation:* Sy.

CYNAN (Welsh) Chief. *Variations:* Cinan, Cinon, Cynon, Cynyn, Kynan.

CYNDEYRN (Welsh) Head chief.

CYPRIAN (Greek) Man from Cyprus. *Variations:* Cipriano, Cyprianus, Cyprien.

CYRANO (Greek) From Cyrene. *Notable:* Literature's Cyrano de Bergerac. *Variation:* Cirano.

CYRIL (Greek) Lordly. *Notables:* Actors Cyril Cusack and Cyril Ritchard. *Variations:* Cirilio, Cirillo, Cirilo, Cyrill, Cyrille, Cyrillus.

CYRUS (Persian) Sun. *Notables:* Inventor Cyrus McCormick; former U.S. Secretary of State Cyrus Vance. *Variations:* Ciro, Cyris, Syris, Syrus.

CYSTENIAN (Welsh) Stable, steady.

CZCIBOR (Polish) Fight with honor. *Variations:* Cibor, Gcibor.

CZESLAW (Polish) Honor and glory. *Variations:* Czech, Czesiek.

DABI (Basque) Beloved. A form of David. *Variations:* Dabee, Dabey, Dabie, Daby.

DABIR (African) Teacher. *Variations:* Dabar, Dabyr.

DACE (English) Noble. *Variations:* Daice, Dayce.

DACEY (Gaelic) A man from the south. *Variations:* Dace, Dacee, Dacia, Dacian, Dacie, Dacy.

DACIAN (Latin) One from Dacia in Rome.

DACSO (Hungarian) God judges.

DADA (African) Child with curly hair.

DAEGAN (Gaelic) Black haired. *Variations:* Daegen, Daegin, Daegon, Daegyn, Daigan, Daigen, Daigin, Daigyn, Daygan, Daygen, Daygin, Daygon, Daygyn.

DAFYDD (Welsh) Beloved. *Variations:* Dafid, Dafidd, Dafyd.

DAG (Scandinavian) Day. *Notable:* Nobel Peace Prize recipient Dag Hammarskjold. *Variations:* Daeg, Dagen, Dagny.

DAGAN (Hebrew) Earth. *Variations:* Dagen, Dagin, Dagon.

DAGDA (Gaelic) Good spirit. *Variation:* Dagdah.

DAGWOOD (English) Bright forest. *Notable:* Dagwood Bumpstead, character in the comic strip *Blondie*.

DAHY (Irish) Capable. *Variations:* Daithi, Daiy.

DAI (Japanese) Large; (Welsh) To shine.

DAIBHIDH (Irish) Beloved. *Variations:* Daibhid, Daith, Daithi, Daithm.

DAIRE (Irish) Last name.

DAIVAT (Hindi) Powerful.

DAIVIK (Hindi) Divine.

DAKARAI (African) Happiness.

DAK-HO (Korean) Deep lake.

DAKOTA (Native American) Friend.

DAKSH (Hindi) Competent.

DALAL (Hindi) Salesman.

DALBERT (English) Bright one. *Variations:* Dalbirt, Dalburt, Delbert.

DALE (English) One who lives in a dale. *Notables:* Self-improvement motivator Dale Carnegie; racecar driver Dale Earnhardt. *Variations:* Dal, Daley, Daly, Dayle.

DALFON (Hebrew) Raindrop. *Variation:* Dalphon.

DALIBOR (Czech) To fight far away. *Variations:* Dal, Dalek.

DALLAN (Irish) Unseeing. *Variations:* Daelan, Daelen, Daelin, Dailan, Dailen, Dailin, Dalan, Dalain, Dallen, Dallin, Dallyn, Dalyn.

DALLAS (Scottish) Waterfall. Town in Scotland. *Variations:* Dalles, Dallis, Dalys.

DALLIN (English) Proud. *Variations:* Dalan, Dallan, Dallen, Dallon, Dalon.

DALTON (English) A town in a valley. *Variations:* Dallton, Dalston, Dalten.

DALY (Irish) To gather together. *Variations:* Dailey, Daley.

DALZIEL (Scottish) A small field. *Variation:* Dalzil.

DAMARCUS (African American) Combination of prefix "Da" and first name "Marcus."

DAMARIO (Spanish) Gentle. *Variation:* Demario.

DAMEK (Czech) Red earth.

DAMIAN (Greek) Tame. *Variations:* Dameon, Damiano, Damien, Damion, Damyan, Damyen, Damyon.

DAMODAR (Hindi) Rope around the abdomen.

DAMON (Greek) Loyal one. *Notable:* Damon Runyon. *Variations:* Daemon, Daimen, Daimon, Daman, Damen, Damone, Daymon.

DAN (Hebrew) God is my judge. Short form of Daniel. *Variation:* Dann.

DANA (English) From Denmark. *Notables:* Comedian Dana Carvey; actor Dana Andrews.

DANAUS (Greek) Ancient mythological king.

DANBY (Norse) From the Dane's settlement.

DANCEL (Dutch) God is my judge. *Variations:* Dansel, Dansil.

DANDIN (Hindi) Holy. *Variations:* Dandan, Danden, Dandon, Dandyn.

DANDRE (French) Courageous. A form of Andre and Andrew. *Variations:* Dandrae, Dandras, Dandray, D'Andre.

DANE (English) From Denmark. *Notable:* Actor Dane Clark. *Variations:* Dain, Dayne.

DANFORTH (English) Town in Britain.

Zodiac Baby: Names by Astrological Sign (Part I)

If you enjoy following your daily horoscope, you might also like to consider a name for your baby that's influenced by the astrological sign under which he (or she) is born.

ARIES

BOYS:	GIRLS:
Benjamin	Rachel
Mark	Scarlett
Simon	Holly

TAURUS

BOYS:	GIRLS:
Edmund	April
Maurice	Lily
Moss	Georgia

GEMINI

BOYS:	GIRLS:
Bernard	Beryl
Albert	Crystal
Robert	Laurel

CANCER

BOYS:	GIRLS:
Andrew	Crystal
Gabriel	Delilah
Matt	Luna

DANG (Vietnamese) Valuable.

DANIEL (Hebrew) God is my judge. *Notables:* American frontiersman Daniel Boone; writer Daniel Defoe; actor Daniel Day-Lewis. *Variations:* Dan, Danakas, Danek, Danel, Danelo, Daniele, Daniels, Danil, Danila, Danilkar, Danilo, Danko, Dannel, Dannie, Danniel, Dannol, Danny, Dano, Danya, Danyel, Danylets, Danylo, Dasco, Donois, Dusan.

DANIOR (Gypsy) Born with teeth. *Variation:* Danyor.

DANLADI (African) Born on Sunday.

DANNO (Japanese) Meeting in a pasture. *Variations:* Danan, Danen, Danin, Dannan, Dannen, Dannin, Dannon, Dano, Danon.

DANNY (Hebrew) God is my judge. Short form of Daniel. *Notables:* Comedians Danny DeVito, Danny Kaye, and Danny Thomas. *Variations:* Danney, Dannie.

DANTE (Latin) Everlasting. *Notables:* Poet Dante Alighieri; artist Dante Gabriel Rossetti. *Variations:* D'Anton, Danton, Dontae, Donte.

DANVEER (Hindi) Benevolent.

DAR (Hebrew) Pearl.

DARA (Cambodian) Stars.

DARBY (English) Area where deer graze. *Variations:* Dar, Darb, Derby.

DARCY (Irish) Dark one. *Variations:* Darce, Darcey, D'Arcy, Darsey, Darsy.

DARD (Greek) Son of Zeus.

DAREH (Persian) Wealthy.

DAREIOS (Greek) Persian king.

DAREN (Nigerian) Born at night.

DARENCE (Irish) Great. *Variations:* Darance, Darrance, Darrence.

DARIN (Greek) Gift. *Variations:* Dare, Daron, Darren, Darrin, Darron.

DARIUS (Greek) Wealthy. *Notable:* Singer Darius Rucker from Hootie & the Blowfish. *Variations:* Dairus, Darieus, Dario, Darioush, Darrias, Darrios, Darrious, Darris, Darrius, Darrus, Darus.

DARNELL (English) Hidden area. *Variations:* Darnal, Darnall, Darnel.

DARRAGH (Irish) Black oak. *Variation:* Darrah.

DARREN (Gaelic) Great. *Notables:* Actor Darren McGavin; Darrin Stephens, husband on TV's *Bewitched*. *Variations:* Daran, Daren, Darian, Darien, Darin, Darion, Daron, Darran, Darrian, Darrien, Darrin, Darrion, Darron, Darrun, Darryn, Darun, Daryn.

DARRICK (English) Ruler of the land. *Variations:* Darik, Darrik.

DARRIE (Irish) Red hair. *Variations:* Darie, Darry.

DARRYL (English; French) Darling. *Notables:* Baseball player Darryl Strawberry; singer Daryl Hall. *Variations:* Daral, Darall, Darel, Darell, Daril, Darile, Darill, Darral, Darrel, Darrell, Darril, Darrill, Darrol, Darryll, Daryl, Daryle, Daryll.

DARSHAN (Hindi) Clarity. *Variation:* Darshon.

DARTON (English) Deer town. *Variations:* Dartan, Darten, Dartin, Dartyn.

DARVELL (English) From the town of eagles. *Variations:* Darvel, Darvil, Darvill, Darvyl.

DARVIN (French) Dearest friend. *Variations:* Darvan, Darven, Darvon, Darvyn.

DARWESHI (African) Devout.

DARWIN (English) Friend. *Variations:* Darvin, Derwin, Derwynn.

DASAN (Native American) Chief. *Variation:* Dassan.

DASHAWN (African American) Combination of prefix "Da" and first name "Shawn."

DASHIELL (French) Page Boy. *Notable:* Writer Dashiell Hammett. *Variation:* Dash.

DATIEL (Hebrew) What God knows.

DAUD (Hindi) Beloved.

DAUDI (African) Beloved.

DAVID (Hebrew) Cherished. *Notables:* Singer David Bowie; TV host David Letterman; soccer star David Beckham. *Variations:* Daeved, Daevid, Daevyd, Daibiah, Daived, Daivid, Daivyd, Dave, Daveed, Davi, Davidas, Davidd, Davidde, Davide, Davidek, Davidos, Davidus, Davie, Daviel, Daviot, Davood, Davy, Davyd, Davydas, Davydd, Davyde, Davydos, Davydus, Davyn, Dawed, Dawfydd.

DAVIN (Scandinavian) Shining. *Variations:* Davan, Daven, Davon, Davyn.

DAVIS (English) Son of David. *Variations:* Davidson, Davies, Davison, Davys.

DAVIT (Armenian) Beloved. Form of David.

DAWSON (English) Son of David. *Variation:* Dawsen.

DAWUD (Arabic) Beloved. *Variation:* Dawudd.

DAX (English) Water.

DAYANAND (Hindi) Compassionate joy.

DAYARAM (Hindi) One who is pleased by being compassionate.

DAYLON (American) Pride. Form of Dallin. *Variations:* Daelon, Dailon, Dallin, Daylen, Delon.

DAYTON (English) Illuminated town.

DE (Chinese) Virtue.

DEACON (Greek) Servant. *Variations:* Deakin, Deke, Dekel, Dekle.

DEAGAN (English) Able. *Variation:* Deegan.

DEAN (English) Valley. *Notable:* Singer Dean Martin. *Variations:* Deane, Dene.

DEANDRE (French) Courageous. Form of Dandre.

DEANGELO (Italian) From the angel. *Variations:* D'Angelo, Dangelo, DiAngelo.

DEARBORN (English) River of deer. *Variations:* Dearbourn, Dearbourne, Deerborn.

DECHA (Thai) Powerful.

DECIMUS (Latin) The tenth.

DECLAN (Irish) Irish saint. *Variations:* Daclan, Deaclan.

DECO (Hungarian) Lord.

DEDRICK (German) Ruler of the people. *Variations:* Deadric, Deadrick, Dederic, Dederick, Dedryk.

DEEMS (English) Child of a judge. *Variation:* Deams.

DEGATAGA (Native American) Gathering.

DEJUAN (African American) Combination of prefix "De" and first name "John." *Variations:* DaJuan, Dawon, Dewaun, Dewon, D'Juan, Dujuan, D'Won.

DEKEL (Arabic) Palm tree.

DEKER (Hebrew) To pierce.

DELANEY (Irish) Child of a competitor. *Variations:* Delaine, Delainey, Delainy, Delane, Delany.

DELANO (Irish) Black man; also could mean "of the night."

DELBERT (English) Sunny day. *Notable:* Singer Delbert McClinton.

DELFINO (Italian) Dolphin. *Variations:* Delfin, Delfine, Delfyn, Delphin, Delphine, Delphino, Delphinus, Delphyn.

DELEWIS (African American) Combination of prefix "De" and first name "Lewis." *Variation:* DLewis.

DELL (English) Valley. *Notables:* Baseball player Del Unser; rock-and-roll singer Del Shannon. *Variation:* Del.

DELLINGER (Scandinavian) Day spring.

DELMAR (Spanish) Oceanside. *Variations:* Delmer, Delmor, Delmore.

DELMON (French) From the mountain. *Variations:* Dalman, Dalmen, Dalmin, Dalmon, Dalmyn, Delman, Delmen, Delmin, Delmyn.

DELON (African American) Unknown definition. *Variations:* Deelon, DeLon, DeLonn, Delonn, Dlon, DLonn.

DELROY (French) Of the king. *Variations:* Dalroi, Dalroy, Delroi.

DELSIN (Native American) He is so. *Variations:* Delsan, Delsen, Delson, Delsy.

DELVIN (English) Good friend. *Variations:* Dalwin, Dalwyn, Delavan, Delevan, Delwyn, Delwynn.

DEMA (Russian) Calm.

DEMARCO (Italian; American) Of Mark. *Variations:* Damarcus, Demarcus, Demario, Demarkis, Demarkus, D'Marcus.

DEMETRIUS (Greek) Lover of the earth. *Variations:* Demeter, Demetre, Demetri, Demetrio, Demetrios, Demetris, Demetrois, Dimetre, Dimitri, Dimitry, Dmitri, Dmitrios, Dmitry.

DEMOS (Greek) People. *Variations:* Demostenes, Demosthenes.

DEMOTHI (Native American) Talks while walking.

DEMPSEY (Irish) Proud. *Variations:* Dempsie, Dempsy.

DEMPSTER (English) Judge.

DENBY (Scandinavian) Denmark village. *Variations:* Danby, Denbey.

DENHAM (English) Town in a dell.

DENHOLM (Scottish) Village in Scotland. *Notable:* Actor Denholm Elliott.

DENIZ (Turkish) Ocean that flows.

DENLEY (English) Meadow near a valley. *Variations:* Denlie, Denly.

DENMAN (English) Dweller of a valley.

DENNIS (Greek) English form of Latin "Dionysius": follower of Dionysos. *Notables:* Actor Dennis Quaid; comedian Dennis Miller. *Variations:* Denas, Denes, Denies, Denis, Denka, Dennas, Dennes, Dennys, Denys.

DENNISON (English) Son of Dennis. *Variations:* Denison, Dennyson, Dyson.

DENNY Short form of Dennis. *Notable:* Singer Denny Doherty of the Mamas and the Papas. *Variations:* Denney, Dennie.

DENTON (English) Valley town. *Variations:* Dent, Denten, Dentin.

DENVER (English) Green valley.

DENZEL (English) From a town in Cornwall, England. *Notable:* Actor Denzel Washington. *Variations:* Denzal, Denzall, Denzell, Denziel, Denzil, Denzill, Denzyl.

DENZO (Japanese) Discreet. *Variation:* Denzio.

DEONTAE (American) Newly created. *Variations:* D'Ante, Deante, Deonte, Diante, Diontay, Dionte, Donte.

DEORSA (Scottish) Farmer.

DEQUAN (Native American) Fragrant.

DERBY (English) Village with deer.

DEREK (German) Gifted ruler. *Notables:* Baseball player Derek Jeter; actor Derek Jacobi. *Variations:* Derec, Dereck, Derick, Derik, Derrec, Derreck, Derrek, Derric, Derrick, Derrik, Deryck, Deryk.

DERMOT (Irish) Free of jealousy. *Notable:* Actor Dermot Mulroney. *Variations:* Dermod, Dermont, Dermott.

DERON (Hebrew) Bird. *Variations:* Daron, Daronn, Dereon, Deronne, Derron.

DEROR (Hebrew) Independence. *Variation:* Derorie.

DERRY (Irish) Redheaded.

DERWARD (English) Deer herder. *Variations:* Derwood, Dirwood, Durward, Durwood.

DERWIN (English) Good friend. *Variations:* Darwin, Darwyn, Derwynn, Durwin.

DESHAD (Hindi) Nation. *Variations:* Deshal, Deshan.

DESHAWN (African American) Combination of prefix "De" and first name "Shawn." *Variations:* DaShaun, Dashawn, DeSean, DeShaun, Deshaun, Dusean, Dushaun, Dushawn.

DESHI (Chinese) Moral.

DESI (Spanish) Desired; (Irish) Short form of Desmond. *Notable:* Actor/singer Desi Arnaz. *Variations:* Desey, Desie, Dezey, Dezi, Dezie.

DESMOND (Irish) From South Munster, a region of Ireland. *Notables:* South African archbishop Desmond Tutu; writer Desmond Morris. *Variations:* Desmund, Dezmond, Dezmund.

DESTIN (French) Fate. *Variations:* Destan, Desten, Deston.

DEUTSCH (German) From Germany. *Variation:* Deutch.

DEVAK (Hindi) God.

DEVAL (Hindi) Divine.

DEVANAND (Hindi) Joy from the gods.

DEVDAS (Hindi) God's servant.

DEVEN (Hindi) God. *Variation:* Diven.

DEVENDRA (Hindi) God of the sky.

DEVERALL (English) Riverbank.

DEVIN (Irish) Poet. *Variations:* Deavin, Dev, Devan, Devon, Devonn, Devyn.

DEVINE (Irish) Ox.

DEVLIN (Irish) Courageous. *Variations:* Devland, Devlen, Devlyn.

DEVMANI (Hindi) Gem from God.

DEVRAJ (Hindi) Ruler of the gods.

DEWAYNE (African American) Combination of prefix "De" and first name "Wayne." *Variations:* DeWayne, D'Wayne.

DEWEY (Welsh) Cherished. *Variations:* Dewi, Dewie, Dewy, Duey.

DEWITT (Flemish) Blond. *Notable:* Politician DeWitt Clinton.

DEXTER (Latin) Right handed. *Variation:* Dex.

DEZYDERY (Polish) To desire.

DHATRI (Sanskrit) Creator.

DHAVAL (Hindi) White. *Variations:* Dhavlen, Dhavlesh.

DHIMANI (Hindi) Smart. *Variations:* Dheemant, Dhimant.

DIALLO (African) Bold.

DIAMOND (English) Jewel.

DIARMAD (Scottish) Freeman.

DIARMAID (Irish) Free. *Variations:* Dermod, Dermot, Dermott.

DIARMUID (Irish) Free of jealousy.

DICHALI (Native American) Speaks later.

DICK (German) Short form of Richard, Frederick. *Notables:* TV hosts Dick Cavett and Dick Clark; U.S. Vice President Dick Cheney; comedian Dick Martin.

DICKENS (English) Last name. *Variations:* Dickon, Dickons.

DIDIER (French) Desired.

DIEDERIK (Scandinavian) Ruler of the people. *Variations:* Diderik, Didrik, Dierk.

DIEGO (Spanish) Form of James. *Notable:* Artist Diego Rivera.

DIETER (German) People's army.

DIETRICH (German) Leader of the people. *Variations:* Detric, Detrich, Detrick, Diedrich, Diedrik.

DIEU HIEN (Vietnamese) Amaryllis flower.

DIGBY (Irish) Village by a ditch. *Variations:* Digbe, Digbee, Digbey, Digbi, Digbie.

DIJON (French) City in France.

DILIP (Hindi) Protector.

DILLON (Irish) Loyal. *Variations:* Dilan, Dilen, Dilin, Dillan, Dillen, Dillin, Dillon, Dillyn, Dilon, Dilyn.

DILWYN (Welsh) Blessed truth. *Variations:* Dilwin, Dillwin, Dillwyn.

DIMA (Russian) Powerful warrior. *Variations:* Dimka, Dyma.

DIMITRI (Russian) Lover of the earth. *Variations:* Dimitr, Dimitre, Dimitrios, Dimitry, Dmitri.

DIN (Vietnamese) Calm. *Variation:* Dinh.

DINESH (Hindi) God of the day.

DINGBANG (Chinese) Protect the country.

DINO (Italian) Small sword. Nickname for Dean. *Variation:* Deno.

DINSMORE (Irish) Fort on the hill. *Variations:* Dinsmoor, Dinsmoore.

DION (Greek) Short form of Dionysus. *Notable:* Football player Deion Sanders. *Variations:* Deion, DeOn, Deon.

DIONYSUS (Latin) God of wine. *Variations:* Dionis, Dionusios, Dionysius.

Begins with "Da" or "De"

For boys, adding "Da" or "De" (or even "D'") to the beginning of a popular name will create a trendy new alternative. "Shawn" can become "Dashawn" or "Deshawn" or "D'Shawn." Here are some popular boys' names to give you some ideas:

Dajohn	Deangelo
Dajuan	Deanthony
Damarcus	Dejuan
Damario	Dejon
Dantrell	Demarco
Daquan	Deonte
(or Daquon)	Dequan
Dashawn	Deshane
(or Dashon)	Deshawn
Davonte	Dewayne
Deandre	

DIPAK (Hindi) Lamp. *Notable:* Motivational speaker/writer Deepak Chopra. *Variation:* Deepak.

DIRK (German) Dagger. *Notable:* Actor Dirk Bogarde.

DISHI (Chinese) Virtuous man.

DISHON (Hebrew) Walk upon.

DIVES (English) Rich man. *Variation:* Divers.

DIVON (Hebrew) To walk gently.

DIVYENDU (Hindi) The moon.

DIWALI (Native American) Bowl.

DIXON (English) Son of powerful ruler. *Variation:* Dickson.

DIYA (Arabic) To shine.

DOANE (English) Hilly area. *Variation:* Doan.

DOB (English) Brilliant.

DOBIESLAW (Polish) Striving for glory.

DOBROMIERZ (Polish) Good and famous.

DOBROMIL (Czech, Polish) Good grace.

DOBROMIR (Czech) Good fame.

DOBROSLAV (Czech) Good glory.

DOBROSLAW (Polish) Good glory.

DOBRY (Polish) Good. *Variations:* Dobri, Dobrie.

DOCTOR (English) Physician. Teacher.

DODEK (Polish) Gift.

DOHASAN (Native American) Cliff. *Variations:* Dohate, Dohosan.

DOHERTY (Irish) Wicked. *Variation:* Dougherty.

DOLAIDH (Scottish) Ruler of the world. *Variation:* Domhnall.

DOLAN (Irish) Dark hair.

DOLPH (German) Short form of Adolph. Fierce wolf. *Notable:* Actor/ martial artist Dolph Lundgren. *Variations:* Dolf, Dolfe, Dolff, Dolffe.

DOM (Latin) Lord. Short form of Dominick. *Variation:* Domm.

DOMINGO (Spanish) Born on Sunday.

DOMINICK (Latin) Lord. *Notables:* Actor Dominic Chianese (Uncle Junior on TV's *The Sopranos*); comedian Dom DeLuise; writer Dominick Dunne. *Variations:* Domek, Domenic, Domenico, Domicio, Domingo, Domingos, Dominic, Dominik, Dominique, Domo, Domokos.

DON (Scottish) Mighty. Short form of Donald. *Variation:* Donn.

DONAGH (Irish) Brown warrior. *Variations:* Donaghy, Donnchadh, Donogh, Donough.

DONAHUE (Irish) Dark fighter. *Variations:* Donahoe, Donohue.

DONAL (Irish) A form of Donald.

DONALD (Scottish) Mighty. *Notables:* Real estate mogul Donald Trump; actors Donald Sutherland and Donald O'Connor; singers Donny Osmond and Donnie Wahlberg. *Variations:* Donaldo, Donalt, Donild, Donnie, Donny.

DONAT (Polish) Given by God. *Variation:* Donatus.

DONATO (Italian) Gift. *Variations:* Donat, Donatello, Donati, Donatien, Donatus.

DONEGAL (Irish) Fort of foreigners. *Variation:* Donigal.

DONG (Korean) East.

DONG-SUN (Korean) Integrity from the East.

DONG-YUL (Korean) Passion from the East.

DONNAN (Irish) Brown.

DONNCHADH (Irish) Brown warrior.

DONNELL (Irish) Brave. *Variations:* Doneal, Donel, Donell, Doniel, Donnel, Donniel, Donnyl, Donyell, Donyl.

DONNELLY (Irish) Dark-skinned man. *Variations:* Don, Donnell.

DONOVAN (Irish) Dark. *Notable:* Singer Donovan Leitch. *Variations:* Donavan, Donaven, Donavin, Donavon, Donoven, Donovin, Donovon.

DOOLEY (Irish) Dark-skinned hero. *Variations:* Dooleigh, Doolie.

DOR (Hebrew) Generation.

DORAN (Irish) Stranger. *Variations:* Doren, Dorin, Doron, Dorran, Dorren, Dorrin, Dorryn.

DORCAS (Greek) Gazelle.

DORIAN (Greek) From Doria, a region in Greece. *Notable:* Dorian Gray, character in Oscar Wilde novel. *Variations:* Dorean, Dorien, Dorion, Dorrian, Dorryen.

DORRELL (Scottish) Keeper of the king's door. *Variations:* Dorrel, Durel, Durell.

DOTAN (Hebrew) Law. *Variation:* Dothan.

DOUG (Scottish) Dark water. Short form of Douglas. *Variations:* Dougie, Dugie.

DOUGAL (Scottish) Dark-skinned stranger. *Variations:* Doogal,

Doogall, Dougald, Dougall, Dugal, Dugald, Dugall.

DOUGLAS (Gaelic) Dark water. *Notables:* General Douglas MacArthur; actor Douglas Fairbanks. *Variations:* Douglass, Duglas.

DOV (Hebrew) Peace.

DOVEV (Hebrew) Whisper.

DOVIDAS (Lithuanian) Friend.

DOW (Irish) Dark hair.

DOWAN (Irish) Black.

DOYLE (Irish) Dark stranger. *Variations:* Doile, Doyal.

DRAGOSLAV (Slavic) Dear glory.

DRAKE (English) Dragon. *Variations:* Drago, Draik.

DRAPER (English) Curtain maker.

DRENG (Scandinavian) Farm hand.

DREW (English) Wise. Form of Andrew. *Notable:* Comedian Drew Carey. *Variations:* Drewe, Dru.

DRISCOLL (Irish) Interpreter. *Variations:* Driscol, Driscole, Dryscol, Dryscoll.

DROGO (German) To carry.

DROVER (Australian) Sheep or cattle herder.

DRUCE (Welsh) Wise man's son.

DRUMMOND (Scottish) Druid's mountain. *Variations:* Drummund, Drumond, Drumund.

DRURY (French) Cherished. *Variations:* Druree, Drurey.

DRYDEN (English) Dry land. *Variations:* Driden, Dridin, Dridyn, Drydan, Drydin, Drydon, Drydyn.

DRYSTAN (Welsh) Sad. *Variation:* Dristan.

DU (Vietnamese) Play.

DUANE (Irish) Dark skinned. *Variations:* Dewain, DeWayne, Duwayne, Dwain, Dwaine, Dwane, Dwayne.

DUARTE (Portuguese) Guardian of the land. *Variation:* Duart.

DUBH (Irish) Black hair. *Variation:* Dubham.

DUBHGHALL (Scottish) Dark-haired stranger.

DUBHGLAS (Irish) Black and gray. *Variation:* Dughlas.

DUBRICK (English) Black ruler. *Variations:* Dubric, Dubrik, Dubryck.

DUC (Vietnamese) Virtuous.

DUCK-HWAN (Korean) Integrity returns.

DUCK-YOUNG (Korean) Integrity lasts.

DUDLEY (English) Field where people gather. *Notable:* Comedian Dudley Moore. *Variations:* Dudlee, Dudleigh, Dudlie, Dudly.

DUDON (Italian) Given from God. *Variations:* Dudan, Duden, Dudin, Dudun, Dudyn.

DUER (Scotttish) Hero.

DUFF (Celtic) Dark skinned. *Variations:* Duffey, Duffy.

DUGAN (Irish) Swarthy. *Variations:* Doogan, Dougan, Dougen, Douggan, Dugen, Duggan.

DUKE (English) Leader. Short version of Marmaduke.

DUKKER (Gypsy) Fortune teller. *Variation:* Duker.

DULANI (African) Cutting. *Variations:* Dulanee, Dulaney, Dulanie, Dulany.

DUMAKA (African) Help out.

DUMAN (Turkish) Smoky or misty. *Variations:* Dumen, Dumin, Dumon.

DUMICHEL (African American) Of Michael.

DUMIN (Czech) Lord.

DUMONT (French) Of the mountains.

DUNCAN (Scottish) Brown-skinned soldier. *Variations:* Dun, Dune, Dunkan, Dunkin, Dunn.

DUNHAM (Celtic) Dark-skinned man.

DUNLEY (Celtic) Meadow on a hill. *Variations:* Dunlee, Dunlie, Dunliegh, Dunly.

DUNLOP (Scottish) Muddy hill.

DUNMORE (Scottish) Fort on a hill. *Variations:* Donmore, Donmorr, Dunmoor.

DUNN (Scottish) Brown. *Variation:* Dunne.

DUNSTAN (English) Rocky hill. *Variations:* Dunsten, Dunstin, Dunston, Dunstyn.

DUNTON (English) Town on a hill. *Variations:* Duntan, Dunten, Duntin, Duntyn.

DUOC (Vietnamese) Ethical.

DUR (Hebrew) To accumulate.

DURAND (Latin) Lasting. *Variations:* Durance, Durant, Durante, Durrant.

DURBIN (Latin) City dweller. *Variations:* Durban, Durben, Derbon, Derbun, Durbyn.

DUREAU (French) Strength. *Variations:* Durea, Duryea.

DURELL (Scottish) Doorman for the King. *Variation:* Durrell.

DURIEL (Hebrew) God is my home.

DURKO (Czech) Farmer.

DURRIKEN (Gypsy) Forecaster.

DURRIL (Gypsy) Gooseberry.

DURWARD (English) Keeper of the door. *Variations:* Derward, Durwood.

DUSAN (Czech) Spirit. *Variations:* Dusa, Dusanek, Duysek.

DUSTIN (English) Warrior. *Notable:* Actor Dustin Hoffman. *Variations:* Dust, Dustan, Duston, Dustyn.

DUSTY (English) Valient. *Variations:* Dustee, Dustey, Dustie.

DUTCH (German) The German.

DWADE (English) Dark traveler. *Variations:* Dwaid, Dwaide, Dwayde.

DWAYNE (Irish) Dark one. Form of Duane.

DWIGHT (English) Blond. *Notable:* U.S. President Dwight D. Eisenhower.

DWYER (Irish) Dark and wise.

DYAMI (Native American) Eagle. *Variation:* Dyani.

DYER (English) One who dyes clothing for a living.

DYLAN (Welsh) Son of the ocean. *Notable:* Poet/writer Dylan Thomas. *Variations:* Dylen, Dylin, Dyllan, Dylon, Dylyn, Dylon.

DYNAWD (Welsh) Donation.

DYRE (Scandinavian: Norwegian) Valuable.

DYSON (English) Short form of Dennison.

DYZEK (Polish) He who loves the earth.

DZIK (Polish) Wild man.

EA (Irish) Fire. *Variations:* Eath, Eth.

EACHANN (Irish) Horse lover. *Variations:* Eachen, Eachin, Eachon, Eachyn.

EADBHARD (Irish) Wealthy protector. *Variation:* Eadbard.

EAIRRDSIDH (Scottish) Genuinely brave. *Variation:* Eairrsidh.

EALAHWEEMAH (Native American) Sleep.

EALLAIR (Scottish) Steward in a monastery. *Variation:* Ellar.

EAMON (Irish) Rich protector. *Variations:* Amon, Eaman, Eamen, Eamin, Eamman, Eammen, Eammin, Eammon, Eammun, Emmyn, Eamonn, Eamun, Eamyn, Eiman, Eimen, Eimin, Eimon, Eimyn, Eymon.

EAN (Irish) God is gracious. Form of Ian. *Variations:* Eaen, Eann, Eion, Eon, Eonn, Eyan, Eyen, Eyon, Eyyn.

EANRAIG (Scottish) Home ruler.

EARDLEY (English) Region in England. Last name. *Variation:* Eardly.

EARL (English) Leader; nobleman. *Notables:* Writer Erle Stanley Gardner; basketball player Earl Monroe, musician Earl Scruggs. *Variations:* Airle, Earld, Earle, Earlie, Earlson, Early, Erl, Erle.

EARNEST (English) Sincere. A form of Ernest.

EARVIN (English) Friend of the sea. A form of Irving. *Variations:* Earvan, Earven, Earving, Earvon, Earvyn.

EASTMAN (English) From the east.

EASTON (English) Eastern town. *Variations:* Eastan, Easten, Eastin, Eastyn.

EATON (English) Town on a river. *Variations:* Eatton, Eton, Eyton.

EBAL (Hebrew) Naked. *Variation:* Ebale.

EBEN (Hebrew) Stone. *Variations:* Eban, Ebin, Ebon, Ebyn, Even.

EBENEZER (Hebrew) Rock foundation. *Notable: A Christmas Carol*'s Ebenezer Scrooge. *Variations:* Ebbaneza, Eben, Ebeneezer, Ebeneser, Ebenezar.

EBERHARD (German) Courageous. *Variations:* Eberhardt, Evard, Everard, Everhardt, Everhart.

EBILO (German) Strong boar. *Variations:* Ebbo, Ebylo.

EBISU (Japanese) The god of labor and luck.

EBNER (Hebrew) Father of light. A form of Abner. *Variations:* Ebnar, Ebnir, Ebnor.

EBO (African) Born on Tuesday.

EBORICO (Spanish) Wild boar king. *Variation:* Eboryco.

EBRULF (German) Fierce wolf.

ECCELINO (Italian) Like his father. *Variation:* Eccelyno.

ECKHARD (German) Brave. *Notable:* Spiritual author Eckhart Tolle. *Variations:* Eckart, Eckhardt.

ED (English) Short form of Edgar, Edmund, Edward. *Notable:* Actor Ed Begley Jr. *Variation:* Edd.

EDAN (Celtic) Fire.

EDDIE (English) Guardian of property. Short form of Edward. *Notables:* Muscians Eddie Van

Halen, Eddie Vedder, and Eddy Arnold; actor Eddie Albert; comedian Eddie Murphy. *Variation:* Eddy.

EDEK (Polish) Guardian of property.

EDEL (German) Noble. *Variations:* Edell, Edelmar.

EDEN (Hebrew) Delight. *Variations:* Eaden, Eadin, Eadon, Eadyn, Edan, Edin, Edon, Edun.

EDENSAW (Native American) Glacier.

EDGAR (English) Wealthy man who holds a spear. *Notables:* "Sleeping Prophet" Edgar Cayce; writer/poet Edgar Allan Poe. *Variations:* Edgaras, Edgard, Edgardo, Edgars, Edger, Edgir, Edgor.

EDISON (English) Edward's son. *Variations:* Eddisen, Eddison, Eddyson, Edisen.

EDMUND (English) Wealthy guardian. *Notable:* Explorer Sir Edmund Hillary. *Variations:* Edman, Edmand, Edmen, Edmon, Edmond, Edmonde, Edmondo, Edmondson, Edmun, Edmundo, Edmunds, Esmond.

EDRED (English) Rich counsel. *Variation:* Edredd.

EDREI (Hebrew) Strong leader.

EDRIC (English) Powerful man who holds property. *Variations:* Eddric, Eddrick, Eddrik, Eddryck, Ederic, Ederick, Ederik, Edrice, Edrick, Edrik, Edris, Edryck.

EDSEL (English) Home of a rich man. *Variation:* Edsell.

EDSON (English) Edward's son. *Variations:* Edsen, Edsin, Edsun.

EDUR (Basque) Snow. *Variation:* Edure.

EDWALD (English) Wealthy ruler. *Variation:* Edwaldo.

EDWARD (English) Guardian of property. *Notables:* Playwright Edward Albee; actors Edward Norton and Edward Burns; artist Edouard Manet. *Variations:* Edoardo, Edouard, Eduard, Eduardo, Edvard, Edvardo, Edvood, Edwardo, Edwood, Edzio.

EDWIN (English) Rich friend. *Notable:* Singer Edwin McCain. *Variations:* Eadwin, Eadwinn, Eduino, Edwan, Edwen, Edwinn, Edwyn.

EDWY (English) War.

EDZARD (Scandinavian) Strong edge.

EFRAIN (Hebrew) Fruitful. *Variations:* Efraine, Efran, Efrane, Efrayne, Efren, Efrin.

EFRON (Hebrew) Bird. *Variation:* Ephron.

EGAN (Irish) Fiery. *Variations:* Egann, Egen, Egin, Egon, Egyn.

EGBERT (English) Bright sword. *Variations:* Egbirt, Egburt, Egbyrt.

EGEDE (Danish) Young goat. *Variations:* Eged, Egide, Egidus.

EGERTON (English) Last name. Region in Britain. *Variations:* Edgarton, Edgartwon, Egeton, Ergeryn.

EGIDIO (Italian) Young goat.

EGIDIUSZ (Polish) Protective shield.

EGIL (Scandinavian) Awe inspiring. *Variations:* Egils, Egyl, Eigel, Eygel.

EGINHARD (German) Power of the sword. *Variations:* Eginhardt, Einhard, Einhardt.

Names for Any Season

Days, months, seasons, holidays —whether your baby arrives when it's snowing or flowers are blooming, the time of year the birth occurs might inspire you to consider one of these names!

BOYS:

August
Christmas
Easter
February
Friday
January
March
Monday
Thursday
Saturday
Sunday
Winter
Valentine

GIRLS:

April
Autumn
July
June
May
November
October
September
Spring
Summer
Tuesday
Wednesday

EGMONT (English) Top of the mountain. *Variation:* Egmount.

EGON (German) Formidable.

EGOR (Russian) Farmer. Form of George. *Variation:* Igor.

EHIOZE (African) Not jealous.

EHREN (German) Honorable. *Variation:* Eren.

EHUD (Hebrew) Praised.

EIDDWEN (Welsh) Fond and faithful. *Variations:* Eiddweyn, Eidwin, Eidwyn, Eyddwyn.

EIDEARD (Scottish) Wealthy protector. *Variation:* Eudard.

EIFAH (Hebrew) Darkness. *Variations:* Efa, Efah, Eifa, Epha, Ephah.

EIFION (Welsh) Last name.

EIGNEACHAN (Irish) Strong man. *Variation:* Ighneachan.

EILAM (Hebrew) Forever. *Variation:* Elam.

EILIF (Scandinavian) Immortal. *Variation:* Eiliv.

EILWYN (Welsh) White brow. *Variation:* Eilwen.

EIMHIN (Irish) Quick.

EINAR (Scandinavian) Leader. *Variations:* Eimar, Ejar, Ejnar, Inar.

EINION (Welsh) Anvil. *Variation:* Einwys.

EINRI (Irish) Ruler at home. *Variations:* Anrai, Hannraoi, Hanraoi.

EIRIG (Welsh) Happy.

EIROS (Welsh) Bright. *Variation:* Eyros.

EISAK (Russian) Laughter. *Variation:* Eysak.

EISENBART (German) Bright iron.

EISENBOLT (German) Iron prince.

EITAN (Hebrew) A form of Ethan. *Variations:* Eithan, Eiton.

EKAANTA (Hindi) Solitude.

EKANA (Hawaiian) Strength. *Variation:* Etana.

EKEKA (Hawaiian) Wealth. *Variation:* Edega.

EKEKIELA (Hawaiian) Powerful god. *Variation:* Ezekiela.

EKELA (Hawaiian) Help. *Variation:* Ezera.

EKEMONA (Hawaiian) Rich protector. *Variations:* Edemona, Edumona, Edwada, Ekewaka, Ekualo, Ekumena.

EKER (Hebrew) Root.

EKON (Nigerian) Strength.

ELAM (Hebrew) Highland.

ELAN (Hebrew) Tree. *Variation:* Ilan.

ELBA (Italian) Area in Italy.

ELBERT (English) Noble; shining. *Variations:* Elbirt, Elburt, Elbyrt.

ELCHANAN (Hebrew) God is good. *Variations:* Elhanan, Elhannan.

ELDAD (Hebrew) Beloved of God.

ELDEN (English) Wise old friend. *Variations:* Eldan, Eldin, Eldun, Eldyn.

ELDER (English) From the elder tree.

ELDON (English) Consecrated hill.

ELDORADO (Spanish) Gilded.

ELDRED (English) Old, wise counsel. *Variations:* Eldrid, Eldryd.

ELDRIDGE (English) Wise leader. *Notable:* Black Panther Eldridge Cleaver. *Variations:* Eldredge, Eldrege, Eldrige.

ELDWIN (English) Old friend. *Variations:* Eldwen, Eldwyn.

ELEAZAR (Hebrew) God helps. *Variations:* Elezar, Eliazar, Eliezer, Elizar.

ELEBERT (English) Noble; shining.

ELEDON (English) Leader's hill.

ELEK (Hungarian) Defender of mankind. Form of Alec. *Variations:* Elec, Eleck, Elic, Elick, Elike, Elyck.

ELENEK (Hawaiian) Eager. *Variations:* Eneki, Eneti, Ereneti.

ELEUTHERIOS (Greek) Liberty. *Variation:* Eleftherios.

ELFIN (Welsh) Elf friend. *Variation:* Elfyn.

ELGAR (German) Noble spear. *Variations:* Elger, Elgir, Elgor.

ELGIN (English) White. *Variations:* Elgan, Elgen, Elgon, Elgyn.

ELI (Hebrew) God is great. *Notables:* Actor Eli Wallach; writer/activist Elie Wiesel. *Variations:* Elie, Ely.

ELIA (Hebrew) The Lord is my God. *Notable:* Film director Elia Kazan. *Variation:* Eliah.

ELIAN (English) Form of Elijah. *Variations:* Elion, Ellian, Ellion.

ELIAS (Greek) Uplifting.

ELIAZ (Hebrew) My God is powerful. *Variation:* Elias.

ELIHU (Hebrew) God.

ELIJAH (Hebrew) The Lord is my God. *Notable:* Actor Elijah Wood. *Variations:* Elek, Elias, Eliasz, Elie, Elija, Eljah, Eliya, Elya.

ELIKAI (Hawaiian) God is my salvation. *Variation:* Elisai.

ELIRAN (Hebrew) My God is song. *Variation:* Eliron.

ELISHA (Hebrew) God is my salvation. *Variations:* Elish, Elisher, Elishua.

ELIYAHU (Hebrew) The Lord is my God.

ELIZUR (Hebrew) God is my rock. *Variation:* Elyzur.

ELJASZ (Polish) God is Lord.

ELJON (Syrian) Ascending.

ELKANAH (Hebrew) God creates. *Variations:* Elkan, Elkin.

ELKI (Native American) To drape over. *Variation:* Elky.

ELLARD (German) Noble. *Variations:* Elard, Ellerd, Ellurd.

ELLERY (English) Elder trees. *Variations:* Elarie, Elary, Elery, Ellarie, Ellary, Ellerie.

ELLIOT (English) God on high. *Notables:* Actor Elliot Gould; law enforcer Eliot Ness. *Variations:* Eliot, Eliott, Eliud, Elliott.

ELLIS (English) Noble. *Variations:* Elis, Ellas, Ellys, Elys.

ELLISON (English) Son of Ellis. *Variations:* Elison, Ellyson, Elson.

ELLISTON (English) Noble town.

ELLMELECH (Hebrew) God is King.

ELLSWORTH (English) Home of a great man. *Variations:* Ellswerth, Elsworth.

ELMAN (German) Elm tree.

ELMER (English) Noble. *Notable:* Cartoon character Elmer Fudd. *Variations:* Aylmar, Aylmer, Aymer, Ellmer, Elmar, Elmir, Ulmer.

ELMO (Italian) Worthy of love.

ELMORE (English) Moor with elm trees. *Notable:* Writer Elmore Leonard. *Variations:* Ellmoor, Ellmoore, Ellmor, Ellmore, Elmoor, Elmoore.

ELOF (Scandinavian) Sole descendant. *Variations:* Elov, Eluf.

ELON (African) Spirit.

ELONI (Polynesian) Lofty.

ELONZO (Spanish) Noble. Form of Alonzo.

ELOY (Spanish) Famous warrior.

ELPIDIOS (Greek) Hope.

ELRAD (Hebrew) God is the king. *Variation:* Elrod.

ELRIC (English) Wise ruler.

ELROY (Latin) King. Form of Leroy. *Variations:* El Roy, Elroi.

ELSDON (English) From the noble's hill. *Variations:* Elsden, Elsdin, Elsdyn.

ELSTON (English) From a noble's town. *Variation:* Ellston.

ELSU (Native American) Falcon in flight.

ELSWORTH (English) From the noble's estate. *Variation:* Ellsworth.

ELTA (Hawaiian) The Lord is my God.

ELTON (English) Ella's town; old town. *Notable:* Singer/songwriter Elton John. *Variations:* Eltan, Elten, Eltin, Eltyn.

ELVERN (Latin) Spring. A form of Alvern. *Variations:* Elverne, Elvirn, Elvirne, Elvyrn, Elvyrne.

ELVET (English) Stream of swans.

ELVIN (English) Old friend. *Notable:* Singer Elvin Bishop. *Variation:* Elvyn.

ELVIS (Scandinavian) Wise sage. *Notables:* Singers Elvis Presley and Elvis Costello. *Variations:* Elviss, Elvys.

ELVY (English) Elf warrior. *Variations:* Elvey, Elvie.

ELWELL (English) Old well.

ELWIN (Welsh) Old friend.

ELWOOD (English) Old wood. *Variation:* Ellwood.

ELWYN (Welsh) Fair.

EMBER (English) Ashes.

EMEK (Hebrew) Valley.

EMERSON (German) Emery's son.

EMERY (German) Ruler of the house. *Variations:* Emmery, Emory.

EMILE (French) Eager to please. *Notable:* Writer Emile Zola. *Variations:* Emil, Emilek, Emiliano, Emilio, Emilo, Emils.

EMLYN (Welsh) Industrious. *Variation:* Emlin.

EMMANUEL (Hebrew) God is among us. *Variations:* Eman, Emanual, Emanuel, Emanuele, Emmanuil, Immanuel, Manuel.

EMMETT (German) Powerful. *Notable:* Clown Emmett Kelly Jr. *Variations:* Emmet, Emmit, Emmitt, Emmot, Emmott.

EMOBI (Polynesian) Birth.

EMRE (Turkish) Brother.

EMRICK (German) Form of Emery. *Variations:* Emric, Emrik.

EMRYS (Welsh) Immortable. Form of Ambrose. *Variation:* Emry.

EMYR (Welsh) Ruler.

ENAM (African) Gift from God.

ENAN (Welsh) Hammer. *Variations:* Enen, Enin, Enon, Enyn.

ENAPAY (Native American) Proceeds with courage.

ENDOR (Hebrew) Endearing.

ENDRE (Greek) Courageous. A form of Andre. *Variations:* Ender, Endres.

ENDRIKAS (Lithuanian) Ruler of the house. A form of Henry. *Variations:* Endrykas.

ENEAS (Greek) Praised. A form of Aeneas.

ENECO (Latin) Fiery. A form of Ignatius.

ENGELBERT (German) Bright as an angel. *Notable:* Singer Engelbert Humperdinck. *Variations:* Engelberte, Engelbirt, Engelburt, Engelbyrt, Englebert, Engleberte, Englebirt, Engleburt, Englebyrt.

ENLAI (Chinese) Appreciation.

ENNIS (Gaelic) Island. *Variations:* Enis, Ennys, Enys.

ENOCH (Hebrew) Dedicated. *Variations:* Enock, Enok, Nucky.

ENOKA (Hawaiian) Learned.

ENOS (Hebrew) Man. *Variations:* Enosa, Enosh.

ENRICO (Italian) Leader of the house. *Notable:* Opera great Enrico Caruso. *Variations:* Enric, Enrick, Enrik, Enrikos, Enrique, Enriquez.

ENRIGHT (Irish) Unlawful son. *Variation:* Enwright.

ENSOR (English) From the blessed bank. *Variations:* Ensar, Enser.

ENVER (Turkish) Handsome.

ENYETO (Native American) Walks like a bear.

ENZI (Swahili) Powerful.

ENZO (Italian) Ruler of the home. Form of Henry. *Variation:* Enzio.

EOCHAIDH (Irish) Horseman.

EOGHAN (Scottish) Youth. *Variation:* Eoghann.

EOIN (Irish) God is good.

EPELAIMA (Hawaiian) Fertile. *Variation:* Eperaima.

EPENA (Hawaiian) Stone. *Variation:* Ebena.

EPHRAIM (Hebrew) Fertile. *Notable:* Actor Efrem Zimbalist Jr. *Variations:* Efraim, Efrain, Efrayim, Efrem, Efren, Ephraim, Ephrain, Ephrayim.

ERAN (Hebrew) Vigilant. *Variation:* Eron.

ERASMUS (Greek) Loved. *Variations:* Erasme, Erasmo, Erastus, Rasmus.

ERASTUS (Greek) Giver of love. *Variation:* Erastos.

ERBERT (German) Glorious warrior. *Variations:* Ebert, Eberto, Erberto, Erbirt, Erbirto, Erburt, Erburto.

ERCOLE (Italian) Gift. *Variation:* Ercol.

ERUBUS (Greek) Dark haired.

EREL (Hebrew) I see God.

ERHARD (German) Determination. *Variations:* Erhardt, Erhart.

ERIC (Scandinavian) Mighty ruler. *Notable:* Singer/guitarist Eric Clapton. *Variations:* Aryk, Ehric, Ehrich, Erek, Erich, Erick, Erico, Erik, Eriks, Erric, Errick, Errik.

ERICKSON (English) Son of Eric. *Variation:* Erikson.

ERLAND (English) Nobleman's land. *Variations:* Earlan, Earland, Erlan, Erlund.

ERLEND (Scandinavian) Stranger. *Variation:* Erlen.

ERLING (English) Son of a nobleman. *Variation:* Erlin.

ERMAN (German) Soldier. Form of Herman. *Variation:* Ermon.

ERNAN (Irish) One who is experienced or wise. *Variations:* Earnan, Ernen, Ernin, Ernon, Ernyn.

ERNEST (English) Earnest. *Notables:* Writer Ernest Hemingway; actor Ernest Borgnine. *Variations:* Erneste, Ernestino, Ernesto, Ernestus, Erneszt, Ernist, Ernst.

ERNIE Short form of Ernest. *Notables:* Singer Tennessee Ernie Ford; comedian Ernie Kovacs. *Variations:* Earnie, Ernee, Erney, Enry.

ERNO (Hungarian) Form of Ernest.

ERRANDO (Basque) Bold. *Variation:* Erando.

ERROL (English) Nobleman. Form of Earl. *Notable:* Actor Errol Flynn. *Variations:* Erel, Erell, Eril, Erill, Erol, Errel, Errell, Erril, Errill, Erroll, Erryl.

ERSKINE (Scottish) High cliff. *Variation:* Erskin.

ERVIN (English; Scottish) Friend of the sea. *Notable:* Basketball great Earvin "Magic" Johnson. *Variations:* Ervan, Erven, Ervine, Erving, Ervon, Ervyn, Ervyne, Ervyng.

ERWIN (English) A boar. *Variations:* Erwinek, Erwinn, Erwyn, Erwynn, Irwin.

ERYX (Greek) The son of Aphrodite and Poseidon.

ESAI (Spanish) God is salvation.

ESAIAS (Greek) God saves.

ESAU (Hebrew) Rough and hairy.

ESBERN (Danish) Holy bear. *Variations:* Esberne, Esbirn, Esbirne, Esburn, Esburne, Esbyrn, Esbyrne.

ESBJORN (Scandinavian) Divine bear. *Variations:* Asbjorn, Ebbe, Esben, Esbern.

ESDRAS (French, Hebrew) Help.

ESKAMINZIM (Native American) Big mouth.

ESKET (Scandinavian) Divine cauldron. *Variation:* Eskil, Eskyl.

ESKO (Finnish) Leader.

ESMOND (English) Rich protector. *Variations:* Esmon, Esmun, Esmund.

ESPEN (Danish) Bear. *Variations:* Espan, Espin, Espon.

ESPOWYES (Native American) Mountain light.

ESSEX (English) Eastern town.

ESSIEN (African) Sixth born.

ESTE (Italian) From the east. *Variation:* Estes.

ESTEBAN (Spanish) Crowned. Form of Stephen. *Variations:* Estabon, Estavao, Estebe, Esteben, Estefan, Estephan, Estevan, Esteven, Estevez, Estiven.

ETHAN (Hebrew) Steadfast. *Notables:* Patriot Ethan Allen; actor Ethan Hawke. *Variations:* Eathan, Eathen, Eathin, Eathon, Eithan, Eithen, Eithin, Eithon, Eithyn, Ethe, Ethen, Ethin, Ethon, Ethyn.

ETHELBERT (English) Highborn.

ETHELRED (English) Noble counsel.

Names from U.S. Cities and States

Place names have become increasingly popular over the last decade.

BOYS:	GIRLS:
Arlington	Alexandria
Austin	Atlanta
Boston	Augusta
Dallas	Charlotte
Denver	Cheyenne
Jackson	Dakota
Laramie	Florida
Montgomery	Georgia
Orlando	Helena
Reno	Madison
Roswell	Montana
Salem	Savannah
Sheridan	

ÉTIENNE (French) Crown. Variation of Stephen.

ETTORE (Italian) Loyal.

ETU (Native American) The sun.

EUAN (Scottish) Young warrior. *Variations:* Euen, Euin.

EUCLID (Greek) Intelligent.

EUFEMIUSZ (Polish) Pleasant voice.

EUGENE (Greek) Well born. *Notables:* Playwright Eugene O'Neill; actor/comedian Eugene Levy; music conductor Eugene Ormandy. *Variations:* Eugeen, Eugen, Eugeni, Eugenio, Eugenios, Eugenius, Eujean, Eujene, Evgeny, Ezven, Gene.

EUKAKIO (Hawaiian) Steady. *Variation:* Eutakio.

EUKEPIO (Hawaiian) To worship well. *Variation:* Eusebio.

EUMANN (Scottish) Wealthy protector.

EUSEBIOS (Greek) To worship well. *Variation:* Eusebius.

EUSTACE (Greek) Productive. *Variations:* Eustache, Eustachio, Eustaquio, Eustatius, Eustazio, Eustis.

EUSTACHY (Polish) Stable, steady.

EUSTON (Irish) Heart. *Variations:* Eustan, Eusten, Eustin, Eustun.

EVAK (Hindi) Equal.

EVAN (Welsh) God is good. *Variations:* Ev, Evann, Evans, Evin, Evon, Evun, Evyn.

EVANDER (Scottish) Good man. *Notable:* Boxer Evander Holyfield.

EVELYN (English) Life. *Notable:* Author Evelyn Waugh.

EVERETT (English) Wild boar. *Variations:* Everard, Everet, Everhard, Everitt.

EVERILD (English) Boar battle.

EVERLEY (English) Boar meadow. *Variations:* Everlea, Everlee, Everleigh.

EVERTON (English) Boar town.

EVZEN (Czech) Well born. *Variations:* Evza, Evzek, Evzenek.

EWALD (English) Powerful in the law. *Variations:* Evald, Evold, Ewold.

EWAN (Scottish) God is good. Form of John. *Notable:* Actor Ewan McGregor. *Variations:* Ewen, Ewin, Ewon, Ewyn.

EWING (English) Lawful. *Variation:* Ewynn.

EYAD (Arabic) Powerful.

EYANOSA (Native American) Big both ways.

EYOTA (Native American) Great.

EYULF (Scandinavian) Lucky wolf. *Variation:* Eyolf.

EZEKIEL (Hebrew) The strength of God. *Variations:* Ezekial, Ezequiel, Zeke.

EZER (Hebrew) Help.

EZRA (Hebrew) Helper. *Notable:* Poet Ezra Pound. *Variations:* Esra, Ezera, Ezri.

FA (Chinese) Beginning.

FAAS (Scandinavian) Firm counsel.

FABIAN (Latin) One who grows beans. *Notable:* Fifties singer

Fabian Forte. *Variations:* Faba, Fabek, Faber, Fabert, Fabiano, Fabien, Fabijan, Fabio, Fabir, Fabius, Fabiyan, Fabyan, Fabyen.

FABRICE (French) One who works with his hands. *Variations:* Fabrizio, Fabrizius.

FABRON (French) Blacksmith. *Variations:* Fabre, Fabriano, Fabroni, Fabryn.

FACHNAN (Irish) Irish saint. *Variations:* Fachtna, Faughnan.

FADEY (Russian) Bold. *Variations:* Faday, Faddei, Faddey, Fadeaushka, Fadeuka, Fadeyka, Fadie, Fady.

FADI (Arabic) Redeemer.

FADIL (Arabic) Generous. *Variations:* Fadal, Fadel, Fadyl.

FADL (Arabic) Grace. *Variation:* Fadhl.

FAGAN (Irish) Fiery child. *Variations:* Faegan, Faegen, Faegin, Faegon, Fagen, Fagin, Fagon, Fagyn, Faigan, Faigen, Faigin, Faigon, Faigyn, Faygan, Faygen, Faygin, Faygon, Faygyn.

FAHD (Arabic) Leopard. *Variation:* Fahad.

FAHEY (English) Joyful. *Variations:* Fahay, Fayey.

FAHIM (Hindi) Intelligent.

FAINGA (Polynesian) Confront.

FAIPA (Polynesian) Bait the hook.

FAIRCHILD (English) Fair-haired child.

FAIRFAX (English) Blond.

FAIRLEIGH (English) Meadow with bulls. *Variations:* Fairlay, Fairlee, Fairlie, Farleigh, Farley.

FAISAL (Arabic) Resolute. *Variations:* Faisel, Fasel, Faysal.

FAKHR (Arabic) Glory. *Variations:* Fakhir, Fakhri.

FAKIH (Arabic) Intelligent.

FALAK (Hindi) Heaven.

FALAN (Hindi) Fertile. *Variations:* Faleen, Falit.

FALCO (Latin) Falcon trainer. *Variations:* Falcko, Falckon, Falcon, Falconn, Falconner, Falconnor, Faulco, Faulconer, Faulconner, Faulconnor.

FALE (Polynesian) House.

FALEAKA (Polynesian) House of plants.

FALKNER (English) Falcon trainer. *Variations:* Falconer, Falconner, Faulkner, Fowler.

FALLON (Gaelic) From a ruling family. *Variations:* Fallan, Fallen.

FANE (English) Happy. *Variations:* Fain, Faine, Fayne.

FANG (Chinese) Wind.

FANGALOKA (Polynesian) Beach.

FANGATUA (Polynesian) Wrestle.

FAOLAN (Irish) Little wolf. *Variations:* Felan, Phelan.

FARAJ (Arabic) Cure. *Variation:* Farag.

FARAJI (Swahili) Consolation.

FARDORAGH (Irish) Dark-skinned man. *Variation:* Feardorcha.

FAREED (Hindi) Unique.

FAREWELL (English) Beautiful spring.

FARID (Arabic) Unrivaled. *Variation:* Farrid.

FARIS (Arabic) Knight.

FARLEY (English) Sheep meadow. *Notable:* Actor Farley Granger. *Variations:* Farlaine, Farlay, Farleigh.

FARMAN (English) Protected traveler. *Variations:* Faramond, Farimond.

FARNELL (English) Hill covered with ferns. *Variations:* Farnall, Farnel.

FARNHAM (English) Meadow of the ferns. *Variations:* Farnhem, Farnam, Farnum, Fernham.

FARNLEY (English) Field with ferns. *Variations:* Farnlea, Farnleigh, Farnlie, Fernleigh, Fernley.

FAROLD (English) Voyager.

FARON (English) Unknown definition. Last name. *Variations:* Faran, Farin, Farran, Farrin, Farron, Farrun, Farun.

FAROUK (Arabic) Truth. *Variations:* Faraq, Faroqh.

FARQUHAR (Scottish) Dear one. *Variations:* Farquar, Farquarson, Farquharson, Fearchar.

FARR (English) Wayfarer.

FARRAR (Irish) Blacksmith. *Variations:* Farar, Farer, Farrer.

FARRELL (Irish) Courageous man. *Variations:* Farall, Farrel, Farrill, Farryll, Ferrel, Ferrell, Ferrill, Ferryl.

FARROW (Irish) Ironsmith.

FARRUCA (Spanish) Freedom. *Variations:* Farruka, Faruca, Frascuelo.

FARUQ (Hindi) Moralist. *Variations:* Farook, Farooq.

FASTE (Norwegian) Firm.

FATHI (Arabic) To win. *Variation:* Fath.

FATIN (Arabic) Clever. *Variation:* Fatine.

FAU (Polynesian) Tree.

FAUIKI (Polynesian) Small trees.

FAUST (Latin) Lucky. *Variations:* Faustin, Faustino, Fausto, Faustus, Fautice.

FAUTAVE (Polynesian) Tall trees.

FAVIAN (Latin) Understanding man. *Variations:* Favien, Favion.

FAWZ (Arabic) To accomplish.

FAXI (Norse) Hair. *Variations:* Faxey, Faxie, Faxy.

FAXON (English) Long haired.

FAYIZ (Arabic) Winner.

FAZIO (Italian) Good worker.

FEAGH (Irish) Raven.

FEARADHACH (Irish) Masculine.

FEARGHALL (Irish) Brave man. *Variations:* Fearghal, Fearghus, Fergal.

FEARGHAS (Scottish) Strong man. *Variations:* Feargus, Fergus.

FEATHERSTONE (English) Town in England.

FEDOR (Greek) Divine gift. *Variations:* Feador, Fidor, Fidore.

FEHIN (Irish) Little raven. *Variations:* Fechin, Feichin.

FEIDHLIM (Irish) Forever good. *Variations:* Fedlim, Feidhelm, Feidhlimidh, Felim, Phelim.

FEILO (Polynesian) Familiar.

FEIVEL (Yiddish) Bright one. *Variation:* Feiwel.

FEKITOA (Polynesian) Two men gather.

The Family Jewels

Each of these gemstones also makes a jewel of a name!

BOYS:
Agate
Alexandrite
Garnet
Iolite
Jasper
Kunzite
Lapis Lazuli
Morganite
Peridot
Tanzanite
Topaz
Zircon

GIRLS:
Amber
Amethyst
Beryl
Citrine
Coral
Emerald
Jade
Onyx
Opal
Pearl
Ruby
Sapphire

FELETI (Polynesian) Peace.

FELICIUS (Latin) Happy.

FELIMY (Irish) Forever good.

FELIPE (Spanish) Form of Philip.

FELIX (Latin) Happy-go-lucky. *Variations:* Felice, Felicio, Feliks, Feliksa, Feliz, Felizio, Filix.

FELTON (English) Field town. *Variations:* Feltan, Felten, Feltin.

FENRIS (Scandinavian) Scandinavian mythological figure.

FENTON (English) Town by a swamp.

FENWICK (English) Farm on a marsh.

FENYANG (African) Conqueror.

FEODOR (Slavic) Gift of God. A form of Theodore. *Variations:* Fedar, Fedinka, Fedor, Fedya, Fiodore.

FEORAS (Irish) Rock.

FERDINAND (German) Brave traveler. *Notables:* Explorer Ferdinand Magellan; actor Fernando Lamas. *Variations:* Ferdinan, Ferdinando, Ferdinandus, Ferdynand, Fernand, Fernando.

FERGAL (Irish) Brave. *Variation:* Forgael.

FERGUS (Scottish) Man of vigor. *Variations:* Ferghas, Ferghus, Fergie, Fergis, Furgus.

FERGUSON (Scottish) Son of Fergus. *Variations:* Fergusen, Firguson, Furguson.

FERMIN (Spanish) Powerful. *Variations:* Firman, Firmin, Furman, Furmin.

FERNLEY (English) Meadow of ferns. *Variation:* Fernleigh.

FEROZ (Persian) Lucky. *Variation:* Firoz.

FERRAN (Arabic) Baker. *Variations:* Feran, Ferin, Feron, Ferren, Ferrin, Ferron.

FERRAND (French) Gray hair. *Variations:* Farand, Farrand, Farrant, Ferrant.

FERRIS (Irish) Rock. *Notable:* Film character Ferris Bueller.

FIACHRA (Irish) Raven. *Variation:* Fiachna.

FIDEL (Latin) Faith. *Notable:* Cuban President Fidel Castro. *Variations:* Fidal, Fidele, Fidelio, Fidelis, Fidello.

FIELDING (English) In the field. *Variations:* Field, Fielder.

FIFE (Scottish) County in Scotland. *Variation:* Fyffe.

FIKRI (Arabic) Smart person.

FILBERT (English) Brilliant. *Variations:* Filberte, Filberti, Filberto, Philbert.

FILIMOEIKA (Polynesian) Shark's enemy.

FILMORE (English) Famous. *Variation:* Fillmore.

FINAN (Irish) Blond child. *Variation:* Fionan.

FINBAR (Irish) Blond hair. *Variation:* Fionnbharr.

FINEEN (Irish) Fair birth. *Variations:* Finghin, Finin, Finneen, Finnin.

FINGALL (Scottish) Fair-haired stranger. *Variation:* Fingal.

FINIAN (Irish) Fair. *Variations:* Finnian, Fionan, Fionn.

FINLAY (Irish) Fair-haired hero. *Variations:* Findlay, Findley, Finleigh, Finley.

FINN (Irish) Short for Finlay or Finnegan. *Variation:* Fionn.

FINNEGAN (Irish) Fair. *Variation:* Finegan.

FIONNLAGH (Scottish) Fair-haired soldier. *Variation:* Fionnla.

FIORELLO (Italian) Little flower. *Notable:* New York City Mayor Fiorello LaGuardia.

FIRDOS (Hindi) Paradise. *Variations:* Firdaus, Firdose, Firdoze.

FIROZ (Hindi) Winner. *Variations:* Feroz, Feroze, Firuz.

FIRTH (English) Forest.

FISHER (English) Fisherman. *Notable:* Actor Fisher Stevens. *Variation:* Fischer.

FISK (English) Fisherman. *Variation:* Fiske.

FITCH (English) Weasel or ferret.

FITZ (English) Son.

FITZGERALD (English) Son of the mighty spear holder.

FITZHUGH (English) Son of an intelligent man.

FITZPATRICK (English) Son of the noble one.

FITZROY (Irish) Son of a king.

FITZWILLIAM (Irish) Son of the soldier.

FLAMINIO (Spanish) Priest.

FLANNERY (Irish) Red hair. *Variations:* Flaine, Flann, Flannan, Flannin.

FLAVIAN (Latin) Blond. *Variations:* Flavia, Flavien, Flavio, Flavius.

FLAWIUSZ (Polish) Blond.

FLEET (Scandinavian) Channel.

FLEMING (English) Man from the valley. *Variation:* Flemming.

FLETCHER (English) One who makes arrows. *Variation:* Fletch.

FLINT (English) Stream. *Variation:* Flynt.

FLIP (American) Horse lover. Short for Philip. *Notable:* Comedian Flip Wilson.

FLORENT (French) Flower. *Variations:* Floranz, Florenz, Florentino, Florenzo.

FLORIAN (Latin) In bloom. *Variations:* Florien, Florino, Floryan.

FLORIS (Scandinavian) Blossoming.

FLOYD (Welsh) Gray haired. *Notable:* Boxer Floyd Patterson.

FLURRY (Irish) In bloom.

FLYNN (Irish) Red-haired-man's son. *Variations:* Flin, Flinn, Flyn.

FOLANT (Welsh) Strong.

FOLAU (Polynesian) Travel.

FOLKE (Scandinavian) People. *Variation:* Folki.

FOLUKE (African) Placed in God's hands.

FOMA (Russian) Twin.

FONDA (Spanish) The earth.

FONSO (Italian) Ready to fight. Short form of Alphonse. *Variations:* Fonzie, Fonzo, Fonzy.

FONTAINE (French) Fountain. *Variation:* Fountain.

FORBES (Scottish) Field.

FORD (English) River crossing.

FORDON (German) Destroyer. *Variations:* Fordan, Forden, Fordin.

FOREST (French) Woods. *Notables:* Film character Forrest Gump; newscaster Forrest Sawyer; actors Forrest Whittaker and Forrest Tucker. *Variations:* Forester, Forrest, Forrester, Forster.

FORTUNÉ (French) Lucky. *Variations:* Fortunato, Fortunatus, Fortunio.

FOSTER (Latin) Woodsman.

FOUAD (Arabic) Heart.

FOWLER (English) Bird trapper.

FOX (English) Fox. *Variation:* Foxx.

FRANCIS (Latin) Frenchman. *Notable:* Lawyer and writer of "The Star Spangled Banner," Francis Scott Key. *Variations:* Fran, Franchot, Francisco, Franco, Francois.

FRANG (Scottish) Frenchman. *Variation:* Frangag.

FRANK (English) Short form of Francis or Franklin. *Notables:* Singers Frank Sinatra, Frank Zappa, and Frankie Valli; architect Frank Lloyd Wright; film directors Frank Capra and Frank Oz. *Variations:* Franc, Frankie.

FRANKLIN (English) A free property owner. *Notable:* U.S. President Franklin D. Roosevelt. *Variations:* Franklyn, Franklynn.

FRANTISEK (Czech) French man. *Variations:* Fanousek, Frana, Franek, Franta, Frantik.

FRANZ (German) Form of Francis. *Notables:* Writer Franz Kafka; composer Franz Liszt. *Variations:* Frans, Franzen, Franzl.

FRASER (French) Strawberry. *Variations:* Frasier, Fraze, Frazer, Frazier.

FRAYNE (English) Foreign. *Variations:* Frain, Fraine, Frayn, Freyne.

FRED (German) Short form of Alfred, Frederick. *Notables:* Dancer Fred Astaire; actor Fred MacMurray; children's TV show host Fred Rogers; singers Fred Durst and Freddie Mercury. *Variations:* Fredd, Freddie, Freddo, Freddy, Fredo.

FREDERICK (German) Merciful leader. *Notables:* Abolitionist Frederick Douglass; composer Frederic Chopin; philosopher Friedrich Nietzsche. *Variations:* Federico, Federigo, Fedrick, Fredek, Frederic, Frederich, Frederico, Frederigo, Frederik, Frederikos, Fredric, Fredrick, Fredrik, Friedrich, Fritz.

FREEBORN (English) Born into freedom.

FREEDOM (English) Liberty.

FREEMAN (English) Free man.

FREMONT (German) Protector of liberty. *Variation:* Fremonte.

FREWIN (English) Free friend. *Variations:* Freewen, Frewen.

FREY (Scandinavian) Supreme Lord.

FRICK (English) Brave.

FRIDMAR (German) Famous peace.

FRIDMUND (German) Peaceful protector. *Variation:* Fridmond.

FRIDOLF (English) Calm wolf.

FRIEND (English) Friend.

FRITJOF (Scandinavian) Peace thief. *Variations:* Fridtjof, Fridtjov, Fritjov.

FRITZ (German) Merciful ruler. Form of Frederick. *Notable:* Film director Fritz Lang. *Variations:* Fritson, Fritt, Fritzchen, Fritzl, Fritzroy.

FRODE (Scandinavian) Wise.

FRODI (Scandinavian) Ancient Danish king.

FU (Chinese) Wealthy.

FUAD (Arabic) Heart. *Variation:* Fouad.

FUANILEVU (Polynesian) Great.

FULBRIGHT (German) Bright.

FULEHEU (Polynesian) A bird.

FULLER (English) One who works with cloth.

FULTON (English) Town settlement.

FULUMIRANI (African) A trip.

FULVIO (Italian) Tawny. *Variation:* Fulvius.

FUNSAN (African) Request.

FUTKEFU (Polynesian) Grass skirt.

FYFE (Scottish) Town in Scotland. *Variations:* Fife, Fyffe.

FYNN (African) River in Ghana.

FYODOR (Russian) Form of Theodore. *Variation:* Feodor.

GABBO (Norse) To scoff.

GABE (Hebrew) Short form of Gabriel. *Notable:* Comedian Gabe Kaplan.

GABRIEL (Hebrew) Man of God. *Notables:* Writer Gabriel Garcia Marquez; actor Gabriel Byrne. *Variations:* Gab, Gabby, Gabel, Gabell, Gabi, Gabirol, Gabko, Gabo, Gabor, Gabriele, Gabrielius, Gabrielli, Gabriello, Gabris, Gabryel, Gabys, Gavi, Gavriel, Gavril.

GADI (Arabic) My fortune. *Variations:* Gad, Gadie, Gady.

GADIEL (Arabic) Fortune from God. *Variation:* Gaddiel.

GAETAN (Italian) An area in Italy.

GAGE (French) Pledge. *Variation:* Gaige.

GAINES (English) To gain. *Variation:* Gaynes.

GAIR (Irish) Small one. *Variations:* Gaer, Geir.

GAIUS (Latin) Rejoice.

GALAHAD (Welsh) Hawk.

GALBRAITH (Irish) Scotsman in Ireland.

GALE (Irish) Foreigner. *Variations:* Gael, Gail.

GALEN (Greek) Healer. *Variation:* Galeno.

GALERAN (French) Healthy ruler. *Variation:* Galerano.

GALEUS (Greek) Lizard.

GALI (Hebrew) Fountain.

GALILEO (Italian) From Galilee. *Notable:* Astronomer Galileo Galilei.

GALLAGHER (Irish) Foreign; helper.

GALLOWAY (Irish) Foreigner. *Variations:* Gallway, Galway.

GALT (Norwegian) From the high ground.

GALTON (English) Landlord. *Variations:* Galtan, Galten, Galtin, Gallton.

GALVIN (Irish) Sparrow. *Variations:* Gallven, Gallvin, Galvan, Galven.

GAMAL (Arabic) Camel. *Variations:* Gamall, Gamil.

GAMBA (African) Warrior.

GAMBLE (Norse) Old. *Variations:* Gambal, Gambel, Gambil, Gambyl.

GAMLIEL (Hebrew) God is my reward. *Variation:* Gamaliel.

GAMLYN (Norse) Little elder. *Variation:* Gamlin.

GAN (Chinese) Adventure.

GANDHI (Sanskrit) Great. *Variation:* Gandhee.

GANDOLF (German) Fierce wolf. *Variation:* Gandolfo.

GANDY (English) A railroad worker who helps to lay tracks.

GANESH (Hindi) Lord of them all.

GANNON (Irish) Light skinned. *Variations:* Ganan, Ganen, Ganin, Gannan, Gannen, Gannin, Gannon, Gannyn, Ganon, Ganyn.

GARAI (African) Settled.

GARBHAN (Irish) Small, tough child. *Variation:* Garvan.

GARCIA (Spanish) Brave spear carrier. A form of Gerald. *Variations:* Garcias, Garcillasso, Garcya, Garcyah, Garcyas, Garsias, Garsya, Garsyah, Garsyas.

GARD (Norse) Dwelling place. *Variations:* Garde, Guard.

GARDNER (English) Gardener. *Variations:* Gardinar, Gardiner, Gardnar, Gardnor.

GAREK (Polish) Wealth with a spear. Variation of Edgar. *Variations:* Garak, Garik, Garreck, Garrik.

GAREN (English) Form of Gary.

GARETH (Welsh) Gentle. *Variations:* Garith, Garreth, Garyth.

GARFIELD (English) Field of spears. *Notable:* Cartoon cat Garfield.

GARIANA (Hindi) Shout.

GARIBALDO (Italian) Prince of war. *Variations:* Garibald, Garybald, Garybaldo.

GARLAND (French) Wreath. *Variations:* Garlan, Garlen, Garlyn.

GARNER (English) To harvest grain. *Variations:* Gar, Garnor.

GARNET (English) Red precious gem. *Variations:* Garnett, Garnier.

GARNOCK (Welsh) River of alder trees. *Variations:* Garnoc, Garnok.

GARRETT (Irish) Brave with a spear. *Variations:* Gared, Garett, Garrad, Garrard, Garrat, Garred, Garret, Garrit, Garritt, Garrod, Gerred.

GARRICK (English) He who rules with a spear. *Variations:* Garic, Garick, Garreck, Garryck, Garyk.

GARRIDAN (Gypsy) He who hides.

GARRIN (English, German) Mighty with a spear. *Variations:* Garan, Garen, Garin, Garon, Garran, Garren, Garron, Garryn, Garyn.

GARRISON (English) Fort.

GARROWAY (English) He who fights with a spear. *Variation:* Garraway.

GARSON (English) Son of Gar.

GARTH (Scandinavian) Gardener. *Notable:* Country singer Garth Brooks.

GARVEY (Irish) Peace. *Variations:* Garvie, Garvy.

GARVIN (English) Friend with a spear. *Variations:* Garvan, Garven, Garvyn.

GARWOOD (English) Evergreen forest.

GARY (English) Spearman. *Notables:* Actor Gary Cooper; cartoonist Garry Trudeau; comedian Garry Shandling. *Variations:* Garey, Garrey, Garrie, Garry.

GASPARD (French) Form of Jasper. *Variations:* Gaspar, Gasper.

GASTON (French) Man from Gascony, France. *Variations:* Gascon, Gascoyne.

GAURAV (Hindi) Pride.

GAUTAMA (Sanskrit) Name of the Buddha.

GAUTE (Norwegian) Great goth. *Variations:* Gaut, Gaunte.

GAUTIER (French) Powerful leader. *Variations:* Gatier, Gauther, Gauthier.

GAUTREK (Swedish) Gothic king.

GAUTULF (Swedish) Gothic wolf.

GAVIN (Welsh) White falcon. *Notable:* Actor Gavin MacLeod. *Variations:* Gavan, Gaven, Gavyn, Gawain, Gawaine, Gawayn, Gawayne, Gawen.

GAVRIEL (Hebrew) Strength of God. Form of Gabriel. *Variations:* Gavra, Gavrel, Gavrie, Gavril, Gavrilo.

GAWATH (Welsh) Hawk of battle.

GAYLORD (French) Lively lord. *Variations:* Gaelord, Gailard, Gailor, Gailord, Gaylor.

GAYNOR (Irish) Son of a pale man. *Variations:* Gaenor, Gainor.

GEARY (English) Changeable. *Variations:* Gearey, Gearie.

GEB (Egyptian) Earth.

GEDALIAH (Hebrew) God is great. *Variations:* Gedalia, Gedaliahu, Gedalya, Gedalyahu.

By George!

Former boxing champ and noted grill-master George Foreman, in an act of paternal pride (or, perhaps, hubris) named all of his five sons "George." There's George Jr., George III, George IV, George V, and George VI. It's interesting to wonder who comes when the name "George" is called in the Foreman household. Like father, like sons.

Junior Leagues

Naming a son after his father is a common practice based on honor and respect. Some sons are real "Juniors," taking their father's entire name: James Daniel Smith Jr. is named for James Daniel Smith Sr. Others are given a different middle name and are frequently called by that middle name. Thus, baby James Dylan Smith is called Dylan.

GEFANIAH (Hebrew) God's orchard. *Variations:* Gefania, Gefanya, Gephania, Gephaniah.

GELASIUS (Greek) Laughter.

GELLIES (Dutch) Warmonger.

GEMALLI (Hebrew) Rider of camels. *Variation:* Gemali.

GEMINI (Latin) Twins.

GENE (English) Short form of Eugene. *Notables:* Dancer/actor Gene Kelly; Kiss member Gene Simmons; comedic actor Gene Wilder; actor Gene Hackman; Star Trek creator/producer Gene Roddenberry. *Variations:* Genek, Genio, Genka, Genya.

GENNARO (Italian) Born in January. *Variation:* Genaro.

GENOS (Phoenician) Sun worshipers.

GENOVESE (Italian) From Genoa.

GENT (English) Gentleman. *Variation:* Gentle.

GENTY (English) Snow.

GEOFFREY (German) Peace. Alternative spelling of Jeffrey. *Variations:* Geff, Geffrey, Geffrie, Geffry, Geof, Geoff.

GEORGE (Greek) Farmer. *Notables:* U.S. Presidents George Washington, George Bush, and George W. Bush; General George Patton; designer Giorgio Armani; actor George Clooney; comedian George Burns. *Variations:* Georg, Georges, Georgi, Georgios, Georgy, Giorgio, Giorgos.

GERAINT (Latin) Old.

GERALD (German) Ruler with a spear. *Notables:* U.S. President Gerald Ford; TV journalist/host Geraldo Rivera. *Variations:* Geralde, Geraldo, Gerrald, Gerrold, Gerry, Jerald, Jeralde, Jeraud, Jerold, Jerrald, Jerrold, Jerry.

GERARD (German) Brave with a spear. *Notable:* Actor Gérard Depardieu. *Variations:* Garrard, Gerardo, Gerhard, Gerrard, Geraud, Gerrit, Gerry.

GERBER (German) Tanner of leather.

GEREMIA (Italian; Hebrew) Chosen by God. A form of Jeremiah.

GERHARD (German) Form of Gerard. *Variation:* Gerhardt.

GERLACH (Scandinavian) Javelin. Spear thrower.

GERMAIN (French) One from Germany. *Variations:* Germaine, German, Germane, Germayn, Germayne, Jermain, Jermaine, Jermane, Jermayn, Jermayne.

GERONIMO (Italian) Form of Jerome.

GERONIMO (Native American) *Notable:* Geronimo, the famous Apache chief.

GERSHON (Hebrew) Exiled. *Variations:* Gersham, Gershom, Gerson.

GERVAISE (French) Honorable. *Variations:* Garvase, Gervase, Gervais.

GERWIN (Welsh) Fair love. *Variations:* Gerwen, Gerwyn.

GESHEM (Hebrew) Rain.

GETHIN (Welsh) Murky. *Variations:* Geth, Gethen.

GEVARIAH (Hebrew) God's might. *Variations:* Gevaria, Gevarya, Gevaryah, Gevaryahu.

GESIO (Portuguese) God will help. A form of Jesus.

GETHIN (Welsh) Dark skinned.

GEYSA (Hungarian) Chief. *Variations:* Geisa, Geza.

GHAFUR (Arabic) One who forgives.

GHALIB (Arabic) Conqueror; dominant.

GHASSAN (Arabic) Young. *Variation:* Ghassam.

GHAYTH (Arabic) Rain. *Variation:* Ghaith.

GHOSHAL (Hindi) Commentator. *Variation:* Ghoshil.

GI (Korean) Brave.

GIACOMO (Italian) Supplanter. Form of Jacob.

GIAN (Italian) God is gracious. Form of Giovanni (John). *Variation:* Gianetto.

GIANCARLO (Italian) Combination of John and Charles. *Notable:* Actor Giancarlo Giannini.

GIANNI (Italian) Short form of Giovanni (John). *Notable:* Designer Gianni Versace. *Variations:* Giannes, Gianni, Giannos.

GIBIDH (Scottish) Famous pledge.

GIBOR (Hebrew) Hero.

GIBSON (English) Son of Gilbert. *Variations:* Gibb, Gibbons, Gibbs, Gibby.

GIDEON (Hebrew) One who cuts down trees. *Variations:* Gideone, Gidon, Gidoni.

GIFFORD (English) Giver. *Variations:* Gifferd, Giffyrd.

GIG (English) Horse carriage. *Notable:* Actor Gig Young.

GIL (Hebrew) Joy.

GILAD (Arabic) Camel's hump. *Variations:* Giladi, Gilead.

GILAM (Hebrew) Joy of a people.

GILBERT (German) Bright pledge. *Notable:* Comedian Gilbert Gottfried. *Variations:* Gil, Gilberto.

GILBY (Norse) Hostage's home. *Variations:* Gilbey, Gillbey, Gillby.

GILCHRIST (Irish) Servant of Christ. *Variation:* Ghilchrist.

GILDEA (Irish) Servant of God. *Variations:* Gildey, Gildy, Giolla Dhe.

GILES (English, French) Bearing a shield. *Variations:* Gilles, Gyles.

GILLANDERS (Scottish) Servant of St. Andrew. *Variations:* Gille Ainndreis, Gille Anndrai.

GILLEAN (Scottish) Servant of Saint John. *Variations:* Gillan, Gillen, Gillian.

GILLEONAN (Scottish) Servant of St. Adomnan. *Variation:* Gille Adhamhnain.

GILLESPIE (Irish) Servant of the bishop. *Variations:* Gilleasbuig, Gillis, Giolla Easpaig.

GILLETT (French) Trusted son. *Variations:* Gelett, Gelette, Gilet, Gilette, Gillette.

GILMORE (Irish) Servant of the Virgin Mary. *Variations:* Gillmoor, Gillmore, Gillmour, Gilmoore, Gilmor, Gilmour, Giolle Maire.

GILON (Hebrew) Joy.

GILROY (Irish) Son of the king's servant. *Variations:* Gilderoy, Gildray, Gildrey, Gildroy, Gillroy.

GILSON (English) Son of Gilbert.

GILUS (Scandinavian) Shield.

GINGER (English) Red haired. *Notable:* Rock drummer Ginger Baker.

GINO (Italian) Noble.

GINTON (Hebrew) Garden.

GIONA (Italian) Italian version of Jonah.

GIORGIO (Italian) Farmer. Form of George. *Notable:* Designer Giorgio Armani.

GIOVANNI (Italian) God is good. Italian version of John. *Variations:* Giovanno, Giovonni.

GIPSY (English) Wanderer. *Variation:* Gypsy.

GIRIOEL (Welsh) Lordly.

GIRVIN (Irish) Small, tough child. *Variations:* Girvan, Girven, Girvon.

GITANO (Spanish) Wanderer.

GIULIO (Italian) Youthful. A form of Jules.

GIUSEPPE (Italian) God will increase. Italian version of Joseph. *Notable:* Composer Giuseppe Verdi.

GIUSTINO (Italian) Righteous. Form of Justin.

GIVON (Hebrew) Hill.

GLADSTONE (Scottish) From the Gledstanes in Scotland.

GLADUS (Welsh) Lame.

GLADWIN (English) Lighthearted. *Variations:* Gladwen, Gladwenn, Gladwinn, Gladwyn, Gladwynn.

GLANVILE (French) Town with oak trees. *Variation:* Glanville.

GLASGOW (Scottish) Capital of Scotland.

GLEN (Irish) Narrow valley. *Notables:* Musician Glenn Miller; actor Glenn Ford; singer Glen Campbell. *Variation:* Glenn.

GLENDON (Scottish) Town in a glen. *Variations:* Glendan, Glenden, Glendin, Glendun, Glendyn, Glenton, Glentworth, Glyndan, Glynden, Glyndin, Glyndon, Glyndyn.

GLENDOWER (Welsh) Valley of water. *Variation:* Glyndwr.

GLENROWAN (Gaelic) From the rowan-tree valley. *Variations:* Glennrowan, Glenrowen, Glenrowin, Glenrowyn, Glynrowan, Glynrowen, Glynrowin, Glynrowyn.

GLENVILLE (English) Town in a valley. *Variation:* Glenvil.

GLYN (Welsh) Small valley. *Variations:* Glin, Glinn, Glynn, Glynne.

GOBIND (Hindi) Cowherder.

GODDARD (German) Firm God. *Variations:* Godard, Godart, Goddart, Godhardt, Godhart, Gothart, Gotthard, Gotthardt, Gotthart.

GODFREY (German) God is peace. Variation of Geoffrey. *Notable:* Comedian Godfrey Cambridge. *Variations:* Goddfrey, Godfried, Gotfrid, Gottfrid, Gottfried.

GODRIC (English) Good ruler.

GODWIN (English) God's friend. *Variations:* Godewyn, Godwinn, Godwyn, Godwynn.

GOEL (Hebrew) The saviour.

GOFRAIDH (Irish) Peaceful God. *Variations:* Gothfraidh, Gothraidh.

GOHACHIRO (Japanese) Thirteenth child.

GOKU (Japanese) Country.

GOLDING (English) Little gold one.

GOLDWIN (English) Golden friend. *Variations:* Goldewin, Goldewyn, Goldwinn, Goldwyn, Goldwynn.

GOLIATH (Hebrew) Exiled. *Variation:* Golliath.

GOMDA (Native American) Wind.

GOMER (English) Good fight. *Notable:* TV's *Gomer Pyle U.S.M.*

GOMEZ (Spanish) Man.

GOMMATA (Sanskrit) Strong armed. *Variation:* Gomata.

GONDOL (Norse) Good.

GONSTAN (Breton) From the hill stone.

GONTHIER (French) War army.

GONZALO (Spanish) Wolf. *Variation:* Gonzales.

GOODMAN (English) Good man.

GOODWIN (English) Good friend.

GORAN (Slavic) From the forest.

GORDON (English) Round hill. *Notables:* Singers Gordon Lightfoot and Gordon Sumner (Sting); hockey player Gordie Howe. *Variations:* Gordan, Gorden, Gordie, Gordy.

GORE (English) Spear.

GORMAN (Irish) Child with blue eyes.

GORO (Japanese) Fifth son.

GOSHEVEN (Native American) Jumper.

GORONWY (Welsh) Old.

GOTAM (Hindi) Best cow. *Variations:* Gautam, Gautama.

GOTEN (Japanese) Palace.

GOTTFRIED (German) Form of Geoffrey.

GOVERT (German) Divine peace.

GOWER (Welsh) Pure. *Notable:* Choreographer Gower Champion.

GOWON (African) Rainmaker.

GOZAL (Hebrew) Bird.

GRADY (Irish) Famous. *Variations:* Gradie, Gradey, Graidey, Graidy, Graydie.

GRAHAM (English) Gray house. *Notables:* Singer Graham Nash; Monty Python comedian Graham Chapman. *Variations:* Graeham, Graeme, Grahame, Gram.

GRANGER (French) Farmer. *Variation:* Grainger.

GRANT (French) Great. *Variation:* Grand.

GRANTLY (English) Gray meadow. *Variations:* Grantlea, Grantleigh, Grantley.

GRANVILLE (French) Big town. *Variations:* Granvil, Granvile, Granvill, Grenville.

GRAY (English) Gray. *Variations:* Grayer, Grey, Greyer.

GRAYDON (English) Son of gray land. *Notable:* *Vanity Fair* editor Graydon Carter. *Variations:* Graydan, Grayden, Graydin, Greydan, Greyden, Greydin, Greydon, Greydyn.

GRAYSON (English) Son of a man with gray hair. *Variations:* Graysen, Graysin, Greysen, Greysin, Greyson.

GREELEY (English) Gray meadow. *Variations:* Greelea, Greeleigh, Greely.

GREENWOOD (English) Green wood. Last name. *Variations:* Green, Greener, Greenshaw.

GREG (English) Observant. Short form of Gregory. *Notables:* Actor Greg Kinnear; diver Greg Louganis. *Variations:* Graig, Graigg, Gregos, Gregus, Gregg, Greig, Greigg.

GREGORY (Latin) Observant. *Notables:* Actor Gregory Peck; actor/dancer Gregory Hines. *Variations:* Greggorie, Greggory, Gregoire, Gregor, Gregorie, Gregorio, Gregorios, Greigor, Gries, Grigor, Grisha.

GREGSON (Latin) Observant son. *Variation:* Greggson.

GRESHAM (English) Last name. *Variation:* Grisham.

GRIFFIN (Latin) One with a hooked nose. *Notable:* Actor Griffin Dunne. *Variations:* Griff, Griffen, Griffon, Griffyn, Gryffin, Gryphon.

GRIFFITH (Welsh) Powerful leader. *Variations:* Griff, Griffyth, Gryffyth.

GRIMSHAW (English) Dark forest.

GRINDAL (English) From the green valley.

GRISWOLD (German) Gray forest. *Variations:* Griswald, Griswaldo, Griswoldo.

GROSVENOR (French) Great hunter.

GROVER (English) Grove of trees. *Notable:* U.S. President Grover Cleveland.

GRUNDE (Norwegian) Contemplative. *Variation:* Grund.

GUGLIELMO (Italian) Determined guardian. Form of William.

GUIDO (Italian) Guide.

GUILFORD (English) Ford with yellow flowers. *Variations:* Gilford, Guildford.

GULSHAN (Hindi) Garden.

GULZAR (Arabic) Blooming.

GUNNAR (Scandinavian) Battle. *Variations:* Gun, Gunder.

GUNTHER (Scandinavian) Warrior. *Variations:* Guenther, Gun, Gunnar, Guntar, Gunter, Guntero, Gunthar.

GUR (Hebrew) Lion cub.

GURION (Hebrew) Strength of a lion. God's dwelling. *Variations:* Guriel, Guryon.

GURPREET (Pakistani) Religious guru.

GURUDATTA (Hindi) Guru's gift.

GURYON (Hebrew) Lion. *Variations:* Garon, Gorion, Gurion.

GUS (English) Short form of Augustus or Gustaf.

GUSTAF (Scandinavian) Staff of the gods. *Notable:* Composer Gustav Mahler. *Variations:* Gustaff, Gustav, Gustave, Gustavo, Gustavs, Gusti, Gustik, Gustus, Gusty.

GUTHRIE (Irish) Windy area. *Variations:* Guthre, Guthry.

GUTIERRE (Spanish) Ruler of the people.

GUY (French) Guide. *Notables:* Designer Guy Laroche; film director Guy Ritchie. *Variations:* Gui, Guion, Guyon.

GUYAPI (Native American) Frank.

GWERB (Welsh) Alder tree.

GWESYN (Welsh) Little friend.

GWIDON (Polish) Life.

GWYNFOR (Welsh) Fair Lord. *Variation:* Gwinfor.

GWYNN (Welsh) Fair. *Variations:* Gwynedd, Gwynne.

Top Names of the 1940s

BOYS:
1. James
2. Robert
3. John
4. William
5. Richard
6. David
7. Charles
8. Thomas
9. Michael
10. Ronald
11. Larry
12. Donald
13. Joseph
14. Gary
15. George
16. Kenneth
17. Paul
18. Edward
19. Jerry
20. Dennis

GIRLS:
1. Mary
2. Linda
3. Barbara
4. Patricia
5. Carol
6. Sandra
7. Nancy
8. Judith
9. Sharon
10. Susan
11. Betty
12. Carolyn
13. Margaret
14. Shirley
15. Judy
16. Karen
17. Donna
18. Kathleen
19. Joyce
20. Dorothy

GWYTHYR (Welsh) Winner. *Variation:* Gwydyr.

GYAN (Hindi) Knowledge. *Variation:* Gyani.

GYANDEV (Hindi) God of knowledge.

GYASI (African) Wonderful.

GYLFI (Scandinavian) Ancient mythological king.

GYULA (Hungarian) Youthful. *Variations:* Gyala, Gyuszi.

HAAKON (Scandinavian) Chosen son. *Variations:* Hagen, Hakan, Haken, Hakin, Hakon.

HABIB (Arabic) Beloved. *Variation:* Habbib.

HABIMANA (African) God exists. *Variation:* Habimama.

HACHEHI (Native American) Wolf.

HACHIUMA (Japanese) Eight horses.

HACKETT (German) Wood cutter. *Variations:* Hacket, Hackit, Hackitt.

HACKMAN (German) Wood cutter.

HADAD (Arabic) Thunder.

HADAR (Hebrew) Glory.

HADAWAKO (Native American) Falling snow.

HADDAD (Arabic) Blacksmith.

HADDEN (English) Hill covered with heather. *Variations:* Haddan, Haddin, Haddon.

HADI (Arabic) Guide. *Variation:* Haddi.

HADLEY (English) Meadow of heather. *Variations:* Hadlea, Hadlee, Hadleigh, -Hadly, Headley, Hedley, Hedly.

HADRIAN (Scandinavian) Black earth. *Variations:* Hadrien, Hadrion, Hadryan.

HADRIEL (Hebrew) God's glory. *Variations:* Hadrial, Hadriell.

HADWIN (English) Friend in war. *Variations:* Hadwen, Hadwinn, Hadwyn, Hadwynne.

HAFIZ (Arabic) Protector.

HAFOKA (Polynesian) Big.

HAGAN (Irish) Home ruler. *Variations:* Hagen, Haggan, Hagin, Hagyn.

HAGAR (Hebrew) Forsaken. *Variations:* Hager, Haggar, Hagger, Haggir, Haggor, Hagir, Hagor.

HAGLEY (English) Surrounded by hedges. *Variations:* Haglea, Haglee, Hagleigh, Haglie, Hagly, Haig.

HAHNEE (Native American) Beggar.

HAI (Vietnamese) Sea.

HAIDAR (Arabic) Lion.

HAILAMA (Hawaiian) Famous brother. *Variations:* Hairama, Hilama, Hirama.

HAJJ (African) Born during the pilgrimage to Mecca. *Variation:* Haji.

HAKADAH (Native American) Last.

HAKAN (Native American) Fiery.

HAKEEM (Arabic) Wise. *Variations:* Hakem, Hakim.

HAKIZIANA (African) God saves.

HAK-KUN (Korean) Foundation.

HAKON (Scandinavian) Of the highest race. *Variations:* Haakon, Hakan, Hakin, Hako.

HAL (English) Army ruler. Short form of Harold. *Notables:* Actors Hal Linden and Hal Holbrook.

HALAPOLO (Polynesian) Place where chili peppers grow.

HALATOA (Polynesian) The grove of trees.

HALBERT (English) Bright hero. *Variations:* Halbirt, Halburt.

HALCYON (Greek) Kingfisher. *Variation:* Halcion.

HALDAN (Scandinavian) Half Danish. *Variations:* Haldane, Halden, Haldin, Haldon, Haldyn.

HALDOR (Scandinavian) Thor's rock. *Variations:* Halldor, Halle.

HALE (English) Healthy. *Variations:* Hael, Haele, Hail, Haile, Hayle.

HALEEM (Arabic) Gentle. *Variation:* Halim.

HALEN (Scandinavian) Hall.

HALEY (Irish) Clover. *Variations:* Hailey, Haily.

HALFORD (English) Ford in a valley. *Variation:* Hallford.

HALI (Greek) Sea.

HALIAN (Native American) Downy.

HALIFAX (English) From the holy field.

HALIL (Turkish) Good friend.

HALIM (Arabic) Gentle.

HALL (English) Worker at the manor.

HALLAM (English) Valley.

HALLAN (English) Manor dweller. *Variations:* Halan, Halen, Halin, Hallen, Hallin, Hallon, Hallyn, Halon, Halyn.

HALLEY (English) Meadow near the manor.

HALLIWELL (English) Holy well. *Variations:* Haliwell, Hallewell, Halliwel, Hallwell, Hellewell.

HALLWARD (English) Protector of the manor. *Variation:* Halward.

HALOLA (Hawaiian) Powerful army. *Variation:* Harola.

HALSE (English) From Hal's land.

HALSEY (English) The island that belongs to Hal. *Variations:* Hallsey, Hallsy, Halsy.

HALSTEAD (English) Grounds of the manor. *Variation:* Halsted.

HALSTEN (Scandinavian) Rock and stone. *Variations:* Hallstein, Hallsten, Hallston, Halston.

HALTON (English) Manor on the hill. *Variations:* Haltan, Halten, Haltin, Haltyn.

HALYARD (Scandinavian) Defender of the rock. *Variations:* Hallvard, Hallvor, Halvar, Halvor.

HAM (English) Town. Also, short form of Hamilton. *Variation:* Hamm.

HAMADI (Arabic) Praised. *Variation:* Hamidi.

HAMAL (Arabic) Lamb. *Variations:* Hamel, Hamil.

HAMER (Norse) Hammer. *Variations:* Hamar, Hammar, Hammer.

HAMFORD (English) Town with a ford.

HAMID (Arabic) Greatly praised. Derivative of Mohammed. *Variations:* Haamid, Hamadi, Hamed, Hameed, Hamidi, Hammad, Hammed.

HAMIDI (African) Admirable.

HAMILL (English) Scarred. *Variations:* Hamel, Hamell, Hamil, Hammill.

HAMILTON (English) Fortified castle. *Notable:* Politician Hamilton Jordan. *Variations:* Hamelton, Hamiltan, Hamilten, Hamiltun.

HAMISH (Scottish) He who removes.

HAMISI (African) Born on Thursday. *Variation:* Hanisi.

HAMLET (English) Village. *Notable:* Hamlet, Shakespeare's tragic Prince of Denmark.

HAMLIN (German) One who loves to stay at home. *Variations:* Hamelin, Hamlen, Hanlon, Hamlyn.

HAMMET (English) Village. *Variations:* Hammett, Hamnet, Hamnett.

HAMMOND (English) Village. *Variations:* Hammon, Hamon, Hamond.

HAMPTON (English) Small town. *Variations:* Hamptan, Hampten, Hamptin.

HAMUND (Scandinavian) Mythological figure.

HAMZA (Arabic) Powerful. *Variations:* Hamzah, Hamzeh.

HANAN (Hebrew) God is good. *Variation:* Hananel.

HANBAL (Arabic) Purity. *Variation:* Hanbel.

HANDEL (German) God is good. *Variations:* Handal, Handol.

HANDLEY (English) Clearing in the woods. *Variations:* Handleigh, Handlie, Handly.

HANEK (Czech) God is good. Variation of John. *Variations:* Hanus, Hanusek, Johan, Nusek.

HANFORD (English) High ford.

HANI (Arabic) Happy.

HANIF (Arabic) Believer. *Variations:* Haneef, Hanef.

HANK (English) Ruler of the estate. *Notables:* Baseball's Hank Aaron; actor Hank Azaria; country singer Hank Williams.

HANLEY (English) Of the high meadow. *Variations:* Hanleigh, Hanlie, Hanly.

HANNES (Scandinavian) God is good. Variation of John. *Variations:* Haensel, Hannu, Hans, Hansel, Hansl.

HANNIBAL (English) With the grace of God. *Notable:* Hannibal Lecter from *The Silence of the Lambs.* *Variation:* Hanibal.

HANRAOI (Irish) Ruler of the home. Variation of Henry.

HANS (Scandinavian) God is gracious. Form of John. *Notable:* Artist Hans Holbein.

HANSEL (Scandinavian) God is gracious. Form of Hans. *Notable:* Fairy tale character from "Hansel and Gretel." *Variation:* Hansil.

HANSON (Scandinavian) Son of Hans. *Variations:* Hansan, Hansen, Hansin, Hanssen, Hansson.

HANSRAT (Hindi) Swan king.

HANUMAN (Hindi) Chief of the monkeys.

HAO (Chinese) Good.

HAOA (Hawaiian) Observer. Hawaiian version of Howard.

HARAL (Scottish) Leader of the army. *Variations:* Arailt, Harall, Harell.

HARAM (Hebrew) Mountaineer.

School Daze: Names from Teachers (Part II)

This selection comes from a third grade class in Newark, New Jersey:

Diamond	Rstee
Jahid	Sherodasia
Kahlil	Tajia
Mykah	Taloupe
Nyasia	Tawuan
Raymear	Tryee

HARATH (Arabic) To provide. *Variation:* Harith.

HARB (Arabic) Warrior.

HARBERT (Scandinavian) Bright army.

HARBIN (French) Little bright warrior. *Variations:* Harban, Harben, Harbon, Harbyn.

HARCOURT (French) Fortified dwelling. *Variation:* Harcort.

HARDEEP (Punjabi) Loves God. *Variation:* Harpreet.

HARDEN (English) Valley of rabbits. *Variations:* Hardan, Hardin, Hardon.

HARDING (English) Hardy.

HARDWIN (English) Brave friend. *Variations:* Hardwen, Hardwyn, Hardwynn.

HARDY (English) Brave. *Variations:* Hardee, Hardie.

HAREL (Hebrew) Mountain of God. *Variations:* Harell, Harrell.

HARFORD (English) Ford of the hares.

HARGROVE (English) Grove of hares. *Variation:* Hargreave.

HARI (Hindi) Tawny.

HARISH (Hindi) Lord. *Variation:* Haresh.

HARITH (Arabic) Plowman. *Variation:* Harithah.

HARJEET (Hindi) Victorious.

HARKIN (Irish) Dark red. *Variations:* Harkan, Harken.

HARLAN (English) Army land. *Notable:* Writer Harlan Coben. *Variations:* Harland, Harlen, Harlenn, Harlin, Harlyn, Harlynn.

HARLEY (English) Rabbit pasture. *Variations:* Arlea, Arleigh, Arley, Harlea, Harlee, Harleiah, Harly.

HARLOW (English) Meadow of the hares.

HARMON (English) Form of Herman. *Variations:* Harman, Harmen, Harmin, Harmyn.

HARO (Japanese) First son of a boar.

HAROLD (English) Army ruler. *Notables:* Playwright Harold Pinter; theater producer/director Harold Prince. *Variations:* Hal, Harailt, Harald, Haraldas, Haraldo, Haralds, Hareld, Harild, Haroldas, Haroldo, Harrel, Harrol.

HAROUN (Arabic) Exalted. *Variations:* Haaroun, Haarun, Harin, Haron, Haroon, Haround, Harron, Harrun, Harun.

HARPER (English) Harp player. *Variation:* Harpo.

HARRINGTON (English) From Harry's town. *Variations:* Harringten, Harringtown.

HARRIS (English) Harry's son. Form of Harrison. *Variations:* Haris, Harrace, Harrice, Harrys.

HARRISON (English) Harry's son. *Notable:* Actor Harrison Ford. *Variations:* Harison, Harrisen, Harryson.

HARRY (English) Ruler at home. Variation of Henry. *Notables:* Britain's Prince Harry; U.S. President Harry Truman; popular literary character Harry Potter. *Variations:* Harrey, Harri, Harrie.

HARSHAD (Hindi) One who gives joy.

HARSHAL (Hindi) Happy. *Variations:* Harshil, Harshul.

HART (English) Stag. *Variation:* Harte.

HARTLEY (English) Deer meadow. *Variations:* Hartleigh, Hartlie, Hartly, Heartly.

HARTMAN (German) Hard man. *Variation:* Hartmann.

HARTWELL (English) Well where stags drink. *Variations:* Harwell, Harwill.

HARTWIG (German) Strong advisor.

HARUE (Japanese) Born in the spring. *Variation:* Haru.

HARVEY (French) Eager for battle. *Notables:* Actor Harvey Fierstein; comedian Harvey Korman. *Variations:* Harv, Herve, Hervey.

HARWOOD (English) Wood of hares.

HASAD (Turkish) Harvest. *Variation:* Hassad.

HASANT (African) Handsome.

HASHIM (Arabic) Destroyer of evil. *Variation:* Hasheem.

HASIM (Arabic) To determine.

HASIN (Hindi) Laughing. *Variation:* Hassin.

HASKEL (Hebrew) Wisdom. *Variations:* Chaskel, Haskell, Heskel.

HASLETT (English) Land of hazel trees. *Variations:* Haslet, Hazlett, Hazlitt.

HASSAN (Arabic) Handsome. *Variations:* Hasan, Hasain, Hasin, Hassan, Hassani, Hassen, Hasson, Husani.

HASSEL (English) From the witches' corner. *Variations:* Hassal, Hassall, Hassell.

HASTIN (Hindi) Elephant.

HASTINGS (English) Son of a miserly man.

HATDAR (Hindi) Lion. *Variations:* Haider, Haydar, Hayder, Hyder.

HATFEZ (Hindi) Protector.

HATIYA (Native American) Bear.

HATIM (Arabic) To decide.

HAU (Vietnamese) Desire.

HAVEA (Polynesian) Chief.

HAVEL (Czech) Small. *Variations:* Hava, Havelek, Havlik.

HAVELOCK (Scandinavian) Sea battler. *Variation:* Haveloch.

HAVEN (English) Sanctuary. *Variations:* Havin, Havon.

HAVIGAN (Celtic) White. *Variations:* Havigen, Havigin, Havigon, Havigun, Havigyn.

HAVIKA (Hawaiian) Beloved. A form of David.

HAWARD (Scandinavian) High defender.

HAWK (English) Falcon.

HAWKINS (English) Little hawk.

HAWLEY (English) Meadow with hedges. *Variations:* Hawleigh, Hawly.

HAWTHORN (English) Where hawthorns grow. *Variation:* Hawthorne.

HAYDEN (English) Hill of heather; (Welsh) Valley with hedges. *Notable:* Actor Hayden Christensen. *Variations:* Aidan, Hadan, Haddan, Haddon, Haden, Hadon, Hadyn, Haydin, Haydn, Haydon, Heydan, Heyden, Heydin, Heydn, Heydon, Heydun, Heydyn.

HAYES (English) Hedges. *Variation:* Hays.

HAYTHAM (Arabic) Proud.

HAYWARD (English) Protector of hedged area.

HAYWOOD (English) Hedged forest.

HEARNE (Scottish) Horse worker. *Variations:* Hearn, Hern, Herne.

HEATH (English) Heath. *Notable:* Actor Heath Ledger. *Variation:* Heathe.

HEATHCLIFF (English) Cliff near an open field. *Notables:* Heathcliff the Cat; Heathcliff, tragic hero of Emily Brontë's *Wuthering Heights*. *Variations:* Heathcliffe, Heathclyffe.

HEATHCOTE (English) Cottage on the heath.

HEATON (English) High town. *Variation:* Heatin.

HEBER (Hebrew) Gathering. *Variation:* Hebor.

HECTOR (Greek) Steadfast. *Notables:* Actor Hector Elizondo; boxer Hector "Macho" Camacho Jr. *Variations:* Heckter, Hecktor, Hectar, Hektor.

HEDDWYN (Welsh) Blessed peace. *Variations:* Hedwen, Hedwin, Hedwyn.

HEDEON (Russian) Logger. *Variations:* Hedion, Hedyon.

HEDLEY (English) Meadow of heather. *Variations:* Heddley, Hedleigh, Hedlie, Hedly.

HEDWIG (German) Fighter. *Variation:* Heddwig.

HEFIN (Welsh) Summer.

HEIMDALL (Scandinavian) White god.

HEINRICH (German) Ruler of the estate. Variation of Henry. *Variations:* Heinrick, Heinrik, Henrik, Henrique, Henryk.

HEINZ (German) Ruler of the house. Form of Henry. *Variations:* Hines, Hynes.

HEKEKA (Hawaiian) To hold fast. *Variation:* Heketa.

HELAKU (Native American) Sunny.

HELEMANO (Hawaiian) Army man. *Variation:* Heremano.

HELEUMA (Hawaiian) Mooring.

HELGI (Scandinavian) Happy. *Variations:* Helge, Helje.

HELI (Greek) Sun. *Variation:* Helio.

HELMUT (French) Warrior. *Notables:* German Chancellor Helmut Kohl; photographer Helmut Newton; fashion designer Helmut Lang. *Variations:* Helmer, Helmuth.

HEMAN (Hebrew) Faithful.

HEMENE (Native American) Wolf.

HENDERSON (English) Son of house ruler.

HENDRICK (Dutch; German) Ruler of the house. *Variations:* Hendric, Hendricks, Hendrickson, Hendrik, Hendriks, Hendrikus, Hendrix.

HENELI (Hawaiian) Ruler of the house. *Variations:* Hanale, Henele, Henely, Heneri.

HENLEY (English) High meadow. *Variations:* Henleigh, Henlie, Henly.

HENNING (German) Ruler of the house. Form of Henry. *Variations:* Hening, Hennings.

HENRICK (Dutch) Ruler of the house. Form of Henry. *Variations:* Henric, Henrik, Henrique, Henryk.

HENRY (German) Ruler of the house. *Notables:* Writers Henry James and Henry David Thoreau; poet Henry Longfellow; actor Henry Fonda; automobile innovator Henry Ford; U.S. Secretary of State Henry Kissinger; explorer Henry Hudson. *Variations:* Arrigo, Eanruig, Enrique, Henery, Henrey, Henri, Henrie.

HERALD (English) Bearer of news.

HERBERT (German) Shining army. *Notables:* U.S. President Herbert Hoover; actor Herbert Lom. *Variations:* Ebert, Hebert, Heibert, Herb, Herbe, Herberte, Herbertus, Herbie, Herbirt, Herburt, Herby.

HERBRAND (German) Army sword. *Variations:* Herbran, Herbrandt, Herbrant.

HERCULES (Greek) Glory. *Variations:* Heracles, Herakles, Hercule.

HEREWARD (English) Military. *Variation:* Herward.

HERLEIF (Scandinavian) Beloved army. *Variations:* Harlief, Herlof, Herluf.

HERMAN (German) Army man. *Notables:* Writers Herman Melville and Hermann Hesse. *Variations:* Armand, Hermando, Hermann, Hermano, Hermanus, Hermi, Hermie, Hermon, Hermy.

HERMES (Greek) Mythological messenger of the Greek gods.

HERN (English) Heron. *Variations:* Hearn, Hearne, Herne.

HERNANDO (Spanish) Brave traveler. *Variations:* Hernandes, Hernandez.

HEROD (Greek) Protector.

HEROMIN (Polish) Estate head.

HERRICK (German) War ruler. *Variations:* Heric, Herick, Herik, Herric, Herrik.

HERSCHEL (Hebrew) Deer. *Notable:* Actor Herschel Bernardi. *Variations:* Hersch, Hersh, Hershel, Hersz, Hertz, Hertzel, Herz, Herzl, Heschel, Hesh, Hirsch, Hirschel.

HERVE (French) Army warrior.

HERZOG (German) Duke. *Variation:* Hertzog.

HESPEROS (Greek) Evening star. *Variation:* Hespero.

HESUTU (Native American) Taking a wasps' nest.

HEVEL (Hebrew) Breath. *Variation:* Hevell.

HEWITT (English) Smart one.

HEWLETT (German) Little Hugh. *Variation:* Hewlitt.

HEWNEY (Irish) Green. *Variations:* Aney, Hewny, Oney, Owney, Oynie, Uaithne.

HEWSON (English) Hugh's son.

HEZEKIAH (Hebrew) God is my strength.

HIALMAR (Scandinavian) Warrior's helmet. *Variation:* Hialmar.

HIAWATHA (Native American) Maker of rivers.

HIBAH (Arabic) Gift.

HIDEAKI (Japanese) Wise.

HIDEO (Japanese) Bet.

HIEN (Vietnamese) Sweet.

HIEREMIAS (Greek) The Lord will uplift.

HIERONYMUS (Latin) Form of Jerome. *Notable:* Artist Hieronymus Bosch.

HIEU (Vietnamese) Respect.

HIFO (Polynesian) Atonement.

HIKILA (Polynesian) To raise the sail.

HIKMAT (Arabic) Knowledge.

HILAL (Arabic) New moon. *Variation:* Hilel.

HILARION (Greek) Cheerful. *Variation:* Ilarion.

HILARY (Greek) Happy. *Variations:* Hilaire, Hilarie, Hillario, Hillary, Hillery.

HILDEBRAND (German) Sword used in battle.

HILDERIC (German) Warrior. *Variations:* Hilderic, Hildrich, Hildriche.

HILLARD (German) Tough soldier. *Variations:* Hilard, Hilliard, Hillier, Hillyer.

HILLEL (Hebrew) Highly praised.

HILMAR (Scandinavian) Renowned nobleman. *Variations:* Hillmar, Hilmer.

HILTON (English) Town on a hill. *Variation:* Hylton.

HIMESH (Hindi) Snow king.

HINTO (Native American) Blue.

HINUN (Native American) God of rain.

HIPPOCRATES (Greek) The father of medicine.

HIPPOLYTE (Greek) Horse.

HIPPOLYTOS (Greek) One who frees horses.

HIRAM (Hebrew) Most noble man. *Variations:* Hirom, Hyrum.

HIROHITO (Japanese) Emperor.

HIROMASA (Japanese) Direct.

HIROSHI (Japanese) Generous.

HIRSH (Hebrew) Deer. *Variations:* Hersch, Herschel, Hersh, Hershel, Hersz, Hertz, Hertzel, Herz, Herzl, Heschel, Hesh, Hirsch, Hirschel.

HISHAM (Arabic) Generosity. *Variation:* Hishim.

HISOKA (Japanese) Restrained.

HITOSHI (Japanese) First.

HIUWE (Hawaiian) Heart. *Variations:* Hiu, Huko.

HJAIMER (Scandinavian) Glorious helmet.

HO (Chinese) Good.

HOA (Vietnamese) Flower.

HOANG (Vietnamese) Completed.

HOBART (German) Brilliant mind. *Variation:* Hobard.

HOBSON (English) Son of the bright and famous one. *Variation:* Hobsen.

HOC (Vietnamese) Learn.

HOD (Hebrew) Wonderful.

HODAKA (Japanese) Mountain.

HODDING (Dutch) Bricklayer.

HODER (Scandinavian) Ancient mythological figure. *Variation:* Hodur.

HODGSON (English) Son of Roger. Renowned spearsman.

HODIAH (Hebrew) God is great. *Variations:* Hodia, Hodiya.

HOENIR (Scandinavian) Ancient mythological figure. *Variation:* Honir.

HOFFMAN (German) Courtier. *Variations:* Hofman, Hoffmann.

Cowboy Names

If you love Westerns, maybe your little pardner might fare well with one of these rugged cowboy names.

Audie	Jesse
Boone	Kidd
Buck	Kit
Butch	Laredo
Cassidy	Ringo
Carson	Roy
Cisco	Slim
Cody	Tex
Dallas	Wyatt
Jack	

Seeing the Forest for the Trees

If you're an outdoorsy type who loves nature, these names will evoke the majesty of forests and trees.

BOYS:	GIRLS:
Ashton	Acacia
Birch	Ashley
Elan	Hazel
Ellery	Ilana
Heath	Juniper
Kirkwood	Keziah
Lyndon	Laurel
Oakley	Lindsay
Oren	Magnolia
Perry	Nara
Shaw	Olivia
Sherwood	Ornella
Sylvester	Rowan
Walden	Sequoia
Waverly	Willow

HOGAN (Irish) Youth. *Variation:* Hogen.

HOHOTS (Native American) Bear.

HOKEA (Hawaiian) Salvation. Hawaiian version of Hosea.

HOKU (Hawaiian) Star.

HOLA (Polynesian) Run away.

HOLAKIO (Hawaiian) Hawaiian version of Horatio. *Variations:* Holeka, Horesa.

HOLATA (Native American) Alligator.

HOLBROOK (English) Brook on a hollow. *Variation:* Holbrooke.

HOLCOMB (English) Deep valley. *Variation:* Holcombe.

HOLDEN (English) Hollow valley. *Notable:* Fictional hero Holden Caulfield from *The Catcher in the Rye. Variations:* Holdan, Holdin, Holdon, Holdun, Holdyn.

HOLGER (German) Rich spear.

HOLIC (Czech) Barber. *Variations:* Holick, Holik.

HOLISI (Polynesian) House built of reeds.

HOLLAND (English) Country.

HOLLEB (Polish) Dove-like. *Variations:* Hollub, Holub.

HOLLIS (English) Near the holly trees.

HOLMAN (Norse) From the hollow. *Variations:* Hollman, Hollmen, Holmen.

HOLMES (English) Islands in a stream.

HOLT (English) Forest. *Variations:* Holtan, Holten, Holtin, Holton.

HOMER (Greek) Hostage. *Notable:* TV cartoon dad Homer Simpson. *Variations:* Homar, Homere, Homero, Homeros, Homerus, Omer.

HONDO (African; Egyptian) War.

HONESTER (English) Stone or tool sharpener.

HONESTO (Filipino) Honest.

HONI (Hebrew) Gracious.

HONOK (Polish) One who leads at home.

HONON (Native American) Bear.

HONORE (Latin) Honored.

HONOVI (Native American) Strong.

HONZA (Czech) God is good.

HOPKIN (English) Bright renown. Last name. Variation of Robert.

HORACE (Latin) Punctual. *Notables:* Educator Horace Mann; newspaper editor/politician Horace Greeley. *Variations:* Horatius, Horats, Horaz.

HORATIO (Latin) Hour. *Notables:* Writer Horatio Alger; British Navy Admiral Horatio Nelson; literary hero Horatio Hornblower. *Variations:* Horacio, Horazio.

HORIMIR (Slavic) From the hill. *Variations:* Horemer, Horemir, Horimer.

HORST (German) Undergrowth.

HORTON (English) Gray town. *Variations:* Horten, Hortin, Hortun, Hortyn.

HORUS (Egyptian) Distant one. God of the sky. *Variation:* Horuss.

HOSA (Native American) Crow.

HOSEA (Hebrew) Salvation.

HOSHAMA (Hebrew) God hears you.

HOSNI (Arabic) Excellence. *Variation:* Husni.

HOSYU (Japanese) Reserved.

HOTA (Native American) White.

HOTAIA (Polynesian) Mine.

HOTOTO (Native American) Whistler.

HOUGHTON (English) Town on the cliff. *Variations:* Houghtan, Houghten, Houghtin.

HOUSTON (English) Town on the hill. *Variations:* Houstan, Housten, Houstin, Houstun, Houstyn, Huston.

HOWARD (English) Observer. *Notables:* Aviator/billionaire/film producer/eccentric Howard Hughes; shock jock Howard Stern; hotelier Howard Johnson. *Variations:* Howey, Howie, Howy.

HOWE (German) High.

HOWELL (Welsh) Remarkable.

HOWIN (Chinese) A swallow.

HOWLAND (English) Land with hills. *Variations:* Howlan, Howlen.

HOYLE (English) From the hollow. *Variations:* Hoil, Hoile, Hoyl.

HOYT (Irish) Spirit. *Notable:* Singer/actor Hoyt Axton.

HU (Chinese) Tiger.

HUANG (Chinese) Wealthy.

HUANU (Hawaiian) God is good.

HUBERT (German) Bright mind. *Notable:* U.S. Senator Hubert Humphrey. *Variations:* Hubbard, Hube, Huber, Huberto, Hubirt, Huburt, Huey, Hugh, Hughes, Hugibert, Hugo, Umberto.

HUDSON (English) Son of a hooded man. *Variations:* Hudsan, Hudsen, Hudsin, Hudsyn.

HUEY (English) Intelligent. Form of Hugh. *Notables:* Singer Huey Lewis; Governor Huey Long; Black Panther Huey Newton.

HUGH (English) Intelligent. *Notables:* Playboy Hugh Hefner; actors Hugh Grant and Hugh Jackman. *Variations:* Aodh, Aoidh, Hew, Huey, Hughes, Hughie, Hugues, Huw.

HUGO (Latin) Intelligent. Form of Hugh. *Notable:* Fashion designer Hugo Boss. *Variations:* Huego, Hughgo, Ugo.

HULA (Native American) Eagle.

HULAMA (Hawaiian) Brilliant.

HULBERT (German) Shining grace. *Variations:* Hulbard, Hulbart, Hulberte, Hulbirt, Hulburt.

HULDA (Scandinavian) Covered.

HULWEMA (Native American) Dead grizzly bear.

HUMAYD (Arabic) To praise.

HUMBERT (German) Famous warrior. *Notable:* Lolita protagonist Humbert Humbert. *Variations:* Humberto, Humbirt, Humburt, Umberto.

HUMPHREY (English) Peaceful. *Notable:* Actor Humphrey Bogart. *Variations:* Humfredo, Humfrey, Humfrid, Humfried, Humphery, Humphry.

HUNG (Vietnamese) Courageous.

HUNT (English) To hunt.

HUNTER (English) Hunter. *Notable:* Gonzo journalist Hunter S. Thompson.

HUNTINGTON (English) Hunting estate. *Variation:* Huntingdon.

HUNTLEY (English) Meadow of the hunter. *Variations:* Huntlea, Huntlee, Huntleigh, Huntly.

HURLBERT (English) Bright army.

HURLEY (Irish) Sea tide. *Variations:* Hurleigh, Hurly.

HURST (English) Grove of trees. *Variations:* Hearst, Hirst.

HUSAM (Arabic) Sword.

HUSANI (Swahili) Handsome.

HUSH (English) Quiet.

HUSNI (Arabic) Perfection.

HUSSEIN (Arabic) Handsome. *Variations:* Husain, Husein, Hussain.

HUTCHINSON (English) Son of a hutch dweller.

HUTTON (English) House on a ledge. *Variations:* Huttan, Hutten, Huttin, Huttun.

HUXFORD (English) Hugh's ford.

HUXLEY (English) Hugh's meadow. *Variations:* Hux, Huxlea, Huxlee, Huxleigh, Huxly.

HUY (Vietnamese) Light.

HUYU (Japanese) Winter.

HY (English) Short form of Hyatt or Hyman.

HYATT (English) High gate. *Variation:* Hiatt.

HYDE (English) Measure of land in England in the Middle Ages.

HYMAN (English) Form of Chaim.

HYO (Korean) Childhood devotion.

HYWEL (Welsh) Famous. *Variation:* Hywell.

IAGAN (Scottish) Little fiery one. *Variation:* Egan.

IAGO (Welsh; Spanish) Supplanter. *Notable:* Character in Shakespeare's Othello.

IAKEKE (Hawaiian) Descendant. *Variation:* Ialekah.

IAKEPA (Hawaiian) Jasper; a semiprecious stone. *Variations:* Iasepa, Kakapa, Kasapa.

IAKONA (Hawaiian) To heal. *Variation:* Iasona.

IAKOPA (Hawaiian) Supplanter. Form of Jacob.

IAKOVOS (Greek; Hebrew) Supplanter. Form of Jacob.

IALEKA (Hawaiian) Descendant. *Variation:* Iareda.

IAN (Scottish) God is good. Form of John. *Notables:* James Bond creator Ian Fleming; Jethro Tull lead singer Ian Anderson; actors Ian McKellen and Ian McShane. *Variations:* Ean, Iain, Iancu, Ianos.

IANTO (Welsh) God is gracious. *Variations:* Ifan, Ifaen.

IAOKIM (Hebrew) God will establish.

IAPETUS (Greek) A titan.

IARLAITH (Irish) Tributary lord. *Variations:* Iarfhlaith, Jarlath.

IASON (Greek) Healer.

IASSEN (Bulgarian) Ash tree.

IAVOR (Bulgarian) Sycamore tree.

IBN (Arabic) Son.

IBRAHIM (Arabic) Father of many. Variation of Abraham. *Variation:* Ibraham.

IBSEN (German) Son of the archer. *Variations:* Ibsan, Ibsin, Ibson, Ibsyn.

IBYCUS (Greek) A bard.

ICARUS (Greek) Follower.

ICHABOD (Hebrew) The glory is no more. *Notable:* Ichabod Crane, character from "The Legend of Sleepy Hollow" by Washington Irving. *Variations:* Ikabod, Ikavod.

ICHIRO (Japanese) First son.

IDAL (English) From the yew tree valley.

IDAN (Hebrew) Era.

IDAS (Greek) An Argonaut.

IDEN (Celtic) Prosperous.

IDI (African) Born during a festival.

IDRIS (Welsh) Impulsive.

IDWAL (Welsh) Lord of the wall.

IEKE (Hawaiian) Wealth. *Variation:* Iese.

IELEMIA (Hawaiian) God will lift up. *Variation:* Ieremia.

IESTYN (Welsh) Moral. *Variation:* Iestin.

IFAN (Welsh) God is gracious. Form of John.

IFOR (Welsh) Archer.

IGAL (Hebrew) God will avenge. *Variations:* Igale, Igeal.

IGASHO (Native American) Wanderer.

IGDALIAH (Israeli) Greatness of the Lord.

IGGY (Latin) Form of Ignatius. *Notable:* Rock singer Iggy Pop.

IGHNEACHAN (Irish) Strong man.

IGNAAS (Scandinavian) Fire.

IGNATIUS (English) Fervent; on fire. *Notable:* St. Ignatius of Loyola. *Variations:* Iggy, Ignac, Ignace, Ignacek, Ignacio, Ignatious, Ignatz, Ignaz, Ignazio, Inigo, Nacek, Nacicek.

IGOR (Russian; Scandinavian) Heroic warrior. *Notables:* Composer Igor Stravinsky; aviation pioneer Igor Sikorsky.

IHAB (Arabic) Present.

IHORANGI (Polynesian) Rain.

IHSAN (Arabic) Benevolence.

IIARI (Spanish) Cheerful.

IIIAN (Spanish) Youth.

IISHIM (Hindi) Spring.

IKAAKA (Hawaiian) Laughter. *Variations:* Aikake, Isaaka.

IKAIA (Hawaiian) God is my savior. *Variation:* Isaia.

IKAIKALANI (Hawaiian) Spiritual power.

IKALE (Polynesian) Eagle.

IKAMALOHI (Polynesian) Fish.

IKANI (Polynesian) Small, hot-headed child.

IKE (English) Short for Isaac. *Notable:* Musician Ike Turner. *Variations:* Ikey, Ikie.

IKENAKI (Hawaiian) Fire.

IKLAL (Arabic) Crown of believers.

ILARIO (Italian) Cheerful. *Variation:* Ilaryo.

ILBERT (German) Distinguished warrior. *Variations:* Ilbirt, Ilburt, Ilbyrt.

ILIAS (Greek) The Lord is my God. Form of Elijah. *Variations:* Ilia, Ilie.

ILKER (Turkish) First man.

ILIAN (Spanish) Youth.

ILLINGWORTH (English) Town in Britain.

ILLTUD (Welsh) Land of many people. *Variation:* Illtyd.

ILLYA (Russian) The Lord is my God. *Variations:* Ilja, Ilya, Ilyah, Ilyas. Ilom (African) My enemies are many.

IL-SUNG (Korean) Superior.

IMAD (Arabic) Pillar of support.

IMAM (African) Religious leader.

IMAROGBE (African) Child born to a good family.

IMBERT (German) Poet. *Variations:* Imbirt, Imburt, Imbyrt.

IMRAN (Arabic) Host. *Variations:* Imren, Imrin, Imryn.

IMRICH (Czech) Strength at home. *Variation:* Imrus.

INAR (English) Individual.

INCE (Hungarian) Innocent.

INCENCIO (Spanish) White one.

INDIANA (American) Land of the Indians. *Notable:* Film hero Indiana Jones.

INDIGO (English) Violet blue.

INDIVAR (Hindi) Blue lotus.

INDRA (Sanskrit) Possessing drops of rain.

INERNEY (Irish) Steward of church land.

INGALL (German) Angel. *Variations:* Ingal, Ingalls, Ingel.

INGELBERT (German) Brilliant angel. *Variations:* Engelbert, Ingleberte, Ingelbirt, Ingelburt, Ingelburte, Ingelbyrt.

INGEMAR (Scandinavian) Famous son. *Notable:* Film director Ingmar Bergman. *Variations:* Ingamar, Inge, Ingemur, Ingmar.

INGER (Scandinavian) Son's army. *Variations:* Ingar, Inghar.

INGO (Scandinavian) Male leader.

INGRAM (English) Raven. *Variations:* Ingraham, Ingrim.

INGVAR (Scandinavian) Ing's protector.

INIGO (Spanish) Ardent. From Ignatius. *Notable:* Architect Inigo Jones.

INIKO (African) Hard times.

INIR (Welsh) Honorable. *Variation:* Inyr.

INMAN (English) Innkeeper.

INNES (Scottish) Island. *Variations:* Inness, Innis, Inniss, Inys.

INNOCENZIO (Italian) Innocent. *Variations:* Inocencio, Inocente.

INOKE (Polynesian) Devoted.

INOKENE (Hawaiian) Innocent.

INRIQUE (Spanish) Ruler of the home.

INTEUS (Native American) Unashamed.

INTREPID (Latin) Fearless.

IOAKIM (Russian) God will judge.

IOAN (Welsh) God is gracious.

IOELA (Hawaiian) God is Lord.

IOKEPA (Hawaiian) God will increase. *Variations:* Iokewe, Iosepa.

IOKIA (Hawaiian) God heals. *Variations:* Iokiah, Iokya, Iokyah.

IOKINA (Hawaiian) God will develop. *Variation:* Wakina.

IOKUA (Hawaiian) God helps.

IOLO (Welsh) Worthy Lord.

ION (Irish) God is good. *Variation:* Ionnes.

IONA (Hawaiian) Dove.

IONAKANA (Hawaiian) God will give. *Variation:* Ionatana.

IONGI (Polynesian) Young.

IORGES (Greek) Farmer. Form of George.

IORWERTH (Welsh) Handsome lord. *Variations:* Iorweth, Yorath.

IOSEPH (Hebrew) God will increase. *Variation:* Iosep.

IOV (Hebrew) God will establish.

IPYANA (African) Grace.

IRA (Hebrew) Observant. *Notables:* Lyricist Ira Gershwin; writer Ira Levin.

IRAM (English) Shining.

IRATEBA (Native American) Pretty bird. *Variations:* Arateva, Yaratev.

IREM (Arabic) Precious tree.

IRMIN (German) Strong and mighty. *Variations:* Irman, Irmen, Irmun, Irmyn.

IROMAGAJA (Native American) Crying. *Variation:* Iromagaju.

IRSHAD (African) Guidance. *Variation:* Irshaad.

IRVIN (Scottish) Beautiful. *Variations:* Irven, Irvine, Irvyn.

IRVING (English) Sea friend. *Notables:* Composer Irving Berlin; writers Irving Stone and Irving Wallace; film producer Irving Thalberg. *Variations:* Irv, Irvyn, Irvyng.

IRWIN (English) Sea friend. Form of Irving. *Notables:* Writer Irwin Shaw; film producers Irwin Winkler and Irwin Allen. *Variations:* Erwin, Irwyn.

ISA (Sanskrit) Lord. *Variation:* Isah.

ISAAC (Hebrew) Laughter. *Notables:* Violinist Isaac Stern; writer and biochemist Isaac Asimov; musician/singer Isaac Hayes; physicist/mathematician Sir Isaac Newton; writer Isaac Bashevis Singer. *Variations:* Isaak, Isaakios, Isak, Itzak, Ixaka, Izaak.

ISAIAH (Hebrew) God helps me. *Notable:* basketball star Isiah Thomas. *Variations:* Isa, Isaia, Isaias, Isia, Isiah, Issiah.

ISAM (Arabic) To safeguard. *Variations:* Isaam, Isamm.

ISAMBARD (Greek; German) Iron giant. *Variations:* Imbard, Imbart, Isambart.

ISAS (Japanese) Valuable.

ISEABAIL (Hebrew) Devoted to God.

ISEN (English) Iron. *Variation:* Isenham.

ISHA (Hindi) Lord.

ISHAAN (Hindi) Sun. *Variation:* Ishan.

ISHAM (English) Area in Britain.

ISHAQ (Arabic) Laughter.

ISHARA (Hindi) Sign.

ISHMAEL (Hebrew) God will hear. *Variations:* Ismael, Ismail, Ismal, Ismale, Yishmael.

ISI (Japanese) Rock.

ISIDORE (Greek) Gift from Isis. *Variations:* Isador, Isadore, Isadorer, Isadoro, Isidor, Isidro, Issy, Izador, Izadore, Izzy.

ISIKELI (Polynesian) God is strong.

ISKANDAR (Arabic) Protector. *Variation:* Iskander.

ISKEMU (Native American) Stream.

ISLWYN (Welsh) Grove.

ISMAH (Arabic) God listens. *Variation:* Ismatl.

ISMAT (Arabic) Protector.

ISRA (Turkish) Freedom.

ISRAEL (Hebrew) Struggle with God. *Variations:* Isreal, Yisrael.

ISSA (African) Protection.

ISSAY (African) Hairy.

ISSUR (Hebrew) From Israel.

ISTU (Native American) Pine sap.

ISTVÁN (Hungarian) Crown. *Variation:* Isti.

ITALO (Italian) Italy.

ITAMAR (Hebrew) Palm-grove island. *Variation:* Ittamar.

ITHEL (Welsh) Charitable lord.

ITHNAN (Hebrew) Strong sailor.

ITIEL (Hebrew) God is with me.

ITZAINA (Basque) Shepherd.

ITZHAK (Hebrew) Form of Isaac. *Notable:* Musician Itzhak Perlman. *Variation:* Yitzhak.

IUKEKINI (Hawaiian) Righteous.

IUKINI (Hawaiian) Well born. *Variation:* Iuaini.

IUSTIG (Welsh) Legendary son of Caw.

IVAN (Czech) God is good. *Notables:* Director Ivan Reitman; arbitrageur Ivan Boesky; tennis pro Ivan Lendl; Russian Czar Ivan the Terrible;

writer Ivan Turgenev. *Variations:* Iva, Ivanchik, Ivanek, Ivankor, Ivano, Ivin, Ivon, Ivun, Ivyn, Yvan, Yvann.

IVANHOE (Hebrew) God's gracious tiller of the soil. *Variations:* Ivanho, Ivanhow.

IVAR (Danish; Scandinavian) Archer with a yew bow. *Variations:* Iver, Iviy, Ivor, Yvon, Yvor.

IVEN (French) Little yew bow.

IVES (English) Yew wood; archer. *Variations:* Ivas, Ivo, Ivon, Yves.

IVOR (Scandinavian) Bow warrior. *Notable:* Welsh entertainer Ivor Novello. *Variations:* Ivar, Iver.

IVORY (African American) *Variations:* Ivoree, Ivorey, Ivori, Ivorie.

IYAPO (African) Tribulation.

IYE (Native American) Smoke.

IZOD (Celtic) Fair haired. *Variations:* Izad, Ized, Izid, Izud, Izyd.

IZZY (Hebrew) Laughter. Short form of Isaac or Isidore.

JA (Korean) Attraction.

JAALI (African) Powerful. *Variation:* Jalie.

JAAN (Estonian) Anointed.

JABARI (Arabic) To comfort; (African) Fearless. *Variations:* Jabare, Jabary, Jabier.

JABBAR (Hindi; Arabic) One who comforts. *Variations:* Jabar, Jabir.

JABEZ (Hebrew) Born in pain. *Variations:* Jabes, Jabesh, Jabus.

JABILO (African) Medicine Man.

JABIN (Hebrew) God has created.

JABULANI (African) Happy.

JACAN (Hebrew) Trouble. *Variation:* Jacon.

JACE (Greek) Healer. Form of Jason. *Variations:* Jacee, Jacey, Jaci, Jacie, Jacy, Jaec, Jaece, Jaic, Jaice, Jaicee, Jaicey, Jaicie, Jaicy, Jayce, Jaycee, Jaycey, Jaycie, Jaycy.

JACHYM (Czech) God will develop. *Variation:* Jach.

JACINTO (Spanish) Hyacinth. *Variations:* Ciacintho, Clacinto, Jacindo.

JACK (American) Familiar form of Jacob, Jackson, John. *Notables:* Actors Jack Nicholson and Jack Lemmon; golfer Jack Nicklaus; CEO Jack Welch; fitness guru Jack LaLanne. *Variations:* Jaac, Jaack, Jaak, Jac, Jacke, Jacki, Jackie, Jacky, Jak, Jakk.

JACKIE (American) Form of Jacob, Jackson, or John. *Notables:* Comedians Jackie Gleason and Jackie Mason. *Variation:* Jacky.

JACKSON (English) Son of Jack. *Notables:* Singer Jackson Browne; artist Jackson Pollock. *Variations:* Jakson, Jaxon.

JACOB (Hebrew) Supplanter or heel. *Notable:* U.S. Senator Jacob Javits. *Variations:* Jaco, Jacobb, Jacobo, Jacobos, Jacobs, Jacobson, Jacobus, Jacoby, Jacopo, Jacquet, Jaecob, Jaekob, Jaicob, Jaikob, Jakab, Jake, Jakie, Jakiv, Jakob, Jakobus, Jakov, Jakub, Jakubek, Jaycob, Jaycobb, Jaykob, Kiva, Kivi.

JACOBSON (English) Son of Jacob.

JACQUES (French) Supplanter. French form of Jacob or Jack.

Variations: Jacot, Jacquet, Jacquez, Jarques, Jarquis.

JACY (Native American) Moon. *Variations:* Jaecee, Jaecey, Jaecie, Jaecy, Jaicee, Jaicey, Jaicie, Jaicy, Jaycee, Jaycey, Jaycie, Jaycy.

JADEN (Hebrew) God has heard. *Variations:* Jadan, Jadin, Jadon, Jadyn, Jaydn.

JADRIEN (American) Combination of Jay and Adrien. *Variations:* Jaedrian, Jaedrien, Jaidrian, Jaidrien, Jaydrian, Jaydrien.

JAEGAR (German) Hunger. *Variations:* Jaager, Jagur, Jaigar, Jaygar.

JAE-HWA (Korean) Wealthy.

JAEL (Hebrew) To ascend. *Variation:* Yael.

JAFAR (Arabic) River. *Variations:* Gafar, Jafari, Jaffar.

JAGANNATH (Hindi) God of all.

JAGGER (English) To haul something. *Variation:* Jaggar.

JAGJIT (Hindi) Victor of the world.

JAGO (English) Supplanter. Form of Jacob, James. *Variations:* Jaego, Jaigo, Jaygo.

JAHAN (Arabic) World.

JAHI (African) Dignity.

JAIDEN (Hebrew) God has heard. Form of Jaden. *Variations:* Jaedan, Jaeden, Jaedin, Jaedon, Jaedyn, Jaidan, Jaidin, Jaidon, Jaidyn.

JAIDEV (Hindi) God of victory.

JAIME (Spanish) Supplanter. A form of James.

JAIMINI (Hindi) Victorious one.

JAINENDRA (Hindi) Victorious lord of the sky. *Variation:* Jinendra.

JAIRAJ (Hindi) Victorious lord.

JAIRUS (Hebrew) God enlightens. *Variations:* Jair, Jairo, Jarrius, Jayro, Jayrus.

JAJA (African) Honor.

JAJUAN (African American) God is gracious.

JAKE (Hebrew) Supplanter. Short form of Jacob. *Notable:* Actor Jake Gyllanhaal.

JAKEEM (Arabic) Noble. *Variation:* Jakim.

JAKUB (Czech) Supplanter. *Variations:* Jakoubek, Kuba, Kubes, Kubicek.

JAL (Gypsy) Wanderer.

JALA (Arabic) Clarity.

JALAAD (Arabic) Glory. *Variation:* Jalad.

JALADHI (Hindi) Ocean.

JALAL (Arabic) Great. *Variation:* Galal.

JALEEL (Hindi) Revered. *Notable:* Jaleel White (Steve Urkel from TV's *Family Matters*). *Variations:* Jahleel, Jahlil, Jaleal, Jalel.

JALEN (African American) Calm. *Variations:* Jalan, Jalin, Jalon, Jalyn.

JAMAINE (Arabic) German. *Variations:* Jamain, Jamayn, Jamayne.

JAMAL (Arabic) Handsome. *Variations:* Gamal, Gamil, Jahmal, Jahmall, Jahmalle, Jahmil, Jahmile, Jahmill, Jamaal, Jamael, Jamahl, Jamail, Jamall, Jameel, Jamel, Jamell, Jamil, Jamill, Jammal, Jemal.

Top Names in Brazil

BOYS:
1. Joao
2. Pedro
3. Lucas
4. Gabriel
5. Miguel
6. Davi
7. Matheus
8. Guilherme
9. Luis
10. Gustavo

GIRLS:
1. Maria
2. Ana
3. Julia
4. Yasmin
5. Beatriz
6. Isabella
7. Vitoria
8. Laura
9. Mariana
10. Leticia

JAMAR (African American) Handsome. Form of Jamal. *Variations:* Jamaar, Jamarr, Jemar, Jimar.

JAMARCUS (African American) Warrior. Combined form of Ja and Marcus. *Variations:* Jarmarc, Jamarco, Jamark, Jamarkus, Jemarcus.

JAMARIO (African American) Sailor. Combined form of Ja and Mario. *Variations:* Jamariel, Jamarius, Jemario.

JAMES (English) He who replaces. Variation of Jacob. *Notables:* Singer James Taylor; actor James Gandolfini. *Variations:* Jacques, Jaimito, Jaymes, Jim, Jimi, Jimmey, Jimmie, Jimmy.

JAMESON (English) Son of James. *Variations:* Jamerson, Jamesen, Jamieson, Jamison, Jaymeson, Jaymison.

JAMIE (English) Supplanter. Familiar form of James. *Notables:* Comedian/actor Jamie Foxx; celebrity chef Jamie Oliver. *Variations:* Jaime, Jaimey, Jaimie, Jamey, Jayme, Jaymie.

JAMIN (Hebrew) Favored one. *Variations:* Jaman, Jamen, Jamon, Jamyn.

JAMOND (African American) Wise protector. Combined form of Ja and Raymond. *Variations:* Jaemond, Jaemund, Jaimon, Jaimond, Jaimun, Jaimund, Jamon, Jamond, Jamun, Jamund, Jaymon, Jaymond, Jaymun, Jaymund.

JAMSHEED (Persian) From Persia.

JAN (Slavic) God is gracious. Form of John. *Variations:* Janco, Jancsi, Jando, Janecek, Janek, Janik, Janika, Jankiel, Janko, Janne, Jano, Janos, Jenda.

JANAKA (Sanskrit) Born of the ancestor.

JANDO (Czech) Defender of mankind. *Variations:* Jandin, Jandino.

JANESH (Hindi) Lord of the people.

JANSON (Scandinavian) Son of Jan. *Variations:* Jansen, Jantzen, Janzen.

JANUS (Latin) Born in January. The first month of the year. *Variations:* Janis, Janiusz, Janiuszek, Januarius, January.

JAPHETH (Hebrew) He increases. *Variations:* Jafet, Japhet, Japeth.

JAQUAN (Native American) Fragrant. *Variations:* Jacquin, Jaquana, Jaquin, Jaquon, Jaqwan.

JARAH (Hebrew) Sweet. *Variations:* Jara, Jarra, Jarrah, Jera, Jerah, Jerra, Jerrah.

JAREB (Hebrew) He struggles. *Variations:* Jarib, Yarev, Yariv.

JARED (Hebrew) Descend. *Notable:* Actor Jared Leto. *Variations:* Jarad, Jarid, Jarod, Jarrad, Jarred, Jerad, Jered, Jerod, Jerrad, Jerrod, Jerryd, Yarden, Yared.

JAREK (Czech) Spring. *Variations:* Jarec, Jareck, Jaric, Jarick, Jarik, Jariusz, Jariuszek, Jarousek.

JARELL (Scandinavian) Brave spear carrier. Form of Gerald. *Variations:* Jairel, Jairell, Jareil, Jarel, Jarrel, Jarrell, Jarryl, Jarryll, Jarul, Jerel, Jerell.

JARETH (African American) Combined form of Ja and Gareth. *Variations:* Jarith, Jarreth, Jarrith, Jarryth, Jaryth, Jerth.

JARIB (Hebrew) Avenger.

JARL (Danish) Noble.

JARMAN (German) German. *Variations:* Jarmen, Jarmin, Jarmon, Jarmyn, Jerman, Jermin, Jermon, Jermyn.

JAROGNIEW (Polish) Spring anger.

JAROMIERZ (Polish) Famous spring.

JAROMIL (Czech) One who loves spring. *Variation:* Jarmil.

JAROMIR (Czech) Great spring.

JARON (Hebrew) To sing or shout. *Variations:* Gerron, Jaran, Jaren, Jarin, Jarran, Jarren, Jarron, Jeran, Jeren, Jeron, Jerrin, Jerron, Yaron.

JAROPELK (Polish) Spring people.

JAROSLAV (Czech) Glorious spring. *Variations:* Jarda, Jaroslaw.

JARRETT (English) Brave with a spear. *Variations:* Jarat, Jaret, Jarit, Jarot, Jarrat, Jarret, Jarrete, Jarrit, Jarritt, Jarrot, Jarrott, Jaryt, Jarytt.

JARVIS (German) Honorable. *Variations:* Jarvice, Jarvise, Jarvys, Jarvyse, Jervis.

JASHA (Russian) He who replaces. Form of Jacob. *Variation:* Jascha.

JASHON (African American) Combined form of Ja and Shawn. *Variations:* JaSean, JaShaun, Jashawn, JaShonn.

JASON (Greek) Healer. *Notables:* Actors Jason Priestley and Jason Biggs. *Variations:* Jace, Jacen, Jacin, Jaeson, Jaison, Jase, Jasen, Jasin, Jasun.

JASPAL (Pakistani) Virtuous.

JASPER (English) Wealthy one. *Variation:* Jaspar.

JASSAN (Native American) Wolf. *Variations:* Jassen, Jasson.

JATINRA (Hindi) Sage plant.

JAVAN (Hebrew) Son of Biblical Japheth; (Latin) Angel of Greece. *Variations:* Jaavon, Jahvon, Javin, Javine, Javion, Javon, Javone, Javoney, Javonie, Javonn, Javyn, Jayvin, Jayvine, Jayvon, Jevan, Jevon.

JAVARIS (Latin) Skilled with a spear. *Variations:* Javar, Javario, Javarius, Javarre, Javarro, Javarus, Javoris.

JAVAS (Hindi) Fast.

JAVIER (Spanish) Homeowner. Variation of Xavier. *Notable:* Actor Javier Bardem.

JAWAHARLAL (Hindi) Victory.

JAWDAT (Arabic) Good. *Variation:* Gawdat.

JAWHAR (Arabic) Jewel.

JAY (French) Blue jay. *Notable:* TV talk-show host Jay Leno. *Variations:* Jae, Jai, Jave, Jaye, Jeays, Jeyes.

JAYAKRISHNA (Hindi) Victorious Krishna.

JAYCE (American) Healer. Form of Jason.

JAYDEN (Hebrew) God listens. Form of Jaden. *Variations:* Jaydan, Jaydin, Jaydon, Jaydyn.

JAYSON (Greek) Healer. Form of Jason. *Variations:* Jayce, Jaycen, Jaysen, Jaysin, Jayson, Jaysun.

JAZEPS (Latvian) God will increase.

JAZON (Polish) Healer. *Variations:* Jazan, Jazen, Jazin.

JAZZ (American) Jazz.

JEAN (French) God is gracious. French version of John. *Notable:* Artist/writer/filmmaker Jean Cocteau. *Variations:* Jean-Francois, Jean-Michel, Jeannot, Jean-Phillipe.

JEB (Hebrew) Beloved of God. Short form of Jebediah.

JEBEDIAH (Hebrew) Beloved of God. Form of Jedidiah. *Variations:* Jebadiah, Jebidia, Jebidiah, Jebidya, Jebodiah, Jebydiah.

JEDIDIAH (Hebrew) Beloved of God. *Variations:* Jed, Jedd, Jedediah, Jedidia, Yedidia, Yedidiah, Yedidya.

JEDREK (Polish) Powerful man. *Variations:* Jedrec, Jedreck, Jedric, Jedrick, Jedrik, Jedrus.

JEFF (English) Peace. Short form of Jefferson, Jeffrey. *Notables:* Racecar driver Jeff Gordon; actors Jeff Goldblum, Jeff Bridges, and Jeff Daniels.

JEFFERSON (English) Son of Jeffrey.

JEFFORD (English) Peaceful ford.

JEFFREY (German) Peace. *Notables:* Film studio chief Jeffrey Katzenberg. *Variations:* Geoff, Geoffrey, Geoffry, Gioffredo, Jeffarey, Jeffarie, Jeffary, Jefferey, Jefferies, Jeffery, Jeffries, Jeffry, Jefry, Joffre, Joffrey.

JEHAN (French) God is good.

JEHIEL (Hebrew) God lives.

JEHU (Hebrew) The Lord is King. *Variation:* Jehudi.

JELANI (African) Strong. *Variations:* Jalani, Jehlani, Jelaney, Jelanie, Jelany.

JEMOND (French) Worldly. *Variations:* Jemon, Jemonde, Jemone, Jemun, Jemund.

JENDA (Czech) God is good.

JENKIN (Flemish) Little John. *Variations:* Jenkins, Jenkyn, Jenkyns.

JENS (Danish) A form of John.

JENSI (Hungarian) Well born. *Variations:* Jenci, Jens, Jensey, Jensie.

JEPHTHA (Hebrew) God sets free.

JERALD (German) Brave spear carrier. A form of Gerald. *Variations:* Jeraldo, Jerold, Jeroldo, Jerrald, Jerraldo, Jerrold, Jerroldo.

JEREMIAH (Hebrew) God will uplift. *Variation:* Jerimiah

JEREMY (Hebrew) The Lord exalts. *Notable:* Actor Jeremy Irons. *Variations:* Jem, Jemmie, Jemmy, Jeramee, Jeramey, Jeramie, Jere, Jereme, Jeremey, Jeremi, Jeremia, Jeremias, Jeremie, Jeromie, Jeromy, Jerr.

JERIAH (Hebrew) God sees.

JERICHO (Arabic) City of the moon. *Variations:* Jericko, Jerico, Jeriko, Jerricko, Jerrico, Jerriko, Jerryko.

JERIEL (Hebrew) Vision of God. *Variations:* Jerial, Jerriel.

JERMAINE (German) German. *Variations:* Jermain, Jermane, Jermayne.

JEROME (Latin) Holy. *Notables:* Choreographer Jerome Robbins; composer Jerome Kern. *Variations:* Gerome, Jarom, Jarome, Jarrome, Jeroan, Jeron, Jerone, Jeronim, Jerrome.

JERRELL (English) Strong. *Variations:* Gerrell, Jarell, Jarrel, Jarrell, Jerel, Jeriel, Jerrel, Jerriel, Jerril, Jerul.

JERRICK (American) Combination of Jerry and Derek. *Variations:* Jeric, Jerick, Jerik, Jerric, Jerrie.

JERRY (English) A familiar form of Gerald or Jerome. *Notables:* Comedians Jerry Seinfeld, Jerry Lewis, and Jerry Stiller; singers Jerry Lee Lewis and Jerry Garcia; talk-show host Jerry Springer. *Variations:* Gerry, Jere.

JERVIS (English) Skilled with a spear. *Variations:* Gervase, Jervice.

JERZY (Polish) Farmer. *Notable:* Writer Jerzy Kosinski. *Variation:* Jersey.

JESSE (Hebrew) God exists. *Notables:* Rev. Jesse Jackson; Western outlaw Jesse James; Olympic track star Jesse Owens. *Variations:* Jesiah, Jess, Jessey, Jessie, Jessy.

JESUS (Hebrew) The Lord is my salvation.

JETHRO (Hebrew) Fame. *Variation:* Jeth.

JETT (English) Airplane. *Variation:* Jette.

JI (Chinese) Order.

JIAO-LONG (Chinese) Dragon.

JIBBEN (Gypsy) Life.

JIBRI (Arabic) Powerful.

JIE (Chinese) Wonderful person.

JIM (English) Supplanter. Short form of James. *Notables:* Comedian Jim Carrey; singer Jim Morrison.

JIMMY (English) Supplanter. Short form of James. *Notables:* Musicians Jimmy Page and Jimi Hendrix. *Variations:* Jimee, Jimi, Jimie, Jimmey, Jimmi, Jimmie, Jimy.

JIMOH (African) Born on Friday.

JIN (Chinese) Gold.

JINAN (Arabic) Garden.

JINDRICH (Czech) Home ruler. *Variations:* Jindra, Jindrik, Jindrisek, Jindrousek.

JING (Chinese) Capital.

JING-QUO (Chinese) Ruler of a nation.

JING-SHENG (Chinese) Born in the capital.

JIRAIR (Armenian) Strong and hard working.

JIRI (Czech) Farmer. *Variations:* Jira, Jiran, Jiranek, Jiricek, Jirik, Jirka, Jirousek.

JIRO (Japanese) Second son.

JITENDRA (Hindi) One who wins over the lord of the sky. *Variations:* Jeetendra, Jitender.

JIVAN (Hindi) Life. *Variations:* Jivin, Jivon.

JOAB (Hebrew) Praise the Lord. *Variation:* Jobe.

JOACHIM (Hebrew) God will determine. *Notable:* Actor Joaquin Phoenix. *Variations:* Joaquim, Joaquin.

JOAH (Hebrew) God is his brother.

JOB (Hebrew) Oppressed. *Variations:* Joab, Jobe, Joby.

JOCK (Scottish) Supplanter. Form of Jack or Jacob. *Variation:* Jacques.

JODY (English) God will increase. Form of Joseph or Jude. *Variation:* Jodie.

JOE (Hebrew) God will increase. Short for Joseph. *Notables:* Baseball legend Joe DiMaggio; football star Joe Montana. *Variations:* Jo, Joey.

JOEL (Hebrew) God is Lord. *Notable:* Actor Joel Grey. *Variation:* Yoel.

JOERGEN (Scandinavian) Farmer.

JOHANN (German) God is gracious. Form of John. *Notables:*

Composers Johann Strauss and Johann Sebastian Bach; inventor Johann Gutenberg.

JOHAR (Hindi) Jewel.

JOHN (Hebrew) God is gracious. *Notables:* Singer John Lennon; actor John Travolta; U.S. President John F. Kennedy. *Variations:* Jack, Jackie, Jacky, Joao, Jock, Jockel, Jocko, Johan, Johann, Johannes, Johnie, Johnnie, Johnny, Jon, Jonam, Jone, Jonelis, Jonnie, Jonny, Jonukas, Jonutis, Jovan, Jovanus, Jovi, Jovin, Jovito, Jovon, Juan, Juanito.

JOHNNY (English) Form of John. *Notables:* TV host Johnny Carson; actor Johnny Depp. *Variations:* Johnie, Johnney, Johnnie, Jonney, Jonnie, Jonny.

JOHNSON (English) Son of John. *Variations:* Johnston, Jonson.

JOJI (Japanese) Farmer.

JOJO (African) Born on Monday.

JOLON (Native American) Valley of the oak trees.

JO-LONG (Chinese) Large dragon.

JOMEI (Japanese) Light.

JON (Scandinavian) Short form of Jonathan; form of John.

JONAH (Hebrew) Dove. Biblical book. *Variations:* Jonas, Yonah, Yonas, Yunus.

JONAS (Greek) Dove. Form of Jonah. *Notable:* Scientist Dr. Jonas Salk.

JONATHAN (Hebrew) Gift from God. *Notables:* Comedian Jonathan Winters; writer Jonathan Swift. *Variations:* Johnathan, Johnathen, Johnathon, Jonathen, Jonathon, Jonnie, Jonny, Jonothon.

JONES (Welsh) Son of John. *Variation:* Jonesy.

JONIGAN (African American) Gift from God.

JONTE (African American) God is gracious. *Variations:* Johatay, Johate, Jontae.

JOOP (Dutch) God will increase. Form of Joseph.

JOOST (Dutch) Just.

JOR-EL (American) Name of Superman's father. *Variations:* Jorel, Jorell, Jorelle, Jorrel, Jorrell, Jorrelle.

JORAM (Hebrew) God is highly praised.

JORDAN (Hebrew) To descend. *Variations:* Jorden, Jordin, Jordy, Jori, Jorrin.

JORGE (Spanish) Farmer. *Variations:* Jorg, Jorgen.

JORMA (Finnish) Farmer. *Notable:* Guitarist Jorma Kaukonen.

JOSE (Spanish) Form of Joseph. *Notables:* Singer José Feliciano; baseball player Jose Canseco.

JOSEPH (Hebrew) God will increase. *Variations:* Josecito, Josef, Joseff, Joselito, Josep, Josephe, Josephus, Josip, Jozef, Jozeff.

JOSH (Hebrew) God is my salvation. Short form of Joshua. *Notables:* Singer Josh Groban; actor Josh Brolin. *Variation:* Joshe.

JOSHA (Hindi) Satisfaction.

JOSHUA (Hebrew) God is my salvation. *Variation:* Joshuah.

JOSIAH (Hebrew) God supports. *Variations:* Josia, Josias, Josua.

Nineteen Kids and Counting

Jim Bob and Michelle Duggar and their nineteen children are the focus of a popular TV reality show. The kids, who span a twenty-one-year range in age, all have names that begin with the letter "J."

Joshua	Jeremiah
Jana	Jason
John-David	James
Jill	Justin
Jessa	Jackson
Jinger	Johannah
Joseph	Jennifer
Josiah	Jordyn-Grace
Joy-Anna	Josie
Jedidiah	

JOSS (Chinese) Fate. *Variations:* Josse, Jossy.

JOTHAM (Hebrew) God is perfect. *Variations:* Jothem, Jothim, Jothom, Jothym.

JOVAN (Latin) Majestic. *Variations:* Jovaan, Jovaann, Jovani, Jovanic, Jovanie, Jovann, Jovanni, Jovannic, Jovannie, Jovannis, Jovanny, Jovany, Jovenal, Jovenel, Jovi, Jovian, Jovin, Jovito, Jovoan, Jovon, Jovonn, Jovonne, Yovan.

JOZA (Czech) God will increase. *Variations:* Jozanek, Jozka.

JUAN (Spanish) Form of John. *Notables:* President of Argentina Juan Peron; Colombian coffee icon Juan Valdez.

JUBAL (Hebrew) Ram's horn.

JUDAH (Hebrew) Praised.

JUDAS (Latin) Praised. Form of Judah.

JUDD (Hebrew) Praised. Form of Judah. *Notables:* Actors Judd Hirsch and Judd Nelson. *Variation:* Jud.

JUDE (Hebrew) Praise God. *Notable:* Actor Jude Law. *Variations:* Juda, Judah, Judas, Judd, Judson.

JUDSON (English) Son of Judd.

JULES (French) Youthful. Form of Julius. *Notable:* Writer Jules Verne. *Variations:* Jools, Jule.

JULIAN (Latin) Youthful. Version of Julius. Saint. *Notable:* Singer Julian Lennon. *Variations:* Julien, Julion, Julyan.

JULIO (Spanish) Form of Julius. *Notable:* Singer Julio Iglesias.

JULIUS (Latin) Young. *Notables:* Roman Emperor Julius Caesar;

basketball star Julius Erving. *Variations:* Giulio, Julio, Julot.

JUMAANE (African) Born on Tuesday.

JUMAH (African) Born on Friday. *Variation:* Juma.

JUN (Chinese) Truth.

JUNG-HWA (Korean) Virtuous.

JUNIOR (English) Young.

JUNIPERO (Spanish) Juniper berry.

JURGEN (German) Farmer. Variation of George.

JURI (Slavic) Farmer. Variation of George.

JUSTICE (Latin) Just. *Variations:* Giustino, Giusto, Justus.

JUSTIN (Latin) Just. *Notable:* Singer Justin Timberlake. *Variations:* Justen, Justino, Justo, Juston, Justyn.

JUVENTINO (Spanish) Youthful. *Variations:* Juventin, Juventine, Juvon, Juvone.

JVALANT (Hindi) Bright. *Variation:* Jwalant.

JYOTISH (Sanskrit) Moon.

KABIL (Turkish) Form of Cain.

KABIR (Hindi) Spiritual leader.

KABR (Hindi) Grass.

KACEY (Irish) Brave. *Variations:* Casey, Kace, Kacy, Kaecey, Kaecie, Kaecy, Kaesie, Kaesy, Kaicey, Kaicie, Kaicy, Kase, Kasey, Kasie, Kasym.

KADAR (Arabic) Powerful. *Variations:* Kade, Kadir, Kador, Kaedar.

KADE (Gaelic) Swamp. *Variations:* Cade, Kaed, Kaid, Kaide, Kayd.

KADEEM (Arabic) Servant. *Notable:* Actor Kadeem Hardison. *Variations:* Kadim, Khadeem.

KADIN (Arabic) Friend. *Variations:* Kadan, Kadeen, Kaden, Kadon.

KADIR (Arabic) Green. *Variation:* Kadeer.

KADISH (Aramaic) Sacred.

KADMIEL (Hebrew) God is first.

KADO (Japanese) Entrance.

KAELAN (Gaelic) Powerful soldier. *Variations:* Kael, Kaelen, Kaelin, Kaelon, Kailan, Kailin, Kalan, Kalen, Kalin, Kalon, Kaylan, Kaylen, Kaylin, Kaylon.

KAEMON (Japanese) Joyful. *Variation:* Kaeman, Kaemin, Kamon, Kaimon, Kaymon.

KAFELE (African) Worth dying for.

KAFIR (Arabic) Nonbeliever.

KAGA (Native American) Writer.

KAGAN (Irish) Form of Keegan.

KAHALE (Hawaiian) Home. *Variation:* Kahail.

KAHANA (Hawaiian) Priest.

KAHANU (Hawaiian) He breathes.

KAHATUNKA (Native American) Raven.

KAHAWAI (Hawaiian) River. *Variation:* Kaheka.

KAHIL (Turkish) Young. *Variations:* Cahil, Kahlil, Kaleel, Khaleel, Khalil.

KAHO (Polynesian) Arrow.

KAHOLO (Hawaiian) Runner.

KAHUA (Hawaiian) Fort.

KAI (Hawaiian) Sea.

KAIHAU (Polynesian) Leader.

KAIHE (Hawaiian) One who throws a spear.

KAIHEKOA (Hawaiian) One who is brave with a spear.

KAIKALA (Hawaiian) Caesar. *Variation:* Kaisara.

KAIKEAPONA (Hawaiian) One who learns.

KAILAHI (Polynesian) To gorge.

KAILEN (Irish) Powerful soldier. Form of Kaelan.

KAIPO (Hawaiian) Lover.

KAISER (German) Emperor.

KAJ (Danish) Earth.

KAJETAN (Polish) From Gaeta. Form of Gaetan.

KAKAIO (Hawaiian) God remembers. *Variations:* Kakalia, Zakaria.

KAKANA (Hawaiian) Powerful.

KAKAU (Polynesian) Swim.

KAKELAKA (Hawaiian) Biblical name.

KAKUMULANI (Hawaiian) Bottom of the sky.

KALA (Hindi) Black.

KALAILA (Hawaiian) Cleansing. *Variation:* Kalaida.

KALAMA (Hawaiian) Torch.

KALANI (Hawaiian) The heavens.

KALAUKA (Hawaiian) Lame. *Variation:* Kalauda.

KALAWINA (Hawaiian) Hairless. *Variation:* Kalavina.

KALE (Hawaiian) Man. *Variations:* Kalolo, Karolo.

KALEA (Hawaiian) Joy.

KALECHI (African) Praise God.

KALEO (Hawaiian) One voice.

KALEOLANI (Hawaiian) Heavenly sounds.

KALEPA (Hawaiian) Faithful. *Variation:* Kaleba.

KALEVI (Finnish) Hero. *Variation:* Kalevy.

KALHANA (Hindi) Poet.

KALID (Arabic) Eternal.

KALIKAU (Polynesian) Athletic.

KALIKIANO (Hawaiian) One who follows God.

KALIL (Arabic) Good friend. *Variation:* Kailil.

KALINGA (Hindi) Bird.

KALINO (Hawaiian) Brilliant.

KALIPEKONA (Hawaiian) Town on a cliff. *Variation:* Kalifetona.

KALIQ (Arabic) Artistic. *Variations:* Kalique, Khaliq.

KALIU (Persian) Maintain well.

KALKIN (Hindi) Tenth.

KALLE (French) Strong and masculine.

KALMIN (Scandinavian) Man. *Variations:* Kalman, Kalmen, Kalmon.

KALOGEROS (Greek) Fair old ace.

KALOOSH (Armenian) Blessed event.

KALU (Hindi) Name of founder of the Sikh religion.

KAMAHA (Hawaiian) Sleeping one.

KAMAKA (Hawaiian) Face.

KAMAKAKOA (Hawaiian) Brave eye.

KAMAKANI (Hawaiian) Wind.

KAMAL (Arabic) Perfect. *Variations:* Kamaal, Kameel, Kamil.

KAMALIELA (Hawaiian) God is my reward.

KAMANGENI (African) Relative.

KAMAR (Arabic) Moon.

KAMAU (African) Warrior.

KAMBAN (Hindi) Twelfth-century poet.

KAMEKONA (Hawaiian) Strong man. *Variation:* Samesona.

KAMERON (Celtic) Crooked nose. *Variations:* Cameron, Kameren, Kamerin.

KAMI (Hindi) Loving. *Variations:* Kamey, Kamie, Kamy.

KAMOKU (Hawaiian) Island.

KAMUELA (Hawaiian) God hears. *Variations:* Kamuele, Samuel.

KAMUZU (African) Medicine.

KANA (Japanese) Powerful. *Variation:* Kanah.

KANAI (Hawaiian) Winner.

KANALE (Hawaiian) Stony meadow. *Variations:* Sanale, Stanley.

KANALOA (Hawaiian) A major Hawaiian god.

KANE (Welsh) Beautiful; (Japanese) Golden. *Variations:* Kaen, Kain, Kaine, Kayne, Keanu.

KANG (Chinese) Healthy.

KANG-DAE (Korean) Powerful.

KANGI (Native American) Raven. *Variation:* Kangee.

Names with "Ja" or "Ke"

Combining "Ja" or "Ke" with boys' names creates interesting new names. Here's a sampling:

"JA" NAMES:
Jajuan
Jalen
Jamarcus
Jamario
Janeil
Jaquan
Jaquarius
Jareth
Jalon
Jashon
Jathan
Javonte

"KE" NAMES:
Keandre
Kechel
Kedarius
Keon
Keshawn (or Keyshawn)
Keshua

KANIEL (Hebrew) Reed. *Variations:* Kan, Kani, Kanniel, Kanny.

KANJI (Japanese) Tin.

KANOA (Polynesian) Freedom.

KANTU (Hindi) Happy.

KANU (Hindi) Handsome

KANUTE (Scandinavian) Knot. Form of Knute.

KANYE (African) City in Botswana. *Notable:* Singer Kanye West.

KAORI (Japanese) Strength.

KAPA (Polynesian) Attack.

KAPALI (Hawaiian) Cliff.

KAPELIEL (Hawaiian) God is my strength. *Variation:* Gabriel.

KAPENI (African) Knife. *Variations:* Kapenie, Kapeny.

KAPILA (Hindi) Monkey.

KAPILDEV (Hindi) Hindi god.

KAPONO (Hawaiian) Righteous.

KARAM (Arabic) Charitable. *Variations:* Kareem, Karim.

KARDAL (Arabic) Mustard seed.

KARDAMA (Hindi) Kapila's father.

KARE (Scandinavian) Large.

KAREEM (Arabic) Noble. *Notable:* Basketball's Kareem Abdul-Jabbar. *Variations:* Karim, Karime.

KAREL (Dutch; French) Manly.

KARIF (Arabic) Born in the fall. *Variations:* Kareef, Kariff, Karriff.

KARIO (African American) Variation of Mario.

KARL (German) Manly. *Notables:* Actor Karl Malden; philosopher and father of Communism, Karl Marx. *Variations:* Carl, Karle, Karlen, Karlens, Karlin, Karlo, Karlton.

KARNAK (Hindi) Heart.

KARNEY (Irish) The winner. *Variations:* Carney, Carny, Karnie, Karny.

KARR (Scandinavian) Swamp.

KARSTEN (Greek) Anointed. *Variations:* Karstan, Karstin, Karston.

KARUN (Hindi) Sympathy.

KASEKO (African) To tease.

KASI (Hindi) Bright.

KASIB (Arabic) Fertile. *Variation:* Kaseeb.

KASIM (Arabic) Divided. *Variation:* Kaseem.

KASIMIR (Slavic) Destroyer of peace.

KASIYA (Egyptian) Departs.

KASPAR (Persian) Protector of wealth. *Variations:* Casper, Kasper.

KASS (German) Blackbird. *Variations:* Kasch, Kase.

KASSIDY (Irish) Clever. *Variations:* Cassidy, Kassadey, Kassadie, Kassady, Kassedy, Kassidey, Kassidie.

KATEB (Arabic) Writer.

KATOA (Polynesian) Complete.

KATSUTOSHI (Japanese) Outsmart.

KAUFANA (Polynesian) Bow.

KAUFMAN (German) Merchant. *Variations:* Kauffman, Kaufmann, Koffman, Koffmann.

KAUL (Arabic) Trustworthy. *Variations:* Kahlil, Kalee, Khaleel, Khalil.

KAULANA (Hawaiian) Famous.

KAULO (Hawaiian) To borrow.

KAURY (Polynesian) Tree. *Variation:* Kaurie.

KAVANAUGH (Irish) Handsome. *Variations:* Kavan, Kavanagh, Kavenagh.

KAVI (Hindi) Poet.

KAVINDRA (Hindi) God of the poets.

KAWA (Native American: Apache) Great.

KAWIKA (Hawaiian) Beloved. *Variations:* David, Kewiki.

KAWIKANI (Hawaiian) Strong man.

KAY (Welsh) Joy.

KAYAM (Hebrew) Stable.

KAYIN (African) Celebrated.

KAYODE (African) Brings joy.

KAZUO (Japanese) Peace. *Notable:* Writer Kazuo Ishiguro.

KEAHI (Hawaiian) Fire.

KEAHILANI (Hawaiian) Heavenly fire.

KEAKA (Hawaiian) God is good.

KEALA (Hawaiian) Fragrant.

KEANE (English) Sharp. *Variations:* Kean, Keen, Keene.

KEANU (Irish) Cool breeze. *Notable:* Keanu Reeves.

KEARN (Irish) Dark. *Variations:* Kern, Kerne.

KEARNEY (Irish) The winner. *Variations:* Karney, Karny, Kearny.

KEATON (English) Hawk nest. *Variations:* Keeton, Keiton, Keyton.

KEAZIAH (African American) Cassia tree.

KEB (Egyptian) Earth.

KEDAR (Hindi) God of mountains.

KEDEM (Hebrew) Old.

KEDRICK (English) Gift of splendor. *Variations:* Keddric, Keddrick, Keddrik, Kedric, Kedrik.

KEEFE (Irish) Beloved. *Variations:* Keefer, Keif, Keifer, Keiff, Keiffer.

KEEGAN (Irish) Small and passionate. *Variations:* Kaegan, Kagen, Keagan, Keagin, Keegen, Keegin, Kegan.

KEELAN (Irish) Small and skinny. *Variations:* Kealan, Kealen, Kealin, Kealon, Keelen, Keelin, Keelon, Keelun, Keelyn, Keilan, Keilen, Keilin, Keilon, Keilyn, Keylen, Keylin, Keylon.

KEELEY (Irish) Handsome. *Variations:* Kealeigh, Kealen, Kealie, Kealy, Keeleigh, Keelen, Keelie, Keely, Keileigh, Keiley, Keilie, Keily, Keyleigh, Keyley, Keylie, Keyly.

KEENAN (Irish) Little ancient one. *Notables:* Comedy writer/producer Keenan Ivory Wayans; actor Keenan Wynn. *Variations:* Cianan, Keanan, Keanen, Keannan, Keannen, Keenen, Keenon, Kenan, Keynan, Keynen, Keynin, Keynon, Kienan, Kienen, Kienon, Keynan, Keynen, Keynin, Keynon, Keynyn, Kienan, Kienen.

KEFENTSE (African) Conqueror.

KEFIR (Hebrew) Lion cub.

KEFU (Polynesian) Blond haired.

KEHINDE (African) Second born of twins. *Variation:* Kehind.

KEIJI (Japanese) Careful.

KEIR (Irish) Dark skinned; swarthy. *Notable:* Actor Keir Dullea. *Variations:* Keiron, Kerr, Kieran, Kieron.

KEITARO (Japanese) Blessed.

KEITH (Scottish) Forest. *Notables:* Rolling Stone Keith Richards; The Who's drummer, Keith Moon.

KEKA (Hawaiian) Appointed.

KEKAPA (Hawaiian) Rebel.

KEKOA (Hawaiian) Courageous.

KEKOANU (Hawaiian) Powerful fighter.

KELALA (Hawaiian) Leader with a spear.

KELAYA (Hebrew) Dry grain.

KELBY (German) A farm by a spring. *Variations:* Kelbey, Kelbie, Kellby.

KELE (Native American) Sparrow. *Variation:* Kelle.

KELEPT (Polynesian) Faithful.

KELILE (Ethiopian) Protected.

KELL (English) Spring. *Variation:* Kel.

KELLAGH (Irish) War.

KELLEN (Irish) Mighty warrior. *Variations:* Keilan, Keillan, Keldan, Kellan, Kellin, Kellyn.

KELLY (Irish) Warrior. *Variations:* Kelley, Kellie.

KELSEY (English) Island. *Notable:* TV's *Frasier*, Kelsey Grammer. *Variations:* Kelsie, Kelsy.

KELTON (English) Town of ships. *Variations:* Keldan, Kelden, Keldin, Keldon, Keltan, Kelten, Keltin.

KELVIN (English) Name of a Scottish River. *Variations:* Keloun, Kelvan, Kelven, Kelvyn.

KELWIN (English) Friend from the ridge. *Variations:* Kelwen, Kelwinn, Kelwyn, Kelwynn.

KEMAL (Turkish) Honor.

KEMIKIUO (Hawaiian) Fertile.

KEMP (English) Fighter.

KEMPTON (English) Military town. *Variations:* Kemptan, Kempten, Kemptin.

KEMUEL (Hebrew) To help God.

KEN (English) Handsome. Short form of Kenneth. *Notables:* Documentary filmmaker Ken Burns; *Jeopardy* champ Ken Jennings. *Variation:* Kenn.

KENAN (Hebrew) To attain. *Variations:* Cainan, Kenen, Kenin, Kenon.

KENDALL (English) Valley of the River Kent. *Variations:* Kendal, Kendale, Kendel, Kendell.

KENDREW (Scottish) Strong and courageous.

KENDRICK (Scottish) Royal hero. *Variations:* Kendric, Kendricks, Kendrik, Kendryck.

KENEKE (Hawaiian) Handsome. *Variations:* Keneki, Kenete, Keneti.

KENELM (English) Brave helmet.

KENIKA (Greek) Strong.

KENJI (Japanese) Second son.

KENLEY (English) Royal meadow. *Variations:* Kenlea, Kenlee, Kenleigh, Kenlie, Kenly.

KENNARD (English) Brave and powerful. *Variations:* Kenard, Kennaird, Kennerd.

KENNEDY (Irish) Armored head. *Variations:* Canaday, Canady, Kennady, Kenneday.

KENNETH (Irish) Handsome. *Notables:* Fashion designer Kenneth Cole; actor Kenneth Branagh. *Variations:* Coinneach, Ken, Kendall,

Kenney, Kennie, Kennith, Kenny, Kenyon.

KENRICK (English) Bold ruler. *Variations:* Kennric, Kennrick, Kennrik, Kenric, Kenricks, Kenrik, Kenryc, Kenryck, Kenryk.

KENT (English) County in England.

KENTARO (Japanese) Big boy.

KENTON (English) From Kent. *Variations:* Kentan, Kenten, Kentin, Kentyn.

KENTRELL (English) Estate of a king. *Variations:* Kentreal, Kentrel.

KENWARD (English) Brave protector.

KENWAY (English) Brave fighter.

KENWOOD (English) From the warrior's forest.

KENYA (African) Mountain of whiteness.

KENYON (Irish) Blond. *Variation:* Kenyan.

KENZIE (Scottish) Wise leader. *Variations:* Kensie, Kensy, Kenzy.

KEO (Hawaiian) God will increase.

KEOIA (Hawaiian) Life.

KEOKI (Hawaiian) Farmer.

KEOKUK (Native American) Alert moves.

KEOLA (Hawaiian) Alive.

KEON (Irish) Well born. *Variations:* Keion, Keone, Keyon, Kian, Kion.

KEONI (Hawaiian) God is good.

KEPAKIANO (Hawaiian) From Sebastia. Hawaiian version of Sebastian. *Variation:* Pakiana.

KEPANO (Hawaiian) Crown. *Variations:* Kekepana, Setepana, Tepano.

KEREL (African) Young man. *Variations:* Kerell, Kerrel, Kerrell.

KEREM (Turkish) Noble and kind.

KERMIT (Irish) Free of jealousy. *Notable:* Muppet Kermit the Frog.

KERN (Irish) Dark-haired child. *Variations:* Kearn, Kearne, Keirn, Keirne.

KERR (Scandinavian) Swamp.

KERRICK (English) King's rule. *Variations:* Keric, Kerick, Kerik, Kerric, Kerrik, Kerryck, Kerryk.

KERRY (Irish) County in Ireland. *Variations:* Kerrey, Kerrie.

KERS (Hindi) Plant.

KERSEN (Indonesian) Cherry. *Variations:* Kersan, Kersin, Kerson, Kersyn.

KERWIN (Irish) Dark. *Variations:* Kerwain, Kerwan, Kerwen, Kerwinn, Kerwon, Kerwyn, Kirwin.

KES (English) Falcon.

KESAVA (Hindi) Hairy.

KESHAWN (American) Combination of prefix "Ke" and first name "Shawn." *Variations:* Keshaun, Keshon, Keyshawn.

KESIN (Hindi) Panhandler with long hair.

KESSE (African) Chubby. *Variations:* Kessey, Kessie, Kessy.

KESTER (English) From the Roman army camp.

KETTIL (Scandinavian) Sacrificial cauldron. *Variations:* Keld, Kjeld, Kjell, Kjetil.

KEVIN (Irish) Handsome. *Notables:* Actors Kevin Kline, Kevin Bacon, and Kevin Costner. *Variations:* Kavan, Kev, Kevan, Keven, Kevon, Kevyn.

KEWINI (Hawaiian) Beautiful birth.

KEY (Gaelic) Son of the fiery one. *Variation:* Keye.

KHALDUN (Arabic) Eternal.

KHALFANI (African) Born to lead.

KHALID (Arabic) Eternal. *Variations:* Khaled, Khaleed.

KHALIL (Arabic) Good friend. *Variations:* Kaleel, Kalil, Khalial.

KHAMISI (African) Born on Thursday. *Variation:* Khamidi.

KHAN (Turkish) Prince.

KHANG (Vietnamese) Strong.

KHARAVELA (Hindi) Name of a king from the area of Kalinga.

KHAYRAT (Arabic) Beneficial act. *Variation:* Khayri.

KHOURY (Arabic) Priest. *Variations:* Khorie, Khory, Khourie.

KIBBE (Native American) Bird of the night.

KIDD (English) Young goat. *Variations:* Kid, Kyd, Kydd.

KIEFER (German) Barrel maker. *Notable:* Actor Kiefer Sutherland. *Variation:* Keefer.

KIEL (Irish) Form of Kyle.

KIERAN (Irish) Dark. *Variations:* Keiran, Keiren, Keiron, Kieron, Kyran.

KIFIMBO (African) A twig.

KIHO (African) Fog.

KIJIH (Native American) Walks quietly.

KIKEONA (Hawaiian) Man who hews. *Variation:* Kileona.

KILAB (Arabic) Dog.

KILEY (English) Narrow land.

KILILA (Hawaiian) Lord. *Variation:* Kirila.

KILIPEKA (Hawaiian) Famous oath. *Variation:* Kilipaki.

KILLIAN (Irish) Conflict. *Variations:* Kilean, Kilian, Kilien, Killean, Killie, Killien, Killy.

KILOHANA (Hawaiian) Supreme.

KIM (Vietnamese) Gold.

KIMBALL (English) Leader in war. *Variations:* Kimbal, Kimbel, Kimbell, Kimble.

KIMEONA (Hawaiian) He has heard. *Variation:* Kimona.

KIMMEL (German) Farmer.

KIMO (Hawaiian) To seize.

KIMOKEO (Hawaiian) Respect God. *Variation:* Timoteo.

KIN (Japanese) Golden.

KINCAID (Celtic) Leader in war. *Variations:* Kincade, Kincaide, Kincayde, Kyncaid.

KING (English) King.

KINGMAN (English) King's man. *Variation:* Kinsman.

KINGSLEY (English) Meadow of the king. *Notable:* Writer Kingsley Amis. *Variations:* Kingslea, Kingsleigh, Kingslie, Kingsly.

KINGSTON (English) Town of the king. *Variation:* Kinston.

KINGSWELL (English) Well of the king.

KINNARD (Irish) Top of the hill. *Variations:* Kinard, Kinnaird.

KINSEY (English) Victorious.

KIPILIANO (Hawaiian) One from Cyprus. *Variation:* Kipiriano.

African Names

BOYS:	GIRLS:
Adisa	Etana
Amadi	Imani
Imamu	Kamaria
Jelani	Malaika
Kgosi	Morowa
Mfalme	Nafisa
Obataiye	Razina
Paki	Sanura
Sefu	Thema
Thabo	Zuri

Extra, Extra: Read All About These Celebrity Baby Names

Sy'rai Iman (Brandy Norwood)

Talula Fyfe, Darby Galen, and Sullivan Patrick (Patrick Dempsey)

Travis Sedgwick and Sosie Ruth (Kevin Bacon and Kyra Sedgwick)

Theo, Sasha Rebecca, Sawyer Avery, Destry Allyn, Mikaela George (Steven Spielberg and Kate Capshaw)

Valentina Paloma (Salma Hayek)

Violet Anne and Seraphina Rose Elizabeth (Ben Affleck and Jennifer Garner)

Walker Nathanial (Idina Menzel and Taye Diggs)

Willow and Jaden (Will Smith and Jada Pinkett Smith)

Wolfgang William (Valerie Bertinelli and Eddie Van Halen)

Zachary Jackson Levon (Elton John)

KIP (English) Hill with a sharp peak. *Variations:* Kipp, Kipper, Kippie, Kippy.

KIRAL (Turkish) King.

KIRAN (Hindi) Ray of light. *Variations:* Kiren, Kirin, Kiron, Kirun, Kiryn, Kyran, Kyren, Kyrin, Kyron, Kyrun.

KIRBY (English) Village of the church. *Variations:* Kerbey, Kerbi, Kerbie, Kirbey, Kirbie.

KIRI (Cambodian) Mountain.

KIRIL (Greek) Ruler. *Variations:* Kirillos, Kyril.

KIRITAN (Hindi) Crown wearer. *Variations:* Kiriten, Kiritin, Kiriton.

KIRK (Scandinavian) Church. *Notables:* Actors Kirk Douglas and Kirk Cameron. *Variations:* Kerk, Kirke.

KIRKLAND (English) Church land.

KIRKLEY (English) Church meadow. *Variations:* Kirklea, Kirklee, Kirkleigh, Kirklie, Kirkly.

KIRKWELL (English) Church spring.

KIRKWOOD (English) Church forest.

KIT (English; American) Short form of Christopher: Christ-bearer.

KITO (African) Jewel.

KITWANA (African) Pledged to live.

KIYIYAH (Native American) Wailing wolf.

KIYOKAYA (Native American) Alert.

KIYOSHI (Japanese) Peaceful.

KIZIL (Turkish) Red.

KIZZA (African) Born after twins.

KLAH (Native American) Left handed.

KLAUS (German) Victorious people. Short for Nicholas. *Notable:* Actor Klaus Kinski. *Variations:* Claes, Claus, Clause, Klaas, Klaes, Klause.

KLEEF (Dutch) Cliff.

KLEMENS (Polish) Mild; compassionate. *Variation:* Klement.

KLENG (Norwegian) Claw. *Variation:* Klen.

KLIMENT (Czech) Gentle.

KLINE (German) Small. *Variations:* Cline, Clyne, Klyne.

KNIGHT (English) Knight. *Variation:* Knightly.

KNOTON (Native American) The wind.

KNOWLES (English) Grassy slope.

KNOX (English) Hills.

KNUD (Danish) Kind.

KNUTE (Scandinavian) Knot. *Notable:* Notre Dame football coach Knute Rockne. *Variations:* Cnute, Knut.

KOAMALU (Hawaiian) Brave peace.

KOBE (Japanese) From Kobe, Japan; (Hebrew) Supplanter; short for Jacob. *Notable:* Hoopster Kobe Bryant. *Variations:* Coby, Kobey, Kobie, Koby.

KODWO (African) Born on Monday.

KOFI (African) Born on Friday.

KOHANA (Native American) Fast.

KOI (Native American) Panther.

KOJI (Japanese) Child.

KOJO (Ghanaian) Born on Monday.

KOKAYI (African) Call the people.

KOKUDZA (African) Short lived.

KOLAIAH (Hebrew) Voice of God. *Variations:* Kolaia, Kolaya, Kolia, Koliya, Kolya.

KOLOMALU (Polynesian) Shelter.

KOLYA (Russian) Victory of the people. Form of Nikolai.

KOMAKI (Hawaiian) Twin. *Variations:* Kamaki, Koma, Toma.

KOMINIKO (Hawaiian) Belonging to God. *Variation:* Dominigo.

KOMOKU (Japanese) God of the south.

KONA (Hawaiian) Leader of the world. *Variation:* Dona.

KONANE (Hawaiian) Bright moonlight.

KONANIAH (Hebrew) God is settled. *Variations:* Konania, Konanya.

KONDO (African) War.

KONDWANI (African) Happy.

KONG (Chinese) Glorious or sky.

KONO (Native American) Squirrel with a pine nut.

KONTAR (African) Only child.

KONUR (Scandinavian) Ancient mythological figure.

KOPANO (African) Union.

KORB (German) Basket.

KORBIN (Welsh) Raven. *Variation:* Korben.

KORDELL (Latin) Warmhearted.

KOREN (Hebrew) Shining. *Variations:* Corin, Korin.

KORESH (Hebrew) To dig. *Variations:* Choreish, Choresh.

KOREY (Irish) From the hollow. *Variation:* Corey.

KORNEL (Czech) Horn. *Variations:* Kornek, Nelek.

KORT (Scandinavian) Wise counselor.

KORUDON (Greek) Man with a helmet.

KOSMY (Polish) Universe.

KOSTI (Scandinavian) Staff of God.

KOSUMI (African) Spear fisher.

KOVAR (Czech) Smith.

KOVIT (Thai) Expert.

KRISHNA (Hindi) Delightful.

KRISTOPHER (Greek) Bearer of Christ. Form of Christopher.

KUBA (Czech) Variation of Jacob. *Variation:* Kubo.

KUKANE (Hawaiian) Masculine.

KULTANO (Hawaiian) Light beard.

KUMAKICHI (Japanese) Lucky.

KUMAR (Hindi) Prince.

KUNAL (Sanskit) Peaceful.

KUNEI (Polynesian) He is present.

KUPAALANI (Hawaiian) Loyal in spirit.

KUPER (Yiddish) Red hair. *Variations:* Kupor, Kupper.

KURAO (Japanese) Mountain.

KURT (German) Courteous. *Notables:* Singer Kurt Cobain; actor Kurt Russell; writer Kurt Vonnegut. *Variations:* Kert, Kirt.

KUZIH (Native American) Fast talker.

KWABENA (African) Born on Tuesday.

KWACHA (African) Morning.

KWAKOU (African) Born on Wednesday. *Variations:* Kwako, Kwaku.

KWAME (African) Saturday born. *Variation:* Kwamin.

KWAN (Korean) Powerful.

KWANG-SUN (Korean) Benevolence.

KWAS (African: Ghanaian) Born on Sunday. *Variations:* Kwasi, Kwesi.

KWAYERA (African) Sunrise.

KWENDE (African) Let's go.

KWINTYN (Polish) Fifth.

KYAN (Irish) Little king. *Notable:* TV's *Queer Eye for the Straight Guy* grooming guru Kyan Douglas.

KYLE (Scottish) Narrow land. *Notable:* Actor Kyle MacLachlan. *Variations:* Kiel, Kile, Ky, Kyele, Kyler.

KYLOE (English) Cow meadow. *Variations:* Kilo, Kiloe, Kilow, Kilowe, Kylo, Kylow, Kylowe.

KYNAN (Welsh) Chief. *Variation:* Kinan.

KYROS (Greek) Master.

KYUBOK (Korean) Blessed.

KYUBONG (Korean) Distinguished.

LA ROY (African American) The king.

LA VONN (African American) The small one. *Variations:* La Vaun, La Voun.

LAAKEA (Hawaiian) Holy light.

LABAN (Hebrew) White. *Variation:* Leban.

LABHRAS (Irish) One from Laurentum. *Variation:* Lubhras.

LABIB (Arabic) Sensible. *Variation:* Labid.

LACH (English) Dweller by the water.

LACHLAN (Scottish) Land of lakes. *Variations:* Lachlann, Laughlin, Lochlain.

LACHTNA (Irish) Gray.

LADAN (Hebrew) Witness.

LADD (English) Young man. *Variations:* Lad, Laddey, Laddie, Laddy.

LADISLAUS (Slavic) Glory. *Variations:* Ladislao, Ladislas, Ladislav, Wladislav, Wladislaw.

LADO (African) Second-born son.

LAEL (Hebrew) Belongs to God.

LAFAYETTE (French) Near the beech tree.

LAFFIT (French) Faithful. *Variation:* Lafitte.

LAFI (Polynesian) Concealed.

LAHAHANA (Hawaiian) Sun's warmth.

LAIONELA (Hawaiian) Lion.

LAIRD (Scottish) Leader of the land.

LAIS (East Indian) Lion.

LAJOS (Hungarian) Holy.

LAKE (English) Body of water.

LAKSHMAN (Hindi) Wealthy.

LAKSHMIDAS (Hindi) Servant of the goddess of beauty.

LAL (Hindi) Lovely.

LALLO (Native American: Kiowa) Little boy.

LALO (Latin) Singing a lullaby. *Notable:* Composer Lalo Schifrin.

LAMAR (German) Land. *Variations:* Lamarr, Lemar, Lemarr.

LAMBERT (German) Bright land. *Variations:* Lambard, Lamberto, Lamberts, Lambirt, Lambirto, Lamburt, Lamburto, Lampard.

LAMECH (Hebrew) Powerful strength.

LAMOND (French) World. *Variations:* Lammond, Lemond.

LAMONT (Scandinavian) Lawyer. *Variations:* Lamond, Lamonte.

LANCE (German) Short form of Lancelot. *Notable:* Tour de France champ Lance Armstrong. *Variations:* Lanz, Launce.

LANCELOT (French) Servant. *Variations:* Lancelott, Launcelot.

LANDER (English) Landlord. *Variations:* Landers, Landor.

LANDIS (French) Grassy plain.

LANDON (English) Grassy meadow. *Variations:* Landan, Landen, Landin.

LANDRY (English) Peaceful ruler. *Variations:* Landre, Landrick.

LANE (English) One who lives near the lane. *Variations:* Laine, Layne.

LANG (Norse) Tall. *Variations:* Laing, Lange.

LANGDON (English) Long hill. *Variations:* Langden, Langsden, Langsdon.

LANGFORD (English) Long ford.

LANGILEA (Polynesian) Thunder.

LANGILOA (Polynesian) Storm.

LANGLEY (English) Long meadow. *Variations:* Langleigh, Langlie, Langly.

LANGSTON (English) Long town. *Notable:* Poet Langston Hughes. *Variations:* Langstan, Langsten, Langstin, Langstyn.

LANGUNDO (Native American) Serene.

LANGWARD (English) Tall protector.

LANGWORTH (English) Long paddock.

LANNY (French) Famous land; (English) Nickname for Landon, Langdon. *Notable:* Golfer Lanny Wadkins. *Variation:* Lannie.

LANTY (Irish) Servant of St. Secundus. *Variations:* Laughun, Leachlainn, Lochlainn, Lochlann.

LANU (Native American) Circle around a pole.

LAOGHAIRE (Irish) One who herds calves.

LAOISEACH (Irish) One from Leix, a county in Ireland. *Variation:* Laoiahseach.

LAP (Vietnamese) Independent.

LAPAELA (Hawaiian) God heals. *Variation:* Lapaele.

LAPHONSO (African American) Noble. *Variations:* Lafonso, LaPhonso.

LAPIDOS (Hebrew) Torches. *Variation:* Lapidoth.

LAQUINTIN (American) Fifth-born child. *Variations:* Laquentin, Laquenton, Laquintas, Laquintise, Laquintiss, Laquinton.

LARAMIE (French) Tears of love. *Variations:* Laramey, Laramy.

LAREDO (Spanish) Place name.

LARKIN (Irish) Fierce. *Variations:* Larkan, Larken, Larkyn.

LARON (French) Thief. *Variations:* Laran, Laronn, Larron.

LARRIMORE (French) One who provides arms. *Variations:* Larimore, Larmer, Larmor.

LARRY (English) Short form of Lawrence. *Notables:* Talk-show host Larry King; basketball great Larry Bird; comedian Larry David; actor Larry Hagman. *Variations:* Larie, Larrie, Lary.

LARS (Scandinavian) Crowned with laurel. *Notable:* Film director Lars von Trier. *Variations:* Larse, Larz.

LARSON (Swedish) Son of Lars. *Variations:* Larsen, Larssen, Larsson.

LASAIRIAN (Irish) Flame. *Variations:* Laisrian, Laserian.

LASALLE (French) Hall. *Variations:* Lasal, Lascelles.

LASH (German) Famous warrior. A form of Louis. *Variations:* Lasher, Lashi, Lasho.

LASHAWN (American) Combination of prefix "La" and first name "Shawn." *Variations:* Lasean, Lashaun, Lashon, Lashun.

LASSE (Finnish) Victory. *Notable:* Writer/director Lasse Hallström.

LASZLO (Hungarian) Famous leader. *Variations:* Laslo, Lazlo, Lazuli.

LATAVAO (Polynesian) Homebody.

LATEEF (Arabic) Gentle. *Variation:* Latif.

LATHAM (Scandinavian) Barn.

LATHROP (English) Farm with barns. *Variations:* Lathe, Lay.

LATIMER (English) Interpreter. *Variations:* Latimor, Latymer.

LATRELL (American) Unknown meaning. *Notable:* Basketball player Latrell Sprewell.

LAUAKI (Polynesian) Best.

LAUDALINO (Portuguese) Praised. *Variations:* Laudalin.

LAUGHLIN (Irish) Servant. *Variations:* Lachlin, Leachlain, Leachlainn.

LAURENCE (Latin) Crown of laurels. Alternate spelling of Lawrence. *Notables:* Actors Laurence Olivier and Laurence Fishburne. *Variations:* Laurance, Laurans, Laurencio, Laurens, Laurenz, Laurie, Lauris, Lauriston, Lauritz, Lauro, Laurus, Laury, Laurynas.

LAURENT (French) Form of Lawrence.

LAVALLE (French) Valley. *Variations:* Laval, Lavall, Lavel, Lavell, Levelle.

LAVAN (Hebrew) White. *Variations:* Lavin, Lavon.

LAVANAA (Hindi) Shining.

LAVESH (Hindi) Crumb.

LAVI (Hebrew) Lion.

LAWFORD (English) Ford on the hill.

LAWLER (Irish) Soft spoken. *Variations:* Lawlor, Lollar, Loller.

LAWRENCE (English; Latin) Crowned with laurel. *Notables:* Band leader Lawrence Welk; film director Lawrence Kasdan. *Variations:* Lawrance, Lawrey, Lawrie, Lawry, Loren, Lorence, Lorencz, Lorens, Lorenzo, Lorin, Lorry, Lowrance.

LAWSON (English) Son of Lawrence. *Variations:* Lawsen, Layson.

LAWTON (English) Town on the hill. *Variation:* Laughton.

LAZAR (Hungarian) Form of Lazarus.

LAZARUS (Hebrew) God's help. *Variations:* Eleazer, Laza, Lazare, Lazaro, Lazzaro.

LEANDER (Greek) Lion man. *Variations:* Leandre, Leandro, Leandros.

LEARY (Irish) Herder.

LEBEN (Hebrew) Life.

LEBRUN (French) Brown haired.

LECH (Polish) From Poland. *Notable:* Polish political leader Lech Walesa.

LECHOSLAW (Polish) Glory of the Poles. *Variations:* Lech, Lechoslav, Leslaw, Leszek.

LEDYARD (German) Guardian of the nation.

LEE (English) Meadow. *Notables:* Actor Lee Marvin; automotive business executive Lee Iacocca; renowned acting teacher Lee Strasberg. *Variation:* Leigh.

LEGGETT (French) Messenger. *Variations:* Legate, Leggitt, Liggett.

LEI (Chinese) Thunder.

LEIBEL (Hebrew) My lion. *Variation:* Leib.

LEIF (Scandinavian) Beloved. *Notables:* Teen idol Leif Garrett; Viking explorer Leif Ericson. *Variations:* Leaf, Lief.

LEIGHTON (English) Town by the meadow. *Variations:* Layton, Leyton.

LEGRAND (French) The great one. *Variations:* Legran, Legrant.

LEITH (Scottish) Broad river.

LEKEKE (Hawaiian) Powerful leader.

Top Names in Chile

BOYS:
1. Benjamin
2. Vicente
3. Martin
4. Matias
5. Joaquin
6. Agustin
7. Maximiliano
8. Cristobal
9. Sebastian
10. Tomas

GIRLS:
1. Martina
2. Sofia
3. Florencia
4. Valentina
5. Isadora
6. Antonella
7. Antonia
8. Emilia
9. Catalina
10. Fernanda

LELAND (English) Meadow land. *Variations:* Layland, Lealan, Leanland, Leelan, Leeland, Leighlan, Leighland, Lelan, Leylan, Leyland.

LEMUEL (Hebrew) Devoted to God.

LEN (German) Short form of Leonard. *Notable:* Actor Len Cariou.

LENNO (Native American) Man.

LENNON (Irish) Cape. *Variations:* Lenon, Lennin.

LENNOX (Scottish) Land with elm trees. *Variation:* Lenox.

LENNY Form of Leonard. *Notable:* Singer Lenny Kravitz. *Variation:* Lennie.

LEO (Latin) Lion.

LEON (French) Lion. *Notables:* Writer Leon Uris; musician Leon Russell. *Variations:* Leonas, Leone, Leonek, Leonidas, Leonis, Leosko, Lyon.

LEONARD (German) Brave lion. *Notables:* Conductor Leonard Bernstein; actor Leonard Nimoy. *Variations:* Leanard, Lenard, Lennard, Leonek, Leonhard, Leonhards, Leonidas, Leontes, Lienard, Linek, Lynnard, Lyonard.

LEONARDO (Italian) Form of Leonard. *Notables:* Artist/architect Leonardo da Vinci; actor Leonardo DiCaprio.

LEONID (Russian) Form of Leonard. *Notable:* Soviet leader Leonid Brezhnev.

LEOPOLD (German) Brave people. *Variations:* Leopoldo, Leupold.

LEPOLO (Polynesian) Attractive.

LERON (Arabic) My song. *Variations:* Lerone, Liron, Lirone, Lyron.

LEROY (French) The king. *Variations:* Le Roy, LeeRoy, Leeroy, LeRoi, Leroi, LeRoy.

LES (English) Short form of Leslie or Lester. *Notable:* Bandleader Les Brown.

LESHAWN (American) God is gracious. A form of Shawn. *Variations:* Lesean, Leshaun, Leshon, Leshonne.

LESHEM (Hebrew) Precious stone.

LESLIE (Scottish) Low meadow. *Notables:* Actors Leslie Nielsen and Leslie Howard. *Variations:* Les, Leslea, Lesley, Lesly, Lezly.

LESTER (English) From Leicester, England. *Variation:* Leicester.

LEV (Hebrew) Heart. *Variations:* Leb, Levko.

LEVERETT (French) Young rabbit. *Variations:* Leveret, Leverit, Leveritt.

LEVERTON (English) Farm town.

LEVI (Hebrew) Pledged. *Variations:* Levey, Levin, Levon, Levy.

LEVON (Armenian) Lion. *Notable:* Musician Levon Helm.

LEWIN (English) Beloved friend. *Variations:* Lewan, Lewen, Lewon, Lewyn.

LEWIS (Welsh) Famous warrior. Form of Louis. *Notable:* Writer Lewis Carroll. *Variation:* Lewys.

LEX (English) Lex, a shortened version of Alexander. *Notable:* Superman's nemesis Lex Luthor.

LEYLAND (English) Uncultivated land.

LEYTON (English) Garden of leeks. *Variation:* Layton.

LI (Chinese) Strength.

LIAM (Irish) Protector. A form of William. *Variation:* Lyam.

LIANG (Chinese) Good.

LIBERIO (Portuguese) Freedom.

LIBOR (Czech) Freedom. *Variations:* Libek, Liborek.

LIEM (Vietnamese) Honest.

LIF (Scandinavian) Life.

LIHAU (Hawaiian) Light rain.

LIKO (Chinese) Buddhist nun.

LI-LIANG (Chinese) Powerful.

LIMU (Polynesian) Seaweed.

LINCOLN (English) Town by a pool. *Variations:* Linc, Link.

LINDBERG (German) Mountain of linden trees. *Variation:* Lindbergh.

LINDBERT (German) From the linden tree hill. *Variations:* Linbert, Linbirt, Linburt, Linbyrt, Lindberg, Lindbirt, Lindburg, Lindburt, Lynbert, Lynbirt, Lynburt, Lynbyrt, Lyndbert, Lyndbirt, Lyndburt.

LINDELL (English) Valley of the linden trees. *Variations:* Lindall, Lindel, Lyndall, Lyndell.

LINDLEY (English) From the meadow with linden or lime trees. *Variations:* Lindlea, Lindleigh, Lindlie, Lindly, Lyndlea, Lyndlee, Lyndleigh, Lyndley, Lyndlie, Lyndly.

LINDSAY (English) Island of linden trees. *Notable:* Musician/singer Lindsey Buckingham. *Variations:* Lindsee, Lindsey, Lindsy, Linsay, Linsey, Lyndsay, Lyndsey.

LINFORD (English) Ford of linden trees. *Variation:* Lynford.

LINFRED (German) Gentle peace. *Variations:* Linfrid, Linfryd, Lynfred, Lynfrid.

LINLEY (English) Meadow of linden trees. *Variations:* Linlea,

Linlee, Linleigh, Linlie, Linly, Lynlea, Lynleigh, Lynley, Lynlie, Lynly.

LINTON (English) Town of lime trees. *Variations:* Lintonn, Lynton, Lyntonn.

LINUS (Greek) Flax. *Variations:* Linis, Lynis, Lynus.

LIONEL (Latin) Little lion. *Notables:* Actor Lionel Barrymore; jazz musician Lionel Hampton. *Variations:* Leonel, Lionell, Lionello, Lonell, Lonnell.

LIOR (Hebrew) Light. *Variation:* Leor.

LIRON (Hebrew) My song. *Variation:* Lyron.

LISIATE (Polynesian) Brave king.

LISIMBA (African) Harmed by a lion.

LISTER (English) A dyer.

LITTON (English) Town on the hill. *Variation:* Lytton.

LIU (African) Voice.

LIVINGSTON (English) Leif's settlement. *Notable:* Singer Livingston Taylor. *Variation:* Livingstone.

LIWANU (Native American) Growling bear.

LLEWELLYN (Welsh) Lionlike. *Variations:* Lewellen, Lewellin, Llewelin, Llewelleyn, Llewelyn.

LLOYD (Welsh) Gray or sacred. *Notable:* Actor Lloyd Bridges. *Variation:* Loyd.

LOBO (Spanish) Wolf.

LOC (Vietnamese) Luck.

LOCH (Irish; Scottish) From the land of the lakes.

LOCHIE (Irish; Scottish) From the land of the lakes. *Variations:* Lachie, Lachy, Lochey, Lochy.

LOCKE (English) Fort. *Variations:* Lock, Lockwood.

LODEWUK (Scandinavian) Famous in war. *Variations:* Lodewijk, Ludovic.

LODUR (Scandinavian) Ancient mythological figure.

LOGAN (Irish) Hollow in a meadow. *Variation:* Logen.

LOKELA (Hawaiian) Famous spear.

LOKENE (Hawaiian) Hawaiian version of Rodney.

LOKNI (Native American) Raining through the roof.

LOMAN (Irish) Little bare one. *Variation:* Lomen.

LOMBARD (Latin) Long beard. *Variations:* Lombardi, Lombardo.

LON (English) Noble and ready. *Notable:* Actor Lon Chaney.

LONATO (Native American) Flint.

LONDON (English) Fortress of the moon. *Variations:* Londen, Lunden.

LONG (Vietnamese) Dragon.

LONNIE (English) Noble and ready. *Variation:* Lonny.

LONO (Hawaiian) God of farming.

LOPAKA (Hawaiian) Bright and famous.

LOPATI (Polynesian) Bright fame.

LORCAN (Irish) Little fierce one.

LORD (English) Lord.

LOREN (English) Short form of Lawrence. *Variations:* Lorren, Lorin, Lorrin.

LORENZO (Spanish; Italian) Form of Lawrence. *Notable:* Actor Lorenzo Lamas. *Variations:* Lorenso, Lorentzo, Lorenz.

LORIMER (Latin) Harness maker. *Variations:* Lorimar, Lorrimer.

LORING (German) Warrior. *Variation:* Lorring.

LORNE (Scottish) Crown of laurels. Form of Lawrence. *Notable: Saturday Night Live* producer Lorne Michaels. *Variation:* Lorn.

LOT (Hebrew) Concealed.

LOTHAR (German) Famous army. *Variations:* Lotario, Lothair, Lothar, Lothario.

LOU (English) Short form of Louis. *Notables:* Singer Lou Rawls; character Lou Grant from TV's *The Mary Tyler Moore Show. Variation:* Lew.

LOUDON (German) A low valley. *Notable:* Singer Loudon Wainwright III. *Variations:* Louden, Lowden, Lowdon.

LOUIS (French; German) Famous warrior. *Notables:* Scientist Louis Pasteur; movie mogul Louis B. Mayer; jazz great Louis Armstrong. *Variations:* Lew, Lewe, Lou, Luigi, Luis.

LOUKANOS (Greek) Man from Lucania, an area in southern Italy. *Variation:* Lukianos.

LOUVAIN (French) City in Belgium.

LOVELL (French) Young wolf. *Variation:* Lovel.

LOWELL (English) Young wolf. *Variation:* Lowel.

LUBOMIERZ (Polish) Great love. *Variation:* Lubomir.

LUBOMIL (Polish) Lover of grace.

LUBORNIR (Czech) Great love. *Variations:* Luba, Lubek, Lubor, Luborek, Lubornirek, Lubos, Lubosek, Lumir.

LUBOSLAW (Polish) Lover of glory. *Variation:* Luboslav.

LUC (French) Light.

LUCAS (Latin) Man from Lucania. *Variations:* Loukas, Luc, Luca, Luka, Lukas, Lukaz, Luke.

LUCIUS (Latin) Light. *Variations:* Luca, Lucan, Lucca, Luce, Lucian, Luciano, Lucias, Lucien, Lucio.

LUCKY (American) Fortunate. *Notable:* Gangster Charles "Lucky" Luciano.

LUDGER (German) Man with spear.

LUDLOW (English) Prince's hill.

LUDOMIERZ (Polish) Famous people.

LUDOMIR (Czech) Famous people. *Variation:* Ludek.

LUDOSLAV (Czech) Great people.

LUDOSLAW (Polish) Glorious people. *Variation:* Lutoslaw.

LUDVIK (Czech) Famous at war.

LUDWIG (German) Famous soldier. *Notable:* Composer Ludwig van Beethoven. *Variations:* Ludovic, Ludovico, Ludvig, Ludvik, Ludwik.

LUFTI (Arabic) Kind friend.

LUGHAIDH (German) Famous fighter.

LUGONO (African) Sleep.

LUIGI (Italian) Form of Louis.

LUISTER (African) One who listens.

LUKE (English) Form of Lucas. *Notable:* Actor Luke Perry. *Variations:* Luc, Luk.

LUKMAN (African) Prophet.

LULANI (Hawaiian) Pinnacle of heaven.

LUNDY (Scottish; Scandinavian) Near an island grove.

LUNGA (African) To be good and kind. *Variation:* Lungani.

LUNN (Irish) Warlike. *Variations:* Lon, Lonn, Lunnie, Lunny.

LUNT (Scandinavian) Of the grove.

LUONG (Vietnamese) Bamboo.

LUTALO (African) Warrior.

LUTHER (German) People's army. *Notable:* Singer Luther Vandross.

LYLE (French) Island. *Notable:* Singer Lyle Lovett. *Variations:* Lisle, Ly, Lyall, Lyell, Lysle.

LYMAN (English) Lives in the meadow. *Variations:* Lymen, Lymon.

LYNCH (Irish) Mariner.

LYNDON (English) Hill with lime trees. *Notable:* U.S. President Lyndon Johnson. *Variations:* Linden, Lydon, Lynden, Lynne.

LYNN (English) Waterfall. *Variation:* Lyn. *Notable:* Writer E. Lynn Harris.

LYNTON (English) Town with lime trees. *Variation:* Linton.

LYSANDER (Greek) Liberator. *Variations:* Lisandro, Sander.

LYSCEUS (Greek) Light. *Variation:* Lycius.

LYTTON (English) Town by the loud stream. *Variations:* Liton, Litton, Lyton.

MAAKE (Polynesian) Warrior.

MAALIN (Hindi) Wreath.

MAASEIYA (Hebrew) God's work. *Variations:* Maaseiah, Masai.

MABON (Celtic) Son. *Variation:* Mabonn.

MABRY (Latin) Worthy of love. *Variation:* Mabrie.

MAC (Scottish) Son of. *Variation:* Mack.

MACADAM (Scottish) Son of Adam. *Variations:* MacAdam, McAdam.

MACALLISTER (Irish) Son of Alistair. *Variations:* MacAlister, McAlister, McAllister.

MACARDLE (Irish) Son of bravery. *Variations:* MacArdell, McCardell.

MACARIO (Spanish) Blessed. *Variation:* Macharios.

MACARTHUR (Scottish) Son of Arthur. *Variations:* MacArthur, McArthur.

MACAULAY (Scottish) Son of the moral one. *Notable:* Actor Macaulay Culkin. *Variations:* Macaulea, Macaulee, Macauleigh, Macauley, Macaulie, Macauly, Mackaulea, Mackaulee, Mackauleigh, Mackauley, Mackaulie, Mackauly, McCaulea, McCaulee, McCauleigh, McCauley, McCaulie, McCauly.

MACBETH (Scottish) Son of Elizabeth. *Variations:* Mackbeth, Makbeth.

MACBRIDE (Irish) Son of Saint Brigid. *Variations:* Macbryde, McBride, Mackbride.

MACCABEE (Hebrew) Hammer. *Variations:* Macabee, Makabi.

MACCOY (Irish) Son of fire. *Variations:* MacCoy, McCoy.

MACCREA (Irish) Son of grace. *Variations:* MacCrae, MacCray, MacCrea, McCrea.

MACDONALD (Scottish) Son of Donald. *Notable:* Actor MacDonald Carey. *Variations:* MacDonald, McDonald.

MACDOUGAL (Scottish) Son of the dark stranger. *Variation:* McDougal.

MACGOWEN (Irish) Son of the blacksmith. *Variations:* MacGowan, Magowan, McGowan.

MACHAR (Scottish) Plain. *Variations:* Machair, Machaire, Machare.

MACHUPA (African) One who likes to drink.

MACK (Celtic) Short form of names beginning with Mac or Mc, meaning "Son of . . . ." *Variations:* Mac, Mc, Mak.

MACKENZIE (Irish) Son of a wise leader. *Variations:* MacKenzie, McKenzie.

MACKLIN (Celtic) Son of Flann. *Variations:* Maclen, Macklinn, Macklyn.

MACKINLEY (Irish) Learned ruler. *Variations:* MacKinley, McKinley.

MACMAHON (Irish) Son of the bear. *Variation:* McMahon.

MACMURRAY (Irish) Son of the mariner. *Variation:* McMurray.

MACON (English) Maker.

MACY (French) Matthew's estate. *Variation:* Macey.

MADAN (Hindi) Cupid.

MADDEN (Celtic) Charitable. *Variations:* Maddan, Maddin, Maddon, Maddyn, Madan, Maden, Madin, Madon, Madyn.

MADDOX (Welsh) Generous. *Variations:* Maddock, Madock, Madox.

MADEEP (Punjabi) Mind that is full of light. *Variations:* Mandeep, Madip.

MADHAV (Hindi) Young.

MADHUR (Hindi) Sweet.

MADISON (English) Son of the mighty warrior. *Variations:* Maddie, Maddison, Maddy, Madisson.

MADZIMOYO (African) Water of life.

MAGAR (Armenian) Attendant of the groom. *Variation:* Magarious.

MAGEE (Irish) Son of Hugh. *Variations:* MacGee, McGee.

MAGNAR (Polish) Strong warrior. *Variation:* Magnor.

MAGNUS (Latin) Great. *Variations:* Magne, Magnes, Magnusson.

MAGUIRE (Irish) Son of the beige man. *Variations:* MacGuire, McGuire, McGwire.

MAGUS (Latin) Sorcerer.

MAHABALA (Hindi) Having great strength.

MAHADEV (Hindi) Great god.

MAHAVIRA (Hindi) Great hero. *Variation:* Mahavir.

MAHENDRA (Hindi) Great god of the sky.

MAHER (Irish) Generous.

MAHESA (Hindi) Great lord. *Variation:* Mahisa.

MAHESH (Hindi) Great ruler.

MAHIR (Arabic) Capable.

MAHKAH (Native American) Earth.

MAHMOUD (Arabic) Form of Mohammed. *Variations:* Mahmed, Mahmood.

Old MacDonald Had a Son

"Mac" or "Mc" at the beginning of a name is the Scottish way of indicating "son of . . ." So, Mac-Adam is "son of Adam." Though mostly known as last names, they are now becoming popular as first names. Each can have several variations, such as Macdonald, Mac-Donald, or McDonald, depending upon tradition or creativity.

Macadam	Macgowan
Macallister	Macgregor
Macalpin	Machenry
Macandrew	Macintosh
Macardle	Macintyre
Macarthur	Mackay
Macauley	Mackendrick
Macauliffe	Mackenna
Macbain	Mackenzie
Macbride	Mackeon
Maccallum	Mackinley
Macclennan	Mackinnon
Maccormack	Maclachlan
Maccoy	Maclaine
Maccrae	Maclaren
Macdonald	Maclean
Macdougal	Macleod
Macdowell	Macmahon
Macduff	Macmillan
Macelroy	Macmurray
Macewen	Macnair
Macfarlane	Macneil
Macgill	Macpherson

MAHON (Irish) Bear.

MAHPEE (Native American) Sky.

MAIDOC (Welsh) Fortunate. *Variations:* Maedoc, Maedock, Maidock, Maidok, Maydoc, Maydock, Maydok.

MAIMON (Arabic) Lucky. *Variations:* Maimun, Maymon.

MAINCHIN (Irish) Little monk.

MAITLAND (English) From the meadowland. *Variations:* Maetland, Maitlan, Mateland, Maytlan, Maytland.

MAJID (Arabic) Magnificent. *Variations:* Magid, Majeed.

MAJOR (Latin) Greater. *Variations:* Majar, Majer, Mayer, Mayor.

MAKAIO (Hawaiian) Gift of God. *Variation:* Makayo.

MAKALANI (Hawaiian) Writer. *Variations:* Makalaaney, Makalanee, Makalanie, Makalany.

MAKANI (Hawaiian) The wind.

MAKARIOS (Greek) Blessed. *Variations:* Macario, Macarios, Maccario, Maccarios, Makar.

MAKIN (Arabic) Strength. *Variation:* Makyn.

MAKIS (Greek) Likeness to God. *Variation:* Makys.

MAKOTO (Japanese) Honesty.

MAKRAM (Arabic) Noble.

MAKSIM (Russian) Greatest. *Variations:* Macka, Makimus, Maks, Maksim, Maksimka, Maksym, Maksymilian, Maxim, Maximilian, Maximillian.

MAKYA (Native American) One who hunts for eagles.

MAL (Irish) Short form of Malcolm.

MALACHI (Hebrew) Messenger. *Notable:* Writer Malachy McCourt. *Variations:* Malach, Malachai, Malachie, Malachy, Malechy.

MALAKI (Hawaiian) Servant. *Variation:* Malakoma.

MALCOLM (Scottish) Follower of St. Columba. *Notables:* Activist Malcolm X; actor Malcolm-Jamal Warner, financier Malcolm Forbes. *Variations:* Malcolum, Malcom, Malkolm.

MALDEN (English) Meeting place in the wood hollow. *Variations:* Maldan, Maldin, Maldon, Maldun, Maldyn.

MALEKO (Hawaiian) Warlike.

MALIK (Arabic) King. *Variations:* Maliq, Mallik.

MALIN (English) Little strong warrior. *Variations:* Mallin, Mallon.

MALKI (Hebrew) My king. *Variations:* Malkia, Malkiah, Malkiya, Malkiyahu.

MALLORY (French) Sad. *Variations:* Mallery, Mallorie, Malory.

MALO (Polynesian) Winner.

MALONEY (Irish) Devoted to God. *Variations:* Malone, Malony.

MALUHIA (Hawaiian) Peaceful. *Variation:* Malulani.

MALVERN (Welsh) Bare hill.

MAMDUH (Arabic) Praised.

MAMUN (Arabic) Trustworthy. *Variations:* Mamoun, Mamoon, Mamnun.

MANASSEH (Hebrew) Forgetful. *Variations:* Manases, Manassas.

MANCHU (Chinese) Pure.

MANCO (Native American) King.

MANDALA (African) Flowers.

MANDEK (Polish) Warrior.

MANDEL (German) Almond. *Variations:* Mandell, Mandy.

MANDER (Gypsy) From me. *Variations:* Mandar, Mandir, Mandor, Mandyr.

MANDHATRI (Hindi) Prince.

MANFORD (English) From the man's river crossing. *Variations:* Manforde, Menford, Menforde.

MANFRED (English) Man of peace. *Notable:* Musician Manfred Mann. *Variations:* Manafred, Manafryd, Manfrid, Manfried, Manfrit, Mannfred, Mannfryd.

MANHEIM (German) Servant.

MANIPI (Native American) Walking wonder.

MANKATO (Native American) Blue earth. *Variations:* Mahecate, Monecato.

MANLEY (English) Man's meadow. *Variations:* Manlea, Manleigh, Manly.

MANNING (English) Son of a man.

MANNIS (Gaelic) Great man. *Variations:* Mannes, Manis, Manus, Manness.

MANNIX (Irish) Monk. *Variations:* Mainchin, Mannox, Mannyx, Manox, Manyx.

MANNY (English) Short form of Emmanuel or Manuel.

MANOACH (Hebrew) To rest. *Variations:* Manoa, Manoah.

MANOLO (Italian) God is with us. *Variation:* Manolys.

MANRICO (Italian) Masculine ruler. *Variations:* Manricko, Manriko, Manrique, Manrycko, Manryco, Manryko.

MANSA (African) King.

MANSEL (English) In a clergyman's house. *Variation:* Mansell.

MANSFIELD (English) Field by a river.

MANSUR (Arabic) Divine assistance. *Variation:* Mansour.

MANTON (English) Man's town. *Variations:* Mannton, Manten.

MANTOTOHPA (Native American) Four bears.

MANU (Hindi) Lawmaker.

MANUEL (Hebrew) God is among us. Form of Emmanuel. *Variation:* Manuelo.

MANVILLE (French) Worker's village. *Variations:* Mandeville, Manneville, Manvel, Manvil, Manvill.

MANZO (Japanese) Third-born son.

MAONA (Native American) Creator.

MAOZ (Hebrew) Strength.

MARAM (Arabic) Desired.

MARC (French) Warlike. *Variation:* Mark.

MARCEL (French) Form of Marcellus. *Notables:* Mime Marcel Marceau; writer Marcel Proust. *Variations:* Marceles, Marcelin, Marcelino, Marcell, Marcelle, Marcellin, Marcellino.

MARCELLO (Italian) Form of Marcellus. *Notable:* Actor Marcello Mastroianni.

MARCELLUS (Latin) Young warrior. *Variations:* Marceau, Marcel, Marcelin.

MARCH (English) One who lives by a border.

MARCO (Italian) Form of Marcus. *Notable:* Explorer Marco Polo.

MARCUS (Latin) Warlike. *Notables:* Social activist Marcus Garvey; TV's *Marcus Welby, M.D.* *Variations:* Marco, Marcos, Markis, Markise, Markos, Markus.

MARDEN (English) From the warrior's valley. *Variations:* Mardan, Mardin, Mardon, Mardun, Mardyn.

MARDONIO (Persian) Male warrior.

MAREK (Czech) Form of Mark. *Variations:* Marecek, Mares, Marik, Marousek.

MARID (Arabic) Defiant.

MARINER (Celtic) Lives by the sea. *Variations:* Marin, Marino, Marinus.

MARIO (Italian) Bitter. *Notables:* Comedian Mario Cantone; chef Mario Batali.

MARION (French) Bitter; defiant. *Variation:* Mariano.

MARIUS (Latin) Male.

MARK (English) Warlike. *Notables:* Writer Mark Twain; actor Mark Wahlberg. *Variations:* Marc, Marco, Marke, Markel, Markell, Markes, Markie, Marko, Markos, Markous, Marku, Markus, Marky, Marq, Marqu, Marque, Marx.

MARKHAM (English) Homestead on the border.

MARLAND (English) Lake land.

MARLEY (English) Meadow near a lake. *Variations:* Marlea, Marleigh, Marlie, Marly.

MARLON (French) Little hawk. *Notables:* Actor Marlon Brando; comedian Marlon Wayans. *Variations:* Marlan, Marlen, Marlin.

MARLOW (English) Hill near a lake. *Variation:* Marlowe.

MARMADUKE (Irish) Servant of Madoc. *Variations:* Marmaduc, Marmaduk, Marmeduke, Melmidoc.

MARMION (French) Small one.

MARO (Japanese) Myself.

MARQUIS (French) Nobleman. *Variations:* Markeece, Markeese, Markese, Marques, Marquez, Marqui, Marquise.

MARS (Latin) God of war. *Variation:* Marz.

MARSDEN (English) Marsh valley. *Variations:* Marsdan, Marsdon.

MARSHALL (French) One who cares for horses. *Notable:* Educator and communications theorist Marshall McLuhan. *Variations:* Marschal, Marsh, Marshal.

MARSTON (English) Town by a marsh.

MARTELL (English) Hammerer. *Variations:* Martal, Martall, Martell, Martellis.

MARTIN (Latin) Warlike. *Notables:* Dr. Martin Luther King Jr.; religious leader Martin Luther; comedian Martin Short; film director Martin Scorsese; U.S. President Martin Van Buren. *Variations:* Maartan, Maarten, Maartin, Maarton, Maartyn, Mart, Martan, Martain, Martainho, Martainn, Martel, Marten, Martese, Martey, Martez, Martie, Martijn, Martili, Martinas, Martine, Martinez, Martinho, Martiniano, Martinka, Martino, Martinos, Martinous, Martins, Martinus, Marto, Marton, Marty, Martyn, Martynas, Martyne, Martynis, Martynos, Martynous, Martynus, Martynys, Mertan, Merten, Mertin, Merton, Mertyn.

MARTY (English) Short form of Martin. *Notable:* Comedian Marty Feldman. Marte, Martee, Martey, Marti, Martie, Martii.

MARUT (Hindi) God of the wind.

MARVIN (English) Mariner. *Notables:* Composer Marvin Hamlisch; singer Marvin Gaye. *Variations:* Marv, Marvan, Marvein, Marven, Marvon, Marvyn.

MARWAN (Arabic) History. *Variations:* Marwen, Marwin, Marwon, Marwyn.

MARWOOD (English) Lake in a forest.

MASAHIRO (Japanese) Broad minded.

MASAMBA (African) Leaves.

MASAO (Japanese) Sacred.

MASATO (Japanese) Justice.

MASHAMA (Native American) Surprise.

MASHEMA (Native American) Elk antlers. *Variation:* Mashumah.

MASIO (African American) Twin. Nickname of Tomasio. *Variation:* Macio.

MASKA (Native American) Powerful.

MASLIN (French) Little twin. *Variations:* Maslen, Masling.

MASON (French) Stone carver or worker. *Variations:* Mace, Maisan, Maisen, Maisin, Maison, Maisun, Maisyn, Masan, Masen, Masin, Masson, Masyn.

MASOU (Native American) Fire god.

MASSEY (English) Twin. *Variation:* Massie.

MASSIMO (Italian) Great one. *Variation:* Massimino.

MASUD (Arabic) Lucky. *Variations:* Masiud, Masood, Masoud.

MATALINO (Filipino) Bright.

MATANIAH (Hebrew) Gift from God. *Variations:* Matania, Matanya, Matitia, Matitiah, Matityah, Matityahu, Mattaniah, Mattathias, Matya.

MATENI (Polynesian) Warrior.

MATHER (English) Mighty army.

MATO (Native American) Bear.

MATOSKAH (Native American) White bear.

MATSON (English) Matt's son. *Variation:* Mattson.

MATT (English) Short form of Matthew. *Notables:* Talk-show host Matt Lauer; actors Matt LeBlanc and Matt Dillon. *Variations:* Mat, Mattee, Mattey, Mattie, Matty, Maty.

MATTAN (Hebrew) Gift. *Variations:* Matan, Matena, Maton, Mattun.

MATTHEW (Hebrew) Gift of the Lord. *Notables:* Actors Matthew Broderick and Matthew Modine. *Variations:* Macias, Macie, Macisk, Mado, Mafew, Maffew, Mafthew, Matausas, Matej, Mateo, Mateoz, Mateus, Mateusz, Matfei, Mathe, Mathes, Mathew, Mathia, Mathias, Mathies, Mathieu, Matias, Matius, Matt, Matta, Mattea, Matteo, Matthaus, Matthes, Matthia, Matthias, Matthieu, Matthiew, Mattias, Mattis, Mattius, Matui, Matya, Matyas.

MAULI (Hawaiian) Dark skinned.

MAURICE (Latin) Dark skinned. *Notables:* Bee Gee Maurice Gibb;

singer Maurice Chevalier. *Variations:* Maurey, Mauricio, Maurie, Mauris, Maurise, Maurizio, Maury, Morey, Morice, Morie, Moris, Moriss, Morrice, Morrie, Morris, Morriss, Morry.

MAURO (Italian) Dark skinned. Form of Maurice. *Variation:* Maurilio.

MAURY (English) Form of Maurice. *Notable:* Talk-show host Maury Povich.

MAVERICK (American) Nonconformist. *Variations:* Maveric, Maverik, Maveryck, Maveryk, Mavric, Mavrick, Mavrik, Mavryc, Mavryck, Mavryk.

MAWULI (African) God exists.

MAX (English) Short for Maximilian or Maxwell. *Notables:* Boxer Max Baer; makeup pro Max Factor.

MAXFIELD (English) Mack's field.

MAXIMILIAN (Latin) Greatest. *Notable:* Actor Maximilian Schell. *Variations:* Maksim, Maksimka, Maksum, Massimiliano, Massimo, Max, Maxi, Maxie, Maxim, Maxime, Maximilano, Maximiliano, Maximillian, Maximino, Maximo, Maximos, Maxy.

MAXWELL (Scottish) Marcus's well.

MAYER (Latin) Larger. *Variations:* Mayor, Meier, Meir, Meirer, Meuer, Myer.

MAYFIELD (English) Strong man's field.

MAYHEW (English) Gift from the Lord. Variation of Matthew.

MAYNARD (English) Hard strength. *Notable:* Jazz legend Maynard Ferguson. *Variations:* Maynhard, Meinhard, Menard.

MAYO (Irish) Plain of yew trees.

MAYON (Hindi) Black god. *Variation:* Maion.

MAZI (African) Sir.

MAZIN (African) Rain cloud.

MBWANA (African) Master.

MEAD (English) Meadow. *Variations:* Meade, Meed.

MEALLAN (Irish) Little pleasant one. *Variations:* Meldan, Mellan.

MEDGAR (German) Form of Edgar. *Notable:* Civil rights activist Medgar Evers.

MEDRIC (English) From the flourishing meadow. *Variations:* Medard, Medford, Medrick, Medrik, Medryc, Medryck, Medryk.

MEDWIN (German) Faithful friend. *Variations:* Medwen, Medwyn.

MEHITABEL (Hebrew) God benefits. *Variation:* Mehetabel.

MEHMET (Turkish) Praised. *Notable:* TV doctor Mehmet Oz.

MEHTAR (Sanskrit) Prince.

MEINHARD (German) Strong. *Variation:* Meinhardt.

MEIR (Hebrew) Bright one. *Variations:* Mayer, Meyer, Myer.

MEL (English) Short for Melvin. *Notables:* Comedian/director Mel Brooks; actor/director Mel Gibson; singer Mel Tormé.

MELBOURNE (English) Mill stream. *Variations:* Melborn, Melburn, Milbourne, Milburn, Millburn, Millburne.

MELCHIOR (Hebrew) King. *Variation:* Melchor.

Seafaring Names

If you love to sail, fish, or swim, or just enjoy the ocean, these names are defined as "from the sea," "friend of the sea," or "protector of the sea."

BOYS:	GIRLS:
Colbert	Chelsea
Dylan	Dylana
Hurley	Marielle
Irving	Marina
Mervin	Marissa
Morgan	Meredith
Murdoch	Meryl
Murphy	Nerida
Murray	Nerissa
Seabert	Ondine
Seward	Pacifica
Zane	Thalassa

Disney Names

Disney films are such family favorites that their characters are bound to inspire parents (or big brothers and sisters) on what to name the new baby.

BOYS:
Aladdin
Chip
Dale
Donald
Eric
Jiminy
Louie
Maurice
Mickey
Naveen
Nemo
Peter
Phillip
Sebastian

GIRLS:
Alice
Ariel
Aurora
Bambi
Belle
Cinderella
Dory
Esmeralda
Jasmine
Lilo
Minnie
Mulan
Tiana
Wendy

MELDON (English) Mill on a hill. *Variation:* Melden.

MELDRICK (English) Boss at the mill. *Variation:* Meldric, Meldrich.

MELVERN (Native American) Great chief. *Variations:* Melverne, Melvirn, Melvirne, Melvyrn, Melvyrne.

MELVILLE (English) Mill town.

MELVIN (Irish) Great chief. *Notables:* Actors Melvin Van Peebles and Melvyn Douglas. *Variations:* Malvin, Malvinn, Malvon, Malvonn, Mel, Melvern, Melvyn, Melwin, Melwinn.

MENACHEM (Hebrew) Comforting. *Notable:* Israeli statesman Menachem Begin. *Variations:* Menahem, Mendel.

MENDEL (Hebrew) Wisdom. *Variations:* Mendeley, Mendell.

MENSAH (African) Third-born son.

MERCER (English) Shopkeeper. *Variation:* Merce.

MERCURY (Latin) Messenger of the gods. *Variations:* Mercurino, Mercurio.

MERED (Hebrew) Rebellion.

MEREDITH (Welsh) Great leader. *Notable:* Broadway composer Meredith Wilson. *Variations:* Meredyth, Merideth, Meridith.

MERIVALE (English) Pleasant valley. *Variations:* Merival, Meryval, Meryvale.

MERLE (French) Form of Merlin or Merrill. *Notable:* Singer Merle Haggard.

MERLIN (English) Falcon. *Notables:* The wizard Merlin from Arthurian legend; actor Merlin Olsen. *Variations:* Marlin, Marlon, Merle, Merlen, Merlinn, Merlino, Merlyn, Merlynn.

MERRICK (English) Ruler of the sea. *Variation:* Merryck.

MERRILL (English) Bright as the sea. *Variations:* Meril, Merill, Merrel, Merrell, Merril, Meryl.

MERRITT (English) Small and famous. *Variations:* Merit, Meritt, Merrett.

MERTON (English) Town by a lake. *Variations:* Mertin, Mirtin, Murton, Myrton.

MERV (Welsh) Short form of Mervyn. *Notable:* TV host/producer Merv Griffin.

MERVILLE (French) Sea village.

MERVYN (Welsh) Sea hill. *Notable:* Film producer/director Mervyn LeRoy. *Variations:* Mervan, Merven, Mervin, Mervon, Mervyn, Merwin, Merwyn, Murvan, Murven, Murvin, Murvine, Murvon, Murvyn, Murwin, Murwyn.

MESHACH (Hebrew) Artist. *Notable:* Actor Meshach Taylor.

MESHULAM (Hebrew) Paid.

MESUT (Turkish) Happy.

METHODIOS (Greek) Fellow traveler. *Variations:* Metodej, Metodek, Metousek.

METHUSHELACH (Hebrew) Messenger. *Variations:* Methuselah, Metushelach.

MEYER (German) Farmer. *Notable:* Gangster Meyer Lansky. *Variations:* Mayer, Meier, Meir.

MICAH (Hebrew) Form of Michael. *Variation:* Micaiah.

MICANOPY (Native American) Chief. *Variation:* Micco.

MICHAEL (Hebrew) Who is like God. *Notables:* Financier Michael Milken; actors Michael J. Fox and Michael Douglas; "King of Pop" Michael Jackson; basketball great Michael Jordan. *Variations:* Makis, Micha, Michak, Michal, Michalek, Michau, Micheal, Michel, Michele, Mick, Mickel, Mickey, Mickie, Micky, Miguel, Mihkel, Mikaek, Mikala, Mike, Mikelis, Mikey, Mikhos, Mikkel, Mikko, Mischa, Misha, Mitch, Mitchel, Mitchell.

MICHELANGELO (Italian) Michael's angel.

MICHIO (Japanese) With the strength of three thousand. *Variation:* Michi.

MICK (English) Short form of Michael. *Notables:* Rolling Stone Mick Jagger; actor Mickey Rooney. *Variations:* Mickey, Micky.

MIDDLETON (English) Town in the middle.

MIDGARD (Norse) From the middle garden. *Variations:* Midgarth, Midrag, Mithgarthr, Mydgard.

MIECZYSLAW (Polish) Glorious sword. *Variations:* Maslaw, Mieszko, Mietek.

MIGUEL (Spanish) Likeness to God. Form of Michael. *Variations:* Migeal, Migeel, Migel, Myguel.

MIKA (Native American) Raccoon. *Variations:* Miika, Myka.

MIKASI (Native American) Coyote.

MIKE (English) Likeness to God. Short form of Michael. *Variations:* Mikey, Myke, Mykey.

MIKHAIL (Russian) Likeness to God. Form of Michael. *Variations:* Michail, Michale, Mihail, Mihailo, Mikael, Mikail, Mikhalis.

MIKOLAS (Czech) Victorious people. *Variation:* Mikuls.

MIKSA (Hungarian) Greatest. Form of Max.

MILAN (Slavic) Beloved.

MILAP (Native American) Giving.

MILBOROUGH (English) Middle borough. *Variation:* Milboro, Milbrough.

MILBURN (English) From the mill stream. *Variations:* Milborn, Milborne, Milbourn, Milbourne, Milburne, Millborn, Millborne, Millbourn, Millbourne, Millburn, Millburne.

MILES (Latin) Soldier. *Notable:* Jazz musician Miles Davis. *Variations:* Milo, Myles.

MILFORD (English) Ford at the mill.

MILILANI (Hawaiian) Heavenly caress. *Variations:* Mililanee, Mililaney, Mililanie, Mililany.

MILLARD (English) Guard of the mill.

MILLER (English) One who mills grain.

MILLS (English) The mills.

MILO (German) Generous. *Notable:* Actor Milo O'Shea. *Variation:* Mylo.

MILOS (Slavic) Pleasant. *Variation:* Mylos.

MILOSLAV (Czech) Glorious love. *Variations:* Milda, Milek, Milon, Milos, Miloslaw, Milosz.

MILSON (English) Son of Miles.

MILTON (English) Mill town. *Notable:* "Mr. Television" Milton Berle. *Variations:* Millton, Myllton, Mylton.

MINGAN (Native American) Gray wolf.

MING-HOA (Chinese) Prestigious.

MINH (Vietnamese) Brilliant.

MINOR (Latin) Younger. *Variation:* Mynor.

MINSTER (English) From the monastery church. *Variation:* Mynster.

MIROSLAV (Czech) Famous glory. *Variation:* Miroslaw.

MIRWAIS (Afghan) Noble ruler.

MISHA (Russian) Form of Michael.

MISTER (English) Man. *Variations:* Mista, Mistah, Mistar, Mistur, Mysta, Mystah, Mystar, Mystur.

MISU (Native American) Flowing water.

MITCH (English) Form of Mitchell. *Notable:* Writer Mitch Albom.

MITCHELL (English) Form of Michael. *Variations:* Mitchel, Mytchel, Mytchell.

MITSU (Japanese) Of the light.

MODESTE (French) Modest. *Variations:* Modestie, Modesto, Modesty.

MOE (English) Form of Moses. *Notable:* "Stooge" Moe Howard.

MOGENS (Dutch) Powerful. *Variation:* Mogen.

MOHAJIT (Hindi) Handsome. *Variations:* Mohan, Mohandas, Mohanshu.

MOHAMMED (Arabic) Greatly praised. *Notable:* Boxer Mohammed Ali. *Variations:* Ahmad, Amad, Amed, Hamdrem, Hamdum, Hamid, Hammad, Hammed, Humayd, Mahamed, Mahammed,

Mahammod, Mahmed, Mahmoud, Mahmud, Mehemet, Mehmet, Mohamad, Mohamed, Mohamet, Mohammad, Mohammod, Mohmmed, Muhamad, Muhamed, Muhammad, Muhammed.

MOHAN (Hindi) Enchanting.

MOJAG (Native American) Noisy. *Variation:* Moiag.

MOLAN (Irish) Servant of the storm.

MOMUSO (Native American) Yellow-jacket nest.

MONAHAN (Irish) Monk. *Variations:* Monaghan, Monohan.

MONFORD (English) From the monk's river crossing. *Variations:* Montford, Mountford.

MONGO (African) Famous.

MONROE (Irish) Mouth of the Roe River. *Variations:* Monro, Munro, Munroe.

MONTAGUE (French) Sharp mountain peak. *Variations:* Montagu, Montaqu, Montaque.

MONTE (Latin) Mountain. *Variations:* Montee, Montey, Monti, Montie, Monty.

MONTEGO (Spanish) From the mountain.

MONTEL (Italian; Spanish) Mountain. *Notable:* TV host Montel Williams.

MONTEZ (Spanish) Dweller at the mountain. *Variations:* Mounteiz, Monteze, Montise, Montiz, Montize, Montyz, Montyze.

MONTGOMERY (English) Rich man's mountain. *Notable:* Montgomery Clift. *Variation:* Montgomerie.

MONTSHO (African) Black.

MONTY (English) Short form of Montgomery or Montague. *Notables:* Game-show host Monty Hall; comedy troupe Monty Python. *Variation:* Monte.

MOORE (French) Dark complexioned. *Variations:* Moar, Moare, Moor, Mor, Morre.

MORAN (Irish) Great.

MORDECAI (Hebrew) Warlike. *Notable:* Writer Mordecai Richler. *Variations:* Mordche, Mordechai, Mordi, Motche.

MORDRED (Latin) Pain. *Variation:* Mordryd.

MORELAND (English) From the marsh meadow. *Variations:* Moarlan, Moraland, Moorelan, Mooreland, Moorlan, Moorland, Morelan, Moreland, Morlan, Morland.

MORELL (French) Dark colored. *Variations:* Morel, Morrel.

MOREY (English) Dark one from the moor. *Variations:* Moree, Mori, Morie, Morrey, Morrie, Morry, Mory.

MORGAN (Welsh) Great and bright. *Notable:* Actor Morgan Freeman. *Variations:* Morgen, Morrgan.

MORIO (Japanese) Woods. *Variation:* Moryo.

MORITZ (German) A form of Maurice. Dark skinned.

MORLEY (English) Meadow on a moor. *Notable:* News reporter Morley Safer. *Variations:* Moorley, Moorly, Morlee, Morleigh, Morly, Morrley.

MORRIS (English) Form of Maurice. *Notable:* Cat-food advertising icon Morris the Cat.

MORRISON (English) Son of Morris. *Variation:* Morrisson.

MORSE (English) Son of Maurice.

MORTIMER (French) Still water. *Variations:* Mort, Mortmer, Mortym.

MORTON (English) Town by a moor. *Notable:* Talk-show host Morton Downey Jr. *Variations:* Mortan, Morten, Mortin, Mortun, Mortyn.

MORVEN (Scottish) Mariner. *Variations:* Morhorven, Morvan, Morvin, Morvinn, Morvyn, Morvynn.

MOSES (Hebrew) Arrived by water. *Notable:* Basketball player Moses Malone. *Variations:* Moise, Moises, Moisey, Mose, Mosese, Mosha, Moshe, Moss, Moyse, Moze, Mozes.

MOSS (Irish) Giving. *Notable:* Playwright Moss Hart.

MOSTYN (Welsh) Fort in a field.

MOSWEN (African) Light colored.

MOTEGA (Native American) New arrow.

MOULTON (English) Mule town. *Variation:* Molton.

MOUSA (Arabic) From water.

MOZART (Italian) Breathless. *Variation:* Mozar.

MUATA (Native American) Yellow jackets.

MUBARAK (Arabic) Blessed.

MUDAWAR (Arabic) Round.

MUHANNAD (Arabic) Sword.

MUHSIN (Arabic) Generous.

MUIR (Scottish) Moor. *Variations:* Muire, Muyr, Muyre.

MUIREADHACH (Irish) Sailor. *Variations:* Murchadh, Murrough.

MUKHTAR (Arabic) To choose.

MUKUL (Sanskrit) Blossom, Soul. *Variation:* Mukull.

MUNCHIN (Gaelic) Little monk.

MUNDAN (African) Garden.

MUNDO (Spanish) Prosperous protector.

MUNDY (Irish) From the Reamonn in Ireland. *Variations:* Mund, Munde, Mundee, Mundey, Mundi, Mundie, Mundo.

MUNGO (Scottish) Friendly. *Variation:* Mongo.

MUNIR (Arabic) Bright.

MUNNY (Cambodian) Smart. *Variations:* Munee, Muney, Muni, Munie, Munnee, Munney, Munni, Muny.

MURACO (Native American) White moon.

MURAT (Turkish) Wish that came true.

MURDOCH (Scottish) Sailor. *Variations:* Murdo, Murdoc, Murdock, Murdox, Murtagh, Mutagh.

MURPHY (Irish) Sea fighter. *Variations:* Murffey, Murffi, Murffie, Murffy, Murphee, Murphey, Murphi, Murphie.

MURRAY (Scottish) Mariner. *Notable:* DJ Murray the K. *Variations:* Murae, Murai, Muray, Murrae, Murrai, Murree, Murrey, Murri, Murrie, Murry.

MUSA (African) Child.

MUSAD (Arabic) Lucky. *Variations:* Misid, Musaed.

MUSTAFA (Arabic) Chosen. *Notable:* Founder of modern Turkey,

Mustafa Kemal Ataturk. *Variations:* Mostafa, Mostafah, Mostaffa, Mostaffah, Moustafa, Mustafah, Mustapha.

MUTAZZ (Arabic) Strong.

MWAMBA (African) Strong.

MYERS (English) One who lives in a swamp. *Variation:* Myer.

MYKAL (Hebrew) Likeness to God. A form of Michael. *Variations:* Mikaal, Mikael, Mikal, Mikall, Mykaal, Mykall, Mykel, Mykell, Mykil, Mykill, Mykyl, Mykyll.

MYLES (Latin) Warrior. *Variation:* Miles.

MYRON (Greek) Fragrant. *Notable:* Comedian Myron Cohen. *Variations:* Miron, Myreon.

NAAL (Gaelic) Birth. *Variation:* Nal.

NAAMAN (Hebrew) Pleasant. *Variation:* Naman.

NABIHA (Arabic) Intelligent. *Variation:* Nabihah.

NABIL (Arabic) Noble. *Variations:* Nabill, Nabyl, Nabyll.

NABOTH (Hebrew) Prophecy.

NACHMAN (Hebrew) Comfort. *Variation:* Nahum.

NACOMA (Native American) Wanderer.

NADIM (Hindi) Friend. *Variation:* Nadeem.

NADIR (Arabic) Precious.

NADISU (Hindi) River of beauty.

NAEEM (Arabic) Benevolent. *Variations:* Naim, Naiym, Nieem.

NAGATAKA (Japanese) Childhood obligation.

NAGID (Hebrew) Leader. *Variation:* Nageed.

NAHELE (Hawaiian) Forest.

NAHMA (Native American) Trout.

NAHOR (Hebrew) Light. *Variations:* Nahir, Nahur, Nehor.

NAHUM (Hebrew) Compassionate. *Variations:* Nahom, Nehemiah, Nemiah.

NAIM (Arabic) Happy. *Variation:* Naeem.

NAIRNE (Scottish) River glade. *Variation:* Nairn.

NAJI (Arabic) Safe. *Variation:* Nagi.

NAJIB (Arabic) Smart. *Variations:* Nagib, Najeeb.

NAKOS (Native American) Sage.

NALDO (Spanish) Strong.

NALIN (Hindi) Lotus.

NALREN (Native American) To thaw.

NAMID (Native American) Star dancer.

NAMIL (Arabic) To achieve.

NAMIR (Hebrew) Leopard.

NANAK (Hindi) Name of the founder of the Sikh religion.

NANDAN (Hindi) Happiness. *Variation:* Nandin.

NANDO (Spanish) Adventurer. Short form of Fernando. *Variation:* Nandor.

NANSEN (Scandinavian) Nancy's son. *Variations:* Nansan, Nansin, Nanson, Nansyn.

NANTAI (Native American) Chief. *Variation:* Nantay.

NANTAN (Native American) Spokesperson. *Variations:* Nanten, Nantin, Nanton, Nantyn.

NAOKO (Japanese) Direct.

NAOMHAN (Irish) Little holy one. *Variation:* Nevan.

NAPIER (English) Keeper of linens.

NAPOLEON (Greek) Lion of the woods; (Italian) From Naples. *Notables:* General Napoleon Bonaparte; speaker/writer Napoleon Hill.

NARAIN (Hindi) Protector.

NARAYANA (Hindi) Man.

NARCISSUS (Greek) Daffodil. *Variations:* Narciso, Narcisse, Narcisso, Narcysse, Narcyssus.

NARD (Persian) Chess game.

NARDO (Spanish) Bold. Short form of Bernard.

NAREN (Hindi) Superior man.

NARESH (Hindi) Ruler of men.

NARVE (Dutch) Healthy strength. *Variation:* Narv.

NASH (English) Ash tree.

NASHASHUK (Native American) Thunder.

NASHOBA (Native American) Wolf. *Variation:* Neshoba.

NASIM (Persian) Breezy. *Variations:* Naseem, Nassim.

NASSER (Arabic) Victory. *Variations:* Naser, Nasir, Nassir, Nassor.

NAT (English) Short form of Nathan and Nathaniel. *Notables:* Singer Nat King Cole; freedom-fighting slave Nat Turner. *Variations:* Natt, Natty.

NATAL (Spanish) Birthday. *Variations:* Natale, Natalino, Natalio.

NATE (English) Giver. Short form of Nathan or Nathaniel.

NATHAN (Hebrew) Giver. *Notables:* American soldier/hero Nathan Hale; actor Nathan Lane. *Variations:* Naethan, Naethen, Naethin, Naethon, Naethun, Naethyn, Naithan, Naithen, Naithin, Naithon, Naithun, Naithyn, Natan, Natham, Nathann, Nathean, Nathen, Nathian, Nathin, Nathon, Nathun, Nathyn, Natthan, Naythan, Naython, Naythun, Naythyn.

NATHANIEL (Hebrew) Gift from God. *Notable:* Writer Nathaniel Hawthorne. *Variations:* Naethanael, Naethanial, Naithanael, Naithanyal, Naithanyel, Natalianou, Nataneal, Nataniel, Nataniello, Nathanael, Nathaneal, Nathaneil, Nathanel, Nathaneol, Nathanial, Nathanie, Nathanielle, Nathanuel, Nathanyal, Nathanyel, Nathinel, Naytanial, Naythaneal, Naythaniel, Nethanial, Nethaniel, Nethanuel.

NAV (Hungarian) Name.

NAVARRO (Spanish) Land. *Variation:* Navarre.

NAVEED (Persian) Good news. *Variation:* Naved.

NAVEEN (Hindi) New. *Notable:* Actor Naveen Andrews. *Variations:* Naven, Navin.

NAWAT (Native American) Left handed.

NAYATI (Native American) Wrestler.

NAYLAND (English) Island resident. *Variations:* Nailan, Nailand, Naylan.

NDALE (African) A trick.

NDULU (African) Dove.

NEAL (Irish) A champion. Form of Neil. *Variations:* Neale, Neall, Nealle, Nealon, Nealy, Neel, Neele, Neell, Neelle.

NEBRASKA (Native American) Flat water. *Variation:* Nebraskah.

NED (English) Short form of Edward or Edwin. *Notable:* Actor Ned Beatty. *Variation:* Nedd.

NEDAVIAH (Hebrew) Charity of the Lord. *Variations:* Nedabiah, Nedavia, Nedavya.

NEFIN (German) Nephew.

NEGASI (Ethiopian) He will become royalty.

NEHAL (Hindi) Rain.

NEHEMIAH (Hebrew) Lord's comfort. *Variations:* Nechemiah, Nechemya.

NEHRU (Hindi) Canal.

NEIL (Irish) Champion. *Notables:* Astronaut Neil Armstrong; playwright Neil Simon; singers Neil Sedaka and Neil Young. *Variations:* Neal, Neale, Neall, Nealle, Nealon, Neile, Neill, Neille, Neils, Niadh, Nial, Niall, Nialle, Niel, Niele, Niell, Nielle, Niels, Nigel, Niles, Nilo.

NELEK (Polish) Like a horn.

NELLO (Spanish) Form of Daniel. *Variation:* Nelo.

NELS (Gaelic) Son of a champion. *Variation:* Nel.

NELSON (English) Son of Neil. *Notables:* South African President Nelson Mandela; New York Governor and U.S. Vice President Nelson Rockefeller; bandleader Nelson Riddle. *Variations:* Nealson, Neilson, Nilson, Nilsson.

NEMESIO (Spanish) Justice.

NEMO (Greek) Glade. *Variations:* Nimo, Nymo.

NEMUEL (Hebrew) The spreading sea of God. *Variations:* Nemuele, Nemuell, Nemuelle.

NEN (Egyptian) Ancient water.

NEPTUNE (Latin) Roman god of the sea.

NEREUS (Greek) Mythological father of the sea nymphs.

NERIAN (English) Protector.

NERO (Latin) Strong. *Notable:* Roman Emperor Nero. *Variations:* Neron, Nerone.

NERVILLE (French) From the sea village. *Variations:* Nervil, Nervile, Nervill, Nervyl, Nervyle, Nervyll, Nervylle.

NESBIT (English) Curve in the road. *Variations:* Naisbit, Naisbitt, Nesbitt, Nisbet, Nisbett.

NESS (Scottish) From the headland.

NESTOR (Greek) Traveler. *Variations:* Nestar, Nester.

NETANIAH (Hebrew) God has given. *Variations:* Netania, Netanya, Nethaniah.

NEVADA (Spanish) Snow covered. *Variations:* Navada, Nevade.

NEVILLE (French) New town. *Notable:* British Prime Minister Neville Chamberlain. *Variations:* Nevil, Nevile, Nevill, Nevyle.

NEVIN (Irish) Holy. *Variations:* Nev, Nevan, Nevins, Niven.

NEWBOLD (English) New tree.

NEWELL (English) New hall. *Variations:* Newall, Newel, Newhall.

NEWLAND (English) New land. *Variation:* Newlan.

Names for Brunettes

BOYS:	GIRLS:
Adrian	Adriana
Bronson	Auburn
Colby	Blake
Donavan	Brunelle
Douglas	Ciara
Duncan	Darcy
Kerwin	Kerry
Kiernan	Kyrie
Lebrun	Melanie
Nigel	Tawny
Sorell	
Tynan	

Names for Redheads

BOYS:	GIRLS:
Clancy	Auburn
Corcoran	Derry
Flynn	Flannery
Reed	Omaira
Rooney	Pyrrha
Rory	Ruby
Rufus	Ruffina
Russell	Scarlett

NEWLIN (Welsh) New lake. *Variations:* Newlun, Newlyn.

NEWMAN (English) Newcomer. *Variations:* Neiman, Neuman, Numan.

NEWTON (English) New town. *Notable:* Politician Newt Gingrich. *Variation:* Newt.

NGAI (Vietnamese) Herb.

NGHIA (Vietnamese) Forever.

NGOZI (African) Good luck.

NHEAN (Cambodian) All seeing.

NIALL (Irish) Champion. Form of Neil and Niles.

NIAZ (Hindi) Gift.

NIBAL (Arabic) Arrow. *Variation:* Nybal.

NIBAW (Native American) To stand up.

NICABAR (Gypsy) Cunning.

NICHOLAS (Greek) Victorious. *Notables:* Actor Nicolas Cage; writer Nicholas Sparks. *Variations:* Niccolo, Nichol, Nickolas, Nickolaus, Nicol, Nicolaas, Nicolas, Nikita, Niklas, Niklos, Niko, Nikolais, Nikolas, Nikolaus, Nikolo, Nikolos, Nikos, Nikula.

NICHOLSON (Greek; English) Nicholas's son. *Variations:* Nickelson, Nickoleson.

NICK (English) Short form of Nicholas or Dominic. *Notables:* Singers Nick Lachey and Nick Carter; actor Nick Nolte; writer Nick Hornby. *Variations:* Nic, Nicki, Nicky, Nik, Nikki.

NICO (Greek) Form of Nicholas. *Variation:* Nicco.

NICODEMUS (Greek) Victory of the people. *Variations:* Nicodem, Nicodemius.

NICOLAI (Russian) Form of Nicholas. *Notable:* Russian writer Nikolai Gogol. *Variation:* Nikolai.

NIEN (Vietnamese) Year.

NIGAN (Native American) In the lead. *Variations:* Ngan, Nigen, Nigin, Nigyn, Nygen, Nygin, Nygon, Nygyn.

NIGEL (Latin) Dark. *Notable:* Actor Nigel Hawthorne. *Variations:* Nigal, Nigiel, Nigil.

NIKE (Greek) Victorious. *Variations:* Nikee, Nikey, Niki, Nikie, Niky, Nyke, Nykee, Nykey, Nyki, Nykie, Nyky.

NIKITA (Russian) Victory of the people. A form of Nicholas. *Variations:* Nakita, Nakitas, Nikula, Nykita, Nykyta.

NIKITI (Native American) Smooth and round. *Variations:* Nikity, Nikyti, Nikyty, Nykiti, Nykity, Nykyty.

NIKODEMOS (Greek) Victory of the people. *Variations:* Nicodemus, Nicomedes, Nikodem, Nikolao, Nikolo, Nikomedes.

NIKOSTRATOS (Greek) Victorious army. *Variation:* Nicostratos.

NILES (English) Champion. Form of Neil. *Variations:* Nial, Niale, Nialle, Niilo, Nile, Nilo, Nyal, Nyale, Nyall, Nyalle, Nyle, Nyles, Nylles.

NILS (Scandinavian) Champion. *Variations:* Nil, Nill, Nille, Nyl, Nyll, Nylle.

NIMROD (Hebrew) Rebel.

NINO (Spanish) Child.

NIPUN (Hindi) Clever.

NIRAM (Hebrew) Fertile meadow.

NIRAN (Thai) Eternal. *Variations:* Niren, Nirin, Nirn, Niron, Nyran, Nyren, Nyrin, Nyron, Nyryn.

NIREL (Hebrew) Ploughed field. *Variations:* Nir, Niral, Niria, Niriel, Nyr, Nyra, Nyral, Nyrel, Nyria, Nyrial.

NIRVAN (Hindi) Bliss.

NISAN (Hebrew) Miracle. *Variation:* Nissan.

NISHAD (Hindi) Seventh note of a scale.

NISHAN (Armenian) Sign or symbol. *Variation:* Nyshan.

NITIS (Native American) Good friend. *Variations:* Netis, Nytis.

NIUTEI (Polynesian) Coconut tree. *Variations:* Niu, Nyu.

NIXON (English) Son of Nicholas. *Variations:* Nixan, Nixen, Nixin, Nixson, Nixun, Nixyn, Nyxan, Nyxen, Nyxin, Nyxon, Nyxyn.

NIZAM (Arabic) Leader.

NJAU (African) Young bull.

NOACH (Hebrew) One who provides comfort.

NOADIAH (Hebrew) Meeting with God. *Variations:* Noadia, Noadya.

NOAH (Hebrew) Comfort. *Notables:* Actor Noah Wyle; dictionary writer Noah Webster. *Variations:* Noach, Noak, Noe, Noi, Noy.

NOAM (Hebrew) Delight. *Notable:* Linguist Noam Chomsky.

NOBLE (Latin) Well bred.

NOBU (Japanese) Truth. *Notable:* Japanese chef Nobu Matsuhisa.

NODIN (Native American) The wind. *Variation:* Noton.

NOE (French) Form of Noah.

NOEL (French) Christmas. *Notable:* Actor/playwright/composer Noel Coward. *Variations:* Natal, Natale, Nowel, Nowell.

NOHEA (Hawaiian) Handsome.

NOLAN (Irish) Little proud one. *Notables:* Fashion designer Nolan Miller; baseball star Nolan Ryan. *Variations:* Noland, Nolen, Nolin, Nollan, Nuallan.

NORBERT (German) Bright. *Variations:* Norberto, Norburt, Norburto, Norbyrt, Norbyrto, Northbert, Northberto, Northburt, Northburto, Northbyrt, Northbyto.

NORCROSS (English) From the north crossroad.

NORIYUKI (Japanese) Filled with happiness.

NORM (English) Short form of Norman. *Notables:* Comedians Norm McDonald and Norm Crosby.

NORMAN (English) Northerner. *Notables:* Writer Norman Mailer; TV producer Norman Lear; clergyman Norman Vincent Peale. *Variations:* Norm, Normand, Normando, Normen, Normie.

NORRIS (French) Northerner. *Variations:* Norice, Noris, Norreys, Norrie, Norriss, Norry, Norrys.

NORTH (English) From the north.

NORTHCLIFF (English) Northern cliff. *Variations:* Northcliffe, Northclyff, Northclyffe.

NORTHROP (English) Northern farm. *Variation:* Northrup.

NORTON (English) Northern town.

NORVILLE (French) North town. *Variations:* Norval, Norvel, Norvil.

NORVIN (English) Northern friend. *Variations:* Norvyn, Norwin, Norwinn, Norwyn, Norwynn.

NORWARD (English) Guardian of the north.

NORWELL (English) From the north stream. *Variations:* Northwel, Northwell, Norwel.

NORWIN (English) Friend of the north.

NORWOOD (English) Northern woods.

NOTAKU (Native American) Growling bear.

NOVA (Latin) New.

NOVAK (Czech) Newcomer.

NOWLES (English) From the grassy slope. *Variations:* Knowles, Nowel, Nowels, Nowl, Nowle.

NSOAH (African) Seventh-born child. *Variation:* Nsoa.

NUHAD (Arabic) Brave. *Variation:* Nouhad.

NULTE (Irish) From Ulster, Northern Ireland.

NUMA (Arabic) Kindness.

NUMAIR (Arabic) Panther.

NUNCIO (Italian) Messenger. *Variation:* Nunzio.

NURI (Arabic) Light. *Variations:* Noori, Nur, Nury.

NURIEL (Hebrew; Arabic) Fire of God. *Variations:* Nuria, Nuriah, Nurial.

NURU (African) Light.

NUSAIR (Arabic) Bird of prey.

NWA (African) Son.

NWAKE (African) Son born on market day.

NYE (Welsh) Noble.

OAKES (English) Oak tree. *Variations:* Oak, Ochs.

OAKLEY (English) Meadow of oak trees. *Variations:* Oaklee, Oakleigh, Oakly.

OBA (African) King.

OBADIAH (Hebrew) Servant of God. *Variations:* Obadias, Obe, Obed, Obediah, Obie, Ovadiach, Ovadiah.

OBASI (African) Honoring God.

OBAYANA (African) The king warms himself at the fire.

OBED (Hebrew) Worshiper. *Variation:* Oved.

OBERON (German) Noble and bear-like. *Variations:* Auberon, Auberron.

OBERT (German) Wealthy and brilliant.

OBI (African) Heart.

OBIKE (African) Dearly loved.

OCEAN (English) Ocean. *Variation:* Oceanus.

OCTAVIUS (Latin) Eighth child. *Variations:* Octave, Octavian, Octavien, Octavio, Octavo, Ottavio.

ODAKOTA (Native American) Friends.

ODELL (English) Forested hill. *Variations:* Ode, Odey, Odi, Odie.

ODHRAN (Irish) Pale green. *Variations:* Odran, Odren, Odrin, Odron, Odryn, Oran.

ODIN (Scandinavian) Supreme ruler.

ODION (African) First born of twins.

ODOLF (German) Wealthy wolf. *Variations:* Adolf, Odolfe, Odolff, Odolph, Odolphe, Odulf, Odulph.

ODOM (African) Oak tree.

ODON (Hungarian) Wealthy protector.

ODWIN (German) Wealthy, noble friend. *Variations:* Odwinn, Odwyn, Odwynn.

ODYSSEUS (Greek) Full of wrath. *Notable:* Trojan War leader Odysseus.

OG (Aramaic) King. *Notable:* Writer/speaker Og Mandino.

OGALEESHA (Native American) Red shirt.

OGDEN (English) Valley of oak trees. *Notable:* Writer Ogden Nash. *Variations:* Ogdan, Ogdon.

OGHE (Irish) Horseman. *Variations:* Oghie, Oho.

OGILVY (Welsh) From the high hill or peak. *Variations:* Ogil, Ogilvey, Ogilvie, Ogyl, Ogylvie.

OGIMA (Native American) Chief. *Variations:* Ogimah, Ogyma, Ogymah.

OGLESBY (English) Awe inspiring. *Variation:* Oglesbie.

OGUN (African) War god. *Variations:* Ogunkeye, Ogunsawo, Ogunsheye.

OHANKO (Native American) Careless.

OHANZEE (Native American) Shadow.

OHIN (African) Chief.

OHIO (Native American) Beautiful river.

OHITEKAH (Native American) Courageous.

OISIN (Irish) Young deer. *Variations:* Ossian, Ossin.

OISTIN (Irish) Respected.

OKE (Hawaiian) Divine spear. A form of Oscar. *Variations:* Okee, Okey, Oki, Okie, Oky.

OKECHUKU (African) Gift from God.

OKELLO (African) Born after twins.

OKEMOS (Native American) Small chief.

OKOTH (African) Born during a rainstorm.

OKPARA (African) First-born son.

OKTAWIAN (African) Eighth.

OLA (African) Wealth.

OLADELE (African) We are honored at home.

OLAF (Scandinavian) Forefather. *Variations:* Olaff, Olav, Olave, Olen, Olin, Olof, Olov, Olyn.

OLAFEMI (African) Fortunate.

OLAKEAKUA (Hawaiian) God lives.

OLANIYAN (African) Surrounded by honor.

OLDRICH (Czech) Noble king. *Variations:* Olda, Oldra, Oldrisek, Olecek, Olik, Olouvsek.

OLEG (Russian) Holy. *Notable:* Fashion designer Oleg Cassini. *Variation:* Olezka.

OLEKSANDR (Russian) Defender of humankind. A form of Alexander. *Variations:* Olek, Oles, Olesandr, Olesko.

OLERY (French) Leader.

OLIN (English) Holly. *Variations:* Olen, Olney.

OLIVER (Latin) Olive tree. *Notables:* Comedian Oliver Hardy; film director Oliver Stone. *Variations:* Oliverio, Olivero, Olivier, Olivor, Olley, Ollie, Olliver, Ollivor, Olly.

OLIWA (Hawaiian) Olive.

OLNEY (English) Town in Britain.

OLORUN (African) Nigerian god.

OLUBAYO (African) Joy.

OLUFEMI (African) God loves me. *Variation:* Olviemi.

OLUGBALA (African) God of the people.

OLUHYODE (African) God makes me happy.

OLUJIMI (African) Given by God.

OLUMIDE (African) God arrives.

OLUMOI (African) God awakens.

OLUSHEGUN (African) God is champion.

OLUSHOLA (African) Blessed by God.

OLUWA (African) Believes in God.

OLUYEMI (African) Pious.

OLYMPOS (Greek) Mountain home of the gods. *Variations:* Olympas, Olympius, Olympus.

OMANAND (Hindi) Joy from a meditation chant.

OMAR (Arabic) High follower of the Prophet. *Notables:* Actor/bridge expert Omar Sharif; General Omar Bradley; poet Omar Khayyam. *Variations:* Omarr, Omer.

OMARI (Arabic) High follower of the prophet. *Variations:* Omaree, Omarey, Omarie, Omary.

OMRI (Hebrew; Arabic) Bundle of grain.

ONACONA (Native American) White owl. *Variation:* Oukounaka.

ONAN (Turkish) Wealthy.

ONANI (African) A glance.

ONAONA (Hawaiian) Sweet smelling.

ONDREJ (Czech) Manly. *Variations:* Ondra, Ondravsek, Ondrejek, Ondrousek.

O'NEIL (Irish) Son of Neil. *Variations:* O'Neal, Oneal, Oneil, O'Neill.

ONKAR (Hindi) Purity.

ONLLWYN (Welsh) Ash grove. *Variations:* Onilwin, Onilwyn, Onllwin.

ONSLOW (English) Fan's hill. *Variation:* Ounslow.

ONUR (Turkish) Honor. *Variation:* Onhur.

OPHIR (Hebrew) Faith. *Variation:* Ofir.

ORAL (Latin) Verbal. *Notable:* Religious leader Oral Roberts.

ORAN (Irish) Green. *Variations:* Orin, Orran, Orren, Orrin.

ORATIO (Latin) Timekeeper. *Variations:* Oratyo, Orazio.

ORBAN (Hungarian) Urbanite.

ORD (English) Spear.

ORDELL (Latin) Beginning. *Variations:* Orde, Ordel, Ordele, Ordelle.

ORDWAY (English) Spear path.

OREN (Hebrew) Pine tree. *Notable:* U.S. Senator Orrin Hatch. *Variations:* Orin, Orran, Orren, Orrin.

ORESTES (Greek) Mountain. *Variations:* Aresty, Oreste.

OREV (Hebrew) Raven. *Variation:* Oreb.

ORFORD (English) Ford of cattle.

ORI (Hebrew) My light. *Variations:* Orie, Oron, Orrie, Orry.

ORION (Greek) Son of fire or light. *Variations:* Orian, Orien, Oryan, Oryen, Oryin, Oryon.

ORLANDO (Italian) Famous land. *Notable:* Actor Orlando Bloom. *Variations:* Ordando, Orlan, Orland, Orlande, Orlo.

ORMAN (English) Spearman.

ORMOND (German) Serpent. *Variations:* Ormand, Ormande, Ormonde, Ormondo.

ORO (Spanish) Gold.

ORON (Hebrew) Light.

ORPHEUS (Greek) Dark of night.

ORRICK (English) Old oak tree. *Variations:* Orec, Oreck, Oric, Orick, Orik, Orric, Orrik, Orryc, Orryck, Orryk, Oryc, Oryck, Oryk.

ORSON (Latin) Bear-like. *Notables:* Actors Orson Welles and Orson Bean. *Variations:* Orsen, Orsin, Orsini, Orsino.

ORTON (English) Shore town.

ORTZI (Basque) Sky. *Variation:* Ortzy.

ORUNJAN (African) Born under the noontime sun.

ORVILLE (French) Golden town. *Notables:* Aviator Orville Wright; popcorn-maker Orville Redenbacher. *Variations:* Orv, Orval, Orvell, Orvelle, Orvil.

ORVIN (English) Friend with a spear. *Variations:* Orwin, Orwynn.

OSAYABA (African) God forgives.

OSBERT (English) Divine and bright.

OSBORN (English) Divine bear. *Variations:* Osborne, Osbourn, Osbourne, Osburn, Osburne.

OSCAR (English) Divine spear. *Notables:* Writer Oscar Wilde; composer Oscar Hammerstein; boxer Oscar De La Hoya; fashion designer Oscar de la Renta. *Variations:* Osgar, Oskar, Oskaras, Osker, Ossie.

OSCEOLA (Native American) Black drink.

OSEI (African) Noble.

OSGOOD (English) Divine and good.

O'SHEA (Irish) Son of Shea. *Variations:* Oshay, Oshea.

OSIRIS (Egyptian) Mythological god of rebirth, resurrection, fertility and the afterlife. *Variations:* Osirys, Osyris.

OSMAN (Turkish) Ruler. *Variations:* Osmanek, Osmen, Osmin, Osmon, Osmyn.

OSMAR (English) Divine and marvelous. *Variations:* Osmer, Osmir, Osmor, Osmyr.

OSMOND (English) Divine protector. *Variations:* Osman, Osmand, Osmonde, Osmont, Osmonte, Osmund, Osmunde, Osmundo, Osmunt, Osmunte.

OSRED (English) Divine adviser.

OSRIC (English) Divine ruler. *Variations:* Osrick, Osrig, Osrik.

OSTIN (Latin) Esteemed. *Variations:* Austin, Ostan, Osten, Oston, Ostun, Ostyn.

OSWALD (English) Divine power. *Variations:* Ossie, Osvald, Oswaldo, Oswall, Osweld, Osweldo, Oswell.

OSWIN (English) Divine friend. *Variations:* Osvin, Oswinn, Oswyn, Oswynn.

OTA (Czech) Wealthy. *Variation:* Otik.

OTADAN (Native American) Abundance.

OTHELLO (Spanish) Wealthy. Form of Otis. *Variation:* Otello.

OTHMAN (German) Rich man.

OTHNIEL (Hebrew) Lion of God. *Variation:* Otniel.

OTIS (English) Son of Otto. *Variation:* Ottis.

OTSKAI (Native American) Leaving.

OTTAH (African) Skinny boy.

OTTAR (Scandinavian) Warrior. Maker of arrows. *Variation:* Otar.

OTTO (German) Wealthy. *Notables:* Film director Otto Preminger; German Chancellor Otto von Bismarck. *Variations:* Odo, Otho, Othon.

OTTOKAR (German) Spirited warrior.

OTTOMAR (Turkish) Ruler. *Variations:* Otman, Otmen, Otomar, Otomars, Ottmar, Ottmer, Ottmen, Ottoma.

OTTWAY (German) Lucky in battle. *Variation:* Otway.

OURAY (Native American) Arrow.

OVERTON (English) From the high town. *Variations:* Overtan, Overten, Overtin, Overtyn.

OVID (Latin) Sheep. *Notable:* Roman poet Ovid. *Variation:* Ovidius.

OWEN (Welsh) Well born. *Notable:* Actor Owen Wilson. *Variations:* Owain, Owaine, Owan, Owin, Owyn.

OWNEY (Irish) Elder. *Variations:* Ownie, Owny.

OXFORD (English) Oxen river crossing.

OXLEY (English) From the meadow of the oxen. *Variations:* Oxleah, Oxlee, Oxleigh, Oxlie, Oxly.

OXTON (English) From the ox town. *Variations:* Oxtan, Oxten, Oxtin, Oxtyn.

OYA (Native American) Talking of the snake.

OZ (Hebrew) Power.

OZIAS (Hebrew) Strength of the Lord. *Variations:* Izia, Oziah, Ozya, Ozyah, Ozyas.

OZNI (Hebrew) To listen to God.

OZURU (Japanese) Stork.

OZZY (English) Short for Osborne or Osgood. *Notables:* Rock singer Ozzy Osborne; actors Ossie Davis and Ozzie Nelson. *Variations:* Osie, Ossie, Ossy, Oz, Ozie, Ozzie.

PAAVO (Finnish) Small. A form of Paul. *Variation:* Paav.

PABLO (Spanish) Form of Paul. *Notable:* Artist Pablo Picasso.

PACE (English) Peace. *Variations:* Paice, Payce.

PACIFICO (Filipino) Peaceful. *Variations:* Pacifica, Pacific.

PACKARD (English) Peddler's pack.

PACO (Spanish) From France. Form of Francisco. *Notable:* Fashion designer Paco Rabanne. *Variations:* Pacorro, Paquito.

PADDY (Irish) Noble. Nickname for Patrick. *Notable:* Dramatist Paddy Chayefsky. *Variations:* Paddey, Paddie.

PADGET (English) Young assistant. *Variations:* Padgett, Paget, Pagett.

PADRE (Spanish) Father; priest.

PADRUIG (Scottish) Noble. A form of Patrick. *Variations:* Padraig, Padraiz.

PAGAN (Latin) Country dweller. *Variations:* Paegan, Paegen, Paegin, Paegon, Paegyn, Paganel, Pagen, Pagin, Pagon, Pagun, Paigan, Paigen, Paigin, Paigon, Paigyn.

PAGE (French) Intern. *Variation:* Paige.

PAGIEL (Hebrew) Worships God. *Variations:* Paegel, Paegell, Pagiell, Paigel, Paigell, Paygel, Paygell.

PAINE (English) Country person. *Variations:* Pane, Pain, Painey, Payn, Payne.

PAINTER (English) Painter.

PAKELIKA (Hawaiian) Nobleman.

PAKI (African) Witness.

PAL (Swedish; Hungarian) Small. A form of Paul. *Variations:* Pali, Palika.

PALAINA (Hawaiian) Strong honor.

PALAKI (Polynesian) Black. *Variations:* Palefu, Peleki.

PALANI (Hawaiian) Free man. *Variation:* Farani.

PALASH (Hindi) Flowery tree.

PALBEN (Basque) Blond haired.

PALLADIN (Native American) Fighter. *Variations:* Pallaten, Pallaton.

PALMER (English) Carrying palm branches. *Variations:* Pallmer, Palmar.

PALMIRO (Latin) Born on Palm Sunday. *Variations:* Palmirow, Palmyro.

PALTI (Hebrew) God frees.

PANAS (Greek) Immortal.

PANCHO (Spanish) Freedom. Nickname for Francisco. *Notable:* Mexican revolutionary Pancho Villa. *Variation:* Panchito.

PANDU (Sanskrit) Pale.

PANOS (Greek) Rock.

PAOLO (Italian) Small. A form of Paul.

PARAMESH (Hindi) Great. *Variation:* Param.

PARIS (Greek) The city. *Variations:* Paras, Parese, Parris.

PARKER (English) Park keeper. *Notable:* Actor Parker Stevenson. *Variations:* Park, Parke, Parkes, Parks.

PARLAN (Scottish) Farmer. *Variations:* Parlen, Parlin, Parlon, Parlyn.

PARNELL (French) Little stone. *Variations:* Parkin, Parnel, Parrnell.

PARR (English) Barn; stable. *Variations:* Parrey, Parrie.

PARRISH (English) County; church area. *Variation:* Parish.

PARRY (Welsh) Son of Harry. *Variations:* Paree, Parey, Pari, Parie, Parree, Parrey, Parri, Parrie, Pary.

PARSONS (English) Clergyman.

PARVAIZ (Persian) Happy. *Variations:* Parvez, Parviz, Parwiz.

PAS (Latin) Dance.

PASANG (Tibetan) Born on a Friday.

PASCAL (French) Easter child. *Variations:* Pascale, Pascalle, Paschal, Pascoe, Pascow, Pasqual, Pasquale.

PASHA (Russian) Form of Paul. *Variation:* Pashka.

PASQUALE (Italian) Form of Pascal. *Variations:* Pasqual, Pasquali.

PAT (Latin) Short form of Patrick. *Notables:* Singer Pat Boone; comedian Pat Cooper.

PATAMON (Native American) Raging man. *Variations:* Pataman, Patamen, Patamin, Patamyn.

PATRICK (Latin) Noble man. *Notables:* Patron saint of Ireland, St. Patrick; basketball player Patrick Ewing; actor Patrick Swayze. *Variations:* Paddey, Paddie, Paddy, Padraic, Padraig, Padruig, Pat, Patek, Patric, Patrice, Patricio, Patricius, Patrik, Patrizio, Patrizius, Patryk.

PATTERSON (English) Son of Pat. *Variation:* Patteson.

PATTON (English) Soldier's town. *Variations:* Paten, Patin, Paton, Patten, Pattin.

PATWIN (Native American) Man. *Variation:* Patwyn.

PAUL (Latin) Small. *Notables:* Singers Paul McCartney and Paul Simon; Revolutionary War hero Paul Revere; actor Paul Newman. *Variations:* Pablo, Pal, Pali, Palika, Pall, Paolo, Pasha, Pashenka, Pashka, Paska, Paulin, Paulino, Paulis, Paulo, Pauls, Paulus, Pauly, Pavel, Pavils, Pavlicek, Pavlik, Pavlo, Pavlousek, Pawel, Pawl, Pol, Poul.

PAVAN (Hindi) Like a breeze. *Variations:* Pavanjeet, Pavanjit, Pavann.

PAVEL (Slavic) Little.

PAVIT (Hindi) Purity. *Variations:* Pavitt, Pavyt, Pavytt.

PAWEL (Polish) Small. A form of Peter. *Variations:* Pawelek, Pawell, Pawl.

PAXTON (English) Peaceful town. *Variations:* Packston, Pax, Paxon, Paxten, Paxx.

PAYAT (Native American) He is coming. *Variations:* Pay, Payatt.

PAYNE (Latin) Countryman. *Variation:* Paine.

PAZ (Spanish) Peace.

PEABO (Irish) Solid as a rock. *Notable:* Singer Peabo Bryson. *Variation:* Peebo.

PEADAR (Irish) Rock. *Variation:* Peadair.

PEALE (English) Ring. *Variations:* Peel, Peele.

PEARSON (English) Son of Piers. *Variation:* Pierson.

PEDAHEL (Hebrew) God redeems. *Variation:* Pedael.

PEDAT (Hebrew) Atonement.

PEDRO (Spanish) Stone. A form of Peter.

Occupations by Name

Some names represent certain skills or professions. These occupational boys' names might determine your son's future calling:

Archer (Archer)
Bailey (Bailiff)
Barry (Marksman)
Baxter (Baker)
Brewster (Beer maker)
Chandler (Candle maker)
Cooper (Barrel maker)
Faulkner (Falcon trainer)
Fletcher (Bow and arrow maker)
Mason (Stoneworker)
Porter (Gatekeeper)
Sawyer (Carpenter)
Squire (Land owner)
Tanner (Leather worker)
Thatcher (Roofer)
Tucker (Cloth cleaner)
Wainwright (Wagon maker)
Waite (Watchman)
Zeeman (Sailor)

PEEL (Celtic) From the castle tower. *Variations:* Peal, Peil.

PEKAR (Czech) Baker.

PEKKA (Finnish) Stone. A form of Peter.

PELAGIOS (Greek) From the sea. *Variation:* Pelagius.

PELEKE (Hawaiian) Wise counselor. *Variation:* Ferede.

PELHAM (English) Region in Britain.

PELI (Basque) Happy. *Variations:* Pelie, Pely.

PELL (English) Parchment paper.

PELLO (Greek) Stone.

PELTON (English) From the town by the pool. *Variations:* Peltan, Pelten, Peltin, Peltyn.

PEMBROKE (Irish) Rocky hill. *Variation:* Pembrook.

PENDLE (English) Hill. *Variations:* Pendal, Pendel, Penndal, Penndel, Penndle.

PENEKIKO (Hawaiian) Blessed. *Variations:* Benedito, Beni, Peni.

PENLEY (English) Fenced meadow. *Variations:* Penlea, Penleigh, Penly, Pennlea, Pennleigh, Pennley.

PENMINA (Hawaiian) Favorite son. *Variation:* Peniamina.

PENN (English) Enclosure. *Notable:* Comedian/magician Penn Gillette. *Variation:* Pen.

PENRITH (Welsh) From the chief river crossing. *Variation:* Penryth.

PENROD (German) Commander.

PENTON (English) From the enclosed town.

PEPE (Spanish) Nickname for Jose. *Variations:* Pepito, Peppe.

PEPIN (German) One who perseveres. *Variations:* Pepi, Peppi, Peppie, Peppy.

PEPPER (English) Pepper.

PER (Scandinavian) Stone. Form of Peter.

PERACH (Hebrew) Flower. *Variation:* Perah.

PERACHIAH (Hebrew) God's flower. *Variations:* Perachia, Perachya.

PERBEN (Danish) Stone. *Variations:* Perban, Perbin, Perbon, Perbyn.

PERCIVAL (French) Pierce the valley. *Variation:* Perceval.

PERCY (French) Valley prisoner. *Notable:* Singer Percy Faith. *Variations:* Pearce, Pearcey, Pearcy, Percey.

PEREGRINE (Latin) Traveler. *Variations:* Pelgrim, Pellegrino, Peregrin, Peregrine, Peregrino, Peregryn, Pilgrim.

PERETZ (Hebrew) Spring forward. *Variations:* Perez, Perezz, Pharez.

PERICLES (Greek) Name of famous Greek orator.

PERKIN (English) Little Peter. *Variations:* Perkins, Perkyn.

PERNELL (French) Form of Parnell. *Notable:* Actor Pernell Roberts.

PERRIN (French) Little stone. *Variation:* Perryn.

PERRY (English) Traveler. *Notables:* Singer Perry Como; fashion designer Perry Ellis. *Variations:* Peree, Perey, Perie, Perree, Perrie.

PERSEUS (Greek) To destroy. *Notable:* In mythology, Perseus was the son of Zeus.

PERSIS (Greek) From Persia.

PERTH (Irish) Thorny bush; (Scottish) From the thorn-bush thicket.

PERVIS (Latin) Passage.

PESACH (Hebrew) One who is spared. The name for Passover. *Variation:* Pessach.

PETE (English) Short form of Peter. *Notables:* Baseball player/manager Pete Rose; singer Pete Seeger.

PETER (Greek) Rock. *Notables:* Actors Peter O'Toole, Peter Sellers, and Peter Ustinov. *Variations:* Pearce, Pears, Pearson, Pearsson, Peat, Peder, Pedro, Peers, Peet, Peeter, Peirce, Petey, Petie, Petras, Petro, Petronio, Petros, Petter, Pierce, Piero, Pierre, Pierrot, Pierrson, Piers, Pierson, Piet, Pieter, Pietro, Piotr, Pyotr.

PETERSON (English) Son of Peter.

PETHUEL (Hebrew) With an open mind toward God.

PETIRI (Native American) Here.

PETON (English) From the warrior's town. *Variations:* Peaten, Peatin, Peaton, Peatun, Peatyn, Petan, Peten, Petin, Petun, Petyn.

PEVERELL (French) Piper. *Variations:* Peverall, Peverel, Peveril.

PEWLIN (Welsh) Small. *Variations:* Peulan, Pewlan, Pewlen, Pewlon, Pewlyn.

PEYTON (English) Warrior's estate. *Notable:* Peyton Manning. *Variations:* Payton, Peyt.

PHARAOH (Egyptian) King. *Variation:* Pharoah.

PHELAN (Irish) Wolf.

PHELPS (English) Son of Philip.

PHIL (American) Short form of Philip. *Notables:* Talk-show host Phil Donahue; TV psychologist Dr. Phil McGraw.

PHILANDER (Greek) Friend of man.

PHILART (Greek) One who loves virtue. *Variations:* Filart, Philaret, Philarte.

PHILEMON (Greek) Kiss. *Variations:* Philamin, Philamine, Philamyn, Philmon, Philmyn, Philmyne, Phylmin, Phylmine, Phylmon, Phylmyn.

PHILIP (Greek) Lover of horses. *Notables:* Prince Philip; writer Philip Roth. *Variations:* Felipe, Felipino, Fil, Filib, Filip, Filipo, Filippo, Fillipek, Fillipp, Fillips, Phil, Philippel, Phill, Phillip, Phillipe, Phillipos, Phillipp, Phillippe, Phillips, Pilib, Pippy.

PHILO (Greek) Loving.

PHINEAS (Hebrew) Oracle. *Notable:* Circus legend Phineas T. Barnum. *Variations:* Pinchas, Pincus.

PHIRUN (Cambodian) Rain.

PHOEBUS (Greek) Radiant.

PHOENIX (Greek) Immortal. *Variation:* Phenix.

PHUOC (Vietnamese) Good. *Variation:* Phuok.

PHUONG (Vietnamese) Destiny.

PICKFORD (English) Ford at a peak.

PICKWORTH (English) From the woodcutter's estate.

PICTON (English) From the town near the pointy hill. *Variations:* Picktown, Pictan, Picten, Pictun, Picktyn, Piktan, Pikten, Piktin, Pikton, Piktown, Piktun, Piktyn, Pyckton, Pyctin, Pycton, Pyctyn, Pyktin, Pykton, Pyktyn.

PIERCE (English) Form of Peter. *Notable:* Actor Pierce Brosnan. *Variations:* Pearce, Piercy, Piercey.

PIERPONT (French) Stone bridge. *Variation:* Pierrepont.

PIERRE (French) Rock. Form of Peter.

PILA (Hawaiian) Hawaiian version of Bill.

PILAR (Spanish) Pillar.

PILI (African) Second born.

PILLAN (Native American) Highest essence. *Variation:* Pilan.

PIN (Vietnamese) Faithful.

PINCHAS (Hebrew) Oracle. *Variations:* Pincas, Pinchos, Pincus, Pinkas, Pinkus, Pynchas.

PINKY (American) Short for Pincus or Phineas. *Notable:* Comedian Pinky Lee.

PINO (Italian) God will add.

PINON (Native American) Constellation.

PIO (Latin) Pious. *Variation:* Pius.

PIPER (English) Bagpipe player.

PIPPIN (German) Father.

PIPPINO (Italian) God will increase. *Variation:* Peppino.

PIRAN (Irish) Prayer. *Variations:* Peran, Pieran, Pieren, Pieryn, Pyran.

PIRRO (Greek) Red hair.

PITNEY (English) Island of a headstrong man. *Variation:* Pittney.

PITT (English) Ditch.

PITTMAN (English) Laborer.

PIUS (Latin) Devout.

PLACIDO (Spanish) Peaceful. *Notable:* Opera singer Placido Domingo. *Variations:* Placid, Placidus, Placyd, Placydo.

PLATO (Greek) Broad shouldered. *Variation:* Platon.

PLATT (French) Flat land. *Variation:* Platte.

POCANO (Native American) Spirits coming.

POLLARD (English) Bald. *Variations:* Poll, Pollerd, Pollurd.

POLLOCK (English) Crowned. *Variations:* Polick, Pollack, Pollick, Polloch, Pollok, Polock, Polok.

POLLUX (Greek) Crown. *Variation:* Pollax.

POLO (Greek) Short form of Apollo.

POMEROY (French) Apple orchard. *Variations:* Pommeray, Pommeroy.

PONCE (Spanish) Fifth. *Notable:* Explorer Ponce de Leon.

PONIPAKE (Hawaiian) Good fortune. *Variations:* Ponipaki, Ponipakia, Ponipakie.

PONTUS (Greek) The sea. *Notable:* Roman statesman Pontius Pilate. *Variation:* Pontius.

PORFIRIO (Greek) Purple stone. *Variations:* Porfiro, Porphirios, Prophyrios.

PORTER (Latin) Gatekeeper.

PORTLAND (English) Town by the port.

POSEIDON (Greek) God of the ocean.

POTTER (English) One who makes pots.

POV (Gypsy) Ground or mud.

POWA (Native American) Rich.

POWELL (Celtic) Alert one. *Variations:* Powal, Powall, Powel, Powil, Powill, Powyl, Powyll

POWHATAN (Native American) From the chief's hill.

PRABHAT (Hindi) Light at dawn.

PRADEEP (Hindi) Light. *Variation:* Prakash.

PRAJIT (Hindi) Kind.

PRAKASH (Sanskrit) Light.

PRAMAN (Polynesian) Wisdom. *Variations:* Pramana, Pramanah.

PRAMOD (Hindi) Joy. *Variation:* Pramad.

PRASAD (Hindi) Brilliant.

PRASHANT (Hindi) Calm and composed.

PRATAP (Hindi) Great and majestic.

PRAVAT (Thai) History

PRAVIN (Hindi) Capable. *Variation:* Praveen.

PRAXEDES (Greek) Active. *Variation:* Praxiteles.

PREM (Hindi) Love.

PRENTICE (English) Apprentice. *Variations:* Pren, Prent, Prentis, Prentiss.

PRESCOTT (English) Priest's cottage. *Variations:* Prescot, Prestcot, Prestcott.

PRESLEY (English) Priest's meadow. *Variations:* Presleigh, Presly, Pressley, Prestley, Priestley, Priestly.

PRESTON (English) Priest's town. *Notable:* Writer/director Preston Sturges.

PREWITT (French) Brave little one. *Variations:* Prewett, Prewit, Pruitt.

PRICE (Welsh) Ardent man. *Variation:* Pryce.

PRIMO (Italian) First son. *Notable:* Writer Primo Levi. *Variations:* Preemo, Premo.

PRINCE (Latin) Prince. *Notable:* The Artist Formerly Known as Prince. *Variations:* Prinz, Prinze.

PRINCETON (English) Princely town.

PROCTOR (Latin) Official. *Variations:* Prockter, Procter.

PROSPER (Latin) Fortunate. *Variation:* Prospero.

PRYDWEN (Welsh) Handsome. *Variation:* Prydwyn.

PRYOR (Latin) Leader of the monastery. *Variation:* Prior.

PUEBLO (Spanish) Town.

PUMEET (Sanskrit) Purity.

PURVIS (English) Purveyor. *Variations:* Purves, Purviss.

PUTNAM (English) From the sire's estate.

QABIL (Arabic) Able. *Variation:* Qaabil.

QADIM (Arabic) Ancient. *Variation:* Qadeem.

QADIR (Arabic) Powerful. *Variations:* Qaadir, Qadeer.

QAHIR (African) Victorious conqueror.

QALATAGA (Native American) Guardian of the people.

QAMAR (Arabic) Moon.

QASIM (Arabic) Provider. *Variation:* Qaseem.

QIANG (Chinese) One who possesses strength.

QIMAT (Hindi) Valuable.

QING-NAN (Chinese) The younger generation.

QUADE (Latin) Fourth. *Variation:* Quaid

QUADREES (African American) Fourth child. *Variation:* Kwadrees.

QUAHHAR (Arabic) Dominant.

QUAN (Vietnamese) Soldier.

QUANAH (Native American) Aromatic.

QUANT (Greek) Quantity.

QUAY (English) From the wharf.

QUDAMAH (Arabic) Courageous. *Variations:* Qudam, Qudama.

QUDDUS (Arabic) Holy. *Variation:* Qudus.

QUED (Native American) Decorated robe.

QUENBY (Scandinavian) From the woman's estate. *Variations:* Quenbey, Quenbie.

QUENNELL (French) Little oak tree. *Variation:* Quennel.

QUENTIN (Latin) Fifth. *Notable:* Film director Quentin Tarantino. *Variations:* Quent, Quenten, Quenton, Quint, Quinten, Quintin, Quinton, Quito.

QUIGLEY (Irish) Untidy. *Variations:* Quigleigh, Quiglie, Quigly.

QUILL (English) Feather. *Variation:* Quil.

QUILLAN (Irish) Cub. *Variation:* Quillen.

QUILLER (English) Writer.

QUILLON (Latin) Sword. *Variation:* Quilon.

QUIMBY (Scandinavian) A woman's house. *Variations:* Quenby, Quim, Quin, Quinby.

QUINCY (French) The estate of the fifth son. *Notable:* Record producer Quincy Jones. *Variation:* Quincey.

QUINLAN (Irish) Strong man. *Variations:* Quindlen, Quinley, Quinlin, Quinly.

QUINN (Irish) Wise. *Notable:* Television producer Quinn Martin. *Variation:* Quin.

QUINNELL (Gaelic) Counsel.

QUINTO (Spanish) Home ruler. *Variations:* Quint, Quiqui.

QUINTON (English) Fifth child. Form of Quentin.

QUINTRELL (French) Fifth.

QUIRIN (English) A magic spell.

QUIRINUS (Latin) Roman god of war.

QUIVER (English) Arrow holder.

QUNNOUNE (Native American) Tall.

QUON (Chinese) Bright.

QUSAY (Arabic) Distant. *Variation:* Qussay.

QUY (Vietnamese) Precious.

RAAMAH (Hebrew) Thunder. *Variations:* Raam, Raamia, Raamiah, Raamya.

RAANAN (Hebrew) Fresh. *Variation:* Ranan.

RABBI (Hebrew) My master.

RABI (Arabic) Breeze. *Variations:* Rabee, Rabie.

RABY (Scottish) Famous and bright. *Variations:* Rab, Rabbie.

RACE (English) One who races. *Variations:* Racel, Racer, Raice.

RACHAM (Hebrew) Compassion. *Variations:* Rachaman, Rachamin, Rachamyn, Rachim, Rachman, Rachmiel, Rachum, Raham, Rahamim, Rahim.

RAD (English) Advisor.

RADBERT (English) Brilliant advisor. *Variations:* Radbirt, Radburt, Radbyrt, Raddbert, Raddbirt, Raddburt.

RADBORNE (English) Red stream. *Variations:* Rad, Radborn, Radbourn, Radbourne, Radburn, Radburne, Radd.

RADCLIFF (English) Red cliff. *Variations:* Radcliffe, Radclyffe.

RADEK (Czech) Famous ruler. *Variations:* Radacek, Radan, Radik, Radko, Radouvsek, Radovs.

RADFORD (English) Red ford or ford with reeds. *Variations:* Rad, Radd, Radferd, Radfurd, Redford.

RADHI (African) Goodwill.

RADIMIR (Russian; Slavic) Happy and famous. *Variations:* Radim, Radmir, Radomir.

Top Names of the 1960s

BOYS:
1. Michael
2. David
3. John
4. James
5. Robert
6. Mark
7. William
8. Richard
9. Thomas
10. Jeffrey
11. Steven
12. Joseph
13. Timothy
14. Kevin
15. Scott
16. Brian
17. Charles
18. Paul
19. Daniel
20. Christopher

GIRLS:
1. Lisa
2. Mary
3. Susan
4. Karen
5. Kimberly
6. Patricia
7. Linda
8. Donna
9. Michelle
10. Cynthia
11. Sandra
12. Deborah
13. Tammy
14. Pamela
15. Lori
16. Laura
17. Elizabeth
18. Julie
19. Brenda
20. Jennifer

RADLEY (English) Red meadow. *Variations:* Radlea, Radlee, Radleigh, Radly.

RADMAN (Slavic) Joy. *Variations:* Radmen, Radmon.

RADNOR (English) Red shore. *Variations:* Radnore, Rednor.

RADOMIL (Slavic) Lover of peace.

RADOSLAV (Czech) Happy and glorious. *Variations:* Raclaw, Radoslaw, Slawek.

RADU (Romanian) Happy. *Notable:* Celebrity fitness trainer Radu Teodorescu.

RADWAN (Arabic) Delight.

RAEDON (English) From the rye hill.

RAFAEL (Spanish) Healed by God. Form of Raphael. *Variations:* Rafaele, Rafaelo, Rafal, Rafello.

RAFAT (Arabic) Merciful.

RAFE (English) Healed by God. Form of Rafferty or Raphael. *Variation:* Raffe.

RAFFERTY (Irish) Prosperous. *Variations:* Rafer, Raferty, Raff, Raffarty, Raffer.

RAFFI (Arabic) Exalted; (Hebrew) Form of Raphael. *Notable:* Children's entertainer Raffi Cavoukian. *Variations:* Rafee, Rafey, Raffee, Raffey, Raffie, Raffin, Raffy, Rafi, Rafie, Rafy.

RAFIQ (Arabic) Friend. *Variations:* Rafeeq, Rafic, Rafikil, Rafique.

RAGHIB (Arabic) Desirous.

RAGHNALL (Irish) Powerful judgment. *Variations:* Ragnal, Ragnall, Rognvaldr.

RAGNAR (Norse) Powerful army. *Variations:* Ragner, Ragnir, Ragnor, Ragnvald.

RAGO (African) Ram.

RAHIM (Arabic) Compassionate. *Variation:* Raheem.

RAHMAN (Arabic) Compassionate. *Variation:* Rahmet.

RAHUL (Arabic) One who travels.

RAIDEN (Japanese) God of thunder. *Variation:* Raidan.

RAINE (English) Form of Rainer.

RAINER (German) Counselor. *Notable:* Monaco's Prince Rainier. *Variations:* Raineiro, Rainier, Rainieri, Rainiero, Rayner, Raynor.

RAJ (Indian) Prince. *Variations:* Raja, Rajah.

RAJAB (Arabic) Seventh month. *Variations:* Ragab, Rajabu.

RAJENDRA (Hindi) King of the sky. *Variations:* Rajender, Rajinder.

RAJESH (Hindi) King of kings.

RAJIV (Hindi) Striped.

RAKESH (Sanskrit) Lord of the full-moon day.

RAKIN (Arabic) Respectable. *Variation:* Rakeen.

RAKTIM (Hindi) Bright red. *Variation:* Raktym.

RALEIGH (English) Deer meadow. *Variations:* Rawleigh, Rawley, Rawly.

RALPH (English) Wolf counselor. *Notables:* Fashion designer Ralph Lauren; consumer advocate Ralph Nader. *Variations:* Ralphie, Raoul, Raul, Raulas, Raulo, Rolf, Rolph.

RALSTON (English) Ralph's town. *Variations:* Ralstone, Ralstyn.

RAMADAN (Arabic) Ninth month of the Muslim year.

RAMBERT (German) Brillliant might. *Variations:* Rambirt, Ramburt, Rambyrt.

RAMESES (Egyptian) Son of Ra. *Notable:* Egyptian pharaoh Rameses. *Variations:* Ramesses, Ramses.

RAMIRO (Portuguese) Great judge. *Variations:* Ramirez, Ramos.

RAMON (Spanish) Wise protection.

RAMSDEN (English) Valley of rams.

RAMSAY (English) Island of rams. *Notable:* Former U.S. Attorney General Ramsey Clark. *Variations:* Ramsey, Ramsy, Ramzey, Ramzie, Ramzy.

RANCE (English) Laurel crowned. Form of Lawrence. *Variations:* Rancel, Rancell, Ransel, Ransell.

RAND (English) Fighter.

RANDALL (English) Wolf with a shield. Form of Randolph. *Notable:* Football quarterback Randall Cunningham. *Variations:* Randal, Randel, Randell, Randil, Randill, Randle, Randol, Randoll, Randyl, Randyll.

RANDOLPH (English) Wolf with a shield. *Notable:* Actor Randolph Scott. *Variations:* Randolf, Randolfe, Randolfo, Randolphe.

RANDY (English) Short form of Randall or Randolph. *Notables:* Record producer and American Idol judge Randy Jackson; singer Randy Travis. *Variations:* Randey, Randie.

RANEN (Hebrew) Joyful. *Variations:* Ranan, Ranin, Ranon, Ranun, Ranyn.

RANGER (French) Protector of the forest. *Variations:* Rainger, Range.

RANIT (Hebrew) Song. *Variation:* Ronit.

RANJAN (Hindi) Delighted.

RANJIT (Indian) Charmed.

RANKIN (English) Shield.

RANON (Hebrew) Joyful song.

RANSFORD (English) Raven's ford.

RANSLEY (English) Raven meadow. *Variations:* Ransleigh, Ransly.

RANSOM (English) Son of the protector. *Variations:* Randsome, Ransome, Ranson.

RAOUL (French) Famous wolf. *Notables:* Celebrity lawyer Raoul Felder; Swedish diplomat Raoul Wallenberg. *Variations:* Raul.

RAPHAEL (Hebrew) God has healed. *Notable:* Italian painter Raphael (Raffaello Sanzio). *Variations:* Raphaele, Raphaello, Raphel, Raphello, Raphiel, Raphiello.

RAPIER (French) As strong as a sword.

RASHAD (Arabic) Moral work. *Variations:* Raashad, Rachad, Rachard, Rachaud, Raeshad, Raishard, Rashaad, Rashaud, Rashid, Rashod.

RASHID (Turkish) Righteous. *Variations:* Rasheed, Rasheid, Rasheyd.

RASHAWN (American) Combination of first names "Ray" and "Shawn." *Variations:* Rachan, Rashaan, Rasham, Rashan, Rashawn, Reshaun, Reshawn.

RASMUS (Greek) Beloved.

RAUF (Arabic) Sympathy.

RAVENEL (English) Raven.

RAVI (Hindi) Sun. *Variation:* Ravee.

RAVINDRA (Hindi) Sun power.

RAVIV (Hebrew) Rain. *Variation:* Ravid.

RAWDON (English) Craggy hill. *Variations:* Rawdan, Rawden, Rawdin, Rawdyn.

RAWLINS (French) Last name. *Variations:* Rawling, Rawlings, Rawlinson, Rawson.

RAY (English) Royal. *Notables:* Comedian Ray Romano; singer Ray Charles; writer Ray Bradbury. *Variations:* Rae, Rayce, Raydell, Rayder, Raydon, Raye, Raylen, Raynell.

RAYBURN (English) Brook for deer. *Variations:* Rayborn, Raybourne, Rayburne.

RAYFIELD (English) From the stream in the field. *Variations:* Raefield, Reyfield.

RAYFORD (English) From the stream ford. *Variations:* Raiford, Raiforde, Reyford, Reyforde.

RAYHAN (Arabic) Favored by God.

RAYMOND (German) Counselor and protector. *Notables:* Actor Raymond Burr; writer Raymond Chandler. *Variations:* Raimondo, Raimund, Raimunde, Raimundo, Rajmund, Ramon, Ramond, Ramone, Ray, Rayment, Raymonde, Raymondo, Raymund, Raymunde, Raymundo, Reimond.

RAZA (Hindi) Content. (Arabic) Hopeful.

RAZIEL (Hebrew) The Lord is my secret. *Variations:* Raz, Razi, Raziel.

READING (English) Son of the red-haired one. *Variations:* Redding, Reeding, Reiding.

REBEL (American) Rebel.

RED (English) Ruddy or red haired. *Notables:* Comedians Red Skelton and Redd Foxx; coach Red Auerbach. *Variation:* Redd.

REDLEY (English) Red meadow. *Variations:* Redleah, Redlee, Redleigh, Redley, Redlie, Redly.

REDFORD (English) Red ford.

REDMOND (Irish) Counselor. Variation of Raymond. *Variations:* Radmond, Radmund, Redmund.

REECE (Welsh) Fiery. *Variations:* Rees, Reese, Reiss, Rhys.

REED (English) Ruddy. *Variations:* Reade, Reed, Reid, Reide, Reyd.

REEVE (English) Bailiff. *Variations:* Reave, Reeves.

REG (English) Strong counselor. Short form of Reginald.

REGAN (Irish) Little king. *Variations:* Reagan, Reagen, Reagin, Regen, Regon, Reigan, Reigen, Reigon.

REGGIE (English) Short form of Reginald. *Notable:* Baseball player Reggie Jackson. *Variations:* Reggy, Regie, Regy.

REGIN (Scandinavian) Judgment. *Variation:* Reigin.

REGINALD (English) Strong counselor. *Variations:* Reg, Reggie, Reginalt.

REGIS (Latin) Regal. *Notable:* Talk show host Regis Philbin. *Variations:* Regiss, Regys, Regyss.

REI (Japanese) Law.

REINHARD (German) Form of Reynard. *Variations:* Reinhardt, Reinhart, Reynhard, Reynhardt, Reynhart.

REMINGTON (English) Family of ravens. *Variations:* Rem, Remee, Remi, Remie, Remmy.

REMUS (Latin) Swift.

REMY (French) From Rheims, a town in central France. *Variations:* Remee, Remi, Remie, Remmy.

RENAUD (French) Powerful. *Variation:* Renard.

RENDOR (Hungarian) Policeman.

RENÉ (French) Reborn. *Notable:* French philosopher René Descartes. *Variations:* Renat, Renato, Renatus, Renne, Rennie, Renny.

RENFRED (English) Strong peace. *Variations:* Ranfred, Ranfrid, Ranfryd, Rinfred, Rinfryd, Ronfred, Ronfryd, Rynfred, Rynfryd.

RENFREW (Welsh) Calm river.

RENJIRO (Japanese) Pure.

RENNY (Irish) Small and mighty. *Variations:* Renie, Renney, Rennie.

RENSHAW (English) Forest of ravens. *Variation:* Renishaw.

RENTON (English) Deer habitat.

RENZO (Italian) Laurel. Diminutive form of Lorenzo.

REUBEN (Hebrew) Behold a son. *Variations:* Reuban, Reubin, Reuven, Reuvin, Rube, Ruben, Rubin, Rubu.

REX (Latin) King. *Notables:* Actor Rex Harrison; film critic Rex Reed.

REXFORD (English) King's ford.

REXTON (English) From the king's town.

REY (Spanish) King. *Variation:* Reyes.

REYHAN (Arabic) God's choice. *Variations:* Reihan, Reyham.

REYNARD (German; English) Brave advisor. *Variations:* Rainard, Reinhard, Renard, Reynard, Reynardo.

REYNOLD (English) Powerful adviser. *Variations:* Ranald, Renald, Renaldo, Renauld, Renault, Reynaldo, Reynaldos, Reynolds, Rinaldo.

REZ (Hungarian) Red hair.

RHETT (Welsh) Fiery. *Notable: Gone with the Wind* hero Rhett Butler. *Variation:* Rhys.

RHODES (Greek) Island of roses. *Variations:* Rhoades, Rhodas, Rodas.

RHODRI (Welsh) Ruler of the wheel.

RHYDDERCH (Welsh) Reddish brown.

RHYS (Welsh) Fiery. A form of Reece.

RICE (English) Form of Reece.

RICH (English) Strong ruler. Short form of Richard. *Notable:* Comedian Rich Little.

RICHARD (German) Strong ruler. *Notables:* Actors Richard Burton, Richard Chamberlain, and Richard Attenborough; comedian Richard Lewis; U.S. President Richard M. Nixon. *Variations:* Ricard, Ricardo, Riccardo, Ricciardo, Rich, Richardo, Richards, Richart, Richerd, Richi, Richie, Rick, Rickard, Rickert, Rickey, Rickie, Ricky, Rico, Rihards, Riki, Riks, Riocard, Riqui, Risa, Ritch, Ritchard, Ritcherd, Ritchie, Ritchy, Rostik, Rostislav, Rostya, Ryszard.

RICHMOND (English) Rich mouth.

RICK (English) Short form of Richard. *Notables:* Singers Rick James, Rik Ocasek, and Rick

Springfield; actor Rick Schroeder. *Variation:* Rik.

RICKWARD (English) Great guardian. *Variations:* Ricward, Ryckward.

RICKY (English) Short form of Richard. *Notable:* Singer Ricky Martin. *Variations:* Rickey, Rickie.

RICO (Spanish) Rich and powerful. Short form of Enrico or Ricardo. *Variation:* Ricco.

RIDA (Arabic) Satisfied. *Variations:* Reda, Rida, Ridha.

RIDDOCK (Irish) Smooth field. *Variations:* Riddick, Ridock, Ridok, Rydock.

RIDER (English) Horseman. *Variations:* Ridder, Ryder.

RIDGE (English) Ridge. *Variation:* Rigg.

RIDGEWAY (English) Road on a ridge.

RIDGLEY (English) Meadow on a ridge. *Variations:* Ridgeleigh, Ridgeley, Ridglea, Ridglee, Ridgleigh.

RIDLEY (English) Reed meadow. *Notable:* Film director Ridley Scott. *Variations:* Riddley, Ridlea, Ridleigh, Ridly.

RIGBY (English) Ruler's valley. *Variations:* Rigbee, Rigbey, Rigbie, Rygbee, Rygbey, Rygbie, Rygby.

RIGEL (Arabic) Foot.

RIGOBERTO (German) Splendid. *Variations:* Rigobert, Rigobirt, Rigoburt, Rigoburto.

RILEY (Irish) Brave. *Variations:* Reilee, Reileigh, Reilie, Reillee, Reilleigh, Reillie, Reilly, Reily, Rylee, Ryleigh, Ryley, Rylie, Ryly.

RIMON (Arabic) Pomegranate.

RINALDO (Italian) Form of Reynold or Ronald.

RING (English) Ring.

RINGO (Japanese) Apple. *Notable:* Beatle Ringo Starr.

RIO (Spanish) River. *Variation:* Reo.

RIORDAN (Irish) Poet and minstrel. *Variations:* Rearden, Reardon.

RIP (Dutch) Ripe. *Notables:* Actor Rip Torn; comedian Rip Taylor.

RIPLEY (English) Shouting man's meadow. *Variations:* Ripleah, Riplee, Ripleigh, Riplie, Riply, Ripp, Ripplee, Rippleigh, Rippley, Ripplie, Ripply, Rypley, Ryplie, Ryply.

RISHI (Hindu) Sage.

RISHON (Hebrew) First.

RISLEY (English) Meadow with shrubs. *Variations:* Rishley, Rislea, Rislee, Risleigh, Risly, Ryslea, Ryslee, Rysleigh, Rysley, Ryslie, Rysly.

RISTON (English) Town near shrubs. *Variation:* Ryston.

RITTER (German) Knight.

RIVE (French) River.

RIVER (English) River. *Notable:* Actor River Phoenix. *Variations:* Rivers, Ryver.

RIYAD (Arabic) Garden. *Variation:* Riyadh.

ROALD (Scandinavian) Famous leader. *Notable:* Children's writer Roald Dahl.

ROAN (English) Rowan tree. Form of Rowan.

ROARK (Irish) Mighty. *Variations:* Roarke, Rork, Rorke, Rourk, Rourke.

Biblical Names

BOYS:	GIRLS:
Abraham	Bathsheba
Aaron	Deborah
Adam	Delilah
Benjamin	Esther
Daniel	Eve
David	Leah
Isaac	Miriam
Jacob	Naomi
Joshua	Rachel
Noah	Rebecca
Samuel	Ruth
Solomon	Sarah

Top Names in the Czech Republic

BOYS:
1. Jan
2. Jakub
3. Tomas
4. Lukas
5. Filip
6. Ondrej
7. Matej
8. Vojtech
9. David
10. Adam

GIRLS:
1. Tereza
2. Anna
3. Eliska
4. Karolina
5. Natalie
6. Adela
7. Kristyna
8. Barbora
9. Lucie
10. Katerina

ROB (English) Bright fame. Short form of Robert. *Notables:* Actor Rob Lowe; director Rob Reiner. *Variation:* Robb.

ROBBIE (English) Bright fame. Form of Robert. *Notables:* Singers Robbie Williams and Robbie Robinson; actor/director Robby Benson. *Variations:* Robbee, Robbey, Robbi, Robbie, Robby, Robee, Robi, Robie, Roby.

ROBERT (English) Bright fame. *Notables:* U.S. Senator Robert Kennedy; actors Robert Taylor, Robert Wagner, Robert Young, Robert Redford, and Robert De Niro; poets Robert Burns and Robert Frost. *Variations:* Bob, Bobbey, Bobbie, Bobby, Riobard, Robbyn, Rober, Robers, Roberto, Roberts.

ROBERTSON (English) Son of Robert.

ROBIN (English) Son of Robert. *Notables:* Actor/comedian Robin Williams; folklore hero Robin Hood. *Variations:* Robbin, Robbyn, Robinet, Robyn.

ROBINSON (English) Son of Robin. *Notable:* Literary hero Robinson Crusoe. *Variations:* Robbinson, Robeson, Robson, Robynson.

ROCCO (Italian) Rest. *Notable:* Chef Rocco DiSpirito. *Variations:* Rock, Rockie, Rocko, Rocky, Rokko.

ROCHESTER (English) Stone fortress.

ROCK (English) Rock. Form of Rocco. *Notable:* Rock Hudson. *Variations:* Roc, Rockie, Rocky, Rok.

ROCKFORD (English) Rocky ford.

ROCKLAND (English) From the stony land. *Variation:* Rocklan.

ROCKLEDGE (English) From the stony ledge.

ROCKLEY (English) Rocky meadow. *Variations:* Rocklee, Rockleigh, Rockly.

ROCKWELL (English) Well by the rocks.

ROCKY (American) Form of Rocco. *Notable:* Boxer Rocky Marciano. *Variations:* Rockee, Rockey, Rocki, Rockie, Rokee, Rokey, Roki, Rokie, Roky.

ROD (English) Short form of Roderick or Rodney. *Notables:* Singer Rod Stewart; hockey player Rod Gilbert; writer/producer Rod Serling; actor Rod Steiger. *Variation:* Rodd.

RODDEN (English) From the reed valley. *Variations:* Rodan, Roden, Rodin, Rodon, Rodyn, Roedan, Roeddan, Roedden, Roeddin, Roeddon, Roeddyn, Roeden, Roedin, Roedon, Roedyn.

RODDY (English) Famous ruler. Form of Roderick. *Notables:* Wrestler "Rowdy" Roddy Piper; writer Roddy Doyle; actor Roddy McDowell. *Variation:* Roddie.

RODEO (Spanish) Round up.

RODERICK (German) Famous ruler. *Variations:* Roderic, Roderich, Roderigo, Rodique, Rodrich, Rodrick, Rodrigo, Rodrique, Rurich, Rurik.

RODMAN (English) Road guard. *Variation:* Rodmann.

RODNEY (English) Island clearing. *Notable:* Comedian Rodney Dangerfield. *Variations:* Rodnee, Rodnie, Rodny.

RODRIQUEZ (Spanish) Son of famous ruler. *Variation:* Rodriguez.

RODWELL (English) Dweller at the cross near the stream. *Variation:* Roddwell.

ROGAN (Irish) Redhead.

ROGER (German) Renowned spearman. *Notables:* Actor Roger Moore; rock singer Roger Daltrey; film critic Roger Ebert. *Variations:* Rodger, Rogelio, Rogerio, Rogerios, Rogers, Ruggerio, Ruggero, Rutger, Ruttger.

ROHAN (Hindi) Sandalwood.

ROHIN (Hindi) Upward path.

ROHIT (Hindi) Big fish.

ROLAND (German) Famous land. *Variations:* Rolando, Rolle, Rolli, Rollie, Rollin, Rollins, Rollon, Rolly, Rolo, Rolon, Row, Rowe, Rowland, Rowlands, Rowlandson.

ROLF (German) Wolf counsel. Form of Ralph.

ROLLE (Scandinavian) Famous land. Form of Roland.

ROLLO (English) Famous land. *Notable:* Psychologist/writer Rollo May.

ROMAN (Latin) One from Rome. *Notable:* Director Roman Polanski. *Variations:* Romain, Romano, Romanos, Romulo, Romulos, Romulus.

ROMANY (Gypsy) Gypsy.

ROMEO (Italian) Pilgrim visiting Rome. *Notable:* Romeo Montague, hero of Shakespearean tragedy *Romeo and Juliet*. *Variations:* Romerio, Romero.

ROMNEY (Welsh) Curving river. *Variations:* Romnie, Romny.

ROMULUS (Latin) Citizen of Rome. *Variations:* Romel, Romele, Romell, Romello, Romelo, Rommel.

RON (English) Short form of Ronald or Aaron. *Notable:* Actor/director Ron Howard. *Variation:* Ronn.

RONALD (English) Powerful adviser. *Notables:* U.S. President Ronald Reagan; McDonald's spokesclown Ronald McDonald. *Variations:* Ranald, Ronaldo, Ronney, Ronnie, Ronny.

RONAN (Irish) Little seal.

RONDEL (French) Poem. *Variations:* Rondal, Rondale, Rondall, Rondeal, Rondell.

RONEL (Hebrew) Song of God.

RONI (Hebrew) Joyful.

RONNIE (English) Powerful advisor. Form of Ronald. *Notables:* Rock musicians Ronnie Van Zant and Ronnie Lane.

RONSON (English) Son of Ronald. *Variations:* Ronsen, Ronsin, Ronsun, Ronsyn.

ROONEY (Irish) Red haired. *Variations:* Roone, Roonie, Roony.

ROOSEVELT (Dutch) Field of roses. *Notable:* Football player Roosevelt Grier.

ROPER (English) Maker of rope.

RORY (Irish) Red king. *Notables:* Irish singer Rory Gallagher; actor Rory Calhoun. *Variations:* Ruaidri, Ruairi, Ruaraidh, Rurik.

ROSARIO (Portuguese) The rosary.

ROSCOE (Scandinavian) Deer forest. *Variations:* Rosco, Roscow, Rosko.

ROSLIN (Scottish) Small redheaded child. *Variations:* Roslyn, Rosselin, Rosslyn.

ROSS (Scottish) Cape. *Variations:* Rosse, Rossie, Rossy.

ROSTISLAV (Czech) Grabs glory. *Variations:* Rosta, Rostecek, Rostek.

ROSWALD (English) Field of roses.

ROSWELL (English) Spring of roses.

ROTH (German) Red.

ROTHWELL (Norse) Red spring.

ROUSSE (French) Red haired.

ROVER (English) Wanderer.

ROWAN (English) Rowan tree. Little red one. *Notable:* Comedic actor Rowan Atkinson. *Variation:* Rowen.

ROWELL (English) Deer spring.

ROWLEY (English) Unevenly cleared meadow. *Variations:* Rowlea, Rowlee, Rowleigh, Rowlie, Rowly.

ROXBURY (English) Raven's fortress.

ROY (Irish) Red; (French) King. *Notables:* Country singers Roy Orbison, Roy Clark, and Roy Rogers. *Variation:* Roi.

ROYAL (French) Royal. *Variations:* Royall, Royle.

ROYCE (English) Prince. *Variations:* Roice, Royse.

ROYD (Scandinavian) Forest clearing.

ROYDON (English) Rye hill. *Variations:* Roidan, Roiden, Roidin, Roidon, Roidyn, Royden, Roydin, Roydun, Roydyn.

ROYSTON (English) Place name: town of Royce. *Variations:* Roiston, Roystan.

BOYS' NAMES

ROZEN (Hebrew) Leader. *Variation:* Rosen.

RUADHAN (Irish) Little red-haired one. *Variation:* Rowan.

RUBE (English) Form of Reuben.

RUBEN (Hebrew) Form of Reuben. *Notables:* Singers Ruben Studdard and Ruben Blades.

RUDD (English) Ruddy skin.

RUDOLPH (German) Famous wolf. *Notables:* New York City mayor Rudolph Giuliani; dancer Rudolf Nureyev; silent-film star Rudolph Valentino. *Variations:* Rodolfo, Rodolph, Rodolphe, Rolf, Rolfe, Rolle, Rollo, Rolph, Rolphe, Rudey, Rudi, Rudie, Rudolf, Rudolfo, Rudolpho, Rudolphus, Rudy.

RUDY (English) Short form of Rudolph or Rudyard. *Variations:* Rudey, Rudie.

RUDYARD (English) Red yard. *Notable:* Writer Rudyard Kipling.

RUFIN (English) Red haired. *Variations:* Ruffin, Ruffino, Rufino.

RUFORD (English) Red ford. *Variation:* Rufford.

RUFUS (Latin) Red haired. *Notable:* Singer/songwriter Rufus Wainwright. *Variations:* Ruffus, Rufo, Rufous.

RUGBY (English) Rock fortress.

RUMFORD (English) Wide river crossing.

RUNAKO (African) Handsome.

RUNE (Scandinavian) Secret.

RUPERT (German) Bright fame. Variation of Robert. *Notable:* Actor Rupert Everett. *Variations:* Rubert, Ruberto, Rudbert, Ruperto, Ruprecht.

RURIK (Scandinavian) Famous king. *Variations:* Roar, Rorek, Roth, Rothrekr.

RUSH (English) Red haired. *Notable:* Radio talk-show host Rush Limbaugh.

RUSHFORD (English) Ford with rushes.

RUSKIN (French) Child with red hair.

RUSS (English) Short form of Russell. *Variation:* Rus.

RUSSELL (French) Small red one. *Notable:* Actor Russell Crowe. *Variation:* Russel.

RUSTY (English) Red haired. *Notable:* Baseball player Rusty Staub. *Variations:* Rustey, Rustie.

RUTGER (Dutch) Form of Roger. *Notable:* Actor Rutger Hauer.

RUTHERFORD (English) Cattle crossing. *Variations:* Rutherforde, Rutherfurd.

RUTLAND (Norse) Red land.

RUTLEDGE (English) From the red ledge.

RUTLEY (English) Red meadow. *Variations:* Rutlea, Rutlee, Rutleigh, Rutlie, Rutly.

RYAN (Irish) Little king. *Notables:* Actors Ryan O'Neal and Ryan Phillippe; singer Ryan Adams. *Variations:* Rian, Rien, Rion, Riun, Riyn, Rhian, Rhien, Rhion, Rhiun, Rhiyn, Ryann, Ryen, Ryin, Ryne, Ryon, Ryun.

RYCROFT (English) Field of rye. *Variations:* Ricroft, Ryecroft.

RYDER (English) Form of Rider.

RYE (English) Strong ruler.

RYERSON (English) Son of Rye or Ryder.

RYLAND (English) Land of rye. *Variations:* Ryeland, Rylan, Rylyn.

RYMAN (English) Rye seller.

RYTON (English) From the rye town.

SAAD (Arabic) Fortunate.

SAARIK (Hindi) Songbird.

SABER (French) Sword. *Variation:* Sabre.

SABIN (Latin) The name of an ancient Roman clan. *Variations:* Sabine, Sabino.

SABIR (Arabic) Patient. *Variations:* Saabir, Sabri.

SABOLA (African) Pepper.

SABURO (Japanese) Third son.

SACHIEL (Hebrew) An archangel.

SADDAM (Arabic) Powerful ruler. *Notable:* Former Iraqi dictator Saddam Hussein.

SADIKI (African) Faithful.

SADLER (English) Saddle maker. *Variation:* Saddler.

SAFAR (Arabic) Devout.

SAFFORD (English) River crossing at the willows.

SAGAR (English) Wise. *Variation:* Sager.

SAGE (English) Wise. *Variations:* Sagen, Saige.

SAHAJ (Hindi) Natural.

SAHALE (Native American) Falcon.

SAHEN (Hindi) Above.

SAHIL (Hindi) Leader.

SAHIR (Arabic) Alert and aware; (Hindi) Friend.

SA'ID (Arabic) Happy. *Variations:* Saeed, Saied, Saiyid, Sayeed, Sayid, Syed.

SAINT (Latin) Holy. *Variations:* Sanche, Sanchez, Sancho, Santo.

SAJAN (Hindi) Beloved.

SAKA (African) Hunter.

SAKARIA (Scandinavian) God remembers. Variation of Zachariah. *Variations:* Sakari, Sakarias.

SAKIMA (Native American) King.

SAL (Italian) Savior. Short form of Salvatore. *Notable:* Actor Sal Mineo.

SALADIN (Arabic) Goodness of faith. *Variations:* Saladine, Saladyn.

SALAH (Arabic) Righteousness. *Variations:* Saladdin, Saladin, Saldin, Saleh, Salih.

SALEHE (African) Good.

SALIH (Arabic) Virtuous.

SALIM (Arabic) Tranquility. *Variations:* Saleem, Salem, Salima, Selim.

SALISBURY (English) From the fort by the willow pool. *Variations:* Salisberie, Salisberrie, Salisberry, Salisbery, Salisburie, Salisburrie, Salisburry, Salysberry, Salysbery, Salysburry, Salysbury.

SALMALIN (Hindi) Taloned.

SALTON (English) Town in the willows.

SALVADOR (Spanish) Form of Salvatore. *Notable:* Artist Salvador Dali. *Variation:* Salvadore.

SALVATORE (Latin) Savior. *Variation:* Salvator.

SAM (English) God listens. Short form of Samuel. *Notables:* Playwright Sam Shepard; singer Sam Cooke; Wal-Mart founder Sam Walton. *Variation:* Samm.

SAMI (Arabic) Exalted.

SAMIR (Arabic) Entertainer.

SAMMAN (Arabic) Grocer. *Variation:* Sammon.

SAMMY (English) Short form of Samuel. *Notables:* Rat Pack singer/dancer Sammy Davis Jr.; rocker Sammy Hagar; baseball player Sammy Sosa. *Variations:* Samee, Samey, Samie, Sammey, Sammie.

SAMOSET (Native American) He who walks a lot. *Variation:* Samaset.

SAMSON (Hebrew) Sun. *Variations:* Sampsan, Sampsen, Sampson, Sampsun, Sampsyn, Sansao, Sansim, Sansom, Sansome, Sanson, Sansón, Sansone.

SAMUEL (Hebrew) God listens. *Notables:* Telegraph inventor Samuel Morse; actor Samuel L. Jackson; American patriot Samuel Adams. *Variations:* Samouel, Samuele, Samuell, Samuello.

SAMURU (Japanese) God listens.

SANAT (Hindi) Ancient.

SANBORN (English) Sandy brook. *Variations:* Sanborne, Sanbourn, Sanbourne, Sanburn, Sanburne, Sandborn, Sandborne, Sandbourn, Sandbourne.

SANCHO (Latin) Sacred. *Notable:* Don Quixote's sidekick Sancho Panza. *Variations:* Sanchaz, Sanchez, Sauncho.

SANDEEP (Punjabi) Enlightened.

SANDER (English) Form of Alexander. *Variations:* Sandar, Sandas, Sanders, Sanderson, Sandor, Sandour, Sandur, Saunder, Saunders, Saunderson.

SANDFORD (English) Sandy crossing. *Variations:* Sandfurd, Sanford.

SANDITON (English) Sandy town.

SANDY (English) Short form of Sander or Alexander. *Notable:* Baseball great Sandy Koufax. *Variations:* Sandey, Sandie.

SANEESH (Hindi) Hindu deity.

SANI (Native American) Old.

SANJAY (Hindi) Winner.

SANJIV (Hindi) Reinvigorate. *Variation:* Sanjeev.

SANSON (Spanish; Italian) Like the sun. *Variation:* Sansone.

SANTA (Italian) Saint. *Variations:* Santana, Santanio, Santanyo.

SANTIAGO (Spanish) Saint.

SANTO (Spanish) Holy. *Variation:* Santos.

SANTOSH (Hindi) Satisfied.

SARAD (Hindi) Born in autumn.

SARGENT (French) Officer. *Notable:* Politician and U.S. Ambassador Sargent Shriver. *Variations:* Sarge, Sergeant.

SARGON (Persian) True king. *Variations:* Sargan, Sargen, Sargin, Sargyn.

SARIK (Hindi) Bird.

SARIYAH (Arabic) Clouds at night time. *Variation:* Sariya.

Top Names in France

BOYS:
1. Lucas
2. Mathis
3. Noah
4. Nathan
5. Mathéo
6. Enzo
7. Louis
8. Raphael
9. Ethan
10. Gabriel

GIRLS:
1. Emma
2. Jade
3. Chloe
4. Sarah
5. Lea
6. Manon
7. Louna
8. Ines
9. Lilou
10. Camille

SARNGIN (Hindi) Protector.

SAROJIN (Hindi) Lotus-like. *Variation:* Sarojun.

SASHA (Russian) Form of Alexander. *Variations:* Sacha, Sascha, Sashka.

SASSACUS (Native American) Wild man.

SATCHEL (Latin) Small sack. *Notable:* Baseball player Satchel Paige.

SATURN (Latin) Saturn, the planet. *Variation:* Saturne.

SAUD (Arabic) Fortunate.

SAUL (Hebrew) Asked for. *Notable:* Writer Saul Bellow.

SAUVEUR (French) Saviour.

SAVILLE (French) Town of willows. *Variations:* Savil, Savile, Savill, Savilla, Savylle.

SAWNEY (Scottish) Protector of men. *Variations:* Sawnie, Sawny.

SAWYER (English) Woodworker. *Variations:* Sayer, Sayers, Sayre, Sayres.

SAXBY (Norse) From the farm of the short sword. *Variations:* Saxbee, Saxbey, Saxbie.

SAXON (English) Swordsman. *Variations:* Saxe, Saxen, Saxin.

SAXTON (English) Swordsman's town. *Variations:* Saxtan, Saxten, Saxtin, Saxtyn.

SAYYID (Arabic) Lord and master.

SCANLON (Irish) Little trapper. *Variations:* Scanlan, Scanlen.

SCHAFER (German) Shepherd. *Variations:* Schaefer, Shaffar, Shaffer.

SCHMIDT (German) Blacksmith. *Variations:* Schmid, Schmit, Schmitt, Schmitz.

SCHNEIDER (German) Tailor. *Variations:* Schnieder, Snider, Snyder, Snydley.

SCHON (German) Handsome.

SCHUMAN (German) Shoemaker. *Variations:* Schumann, Schumen, Schumenn, Shueman, Shuemann, Shuemen, Shuemenn, Shuman, Shumann, Shumen, Shumenn.

SCHUYLER (Dutch) Scholar. *Variations:* Schuylar, Skuyler, Skylar, Skyler.

SCOEY (French) Scottish village. *Variations:* Scoee, Scoie, Scowie, Scowy.

SCORPIO (Latin) Scorpion.

SCOTT (English) One from Scotland. *Notable:* Musician Scott Weiland. *Variations:* Scot, Scottie, Scotto, Scotty.

SCRIBE (Latin) Writer. *Variations:* Scribner, Scrivener, Scrybe.

SCULLY (Irish) Town crier. *Variations:* Scullee, Sculleigh, Sculley, Scullie.

SEABERT (English) Bright sea. *Variations:* Seabirt, Seaburt, Seabyrt, Seebert, Seebirt, Seeburt, Seebyrt, Seibert, Seibirt, Seiburt, Seibyrt, Seybert, Seybirt, Seyburt, Seybyrt.

SEABRIGHT (English) From the shining sea.

SEABROOK (English) River running to the sea. *Variation:* Seabrooke.

SEAFRA (Irish) Peace. *Variations:* Seafraid, Seartha, Seathra.

SEAMUS (Irish) He who supplants. Variation of James. *Variation:* Shamus.

SEAN (Irish) God is good. Variation of John. *Notables:* Actors Sean Penn and Sean Connery. *Variations:*

Seann, Shaine, Shane, Shaughn, Shaun, Shawn, Shayn, Shayne.

SEANAN (Irish) Old and wise. *Variations:* Senan, Sinan, Sinon.

SEARLE (English) Armor. *Variations:* Searl, Searlas, Serl, Serle, Serlo.

SEATON (English) Town by the sea. *Variations:* Seeton, Seton.

SEBASTIAN (Greek) Revered. *Variations:* Seb, Sebastao, Sebaste, Sebastiano, Sebastiao, Sebastien, Sebastion, Sebastyn, Sebbie, Sebestyen, Sepasetiano.

SEDGLEY (English) Sword meadow. *Variations:* Sedgeleigh, Sedgeley, Sedgly.

SEDGWICK (English) Sword place. *Variations:* Sedgewick, Sedgewyck, Sedgwyck.

SEELEY (English) Blessed. *Variations:* Sealee, Sealeigh, Sealey, Sealie, Sealy, Seeleigh, Seelie, Seely, Seilee, Seileigh, Seiley, Seilie, Seily.

SEF (Egyptian) Yesterday.

SEFTON (English) Town in the rushes. *Variations:* Seftan, Seften, Seftin, Seftun, Seftyn.

SEFU (African) Sword.

SEGER (English) Sea warrior. *Variations:* Seager, Seeger.

SEGUNDO (Spanish) Second-born child.

SEIF (Arabic) Religion's sword.

SEKANI (Egyptian) Laughter.

SEKAR (Hindi) Peak. *Variation:* Shekhar.

SELAH (Hebrew) Song.

SELBY (English) Manor in the village. *Variations:* Selbee, Selbey, Selbi, Selbie, Shelby.

SELDON (English) Willow valley. *Variations:* Selden, Seldin, Seldyn, Sellden.

SELIG (German) Blessed.

SELWYN (English) From the manor. *Variations:* Selvin, Selwin, Selwinn, Selwynn, Selwynne.

SEMI (Polynesian) Character.

SEN (Japanese) Wood sprite.

SENIOR (French) Lord.

SENNETT (French) Venerable. *Variations:* Senett, Senit, Senitt, Sennet, Sennit.

SENWE (African) Grain stalk.

SEOIRSE (Irish) Farmer. *Variation:* Searsa.

SEOSAMH (Irish) He will add. *Variations:* Sedsap, Sedsaph.

SEPP (German) God will add. Form of Joseph. *Variations:* Seppe, Seppey, Seppie, Seppy.

SEPTIMUS (Latin) Seventh.

SEQUOIA (Native American) Large tree.

SERAPHIM (Greek) The angels; (Hebrew) Fiery. *Variations:* Serafin, Serafino, Seraphimus.

SERENO (Latin) Calm. *Variation:* Serino.

SERGE (Latin) Servant. *Variations:* Serg, Sergi, Sergie.

SERGEI (Russian) Form of Sergius. *Notable:* Russian composer Sergei Prokofiev. *Variation:* Sergey.

SERGIO (Italian) Form of Sergius. *Notables:* Spaghetti-Western film director Sergio Leone; musician Sergio Mendes. *Variation:* Sirgio.

SERGIUS (Latin) Servant. *Variations:* Serg, Serge, Sergey, Sergi, Sergie.

SERVAAS (Scandinavian) Saved.

SETH (Hebrew) To appoint. *Notables:* Actor Seth Greene; TV animator Seth MacFarlane.

SETON (English) Sea town. *Variations:* Seatan, Seaten, Seatin, Seaton, Seatun, Seatyn, Setan, Seten, Setin, Setun, Setyn.

SEVERIN (French) Strict. *Variation:* Severen.

SEVERN (English) Boundary.

SEWARD (English) Protector of the sea. *Variation:* Sewerd.

SEWATI (Native American) Bear claw.

SEWELL (English) Strong at sea. *Variations:* Sewald, Sewall.

SEXTON (English) Church custodian. *Variations:* Sextan, Sexten, Sextin, Sextyn.

SEXTUS (Latin) Sixth. *Variation:* Sixtus.

SEYMOUR (French) From St. Maur, a village in France. *Variations:* Seamoor, Seamoore, Seamor, Seamore, Seamour, Seamoure, Seemoor, Seemoore, Seemor, Seemore, Seemour, Seemoure, Seimoor, Seimoore, Seimor, Seimore, Seimour, Seymoor, Seymore, Seymoure.

SHACHAR (Hebrew) Sunrise.

SHADI (Arabic) Singer.

SHADMON (Hebrew) Farm.

SHADRACH (Babylonian) Under the command of Aku (the Babylonian god of the moon). *Variations:* Shad, Shadrack.

SHAFIR (Hebrew) Handsome.

SHAFIQ (Arabic) Compassionate. *Variations:* Shafeek, Shafeeq, Shaff, Shafi, Shafik.

SHAH (Persian) King.

SHAHZAD (Arabic) Son of the king.

SHAI (Hebrew) Gift.

SHAKIL (Hindi) Attractive. *Notable:* Basketball great, Shaquille O'Neal. *Variations:* Shakeel, Shaquille.

SHAKIR (Arabic) Grateful. *Variations:* Shakur, Shukri.

SHALEV (Hebrew) Calm.

SHALOM (Hebrew) Peace. *Notable:* Writer Sholem Aleichem. *Variations:* Sholem, Sholom.

SHAMAN (Native American) Medicine man. *Variations:* Shaiman, Shaimen, Shamen, Shayman, Shaymen.

SHAMIR (Hebrew) Flint. *Variation:* Shamur.

SHANAHAN (Irish) Wise one.

SHANDAR (Pakistani) Fabulous.

SHANDY (English) Noisy. *Variations:* Shandey, Shandie.

SHANE (Irish) God is gracious. Form of Sean. *Variations:* Shaine, Shayn, Shayne.

SHANKARA (Hindi) Bringing luck. *Variations:* Sankar, Sankara, Shankar.

SHANLEY (Irish) Small and ancient. *Variations:* Shanleigh, Shanlie, Shanly, Shannleigh, Shannley.

SHANNON (Irish) Wise river. *Variations:* Shannan, Shannen.

SHAQUILLE (Arabic) Handsome. *Variations:* Shakil, Shaq, Shaquan.

SHARAD (Pakistani) Autumn.

SHARIF (Arabic) Virtuous. *Variations:* Shareef, Shereef, Sherif.

SHATTUCK (Irish) Little fish.

SHAW (English) Grove of trees.

SHAWN (Irish) Form of Sean. *Variation:* Shaun.

SHEA (English) Requested. *Variations:* Shae, Shai, Shay, Shaye.

SHEEHAN (Irish) Calm.

SHEFFIELD (English) Uneven field.

SHELBY (English) Village on the ledge. *Variations:* Shelbey, Shelbie.

SHELDON (English) Steep valley. *Variations:* Shelden, Sheldin.

SHELLEY (English) Meadow on a ledge. *Notable:* Comedian Shelley Berman. *Variation:* Shelly.

SHELTON (English) Town on a ledge.

SHEM (Hebrew) Famous.

SHEMAIAH (Hebrew) God has heard. *Variations:* Shemaia, Shemaya.

SHEN (Chinese) Meditation.

SHENG (Chinese) Victory.

SHEPHERD (English) Sheepherder. *Variations:* Shep, Shepard, Shephard, Shepp, Sheppard, Shepperd.

SHEPLEY (English) Sheep meadow. *Variations:* Sheplea, Shepleigh, Sheply.

SHERBORN (English) Clear brook. *Variations:* Sherborne, Sherbourn, Sherburn, Sherburne.

SHERIDAN (Irish) Wild man. *Variations:* Sheredan, Sheridon, Sherridan.

SHERLOCK (English) Bright hair. *Notable:* Fictional detective Sherlock Holmes. *Variations:* Sherlocke, Shurlock.

SHERMAN (English) One who cuts cloth. *Notable:* Actor Sherman Hemsley. *Variations:* Scherman, Schermann, Shermann.

SHERROD (English) Land clearer. *Variation:* Sherod.

SHERWIN (English) Bright friend. *Variations:* Sherwind, Sherwinn, Sherwyn, Sherwynne.

SHERWOOD (English) Shining forest. *Variations:* Sherwoode, Shurwood.

SHET (Hebrew) Chosen.

SHILIN (Chinese) Intellectual.

SHILOH (Hebrew) Gift from God. *Variation:* Shilo.

SHIMON (Hebrew) Heard. *Variation:* Simeon.

SHIMSHON (Hebrew) Sun.

SHIN (Japanese) True.

SHING (Chinese) Victorious.

SHIPLEY (English) Dweller at the sheep meadow. *Variations:* Shiplee, Shipleigh, Shiplie, Shiply.

SHIPTON (English) Sheep town. *Variations:* Shiptan, Shipten, Shiptin, Shiptun, Shiptyn, Shyptan, Shypten, Shyptin, Shypton, Shyptyn.

SHIRO (Japanese) Fourth son.

SHIVA (Hindi) Fortunate. *Variations:* Sheo, Shiv, Sib, Siva.

SHLOMO (Hebrew) Peace.

SHMUEL (Hebrew) Form of Samuel.

SHOMER (Hebrew) Guardian.

SHONI (Hebrew) Changing.

SHUZO (Japanese) Third son.

SHYAM (Hindi) Dark blue. *Variation:* Sham.

SIARL (Welsh) Man.

SID (English) From St. Denis, France. Short form of Sidney. *Notables:* Comedian Sid Caesar; singer Sid Vicious. *Variations:* Sidd, Syd, Sydd.

SIDDHARTHA (Sanskrit) Accomplishment. *Variations:* Siddartha, Sidharth, Sidhartha, Syddhartha.

SIDNEY (English) One from Saint Denis, a town in France. *Notables:* Film director Sidney Lumet; actor Sidney Poitier; writer Sidney Sheldon. *Variations:* Sid, Siddie, Sidon, Sidonio, Syd, Sydney.

SIDONIUS (Latin) From Sidon. *Variations:* Sidonis, Sydonis, Sydonius.

SIDWELL (English) Wide brook. *Variations:* Siddwal, Siddwall, Siddwel, Siddwell, Sidwal, Sidwall, Sidwel, Sydwal, Sydwall, Sydwel, Sydwell.

SIEGFRIED (German) Victory and peace. *Variations:* Siegfrid, Siffredo, Sifredo, Sigfredo, Sigfrido, Sigfried, Sigfroi, Sigifredo, Sigvard.

SIGBJORN (Scandinavian) Victory bear. *Variations:* Sigge, Sikke.

SIGMUND (German) Victory shield. *Notable:* Founder of psychoanalysis Sigmund Freud. *Variations:* Siegmund, Sigismund, Sigmond, Sygmond.

SIGURD (Scandinavian) Guardian of victory. *Variations:* Sjurd, Sygurd.

SIGWALD (German) Victorious leader. *Variation:* Siegwald.

SILAS (English) Forest.

SILVAN (Latin) Forest. *Variations:* Silva, Silvain, Silvano, Silvanus, Silvio, Sylas, Sylvain, Sylvan, Sylvanus.

SILVESTER (English) From the forest. Form of Sylvester. *Variations:* Sailbheastar, Silvestre, Silvestro.

SIMA (Hebrew) Treasure.

SIMBA (African) Lion.

SIMCHA (Hebrew) Joy.

SIMON (Hebrew) God hears. *Notables:* American Idol judge Simon Cowell; South American Revolutionary leader Simon Bolivar. *Variations:* Simeon, Simion, Simm, Simms, Simone, Symms, Symon.

SIMPSON (English) Son of Simon. *Variations:* Simpsan, Simpsen, Simpsin, Simpsyn, Simson, Sympsan, Sympsen, Sympsin, Sympson.

SINBAD (German) Prince. *Notable:* Comedian Sinbad; fictional adventurer Sinbad the Sailor.

SINCLAIR (French) From St. Clair, a town in France. *Variations:* Sinclaire, Sinclar, Sinclare, Synclair.

SINGER (English) A singer.

SINJIN (English) From St. John. *Variations:* Sinjon, Sinjun.

SIOR (Welsh) Farmer. *Variations:* Siors, Siorys.

SIPHO (African) Gift.

SIRAJ (Arabic) Light.

SIRIUS (Greek) Dog star. *Variations:* Sirios, Syrios, Syrius.

SIROSLAV (Slavic) Famous glory.

SISTO (Italian) Sixth-born child.

SITRIC (Norse) Conqueror. *Variations:* Sitrick, Sitrik, Sytric, Sytrick.

Top Names in Austria

BOYS:
1. Lukas
2. Tobias
3. Maximilian
4. Alexander
5. Simon
6. David
7. Jonas
8. Sebastian
9. Felix
10. Julian

GIRLS:
1. Sarah
2. Anna
3. Leonie
4. Lena
5. Hannah
6. Sophie
7. Julia
8. Laura
9. Marie
10. Katharina

SIVAN (Hebrew) Ninth month of the Jewish year.

SIWILI (Native American) Fox tail.

SKEETER (English) Swift. *Variation:* Skeet.

SKELLY (Irish) Storyteller. *Variations:* Scully, Skelley, Skellie.

SKERRY (Scandinavian) Island of stones.

SKIP (Scandinavian) Boss of a ship. *Variations:* Skipp, Skipper, Skippie, Skippy.

SKIPTON (English) From the ship town. *Variations:* Skippton, Skyppton, Skypton.

SKY (English) Sky.

SKYLAR (Dutch) Form of Schuyler, meaning scholar. *Variation:* Skyler.

SLADE (English) Valley. *Variations:* Sladen, Slaide, Slaiden, Slayde.

SLANE (Czech) Salty. *Variations:* Slaine, Slayne.

SLATER (English) Slater of roofs.

SLAVIN (Irish) Mountain man. *Variations:* Slaven, Slavon, Slawin, Sleven.

SLAVOMIR (Slavic) Great peace. *Variation:* Slavomil.

SLAWOMIERZ (Polish) Great glory.

SLOAN (Irish) Soldier. *Variation:* Sloane.

SMEDLEY (English) Flat meadow. *Variations:* Smedlee, Smedleigh, Smedly.

SMITH (English) Blacksmith. *Variations:* Smithy, Smitty, Smyth, Smythe.

SNOWDEN (English) Snowy mountain. *Variation:* Snowdon.

SOBESLAW (Czech) Usurps glory. *Variations:* Sobes, Sobik. Sobieslav.

SOCRATES (Greek) Whole power. *Notable:* Greek philosopher Socrates. *Variations:* Socratis, Sokrates.

SOFIAN (Arabic) Devoted.

SOHAN (Hindi) Charming.

SOL (Hebrew) Short form of Solomon; (Latin) Sun. *Notable:* Music impresario Sol Hurok.

SOLOMON (Hebrew) Peaceable. *Notable:* Solomon Schechter, founder of Conservative Judaism. *Variations:* Salamen, Salamon, Salamun, Salaun, Salman, Salmon, Salom, Salomo, Salomon, Salomone, Selim, Shelomoh, Shlomo, Sol, Solaman, Sollie, Solly, Soloman, Solomo, Solomonas, Solomone.

SOMERLED (Norse) Summer wanderer.

SOMERSET (English) Summer estate. *Notable:* Writer W. Somerset Maugham. *Variations:* Sommerset, Summerset.

SOMERTON (English) Summer town. *Variations:* Somervile, Somerville.

SONGAN (Native American) Strong. *Variation:* Songaa.

SONNY (English) Son. *Notables:* Singer Sonny Bono; boxer Sonny Liston; musician Sonny Rollins. *Variations:* Sonni, Sonnie.

SOREN (Scandinavian; Danish) Stern. *Variation:* Sorenson.

SORLEY (Scottish) Viking. *Variations:* Sorlee, Sorleigh, Sorlie, Sorly.

SORRELL (French) Reddish brown. *Notable:* Actor Sorrell Booke. *Variations:* Sorrel, Sorrelle.

SOTERIOS (Greek) Saviour.

SOUTHWELL (English) Southern well.

SOVANN (Cambodian) Gold.

SPALDING (English) Divided field. *Notable:* Writer/actor Spalding Gray. *Variation:* Spaulding.

SPANGLER (German) Tinsmith.

SPEAR (English) Man with a spear. *Variations:* Speare, Spears, Speer, Speers, Spiers.

SPENCER (English) Seller of goods. *Notables:* Actor Spencer Tracy; musician Spencer Davis. *Variations:* Spence, Spense, Spenser.

SPIKE (English) One with spiky hair. *Notables:* Film directors Spike Lee and Spike Jonze; bandleader and comedian Spike Jones.

SPIRO (Greek) Spirit. *Notable:* U.S. Vice President Spiro Agnew. *Variations:* Spiridion, Spiridon, Spiros, Spyridon, Spyro, Spyros.

SQUIRE (English) Shield bearer.

STACY (Greek) Fertile. *Notable:* Actor Stacy Keach. *Variation:* Stacey.

STAFFORD (English) Landing with a ford. *Variations:* Stafforde, Staford.

STAMOS (Greek) Crown.

STAN (English) Stony meadow. Short form of Stanley. *Notables:* Comedian Stan Laurel; jazz musician Stan Getz.

STANBURY (English) Fort made of stone. *Variations:* Stanberry, Stanbery.

STANCLIFF (English) Stony cliff. *Variation:* Stancliffe.

STANDISH (English) Stony park.

STANFIELD (English) Stony field. *Variation:* Stansfield.

STANFORD (English) Stony ford. *Variations:* Stamford, Stan, Standford, Stanforde.

STANHOPE (English) Stony hollow.

STANISLAUS (Polish) Glorious camp. *Variations:* Stach, Stanislao, Stanislas, Stanislau, Stanislav, Stanislaw, Stanislus, Stas, Stash, Stashko, Stasio.

STANLEY (English) Stony meadow. *Notable:* Director Stanley Kubrick. *Variations:* Stan, Stanlea, Stanlee, Stanleigh, Stanly.

STANMORE (English) Stony moor. *Variation:* Stanmoore.

STANNARD (English) Hard as a stone. *Variation:* Stanard.

STANTON (English) Stony town. *Variations:* Stanten, Staunton.

STANWAY (English) Stony road. *Variations:* Stanaway, Stannaway, Stannway.

STANWICK (English) Stone village. *Variation:* Stanwyck.

STANWOOD (English) Stony woods.

STARBUCK (English) Challenger of fate.

STARR (English) Star.

STAVROS (Greek) Crowned.

STEADMAN (English) One who lives on a farm. *Notable:* Speaker/writer Stedman Graham. *Variations:* Steadmann, Stedman.

STEELE (English) One who resists. *Variation:* Steel.

STEFAN (Scandinavian) Crowned. Form of Stephen. *Variations:* Stefan, Stefano, Stefanos, Stefans, Steffan, Steffel, Steffen, Stefos.

STEIN (German) Stone. *Variations:* Steen, Steine, Steiner, Styne.

STEPHEN (Greek) Crowned. *Notables:* Composer Stephen Sondheim; writer Stephen King; physicist Stephen Hawking. *Variations:* Stepa, Stepan, Stepanek, Stepek, Stephan, Stephane, Stephano, Stephanos, Stephanus, Stephens, Stephenson, Stepka, Stepousek.

STERLING (English) First class. *Variation:* Stirling.

STERNE (English) Austere and unyielding. *Variations:* Stearn, Stearne, Stearns, Stern, Sturn, Sturne.

STEVE (English) Short form of Steven. *Notables:* Actor Steve McQueen; comedian Steve Martin. *Variation:* Steeve.

STEVEN (English) Form of Stephen. *Notables:* Film director Steven Spielberg; Aerosmith lead singer Steven Tyler. *Variations:* Stevan, Stevenson, Stevie, Stevin, Stevon, Stevyn.

STEWART (English) Steward. *Notables:* Actor Stewart Granger; musician Stewart Copeland. *Variations:* Stew, Steward, Stu, Stuart.

STIG (Scandinavian) Wanderer. *Notable:* Author Stieg Larsson. *Variations:* Stieg, Stigandr, Stigr, Styge, Stygge.

STILLMAN (English) Silent man.

STOCKLEY (English) Meadow of tree stumps. *Variations:* Stocklea, Stocklee, Stockleigh.

STOCKTON (English) Town of tree stumps.

STOCKWELL (English) Spring with tree stumps.

STODDARD (English) Protector of horses.

STORM (English) Storm. *Notable:* TV weatherman Storm Field.

STOVER (English) Keeper of the stove.

STOWE (English) Hidden. *Variation:* Stow.

STRAHAN (Irish) Minstrel. *Variation:* Strachan.

STRATFORD (English) River crossing near a street.

STRATTON (Scottish) River town.

STROM (German) River. *Notable:* U.S. Senator Strom Thurmond.

STRUTHERS (Irish) Brook.

STUART (English) Caretaker. Form of Stewart. *Notables:* Shoe designer Stuart Weitzman; children's book character, mouse Stuart Little. *Variation:* Stu.

STURE (Scandinavian) To be contrary.

STYLES (English) Stile, or stairs that go over a wall.

SUBHASH (Hindi) Speaks well.

SUDHIR (Hindi) Wise and considerate.

SUDI (African) Fortune.

SUFFIELD (English) Southern field.

SUHAYL (Arabic) Star. *Variation:* Suhail.

SUIBHNE (Irish) Going well. *Variation:* Sivney.

SUJAY (Hindi) Successful victory.

SULEYMAN (Turkish) Peaceful. *Variations:* Shelomon, Siliman, Sulaiman, Sulayman, Suleiman.

SULLIVAN (Irish) Black eyed. *Variations:* Sullavan, Sullevan, Sulliven.

SULLY (English) Southern meadow. *Variations:* Sulleigh, Sulley.

SULTAN (Arabic) Ruler.

SULWYN (Welsh) Bright sun. *Variation:* Sulwyn.

SUMAN (Hindi) Smart.

SUMANTRA (Hindi) Good advice.

SUMNER (English) Summoner. *Notable:* Communications CEO Sumner Redstone.

SUNDAR (Hindi) Beautiful. *Variations:* Sundara, Sundarama, Sunder.

SUNDEEP (Punjabi) Enlightened being.

SUNIL (Hindi) Dark blue.

SURAJ (Sanskrit) Born of the gods.

SUTCLIFF (English) Southern cliff.

SUTHERLAND (Scandinavian) Southern land. *Variation:* Southerland.

SUTTON (English) Southern town.

SVATOPULK (Slavic) Bright people.

SVATOSLAV (Slavic) Glorious and holy.

SVEN (Scandinavian) Youth.

SVENBJORN (Norse) Young bear. *Variation:* Sveniborn.

SWAIN (English) Herdsman or knight's attendant. *Variations:* Swaine, Swayne.

SWALEY (English) Winding stream. *Variations:* Swailey, Swale, Swales.

SWEENEY (Irish) Small hero. *Variation:* Sweeny.

SWIETOMIERZ (Polish) Holy and famous.

SWIETOPELK (Polish) Holy people.

SWIETOSLAW (Polish) Holy glory. *Variations:* Swietoslav, Svyatoslav.

SWINBOURNE (English) Brook used by swine. *Variations:* Swinborn, Swinborne, Swinburn, Swinbyrn, Swynborne.

SWINDEL (English) Swine valley. *Variations:* Swyndel, Swyndell, Swyndelle.

SWINTON (English) Swine town.

SY (English) Short form of Sydney or Sylvester. *Notable:* Hair Club for Men founder Sy Sperling.

SYDNEY (English) Form of Sidney. *Notable:* Director Sydney Pollack.

SYLVESTER (Latin) Forested. *Notable:* Actor Sylvester Stallone. *Variations:* Silvester, Silvestre, Silvestro, Sly.

SZCZESNY (Polish) Lucky.

TAB (German) Brilliant. *Notable:* Actor Tab Hunter. *Variation:* Tabb.

TABARI (Arabic) Remember. *Variations:* Tabaris, Tabarus, Tabary.

TABBAI (Hebrew) Good.

TABBEBO (Native American) Man of the sun.

TABIB (Turkish) Doctor. *Variation:* Tabeeb.

TABOR (Hungarian) Encampment.

TAD (Welsh) Father. *Variation:* Tadd.

TADAN (Native American) Plentiful. *Variations:* Taden, Tadin, Tadon, Tadyn.

TADAO (Japanese) Self-satisfying.

TADASHI (Japanese) Serves faithfully. *Variations:* Tadashie, Tadashy.

TADE (Croation) Strong.

TADHG (Irish) Poet. *Variations:* Taidhgin, Teague, Teige.

TADI (Native American) Wind.

TADLEIGH (Irish) Poet from the meadow. *Variations:* Tadleah, Tadlee, Tadley, Tadlie, Tadly.

TADZI (Native American) Loon.

TAFT (English) River.

TAGE (Danish) Day. *Variations:* Tag, Taig, Taige, Tayge.

TAGGART (Irish) Son of a priest. *Variations:* Tagart, Tagert, Taggert, Taggirt, Taggurt, Taggyrt, Tagirt, Tagurt.

TAGHEE (Native American) Chief. *Variations:* Taighe, Taihee, Tyee, Tyhee.

TAHA (Polynesian) One.

TAHATAN (Native American) Hawk.

TAHETON (Native American) Crow.

TAHI (Polynesian) Ocean.

TAHIR (Arabic) Pure

TAHOMA (Native American) Shoreline. *Variation:* Tohoma.

TAI (Vietnamese) Skilled.

TAIMAH (Native American) Thunder. *Variations:* Taima, Taiomah, Tama, Tamah.

TAIN (Gaelic) Stream. *Variations:* Taine, Tayne.

TAIWO (African) First-born twin.

TAIZO (Japanese) Third son.

TAJ (Hindi) Crown.

TAKEO (Japanese) Strength. *Variation:* Takeyo.

TAKESHI (Japanese) Bamboo.

TAKIS (Greek) Form of Peter.

TAKLISHIM (Native American) Gray.

TAKODA (Native American) Friends.

TAJUAN (African American) God is gracious.

TAL (Hebrew) Rain.

TALBOT (English) From the valley. *Variations:* Talbert, Talbott, Tallbot, Tallbott.

TALCOTT (English) From the tall cottage. *Variations:* Talcolt, Talcot, Taldon, Talmadge.

TALE (African) Green.

TALFRYN (Welsh) High hill. *Variation:* Talfrin.

TALIB (Arabic) Searcher.

TALIESIN (Welsh) Radiant brow. *Variations:* Taliesen, Talieson, Taliesyn, Talisan, Tallas, Tallis, Tallys, Taltesin, Talyesin, Talyesyn, Tayliesin, Tayliesyn.

TALMAI (Hebrew) Furrow. *Variation:* Talmi.

TALMAN (Aramaic) To injure or oppress. *Variations:* Tallie, Tally, Talmen, Talmin, Talmon, Talmyn.

TALON (Hebrew) Claw.

TALOR (Hebrew) Morning dew.

TALUT (Arabic) Borrowed. *Variation:* Talu.

TAM (Scottish) Form of Thomas.

TAMAN (Serbo-Croatian) Black.

TAMAR (Hebrew) Palm tree. *Variations:* Tamer, Tamir, Tamor, Tamyr.

TAMBO (African) Vigorous.

TAMIR (Arabic) Tall as a tree.

TAMMANY (Native American) Friendly. *Variation:* Tamanend.

TAMSON (Scandinavian) Son of Thomas. *Variations:* Tamsan, Tamsen, Tamsin, Tamsun, Tamsyn.

TAN (Vietnamese) New.

TANAFA (Polynesian) Drumbeat.

TANAKI (Polynesian) Keep score. *Variations:* Tanakie, Tanaky.

TANAY (Hindi) Son.

TANCRED (German) Counselor. *Variation:* Tancrid.

TANDIE (African American) Masculine.

TANEK (Greek) Immortal.

TANELI (Finnish) God is my judge. *Variations:* Tanel, Tanelie, Tanell, Tanely.

TANH (Vietnamese) Attitude.

TANI (Japanese) Valley.

TANIEL (Estonian) God is my judge. *Variations:* Taniell, Tanyel, Tanyell.

TANJIRO (Japanese) Second-born son who is highly valued.

TANK (Polynesian) God of the sky.

Baby Bottoms Up!

If you love a celebration but, as a new parent, your nights out drinking with the girls or boys are behind you, these sparkling names will have great associations!

BOYS:

Belvedere
Dom Perignon
Frangelico
Galliano
Glenfiddich
Guinness
Hennessy
Hiram Walker
Jack Daniel
Jagermeister
Jim Beam
Johnnie
Walker
Jose Cuervo
Martell
Mojito
Negroni
Pernod
Remy Martin
Ron Rico
Tom Collins

GIRLS:

Alize
Amaretto
Amarone
Anisette
Bellini
Brandy
Carolans
Chablis
Champagne
Chartreuse
Kahlua
Lillet
Margarita
Merlot
Midori
Mimosa
Sherry
Syrah
Tia Maria
Tuaca

TANNER (English) One who tans leather. *Variations:* Tan, Tanier, Tann, Tanney, Tannie, Tanny.

TANTON (English) Town on a silent river.

TANO (African) River. *Variation:* Tanno.

TANTON (English) From the quiet river estate or town. *Variations:* Tantin, Tantun, Tantyn.

TARHE (Native American) Tree.

TARIK (Arabic) Nocturnal visitor. *Variations:* Taril, Tarin, Tariq.

TARLETON (English) Thor's town. *Variation:* Tareton.

TARO (Japanese) First male.

TARQUIN (Latin) Etruscan king.

TARRANT (Welsh) Thunder. *Variations:* Tarant, Tarent, Tarrent.

TARRIL (Scandinavian) Belonging to Thor. Form of Terrell. *Variation:* Tarell.

TAS (Gypsy) Bird's nest.

TASHUNKA (Native American) Horse. *Variation:* Tasunke.

TATANKA (Native American) Walking bull.

TATE (English) Happy. *Notable:* Actor Tate Donovan. *Variations:* Tait, Taite, Taitt, Tayte.

TATIUS (Latin) Ruler. *Variations:* Tatianis, Tatianus, Tytius.

TATONGA (Native American) Male deer.

TATUM (English) From Tate's homestead. *Variations:* Taitam, Taitim, Taitom, Taitum, Taitym, Tatam, Tatem, Tatim, Tatom, Taytam,

Taytem, Taytim, Taytom, Taytum, Taytym.

TAU (African) Lion.

TAVA (Polynesian) Tree with fruit.

TAVARIS (Aramaic) Misfortune. *Variations:* Tavar, Tavares, Tavarian, Tavarius, Tavor.

TAVED (Estonian) Beloved. *Variations:* Tavad, Tavid, Tavod.

TAVEY (Latin) Eighth-born child. The short form of Octavio. *Variations:* Tavee, Tavie, Tavy.

TAVI (Hebrew) Good.

TAVIS (Scottish) Twin. *Variation:* Tevis.

TAVISH (Irish) Twin.

TAWA (Native American) The sun.

TAWANIMA (Native American) Movement of the sun. *Variation:* Tewanima.

TAWFIQ (Arabic) Good luck. *Variation:* Tawfi.

TAWNO (Gypsy) Small.

TAYIB (Arabic) Good.

TAYLOR (English) Tailor. *Notable:* Film director Taylor Hackford. *Variations:* Tailer, Tailor, Talor, Tayler, Taylour.

TAZ (Persian) Goblet. *Variations:* Tas, Tass, Tazz.

TEAGAN (Irish) Poet. Form of Teague. *Variations:* Teegan, Tegan, Teigen, Teirgan.

TEAGUE (Irish) Poet. *Variations:* Teig, Teige, Teigue, Tighe.

TEARLACH (Scottish) Man.

TEASDALE (English) Dweller at the river valley. *Variation:* Teesdale.

TECHOMIR (Czech) Great consolation.

TECHOSLAV (Czech) Glorious consolation.

TECUMSEH (Native American) Traveler.

TECWYN (Welsh) White-haired friend.

TED (English) Short form of Edward or Theodore. *Notables:* News anchorman Ted Koppel; singer Ted Nugent; media entrepreneur Ted Turner. *Variation:* Tedd.

TEDDY (English) Short form of Edward or Theodore. *Notable:* Singer Teddy Pendergrass. *Variations:* Teddey, Teddie, Tedey, Tedi, Tedie, Tedy.

TEDMUND (English) Watcher over land. *Variation:* Tedmond.

TEDRICK (English) Powerful ruler. *Variations:* Tedric, Tedrik.

TEFERE (African) Seed. *Variation:* Tefer.

TEGAN (Irish) Doe.

TEIJI (Japanese) Second son who is righteous.

TEJOMAY (Hindi) Glorious. *Variation:* Tej.

TEKEA (Polynesian) King of the sharks.

TEKONSHA (Native American) Little caribou.

TELAMON (Greek) Father of Ajax, an ancient mythological figure.

TELEK (Polish) Ironworker.

TELEM (Hebrew) Furrow. *Variation:* Tellem.

TELESPHOROS (Greek) To bring the end of an event.

TELFORD (French) One who works with iron. *Variations:* Telfer, Telfor, Telfour.

TELLER (English) Storyteller.

TELLY (Greek) Short form of Teller or Theodore. *Notable:* Actor Telly Savalas.

TEM (Gypsy) Country.

TEMAN (Hebrew) On the right.

TEMBO (African) Elephant.

TEMPEST (French) Storm.

TEMPLE (English) Temple.

TEMPLETON (English) Town near the temple. *Variations:* Temple, Templeten.

TENDOY (Native American) To climb. *Variation:* Tendoi.

TENNANT (English) Tenant. *Variations:* Tenant, Tennent.

TENNESSEE (Native American) The state. *Notable:* Playwright Tennessee Williams.

TENNYSON (English) Son of Dennis. *Variations:* Tenney, Tennie, Tennison, Tenny.

TEO (Polynesian) Gift from God.

TENZIN (Tibetan) Keeper of the teachings.

TERACH (Hebrew) Goat. *Variations:* Tera, Terah.

TERENCE (Latin) Smooth, tender. *Notables:* Actor Terence Stamp; playwright Terrence McNally. *Variations:* Tarrance, Terance, Terencio, Terrance, Terrence.

TERRELL (German) Follower of Thor. *Variations:* Terrall, Terrel, Terrill, Terryl, Terryll, Tirrell, Tyrrell.

TERRY (English) Short form of Terence. *Notables:* Football player Terry Bradshaw; director/animator and Monty Python member Terry Gilliam. *Variations:* Tere, Terie, Terre, Terrey, Terrie, Tery.

TESHER (Hebrew) Donation.

TET (Vietnamese) Festival.

TETLEY (English) From Tate's meadow. *Variations:* Tetleigh, Tetlie, Tetly.

TEVA (Hebrew) Nature.

TEVEL (Yiddish) Beloved. *Variations:* Tevell, Tevil, Tevill.

TEVIN (African American) Variation of Kevin.

TEVIS (Scottish) Form of Thomas.

TEX (American) Nickname for Texas. *Notables:* Country singer and actor Tex Ritter.

THABITI (African) A man.

THADDEUS (Aramaic) Brave. *Notable:* Polish patriot and soldier, Thaddeus Kosciuszko. *Variations:* Taddeo, Tadeo, Tadio, Thad, Thadd, Thaddaus, Thaddej, Thaddeo, Thaddeos, Thaddeys, Thadeas, Thadeis, Thadeos, Thadeus, Thadeys, Thadias, Thadios, Thadius.

THAI (Vietnamese) Many.

THANDIWE (African) Beloved.

THANE (English) Warrior. *Variations:* Thain, Thaine, Thayn, Thayne.

THANG (Vietnamese) Conquer.

THANH (Vietnamese) End.

THANIEL (Hebrew) Gift of God. Form of Nathaniel.

THANOS (Greek) Nobleman. *Variations:* Athanasios, Thanasis, Thanus.

THATCHER (English) Roof thatcher. *Variations:* Thacher, Thatch, Thaxter.

THAW (English) Melt.

THAYER (German) Of the army.

THEMBA (African) Hope.

THEO (German; Greek) Short form of Theobald or Theodore.

THEOBALD (German) Brave people. *Variations:* Teobald, Teobaud, Thebaud, Thebault, Theobaldo, Thibault, Thibaut, Tibold, Tiebold.

THEODORE (Greek) Gift from God. *Notable:* U.S. President Theodore Roosevelt. *Variations:* Teador, Tedor, Teodor, Teodoro, Theo, Theodor.

THEODORIC (German) Leader of the people. *Variations:* Teodorico, Theodorik, Theodorio, Thierry.

THEOPHILUS (Greek) Dear to God. *Variations:* Teofil, Theophile.

THERON (Greek) Hunter.

THESEUS (Greek) Ancient mythological figure.

THIASSI (Scandinavian) Ancient mythological figure. *Variations:* Thiazi, Thjazi.

THIERRY (French) Form of Theodore. *Notable:* Fashion designer Thierry Mugler.

THO (Vietnamese) Long life.

THOMAS (Aramaic) Twin. *Notables:* U.S. President Thomas Jefferson; inventor Thomas Edison; writer Thomas Hardy. *Variations:* Tam, Tameas, Thom, Thoma, Thompson, Thomson, Thumas, Thumo, Tom, Tomas, Tomaso, Tomasso, Tomaz, Tomcio, Tomek, Tomelis, Tomi, Tomie, Tomislaw, Tomm, Tommy, Tomsen, Tomson, Toomas, Tuomas, Tuomo.

THOMPSON (English) Son of Thomas.

THONG (Vietnamese) Smart.

THOR (Scandinavian) Thunder. *Notables:* Thor, mythological god of thunder; Norwegian explorer Thor Heyerdahl. *Variations:* Thordis, Thore, Thorin, Thorley, Thorr, Thorsson, Tor, Torr.

THORALD (Scandinavian) One who follows Thor. *Variations:* Thorold, Thorvald, Torald, Torvald.

THORBERT (Scandinavian) Thor's brightness. *Variation:* Thorburt, Torbert, Torburt.

THORBURN (Scandinavian) Thor's bear. *Variations:* Thorburne, Thorbyrne.

THORER (Scandinavian) Thor's warrior.

THORGOOD (English) Thor is good. *Notable:* Civil-rights leader Thurgood Marshall. *Variation:* Thurgood.

THORLEIF (Scandinavian) Thor's beloved.

THORLEY (English) Thor's meadow. *Variations:* Thorlea, Thorlee, Thorleigh, TorleyThorly.

THORMOND (English) Defended by Thor. *Variations:* Thormon, Thurmond, Thurmund.

THORNDIKE (English) Thorny riverbank. *Variations:* Thorndyck, Thorndyke.

THORNE (English) Thorn. *Variation:* Thorn.

THORNLEY (English) Thorny meadow. *Variations:* Thornlea, Thornleigh, Thornly.

THORNTON (English) Thorny town. *Notable:* Writer Thornton Wilder.

THORPE (English) Village. *Variation:* Thorp.

THU (Vietnamese) Autumn.

THUC (Vietnamese) Alert.

THUONG (Vietnamese) Chase.

THURLOW (English) Thor's hill. *Variation:* Thurlo.

THURMOND (English) Defended by Thor. *Notable:* Baseball player Thurman Munson. *Variations:* Thurman, Thurmon.

THURSTON (Scandinavian) Thor's stone. *Variations:* Thorstan, Thorstein, Thorsteinn, Thorsten, Thurstain, Thurstan, Thursten, Torstein, Torsten, Torston.

THUY (Vietnamese) Tender.

TIARNACH (Irish) Devout. *Variation:* Tighearnach.

TIBOR (Slavic) Sacred place. *Variations:* Tiebout, Tybald, Tybalt, Tybault.

TIERNAN (Irish) Little lord. *Variations:* Tierney, Tighearnach, Tighearnan.

TIERNEY (Irish) Lordly.

TIGER (American) Tiger. *Notable:* Golfer Tiger Woods. *Variations:* Tige, Tyger.

TIKI (Polynesian) The first man. *Notable:* Football player Tiki Barber.

TILDEN (English) Fertile valley. *Variations:* Tildan, Tildin, Tildon, Tildyn.

TILFORD (English) Fertile ford. *Variations:* Tilforde, Tillford.

TILL (German) Leader of the people. *Variations:* Til, Tyl, Tyll.

TILON (Hebrew) Hill.

TILTON (English) Fertile town.

TIM (Greek) Honoring God. Short form of Timothy. *Notables:* Comedian Tim Allen and Tim Conway; film director Tim Burton. *Variations:* Timm, Tym, Tymm.

TIMIN (Arabic) Sea serpent.

TIMMY (Greek) Short form of Timothy. *Variations:* Timee, Timey, Timie, Timmee, Timmey, Timmi, Timmie, Timmo, Tymee, Tymey, Tymi, Tymie, Tymmee, Tymmey, Tymmie, Tymmo, Tymmy, Tymy.

TIMON (Greek) Honorable. *Variations:* Timan, Timen, Timin.

TIMOTHY (Greek) Honoring God. *Notables:* Actors Timothy Hutton and Timothy Dalton. *Variations:* Timathey, Timathy, Timmothy, Timo, Timofeo, Timon, Timoteo, Timothe, Timotheo, Timotheus, Timothey, Tymmothy, Tymothy.

TIMUR (Hebrew) Tall.

TIN (Vietnamese) Thinker.

TINO (Italian) Small.

TINSLEY (English) Defender of the meadow. *Variations:* Tinsleigh, Tinslie, Tinsly, Tynslee, Tynsleigh, Tynsley, Tynslie, Tynsly.

TIPU (Hindi) Tiger.

TIRU (Hindi) Devoted.

TITO (Spanish) To honor. *Notable:* Musician Tito Puente.

TITUS (Greek) Of the giants. *Variations:* Tito, Titos, Tytus.

TIVON (Hebrew) Lover of nature.

TOA (Polynesian) Brave.

TOAFO (Polynesian) Forest.

TOAL (Irish) Strong people. *Variations:* Tuathal, Tully.

TOBAR (Gypsy) Road.

TOBIAS (Hebrew) God is good. *Variations:* Tobej, Tobia, Tobiah, Tobiasz, Tobin.

TOBIKUMA (Japanese) Cloud.

TOBY (English) Short form of Tobias. *Notables:* Country singer Toby Keith; actor Tobey McGuire. *Variations:* Tobe, Tobey, Tobie, Toby.

TODD (English) Fox. *Notable:* Chef Todd English. *Variation:* Tod.

TOHON (Native American) Cougar.

TOHYAH (Native American) Walking by a stream.

TOIRDEALBHACH (Irish) Like Thor, the Norse god of thunder. *Variations:* Tirloch, Turlough.

TOIVO (Finnish) Hope. *Variation:* Toyvo.

TOKALA (Native American) Fox.

TOKUTARO (Japanese) Virtuous.

TOLAN (English) Taxed land. *Variations:* Toland, Tolen, Tolin, Tollan, Tolland, Tolon, Tolun, Tolyn.

TOLBERT (English) Bright tax collector. *Variations:* Talbert, Talberte, Talbirt, Talburt, Talburte, Tolberte, Tolbirt, Tolburt, Tolburte.

TOLER (English) Tax collector. *Variation:* Toller.

TOLMAN (English) Tax man. *Variations:* Tollman, Tollmen.

TOM (English) Twin. Short form of Thomas. *Notables:* Actors Tom Cruise and Tom Hanks; rocker Tom Petty. *Variations:* Thom, Tomm.

TOMER (Hebrew) Tall.

School Daze: Names from Teachers (Part III)

This selection comes from an elementary school in Santa Barbara, California:

Advil	Otniel
Anjama	Perlonia
Bolden	Philinda
Champagne	Rashon
Deejonay	Shenique
Emari	Shenoa
Fantasee	Sheona
Fuk	Sulem
Jome	Synge
Jyl	Torston
Lan	Tranquilino
Klinsmann	Twyla
Marassa	Vianey
Mazulabelle	Yovanka
Mozelle	Zern
Myrt	Zuleika
Mysterium	Zulema
Ooanh	

Top Arabic Names

BOYS:
1. Mohamed
2. Ahmed
3. Omar
4. Yousef
5. Ali
6. Abdallah
7. Adam
8. Abdul Rahman
9. Khaled
10. Hamzah

GIRLS:
1. Jana
2. Mariam
3. Malak
4. Sara
5. Nour
6. Hala
7. Yara
8. Liane
9. Fatima
10. Leen

TOMI (Japanese) Wealthy.

TOMKIN (English) Little twin. *Variations:* Tomken, Tomkins.

TOMLIN (English) Little twin. *Variation:* Tomlinson.

TOMMY (English) Twin. Short form of Thomas. *Notables:* Fashion designer Tommy Hilfiger; choreographer Tommy Tune; comedian Tommy Chong. *Variations:* Thomee, Thomey, Thomie, Thommee, Thommey, Thommie, Thommy, Tomee, Tomey, Tomie, Tommee, Tommie, Tomy.

TOMOCHICHI (Native American) To fly up. *Variation:* Tomocheechee.

TONDA (Czech) Priceless. *Variations:* Tondek, Tonneli.

TONG (Vietnamese) Aromatic.

TONY (Latin) Nickname for Anthony. *Notables:* Singer Tony Orlando; actor Tony Curtis. *Variations:* Toney, Tonie, Tonio.

TOPHER (English) Christ bearer. Form of Christopher. *Notable:* Actor Topher Grace.

TOPPER (English) Top of the hill.

TOPWE (African) Vegetable.

TOR (Celtic) Rock. *Variation:* Torr.

TORAN (Gaelic) From the craggy hills. *Variation:* Torran.

TORAO (Japanese) Tiger.

TORBEN (English) Thor's bear. *Variation:* Torbjörn.

TORBERT (English) Rocky hilltop. *Variations:* Thorbet, Thorbirt, Thorburt, Torbirt, Torburt.

TORD (Scandinavian) Peace of Thor.

TORGER (Scandinavian) Thor's spear. *Variations:* Terje, Torgeir.

TORIL (Hindi) Attitude.

TORIN (Irish) Chief. *Variations:* Thorfin, Thorin, Thorstein, Thoryn, Toren, Torine, Torren, Torrin, Torrine, Torryn, Torryne, Toryn.

TORIO (Japanese) Bird's tail.

TORKEL (Scandinavian) Thor's cauldron. *Variations:* Thorkel, Torkil, Torkild, Torkjell, Torquil.

TORMOND (Scottish) Man from the North. *Variations:* Thormon, Thormond, Thormondo, Thormun, Thormund, Thormundo, Tormon, Tormondo, Tormun, Tormund, Tormundo.

TORNA (Irish) Prince.

TOROLF (Scandinavian) Thor's wolf. *Variations:* Thorolf, Tolv, Torolv, Torulf.

TORRANCE (Irish) From the craggy hills. *Variations:* Torrence. Tawrence, Torance, Torence.

TORSTEN (Norse) Thor's stone. *Variations:* Torstan, Torstin, Torston.

TORU (Japanese) Ocean.

TORY (English) From the craggy hills. Short form of Torrance. *Variations:* Torey, Torie, Torrey, Torry.

TOSHIRO (Japanese) Skillful. *Variations:* Toshi, Toshihiro.

TOSTIG (Norse) Harsh day.

TOV (Hebrew) Good. *Variations:* Tovi, Toviel, Toviya, Tuvia, Tuviah, Tuviya.

TOVE (Scandinavian) Thor's rule. *Variation:* Tuve.

TOWNLEY (English) Town meadow. *Variations:* Townlea, Townlee, Townleigh, Townlie, Townly.

TOWNSEND (English) Town's end.

TRACY (Greek) Brave warrior. *Variations:* Trace, Tracey, Tracie, Treacy.

TRADER (English) Skilled worker.

TRAHERN (Welsh) Strong as iron. *Variations:* Trahaern, Trahearn, Trahearne, Trahern, Traherne.

TRAI (Vietnamese) Pearl.

TRANT (German) Cunning.

TRAUGOTT (German) Trust in God. *Variation:* Traugot.

TRAVELL (English) Traveler. *Variations:* Traveler, Travelis, Travell, Travelle, Travil, Travill, Traville, Travyl, Travyll, Trevel, Trevell, Trevil, Trevill, Trevyl, Trevyll.

TRAVERS (French) Crossroads. *Variations:* Travaris, Travarius, Travarus, Traver, Traveress, Traverez, Travoris, Travorus.

TRAVIS (French) Toll taker. *Notable:* Singer Travis Tritt. *Variations:* Traves, Travess, Traviss, Travus, Travys.

TRAVON (English) Fair town. *Variations:* Travaughn, Traveon, Travion, Trayvon, Trevin, Trevonn.

TRAYLOR (English) Crowned with trees. *Variations:* Trailor, Trayler, Treilor, Treyler, Treylor.

TRAYTON (English) Town near trees. Traiton, Treiton, Treyton.

TREAT (Latin) Swiftly moving stream. *Variations:* Treet, Treit, Trentan, Trenten, Trentin, Trenton.

TREDWAY (English) Mighty warrior. *Variation:* Treadway.

TREMAIN (Celtic) Stone town. *Variations:* Tramain, Tramaine, Tramayne, Tremaine, Tremayne.

TRENT (Latin) Rushing waters. *Notable:* Singer Trent Reznor. *Variations:* Trentan, Trenten, Trentin, Trenton.

TREVELYAN (Gaelic) From the lively homestead. *Variation:* Trevelian.

TREVIN (Welsh) From the lively village. *Variations:* Travan, Traven, Traveon, Travien, Travin, Travion, Trevan, Treven, Trevian, Trevion, Trevyn.

TREVOR (Welsh) Large homestead. *Notable:* Actor Trevor Howard. *Variations:* Trefor, Trev, Trevar, Trever, Trevis.

TREY (English) Three. *Notable: South Park* creator Trey Parker. *Variations:* Trae, Tray, Traye, Tre, Trei, Treye.

TRIG (Scandinavian) Trusty. *Variation:* Trigg.

TRINI (Latin) Three. Short form of Trinity. *Notable:* Singer Trini Lopez. *Variation:* Triny.

TRINITY (Latin) Three; the Holy Trinity.

TRIPP (English) Traveler. *Variations:* Trip, Trypp.

TRISHUL (Sanskrit) Trident.

TRISTAN (Welsh) Outcry. *Variations:* Tris, Tristen, Tristian, Triston, Trystan, Trysten, Trystin, Tryston.

TRISTRAM (Welsh) Sorrowful. *Notable:* Literary character Tristram Shandy. *Variations:* Tristam, Trystam, Trystram.

TROND (Scandinavian) From Trondelag, an area in central Norway.

TROWBRIDGE (English) Bridge by a tree.

TROY (Irish) Soldier. *Notable:* Actor Troy Donahue. *Variations:* Troi, Troye.

TRUITT (English) Small and sincere. *Variations:* Truet, Truett, Truit.

TRUMAN (English) Loyal one. *Notable:* Writer Truman Capote. *Variations:* Trueman, Trumaine, Trumann.

TRUMBALL (English) Strong. *Variations:* Trumbell, Trumbull.

TRYG (Scandinavian) Truth. *Variations:* Trig, Trigg, Trygg.

TRYGVE (Scandinavian) Protector.

TSALANI (African) Goodbye.

TSATOKE (Native American) Horse who hunts.

TSELA (Native American) Stars lying down.

TSIN (Native American) Canoe.

TSOAI (Native American) Rock tree.

TSOTOHAH (Native American) Red cliff.

TU (Vietnamese) Four.

TUAN (Vietnamese) Unimportant.

TUARI (Native American) Young eagle. *Variations:* Tuarie, Tuary.

TUCKER (English) One who works with cloth. *Notable:* TV news commentator Tucker Carlson.

TUDOR (Welsh) Divine gift.

TUG (Scandinavian) Pull. *Notable:* Baseball player Tug McGraw.

TULLY (Irish) Peaceful. *Variations:* Tull, Tulley, Tullie.

TULSI (Hindi) Basil.

TUMAINI (African) Hope.

TUNG (Vietnamese) Peace.

TUNU (Native American) Deer eating wild onions.

TUONG (Vietnamese) Everyone.

TUPI (Native American) To pull a salmon onto the river bank.

TUPPER (English) One who keeps rams.

TURK (English) From Turkey.

TURLOUGH (Celtic; Scandinavian) Shaped like Thunder. *Variations:* Thorlough, Torlough.

TURNER (English) Woodworker.

TURPIN (Scandinavian) Man of Thor. *Variations:* Thorpin, Torpin.

TUT (Egyptian) Strong.

TUXFORD (Scandinavian) From the spear ford. *Variation:* Tuxforde.

TUYEN (Vietnamese) Angel.

TWAIN (English) Split in two. *Variations:* Twaine, Twayn, Twayne.

TWITCHELL (English) Narrow alley. *Variations:* Twitchel, Twytchel, Twytchell.

TWYFORD (English) Place where rivers converge. *Variations:* Twiford, Twiforde, Twyforde.

TY (English) Short form of Tyler or Tyrone. *Notables:* TV fix-it man Ty Pennington; baseball player Ty Cobb. *Variation:* Tye.

TYBALT (English) Bold. *Variations:* Tibalt, Tibolt, Tybolt.

TYCHO (Scandinavian) On the mark. *Variations:* Tyge, Tyko.

TYDEUS (Greek) Ancient mythological figure.

TYEE (Native American) Chief.

TYKE (Native American) Captain.

TYLER (English) Tile maker. *Variations:* Ty, Tylar, Tylor.

TYMON (Greek) Worthy.

TYMOTEUSZ (Polish) To honor God. *Variations:* Tomek, Tymek, Tymon.

TYNAN (Irish) Dark.

TYR (Scandinavian) God of war.

TYREE (Scottish) Island dweller. *Variation:* Tyrie.

TYRRELL (French) To pull. *Variations:* Terrell, Tirell, Tyrrell.

TYRONE (Irish) Land of Owen. *Notable:* Actor Tyrone Power. *Variations:* Tiron, Tirone, Tirown, Tyron.

TYRUS (English) Strength. *Variation:* Tirus.

TYSON (English) Firebrand. *Notable:* Model Tyson Beckford. *Variations:* Tieson, Tison, Tysen.

TZACH (Hebrew) Clean. *Variations:* Tzachai, Tzachar.

TZADIK (Hebrew) Virtuous. *Variations:* Tzadok, Zadik, Zadoc, Zadok, Zaydak.

TZADKIEL (Hebrew) Virtuous with God. *Variation:* Zadkiel.

TZALMON (Hebrew) Dark. *Variation:* Zalmon.

TZEPHANIAH (Hebrew) God protects. *Variations:* Tzefanya, Zefania, Zefaniah, Zephania, Zephaniah.

TZEVI (Hebrew) Deer. *Variations:* Tzeviel, Zevi, Zeviel.

TZURIEL (Hebrew) God is my rock. *Variation:* Zuriel.

UALAN (Scottish) Valentine.

UALTAR (Irish) Ruler of the army. *Variations:* Uaitcir, Ualteir.

UANG (Chinese) Great.

UATA (Polynesian) Army leader. *Variation:* Uate.

UBA (African) Wealthy.

UBADAH (Arabic) He who serves God.

UBALD (German) Peace of mind. *Variations:* Ubaldas, Ubalde, Ubaldo, Ubaldus, Ubold, Uboldas, Uboldo, Uboldus.

UBERTO (Italian) Form of Herbert.

UCAL (Hebrew) Powerful.

UCELLO (Italian) Bird. *Variation:* Ucelo.

UCHECHI (African) God's will.

UDAY (Hindi) To rise. *Variation:* Udayan.

UDELL (English) Yew grove. *Variations:* Dell, Eudel, Udall, Udel.

UDO (German) Prosperity.

UDOLF (English) Wealthy wolf. *Variations:* Udolfo, Udolph.

UELI (Swiss) Noble ruler. *Variations:* Uelie, Uely.

UFFE (Scandinavian) Wolf. *Variation:* Ulfr.

UFFO (German) Wild bear. *Variation:* Ufo.

UGGIERI (Italian) Holy. *Variation:* Ugieri.

UGO (Italian) Intellect. Form of Hugo.

UHILA (Polynesian) Lightning.

UHURU (African) Freedom.

UILLEOG (Irish) Small protector. *Variations:* Uilleac, Uillioc.

UILLIAM (Irish) Form of William.

UINSEANN (Irish) One who conquers. *Variation:* Uinsionn.

UJALA (Hindi) Shining. *Variation:* Ujaala.

UKIAH (Native American) Deep valley.

ULAN (African) First born of twins.

ULAND (English) Noble country.

ULBRECHT (German) Grandeur.

ULDERICKS (Latvian) Noble ruler. *Variations:* Uldric, Uldrics, Uldrik, Uldryck.

ULEKI (Hawaiian) Hawaiian version of Ulysses. *Variation:* Ulesi.

ULF (Scandinavian) Wolf. *Variations:* Uffe, Ulf, Ulff, Ulfr, Ulfur, Ulph, Ulv, Ulve, Ulvur.

ULFER (Scandinavian) Wolf peace. *Variations:* Ulfred, Ulfrid, Ulfryd, Ulpher, Ulphrid, Ulphryd.

ULGER (English) Wolf spear. *Variations:* Ulga, Ulgah, Ulgar.

ULICK (Scandinavian) Rewarding mind. *Variations:* Ulic, Ulik, Ulyck.

ULL (Scandinavian) Glory.

ULLIVIERI (Italian) Olive tree. *Variation:* Ulivieri.

ULLOCK (English) Wolf sport. *Variations:* Uloc, Uloch, Uloche, Ulock, Ulok, Uloke, Ulloc, Ulloch, Ulloche, Ullok, Ulloke.

ULMER (English) Famous wolf. *Variations:* Ullmar, Ulmar.

ULRIC (German) Wolf power; (Scandinavian) Noble ruler. *Variations:* Ulrich, Ulrick, Ulrik, Ulrike.

ULTAN (German) Noble stone. *Variations:* Ulten, Ultin, Ulton, Ultyn.

ULTIMO (Latin) The last.

ULTRA (Latin) Extreme.

ULUKA (Sanskrit) Owl.

ULYSSES (Latin) Wrathful. *Notable:* U.S. President Ulysses S. Grant. *Variations:* Ulises, Ulisse.

UMAR (Arabic) To bloom.

UMBERTO (Italian) Famous German. Variation of Humbert. *Notable:* Writer Umberto Eco.

UMBRA (Latin) Shadow cast during an eclipse.

UMED (Hindi) Desire.

UMI (African) Life.

UNADUTI (Native American) Woolly head.

UNCAS (Native American) Fox. *Variations:* Unkas, Wonkas.

UNER (Turkish) Famous.

UNGER (German) From Hungary.

UNIKA (African) Shining; to shine.

UNITY (Latin) Oneness. *Variations:* Unitee, Unitey, Uniti, Unitie.

UNO (Latin) First.

UNWIN (English) Enemy. *Variations:* Unwinn, Unwyn.

UPDIKE (English) Upper bank.

UPRAVDA (Slavic) Upright.

UPSHAW (English) Upper forest.

UPTON (English) Hill town. *Notable:* Writer Upton Sinclair.

UPWOOD (English) Forest on a hill.

URBAN (Latin) Man from the city. *Variations:* Urbain, Urbaine, Urbane, Urbano, Urbanus, Urvan.

URI (Hebrew) God's light. *Notable:* Paranormalist Uri Geller. *Variations:* Uria, Uriah, Urias, Urie.

URIAH (Hebrew) My light.

URIAN (Greek) Heaven.

URIEL (Hebrew; Russian) God's light. *Variations:* Yuriel, Yuryel.

URIEN (Welsh) Privileged birth.

URJASZ (Polish) God is light.

URSA (Latin) Bear. *Variations:* Ursah, Ursan, Ursel, Ursen, Urshell, Ursin, Ursine, Ursus.

URSON (French) Spearman's son. *Variation:* Orson.

URVIL (Hindi) The sea.

USAMA (Arabic) Lion. *Variation:* Usamah.

USENI (African) Tell me.

USENKO (Russian) Son of the man with the moustache.

USHER (Latin) River mouth. *Notable:* R&B singer Usher Raymond.

USI (African) Smoke.

USMAN (Arabic) Owner of two lights.

USTIN (Russian) Just.

UTHER (English) From Arthurian legend, King Arthur's father.

UTHMAN (Arabic) Bird. *Variations:* Othman, Usman.

UTTAM (Hindi) Best.

UTU (Polynesian) Returning.

UWE (German) Inherited from birth.

UYEDA (Japanese) Field of rice.

UYENO (Japanese) Upper field.

UZAIR (Arabic) Helper. *Variations:* Uzaire, Uzare, Uzayre.

UZI (Hebrew) My strength.

UZIAH (Hebrew) God is my strength. *Variations:* Uzia, Uziya, Uzziah.

UZIEL (Hebrew) Powerful. *Variation:* Uzziel.

UZOMA (African) Born on a trip.

VAAL (Dutch) Valley.

VACHEL (French) Small cow. *Variation:* Vachell.

VACLAV (Czech) Glory. *Notable:* Writer/dramatist Vaclav Havel.

VADIN (Hindi) Educated orator.

VAIL (English) From the valley. *Variations:* Vaile, Vale, Vayle.

VAINO (Scandinavian) Wagon builder.

VAL (English) Strong. Short form of Valentine. *Notable:* Actor Val Kilmer.

VALA (Polynesian) Loincloth.

VALBORG (Scandinavian) Protection from the slaughter. *Variation:* Valbor.

VALDEMAR (German) Famous leader.

VALDUS (German) Possessor of power. *Variations:* Valdis, Valdys.

VALE (French) Dweller in the valley. *Variations:* Vael, Vaiel, Vail, Vayel, Vayle.

VALENTINE (Latin) Strong. *Variations:* Val, Valentin, Valentino, Valentyn.

VALERIAN (Latin) Healthy. *Variations:* Valerie, Valerien, Valerio, Valery, Valeryan.

VALI (Scandinavian) Ancient mythological figure.

VALIN (Hindi) Mighty soldier. *Variations:* Valen, Valyn.

VALMIKI (Hindi) Ant hill.

VALU (Polynesian) Eight.

VAMANA (Sanskrit) One who deserves praise. *Variation:* Vamanah.

VAN (Dutch) Short form of Vandyke. *Notables:* Actor Van Johnson; pianist Van Cliburn.

VANCE (English) Swampland. *Variations:* Van, Vancelo, Vann.

VANDA (Lithuanian) Ruling people. *Variation:* Vandele.

VANDAN (Hindi) Salvation. *Variations:* Vanden, Vandin, Vandon, Vandyn.

VANDYKE (Dutch) From the dyke. *Notable:* Songwriter Van Dyke Parks. *Variations:* Van Dyck, Vandike.

VANE (English) Banner. *Variations:* Vain, Vaine, Vayne.

VANYA (Russian) God is good. Variation of Ivan. *Variations:* Vanek, Vanka.

VARAD (Hungarian) Belonging to the fortress. *Variations:* Vared, Varid, Varod.

VARDEN (French) Green mountains. *Variations:* Vardon, Verden, Verdon, Verdun.

VARDHAMMA (Hindi) Growth. *Variation:* Vardhaman.

VAREN (Hindi) Superior. *Variations:* Varan, Varin, Varon, Varyn.

VARESH (Hindi) God is superior.

VARICK (German) Defending ruler. *Variations:* Varic, Varik, Varrick.

VARIL (Hindi) Water. *Variations:* Varal, Varel.

VARTAN (Armenian) Rose grower. *Variations:* Vartin, Varton, Vartyn.

VARUN (Hindi) God of rain. *Variations:* Varin, Varoon.

VASANT (Hindi) Spring.

VASILIS (Greek) Kingly. *Variations:* Vasile, Vasilek, Vasili, Vasilios, Vasilis, Vasilos, Vasily, Vassily.

VASIN (Hindi) Leader. *Variations:* Vasan, Vasen, Vason, Vasun, Vasyn.

VASU (Hindi) Prosperous.

VAUGHN (Welsh) Small. *Variation:* Vaughan.

VEA (Polynesian) Chief. *Variations:* Veamalohi, Veatama.

VEASNA (Cambodian) Lucky.

VEIKO (Finnish) Brother. *Variation:* Veyko.

VEIT (German) Wide. *Variation:* Veyt.

VEKOSLAV (Slavic) Eternal glory.

VELESLAV (Czech) Great glory. *Variations:* Vela, Velek, Velousek.

VENCEL (Hungarian) Wreath.

VENCESLAV (Czech) Glorious government.

VENEDICT (Russian) Blessed. Variation of Benedict. *Variations:* Venedikt, Venka, Venya.

VENN (Gaelic) Dweller at the marsh. *Variation:* Ven.

VERDUN (French) From the hill fort. *Variations:* Verdon, Virdun.

VERE (French) True.

VERED (Hebrew) Rose.

VERLIE (French) Town in France. *Variation:* Verley.

VERLIN (Latin) Spring. *Variations:* Verlan, Verlain, Verle, Verlinn, Verlon, Verlyn.

VERN (Latin) Youthful. Short form of Vernon. *Notable:* "Mini-Me" actor Verne Troyer. *Variations:* Verne.

VERNER (German) Defense army.

VERNEY (French) Belonging to the alder grove. *Variations:* Vernee, Vernie, Verny, Virnee, Virney, Virnie, Virny, Vurnee, Vurney, Vurnie, Vurny, Vyrnee, Vyrney, Vyrnie, Vyrny.

VERNON (Latin) Youthful. *Variations:* Vern, Verne.

VERRILL (French) Loyal. *Variations:* Verill, Verrall, Verrell, Verroll, Veryl.

VESTON (English) From the town of churches. *Variations:* Vestan, Vesten, Vestin, Vestun, Vestyn.

VIAN (English) Lively.

VIBERT (French) One who is shining brightly. *Variations:* Viberte, Viburt, Viburte.

VIC (Latin) Short form of Victor. *Notable:* Actor Vic Morrow. *Variations:* Vick, Vyck, Vyk.

VICAR (English) Clergy member. *Variations:* Vica, Vicka, Vickar, Vicker, Vickor.

VICTOR (Latin) Conqueror. *Notables:* Musician Victor Borge; actor Victor Mature. *Variations:* Victoir, Victorien, Victorino, Victorio, Viktor, Vitenka, Vitor, Vittore, Vittorio, Vittorios, Vyctor, Wiktor.

VIDAL (Spanish) Vital. *Notable:* Hair stylist Vidal Sassoon. *Variation:* Vidale.

VIDAR (Scandinavian). Strong and silent.

VIDKUN (Scandinavian) Vast experience.

VIDOR (Hungarian) Happy. *Variation:* Vidore.

VIDYA (Sanskrit) Wisdom. *Variation:* Vidyah.

VIGGO (Scandinavian) Warrior. *Notable:* Actor Viggo Mortensen.

VIJAY (Hindi) Victory. *Variations:* Bijay, Vijen, Vijun.

VIJAYA (Sanskrit) Strength. *Variations:* Vijayah, Vyjaya.

VIJAYENDRA (Hindi) Victorious god of the sky. *Variation:* Vijendra.

VIJNANA (Sanskrit) Intelligent. *Variations:* Vijnan, Vijnanah.

VILA (Czech) From William. Combination of will and helmet. *Variations:* Vilek, Vilem, Vilhelm, Vili, Viliam, Vilko, Ville, Vilmos.

VILHELM (German) Form of William. *Variations:* Vilem, Vilhelms, Villem, Vilmos.

VILIAMI (Polynesian) Protector.

VILJO (Scandinavian) Guardian.

VILMAR (German) Famous.

VILMOS (German) Steady soldier.

VILOK (Hindi) To see.

VIMAL (Hindi) Pure.

VIN (English) Short form of Vincent. *Notable:* Actor Vin Diesel.

VINAY (Hindi) Courteous.

VINCE (English) Short form of Vincent. *Notables:* Football coach Vince Lombardi; country singer Vince Gill.

VINCENT (Latin) To conquer. *Notables:* Actor Vincent Price; artist Vincent van Gogh. *Variations:* Vicen, Vikent, Vikenti, Vikenty, Vikesha, Vincante, Vincence, Vincencio Vincente, Vincentij, Vincentius, Vincenty, Vincentz, Vincenz, Vincenzio, Vincenzo, Vinci, Vinco, Vinn, Vinnie, Vinny, Vinsin, Vinsint, Vinson, Vinsynt, Vyncent, Vyncint.

VINE (English) One who works in a vineyard.

VINNY (English) Short form of Vincent. *Notable:* Football player Vinny Testaverde. *Variation:* Vinnie.

VINOD (Hindi) Joyful.

VINSON (English) Son of a conqueror. *Variations:* Vinsan, Vinsen, Vinsin, Vinson.

VINTON (English) Vineyard settlement.

VIRGIL (Latin) Staff bearer. *Notable:* Roman poet Virgil. *Variations:* Vergel, Vergil, Virgilio, Virgille, Virgillion.

VISHAL (Hindi) Great.

VISHESH (Sanskrit) Special.

VISHNU (Hindi) Protector.

VISHVA (Sanskrit) One who has everything.

VISHWESH (Sanskrit) The Lord Almighty.

VISVALDIS (Latvian) Ruler of all.

VITALE (Italian) Life. *Variations:* Vital, Vytal.

VITALIS (Latin) Life. *Variations:* Vitalys, Vytalis.

VITAS (Latin) Vital. *Notable:* Tennis player Vitas Gerulaitis. *Variation:* Vitus.

VITO (Latin) Alive. *Variations:* Vital, Vitale, Vitalis.

VITTORIO (Italian) Conqueror. Form of Victor. *Variation:* Vitorio.

VITUS (French) Forest. *Variation:* Vitya.

VIVEK (Hindi) Wisdom. *Variations:* Vivekanand, Vivekananda.

VIVIAN (Latin) Full of life.

VLAD (Slavic; Russian) Prince or ruler. Short form of Vladimir or Vladislav.

VLADIMIR (Russian) Famous prince. *Notables:* Russian revolutionary Vladimir Lenin; Lolita writer Vladimir Nabokov. *Variations:* Vlad, Vladamir, Vladimeer, Vladko, Vladlen, Vladmir, Vlado.

VLADISLAV (Czech) Glorious ruler. *Variation:* Ladislav.

VOGEL (German) Bird. *Variations:* Vogal, Vogil, Vogol, Vogyl.

VOITTO (Finnish) Winner. *Variation:* Voytto.

VOJTECH (Czech) Comforting soldier. *Variations:* Vojciech, Vojta, Vojtek, Vojtresek.

VOLKER (German) Protector of the people.

VOLNEY (German) Spirit of the people. *Variations:* Volni, Volnie, Volny.

VOLYA (Russian) Ruler of the people. Variation of Walter. *Variations:* Vova, Vovka.

VON (Scandinavian) Hope.

VOSHON (African American) God's grace.

VUC (Slavic) Wolf. *Variation:* Vuk.

VUI (Vietnamese) Cheerful.

VUKMIL (Slavic) Wolf of love. *Variations:* Vucmil, Vukmyl.

VYASA (Sanskrit) Order. *Variation:* Viasa.

WABAN (Native American) Easterly wind.

WABANAQUOT (Native American) White cloud.

WABAUNSEE (Native American) Sunrise.

WABONISHI (Native American) Winter survival.

WACHIRU (African) Son of a lawmaker.

WACLAW (Polish) Crowning glory. *Variations:* Vaclav, Waclav.

WADE (English) To cross a river. *Notable:* Baseball player Wade Boggs.

WADLEY (English) Meadow near a river crossing. *Variations:* Wadleigh, Wadly.

WADSWORTH (English) Village near a river crossing. *Variation:* Waddsworth.

WADUD (Arabic) Loving.

WAGNER (German) Wagon maker. *Variation:* Waggoner.

WAHCHUMYUS (Native American) Rainbow.

WAHHAB (Arabic) One who gives. *Variations:* Wahad, Wahib.

WAHID (Arabic) Unique. *Variation:* Waheed.

WAHKAN (Native American) Sacred.

WAHNAHTAH (Native American) Pursuer. *Variation:* Wahnata.

WAHOTKONK (Native American) Black eagle.

WAHTSAKE (Native American) Eagle.

WAIL (Arabic) One who returns to Allah.

WAINWRIGHT (English) Wagon maker. *Variations:* Wainright, Waynewright, Waynright.

WAITE (English) Watchman. *Variations:* Waits, Wayte.

WAJID (Arabic) Finder.

WAJIH (Arabic) Extraordinary.

WAKEFIELD (English) Damp field. *Variation:* Wake.

WAKELEY (English) Damp meadow. *Variations:* Wakelea, Wakeleigh, Wakely.

WAKEMAN (English) Watchman.

WAKIL (Arabic) Advocate.

WAKIZA (Native American) Bold warrior.

WALAKA (Hawaiian) Ruler of the people. *Variation:* Walata.

WALBY (English) From the home near the wall. *Variations:* Walbey, Walbie.

WALCOTT (English) Cottage by the wall. *Variations:* Wallcot, Wallcott, Wolcott.

WALDEMAR (German) Famous ruler. *Variations:* Valdemar, Waldermar.

WALDEN (English) Forested valley. *Variations:* Waldan, Waldin, Waldon.

WALDO (German) Strong.

WALDRON (German) Strong raven. *Variations:* Waldran, Waldrin, Waldryn.

WALELIANO (Hawaiian) Strong.

WALENA (Hawaiian) Defender.

WALENEKINO (Hawaiian) Strong. *Variations:* Walakino, Walekino.

WALERIAN (Polish) Strong. *Variations:* Walenty, Waleran.

WALFORD (English) River crossing.

WALFRED (German) Peaceful ruler.

WALI (Arabic) Servant of Allah. *Variations:* Walea, Walee, Waley, Walie.

WALID (Arabic) Newborn. *Variation:* Waleed.

WALKARA (Native American) Yellow. *Variation:* Wakara.

WALKER (English) Cloth walker.

WALLACE (Scottish) One from Wales. *Notables:* Actors Wallace Shawn and Wallace Beery. *Variations:* Walice, Walise, Wallach, Wallice, Wallie, Wallis, Wallise, Walsh, Welch, Welsh.

WALLACH (German) Form of Wallace. *Variations:* Walach, Walloch, Waloch.

WALLER (English) Wall maker.

WALLINGFORD (Welsh) From the wall near the ford. *Variation:* Walingford.

WALLY (English) Short form of Wallace or Walter. *Notables:* Writer Wally Lamb; cookie-maker Wally "Famous" Amos. *Variations:* Waley, Walleigh, Walley, Wallie.

WALMOND (German) Mighty or ruling protector.

WALSH (English) Form of Wallace.

WALT (German) Short form of Walter or Walton. *Notable:* Film and theme-park legend Walt Disney.

WALTER (German) Ruler of the people. *Notables:* Newscaster Walter Cronkite; actor Walter Pidgeon. *Variations:* Walt, Walther, Waltier, Waltir, Waltor, Waltr, Watkin.

WALTON (English) Walled town.

WALWORTH (English) Walled farm.

WALWYN (English) Welsh friend. *Variations:* Walwin, Walwinn, Walwynn, Walwynne.

WAMBLEE (Native American) White eagle. *Variations:* Wamblea, Wambley, Wamblie, Wambly.

WAMBUA (African) Born during the rainy season.

WANEKIA (Native American) Creator of life. *Variation:* Wanikiya.

WANETA (Native American) He who charges another.

WANG (Chinese) Hope.

WANJOHI (African) Brewer.

WANONCE (Native American) Place of attack.

WAPASHA (Native American) Red leaf. *Variations:* Wabasha, Wapusha.

WAPI (Native American) Lucky.

WARBURTON (English) Old fortress.

WARD (English) Guardian. *Variations:* Warde, Warden, Worden.

WARDELL (English) Watchman's hill.

WARDLEY (English) Watchman's meadow. *Variations:* Wardlea, Wardleigh, Wardlie, Wardly.

WARE (English) Cautious.

WARFIELD (English) Field by the weir.

WARFORD (English) River crossing by the weir.

WARING (German) Shelter of protection. *Variations:* Warrin, Warring.

WARLEY (English) Meadow by the weir.

WARNER (German) Army guard.

WARREN (German) Protector. *Notables:* Actor Warren Beatty; U.S. President Warren Harding. *Variations:* Warrin, Warriner.

WARRICK (English) Hero of the village. *Variations:* Waric, Warick, Warik, Warric, Warrik, Warryck, Waryck.

WARWICK (English) House near a dam.

WASHAKIE (Native American) Gourd.

WASHBURN (English) Flooded river. *Variations:* Washbern, Washberne, Washbirn, Washbirne, Washborn, Washborne, Washbourn, Washbourne, Washburne, Washbyrn, Washbyrne.

WASHINGTON (English) Town of smart men. *Notable:* Writer Washington Irving. *Variations:* Washingten, Washingtin.

WASI (Arabic) Understanding. *Variations:* Wasie, Wasy.

WASIL (Arabic) Divine.

WASILY (Russian) Form of Basil. *Variations:* Wasili, Wassily, Wasyl.

WASIM (Arabic) Attractive. *Variations:* Waseem, Wassim.

WASSAJA (Native American) Indication. *Variation:* Wasagah.

What Celebrities Are Naming Their Babies

Here's a list of what some notables have selected:

Alabama Gypsyrose and Wayland Albert "Blackjack" (Drea de Matteo and Shooter Jennings)

Apple Blythe Alison and Moses Bruce Anthony (Gwyneth Paltrow and Chris Martin)

Archibald William Emerson and Abel James (Amy Poehler and Will Arnett)

Arpad Flynn Alexander and Aurelius Cy Andrea (Elle Macpherson)

August Miklos Friedrich and Amaya Josephine (Mariska Hargitay)

Ava Elizabeth and Deacon Reese (Reese Witherspoon and Ryan Phillippe)

Aviana Olea (Amy Adams)

Banjo Patrick, Adelaide Rose, and Clementine Grace (Rachel Griffiths)

Beatrice Milly (Paul McCartney and Heather Mills)

Billie Beatrice (Eric Dane and Rebecca Gayheart)

WATENDE (African) Vengeful. *Variation:* Watend.

WATERMAN (English) Works on the water.

WATFORD (English) Wattle ford. *Variation:* Wattford.

WATKINS (English) Son of Walter. *Variations:* Watkin, Watkyn, Watkyns, Wattkin, Wattkins, Wattkyn, Wattkyns.

WATSON (English) Son of Walter.

WATTAN (Native American) Black. *Variation:* Waatina.

WAUNAKEE (Native American) Peaceful.

WAVERLY (English) Meadow of aspen trees. *Variations:* Waverlee, Waverleigh, Waverley, Waverlie.

WAYA (Native American) Wolf. *Variations:* Waia, Waiah, Wayah.

WAYLAND (English) Near the pathway. *Variations:* Wailan, Wailand, Whalan, Whalen, Whalin, Whalon, Whalyn.

WAYLON (English) Roadside land. *Notables:* Singer Waylon Jennings; ventriloquist Wayland Flowers. *Variations:* Way, Waylan, Wayland, Waylen, Waylin.

WAYNE (English) Wagon maker. *Notables:* Singer Wayne Newton; TV host/comedian Wayne Brady; motivational writer/speaker Wayne Dyer. *Variations:* Wain, Waine, Wayn.

WAZIRE (Arabic) Minister. *Variations:* Wazir, Wazyr.

WEAVER (English) Weaver.

WEBB (English) Weaver.

WEBLEY (English) Weaver's meadow. *Variations:* Webbley, Webbly, Webly.

WEBSTER (English) Weaver. *Variations:* Web, Webb, Weber.

WEDDELL (English) From the advancer's hill. *Variations:* Weddel, Wedel, Wedell.

WEI-QUO (Chinese) Leader of a nation.

WEISS (German) White. *Variations:* Weis, Weise, Weisse, Weyss, Weysse.

WEKESA (African) Born during the harvest. *Variation:* Wekeasa.

WELBORNE (English) Spring-fed river. *Variations:* Welbern, Welberne, Welbirn, Welbirne, Welborn, Welbourne, Welburn, Welburne, Wellborn, Wellborne, Wellbourn, Wellbourne, Wellburn, Wellburne, Wellbyrne.

WELBY (English) Waterside farm. *Variations:* Welbey, Welbie, Wellbey, Wellby.

WELDON (English) Well near a hill. *Variations:* Welden, Weldin, Weldyn, Welldon.

WELFORD (English) Well near a river crossing. *Variation:* Wellford.

WELLINGTON (English) Temple in a clearing.

WELLS (English) Source of water.

WELSH (English) Man from Wales.

WELTON (English) Well for a town.

WEMILAT (Native American) He has everything.

WEMILO (Native American) Everyone talks to him.

WEN (Chinese) Refined.

WEN HU (Chinese) Educated.

WENCESLAUS (Slavic) Glorious garland. *Variations:* Wenceslas, Wenzel.

WENDELL (German) Wanderer. *Variations:* Wendel, Wendle.

WENLOCK (Welsh) From the lake at the holy monastery. *Variations:* Wenloc, Wenloch, Wenlok.

WENSLEY (English) From the meadow with the wood clearing. *Variations:* Wenslee, Wensleigh, Wenslie, Wensly.

WENTWORTH (English) White man's town.

WENUTU (Native American) Sky clearing.

WERNER (German) Defending army. *Notable:* Film director Werner Herzog. *Variations:* Warner, Wernher.

WES (English) Short form of Wesley or Weston. *Notable:* Film director Wes Craven.

WESH (Gypsy) Forest.

WESLEY (English) Western meadow. *Notable:* Actor Wesley Snipes. *Variations:* Weslie, Wesly, Wessley, Westleigh, Westley.

WESTBROOK (English) Western stream. *Variations:* Wesbrook, West, Westbrooke.

WESTBY (English) Western farm.

WESTCOTT (English) Western cottage. *Variations:* Wescot, Wescott, Westcot.

WESTON (English) Western town. *Variations:* Westen, Westin.

WETHERBY (English) Form of male sheep, known as a wether. *Variations:* Weatherbey, Weatherbie, Weatherby, Wetherbey, Wetherbie.

WETHERELL (English) Sheep corner. *Variations:* Weatherell, Weatherill, Wetherill, Wethrill.

WETHERLY (English) Sheep meadow. *Variations:* Weatherley, Weatherly, Wetherleigh, Wetherley.

WHALLEY (English) Forest by a hill. *Variations:* Whaleigh, Whaley, Whalie, Whallie.

WHARTON (English) Town on a river bank. *Variation:* Warton.

WHEATLEY (English) Wheat field. *Variations:* Wheatlea, Wheatleigh, Wheatlie, Wheatly.

WHEATON (English) Town of wheat. *Variation:* Wheaten.

WHEELER (English) Wheel maker.

WHISTLER (English) Occupational name: whistler or piper.

WHIT (English) Short form of Whitney.

WHITAKER (English) From the white field. *Variation:* Whittaker.

WHITBY (English) Farm with white walls. *Variations:* Whitbey, Whitbie.

WHITCOMB (English) White valley. *Variation:* Whitcombe.

WHITELAW (English) White hill. *Variation:* Whitlaw.

WHITEY (English) Fair-skinned; white-haired. *Notable:* Baseball player Whitey Ford.

WHITFIELD (English) White field.

WHITFORD (English) White ford.

WHITLEY (English) White meadow. *Variations:* Whitleigh, Whitlie, Whitly.

WHITLOCK (English) White-haired one. *Variation:* Whitloch.

WHITMAN (English) White-haired man.

WHITMORE (English) White moor. *Variations:* Whitmoor, Whitmoore, Whittemore, Witmoor, Witmore, Wittemore.

WHITNEY (English) White island.

WHITTAKER (English) White field. *Variations:* Whitacker, Whitaker.

WICASA (Native American) Man.

WICHADO (Native American) Compliant.

WICK (English) From the dairy farm. *Variations:* Wic, Wik, Wyc, Wyck, Wyk.

WICKHAM (English) Village paddock. *Variation:* Wyckham.

WICKLEY (English) From the willow meadow in the village. *Variations:* Wickleah, Wicklee, Wickleigh, Wicklie, Wickly, Wycklea, Wyckleah, Wycklee, Wyckleigh, Wyckley, Wycklie, Wyckly, Wykleigh, Wyklie, Wykly.

WIELISLAW (Polish) Glory is great. *Variations:* Wiesiek, Wiesiulek, Wiestaw.

WIES (German) Warrior who is famous. *Variation:* Wiess.

WIKOLI (Hawaiian) Conqueror. Hawaiian version of Victor. *Variation:* Vitori.

WIKTOR (Polish) Victorious. *Variations:* Wicktor, Wycktor, Wyktor.

WILANU (Native American) Mixing water with flour.

WILBERT (German) Brilliant. *Variations:* Wilbirt, Wilburt, Wilbyrt, Wylbery, Wylbirt, Wylburt, Wylbyrt.

WILBUR (German) Brilliant. *Notable:* Aviator Wilbur Wright. *Variations:* Wilber, Wilburn, Wilburt, Willbur.

WILDER (English) Wilderness. *Variations:* Wild, Wilde, Wyld, Wylde.

WILDON (English) Wild valley. *Variations:* Wildan, Wilden, Wildin, Wildyn, Willdan, Willden, Willdin, Willdon, Willdyn, Wyldan, Wylden, Wyldin, Wyldon, Wyldyn, Wylldan, Wyllden, Wylldin, Wylldon, Wylldyn.

WILEY (English) Water meadow. *Variations:* Wileah, Wilee, Wileigh, Wilie, Willey, Wily, Wylea, Wyleah, Wylee, Wyleigh, Wyley, Wylie, Wyly.

WILFORD (English) River crossing by willow trees. *Notable:* Character-actor Wilford Brimley. *Variation:* Wylford.

WILFRED (English) Purposeful peace. *Variations:* Wilfredo, Wilfrid, Wilfried, Wilfryd.

WILHELM (German) Guardian. *Variations:* Wilhelmus, Willem, Wylhelm.

WILKINS (English) Kin of William. *Variations:* Wilken, Wilkens, Wilkes, Wilkie, Wilkin, Wilikes, Wilikins, Wylkin, Wylkins, Wylkyn, Wylkyns.

WILKINSON (English) Son of little Will. *Variations:* Wilkenson, Wilkes, Wilkie, Wilkins, Willkins, Willkinson, Wylkenson, Wylkinson.

WILL (German) Short form of William. *Notables:* Comedians/actors Will Farrell and Will Smith; humanitarian Will Rogers. *Variation:* Wil.

WILLARD (German) Determined. *Notable:* Weatherman Willard Scott. *Variations:* Wilard, Wylard, Wyllard.

WILLIAM (German) Constant protector. *Notables:* Playwright William Shakespeare; actors William Shatner and William Holden. *Variations:* Bill, Billy, Guillaume, Guillaums, Guillermo, Vila, Vildo, Vilek, Vilem, Vilhelm, Vili, Viliam, Vilkl, Ville, Vilmos, Vilous, Willil.

WILLIAMSON (English) Son of William.

WILLIE (German) Short form of William. *Notable:* Singer Willie Nelson. *Variations:* Willi, Willy.

WILLIS (English) Form of William. *Variations:* Wilis, Williss, Wylis, Wyliss, Wylyss.

WILLOUGHBY (English) Willow tree farm. *Variations:* Willobee, Willobey, Willoughbey, Willoughbie, Willowby.

WILMER (German) Resolute fame. *Notable:* Actor Wilmer Valderrama. *Variations:* Willimar, Willmer, Wylmer.

WILMOT (German) Resolute. *Variation:* Wilmott.

WILNY (Native American) Screaming eagle. *Variations:* Wilni, Wilnie, Wylni, Wylnie, Wylny.

WILSON (English) Son of Will. *Notable:* R&B singer Wilson Pickett. *Variations:* Willsen, Willsin, Willson, Willsun, Willsyn, Wilsen, Wilsin, Wilsun, Wylsen, Wylsin, Wylson, Wylsun.

WILTON (English) Town with a well. *Variations:* Wilt, Willtan, Willten, Willtin, Willton, Willtown, Willtyn, Wiltan, Wilten, Wiltin, Wiltown, Wiltyn, Wyltan, Wylten, Wyltin, Wylton.

WILU (Native American) Warbling chicken hawk.

WINCHELL (English) Road bend. *Variations:* Winchel, Wynchel, Wynchell.

WINDHAM (English) Friend of the town. *Variations:* Win, Winn, Wyndham, Wynne.

WINDSOR (English) From Windsor. *Variation:* Wyndsor.

WINFIELD (English) Friend's field. *Variations:* Winnfield, Wynfield, Wynnfield.

WINFRIED (German) Peaceful friend. *Variations:* Winfredd, Winfrid, Winfryd.

WING (Chinese) Glory.

WINGATE (English) Winding gate.

WINGI (Native American) Willing. *Variations:* Wingie, Wingy, Wyngie, Wyngy.

WINIKENEKE (Hawaiian) To conquer.

WINNEMUCCA (Native American) Chief.

WINSLOW (English) Friend's hill. *Notable:* Artist Winslow Homer. *Variations:* Winslowe, Wynslow.

WINSTON (English) Friend's town. *Notable:* British Prime Minister Winston Churchill. *Variations:* Winstan, Winsten, Winstin, Winstone, Winstonn, Winton, Wynstan, Wynston.

WINTER (English) Born at winter time. *Variations:* Winterford, Winters, Wynter, Wynters.

WINTHROP (English) Friend's village. *Variation:* Wynthrop.

WINWARD (English) My brother's forest. *Variation:* Wynward.

WIREMU (Polynesian) Willful.

WISTAN (German) Wise stone.

WIT (Polish) Life. *Variations:* Witt, Wyt, Wytt.

WITEK (Polish) Victory. *Variation:* Wytek.

WITHA (Arabic) Handsome.

WITTER (English) Wise warrior. *Variations:* Whiter, Whitter.

WITTON (English) From the wise man's town. *Variations:* Whiton, Whytton.

WLADISLAV (Polish) Glorious ruler. *Variations:* Wladislaw, Wladyslav, Wladyslaw, Wtodzistaw.

WLODZIMIERZ (Polish) Famous ruler.

WOJTEK (Polish) Soldier of consolation. *Variation:* Wojteczek.

WOLCOTT (English) Wolf's cottage.

WOLFE (English) Wolf. *Variations:* Wolf, Woolf.

WOLFGANG (German) Wolf fight. *Notables:* Chef Wolfgang Puck; composer Wolfgang Amadeus Mozart.

WOLFRAM (German) Wolf raven. *Variation:* Wolfrem.

WOODFIELD (English) Field in the forest.

WOODFORD (English) River crossing in the forest. *Variation:* Woodforde.

WOODROW (English) Row in the woods. *Notable:* U.S. President Woodrow Wilson.

WOODRUFF (English) Ranger from the forest.

WOODVILLE (English) Forest town.

WOODWARD (English) Protector of the forest. *Variation:* Woodard.

WOODY (American) Short form of Woodrow, Woodward. *Notables:* Writer/director Woody Allen; actor Woody Harrelson. *Variations:* Wood, Woodie, Woodey.

WORTH (English) Enclosed farm. *Variations:* Worthy, Worthey, Worthington.

WRIGHT (English) Carpenter.

WUIRTON (Native American) Thrive.

WULITON (Native American) To succeed.

WUNAND (Native American) God is good.

WUYI (Native American) Flying turkey vulture.

WYANDANCH (Native American) Wise orator. *Variation:* Wiantance.

WYATT (French) Little fighter. *Notable:* Cowboy Wyatt Earp. *Variations:* Wiatt, Wyat.

WYBERT (English) Brilliant at war. *Variations:* Wibert, Wibirt, Wiburt, Wibyrt, Wybirt, Wyburt, Wybyrt.

WYBORN (Norse) War bear. *Variations:* Wibjorn, Wiborn.

WYCLIFF (English) White cliff. *Notable:* Musician Wyclef Jean. *Variations:* Wycliffe, Wyclef.

WYLIE (English) Charming.

WYMAN (English) Warrior. *Variation:* Wymann.

WYNDHAM (English) Town near the path. *Variation:* Windham.

WYNTON (English) Friend. *Notable:* Musician Wynton Marsalis. *Variation:* Winton.

WYNN (English) Friend. *Variations:* Win, Winn, Wynne.

WYNONO (Native American) First-born son.

WYSTAN (English) Battle stone. *Variation:* Wistan.

WYTHE (English) Willow-tree dweller. *Variation:* Withe.

Zodiac Baby: Names by Astrological Sign (Part II)

LEO

BOYS:	GIRLS:
Adam	Judy
Leo	Leona
Rex	Rose

VIRGO

BOYS:	GIRLS:
August	Celeste
Jasper	Elizabeth
Philip	Stella

LIBRA

BOYS:	GIRLS:
Charles	Grace
Nathaniel	Jewel
Luke	Venus

SCORPIO

BOYS:	GIRLS:
Alexander	Alexandra
Daniel	Danielle
Thomas	Topaz

XAN (English) Short form of Alexander.

XANDER (Dutch) Form of Alexander.

XANTHIPPUS (Greek) Light-colored horse. *Variations:* Xanthyppus, Zanthippus, Zanthyppus.

XANTHUS (Greek) Blond. *Variation:* Xanthos.

XANTO (Greek) Blond haired.

XAVER (Spanish) Brilliant. *Variations:* Saveri, Savero, Xavery, Xaviero, Xavyer, Xever, Zabyer, Zavier, Zever.

XAVIER (English; Spanish) New house. *Notable:* Musician Xavier Cugat. *Variations:* Javer, Javerri, Javier, Saveri, Saverio, Savero, Xaver, Xavery, Xaviero, Xavyer, Xever, Zabyer, Zavier, Zever.

XAYVION (African American) The new house. *Variations:* Savion, Sayveon, Sayvion, Xavion, Xayveon, Zayvion.

XENON (Greek) Stranger.

XENOPHON (Greek) Foreign voice.

XENOS (Greek) Guest. *Variations:* Xeno, Zenos.

XERXES (Persian) Ruler. Jerez, Xeres, Xerus, Zerk, Zerzes.

XERYUS (Greek) The name of a bright star. *Variation:* Xeyrus.

XEVACH (Hebrew) Sacrifice. *Variation:* Zevach.

XEVADIAH (Hebrew) God will live. *Variations:* Xevadia, Zevadia, Zevaddiah.

XEVEN (Slavic) Lively. *Variations:* Xyven, Ziven, Zyven, Zyvyn.

XEVULUM (Hebrew) Home. *Variation:* Zevulum.

XIANG (Chinese) To soar. Fragrant.

XIAOPING (Chinese) Small bottle.

XIMEN (Spanish) Obedient. *Variations:* Ximenes, Ximon, Ximun.

XIMENES (Spanish) Listening. A form of Simon. *Variations:* Ximene, Xymen, Xymenes, Xymon, Zimene, Zimenes, Zimon, Zymen, Zymene, Zymenes.

XIMON (Spanish) Simon.

XIMRAAN (Arabic) Celebration. *Variations:* Zimraan, Zymraan.

XIMRAN (Hebrew) Sacred. *Variations:* Xymran, Zimran, Zymran.

XINDEL (Hebrew) Protector of humankind. *Variations:* Xyndel, Zindel, Zyndel.

XING-FU (Chinese) Happiness.

XION (Hebrew) From the guarded land. *Variations:* Xyon, Zion, Zyon.

XITOMER (Czech) Living fame. *Variations:* Xytomer, Zitomer, Zytomer.

XI-WANG (Chinese) Desire.

XOLANI (African) You all have peace. Take it easy.

XOWIE (Greek) Life. *Variations:* Xoe, Xowy, Zoe, Zoey.

XUAN (Vietnamese) Spring.

XUN (Chinese) Fast.

XYLON (Greek) One who lives in the forest.

YAAR (Hebrew) Forest.

YADAVA (Sanskrit) Descended. *Variation:* Yadav.

YADID (Hebrew) Beloved.

YADIN (Hebrew) God will judge. *Variation:* Yadon.

YAFEU (African) Bold.

YAGEL (Hebrew) Happiness. *Variations:* Yagil, Yagyl, Yogil, Yogyl.

YAHOLO (Native American) One who hollers.

YAHYA (Arabic) God is good. *Variation:* Yihya.

YAIR (Hebrew) God will teach. *Variation:* Jair.

YAJNA (Sanskrit) Sacrifice. *Variation:* Yajanah.

YAKAR (Hebrew) Dear. *Variation:* Yakir.

YAKECEN (Native American) Song from the sky.

YAKEZ (Native American) Heaven.

YAKIM (Hebrew) God develops. *Variation:* Jakim.

YAKOV (Russian) Form of Jacob. *Notable:* Comedian Yakov Smirnoff. *Variation:* Yankov.

YAKIR (Hebrew) Honored. *Variation:* Yakire.

YALE (Welsh) Fertile moor.

YAMA (Sanskrit) God of the setting sun. *Variation:* Yamah.

YAMAL (Hindi) One of a twin.

YAMIN (Hebrew) Right hand. *Variation:* Jamin.

YANA (Hebrew) He answers. *Variations:* Janai, Jannai, Yan, Yannai.

YANCY (Native American) Englishman. *Variations:* Yance, Yancey, Yantsey.

YANDACH (Hebrew) Restful.

YANEK (Dutch) God is gracious.

YANKA (Russian) God is good.

YANKEL (Yiddish) Form of Jacob.

YANNIS (Greek) God is good. Variation of John. *Variations:* Yannakis, Yanni, Yiannis.

YANOACH (Hebrew) Rest.

YAPHET (Hebrew) Attractive. *Notable:* Actor Yaphet Kotto. *Variations:* Japhet, Japheth, Yapheth.

YAQUB (Arabic) Supplanter. Form of Jacob. *Variation:* Yaqoob.

YARB (Gypsy) Herb.

YARDAN (Arabic) King.

YARDLEY (English) Enclosed meadow. *Variations:* Yardlea, Yardlee, Yardleigh, Yardly.

YARIN (Hebrew) To understand.

YARON (Hebrew) To sing.

YASAHIRO (Japanese) Peaceful.

YASAR (Arabic) Wealth. *Variations:* Yaser, Yasir, Yasser, Yassir.

YASH (Hindi) Glorious.

YASHAR (Hebrew) Honorable and moral. *Variations:* Yesher, Yeshurun.

YASHASKAR (Hindi) One who brings fame.

YASIN (Arabic) Prophet.

YASUO (Japanese) Calm.

YATES (English) Gates. *Variation:* Yeats.

YAVIN (Hebrew) God is understanding. *Variation:* Yavnie.

YAZID (African) To increase.

YE (Chinese) Universe.

YECHEZKEL (Hebrew) God strengthens. *Variations:* Chaskel, Chatzkel, Keskel.

YEHOCHANAN (Hebrew) God is good. *Variations:* Yochanan, Yohannan.

YEHONATAN (Hebrew) God provides.

YEHORAM (Hebrew) God will praise. *Variation:* Yoram.

YEHOSHUA (Hebrew) God is salvation. *Variation:* Yeshua.

YEHOYAKIM (Hebrew) God will establish. *Variations:* Jehoiakim, Yehoiakim, Yoyakim.

YEHUDI (Hebrew) A man from Judah; someone who is Jewish. *Notable:* Violinist Yehudi Menuhin. *Variations:* Yechudi, Yechudil, Yehuda, Yehudah.

YELUTCI (Native American) Quiet bear.

YEMON (Japanese) Guardian.

YEN (Vietnamese) Calm.

YEOMAN (English) Servant.

YERED (Hebrew) To come down. *Variation:* Jered.

YERIEL (Hebrew) Founded by God. *Variation:* Jeriel.

YERIK (Russian) God is exalted. *Variation:* Yeremey.

YESHAYAHU (Hebrew) God saves. *Variation:* Yeshaya.

YESHE (Tibetan) Wise one.

YESTIN (French) Righteous. *Variations:* Yestan, Yesten, Yeston, Yestyn.

YEVGENI (Russian) Well born. *Variations:* Yevgeniy, Yevgeny.

YIGAEL (Hebrew) God will redeem. *Variations:* Yagel, Yigal.

YIN-HSIN (Chinese) The one force.

YIRMEYAHU (Hebrew) God will restore.

YISHACHAR (Hebrew) Reward. *Variations:* Issachar, Sachar, Yisaschar.

YISRAEL (Hebrew) Israel.

YITRO (Hebrew) Plenty. *Variation:* Yitran.

YITZCHAK (Hebrew) Laughter. *Notable:* Israeli statesman Yitzhak Rabin. *Variations:* Itzhak, Yitzaac, Yitzaack, Yitzaak, Yitzack, Yitzak, Yitzhak.

YMIR (Scandinavian) Ancient mythological figure.

YO (Chinese) Bright.

YOAKIM (Slavic) Form of Jacob.

YOGI (Sanskrit) One who practices yoga. *Variations:* Yogee, Yogey, Yogie, Yogy.

YOHAN (Hebrew) God is gracious. *Variation:* Yohann.

YONA (Native American) Bear; (Hebrew) Dove. *Variations:* Yonah, Yonas.

YONATAN (Hebrew) Gift from God.

YONG (Chinese) Brave.

YONG-SUN (Korean) Courageous.

YORA (Hebrew) Teacher. *Variation:* Yorah.

YORATH (English) Worthy god. *Variations:* Iolo, Iorwerth.

YORICK (English) Farmer.

YORK (English) Yew tree. *Variations:* Yorick, Yorke, Yorrick.

YOSEF (Hebrew) God increases. *Variations:* Yoseff, Yosif, Yousef, Yusef, Yusif, Yusuf, Yuzef.

YOSHA (Hebrew) Wisdom.

YOSHI (Japanese) Quiet.

YOSHIRO (Japanese) Good son.

YOTIMO (Native American) Bee flying to its hive.

YOTTOKO (Native American) Mud from the river.

YOUKIOMA (Native American) Flawless. *Variations:* Youkeoma, Yukeoma, Yukioma.

YOUNG (Korean) Forever.

YOUNG-JA (Korean) Forever stable.

YOUNG-JAE (Korean) Forever prosperous.

YOUNG-NAM (Korean) Forever south.

YOUNG-SOO (Korean) Forever rich.

YOUSEF (Arabic) Form of Joseph. *Variation:* Youssef.

YUAN (Chinese) Round.

YUCEL (Turkish) Noble.

YUKIKO (Japanese) Snow. *Variations:* Yuki, Yukio.

YUL (Chinese) Past the horizon. *Notable:* Actor Yul Brynner.

YULE (English) Christmas.

YUMA (Native American) Son of the chief.

YUNIS (Arabic) Dove. *Variations:* Younis, Yunus.

YURCHIK (Russian) Farmer. Variation of George. *Variations:* Yura, Yuri, Yurik, Yurko, Yurli, Yury.

YURI (Russian) Farmer.

YUSHUA (Arabic) God's help. *Variation:* Yusha.

YUSTYN (Russian) Just.

YUSUF (Arabic) God will increase. *Variations:* Youssef, Yousuf, Yusef, Yusif, Yussef.

YUTU (Native American) Coyote hunting.

YUVAL (Hebrew) Brook. *Variation:* Jubal.

YVAN (Russian) God is gracious. *Variations:* Yven, Yvin.

YVES (French) Yew wood. *Notables:* Designer Yves St. Laurent; actor Yves Montand. *Variations:* Evo, Iveo, Ives, Yvo, Yvon.

YWAIN (Welsh) Well born.

ZABDIEL (Hebrew) Gift. *Variations:* Zabdi, Zabdil, Zavdiel, Zebdiel.

ZACCHEUS (Hebrew) Pure.

ZACH (American) God remembers. Short form of Zachary or Zachariah. *Notable:* Actor Zach Braff. *Variations:* Zac, Zacher, Zack, Zacker, Zak, Zaker, Zako.

ZACHARIAH (Hebrew) God remembers. *Variations:* Zacaria, Zaccaria, Zacchaeus, Zacharia, Zackaria, Zackariah.

ZACHARIAS (German) God remembers. Form of Zachariah. *Variations:* Zacarias, Zacharyasz, Zackerias, Zakarias, Zakarius, Zakaryas, Zakarys, Zakaryus.

ZACHARY (Hebrew) God remembers. Popular form of Zachariah. *Notable:* U.S. President Zachary Taylor. *Variations:* Zacarey, Zacary, Zaccarie, Zaccary, Zachaery, Zacharay, Zacharey, Zacharie, Zacharry, Zachery, Zachory, Zachry, Zackary, Zackery, Zackory, Zackury, Zakarie, Zakary, Zakerie, Zakery.

ZADOK (Hebrew) Righteous. *Variations:* Zadak, Zadoc, Zadock.

ZAFAR (Arabic) To win. *Variation:* Zafir.

ZAHAVI (Hebrew) Gold.

ZAHID (Arabic) Strict.

ZAHIR (Hebrew) Bright. *Variations:* Zaheer, Zahur.

ZAHUR (Arabic) Flower.

ZAIDE (Hebrew) Aging. *Variations:* Zaid, Zaiden.

ZAIM (Arabic) General.

ZAKAI (Hebrew) Pure. *Variation:* Zakkai.

ZAKARIYYA (Arabic) God knows.

ZAKI (Arabic) Smart. Full of virtue.

ZAKUR (Hebrew) Masculine. *Variation:* Zaccur.

ZALE (Greek) Strength from the sea. *Variations:* Zail, Zaile, Zayle.

ZALMAN (Hebrew) Peaceful. *Variations:* Zalmen, Zalmin, Zalmon, Zalmyn.

ZAMIEL (German) God has heard. Variation of Samuel.

ZAMIR (Hebrew) Song. *Variations:* Zamar, Zameer, Zamer, Zamyr.

ZAN (Hebrew) Well fed.

ZANDER (Greek) Defender of mankind. Short form of Alexander. *Variations:* Zandar, Zandor, Zandyr.

ZANE (English) God is good. Variation of John. *Notable:* Writer Zane Grey. *Variations:* Zain, Zaine, Zayne.

ZANTHUS (Greek) Blond.

ZAREB (African) Guardian.

ZARED (Hebrew) Trap. *Variations:* Zarad, Zarid, Zarod.

ZAREK (Polish) May God protect the king. *Variations:* Zarec, Zareck, Zaric, Zarick, Zaryck, Zaryk.

ZAVAD (Hebrew) Present. *Variation:* Zabad.

ZAVDIEL (Hebrew) Gift from God. *Variations:* Zabdiel, Zebedee.

ZAVIER (Arabic) Brilliant. Form of Xavier.

ZAYD (Arabic) To increase. *Variations:* Zaid, Zayed, Ziyad.

ZAYN (Arabic) Beauty.

ZBIGNIEW (Polish) To get rid of anger. *Notable:* Political scientist Zbigniew Brzezinski. *Variations:* Zbyszek, Zbyszko.

ZBYHNEV (Czech) Rid of anger. *Variations:* Zbyna, Zbynek, Zbysek.

ZDENEK (Czech) God of wine. *Variations:* Zdenecek, Zdenko, Zdenousek, Zdicek.

ZDESLAV (Czech) Glory is here. *Variations:* Zdik, Zdisek, Zdislav.

ZDZISLAW (Polish) Glory is here. *Variations:* Zdzich, Zdziech, Zdziesz, Zdzieszko, Zdzis, Zdzisiek.

ZEBADIAH (Hebrew) Gift from God. *Variations:* Zeb, Zebediah.

ZEBEDEE (Hebrew) God's gift. Form of Zebadiah.

ZEBULON (Hebrew) To exalt. *Variations:* Zebulen, Zebulun.

ZEDEKIAH (Hebrew) God is just. *Variations:* Tzedekia, Tzidkiya, Zed, Zedechiah, Zedekia, Zedekias.

ZEEMAN (Dutch) Seaman. *Variations:* Zeaman, Zeman, Zemen, Ziman, Zimen.

ZE'EV (Hebrew) Wolf.

ZEHARIAH (Hebrew) Light of God. *Variations:* Zeharia, Zeharya.

ZEHEB (Turkish) Gold.

ZEIRA (Aramaic) Small. *Variations:* Zeirah, Zeyra, Zeyrah.

ZEKE (Hebrew) The strength of God.

ZEKI (Turkish) Smart.

ZELFIRINO (Greek) Spring wind.

ZELIG (Hebrew) Holy.

ZELIMIR (Slavic) Desires peace.

ZEMARIAH (Hebrew) Song. *Variations:* Zemaria, Zemarya.

ZENAS (Greek) Generous. *Variations:* Zeno, Zenon.

ZENDA (Czech) Well born.

ZENO (Greek) From Zeus.

ZENOBIAS (Greek) Given life by Zeus. *Variations:* Zenobia, Zenobiah, Zenobio.

ZEPHANIAH (Hebrew) Protection. *Variations:* Zenphan, Zenphaniah, Zeph, Zephan.

ZEPHYR (Greek) West wind. *Variation:* Zephyrus.

ZERACH (Hebrew) Light. *Variations:* Zerachia, Zerachya, Zerack, Zerah, Zerak.

ZEREM (Hebrew) Stream.

ZERIKA (Hebrew) Rain shower.

ZERO (Arabic) Worthless. *Notable:* Actor Zero Mostel.

ZEROUN (Armenian) Respected.

ZESIRO (African) First born of twins.

ZETH (Greek) Investigator.

ZETHAN (Hebrew) Shining. *Variations:* Zethen, Zethin, Zethon, Zethyn.

ZETHUS (Greek) Son of Zeus.

ZEUS (Greek) Living. King of the gods. *Variations:* Zeno, Zenon, Zinon.

ZEV (Hebrew) Short form of Zevach, Zevariah, Zeviel.

ZEVACH (Hebrew) Sacrifice. *Variations:* Zevachia, Zevachtah, Zevachya, Zevah.

ZEVADIAH (Hebrew) God bestows. *Variations:* Zevadia, Zevadya, Zevaria, Zevariah.

ZEVID (Hebrew) Present.

ZEVIEL (Hebrew) Gazelle of God. *Variations:* Zevial, Zevyel.

ZEVULUN (Hebrew) House. *Variations:* Zebulon, Zebulun, Zevul.

ZHIXIN (Chinese) Ambitious.

ZHONG (Chinese) Second brother.

ZHU (Chinese) Wish.

ZHUANG (Chinese) Strong.

ZIGFRIED (Russian) Victory and peace. Form of Siegfried.

ZIGGY (American) Victory. Form of Siegfried or Sigmund.

ZIGMUND (Russian) Victory shield. Form of Sigmund.

ZIKOMO (African) Thank you.

ZILPAH (Hebrew) Trickling water. *Variations:* Zilpa, Zylpa, Zylpah.

ZIMEN (Spanish) Obedient. *Variations:* Ziman, Zimin, Zimyn, Zymen, Zymin.

ZIMON (Hebrew) Listening. A form of Simon. *Variation:* Zymon.

ZIMRA (Hebrew) Sacred. *Variations:* Zemora, Zimrat, Zimri, Zimriah.

ZIMRAAN (Arabic) Celebrated.

ZIMRI (Hebrew) Valuable.

ZINAN (Japanese) Second son.

ZINDEL (Hebrew) Protector of mankind. *Variations:* Zindell, Zindil, Zyndel.

ZION (Hebrew) Guarded land. *Variations:* Tzion, Zyon.

ZIPKIYAH (Native American) Big bow. *Variations:* Zipkoeete, Zipkoheta.

ZISKIND (Yiddish) Sweet child.

ZITKADUTA (Native American) Red bird.

ZITOMER (Czech) To live in fame. *Variations:* Zitek, Zitousek.

ZIV (Hebrew) To shine. *Variations:* Zivan, Zivi.

ZIVAN (Czech) Alive. *Variations:* Zivanek, Zivek, Zivko.

ZIVEN (Slavic) Lively. *Variations:* Ziv, Zivon.

ZIYA (Arabic) Light. *Variations:* Zia, Ziah, Ziyah, Zya, Zyah.

ZIYAD (Arabic) To increase.

ZLATAN (Czech) Golden. *Variations:* Zlatek, Zlaticek, Zlatik, Zlatko, Zlatousek.

ZOHAR (Hebrew) Bright light.

ZOILO (Greek) Lively.

ZOIS (Greek) Life.

ZOLA (German) Prince. *Variations:* Zolah, Zolla.

ZOLLY (Hebrew) Peace. Form of Sol. *Variations:* Zollie, Zolio.

ZOLTIN (Hungarian) Life. *Variations:* Zsolt, Zsoltan, Zoltan, Zolten, Zoltin, Zoltun, Zoltyn.

ZOMEIR (Hebrew) One who prunes trees. *Variation:* Zomer.

ZOMELIS (Lithuanian) Asked of God.

ZORBA (Greek) Live to fullest.

ZORO (Persian) Star. *Variation:* Zorro.

ZORYA (Slavic) Star.

ZOSIMO (Greek) Lively. *Variations:* Zosime, Zosimos, Zosimus, Zosyme.

ZOTOM (Native American) One who bites.

ZOWIE (Greek) Life.

ZSIGA (Hungarian) Victorious. *Variations:* Zsigah, Zsyga, Zyga.

ZSOLT (Polish) Ruler.

ZUBERI (African) Strong.

ZUBIN (Russian) Toothy. *Notable:* Music conductor Zubin Mehta. *Variations:* Zuban, Zuben, Zubon, Zubyn.

ZUHAYR (Arabic) Young flowers. *Variation:* Zuhair.

ZURIEL (Hebrew) The Lord is my rock.

ZVI (Hebrew) Deer.

ZWI (Scandinavian) Gazelle.

ZYGMUNT (Polish) Victorious protection.

ZYLON (Greek) Forest dweller. *Variations:* Xylon, Zilon.

CHAPTER 3

Girls' Names

AADI (Hindi) Child of the beginning. *Variations:* Aadie, Aady, Aadee, Aadea.

AALIYAH (Hebrew) To ascend. Form of Aliya. *Notable:* R&B singer/ actress Aaliyah.

AANANDINI (Hindi) Happy. *Variation:* Ananda.

AARALYN (American) Woman with song. *Variations:* Aaralin, Aralyn.

AARTI (Hindi) Prosperous. *Variation:* Arti.

AASE (Norse) From the tree-covered mountain.

ABA (African) Born on Thursday.

ABABUO (African) A child who keeps coming back.

ABAGBE (African) Much-desired child.

ABAM (African) Second child born after twins.

ABARRANE (Hebrew) Mother of nations. *Variation:* Abarane.

ABAYOMI (African) Happiness.

ABBY (English) Short form of Abigail. *Variations:* Abbe, Abbey, Abbi, Abbie, Abi, Aby.

ABEBI (African) We asked for her and she came to us. *Variations:* Abeje, Abeni.

ABEDA (African) Delicate woman. *Variations:* Abedah, Abeeda, Abeedah, Abeida, Abieda, Abiedah.

ABELA (French) Breath, sigh. *Variations:* Abelah, Abella, Abelia, Abellah.

ABELARDA (German) Feminine form of Abelard. Highborn.

ABELIA (Hebrew) A sigh. Feminine version of Abel. *Variations:* Abella, Abelle.

ABELLONA (Danish) Feminine version of Apollo. *Variations:* Abbelina, Abbeline, Abelone, Apolline, Apollinia, Appoline, Appolinia.

ABENA (African) Born on Tuesday. *Variations:* Abenah, Abeena, Abina, Abyna.

ABERDEEN (Scottish) Woman from Aberdeen. *Variation:* Aberdine.

ABERTHA (Welsh) Sacrificed.

ABHA (Hindi) Light. *Variations:* Aabha, Aabhaa, Abhaa.

ABIA (Arabic) Great.

ABIAH (Hebrew) God is my father. *Variations:* Abia, Abiya, Avia, Aviah, Aviya.

ABICHAYIL (Hebrew) Strong father. *Variations:* Avichayil, Avihayil.

ABIDA (Hebrew) Of knowledge. *Variations:* Abeeda, Abeida, Abidah, Abieda.

ABIELA (Hebrew) My father is the Lord. *Variations:* Abiella, Aviela, Aviella.

ABIGAIL (Hebrew) Father's joy. *Notables:* Advice columnist Abigail Van Buren (more commonly known as Dear Abby); second U.S. First Lady, Abigail Adams. *Variations:* Abagael, Abagail, Abagale, Abbey, Abbi, Abbie, Abbiegayle, Abbigael, Abbigail, Abbigale, Abby, Abbye, Abbygael, Abbygail, Abbygale, Abigaille, Abigale, Abigayle, Avigail.

ABELIA (Hebrew) A sigh. *Variations:* Abela, Abella, Abelle.

ABELINA (American) Feminine version of Abel.

ABILA (Spanish) Beautiful one. *Variation:* Abyla.

ABILENE (American) From a town in Texas. *Variations:* Abalene, Abilena, Abilyn.

ABIONA (African) Born during a trip.

ABIR (Arabic) Fragrant. *Variations:* Abyr, Abhir.

ABIRA (Hebrew) Strong. *Variations:* Abirah, Abeera, Abeerah.

ABITAL (Hebrew) My father is the dew. *Variation:* Avital.

ABRA (Hebrew) Mother of many children. *Variations:* Abriana, Abrietta.

ABRIANA (Italian) Mother of nations. *Variations:* Abrianna, Abrianne.

ABRIELLE (French) Protection. *Variations:* Abriella, Abrial, Abriel.

ABRIL (Spanish) April. Spring.

ACACIA (Greek) Of the acacia tree. *Variations:* Cacia, Casia.

ACADIA (Native American) Village.

ACANTHA (Greek) Thorny.

ACCALIA (Latin) In mythology, foster mother of Romulus and Remus. *Variations:* Acalia, Acalya, Ackalia.

ACELINE (French) Highborn woman. *Variations:* Acela, Acelin, Asceline, Acelynn.

ACENITH (African) Goddess of love.

ACHALA (Hindi) Steady. *Variation:* Achalaa.

ACHAVA (Hebrew) Friendship.

ACHSAH (Hebrew) Ankle bracelet.

ACIMA (Hebrew) God will judge. *Variations:* Achima, Achimah.

ACTON (English) A town in England.

ADA (German) Nobility. *Variations:* Adah, Aida, Aidah.

ADABELLE (American) Combined form of Ada and Belle. *Variations:* Adabel, Adabella.

ADAIR (Scottish) The oak-tree ford. *Variations:* Adaira, Adaire, Adare.

ADALEE (American) Combined form of Ada and Lee. *Variation:* Adaley.

ADALHEIDIS (Scandinavian) Noble one. *Variations:* Aalt, Aaltje, Adalheid, Adelheid, Aleida, Alida.

ADALIA (Hebrew) God as protector.

ADAMA (African) Majestic and regal. *Variations:* Adamah, Adamma.

ADAMINA (Hebrew) Woman of the earth. Feminine version of Adam. *Variations:* Adameena, Adamia.

ADANNA (African) Mother's pride. *Variations:* Adana, Adanne, Adanya.

ADARA (Greek) Lovely woman.

ADDIE (American) Nickname for Adelaide, Addison, et. al. *Variations:* Adi, Addee, Addi, Addy.

ADDILYN (American) Form of Adeline. *Variations:* Adalyn, Adalynn, Addalyn, Adelin, Adelyn.

ADDISON (English) Daughter of Adam. *Variations:* Addisyn, Adison, Adisyn, Addyson.

ADEEN (Irish) Bright little fire. *Variations:* Adeane, Adeyn.

ADELAIDE (English) Nobel and quiet. *Variations:* Adal, Adala, Adalaid, Adalaide, Adalee, Adali,

Adalie, Adalley, Addal, Adelaida, Adele, Adelia, Adelice, Adelicia, Adeline, Adelis, Adell, Adella, Adelle, Della, Edeline, Eline.

ADELE (French) Form of Adelaide. *Variations:* Adela, Adelia, Adelie, Adell, Adella, Adelle.

ADELEKE (African) The crown brings happiness.

ADELINE (German) Noble. *Variations:* Adalina, Adaline, Adelaine, Adelina, Adoline.

ADELISE (German) Form of Adeline. *Variations:* Adelisa, Adelita, Adeliza.

ADELPHA (Greek) Caring sister. *Variation:* Adelfa.

ADEOLA (African) Crown. *Variations:* Adola, Dola.

ADERES (Hebrew) Cape. *Variations:* Aderet, Aderetz.

ADERYN (Welsh) Bird-like child. *Variations:* Aderin, Aderine.

ADESIMBO (African) Noble birth.

ADESINA (African) Child of many more to come.

ADHIKA (Hindi) Increase.

ADHITA (Hindi) Student. *Variations:* Adhita, Adita, Aditi.

ADIA (English) Wealthy. *Variations:* Adea, Adiah, Adiana.

ADIANCA (Native American) Bringing peace. *Variation:* Adianka.

ADIBA (Arabic) Cultured, refined. *Variation:* Adibah.

ADIELA (Hebrew) Adornment of God. *Variation:* Adiella.

ADIENA (Welsh) Woman of beauty. *Variations:* Addiena, Adienne.

ADILA (Arabic) Just. *Variation:* Adilah.

ADINA (Hebrew) Delicate. *Variations:* Adeana, Adin, Adine.

ADIRA (Hebrew) Powerful woman. *Variations:* Adiera, Adirah, Adyra.

ADISHREE (Hindi) Exhalted.

ADIVA (Arabic) Gentle.

ADMINA (Hebrew) Daughter of red earth. *Variation:* Adminah.

ADOLPHA (German) Noble wolf. Feminine version of Adolph. *Variation:* Adolfa.

ADONIA (Greek) Beauty. *Variations:* Adona, Adoniah, Adonna.

ADONCIA (Spanish) Sweet.

ADORA (Latin) Much adored. *Variations:* Adoree, Adoria, Adorlee, Dora, Dori, Dorie, Dorrie.

ADORABELLA (Latin) Beautiful woman.

ADORACION (Spanish) One who is adored.

ADRA (Arabic) Virginal.

ADRIA (Latin) Dark. From the sea. *Variations:* Adrea, Adreea, Adria, Adriah, Adrie.

ADRIANA (Italian; Spanish; English) Dark, exotic one. *Variations:* Adrian, Adriane, Adrianna, Adriannah, Adrianne, Adrien, Adriena, Adrienah, Adrienne.

ADRIEL (Hebrew) God's flock. *Variations:* Adriela, Adriella, Adrielle.

ADRINA (Italian) Having great happiness. *Variations:* Adreen, Adreena, Adrinna.

ADRITA (Sanskrit) Respected woman.

Top Names of the 1950s

BOYS:
1. James
2. Michael
3. Robert
4. John
5. David
6. William
7. Richard
8. Thomas
9. Mark
10. Charles
11. Steven
12. Gary
13. Joseph
14. Donald
15. Ronald
16. Kenneth
17. Paul
18. Larry
19. Daniel
20. Stephen

GIRLS:
1. Mary
2. Linda
3. Patricia
4. Susan
5. Deborah
6. Barbara
7. Debra
8. Karen
9. Nancy
10. Donna
11. Cynthia
12. Sandra
13. Pamela
14. Sharon
15. Kathleen
16. Carol
17. Diane
18. Brenda
19. Cheryl
20. Janet

ADSILA (Native American) Blossom.

ADYA (Hindi) Born on Sunday.

AE-CHA (Korean) Loving daughter.

AEGINA (Greek) Ancient mythological figure. Sea nymph. *Variations:* Aegea, Aegena.

AELWEN (Welsh) Woman with fair brow. *Variations:* Aelwin, Aelwyn.

AELWYD (Welsh) From the hearth.

AENEA (Greek) Worthy.

AEOLA (Greek) Goddess of the winds.

AERIN (Irish) Form of Erin. *Variation:* Aerinn.

AERONA (Welsh) From the river.

AERWYNA (English) Friend of the ocean.

AETHRA (Greek) Ancient mythological figure.

AFAF (Arabic) Virtuous. *Variations:* Afifa, Afifah.

AFAFA (African) First child from second husband.

AFEI (Polynesian) Wrap around.

AFINA (Hebrew) Young doe. *Variation:* Aphina.

AFIYA (African) Health.

AFRA (Hebrew) Young doe. *Variation:* Aphra.

AFRAIMA (Hebrew) Fertile.

AFREDA (English) Elf counselor. *Variations:* Afreida, Afrieda.

AFRICA (Celtic) Pleasant. *Variation:* Afrika.

AFTON (English) From Afton, England. *Variations:* Aften, Aftin.

AGAPI (Greek) Affectionate. *Variations:* Agape, Agappe.

AGATE (English) Semiprecious stone.

AGATHA (Greek) Good. *Notable:* Mystery writer Agatha Christie. *Variations:* Aga, Agace, Agacia, Agafia, Agasha, Agata, Agate, Agathe, Agathi, Agatta, Ageneti, Aggi, Aggie, Aggy, Akeneki.

AGAVE (Greek) Noble.

AGHAMORA (Irish) From the vast meadow.

AGLAIA (Greek) Splendor and glory. *Variation:* Agalia.

AGNES (English; German; French; Scandinavian) Chaste. *Notable:* Actress Agnes Moorehead. *Variations:* Agnella, Agnesa, Agnesca, Agnese, Agnesina, Agneska, Agness, Agnessa, Agneta, Agnetha, Agneti, Agnetta, Agnieszka, Agnola, Agnolah, Agnolla, Agnolle, Nesa, Ness, Nessa, Nessi, Nessia, Nessie, Nessy, Nesta, Senga, Ynes, Ynesita, Ynez.

AGOSTINA (Latin) August.

AGRACIANA (Spanish) Forgiving. *Variation:* Agracianne.

AGRIPPINA (Latin) Born feet first. *Variations:* Agrafina, Agrippa, Agrippine.

AGRONA (Celtic) Goddess of war and death. *Variations:* Agronia, Agronna.

AHALYA (Hindi) Beautiful.

AHAVA (Hebrew) Beloved. *Variations:* Ahavah, Ahavat, Ahouva, Ahuda, Ahuva.

AHELIA (Hebrew) Breath. *Variations:* Ahelea, Ahelya.

AHELLONA (Greek) Woman with masculine qualities. *Variation:* Ahelona.

AHINOAM (Hebrew) Biblical: One of David's wives.

AHLADITA (Indian) Cheerful.

AHULANI (Hawaiian) Heavenly shrine.

AHUVA (Hebrew) Dearly loved. *Variations:* Ahuda, Ahuva.

AI (Japanese) One who is loved.

AIDA (Arabic) Reward. *Notable:* Actress Aida Turturro. *Variations:* Ayda, Aidee.

AIDAN (Irish) Fire. *Variations:* Aidana, Aydana, Edana.

AIDEEN (Irish) Unknown definition. *Variations:* Adene, Etain.

AIKEN (English) Oak tree.

AIKO (Japanese) Little one.

AILA (Scottish) Protected place. *Variation:* Aili.

AILAINA (Scottish) Rock. *Variations:* Alaine, Alanis.

AILBHE (Irish) Of noble character. *Variations:* Ailesh, Ailish, Ailith.

AILEEN (Scottish) Light. *Variations:* Ailee, Ailene, Ailey, Aleen, Alene, Aline, Alleen, Allene, Alline, Eileen, Ilene.

AILIS (Irish) Noble and kind.

AILLA (Gaelic) Great beauty. *Variation:* Aille.

AILNA (German) Sweet and pleasant. *Variation:* Ailne.

AILSA (Gaelic) Scottish island.

AIMEE (French) Beloved. Form of Amy. *Variations:* Aimie, Amie.

AIMILIONA (Irish) Hard working.

AINAKEA (Hawaiian) Fair earth.

AINALAN (Hawaiian) Heavenly earth.

AINANANI (Hawaiian) Beautiful earth.

AINARA (Basque) Swallow.

AINE (Celtic) Brightness and joy.

AINHOA (Basque) Chaste.

AINSLEY (Scottish) A meadow. *Variations:* Ainslee, Ainsleigh, Ainslie, Ansley, Aynslee, Aynsley.

AIONIA (Greek) Everlasting life. *Variations:* Aionea, Ayonia.

AIRIC (Celtic) Pleasant and agreeable. *Variation:* Aeric.

AIRLIA (Greek) Ethereal. *Variations:* Airlea, Airlie.

AISHA (Arabic; African) Life. *Notable:* TV personality Aisha Tyler. *Variations:* Aishah, Aisia, Aisiah, Asha, Ashah, Ashia, Ashiah, Asia, Asiah, Ayeesa, Ayeesah, Ayeesha, Ayeeshah, Ayeisa.

AISLING (Irish) Dream. *Variations:* Aesling, Aislin, Aislinn, Aislyn, Aislynn, Ashling, Isleen.

AITANA (Portuguese) Glorious one.

AITHERIA (Greek) Of the wind. *Variation:* Aytherea.

AITHNE (Irish) Small fire. Feminine version of Aidan. *Variations:* Aithnea, Eithne, Ethnah, Ethnea, Ethnee.

AIYANA (Native American) Eternally beautiful.

AJA (Hindi) Goat. *Variations:* Aija, Ajia.

AJAYA (Hindi) Invincible. *Variations:* Ajay Ajeya.

AKAKA (Hawaiian) Good. Hawaiian version of Agatha.

AKAKO (Japanese) Red.

AKALA (Hawaiian) Raspberries.

AKAMAI (Hawaiian) Wise.

AKAULA (Hawaiian) Sunset.

AKELA (Hawaiian) Noble. *Variations:* Akala, Akayla.

AKI (Japanese) Born in autumn.

AKIA (African) First born. *Variation:* Akiah.

AKIKO (Japanese) Bright light.

AKILAH (Arabic) Wise and logical. *Variations:* Akeela, Akeelah, Akila.

AKILI (Tanzanian) Possessing great wisdom. *Variations:* Akilee, Akilli, Akylie.

AKILINA (Latin) Like an eagle. *Variations:* Akileena, Akiline, Akylina.

AKINA (Japanese) Spring flower. *Variation:* Akeena.

AKIRA (Japanese) Intelligent.

AKIVA (Hebrew) Shelter. *Variations:* Kiba, Kibah, Kiva, Kivah.

AKSANA (Russian) Hospitality. *Variation:* Oksana.

ALA (Hawaiian) Fragrant.

ALABAMA (American) From Alabama.

ALAIA (Arabic) Virtuous.

ALAIR (French) Cheerful disposition. *Variations:* Alaire, Alare.

ALALA (Greek) Protected.

ALAMEDA (Spanish) Poplar tree.

ALANA (English) Pretty. *Notable:* TV personality Alana Stewart. *Variations:* Alaina, Alane, Alanna, Alannah, Alayna, Alayne, Alena, Alene, Alenne, Aleyna, Aleynah, Aleyne, Allaine, Allayne, Alleen, Alleine, Allena, Allene, Alleynah, Alleyne, Allina, Allinah, Allyna, Allynn, Allynne, Alynne.

ALANI (Hawaiian) Orange.

ALANIS (English) Form of Alana. *Notable:* Singer Alanis Morissette. *Variation:* Alannis.

ALANZA (Spanish) Feminine form of Alonzo.

ALARICE (Greek) Noble. *Variations:* Alara, Alarica.

ALASKA (Native American) From the great land.

ALASTRINA (Scottish) Defender of mankind. *Variations:* Alastriana, Alastrin, Alastriona.

ALAUDA (French) Lark.

ALAULA (Hawaiian) Dawn.

ALAURA (Latin) Form of Laura. A laurel.

ALBA (Latin) White. *Variations:* Albane, Albina, Albine, Albinia, Albinka, Alva.

ALBANY (Latin) From the white hill.

ALBERGA (Latin) Noble. Inn. *Variation:* Alberge.

ALBERTA (English) Noble. *Variations:* Albertha, Albertina, Albertine, Albertyna, Elberta, Elbertina, Elbertine.

ALBINA (Italian) White. *Variations:* Albi, Albia, Albinia, Albinka, Alverta, Alvinia, Alwine, Elbi, Elbie, Elby.

ALBREDA (German) Counselor for elves.

ALCINA (Greek) A sorceress. *Variations:* Alcine, Alcinia, Alsina, Alsinia, Alsyna, Alzina.

ALDA (Italian) Old. *Variations:* Aldabella, Aldea, Aldina, Aldine.

ALDARA (Greek) A winged gift. *Variation:* Aldora.

ALDEN (English) Old friend. *Variations:* Aldena, Aldin, Aldina.

ALDIS (English) From the ancient house. *Variation:* Aldys.

ALDORA (English) Noble and superior. *Variations:* Aldorah, Aldorra.

ALDONZA (Spanish) Sweet.

ALDREDA (English) Elder counselor.

ALEA (Arabic) Honorable. *Variation:* Aleah.

ALEEKA (African) Pretty girl.

ALEGRIA (Spanish) Joy. *Variations:* Alegra, Allegria.

ALEI (Hebrew) Leaf.

ALEKA (Hawaiian) Noble.

ALEMA (Hawaiian) Soul.

ALERA (Latin) Eagle-like. *Variation:* Aleria.

ALESA (Hawaiian) Noble one.

ALETA (Greek) Truth. *Notable:* Singer Oleta Adams. *Variations:* Aleda, Aleida, Aletta, Alette, Alida, Alita, Oleta.

ALETHEA (Greek) Truth. *Variations:* Alathea, Alathia, Aleethia, Aletea, Aletha, Alethia, Alithea, Alithia.

ALEX (Greek) Short form of Alexandra or Alexis.

ALEXA (Greek) Short form of Alexis. *Variations:* Alexia, Alexina.

ALEXANDRA (Greek) One who defends. *Variations:* Alejandrina, Aleka, Aleksasha, Aleksey, Alesia, Aleska, Alessa, Alessandra, Alessi, Alexanderia, Alexanderina, Alexandrea, Alexandria, Alexena, Alexene, Alexina, Alexiou, Alixandra.

ALEXIS (Greek) Helper. *Notable:* Actress Alexis Bledel. *Variations:* Aleksi, Alessa, Alexa, Alexi, Alexia, Alexius, Alexys, Lexi, Lexy.

ALFONSA (Spanish) Feminine form of Alfonso. Noble. *Variations:* Alfonsia, Alfonsine, Alphonsa, Alphonsia, Alphonsina, Alphonsine.

ALFREDA (English) Wise counselor. Feminine version of Alfred. *Variations:* Alfre, Alfredah, Alfredda, Alfreeda, Alfrieda, Alfryda, Allfrieda, Allfry, Allfryda, Elfre, Elfrea, Elfrida, Elfrieda, Elva, Freda, Freddi, Freddie, Freddy, Fredi, Fredy, Freeda, Freedah, Frieda, Friedah, Fryda, Frydah.

ALHENA (Arabic) Star.

ALI (Greek) Short for Alexandra, Alexis, Allison. *Variations:* Allee, Alley, Allie, Ally, Aly.

ALIANA (English) The Lord answers our prayers. *Variations:* Alianna, Aliannah.

ALICE (Greek) Truthful; (German) Noble. *Notable:* Writer Alice Walker. *Variations:* Alis, Alles, Allice, Allis, Allyce, Alyce, Alyss.

ALICIA (English; Spanish) Truthful. Form of Alice. *Notable:* Singer Alicia Keyes; actress Alicia Silverstone. *Variations:* Alesha, Alesia, Aliciana, Alisha, Alissa, Alycia, Alysha, Alyshia, Alysia, Ilysha.

ALIDA (Spanish) Winged. *Variations:* Alaida, Alda, Aldina, Aldine, Aldyne, Aleda, Alidah, Alidia, Alita, Allda, Alleda, Allida, Allidah, Allidia, Allidiah, Allyda, Allydah, Alyda, Alydah.

ALIKA (Hawaiian) Honest.

ALIMA (Arabic) Sea maiden. *Variations:* Alema, Aleema, Alyma.

ALINA (Dutch; English) Fair and bright. *Variations:* Aleen, Aleena,

Alenah, Aline, Alinea, Alline, Allyna, Alyna, Alynah, Alyne, Leena, Leenah, Lena, Lenah, Lina, Lyna, Lynah.

ALISA (Hebrew) Happiness. *Variations:* Alisah, Alisanne, Alissa, Alissah, Aliza, Allisa, Allisah, Allissa, Allissah, Allyea, Allysah, Alyssa, Alyssah.

ALITA (Spanish) Nobility.

ALITZAH (Hebrew) Happy. *Variations:* Aleetza, Alitza.

ALIYAH (Hebrew; Arabic) Exalted. *Variations:* Aaliyah, Aliya, Aliye, Allyah, Alya.

ALIZA (Hebrew) Joyful. *Variations:* Aleaza, Aleeza, Alieza, Alitza, Alitzah, Aliz, Alizka.

ALLEGRA (Latin; Italian) Joyful.

ALLISON (German) A form of Alice. *Notable:* Actress Allison Janney. *Variations:* Alisann, Alisanne, Alison, Alisoun, Alisun, Allcen, Allcenne, Allicen, Allicenne, Allie, Allisann, Allisanne, Allisoun, Ally, Allysann, Allysanne, Allyson, Alyeann, Alysanne, Alyson.

ALLYRIANE (French) A lyre.

ALMA (Latin) Nurturing one. *Variations:* Allma, Almah.

ALMEDA (Latin) Determined. Destined for success. *Variations:* Allmeda, Allmedah, Allmeta, Almedah, Almeta, Almetah, Almida, Almidah, Almita.

ALMERA (Arabic) Refined woman. *Variations:* Allmeera, Allmera, Almeria, Almira, Almyra, Elmerya, Elmyrah, Meera, Merei, Mira, Mirah, Myra, Myrah.

ALMODINE (Latin) Stone.

ALMOND (English) Nut name. *Variations:* Almondine, Almondina.

ALOHA (Hawaiian) Kind, loving, and compassionate. *Variations:* Alohalani, Alohi, Alohilani, Alohinani.

ALOMA (Spanish) Dove-like.

ALONA (Hebrew) Oak tree. *Variations:* Allona, Allonia, Alonia, Eilona.

ALONSA (Spanish) Ready to fight. *Variation:* Alonza.

ALOUETTE (French) Lark. *Variations:* Allouette, Alouetta.

ALPANA (Indian) Beautiful decoration. *Variations:* Alpanah, Alpanna.

ALPHA (Greek) First letter of the Greek alphabet. *Variation:* Alfa.

ALPHONSINE (French) Feminine form of Alphonse. *Variation:* Alphonsina.

ALPINA (Scottish) Blond. *Variations:* Alpena, Alpeena.

ALTA (Latin) High. *Variation:* Allta.

ALTAGRACIA (Spanish) High grace.

ALTAIR (Arabic) Bird. *Variations:* Altaire, Altara.

ALTHEA (Greek) Healer. *Notable:* Tennis player Althea Gibson. *Variations:* Altha, Althaia, Altheta, Althia.

ALTHEDA (Greek) Blossom.

ALUDRA (Arabic) Maiden.

ALULA (Latin) Delicate.

ALUMINA (Latin) Surrounded by light. *Variations:* Allumina, Alumeena.

ALURA (English) Divine counselor. *Variation:* Allura.

ALVA (Spanish) Fair skinned. *Variations:* Alvah, Alvy, Elva, Elvy.

Wiccan Baby Names

Forget Samantha, Serena, Tabitha, and Endora! Real Wiccans have far-more-bewitching names to offer!

BOYS:
Angel
Forest
Hawk
Mars
Puck
Ocean
Sage
Silver
Spider

GIRLS:
Bree
Cerridwen
Coventina
Erba
Freya
Gaia
Marah
Pandora
Raven
Rhiannon

ALVINA (English) Noble friend. *Variations:* Alvedine, Alveena, Alveene, Alveenia, Alverdine, Alvine, Alvineea, Alvinia, Alwinna, Alwyna, Alwyne, Elveena, Elvena, Elvene, Elvenia, Elvina, Elvine, Elvinia.

ALVITA (Latin) Energetic.

ALYA (Arabic) To rise up.

ALYSSA (Greek) To flourish. *Variations:* Alissa, Elyssa, Ilyssa, Lyssa.

ALZBETA (Czech) Consecrated.

ALZENA (Arabic) Lovely woman. *Variation:* Alzina.

AMABEL (Latin) Lovable. *Variations:* Ama, Amabelle.

AMADA (Spanish) Loved by all. *Variation:* Amadah.

AMADEA (Latin) Lover of god. *Variations:* Amadee, Amadia, Amedee.

AMADI (African) Rejoice. *Variation:* Amadie.

AMADORE (Italian) Gift of love. *Variation:* Amadora.

AMAL (Arabic) Hope. *Variations:* Amahl, Amahla, Amala.

AMALA (Hindi) Pure. *Variation:* Amalah.

AMANA (Hebrew) Loyal. *Variations:* Amania, Amaniah, Amanya.

AMANDA (Latin) Loved. *Notables:* Actresses Amanda Peet and Amanda Bynes. *Variations:* Amandi, Amandie, Amandine, Amandy, Amata, Manda, Mandaline, Mandee, Mandi, Mandie, Mandy.

AMANI (Arabic) To want. *Variation:* Amany.

AMARA (Greek) Forever lovely. *Variations:* Amarande, Amaranta, Amarante, Amarantha, Amarinda, Amarra, Amarrinda, Mara, Marra.

AMARINA (Australian) Bring the rain. *Variations:* Amaine, Amareena, Amarin, Amaryn.

AMARIS (Hebrew) Covenant with God. *Variations:* Amaria, Amariah.

AMARJAA (Hindi) Everlasting.

AMARYLLIS (Greek) Fresh flower. *Variation:* Amarillis.

AMATA (Spanish) Dearly loved.

AMAUI (Hawaiian) A bird.

AMAYA (Japanese) Night rain.

AMBER (French) Semiprecious stone. *Notable:* Actress Amber Tamblyn. *Variations:* Ambar, Amberetta, Amberlee, Amberley, Amberly, Ambur.

AMBIKA (Hindi) God of fertility.

AMBROSIA (Greek) Food of the gods. *Variation:* Ambrozia.

AMBROSINE (Greek) Immortal. *Variations:* Ambrosina, Ambrosinetta, Ambrosinette, Ambroslya, Ambrozetta, Ambrozine.

AMELIA (Latin) Hard working. *Notable:* Aviatrix Amelia Earhart. *Variations:* Amalea, Amalie, Amelcia, Ameldy, Amelie, Amelina, Amelinda, Amelita, Amella.

AMENTI (Egyptian) Goddess of the west. *Variations:* Ament, Iment.

AMERICA (Latin) Powerful ruler. *Notable:* Actress America Ferrera. *Variation:* Amerika.

AMETHYST (English) Semiprecious violet quartz stone.

AMICA (Italian) Close friend. *Variations:* Amice, Amici.

AMIDA (Hebrew) Moral. *Variation:* Amidah.

AMINA (Arabic) Honest. *Variations:* Ameena, Aminah, Amine, Amineh, Amna.

AMIRA (Arabic) Highborn. *Variations:* Amera, Ameera, Amyra, Merah, Mira.

AMISSA (Hebrew) Honest friend. *Variations:* Amisa, Amise, Amisia, Amiza.

AMITA (Indian) Without limits. *Variation:* Ameeta.

AMITOLA (Native American) Rainbow.

AMITY (Latin) Friendship. *Variations:* Amitie, Amiti.

AMMA (Scandinavian) Grandmother.

AMOKE (African) To know her is to love her.

AMOLI (Hindi) Valuable.

AMOR (Spanish) Love. *Variations:* Amora, Amoreena, Amoretta, Amorette, Amorina, Amorine, Amorita.

AMRITA (Hindi) Immortal. *Variation:* Amreeta.

AMY (English) Loved. *Notables:* Singer Amy Grant; actress Amy Brenneman. *Variations:* Aimee, Aimie, Amada, Amata, Ami, Amice, Amie, Amil.

ANA (Spanish) Form of Anna.

ANABA (Native American) Returning from battle. *Variation:* Annaba.

ANADARIA (Hawaiian) Woman. *Variation:* Anakalia.

ANAHID (Armenian) Goddess of water and fertility.

ANAHITA (Persian) Immaculate one. *Variation:* Anahit.

ANAIS (French) Grace. *Notable:* Writer Anaïs Nin.

ANAKA (African American) Sweet face. *Variations:* Anaca, Anika, Anikee.

ANAKONIA (Hawaiian) Valuable. *Variation:* Anatonia.

ANALA (Hindi) Fire. *Variation:* Analaa.

ANAMOSA (Native American) White fawn.

ANANDA (Hindi) One who brings happiness.

ANANDITA (Hindi) Happy.

ANANI (Hawaiian) From the orange tree. *Variations:* Ananee, Ananie.

ANASTASIA (Greek) Resurrection. *Variations:* Anastace, Anastacia, Anastacie, Anastase, Anastasie, Anastasija, Anastasiya, Anastassia, Anastatia, Anastazia, Anastice, Anastyce.

ANAT (Hebrew) To sing.

ANATOLA (Greek) Easterly.

ANBAR (Arabic) Fragrant woman. *Variation:* Anbarre.

ANCI (Hungarian) Grace of God.

ANCINA (Latin) Graced with God's favor. *Variations:* Ancena, Ancine, Ancyna.

ANDEANA (Spanish) One who is leaving. *Variation:* Andiana.

ANDELA (Czech) Angel. *Variations:* Andel, Andelka.

ANDIE (American) Short form of Andrea. *Notable:* Actress Andie MacDowell.

ANDREA (Latin) Womanly. *Notable:* Actress/comedian Andrea Martin. *Variations:* Andera, Andra, Andreana, Andree, Andreea, Andrene, Andrette, Andria, Andriana, Andrianna, Andrienne, Andrietta, Andrina, Andrine.

ANDROMEDA (Greek) One who ponders.

ANDULA (Czech) Grace of God. *Variation:* Andulka.

ANEIRA (Welsh) Golden woman. *Variations:* Aneara, Aneera, Aneira.

ANEKA (Hawaiian) Grace. *Variation:* Aneta.

ANEKO (Japanese) Older sister. *Variation:* Aniko.

ANELA (Hawaiian) Messenger of heaven. *Variations:* Anella, Anelle.

ANEMONE (Greek) Windflower.

ANESH (Czech) Virginal, pure. *Variations:* Anesa, Anezka, Neska.

ANEVAY (Native American) Superior.

ANGANAA (Hindi) Beautiful. *Variation:* Angana.

ANGELA (Greek) Messenger of God. Angel. *Notables:* Actresses Angela Lansbury and Angela Bassett. *Variations:* Aingeal, Ange, Angel, Angele, Angelene, Angelia, Angelita, Angie, Angiola, Anngilla.

ANGELICA (Latin) Angelic. *Notable:* Actress Anjelica Huston. *Variations:* Angelika, Angelique, Anjelica.

ANGELINA (Italian) Form of Angela. *Notable:* Actress Angelina Jolie. *Variations:* Angeline, Anjolina.

ANGEVIN (French) Angel of wine.

ANGHARAD (Welsh) One who is greatly loved. Beloved.

ANGIE (Greek) Short form of Angela. *Notable:* Actress Angie Dickinson.

ANGUSINA (Gaelic) Feminine form of Angus.

ANI (Hawaiian) Beautiful.

ANIANI (Hawaiian) Clear.

ANILA (Hindi) Child of the wind. *Variations:* Anilla, Anillah, Anylla.

ANIMA (Hindi) Small.

ANINA (Hebrew) Answer to a prayer.

ANISAH (Arabic) Friendly. *Variations:* Anisa, Anise, Anisha, Anissa, Annissa.

ANISHA (Hindi) Born at the end of the night. *Variations:* Anesha, Aneisha, Anicia.

ANITA (Spanish) Form of Anna. *Notable:* Singer Anita Baker. *Variations:* Aneata, Aneeta, Anyta.

ANITARA (Hawaiian) Hawaiian version of Anitra. *Variation:* Anikala.

ANITRA (Norwegian) Literary name of princess in Ibsen's "Peer Gynt."

ANJALI (Indian) Offering with both hands. *Variations:* Anjalee, Anjalie.

ANJU (Hindi) Glory.

ANKINE (Armenian) Valuable.

ANN (English) Grace. *Notables:* Advice columnist Ann Landers; fashion designer Ann Taylor. *Variations:* Ana, Anita, Anitra, Anitte, Anna, Annah, Anne, Annie, Annita, Annitra, Annitta, Hannah, Hannelore.

ANNA (English) Form of Ann. *Notable:* Actress/model Anna Nicole Smith.

ANNABELLE (English) Graceful and beautiful. *Notable:* Actress Annabella Sciorra. *Variations:* Anabel, Anabele, Anabell, Anabelle, Annabel, Annabell, Annabella.

ANNABETH (English) Combined form of Ann and Beth. *Variations:* Anabeth, Annabetta.

ANNALISA (English) Combined form of Ann and Lisa. *Variation:* Annalise.

ANNALYNN (English) Combined form of Ann and Lynn. *Variations:* Analin, Analyn, Annaline, Annalyn.

ANNEMARIE (English) Combination of first names "Anne" and "Marie."

ANNETTE (French) Form of Ann. *Notables:* Actresses Annette Bening and Annette Funicello.

ANNIE (English) Gracious. Form of Ann. *Variations:* Annee, Anni, Anny.

ANNISA (Arabic) Friendly. *Variations:* Anisa, Anissa, Annamaria, Annamarie, Annissa, Annmarie.

ANNORA (Latin) Having great honor. *Variations:* Anora, Anorah, Anoria, Annore.

ANNUNCIATA (Latin) The Annunciation. *Variations:* Annunziate, Anonciada, Anunciacion, Anunciata, Anunziata.

ANOI (Hawaiian) Desire.

ANONA (Latin) Pineapple. *Variation:* Anonna.

ANOUSH (Armenian) Of sweet disposition. *Variation:* Anousha.

ANSLEY (English) Form of Ainsley. Meadow. *Variations:* Ansleigh, Anslie, Ansliee.

ANSONIA (Greek) Child of the divine.

ANTALYA (Russian) Born during the first light of morning.

ANTHEA (Greek) Flower. *Variations:* Annthea, Anthe, Anthia, Antia.

ANTIGONE (Greek) In mythology, daughter of Oedipus.

ANTJE (German) Graceful woman.

ANTOINETTE (French) Priceless. *Notable:* Actress/director Antoinette Perry, for whom theater's Tony Award is named. *Variations:* Antonella, Antonetta, Antonette, Antonia, Antonie, Antonieta, Antonietta, Antonina, Antonine, Tonelle, Tonette, Toney, Toni, Tonia, Tonie, Tony.

ANTONIA (Latin) Priceless. *Variation:* Antonea.

ANUHEA (Hawaiian) Fragrant.

ANUKA (Hindi) Envious.

ANULI (African) Joyous.

ANUMATI (Hindi) Moon goddess of wealth, intellect, children, and spirituality.

ANUPA (Hindi) Unique. *Variation:* Anupaa.

ANUPRIYAA (Hindi) Exceptional.

ANURA (Hindi) Information.

ANUSHEELA (Hindi) Fan.

ANWEN (Welsh) Fair, beautiful. *Variation:* Anwyn.

ANYA (Russian) Grace of God. *Variation:* Anyuta.

AOI (Japanese) Hollyhock.

AOIBHEANN (Irish) Beautiful. *Variations:* Aibfinnia, Aoibh, Aoibhinn, Eavan.

AOIFE (Irish) In mythology, a warrior princess. *Variation:* Aoiffe.

AOLANI (Hawaiian) Cloud from heaven. *Variations:* Aolanea, Aolanee, Aolania.

AONANI (Hawaiian) Beautiful light.

APALA (African) Creator of music. *Variations:* Apalah, Apalla, Appalla.

APERILA (Hawaiian) April. *Variation:* Apelila.

APHRA (Hebrew) Dust. *Variations:* Affery, Afra, Afrat, Afrit, Aphrah, Aphrat, Aphrit, Aprah.

APHRODITE (Greek) The goddess of love and beauty.

APOLLONIA (Greek) Strength. *Variations:* Apolinara, Apolinia.

APONA (Hawaiian) Encompassing.

APONI (Native American) Butterfly.

APPLE (English) Apple. *Variation:* Appell.

APRIA (Latin) Apricot. *Variations:* Aprea, Apriah, Aprya.

APRIL (Latin) To open up. Springlike. *Variations:* Abrial, Abril, Aprilete, Aprilette, Aprili, Aprille, Apryl.

APSARA (Hindi) Heavenly woman.

AQUA (Greek) Water. *Variations:* Acqua, Aquanetta, Aquanette.

AQUARIUS (Latin) Constellation of the water bearer.

AQUENE (Native American) Peace.

AQUILA (Latin) Eagle. *Variations:* Aquil, Aquilla, Aquilina, Aquiline.

AQUINNAH (Native American) High hill. *Variations:* Aquina, Aquinna.

ARA (Arabic) Opinionated woman. *Variations:* Arah, Araya.

ARABELLA (English) Answered in prayer. *Variations:* Arabel, Arabela, Arbell, Arbella, Bel, Bella, Belle, Orabella, Orbella.

ARACELI (Spanish) Altar of heaven. *Variation:* Aricela.

ARACHNE (Greek) Mythological woman turned into a spider by Athena.

ARADHANA (Hindi) Devotion.

ARAMINTA (English) Literary name created in the eighteenth century.

ARANKA (Hungarian) Golden child.

ARASHEL (Hebrew) Strong and protected hill. *Variation:* Arashela.

ARAVA (Hebrew) Arid land. *Variation:* Aravah.

ARAXIE (Armenian) River of inspiration. *Variations:* Araxa, Araxea, Araxia.

ARCADIA (Greek) Pastoral. *Variations:* Arcadie, Arkadia.

ARCANGELA (Greek) High angel. *Variation:* Archangela.

ARCELIA (Spanish) Treasure chest.

ARDA (English) Warm and friendly. *Variations:* Ardi, Ardine.

ARDALA (Irish) Woman of high honor. *Variations:* Ardalia, Ardalla, Ardalle.

ARDARA (Gaelic) Stronghold on the hill.

ARDELLE (Latin) Enthusiastic. *Variations:* Arda, Ardel, Ardelia, Ardelis, Ardella, Ardia, Ardra.

ARDEN (Latin) Excited. *Variations:* Ardan, Ardana, Ardena, Ardin, Ardyn.

ARDITH (Hebrew) Field of flowers. *Variations:* Ardath, Ardise.

ARELLA (Hebrew) Angel. *Variation:* Arela.

ARETHA (Greek) Virtuous. *Notable:* Singer Aretha Franklin. *Variations:* Areta, Arete, Arethi, Arethusa, Aretina, Aretta, Arette.

Pharmaceutical Names

Believe it or not, names of popular prescription and over-the-counter drugs have been making their way to babies. Perhaps that's because some of these names sound exotic enough to be appealing. Or perhaps they are used (with doctor's approval, of course) to successfully treat a condition!

Advil	Kadian
Advair	Kalestra
Aleve	Levitra
Allegra	Lunesta
Ambien	Marinol
Amaryl	Nexium
Astelin	Paxil
Avandia	Solodyn
Boniva	Valium
Celexa	Viagra
Chantix	Vytorin
Cialis	Xalatan
Cymbalta	Xanax
Flomax	Yasmin
Flonase	Zetia
Januvia	Zyprexa

Chinese Names

BOYS:	GIRLS:
An	Ai
Cheng	Bao
Ho	Chan
Hu	Dai
Jin	Hua
Kong	Jiao
Li	Jun
Liang	Li
Ning	Lin
Po	Ling
Qiang	Mei
Shing	Ping
Wen	Qian
Wing	Ting
Yong	Xian
Yu	Yan

ARGEL (Welsh) Providing refuge. *Variations:* Argella, Argelle.

ARGENTA (Latin) Silver. *Variations:* Argena, Argentia, Argentina.

ARIA (Italian) Melody. *Variation:* Ariah.

ARIADNE (Greek) Most holy. *Variation:* Ariadna.

ARIANA (Greek) Holy. *Notable:* Blogger and media mogul Arianna Huffington. *Variations:* Ariane, Arianie, Arianna, Arianne.

ARIEL (Hebrew) Lioness of God. *Notable:* Ariel the Mermaid from the film *The Little Mermaid*. *Variations:* Aeriel, Aeriela, Ari, Ariela, Ariella, Arielle, Ariellel.

ARIETTA (Italian) Short melody. *Variations:* Arieta, Ariette.

ARIN (English) Form of Erin. Woman of Ireland. *Variation:* Aryn.

ARISSA (Greek) Feminine form of Aris. Superior. *Variations:* Aris, Arisa, Aryssa.

ARISTA (Greek) Harvest.

ARIZONA (Native American) From the little spring.

ARLAIS (Welch) From the temple.

ARLEIGH (English) From the meadow. *Variations:* Arleah, Arlee, Arlia.

ARLEN (Irish) Devoted. *Variations:* Arlin, Arlyn.

ARLENE (English) Pledge. *Notables:* Actresses Arlene Francis and Arlene Dahl. *Variations:* Arleen, Arlena, Arlie, Arliene, Arlina, Arline, Arlise, Arlys.

ARLETTE (French) Devoted. *Variations:* Arlet, Arletta.

ARLISS (Irish) From a high fortress. *Variations:* Arlissa, Arlisse, Arlyssa.

ARIZA (Hebrew) Made from cedar wood.

ARMANDA (Spanish) Feminine form of Armando. Battle maiden.

ARMANI (Persian) Desired. *Variations:* Arman, Armania, Armany.

ARMELLE (French) Royally born. *Variation:* Armella.

ARMILLA (Latin) Decorative bracelet.

ARMINA (German) Woman of war. *Variations:* Armida, Armine, Armini.

ARNA (Scandinavian) Eagle. *Variations:* Arni, Arnice, Arnit.

ARNALDA (German) Eagle rule. *Variation:* Arnolda.

ARNELLE (German) Eagle. *Variations:* Arnell, Arnella.

ARNETTE (English) Small eagle. *Variation:* Arnet.

ARNINA (Hebrew) Enlightened one.

ARONA (Maori) Vivacious and colorful.

ARPANA (Hindi) Devoted one.

ARROSA (Spanish) Of the rose. *Variation:* Arosa.

ARTEMISIA (Greek) Perfection. *Variation:* Artemesia.

ARTHA (Hindi) Great wealth.

ARTHURINA (Gaelic) Rock. Nobility. *Variations:* Artheia, Arthelia, Arthene, Arthuretta, Arthurine, Artina, Artis, Artri.

ARTOIS (French) Of the Netherlands.

ARUNA (Hindi) Reddish brown in color. *Variations:* Arunika, Arunima.

ARVIDA (English) From the eagle tree.

ARVINDA (Hindi) Lotus.

ASABI (African) Of select birth.

ASELA (Spanish) Small donkey.

ASELMA (Gaelic) Fair skinned.

ASENA (Turkish) She-wolf. *Variation:* Asenna.

ASENATH (Egyptian) A father's daughter.

ASENKA (Hebrew) Graceful woman.

ASHA (Sanskrit) Hope. *Variation:* Ashia.

ASHANTI (African) African tribal name. *Notable:* Singer Ashanti. *Variations:* Ashantee, Ashaunta, Ashuntae.

ASHBY (English) Ash trees.

ASHERAT (Syrian) Goddess of the sea.

ASHIMA (Hebrew) Deity worshipped at Hamath. *Variation:* Ashimah.

ASHIRA (Hebrew) Wealthy. *Variations:* Asheera, Asherea, Ashirah, Ashra.

ASHLEY (English) Ash-tree meadow. *Notables:* Actresses Ashley Judd and Ashley Olsen. *Variations:* Ashely, Ashla, Ashlan, Ashlea, Ashlee, Ashleigh, Ashlie, Ashly.

ASHLYN (Irish) Dream. *Variations:* Aislinn, Ashlin, Ashlynn.

ASHNI (Hindi) Lightning.

ASHTON (English) Ash-tree town. *Variations:* Ashten, Ashtin, Ashtine.

ASIA (Greek) Reborn. *Variations:* Aisia, Asiah, Asya, Aysia.

ASIMA (Arabic) Offering protection. *Variations:* Ashimah, Asyma, Azima.

ASISA (Hebrew) Ripe.

ASISYA (Hebrew) Juice of God. *Variation:* Asisia.

ASLAUG (Scandinavian) Consecrated to God. *Variation:* Aslog.

ASMA (Arabic) Renown.

ASMEE (Hindi) Confident.

ASOKA (Hindi) Flower.

ASPASIA (Greek) Welcome. *Variations:* Aspa, Aspia.

ASPEN (English) Tree name. *Variation:* Aspin.

ASPHODEL (Greek) Lily.

ASSANA (Irish) Waterfall. *Variations:* Asana, Asanna.

ASTERA (Hebrew) Star. *Variations:* Asta, Asteria, Asteriya, Astra.

ASTRAEA (Greek) Starry skies. *Variation:* Astrea.

ASTRID (Scandinavian) Godlike beauty and strength. *Notable:* Jazz singer Astrud Gilberto. *Variations:* Astrud, Astryd.

ASUNCION (Spanish) Ascension.

ASURA (African) Born during month of Ashur.

ATALANTA (Greek) Athletic hunter. *Variation:* Atlanta.

ATALAYA (Spanish) Watch tower.

ATARA (Hebrew) Crown. *Variations:* Atarra, Atera.

ATHALIA (Hebrew) Praise the Lord. *Variations:* Atalia, Ataliah, Atalie, Atalya, Athalee, Athalie, Athalina.

ATHENA (Greek) Goddess of wisdom. *Variations:* Athene, Athina.

ATHILDA (English) Elder tree. *Variations:* Athide, Athild, Atilda, Atilde.

ATIA (Arabic) Of an ancient line.

ATIFA (Arabic) Showing affection and sympathy. *Variations:* Afteefa, Ateifa.

ATIRA (Hebrew) Bowing in prayer. *Variations:* Ateera, Atirah.

ATIYA (Arabic) Present.

ATRINA (Hawaiian) Peaceful.

AUBREY (German) Noble; (French) Blond leader. *Variations:* Aubre, Aubree, Aubri, Aubria, Aubrianna, Aubrie.

AUBURN (Latin) Having reddish-brown hair.

AUDHILD (Scandinavian) Prosperous in battle. *Variations:* Aud, Audny.

AUDREY (English) Nobility and strength. *Notable:* Actress Audrey Hepburn. *Variations:* Audey, Audi, Audie, Audra, Audre, Audree, Audri, Audria, Audrie, Audris, Audrisa, Audrissa, Audry, Audrye, Audy.

AUDRINA (English) Noble strength. *Notable:* Actress Audrina Patridge. *Variations:* Audreen, Audreena, Audrinah, Audryna.

AUGUSTA (Latin) Majestic. *Variations:* Agusta, Augustia, Augustina, Augustine, Augustyna, Augustyne, Austina, Austine, Austyna, Austyne.

AULANI (Hawaiian) King's messenger. *Variations:* Aulania, Aulanie.

AULII (Hawaiian) Delicate.

AURA (Greek) Slow breeze. *Variations:* Aure, Aurea, Auria.

AURELIA (English) Golden haired. *Variations:* Arela, Arella, Aurella, Aurene, Aureola, Aureole, Auriel, Aurielle.

AURORA (Latin) Roman goddess of dawn. *Variation:* Aurore.

AUSTINA (French) Feminine form of Austin. *Variation:* Austine.

AUTUMN (English) Autumn.

AVA (English) Life. *Notable:* Actress Ava Gardner. *Variations:* Aualee, Avah, Avelyn, Avia, Aviana, Aviance, Avilina, Avis, Aviva.

AVALON (Gaelic) Island paradise.

AVANI (Hindi) From the earth.

AVELINE (French) Bird-like. *Variations:* Avalina, Avaline, Avelina.

AVENA (Latin) Oat field.

AVERY (English) Noble leader. *Variations:* Avary, Averi, Averie.

AVIANA (Latin) Gracious life. *Variations:* Avianna, Avianne.

AVIVA (Hebrew) Spring. *Variations:* Abiba, Abibah, Abibi, Abibit, Avivah, Avivi, Avivit.

AVONMORA (Irish) From the great river.

AVRIL (English) Form of April. *Notable:* Singer Avril Lavigne. *Variations:* Averil, Averill. Averille.

AWENA (Welsh) Seer. *Variations:* Awen, Awina, Awynna.

AWENDELA (Native American) Sunrise.

AWINITA (Native American) Fawn. *Variation:* Awenita.

AXELLE (German) Peace. *Variations:* Axelia, Axella.

AYALA (Hebrew) Gazelle.

AYANNA (Hindi) Innocent. *Variation:* Ayana.

AYELET (Hebrew) Deer.

AYLA (Hebrew) Oak tree.

AYLIN (Gaelic) Form of Helen. Pleasant.

AYONDELA (African) Bending tree.

AZALEA (Latin) Flower name. *Variation:* Azalia.

AZAMI (Japanese) Flower.

AZANA (African) Superior. *Variation:* Azanna.

AZARIA (Hebrew) Helped by God. *Variations:* Azariah, Azelia.

AZIZA (African) Beloved.

AZRA (Hebrew) Chaste.

AZRIELA (Hebrew) God is my strength. *Variations:* Azriel, Azriella, Azrielle.

AZUCENA (Arabic) Lily. *Variations:* Asucena, Asusena, Azusena, Azuzena.

AZURA (French) Blue. *Variations:* Azor, Azora, Azure, Azzura, Azzurra.

AZUSA (Arabic) Variation of Azucena. Lily.

BABA (African) Born on Thursday.

BABE (Latin) Short form of Barbara. Nickname of endearment. *Notable:* Olympic athlete Babe Didrikson Zaharias.

BABETTE (French) Little Barbara.

BABS (American) Familiar form of Barbara.

BABY (American) Baby.

BACHIKO (Japanese) Happy child.

BADIA (Arabic) Elegant woman.

BADU (African) Tenth-born child.

BAHAR (Arabic) Born in spring. *Variation:* Bahaar.

BAHIRA (Arabic) Sparkling and brilliant.

BAILA (Spanish) To dance. *Variations:* Bayla, Beyla, Byla.

BAILEY (English) Bailiff. *Variations:* Baeley, Baelyn, Bailee, Baylee, Bayley, Baylie, Baylin.

BAISLEY (English) Variation of Bailey. *Variations:* Baislee, Baisly.

BAKA (Indian) A crane. *Variations:* Bacca, Bakka.

BAKUL (Hindi) Flower. *Variation:* Bakula.

BAKURA (Hebrew) Ripened fruit.

BALANIKI (Hawaiian) White.

BALBINA (Latin) Strong woman.

BALLAD (English) Poetic song. *Variation:* Ballade.

BAMBI (Italian) Child. *Variations:* Bambie, Bambina, Bamby.

BANDANA (Spanish) Colored headscarf.

BANITA (Hindi) Woman.

BAO (Chinese) Precious.

BAO-YO (Chinese) Precious jade.

BAPTISTA (Latin) One who baptizes. *Variations:* Baptiste, Batista, Battista, Bautista.

BARA (Hebrew) To choose. *Variations:* Bari, Barra.

BARB (American) Short form of Barbara.

BARBARA (Greek) Foreign. *Notables:* U.S. First Lady Barbara Bush; actresses Barbara Stanwyck and Barbra Streisand. *Variations:* Babb, Babbett, Babbette, Babe, Babett, Babette, Babita, Babs, Barb, Barbary, Barbe, Barbette, Barbey, Barbi, Barbie, Barbra, Barby, Basha, Basia, Vaoka, Varenka, Varina, Varinka, Varka, Varvara, Varya, Vava.

BARBIE (American) Short form of Barbara. *Notable:* Former Playboy model/singer Barbi Benton.

BARIAH (Arabic) To succeed.

BARIKA (African) Successful woman.

BARKAIT (Hebrew) Morning star. *Variation:* Barkat.

BARRAN (Irish) Little top.

BARRIE (Irish) Spear. Feminine version of Barry. *Variations:* Bari, Barri.

BASANTI (Indian) Born in springtime.

BASHIRA (Arabic) Joyful. *Variations:* Basheerah, Bashirah.

BASIA (Hebrew) Daughter of God. *Notable:* Singer Basia. *Variations:* Basha, Basya.

BASILIA (Greek) Royal. *Variations:* Basila, Basilea, Basilie.

BASIMA (Arabic) To smile. *Variations:* Basimah, Basma.

BATHIA (Hebrew) Daughter of God. *Variations:* Basha, Baspa, Batia, Batya, Bitya, Peshe, Pessel.

BATHILDA (German) Female soldier. *Variations:* Bathild, Bathilde, Berthilda, Berthilde.

BATHSHEBA (Hebrew) Daughter of Sheba. *Notable:* Mistress/wife of King David. *Variations:* Bathseva, Batsheba, Batsheva, Batshua, Sheba.

BATHSHIRA (Arabic) Seventh daughter. *Variation:* Bathsheera.

BATYA (Hebrew) Daughter of God.

BAY (French) Berry.

BEA (English) Short form of Beatrice. *Notable:* Actress Bea Arthur. *Variation:* Bee.

BEATA (Latin) Blessed. *Variation:* Beate.

BEATHA (Irish) Life. *Variation:* Betha.

BEATRICE (Latin) Bringing joy. *Notable:* Writer Beatrix Potter. *Variations:* Bea, Beatrisa, Beatrise, Beatrix, Beatriz, Beattie, Bebe, Bee, Beitris, Beitriss.

BEBE (Spanish) A form of Beatrice. *Variation:* Bibi.

BEBHINN (Irish) Sweet woman. *Variations:* Bebhinn, Bebhionn, Bebinn.

BECCA (Hebrew) Short form of Rebecca. *Variation:* Bekka.

BECHIRA (Hebrew) Chosen.

BECKY (American) Short form of Rebecca. *Variations:* Beckey, Becki, Beckie, Bekki.

BEDA (German) Goddess warrior.

BEDELIA (Irish) Form of Bridget. *Variations:* Bidelia, Delia.

BEDRISKA (Czech) Peaceful ruler.

BEEJA (Hindi) Beginning. *Variation:* Beej.

BEGONIA (Spanish) Flower name.

BEHIRA (Hebrew) Bright light.

BEL (Hindi) From the sacred wood.

BELDA (French) Fair maiden.

BELÉN (Spanish) From Bethlehem.

BELIA (Spanish) Oath of God. *Variations:* Belica, Belicia.

BELICA (Hebrew) God is perfection. *Variations:* Belica, Belicka.

BELINDA (English) Dragon. *Notable:* Singer Belinda Carlisle. *Variation:* Belynda.

BELITA (Spanish) Little beauty.

BELLA (Italian) Beautiful. *Variation:* Bellissima.

BELLE (French) Beautiful. *Variations:* Bela, Bell, Bella, Belva, Belloma.

BELVA (Latin) Beautiful view. *Notable:* Writer Belva Plain.

BEMEDIKTA (Scandinavian) Blessed. Feminine version of Benedict. *Variation:* Benedikte.

BENA (Hebrew) Wise.

BENEDETTA (Italian) Blessed. *Variations:* Benedicta, Benedicte, Benedikta, Benetta, Benita, Benni, Benoite.

BENEDICTA (Latin) Blessed. *Variation:* Benedictine.

BENIGNA (Italian) Feminine form of Benigno. Kind.

BENITA (Latin) God has blessed. *Variations:* Bena, Benitri, Bennie, Binnie.

BENJAMINA (Hebrew) Feminine form of Benjamin. Child of my right hand.

BENNIE (American) Nickname for Benedicta.

BENTLEY (English) Meadow of grass. *Variations:* Bentlea, Bentlee, Bentleigh, Bently.

BERA (German) Bear.

School Daze: Names from Teachers (Part IV)

Here's another selection of names from an elementary school in Santa Barbara, California:

Acachia
Adagio
Adonis
Alitha
Allondra
Amairani
Aradia
Flora and
Fauna (Twins)
Gennipher
Herculana
Jazzman
Kathe
Keyani
Lemongelo
and Organelo
(Twins)
Mali
Maralisbeth
Mweya
Omigali
Ona
Oona
Orion
Remington
Seita
Seneca
Seven
Shadean
Shale
Shama
Shamsedeen
Shyama
Soxchil
Tombe
Torin
Uriah
Usmail

BERACHAH (Hebrew) Benediction. *Variations:* Beracha, Berucha, Beruchiya, Beruchya.

BERDINE (Greek) Bright maiden. *Variations:* Berdie, Berdina, Berdine, Burdine.

BERIT (Scandinavian) Magnificent. *Variations:* Beret, Berette.

BERKLEY (Scottish) Birch-tree meadow. *Variations:* Berkeley, Berkly.

BERLYN (English) Combination of Bertha and Lynn. *Variation:* Berlynn.

BERNADETTE (French) Brave as a bear. *Notable:* Actress Bernadette Peters. *Variations:* Berna, Bernadene, Bernadett, Bernadina, Bernadine, Bernarda, Bernardina, Bernardine, Bernetta, Bernette, Berni, Bernie, Bernita, Berny.

BERNEEN (Irish) Strong as a bear. *Variation:* Bernine.

BERNICE (Greek) Bringing victory. *Variations:* Berenice, Bernelle, Bernetta, Bernette, Bernicia, Bernie, Bernyce.

BERNIE (English) Form of Bernice. *Variations:* Bernee, Berni, Berney.

BERNITA (African) Form of Bernice.

BERONICA (English) Showing a true image.

BERRY (American) Berry. *Variations:* Berri, Berrie.

BERTHA (German) Bright. *Variations:* Berta, Berthe, Berti, Bertie, Bertilda, Bertilde, Bertina, Bertine, Bertuska, Bird, Birdie, Birdy, Birtha.

BERTILDE (German) Bright warrior. *Variations:* Bertilda, Bertille.

BERTINA (German) Bright.

BERURIA (Hebrew) Chosen by God. *Variation:* Berura.

BERYL (Greek) Green gemstone. *Variations:* Beril, Berrill, Berry, Beryla, Beryle.

BESS (English) Short form of Elizabeth. *Notable:* U.S. First Lady Bess Truman. *Variation:* Bessie.

BETA (Czech) Grace of God. *Variations:* Betka, Betuska.

BETH (Hebrew) House of God. *Notable:* Singer Beth Nielsen Chapman.

BETHANY (English) House of God. *Variations:* Bethanee, Bethani, Bethanie, BethAnn, Bethann, Bethanne, Bethannie, Bethany.

BETHEL (Hebrew) Temple.

BETHESDA (Hebrew) House of mercy.

BETHIA (Hebrew) Daughter of Jehovah. *Variations:* Betia, Bithia.

BETSY (American) Short form of Elizabeth. *Notables:* American flag seamstress Betsy Ross; fashion designer Betsey Johnson. *Variations:* Betsey, Betsi, Betsie.

BETTE (French) Form of Betty. *Notables:* Actress Bette Davis; singer/actress Bette Midler.

BETTINA (English) Form of Betty. *Variation:* Bettine.

BETTY (English) Short form of Elizabeth. *Notables:* Actress Betty White; cartoon siren Betty Boop. *Variations:* Betti, Bettie.

BETUEL (Hebrew) Daughter of God. *Variation:* Bethuel.

BETULAH (Hebrew) Dedicated. *Variations:* Bethula, Bethulah, Betula.

BEULAH (Hebrew) Married. *Variations:* Bealah, Beula.

BEV (English) Short form of Beverly.

BEVERLY (English) Beaver meadow. *Notables:* Actress Beverly D'Angelo; model Beverly Johnson. *Variations:* Bev, Beverelle, Beverle, Beverlee, Beverley, Beverlie, Beverlye.

BEVIN (Gaelic) Singer. *Variations:* Bevan, Beven, Bevena, Bevina, Bevinn.

BEYLA (Norse) Mythological elf. *Variations:* Bayla, Beylah.

BEYONCE (African) Beyond others. *Notable:* Singer Beyonce Knowles.

BHAMINI (Hindi) Beautiful lady.

BHANUMATI (Hindi) Sunlight.

BHARATI (Hindi) Goddess of sacrifice.

BHAVIKA (Hindi) Devoted.

BHUMA (Hindi) Earth. *Variation:* Bhumika.

BIANCA (Italian) White. *Notable:* Former model Bianca Jagger. *Variations:* Beanka, Biancha, Bianka, Bionca, Bionka.

BIBI (Arabic) Lady. *Notable:* Actress Bibi Andersson. *Variation:* Bebe.

BIBIANA (Latin) Lively. *Variations:* Bibiane, Bibianna, Bibianne, Bibyana.

BICE (Italian) Nickname for Beatrice. Life voyager.

BIDDY (Irish) Short form of Bridget. *Variations:* Biddi, Biddie.

BIDELIA (Irish) Strong. *Variations:* Bedilia, Bidina.

BIENVENIDA (Spanish) Welcome.

BIJOU (French) Sassy. *Notable:* Hollywood "Wild Child" Bijou Phillips. *Variations:* Bejeaux, Bejou, Bijue.

BILLIE (English) Constant protector. *Notables:* Singer Billie Holiday; tennis champ Billie Jean King. *Variations:* Billa, Billee, Billey, Billi, Billy.

BINA (Hebrew) Knowledge. *Variations:* Bena, Binah, Byna.

BINALI (Hindi) Musical instrument.

BINDI (Aboriginal) Little girl. *Notable:* Australian TV child star, Bindi Irwin. *Variations:* Bindee, Bindie, Bindy.

BINTI (African) Daughter.

BINYAMINA (Hebrew) Right hand. Feminine form of Benjamin.

BIRA (Hebrew) Fortress. *Variations:* Biria, Biriya.

BIRCIT (Scandinavian: Norwegian) Power. *Variation:* Birgit.

BIRDIE (English) *Variations:* Bird, Birdey, Byrd, Byrdie.

BIRGITTE (Scandinavian) Bridget. *Variations:* Birget, Birgetta, Birgit, Birgitta.

BIRKITA (Celtic) Woman of great strength.

BISA (African) Greatly loved daughter.

BITHIA (Hebrew) Daughter of God.

BITHRON (Hebrew) Daughter of song.

BITKI (Turkish) A type of plant.

BITSIE (American) Small. Short form of Elizabeth. *Variations:* Bitzee, Bitzi, Bitzie, Bitsy.

BITTAN (Scandinavian) Strength.

BIXENTA (Basque) Victorious woman.

BJORK (Icelandic) One of a kind. *Notable:* Singer Bjork.

BLAINE (Gaelic) Thin. *Variations:* Blane, Blayne.

BLAIR (English) A flat piece of land. *Variations:* Blaire, Blayre.

BLAISE (Latin) One who stutters. *Variations:* Blaize, Blase, Blaze.

BLAKE (English) Dark. *Variations:* Blakeley, Blakely.

BLANCA (Italian) White.

BLANCHE (English) White. *Notable:* Blanche DuBois, character in the play *A Streetcar Named Desire*. *Variations:* Blanch, Blancha, Blanka, Blanshe, Blenda.

BLANCHEFLEUR (French) White flower.

BLANDA (Latin) Seductive. *Variations:* Blandina, Blandine.

BLASIA (Latin) Stutterer. *Variation:* Blaise.

BLATH (Irish) Flower. *Variations:* Blaithin, Blaithm, Blathnaid, Blathnait.

BLESSING (English) To sanctify. *Variation:* Bless.

BLIMA (Hebrew) Blossom. *Variations:* Blimah, Blime.

BLISS (English) Joy. *Variations:* Blisse, Blyss, Blysse.

BLODWEN (Welsh) White flower. *Variations:* Blodwedd, Blodwyn, Blodyn.

BLONDELLE (French) Blond one. *Variation:* Blondell.

BLONDIE (American) Blond haired. *Variations:* Blondee, Blondi, Blondy.

BLOSSOM (English) Flower. *Notable:* TV character Blossom Russo.

BLUE (American) Like the color blue. *Variation:* Blu.

BLUEBELL (English) Flower name. *Variation:* Bluebelle.

BLUM (Hebrew) Flower. *Variations:* Blom, Bluma.

BLYTHE (English) Happy. *Variations:* Blithe, Blyth.

BO (Chinese) Precious. *Notable:* Actress Bo Derek.

BO-BAE (Korean) Treasured child.

BOBBI (English) Bright fame. Feminine version of Robert. *Notable:* Cosmetics queen Bobbi Brown. *Variations:* Bobbee, Bobbette, Bobbie, Bobby, Bobbye, Bobina.

BODIL (Scandinavian) Battle. *Variations:* Bothild, Botilda.

BOGDANA (Polish) Gift from God. *Variations:* Boana, Bocdana, Bogna, Bohdana, Bohna.

BOGUMILA (Polish) Grace of God.

BOLADE (African) Honor is here.

BOLANILE (African) Wealth in our house.

BONAMI (French) Good friend. *Variations:* Bonamie, Bonamy.

BONFILIA (Italian) Good daughter.

BONG-CHA (Korean) Best daughter.

BONITA (Spanish) Pretty. *Variations:* Bo, Boni, Bonie, Nita.

BONNIE (English) Pretty. *Notable:* Singer Bonnie Raitt. *Variations:* Boni, Bonie, Bonne, Bonnebell, Bonnee, Bonni, Bonnibel, Bonnibell, Bonnibelle, Bonny.

BORBALA (Hungarian) From a foreign land.

BORGHILD (Scandinavian) Fortified for battle.

BORGNY (Norwegian) Offering help. *Variation:* Borgni.

BOSKE (Hungarian) Lily.

BOSMA (Hebrew) Perfumed. *Variations:* Bosmat, Bosmath.

BOTAN (Japanese) Fresh as a blossom.

BOUDICCA (Celtic) Victorious queen. *Variation:* Bodicea.

BOZICA (Slavic) Born during Christmas. *Variations:* Bozicka, Bozika.

BOZIDARA (Czech) Divine gift. *Variations:* Boza, Bozena, Bozka.

BRACHA (Hebrew) Blessing. *Variation:* Brocha.

BRACKEN (English) A large fern.

BRADLEY (English) Wide meadow. *Variations:* Bradlee, Bradleigh, Bradlie, Bradly.

BRADY (English) Broad clearing. *Variations:* Bradee, Bradi, Bradie, Braedy.

BRAEDEN (English) Broad hill.

BRIATH (Welsh) Woman with freckles. *Variations:* Braithe, Brayth.

BRANCA (Portuguese) White.

BRANDA (Hebrew) Blessing.

BRANDY (English) A liquor. *Notable:* Singer/actress Brandy Norwood. *Variations:* Brandais, Brande, Brandea, Brandee, Brandi, Brandice, Brandie, Brandye, Branndea.

BRAZIL (Spanish) Of the ancient tree. *Variations:* Brasil, Brasille, Brazille.

BREANA (Celtic) Strong. Feminine version of Brian. *Variations:* Breann, Breanna, Breanne, Briana, Briane, Briann, Brianna, Brianne, Briona, Bryanna, Bryanne.

BRECK (Gaelic) Freckled.

BREE (Irish) Uplifting. *Variations:* Brea, Bria, Brie.

BRENDA (English). Sword. *Notable:* Comic-strip heroine Brenda Starr. *Variations:* Bren, Brendalynn, Brenn, Brennda, Brenndah.

BRENNA (English) Raven. Black hair. *Variation:* Brennan.

BRETISLAVA (Czech) Glorious noise. *Variations:* Breeka, Breticka.

BRETT (Latin) From Britain. *Notable:* Comedian Brett Butler. *Variation:* Brette.

BRIA (Irish) Form of Brianna.

BRIANNA (English) Noble. *Variations:* Briana, Bryana, Bryanna.

BRIAR (English) Thorny plant.

BRICE (English) Quick. *Variation:* Bryce.

BRIDGET (Irish) Strength. *Notables:* Actress Bridget Fonda; fictional diary writer Bridget Jones. *Variations:* Birgit, Birgitt, Birgitte, Breeda, Brid, Bride, Bridgett, Bridgette, Bridgitte, Brigantia, Brighid, Brigid, Brigida, Brigit, Brigitt, Brigitta, Brigitte, Brygida, Brygitka.

BRIDIE (Irish) Form of Bridget. *Variation:* Bridey.

BRIELLE (Hebrew) Form of Gabrielle. Strength is God. *Variations:* Briella, Bryelle.

BRIER (French) Heather.

BRIGITTE (French) Bridget. *Notables:* Actresses Brigitte Bardot and Brigitte Nielsen. *Variation:* Brigitta.

BRINA (Slavic) Defender. *Variations:* Breena, Brena, Brinna, Bryn, Bryna, Brynn, Brynna, Brynne.

BRISA (Spanish) Beloved. *Variations:* Breezy, Brisha, Brisia, Brissa, Briza, Bryssa.

BRISTOL (English) From the town of Bristol. *Notable:* Political daughter Bristol Palin. *Variations:* Bristel, Bristelle, Bristyl.

BRITT (English) From Britain. *Variations:* Brit, Britty.

BRITTA (Swedish) Strong. *Variation:* Brita.

BRITTANY (English) From Brittany, France. *Notable:* Singer Britney Spears. *Variations:* Brinnee, Britany, Britney, Britni, Brittan, Brittaney, Brittani, Brittania, Brittanie, Brittannia, Britteny, Brittni, Brittnie, Brittny.

BROGAN (Irish) Shoe.

BRONA (Czech) She who wins.

BRONISLAWA (Polish) Glorious protection. *Variation:* Bronya.

BRONTE (Irish) Generous person.

BRONWYN (Welsh) Pure of breast. *Variation:* Bronwen.

BROOKE (English) One who lives by a brook. *Notable:* Actress and child model Brooke Shields. *Variations:* Brook, Brookelle, Brookette.

BROOKLYN (American) Combination of Brooke and Lynn. *Variations:* Brooklan, Brooklynn.

BRUCIE (French) Thick brush. Feminine version of Bruce. *Variations:* Brucee, Brucia, Brucina, Brucine.

BRUNA (Italian) Having brown skin or brown hair. Feminine version of Bruno.

BRUNELLE (French) Little brown-haired girl. *Variations:* Brunella, Brunetta, Brunette.

BRUNHILDA (German) Armor-clad maiden who rides into battle. *Variations:* Brunhild, Brunhilde, Brunnhilda, Brunnhilde, Brynhild, Brynhilda.

BRYLEY (English) *Variations:* Briley, Brylee, Bryleigh, Brylie.

BRYNN (Welsh) Hill. *Variations:* Brinn, Bryn, Brynne.

BRYONY (English) Vine. *Variations:* Briony, Bronie, Bryonie.

BUA (Vietnamese) Good-luck charm.

BUBBLES (American) Effervescence.

BUENA (Spanish) Very good.

BUFFY (American) Form of Elizabeth. *Variations:* Buffee, Buffey, Buffi, Buffie.

BUNNY (English) Rabbit. *Variations:* Bunni, Bunnie.

BURGUNDY (French) Wine. *Variation:* Burgandy.

BURNETTE (French) Brown.

BUTTERCUP (American) A flower.

BUTTERFLY (American) A butterfly.

CABRINA (American) Legendary princess. *Variations:* Cabreena, Cabreene, Cabreina, Cabriena, Cabrinah, Cabrinna, Cabryna, Cabrynna.

CABRIOLE (French) Adorable girl. *Variations:* Cabriola, Cabriolla, Cabriolle, Cabryola, Cabryole.

CACALIA (Latin) Resembling the flowering plant. *Variations:* Cacalea, Cacaliah.

CACHET (French) Distinguished woman. *Variations:* Cachay, Cache, Cachette.

CACIA (Greek) Form of Acacia. Thorny treee. *Variations:* Cacea, Caciah.

CADEN (English) Battle maiden. *Variations:* Cadan, Cadenne, Cadin, Cadon.

CADENCE (Latin) Rhythmic. *Variations:* Cadena, Cadenza, Caydence, Kade, Kadena, Kadence, Kadenza.

CADHLA (Irish) Beautiful woman.

CADIS (Greek) Sparking young girl. *Variation:* Cadys.

CADWYN (Welsh) A strong chain. *Variations:* Cadwen, Cadwin, Cadwynn.

CADY (English) Happiness. *Variations:* Cade, Cadee, Cadey, Cadie, Kade, Kadee.

CAEL (Celtic) Victorious person. *Variation:* Caelle.

CAESARIA (Greek) Ruler. Feminine form of Caesar. *Variations:* Cesaria, Cesarina.

CAFELL (Welsh) Oracle priestess.

CAFFARIA (Irish) Helmeted one. *Variations:* Caffara, Caffariah.

CAHIRA (Irish) Woman warrior. *Variations:* Caheera, Cahirah, Cahyra.

CAI (Vietnamese) Girl.

International Place Names

BOYS:
Chad
Cuba
Donegal
Israel
Jordan
London
Melbourne
Oman
Troy
Wellington

GIRLS:
China
Florence
Geneva
India
Ireland
Jamaica
Kenya
Paris
Sydney
Victoria

CAIA (Latin) Rejoice.

CAILIDA (Spanish) Adoring.

CAILIDORA (Greek) Gift of beauty.

CAILIN (Scottish) Triumphant people. *Variations:* Caelan, Caileen, Cailyn, Calunn, Cauleen, Caulin.

CAINELL (Welsh) A beautiful young girl. *Variations:* Cainelle, Caynelle.

CAINWEN (Welsh) Beautiful treasure. *Variation:* Cainwyn.

CAIRO (Egyptian) From Cairo (Egypt).

CAITLIN (Irish) Pure. *Variations:* Caitilin, Caitlan, Caitlion, Caitlon, Caitlyn, Caitlynne, Catlin, Kaitlin, Kaitlyn, Kaitlynn, Kaitlynne, Katelin, Katelynn.

CAITRIA (Gaelic) Pure. *Variations:* Caitrin, Caitriona.

CALA (Arabic) Fortress.

CALAIS (French) From Calais in France.

CALANDRA (Greek) Lark. *Variations:* Cal, Calandria, Calendra, Calendre, Calinda, Kalandra.

CALANTHA (Greek) Flower. *Variations:* Calanth, Calantha, Calanthe.

CALATEA (Greek) Flowering woman. *Variation:* Calatia.

CALDWELL (English) Of the cold well.

CALEDONIA (Latin) From Scotland.

CALIDA (Greek) Most beautiful; (Spanish) Affectionate, warm. *Variation:* Callida.

CALIFORNIA (Spanish) Paradise.

CALISTA (Greek) Beautiful. *Notable:* Actress Calista Flockhart. *Variations:* Cala, Calesta, Cali, Calise, Calissa, Calisse, Calisto, Callie, Callista, Cally, Callysta, Calysta, Kala, Kallie.

CALLA (Greek) Lily. *Variations:* Cala, Callah.

CALLAN (Gaelic) Powerful in battle. *Variations:* Callen, Callon, Callyn.

CALLIDA (Latin) Fiery young girl.

CALLIDORA (Greek) Beautiful gift.

CALLIE (Greek) Lovely. *Variations:* Caleigh, Caley, Cali, Callee, Calleigh, Calley, Calli, Cally, Kali, Kallee, Kalley, Kallie.

CALLIGENIA (Greek) Ancient mythological figure.

CALLIOPE (Greek) Pretty muse. *Variations:* Kalliope, Kallyope.

CALLULA (Latin) Little beauty.

CALOGERA (Italian) Beautiful elder.

CALPURNIA (Latin) Woman of power.

CALTHA (Latin) Yellow flower. *Variation:* Kaltha.

CALUMINA (Scottish) Peaceful woman.

CALVINA (Latin) Without hair. Feminine version of Calvin. *Variation:* Calvine.

CALYPSO (Greek) Girl in hiding.

CAMBRIA (Welsh) From Wales. *Variations:* Cambrie, Cambry, Cambrya.

CAMDEN (English) From the enclosed valley. *Variations:* Camdin, Camdyn.

CAMELLIA (Italian) Flower name. *Variations:* Camalia, Camela, Camelia, Kamelia.

CAMEO (Italian) A piece of profile jewelry. *Variation:* Cammeo.

CAMERON (Scottish) Crooked nose. *Notable:* Actress Cameron Diaz. *Variations:* Camaran, Camaron, Camren, Camron, Camryn.

CAMI (American) Short form of Cameron or Camille. *Variations:* Camey, Camie, Cammie, Cammy.

CAMILLE (French) Assistant in the church. *Notable:* Feminist/writer Camille Paglia. *Variations:* Cam, Cama, Camala, Cami, Camila, Camile, Camilia, Camilla, Cammi, Cammie, Cammy, Cammylle, Camyla, Kamila, Kamilka.

CAMPBELL (Scottish) Having a crooked mouth. *Notable:* News reporter Campbell Brown.

CANA (Turkish) Beloved daughter.

CANACE (Greek) Born of the wind.

CANADA (Native American) Horizon. *Variations:* Caneadea, Kanada.

CANDACE (Latin) White. *Notables:* Writer Candace Bushnell; actress Candice Bergen. *Variations:* Candice, Candie, Candis, Candiss, Candyce, Kandace, Kandice, Kandyce.

CANDELARA (Spanish) Spiritual woman.

CANDIDA (Latin) White. *Variation:* Candide.

CANDRA (Latin) Radiant. *Variations:* Candria, Kandra.

CANDY (English) Short form of Candace. *Variations:* Candee, Candi, Candie, Kandee, Kandi, Kandie, Kandy.

CANISA (Greek) Very much loved. *Variations:* Caneesa, Canissa, Canyssa.

CANNELITA (Italian) From a beautiful garden. *Variation:* Canelita.

CANTARA (Arabic) Small bridge. *Variation:* Kantara.

CAOILFHIONN (Irish) Slender and fair. *Variations:* Caoilainn, Caoilinn, Caoilfhinn, Caoimhe.

CAPRICE (Italian) On a whim. *Variations:* Caprece, Capricia, Caprie, Kapri, Kaprice, Kapricia, Kaprisha.

CAPRINA (Italian) From Capri. *Variation:* Capreena, Capriana, Caprinna.

CAPUCINE (French) Collar. *Variations:* Cappucine, Capucina.

CARA (Italian) Dear. *Variations:* Caralea, Caralee, Caralisa, Carella, Carita, Carra, Kara, Karah, Karry.

CAREN (Greek) Pure. Form of Karen. *Variations:* Carin, Carine, Carrin, Caron, Caryn, Karen, Karena, Karin, Karina, Karine, Karon, Karyn, Karyna, Karynn.

CARESSA (French) Loving touch. *Variations:* Caresa, Caress, Caresse.

CAREY (Welsh) Near a castle. *Notable:* Actress Carey Lowell. *Variations:* Caree, Carree, Carrie.

CARIDAD (Spanish) Generous love.

CARINA (Italian) Darling. *Variations:* Carena, Careena, Cariana, Carin, Carinna, Karina.

CARISSA (Greek) Refined. *Variations:* Carisa, Carisse, Karissa.

CARITA (Italian) Charity. *Variations:* Caritta, Carrita.

CARLA (Italian) Woman. Feminine version of Carl, Carlo, or Charles. *Notable:* Actress Carla Gugino. *Variations:* Carlesssa, Carlisa, Karla.

CARLENE (English) Woman. Form of Caroline. *Notable:* Singer Carlene Carter. *Variations:* Carleen, Carlina, Carline, Karleen, Karlene.

CARLIN (Irish) Little champion. *Variations:* Carlinn, Carlyn, Carlynn, Carlynne.

CARLISLE (English) From Carlisle. *Variation:* Carlyle.

CARLOTTA (Italian; Spanish) Form of Charlotte. *Variations:* Carletta, Carlette, Carlita, Carlota, Karlotta.

CARLY (English) Feminine form of Carl or Charles. *Notable:* Singer Carly Simon. *Variations:* Carlee, Carley, Carli, Carlie, Carlye, Karlee, Karli, Karlie, Karley.

CARMEL (Hebrew) Garden. *Variations:* Carmeli, Carmelina, Carmelita, Carmia, Carmiela, Carmit, Carmiya, Karmel, Karmeli, Karmia, Karmit, Karmiya.

CARMELA (Italian) Form of Carmel. *Variations:* Carmelia, Carmella, Karmela, Karmella.

CARMEN (Latin) Song. *Notable:* Actress Carmen Electra. *Variations:* Carma, Carman, Carmena, Carmencita, Carmenta.

CARNA (Arabic) Horn. *Notable:* Singer Carnie Wilson. *Variations:* Carney, Carni, Carnia, Carnie, Carniela, Carniella, Carniya, Carny, Karni, Karnia, Karniela, Karniella, Karniya.

CARNATION (Latin) Like the carnation flower.

CARNI (Hebrew) Horn. *Variations:* Carna, Carney, Carnia, Carnie, Carniela, Carniella, Carniya, Carny, Karni, Karnia, Karniela, Karniella, Karniya.

CAROL (German) Woman. *Notables:* Comedian Carol Burnett; singer Carole King. *Variations:* Carel, Carelle, Caro, Carola, Carole, Carolee, Caroll, Carrelle, Carroll, Caru, Caryl, Caryle, Caryll, Carylle, Karel, Karil, Karol, Karole, Karyl.

CAROLINE (German) Woman. *Notables:* Presidential "First Daughter" Caroline Kennedy; Princess Caroline of Monaco. *Variations:* Carilyn, Carilynn, Carlyn, Carlynn, Carolenia, Carolin, Carolina, Karolin, Karolina, Karoline.

CAROLYN (English) Women. Form of Caroline. *Notable:* Medical intuitive/writer Carolyn Myss. *Variations:* Carolynn, Carolynne, Karolyn, Karolyna, Karolyne, Karolynn, Karolynne.

CARON (Welsh) Love. *Variations:* Carren, Carrin, Carron, Carrone, Caryn, Carynn.

CARRIE (English) A form of Caroline. *Notable:* Writer Carrie Fisher. *Variations:* Carey, Cari, Carri, Carrie, Carry, Cary, Kari, Karie, Karri, Karrie, Karry, Karrye.

CARRINGTON (English) Woman from Carrington.

CARSON (Scottish) Child of Carr. *Variations:* Carsan, Carsen, Carsin.

CARYS (Welsh) Loved. *Variations:* Caris, Cariss, Carisse, Caryss, Carysse.

CASCADIA (Latin) Of the waterfall. *Variation:* Cascadea.

CASEY (Irish) Observant. *Variations:* Cacia, Casee, Casie, Cassie, Caycey, Caysey, Kacey, Kacia, Kasee, Kasie, Kaycey, Kaysey.

CASILDA (Latin) House. *Variations:* Casild, Casildah, Casilde.

CASS (English) Short form of Cassandra. *Notable:* Singer Mama Cass Elliot. *Variation:* Kass.

CASSANDRA (Greek) Protector. *Variations:* Casandera, Casandra, Cassandre, Cassaundra, Casson, Cassondra, Kasandera, Kasandra, Kassandra, Kassandre, Kassaundra, Kassie, Kasson, Kassondra.

CASSIA (Greek) Cinnamon.

CASSIE (English) Short form of Cassandra. *Variations:* Cassee, Casi, Cassi, Cassielle, Cassey, Cassy.

CASSIDY (Irish) Clever. *Variations:* Cassidee, Cassidey, Cassidi, Cassidie, Kasady, Kassidey, Kassidi, Kassidie, Kassidy.

CASTA (Spanish) Pure.

CASTALIA (Greek) Mythological nymph.

CATALINA (Spanish) Pure.

CATAVA (African) Sleep.

CATE (English) Short form of Catherine. *Notable:* Actress Cate Blanchett. *Variations:* Cait, Caty, Kate, Katee, Katey, Kait, Kati, Katie, Katy.

CATHERINE (English) Pure. *Notable:* Actress Catherine Zeta Jones. *Variations:* Catalina, Catarina, Catarine, Cateline, Catharin, Catharine, Catharyna, Catharyne, Cathee, Cathelin, Cathelina, Cathelle, Catherin, Catherina, Catrin, Catrina, Catrine, Catryna, Kai, Kaila, Kaitlin, Kata, Kataleen, Katalin, Katalina, Katarina, Kateke, Katerina, Katerinka, Katharin, Katharina, Katharine, Katharyn, Kathereen, Katherin, Katherina, Kathren, Kathrine, Kathryn, Kathryne, Katia, Katica, Katina, Katrina, Katrine, Katriona, Katryna, Kattrina, Katushka, Katya, Kay,

Kisan, Kit, Kitti, Kittie, Kitty, Kotinka, Kotryna.

CATHLEEN (Irish) Pure. Form of Catherine. *Variations:* Cathelin, Cathlene, Cathlyn, Kathleen, Kathlyn, Kathlynn.

CATHY (English) short form of Catherine. *Notable:* Cartoonist Cathy Guisewite. *Variations:* Cathe, Cathee, Cathey, Cathi, Cathie, Kaethe, Kathe, Kathey, Kathi, Kathie, Kathy.

CATRICE (Greek) Wholesome woman. *Variations:* Catreese, Catrysse.

CATRIONA (Irish) Pure. *Variations:* Catraoine, Catrina.

CAVANA (Irish) From the hallow. *Variations:* Cavanna, Cavannah.

CECE (Latin) Blind. Short form of Cecilia. *Variations:* CeeCee, Ceci.

CECILIA (Latin) Blind. Feminine version of Cecil. *Notable:* Opera singer Cecilia Bartoli. *Variations:* Cacilia, C'Ceal, Cecely, Ceci, Cecia, Cecile, Cecilie, Cecille, Cecilyn, Cecyle, Cecylia, Ceil, Cele, Celenia, Celia, Celie, Celina, Celinda, Celine, Celinna, Celle, Cesia, Cespa, Cicely, Cicilia, Cycyl, Seslia, Sessaley, Sessile, Sessilly, Sheelagh, Sheelah, Sheila, Sheilagh, Sheilah, Shela, Shelah, Shelia, Shiela, Sisely, Sissie, Sissy.

CEDRICA (English) Chief. *Variation:* Cedricka.

CEIL (Latin) Short form of Cecilia. *Variation:* Ciel.

CEINWYN (Welsh) Blessed with beauty. *Variations:* Ceinwen, Ceinwenn, Ceinwynne.

CEITEAG (Scottish) Pure.

CELANDINE (Greek) Yellow flower. A swallow. *Variations:* Celand, Celandina, Celanda.

CELENA (Greek) Moon goddess. *Notable:* Singer Celine Dion. *Variations:* Celina, Celene, Celine, Selena.

CELESTE (Latin) Heavenly. *Variations:* Cela, Celesse, Celesta, Celestia, Celestiel, Celestina, Celestine, Celestyn, Celestyna, Celinka, Celisse, Cesia, Seleste, Selestia, Selinka.

CELIA (Italian; Spanish) Heaven. *Notable:* Queen of Salsa, Celia Cruz.

CELISHA (Greek) Passionate woman. *Variations:* Celeesha, Celeisha.

CELOSIA (Greek) Aflame.

CENOBIA (Spanish) Sign or symbol. *Variation:* Zenobia.

CERA (French) Colorful.

CERELIA (Latin) In springtime. *Variation:* Cerella.

CERES (Latin) Roman goddess of agriculture.

CERIDWEN (Celtic) Goddess of poetry. *Variation:* Ceridwyn.

CERINA (Latin) Form of Serena.

CERISE (French) Cherry. *Variations:* Cherice, Cherise, Cherrise, Sarise, Sharise, Sherice, Sherise, Sheriz.

CERYS (Welsh) Love. *Variations:* Ceri, Ceries, Cerri, Cerrie.

CESARINA (Latin) Hairy. Feminine version of Cesar. *Variations:* Cesarea, Cesarie, Cesarin.

CHABLIS (French) White wine.

CHAHNA (Hindi) Love.

CHAILYN (American) Waterfall.

CHAITALI (Hindi) Active.

CHAKA (Sanskrit) Energy. *Notable:* Singer Chaka Khan.

CHAKRA (Sanskrit) Circle of energy.

CHALICE (French) Goblet. *Variations:* Chalace, Chalissa, Chalisse, Chalyse.

CHALINA (Spanish) A rose.

CHAMANIA (Hebrew) Sunflower. *Variations:* Chamaniya, Hamania, Hamaniya.

CHAMELI (Hindi) Jasmine.

CHAMPAGNE (French) Sparkling wine.

CHANA (Hebrew) Grace. *Variations:* Chanah, Chani, Channa, Channah, Hannah.

CHANDAA (Hindi) Moon. *Variations:* Chanda, Chandra, Chandrakanta.

CHANDANI (Hindi) Moonlight. *Variations:* Chandni, Chandree, Chandrika, Chandrima, Chandrimaa, Chandrjaa.

CHANDELLE (French) Candle. *Variations:* Chandal, Chandell, Shan, Shandell, Shandelle.

CHANDLER (English) Candle maker.

CHANDRA (Sanskrit) Moonlike. *Variations:* Chandre, Shandra, Shandre.

CHANEL (French) Name inspired by the French designer Coco Chanel. *Variations:* Chanell, Chanelle, Channell, Channelle, Shanell, Shanelle, Shannelle.

CHANIA (Hebrew) Grace of the lord. *Variations:* Chanina, Chaniya, Hania, Haniya.

Aromatic Names

Designer fragrances not only delight our senses; they often have names as captivating as their scents, especially when the creators honor themselves with an eponymous product.

BOYS:	GIRLS:
Adolfo	Anais
Aramis	Arpege
Armani	Cacharel
Bijon	Calandre
Boucheron	Chanel
Casmir	Chantilly
Claiborne	Chloe
Cristobal	Coriandre
Dior	Desirade
Giorgio	Detchema
Givenchy	Escada
Guerlain	Jontue
Halston	Katia
Jivago	Kantara
Jovan	Mahora
Lanvin	Norell
Tresor	Pavlova
Valentino	Sirene
Versace	Shalimar
Xeryus	Tiffany

Top Names of the 1980s

BOYS:

1. Michael
2. Christopher
3. Matthew
4. Joshua
5. David
6. James
7. Daniel
8. Robert
9. John
10. Joseph
11. Jason
12. Justin
13. Andrew
14. Ryan
15. William
16. Brian
17. Brandon
18. Jonathan
19. Nicholas
20. Anthony

GIRLS:

1. Jessica
2. Jennifer
3. Amanda
4. Ashley
5. Sarah
6. Stephanie
7. Melissa
8. Nicole
9. Elizabeth
10. Heather
11. Tiffany
12. Michelle
13. Amber
14. Megan
15. Amy
16. Rachel
17. Kimberly
18. Christina
19. Lauren
20. Crystal

CHANIT (Hebrew) Spear. *Variations:* Chanita, Hanit, Hanita.

CHANNA (Hindi) Chickpea.

CHANNING (English) Church official.

CHANTAL (French) Song. *Variations:* Chandal, Chantala, Chantale, Chantalle, Chante, Chantel, Chantele, Chantelle, Shanta, Shantae, Shantal, Shantalle, Shantay, Shante, Shanteigh, Shantel, Shantell, Shantella, Shantelle, Shontal, Shontalle, Shontelle.

CHANTERELLE (French) Cup. *Variation:* Chantrelle.

CHANTEUSE (French) Singer.

CHANTILLY (French) Lace. *Variation:* Chantille.

CHANTOU (Cambodian) Flower.

CHANTREA (Cambodian) Moonlight.

CHANYA (Hebrew) God's grace. *Variation:* Hanya.

CHARA (Spanish) Rose. *Variation:* Charo.

CHARDONNAY (French) White wine. *Variations:* Chardonnae, Shardonnay.

CHARILLE (French) Womanly. *Variations:* Charil, Charila, Charile, Charyl.

CHARIS (Greek) Grace. *Variations:* Chara, Charece, Charice, Charisse.

CHARISMA (Latin) Charismatic. *Notable:* Actress Charisma Carpenter. *Variations:* Carisma, Karisma.

CHARITA (Spanish) Princess.

CHARITY (Latin) Kindness. *Variations:* Charita, Charitee, Charitey, Sharitee.

CHARLENE (English) Womanly. Feminine version of Charles. *Variations:* Charla, Charlaine, Charlayne, Charlena, Charli, Charlie, Charlina, Charline, Cherlene, Cherline, Sharlayne, Sharleen, Sharlene.

CHARLIZE (French) Womanly. *Notable:* Actress Charlize Theron. *Variations:* Charlisa, Charlisse.

CHARLOTTE (French) Small beauty. Variant of Charles. *Notable:* Writer Charlotte Brontë. *Variations:* Carlotta, Charlet, Charlett, Charletta, Charlette, Charlot, Charlotta.

CHARMAINE (French) Song. *Variations:* Charma, Charmagne, Charmain, Charmane, Charmayne, Charmin, Charmine.

CHARMIAN (Greek) Joy. *Variation:* Charmion.

CHARNA (Yiddish) Dark. *Variation:* Charnette.

CHARO (Spanish) Rose. *Notable:* Singer/actress Charo. *Variation:* Charro.

CHARU (Hindi) Attractive.

CHARUMAT (Hindi) Wise mind.

CHASHMONA (Hebrew) Princess. *Variation:* Chashmonit.

CHASIA (Hebrew) Protected by God. *Variations:* Chasya, Hasia, Hasya.

CHASIDA (Hebrew) Righteous. *Variation:* Chasidah.

CHASINA (Hebrew) Strong. *Variation:* Hasina.

CHASTITY (Latin) Purity. *Variations:* Chasta, Chastina, Chastine.

CHAU (Vietnamese) Pearl.

CHAVA (Hebrew) Life. *Variations:* Chabah, Chapka, Chavah, Chavalah, Hava.

CHAVIVA (Hebrew) Beloved.

CHAVON (Hebrew) God is good. *Variations:* Chavona, Chavonna, Chavonne, Shavon.

CHAYA (Hebrew) Life. *Variations:* Chayah, Haya.

CHAZMIN (American) Form of Jasmine.

CHEDRA (Hebrew) Happiness. *Variation:* Hedra.

CHEFTZIBA (Hebrew) I am delighted by her. *Variations:* Cheftzibah, Cheftziya, Hefibah, Hefzi, Hefzia, Hefziba, Hephziba, Hephzibah, Hepzi, Hepzia, Hepziba, Hepzibah.

CHEIFA (Hebrew) Haven. *Variations:* Chaifa, Haifa, Heifa.

CHELO (Spanish) Nickname for Consuelo; consolation.

CHELSEA (English) Ship port. *Notables:* Presidential "First Daughter" Chelsea Clinton; talk-show host Chelsea Handler. *Variations:* Chelcy, Chelsa, Chelsee, Chelsey, Chelsi, Chelsie, Chelsy.

CHEMDA (Hebrew) Charm. *Variation:* Hemda.

CHEMDIAH (Hebrew) God is my hope. *Variations:* Chemdia, Chemdiya, Hemdia, Hemdiah.

CHEN (Chinese) Morning.

CHENGUANG (Chinese) Morning glory.

CHENIA (Hebrew) Grace of God. *Variations:* Chen, Chenya, Hen, Henia, Henya.

CHENOA (Native American) White dove. *Variation:* Shonoa.

CHER (French) Dearest. *Notable:* Singer/actress Cher. *Variations:* Cherise, Sher, Shereen, Shereena, Sherena, Sherene, Sheri, Sherianne, Sherina, Sherry.

CHERIE (French) Dear. *Variations:* Chere, Cherey, Cheri, Cherice, Cherie, Sheree, Sheri, Sherry.

CHERILYN (American) Combination of Cher or Cheryl and Lynn. *Variations:* Cheralyn, Cherilin, Cherilynn, Cherilynne, Cherlin, Cherlyn, Cherylin, Sheralynne, Sherilin, Sherralin, Sherrilyn, Sherrylene, Sherryline, Sherrylyn, Sherylin, Sherylyn.

CHERISH (English) To treasure. *Variations:* Charish, Charisha, Cherrish.

CHERMONA (Hebrew) Holy mountain. *Variation:* Hermona.

CHERRY (French) Cherry. *Notable:* Actress Cherry Jones. *Variations:* Chere, Cheree, Cherey, Cherida, Cherise, Cherita, Cherreu, Cherri, Cherrie.

CHERUT (Hebrew) Freedom. *Variation:* Cheruta.

CHERYL (French) Beloved. *Notable:* Actress Cheryl Ladd. *Variations:* Cherill, Cherrill, Cherryl, Cheryle, Cheryll, Sherill, Sherryll, Sheryl.

CHESLEY (English) From the meadow. *Variations:* Cheslea, Chesley, Chesly.

CHESNA (Slavic) Peaceful.

CHEYENNE (Native American) Red talker. *Variations:* Cheyanna, Cheyanne, Chiana, Chianna, Shayann, Sheyenne.

CHEYNE (English) From the oak grove. *Variation:* Chaney.

CHIANTI (Italian) Like chianti wine.

CHIARA (Italian) Light. *Variations:* Cheara, Chiarra, Chiarina.

CHIASA (Japanese) A thousand mornings.

CHIBA (Hebrew) Love.

CHICA (Spanish) Girl. *Variations:* Chickie, Chicky.

CHIDORI (Japanese) A bird.

CHIEKO (Japanese) Wise child.

CHIHARU (Japanese) A thousand springs.

CHIKAKO (Japanese) Intelligence.

CHILALI (Native American) Snowbird.

CHIMALIS (Native American) Bluebird.

CHIMENE (French) Listening.

CHINA (English) Country. *Notable:* Singer Chynna Phillips. *Variations:* Chinah, Chinna, Chyna, Chynna.

CHIQUITA (Spanish) Little girl. *Variations:* Chaqueta, Chaquita, Chiqueta.

CHISLAINE (French) Faithful.

CHITA (Italian) Pearl. *Notable:* Actress/singer Chita Rivera.

CHIVONNE (American) Form of Siohban. God is gracious. *Variations:* Chevonna, Chevonne, Chivon, Chivonna, Chivonni.

CHIYO (Japanese) A thousand generations. *Variation:* Chiyoko.

CHLOE (Greek) Young blade of grass. *Notable:* Actress Chloe Sevigny. *Variations:* Clo, Cloe.

CHO (Japanese) Butterfly. *Variation:* Chou.

CHOLENA (Native American) Bird.

CHOON-HEE (Korean) Daughter of spring.

CHRIS (English) Short form of Christina. *Notable:* Tennis champ Chris Evert. *Variations:* Chrissie, Chrissy, Cris, Kris.

CHRISTABEL (Latin) Fair Christian. *Variations:* Christabella, Christabelle, Cristabel.

CRISTAL (Latin) Form of Crystal. *Variations:* Christel, Christelle.

CHRISTINA (Greek) Anointed one. *Variations:* Chris, Chrissa, Chrissy, Christa, Christen, Christi, Christiana, Christiane, Christiann, Christianna, Christie, Christina, Christy, Krista, Kristina, Kristine, Kristy, Teena, Teina, Tena, Tina, Tinah.

CHRYSALIS (Latin) Butterfly.

CHRYSANTHEMUM (Latin) Daisy-like flower.

CHULDAH (Hebrew) Mole or weasel. *Variation:* Chulda.

CHUMANI (Native American) Dew.

CHUN (Chinese) Spring.

CHUNG-AE (Korean) Virtuous love.

CHUNG-CHA (Korean) Virtuous daughter.

CHUNHUA (Chinese) Spring flowers.

CHUNTAO (Chinese) Spring peach.

CHYNNA (English) China, the country. *Variation:* China.

CIANDRA (Italian) Surrounded by light.

CIANNAIT (Irish) Ancient. *Variation:* Ciannata.

CIARA (Irish) Black. *Variations:* Ceara, Ciarra, Ciera, Cierra.

CICELY (Latin) Form of Cecilia. *Variations:* Cicelie, Cicilie, Cicily, Cilla, Sicely.

CINDY (Greek) Moon goddess. Short form of Cynthia. *Notables:* Columnist Cindy Adams; supermodel Cindy Crawford; singer Cyndi Lauper. *Variations:* Cinda, Cindee, Cindi, Cindie, Cyndee, Cyndi, Cyndie, Cyndy, Sindee, Sindi, Sindie, Sindy, Syndi, Syndy.

CINZIA (Italian) Form of Cynthia.

CIPRIANA (Greek) From Cyprus. *Variations:* Cipriane, Ciprianna, Cypriana, Cyprienne.

CIRCE (Greek) Mythological goddess of magic.

CISSY (American) Short form of Cecilia. *Variations:* Ciss, Cissey, Cissi, Cissie, Sissi, Sissy.

CITARA (Greek) Harp. *Variation:* Citare.

CLAIRE (Latin; French) Bright. *Notable:* Actress Claire Danes. *Variations:* Clair, Clairette, Clairine, Clairy, Clare.

CLANCEY (Irish) Red-headed soldier. *Variations:* Clancy, Clancie.

CLARA (English) Bright. *Notable:* Red Cross founder Clara Barton. *Variations:* Claramond, Claresta, Clareta, Clarette, Clarice, Clarie, Clarinda, Clarine, Claris, Clarisa, Clarissa, Clarisse, Clarita, Klara, Klari.

CLARICE (French) Clear. *Variations:* Clairice, Clareece, Clarise, Clarisse, Claryce, Cleryce, Clerysse, Klarice, Klarissa, Klaryce, Klaryssa.

CLARISSA (Latin) Brilliant. *Variations:* Clairissa, Claressa, Clarisa, Clarissa, Clarista, Claritza, Klarissa.

CLAUDETTE (French) French form of Claudia. *Notable:* Actress Claudette Colbert. *Variation:* Claudet.

CLAUDIA (Latin) Lame. Feminine version of Claude. *Notable:* Cover girl Claudia Schiffer. *Variations:* Claudelle, Claudette, Claudina, Claudine.

CLELIA (Latin) Glorious.

CLEMATIS (Greek) Vine or flower name. *Variation:* Clematia.

CLEMENTINE (English) Gentle. *Variations:* Clementia, Clementina, Clemenza.

CLEO (Greek) Acclaim. Short form of Cleopatra. *Variation:* Clea.

CLEOPATRA (Greek) Her father's renown. *Notable:* Cleopatra, Queen of the Nile. *Variations:* Clea, Cleo.

CLEVA (English) One who lives on a hill.

CLIANTHA (Greek) Flower. *Variations:* Cleantha, Cleanthe, Clianthe.

CLIO (Greek) Proclaimer. *Variation:* Klio.

CLODAGH (Irish) A river.

CLORIS (Latin) White, pure. *Notable:* Actress Cloris Leachman. *Variation:* Chloris.

CLOTILDA (German) Famous in battle. *Variations:* Clothilda, Clothilde, Clotilde, Tilda, Tilly.

CLOVER (English) Flower name.

CLYMENE (Greek) Goddess of fame and infamy. *Variation:* Clymena.

CLYTIE (Greek) Lovely. *Variations:* Clyte, Clytia.

COAHOMA (Native American: Choctaw) Red panther.

COBIE (English) Protected. *Notable:* Actress Cobie Smulders. *Variations:* Cobey, Cobi, Coby.

COCHAVA (Hebrew) Star.

COCHETA (Native American) Foreign.

COCO (Spanish) Coconut. *Notable:* Fashion designer Coco Chanel. *Variation:* Koko.

CODY (English) Cushion. *Variations:* Codee, Codi, Codie, Kodi, Kodie.

COKIE (American) Nickname for Corinne. *Notable:* Reporter Cokie Roberts. *Variations:* Cokey, Cokee, Coki.

COLANDA (African American) Variation of Yolanda.

COLBY (English) Coal village. *Notable:* Singer Colbie Caillat. *Variations:* Colbey, Colbi, Colbie.

COLETTE (French) Triumphant people. *Notable:* French novelist Colette. *Variations:* Coletta, Collet, Collete, Collett.

COLISA (English) Wonderful. *Variations:* Coleesa, Colissa.

COLLEEN (Irish) Young girl. *Variations:* Coleen, Colene, Colina, Coline, Colline, Kolleen.

COLMCILLA (Irish) Dove of the church.

COLMYNA (Irish) Shrewd. *Variation:* Colmina.

COLUMBA (Latin) Dove. *Variations:* Colombe, Columba, Columbia, Columbina, Columbine.

COLWYN (Welsh) From the river. *Variations:* Colwen, Colwyn.

COMFORT (English) To comfort.

CONCEPCION (Latin) Conception.

CONCHA (Spanish) Nickname for Concepcion.

CONCHETTA (Spanish) Pure. *Variations:* Concetta, Concettina, Conchita.

CONCORDIA (Greek) Harmonious.

CONDOLEEZZA (Italian) Musical term "con dolcezza," which means "with sweetness." *Notable:* Former U.S. Secretary of State Condoleezza Rice. *Variations:* Condoleeza, Condi.

CONGALIE (Irish) Constant. *Variation:* Congolia.

CONNIE (English) Short form of Constance. *Notables:* Actress Connie Stevens; singer Connie Francis. *Variations:* Conni, Conny.

CONNOR (Irish) Praised. *Variations:* Connar, Conner, Connery, Conor.

CONRADINE (German) Bold counsel. *Variation:* Conradina.

CONSTANCE (Latin) Steady. *Variations:* Connie, Constancia, Constancy, Constanta, Constantia, Constantina, Constanza, Constanze.

CONSUELA (Spanish) Consolation. *Variations:* Consolata, Consuelo.

CONTESSA (Italian) A countess.

COOKIE (American) Cookie. *Variations:* Cookee, Cooki, Cooky.

CORA (Greek) Maiden. *Variations:* Corah, Coralee, Coralie, Coretta, Corissa, Corra.

CORAL (English) Coral. *Variations:* Corall, Coralle, Corel, Coryl, Koral.

CORAZON (Spanish) Heart.

CORBY (English) Town in Great Britain. *Variations:* Corbee, Corbi, Corbie.

CORDELIA (English) Warm hearted. *Variations:* Cordalia, Cordella, Cordelle, Cordi, Cordilia, Cordy.

COREY (Irish) The hollow. *Variations:* Cori, Corie, Corri, Corrie, Corry, Khori, Kori, Korie, Korey.

CORIANDER (Greek) Like the herb, coriander.

CORINNE (French) Maiden. *Variations:* Carine, Carinna, Carinne, Carynna, Corina, Corine, Corinna, Correna, Corrianne, Corrienne, Corrine, Corrinn, Korina, Korinne, Korrina.

CORINTHIA (Greek) Woman from Corinth. *Variation:* Corinthe.

CORKY (American) Sprite. *Variations:* Corkee, Corkey, Corki, Corkie, Korky.

CORLISS (English) Generous. *Variation:* Corlyss.

CORNELIA (English) Horn. Feminine version of Cornelius. *Variations:* Cornela, Cornelie, Cornella, Corney, Neelia, Neely, Neelya, Nela, Nelia, Nila.

CORONA (Spanish) Crown. *Variation:* Coronetta.

CORVINA (Latin) A raven.

COSETTE (French) Victorious. *Variations:* Cosetta, Cossette, Cozette.

COSIMA (Greek) Order. Feminine version of Cosmo. *Variations:* Cosma, Kosima.

COTY (French) Slope. *Variations:* Cotee, Coti, Cotie.

COURTNEY (English) Dweller in the court. *Notables:* Singer Courtney Love; actress Courteney Cox. *Variations:* Cortney, Courtenay, Courteney, Courtnie, Courtny.

COVENTINA (Celtic) Water goddess. *Variations:* Coventeena, Coventine, Covintina.

CREE (Native American) Tribal name. Girl's nickname. *Notable:* Actress Cree Summer. *Variations:* Crea, Crigh.

CREIRWY (Welsh) Jewel.

CRESCENT (French) Crescent shaped. *Variations:* Crescencia, Crescentia, Cressant, Cressent, Cressentia.

CRESSIDA (Greek) Gold. *Variations:* Cressa, Cressie.

CRICKET (American) Insect. Pet name.

CRISPINA (Latin) Curly hair. Feminine version of Crispin. *Variation:* Crispa.

CROCETTA (Italian) Way of the cross. *Variation:* Crocifissa.

CRUZ (Spanish) Cross. *Variation:* Cruzita.

CRYSTAL (Latin) Clear. *Variations:* Christal, Chrystal, Cristal, Cristalle, Cristel, Crystol, Kristal, Kristle, Kristol, Krystal, Krystalle, Krystel, Krystle.

CULLEN (Irish) Pretty. *Variations:* Cullan, Cullin.

CUSTODIA (Spanish) Guardian.

CYANEA (Greek) Blue as the sky. *Variations:* Cyan, Cyanna, Cyanne.

CYBELE (Greek) Goddess of nature.

CYBILL (Latin) Prophet. *Notable:* Actress Cybill Shepherd. *Variations:* Cybil, Cybilla, Cybille, Sibyl, Sibil.

CYDELL (English) Form of Sydell. Wide valley. *Variations:* Cydel, Cydela, Cydele, Cydella, Cydelle, Sidel, Sydell.

CYDNEY (English) Form of Sydney. *Notable:* Dancer Cyd Charisse. *Variations:* Cidnee, Cidney, Cidni, Cyd, Cydnee, Cydney, Cydni, Cydny.

CYMA (Greek) Blossoming. *Variation:* Syma.

CYNARA (Greek) Thistle plant. *Variations:* Cynarra, Zinara.

CYNTHIA (Greek) Goddess of the moon. *Notable:* Actress Cynthia Nixon. *Variations:* Cindi, Cindie, Cindy, Cinthea, Cinthia, Cintia, Cyndi, Cynth, Cynthea, Cynthie, Cyntia, Cyntie, Synthia, Syntia.

CYPRIS (Greek) From Cyprus. *Variations:* Cypress, Cypriss, Cyprus.

CYRA (Persian) Sun. *Variation:* Cyrah.

CYRENE (Greek) Siren. *Variations:* Cyreen, Cyren, Cyrena.

CYRILLA (Latin) Godly. Feminine version of Cyril. *Variation:* Cirilla.

CYTHEREA (Greek) From the island of Cythera. *Variation:* Cytheria.

CZARINA (Russian) Empress. *Variations:* Cyzarina, Cyzarine.

CZIGANY (Hungarian) Gypsy girl. *Variations:* Czigani, Cziganie.

DABORA (Czech) To fight far away. *Variations:* Dalena, Dalenka.

DABRIA (Latin) Angel. *Variations:* Dabrea, Dabriah, Dabrya.

DACEY (Irish) From the south. *Variations:* Dacee, Daci, Dacia, Dacie, Dacy, Daicee, Daicy.

DAFFODIL (French) Flower name. *Variations:* Daffi, Daffie, Daffy.

DAGANA (Hebrew) Grain. *Variations:* Dagan, Dagania, Daganya, Degana, Degania, Deganiah, Deganit, Deganiya, Deganya.

DAGMAR (German) Glory. *Variations:* Daga, Daggi, Dagi, Dagmara, Dagmari, Dagmarie, Dagomar.

DAGNY (Scandinavian) New day. *Variations:* Dagna, Dagne, Dagney.

DAHLIA (Scandinavian) Flower name. *Variations:* Dahla, Dalia, Daliah.

DAI (Japanese) Grand.

DAILA (Latvian) Beautiful. *Variations:* Daela, Daelah, Dailah, Dayla, Daylah.

DAIRA (Greek) Well informed. *Variation:* Daeira.

DAIRINE (Irish) Fertile.

DAISY (English) Flower name. *Notable:* TV personality Daisy Fuentes. *Variations:* Dacey, Dacia, Dacy, Daisey, Daisha, Daisi, Daisie, Daizy, Daysi, Deyci.

DAIYA (Polish) Gift. *Variations:* Daia, Daiah, Daiyah, Daya, Dayah.

DAIYU (Chinese) Black jade.

DAKINI (Sanskrit) Sky dancer. *Variations:* Dakinee, Dankinie.

DAKOTA (Native American) Friend. *Notable:* Child actress Dakota Fanning. *Variations:* Dakoda, Dakotah.

DALAL (Arabic) To flirt. *Variation:* Dhelal.

DALE (English) Valley. *Notable:* Country/Western actress/singer Dale Evans. *Variations:* Dael, Daelyn, Dahl, Dalena, Dalene, Dalenna, Dalina, Dallana, Daly, Dayle.

DALILA (African) Gentle. *Variations:* Dahlila, Dalia, Dalice, Dalilah.

DALIT (Hebrew) Running water.

DALLAS (Scottish) From the valley meadow. *Variations:* Dallis, Dallys.

DALMATIA (Latin) From Dalmatia in Italy. *Variations:* Dalma, Dalmace, Dalmassa.

DALYA (Hebrew) Branch. *Variations:* Dalia, Daliya.

DAMALI (Arabic) Beautiful vision. *Variations:* Damalea, Damalee, Damalie.

DAMARIS (Greek) Calf. *Variations:* Damara, Damaress, Damarys, Dameris, Dameryss, Damiris.

DAMAYANT (Hindi) Flirt.

DAMHNAIT (Irish) Poet. *Variations:* Deonet, Devnet, Downet, Downett, Dympha.

DAMIA (Greek) To tame.

DAMIANA (Greek) To tame. *Variations:* Damian, Damiana.

DAMITA (Spanish) Princess. *Variations:* Damitah, Damyta.

DANA (English) From Denmark. *Notable:* Actress Dana Delany. *Variations:* Daina, Danay, Danaye, Dane, Danee, Danet, Danna, Dayna, Denae.

DANAE (Greek) Pure and bright. *Variations:* Danay, Danea, Denae.

DANI (Hebrew) Short for Danielle. *Variations:* Danee, Danie, Danni, Dannie.

DANIAH (Hebrew) God's judgment. *Variations:* Dania, Daniya, Danya.

DANICA (Slavic) Morning star. *Notable:* Racecar driver Danica Patrick. *Variations:* Danika, Dannica, Dannika.

DANIELLE (French) God is my judge. Feminine version of Daniel. *Notable:* Writer Danielle Steele. *Variations:* Danee, Danela, Danele, DaNell, Danella, Danette, Daney, Dani, Dania, Danica, Danice, Danie, Daniela, Daniella, Danila, Danita, Daniya, Danya, Danyelle.

DANU (Welsh) The mother of the gods.

DANUTA (Polish) Given by God.

DAO-MING (Chinese) The right path.

DAPHNE (Greek) Ancient mythological nymph who was transformed into a laurel tree. *Notable:* Writer Daphne du Maurier. *Variations:* Dafne, Daphney, Daphny.

DARA (Hebrew) Wisdom. *Variations:* Dahra, Dareen, Darice, Darissa, Darra, Darrah.

DARALIS (English) Cherished. *Variation:* Daralice.

DARBY (English) A place where deer graze. *Variations:* Darbi, Darbie.

DARCIE (Irish) Dark one. *Variations:* Darcee, Darcey, Darci, D'Arcy, Darcy, Darsi, Darsie.

DARDA (Hebrew) Pearl of wisdom.

DARIA (Greek) Luxurious. *Variations:* Darea, Dari, Darian, Darianna, Dariele, Darielle, Darienne, Darrelle.

DARIAN (English) Precious. *Variations:* Darien, Darienne, Derian.

DARLA (English) Short form of Darlene. *Variation:* Darly.

DARLENE (English) Darling. *Variations:* Darla, Darleane, Darleen, Darleena, Darlena, Darlina, Darline.

DARNELLE (English) Hiding place. *Variations:* Darnel, Darnell, Darnella, Darnetta.

Flower Names for Girls

There are lovely associations with names that evoke the scents and colors of flowers.

Blossom	Jasmine
Clover	Lily
Dahlia	Marigold
Daisy	Pansy
Flora	Petunia
Heather	Poppy
Holly	Posey
Hyacinth	Rose
Iris	Violet
Ivy	Zinnia

DARING (American) One who takes risks. *Variation:* Derring.

DARON (Irish) Great. *Variations:* Daren, Darian, Darron.

DARSHA (Hindi) Sighted. *Variations:* Darshika, Darshina, Darshini, Darshna.

DARU (Hindi) Cedar tree.

DARVA (American) Unknown definition. *Variations:* Darvah, Darvy.

DARYL (French) Beloved. *Notable:* Actress Daryl Hannah. *Variations:* Darel, Darielle, Darrel, Darrell, Darrelle, Darryl, Darrylene, Darrylin, Darryline, Darrylyn, Darylin, Daryline, Darylyne.

DARYN (Greek) Gift. *Variations:* Darin, Daryan, Darynne.

DASHA (Russian) Dear one. *Variations:* Dashia, Dasia.

DASHIKI (African) Loose shirt. *Variations:* Dashi, Dashka, Deshiki.

DATIAH (Hebrew) God's law. *Variations:* Datia, Datiya, Datya.

DAVIDA (Hebrew) Beloved. Feminine version of David. *Variations:* Daveen, Davene, Davia, Daviana, Daviane, Davianna, Davidine, Davina, Davine, Davinia, Davita, Davonna, Davy, Davynn.

DAVINA (Scottish) Form of Davida. *Variations:* Dava, Davean, Daveen, Daveena, Davene, Davi, Davianna, Davin, Davinia, Davinna, Davonna, Deveen, Devina.

DAWN (English) Sunrise; the dawn. *Variations:* Dawna, Dawne, Dawnelle, Dawnetta, Dawnette, Dawnielle, Dawnika, Dawnn.

DAY (English) Day. *Variation:* Dae.

DAYANA (Arabic) Divine. *Variations:* Daya, Dayanara, Dayani, Dayanna, Dayo, Dyana.

DAYTONA (English) Bright town. *Variations:* Dayton, Daytonia.

DEA (Greek) Like a goddess; (Latin) Goddess.

DEANA (English) Valley. Feminine version of Dean. *Variations:* Deane, Deanna, Deena, Dene, Denna.

DEANDRA (American) Divine. Form of Diana. *Variations:* Deanda, Deandrea, Deandria, Deeandra, Dianda, Diandra, Diandre.

DEANNA (English) Valley. *Notable:* Actress Deanna Durbin. *Variations:* Deana, Deane, Deanie, Deann, Deanne, Deeana, Deeann, Deeanna, Deena, Deona, Deondra, Deonna, Deonne.

DEARBHAIL (Gaelic) Daughter of destiny.

DEARBHLA (Gaelic) True poet.

DEBBIE (American) Short form of Deborah. *Notables:* Actress Debbie Reynolds; singer Debbie Gibson. *Variations:* Deb, Debi, Debbi, Debby, Debbye.

DEBORAH (Hebrew) Bee. *Notable:* Blondie lead singer Deborah Harry. *Variations:* Deb, Debbi, Debbie, Debby, Debi, Debora, Deborrah, Debra, Debrah, Devora, Devorah, Devra.

DEBRA (Hebrew) Variation of Deborah. *Notables:* Actresses Debra Winger and Debra Messing.

DECEMBER (Latin) Tenth.

DECIMA (Latin) Tenth.

DECLA (Irish) Of the family. Feminine version of Declan.

DEE (Welsh) Black.

DEEDEE (English) Nickname for girls' names beginning with "D." *Variations:* D.D., Didee, Didi.

DEIANIRA (Greek) Ancient mythological figure.

DEIFILIA (Spanish) Daughter of God.

DEIRBHILE (Irish) Poet's daughter. *Variations:* Dervila, Dervla.

DEIRDRE (Irish) Sorrow. *Notable:* Soap opera actress Deidre Hall. *Variations:* Dedra, Deidra, Deirdra, Deirdre, Deirdrie, Diedre, Dierdre.

DEITRA (Greek) Earth mother. Short form of Demetria. *Variations:* De'Atra, Deetra, Detria.

DEJA (French) Seen before. Dejah, Dejanae, Dejon.

DEKLA (Latvian) Trinity goddess.

DELANCEY (Irish) Child of defiance. *Variations:* Delancie, Delancy.

DELANEY (Irish) Child of a competitor. *Variations:* Delaina, Delaine, Delana, Delane, Delayna, Delayne.

DELBINA (Greek) Flower. *Variations:* Delbin, Delbine.

DELIA (Greek) From Delos. *Notable:* Writer Delia Ephron. *Variations:* Del, Delise, Delya, Delys, Delyse.

DELICIA (Latin) Delight. *Variations:* Daleesha, Dalicia, Dalisia, Delcia, Delcina, Delcine, Deleesha, Delesha, Delesia, Delice, Delisa, Delise, Delisha, Delisia, Delys, Delyse.

DELILAH (Hebrew) Delicate. *Notable:* Radio personality Delilah. *Variations:* Dalila, Delila, Deliylah.

DELINE (French) Noble.

DELJA (Polish) Daughter of the sea.

DELLA (English) Noble. *Notable:* Actress Della Reese. *Variations:* Del, Dela, Dell, Delle.

DELMA (German) Noble protector. *Variations:* Delmar, Delmara, Delmia, Delmira.

DELORA (Spanish) From the ocean.

DELPHINE (Greek) From Delphi. *Variations:* Delfina, Delpha, Delphe, Delphi, Delphia, Delphina.

DELTA (Greek) Fourth letter of the Greek alphabet. *Notable:* Actress Delta Burke.

DELWYN (Welsh) Pretty and fair.

DELYTH (Welsh) Pretty. *Variation:* Delythe.

DEMELZA (Cornish) From the fortress.

DEMETRIA (Greek) Earth mother. *Variations:* Demeter, Demetra, Demetris, Demitra, Demitras, Dimetria.

DEMI (Greek) Short form of Demetria. *Notable:* Actress Demi Moore.

DENAE (Hebrew) Innocent.

DENALI (Indian) Superior woman. *Variations:* Denalee, Denalie, Denalli, Denaly.

DENDARA (Egyptian) Town on the river. *Variations:* Dendaria, Dendera.

DENISE (French) Wine goddess. Feminine version of Dennis. *Notables:* Fitness guru Denise Austin; actress Denise Richards. *Variations:* Denese, Deni, Denice, Deniece, Denisha, Denize, Dennise, Denyce, Denys.

DENISHA (American) Form of Denise. *Variations:* Deneesha, Deneisha, Denesha, Deneshia, Denishia.

DEOIRIDH (Scottish) Gazelle.

DEOLINDA (Portuguese) God is beautiful. *Variations:* Deolenda, Deolynda.

DEONAID (Scottish) God is gracious.

DERIKA (German) Ruler. *Variations:* Dereka, Derica, Derrica.

DERINA (German) Ruler. *Variations:* Dereena, Derine.

DERINDA (English) Ruler of the people. *Variation:* Darinda.

DERORA (Hebrew) Free as a bird. *Variations:* Derorah, Derorra, Derorit.

DERRY (Irish) Red haired. *Variations:* Deri, Derrie.

DERYN (Welsh) Bird. *Variations:* Derren, Derrin, Derrine, Derron, Deryn.

DESDEMONA (Greek) Misery. *Variation:* Desdemonia.

DESIDERIA (Italian; Spanish) Longing.

DESIRE (English) Desired.

DESIRÉE (French) Desired. *Variations:* Desarae, Desira, Desyre, Dezarae, Dezirae, Diseraye, Diziree, Dsaree.

DESMA (Greek) Binding oath. *Variation:* Dezma.

DESPINA (Greek) Lady. *Variation:* Despoina.

DESSA (Greek) One who wanders.

DESTINY (French) Fate. *Variations:* Destanee, Destina, Destine, Destinee, Destini, Destinie.

DEVA (Hindi) Divine. *Variations:* Devanee, Devee, Devi, Devika.

DEVANA (Hindi) Divine love. *Variations:* Devanah, Devanna, Devannah.

DEVANY (Gaelic) Dark haired. *Variations:* Davane, Devaney, Devenny, Devinee, Devony.

DEVASHA (Hebrew) Honey. *Variation:* Devash.

DEVENE (Scottish) Beloved. Feminine version of David. *Variations:* Devean, Deveen.

DEVERA (Latin) Sweep away. *Variation:* Deverra.

DEVERELL (Welsh) From the riverbank. *Variations:* Deverel, Deverella, Deverelle.

DEVI (Hindi) Goddess. *Variations:* Devia, Devie, Devri.

DEVIKA (Indian) Little goddess. *Variation:* Devica.

DEVIN (Irish) Poet. *Variations:* Deva, Devan, Devinne.

DEVON (English) From Devon, a region in southern England. *Variations:* Devan, Devana, Devanna, Devona, Devondra, Devonna, Devonne, Devyn, Devynn.

DEVORA (Hebrew) Form of Deborah. *Variations:* Devorah, Devore, Devra.

DEWANDA (African American) Combination of prefix "De" and first name "Wanda."

DEXTRA (Latin) Skilled. *Variations:* Dexter, Dexy.

DHARA (Hindi) Earth. *Variations:* Dharinee, Dharitri, Dharti.

DHARMA (Hindi) Believe. *Variation:* Darma.

DHAVALA (Hindi) White.

DHISANA (Hindi) Goddess of prosperity.

DHYANA (Hindi) One who meditates.

DI (Latin) Short form of Diana or Diana. *Variation:* Dy.

DIAMOND (English) Jewel. *Variations:* Diamanda, Diamanta, Diamante, Diamonique, Diamontina.

DIANA (Latin) Divine. *Notables:* Great Britain's Princess Diana; singer Diana Ross. *Variations:* Dee, Dianna, Didi, Dyana.

DIANE (Latin) Divine. Form of Diana. *Notables:* TV news personality Diane Sawyer; fashion designer Diane von Furstenberg; actresses Diahann Carroll, Diane Lane, and Dyan Cannon. *Variations:* Diahann, Dian, Dianne, Dyan.

DIATA (African) Like a lioness. *Variation:* Dyata.

DIANTHA (Greek) Divine flower. *Variations:* Diandre, Dianthe, Dianthia.

DIDIANE (French) Longing.

DIDO (Greek) Ancient mythological figure. *Notable:* British singer Dido Armstrong.

DIEGA (Spanish) Feminine form of Diego. Supplanter.

DIELLE (French) God. *Variation:* Diella.

DIETRICHA (German) First of the people. *Variations:* Didrika, Diedricka.

DIGNA (Latin) Valuable. *Variation:* Dinya.

DILWEN (Welsh) Genuine and blessed.

DILYS (Welsh) Faithful. *Variations:* Dylis, Dyllis, Dylys.

DIMA (Arabic) Rain.

DIMONA (Hebrew) From the south. *Variations:* Dimonah, Dymona.

DINAH (Hebrew) God will judge. *Notable:* Singer/TV host Dinah Shore. *Variations:* Deena, Denora, Dina, Dinorah, Diondra, Diynah, Dyna, Dynah.

DINIA (Hebrew) Wisdom of God. *Variation:* Dinya.

DIONNE (Greek) Divine ruler. *Notable:* Singer Dionne Warwick. *Variations:* Deonne, Dion, Diona, Dione, Dionia, Dionna, Dionysia.

DISA (Scandinavian) Sprite.

DISCORDIA (Latin) Goddess of strife.

DITA (English; Spanish) Derivative of Edith. *Notable:* Burlesque artist and model Dita Von Teese. *Variations:* Deeta, Ditka.

DITI (Hindi) Earth goddess. *Variation:* Dity.

DIVINE (Latin) Divine. *Variations:* Divina, Divinia.

DIVONAH (Hebrew) South. *Variations:* Dimona, Dimonah, Divona.

DIVYA (Hindi) Brilliant.

DIXIE (French) Tenth. *Notable:* Actress Dixie Carter. *Variations:* Dix, Dixee, Dixy.

DIZA (Hebrew) Joy. *Variations:* Ditza, Ditzah.

DOBRILA (Czech) Good.

DOBROMILA (Czech) Good grace.

DOBROMIRA (Czech) Good and famous.

DOBROSLAVA (Czech) Good and kind.

DODIE (Hebrew) Beloved. *Variations:* Dodee, Dodi, Dody.

DOLLY (English) Doll. *Notables:* U.S. First Lady Dolly Madison; country singer Dolly Parton. *Variations:* Doll, Dollee, Dolley, Dollie.

DOLORES (Spanish) Sorrow. *Notable:* Actress Dolores Del Rio. *Variations:* Delores, Doloras, Doloris, Doloritas.

DOMINA (Latin) Woman. *Variation:* Domini.

DOMINIQUE (French) Of the Lord. *Notable:* Actress Dominique Sanda. *Variations:* Domenica, Dominica, Domini, Dominika.

DOÑA (Spanish) Lady. *Variations:* Donella, Donelle, Donetta.

DONALDA (Scottish) Feminine form of Donald. Ruler of the world. *Variation:* Donaldina.

DONATA (Latin) Given. *Variations:* Donada, Donatha, Donatta.

DONATELLA (Italian) Given. *Notable:* Fashion designer Donatella Versace. *Variation:* Donatienne.

DONCIA (Spanish) Sweet.

DONELLE (Irish) Ruler of the world. *Variation:* Donla.

DONNA (Italian) Woman of the home. *Notables:* Actress Donna Reed; disco songstress Donna Summer; fashion designer Donna Karan. *Variations:* Dahna, Donetta, Donielle, Donisha, Donnalee, Donnalyn, DonnaMarie, Donni, Donnie, Donya.

DONNAG (Scottish) World ruler. *Variations:* Doileag, Dolag, Dollag.

DONOMA (Native American) Sight of the sun.

DORA (Greek) Gift. *Notable:* Children's TV character Dora the Explorer. *Variations:* Doralia, Doralyn, Doralynn, Doreen, Dorelia, Dorelle, Dorena, Dorenne, Dorette, Dori, Dorie, Dorinda, Dorita, Doru.

DORCAS (Greek) Gazelle. *Variation:* Doreka.

DOREEN (Irish) Gloomy. *Variations:* Doireann, Dorene, Dorine, Dorinnia, Doryne.

DORIAN (Greek) A region in Greece. *Variations:* Doriana, Dorianne, Dorrian, Dorryen.

DORINDA (Spanish) Form of Dora.

DORIS (Greek) From Doria, a region in Greece. *Notables:* Actresses Doris Day and Doris Roberts. *Variations:* Dorice, Dorisa, Dorlisa, Dorolice, Dorosia, Dorrie, Dorrys, Dorys, Doryse.

DORIT (Hebrew) Generation. *Variations:* Dor, Dorrit.

DOROTHY (Greek) Gift from God. *Notable:* Writer Dorothy Parker. *Variations:* Dollie, Dolly, Dorethea, Doro, Dorotea, Dorotha, Dorothea, Dorothee, Dorothia, Dorrit, Dortha, Dorthea, Dot, Dottie, Dotty.

DORY (English) Yellow-haired girl. *Variations:* Dori, Dorri, Dorrie, Dorry.

DOTTIE (English) Nickname for Dorothy. *Notable:* Singer Dottie West. *Variations:* Dot, Dotty.

DOUCE (French) Sweet.

DOVE (American) Bird of peace.

DOVEVA (Hebrew) Limber. *Variations:* Dovevet, Dovit.

DRAHOMIRA (Czech) Dearly beloved.

DREA (Greek) Courageous. *Variation:* Dree.

DREW (Greek) Strong. Diminutive of Andrew. *Notable:* Actress Drew Barrymore. *Variations:* Dru, Drue.

DRINA (Greek) Protector. *Variations:* Dreena, Drena.

DRISANA (Indian) Daughter of the sun. *Variations:* Drisanna, Drysana, Drysanna.

Last Names as First Names

Rising in popularity, last names are making for trendy first names. Many of these work for either boys or girls!

BOYS:	GIRLS:
Campbell	Arden
Carter	Bailey
Cooper	Emerson
Dawson	Flynn
Hamilton	Harper
Hudson	Logan
Kennedy	Mackenzie
Mason	Macy
Parker	Mallory
Payton	Murphy
Porter	Piper
Sawyer	Quinn
Truman	Schuyler
Tucker	Tierney
Walker	Waverly

DRISILLA (Latin) Strong. *Variations:* Drewsila, Drucella, Drucie, Drucilla, Drucy, Druscilla.

DUA (Arabic) To pray.

DUANA (Irish) Dark skinned. Feminine version of Duane. *Variations:* Duna, Dwana.

DUENA (Spanish) Chaparone.

DULCIE (Latin) Sweet. *Variations:* Delcina, Delcine, Delsine, Dulce, Dulcea, Dulci, Dulcia, Dulciana, Dulcibella, Dulcibelle, Dulcina, Dulcine, Dulcinea.

DUMIA (Hebrew) Quiet. *Variation:* Dumiya.

DURGA (Hindi) Unreachable.

DURVA (Hindi) Grass.

DUSANA (Czech) Spirit. *Variations:* Dusa, Dusanka, Dusicka, Duska.

DUSCHA (Russian) Sweet.

DUSTINE (English) Dusty place. Feminine version of Dustin. *Variations:* Dusteen, Dustyne.

DUSTY (English) Feminine form of Dustin. *Notable:* Singer Dusty Springfield. *Variations:* Dustee, Dusti, Dustie.

DUVESSA (Irish) Dark beauty. *Variation:* Duvesa.

DUYEN (Vietnamese) Charming and graceful.

DWYNWEN (Welsh) White wave.

DYANI (Native American) Deer.

DYLAN (Welsh) Born of the sea. *Variation:* Dylana.

DYMPNA (Irish) Fawn.

DYSIS (Greek) Born at sunset. *Variation:* Dysisse.

EADA (English) Prosperous. *Variations:* Eadah, Eadda, Eaddah, Eadea.

EADLIN (English) Born into royalty. *Variations:* Eadlen, Eadlina, Eadlyn.

EADOIN (English) Having many friends. *Variation:* Eadiyn.

EALGA (Irish) Born into nobility. *Variation:* Ealgah.

EARA (Scottish) From the East. *Variations:* Earah, Earea, Earey, Earie.

EARLENE (English) Leader. Feminine version of Earl. *Variations:* Earla, Earleen, Earley, Earlie, Earlinda, Earline, Erlene, Erlina, Erline.

EARTHA (English) Earth. *Notable:* Singer Eartha Kitt. *Variations:* Erta, Ertha, Hertha.

EASTER (English) Named for the holiday.

EASTON (English) From the East. *Variations:* Eastan, Easten, Eastin.

EAVAN (Irish) Fair haired. *Varations:* Eavana, Eavane, Eavannah.

EBBA (English) Flowing tide. *Variations:* Eba, Ebah, Ebbah.

EBERTA (German) Bright. *Variations:* Ebertah, Eberte, Ebirta, Eburta, Ebyrta.

EBONY (English) Black wood. *Variations:* Ebbony, Eboney, Eboni, Ebonie.

EBREL (Cornish) Born in April. *Variation:* Ebril.

ECATERINA (Romanian) Form of Katherine. *Variation:* Ekaterina.

ECHIDNA (Greek) She-viper.

ECHO (Greek) Sound.

ECSTASY (Greek) Overwhelming happiness. *Variations:* Ecstasea, Esctasie, Ekstasy.

EDA (English) Happy. *Variations:* Edah, Ede.

EDANA (Celtic) Desired one. *Variations:* Edanah, Edanna, Edannah.

EDDA (Scandinavian) Ancient mythological figure. *Variations:* Eddah, Edde.

EDDIE (English) Protector of property. Feminine version of Edward. *Variations:* Eddi, Eddy, Eddye.

EDEEN (Scottish) From Edinburgh. *Variations:* Edean, Edeene, Edine, Edyne.

EDELINE (German) Noble. *Variations:* Edalene, Edalyne, Edel, Ediline, Lena.

EDELMIRA (Spanish) Noble and famous.

EDEN (Hebrew) Place of pleasure. *Variations:* Eaden, Eadin, Edana, Edena, Edenia, Edin.

EDIAH (Hebrew) Decoration for God. *Variations:* Edia, Ediya, Edya, Edyah.

EDIE (English) Form of Edith. *Notable:* Actress Edie Falco. *Variations:* Eadee, Eadie, Eady, Eydie.

EDINA (English) One from Edinburgh, capital of Scotland. *Variations:* Edeena, Edena, Edyna, Idina.

EDITH (English) Prosperity in war. *Notables:* Novelist Edith Wharton; costume designer Edith Head.

Variations: Edie, Edita, Edithe, Edy, Edyth, Edytha, Edythe, Eydie, Eydith.

EDLA (Scandinavian) Princess. *Variations:* Edlah, Edela.

EDLYN (English) Small noble girl. *Variations:* Edlan, Edland, Edlin.

EDMEE (Scottish) To love. *Variation:* Edme.

EDMONDA (English) Rich protector. Feminine version of Edmund. *Variations:* Edmona, Edmunda.

EDNA (Hebrew) Youthful. *Notable:* Writer Edna St. Vincent Millay. *Variation:* Ednah.

EDRA (English) Powerful and mighty. *Variations:* Edrah, Edrea, Edria, Edriah.

EDRICE (English) Strong property owner. Feminine version of Edric. *Variations:* Edris, Edryce, Edrys, Eidris, Eydris.

EDRINA (English) Wealthy ruler. *Variations:* Edreena, Edrinah, Edryna.

EDUARDA (Spanish) Guardian of prosperity. *Variation:* Eduardia.

EDUSA (Latin) Goddess of nourishment. *Variation:* Edulica.

EDWARDINE (English) Rich protector. Feminine version of Edward. *Variations:* Edwarda, Edwardeen, Edwardene, Edwardina, Edwardyne.

EDWIGE (French) Joyful war. *Variations:* Edvig, Edvige, Edwig, Hedwig, Hedwige, Yadwigo.

EDWINA (English) Rich friend. Feminine version of Edwin. *Variations:* Edween, Edweena, Edwena, Edwiena, Edwuna, Edwyna.

EFA (Hebrew) Gloomy. *Variations:* Efah, Eifa.

EFFIE (Greek) Singing talk. *Variations:* Eff, Effy, Ephie, Eppie, Euphemia, Euphemie, Euphie.

EFRATA (Hebrew) Fertile. *Variations:* Efrat, Ephrat, Ephrata.

EGA (Nigerian) Bird. *Variation:* Egah.

EGBERTA (English) Bright sword. *Variations:* Egberte, Egbirte.

EGIDIA (Scottish) Young goat.

EGLAH (Hebrew) Cow. *Variation:* Egla.

EGLANTINE (English) Sweetbriar. *Variations:* Eglantilne, Eglantyne.

EGYPT (English) The country Egypt.

EHANI (Hindi) Desired. *Variations:* Ehanee, Ehanie, Ehany.

EHAWEE (Native American) Laughter. *Variations:* Ehawey, Ehawi.

EIBHLIN (Irish) Shining, bright. Derivative of Helen. *Variations:* Eibhleann, Eibhlhin.

EIDEL (Yiddish) Delicate.

EIDDWEN (Welsh) Fond and blessed.

EIDOTHEA (Greek) Knowing one.

EIFIONA (Welsh) From Wales. *Variation:* Eifionah.

EILAH (Hebrew) Oak tree. *Variations:* Aila, Ailah, Ala, Alah, Ayla, Eila, Eilia, Eilya, Eilyah, Eilona, Ela, Elah, Elona, Eyla.

EILEEN (Irish) Shining, bright. Familiar version of Helen. *Variations:* Aileen, Ailene, Alene, Aline, Ayleen, Eilean, Eilleen, Ilene.

EILEITHYIA (Greek) Goddess of childbirth.

EILISH (Gaelic) God is my oath. *Variations:* Eilis, Eilisha, Elish.

EILUNED (Welsh) Idol.

EILWEN (Welsh) Fair friend. *Variations:* Eilwena, Eylwen, Eylwena.

EIR (Norse) Peaceful healer. *Variation:* Eyr.

EIRA (Welsh) Snow. *Variations:* Eirah, Eiralys, Eyra, Eyrah.

EIRALYS (Welsh) Snowdrop. *Variation:* Eirlys.

EIRENE (Greek) Peace.

EIRIAN (Welsh) Bright and beautiful. *Variations:* Eiriana, Eirianne.

EIRWEN (Welsh) Fair. *Variation:* Eirwyn.

EISA (Scandinavian) Ancient mythological figure.

EITHNE (Celtic) Fiery. Variations Ethne.

EKALA (Australian) Lake. *Variation:* Ekalah.

EKELA (Hawaiian) Noble. *Variation:* Etela.

ELA (Hebrew) Oak tree. *Variation:* Eila.

ELAINE (French) Bright, shining. Derivative of Helen. *Notables:* Actress Elaine Stritch; writer/director Elaine May. *Variations:* Alaina, Alayna, Alayne, Allaine, Elaina, Elayn, Elayne, Eleana, Elena, Eleni, Ellaina, Ellaine, Ellane, Ellayne.

ELAMA (Hebrew) God's people.

ELAMMA (Hindi) Mother goddess. *Variation:* Ellama.

ELANA (Hebrew) Oak tree. *Variations:* Elane, Elanna.

ELATA (Latin) Held in high esteem. *Variations:* Elatah, Elatt, Elatta, Elota.

ELBERTA (English) Noble. Shining. Feminine version of Elbert. *Variations:* Elbertina, Elbertine, Elbie.

Top Names of the 1970s

BOYS:

1. Michael
2. Christopher
3. Jason
4. David
5. James
6. John
7. Robert
8. Brian
9. William
10. Matthew
11. Joseph
12. Daniel
13. Kevin
14. Eric
15. Jeffrey
16. Richard
17. Scott
18. Mark
19. Steven
20. Thomas

GIRLS:

1. Jennifer
2. Amy
3. Melissa
4. Michelle
5. Kimberly
6. Lisa
7. Angela
8. Heather
9. Stephanie
10. Nicole
11. Jessica
12. Elizabeth
13. Rebecca
14. Kelly
15. Mary
16. Christina
17. Amanda
18. Julie
19. Sarah
20. Laura

ELDA (Italian) Battle.

ELDEAN (English) Old one. *Variations:* Eldeana, Eldene, Eldina, Eldine.

ELDORA (Spanish) Coated by gold. *Variations:* Eldoree, Eldoria, Eldoris.

ELDREDA (English) Elderly counselor. *Variations:* Eldridah, Eldryda.

ELEANOR (English) Light. Derivative of Helen. *Notable:* U.S. First Lady Eleanor Roosevelt. *Variations:* Eleanora, Eleanore, Elenore, Eleonora, Eleonore, Elinor, Ellinor.

ELEBANA (Australian) Beautiful. *Variations:* Elebanna, Eleebana.

ELECTRA (Greek) Shining one. *Variations:* Elektra, Eletra.

ELENA (Greek; Spanish; Russian) Light. Form of Helen. *Variations:* Elana, Eleana, Eleni, Ilena.

ELENOLA (Hawaiian) Bright. *Variations:* Elenoa, Elenora, Elianora.

ELERI (Welsh) Smooth. *Variations:* Eleree, Elleri, Ellery.

ELETTA (English) Elf. *Variations:* Eleta, Elette.

ELEU (Hawaiian) Alive.

ELEXIS (English) Form of Alexis. Helper. *Variations:* Elexa, Elexea, Elexee, Elexi, Elexia, Elexina, Elexys.

ELFREDA (English) Strong as an elf. *Variations:* Elfrida, Elfrieda, Elfryda.

ELGA (Slavic) Holy. *Variations:* Elgana, Elgania.

ELGIVA (English) Noble elf. *Variation:* Elgivah.

ELI (Scandinavian) Light. *Variations:* Elie, Ely.

ELIANA (Hebrew) God has answered my prayers. *Variations:* Eliane, Elianna, Elianne.

ELICIA (Greek) Form of Alicia. Truthful. *Variation:* Elisha.

ELIDA (English) With wings. *Variations:* Eleda, Eleeda, Elidah, Elyda.

ELIDI (Greek) Gift from the sun.

ELIEZRA (Hebrew) God is salvation.

ELIKA (Hawaiian) Forever ruler. *Variations:* Elikah, Elyka.

ELILI (Polynesian) Periwinkle.

ELIORA (Hebrew) God is light. *Variation:* Eleora.

ELISA (Hebrew; Spanish) Form of Elizabeth. *Variations:* Elesa, Elysa.

ELISE (English) Form of Elizabeth. *Variations:* Elisse, Elyse, Elysse.

ELISHA (Hebrew) Consecrated to God. *Variations:* Eleasha, Elecia, Eleesha, Elesha.

ELISHEBA (Hebrew) God is my oath. *Variation:* Elisheva.

ELISKA (Slavic) Truthful.

ELITA (Latin) Chosen. *Variations:* Elida, Ellita, Ilita.

ELIVAH (Hebrew) God is able. *Variation:* Eliava.

ELIZA (English) Form of Elizabeth.

ELIZABETH (Hebrew) Pledged to God. *Notables:* Actress Elizabeth Taylor; Great Britain's Queen Elizabeth. *Variations:* Alzbeta, Babette, Bess, Bessey, Bessi, Bessie, Bessy, Bet, Beta, Beth, Betina, Betine, Betka, Betsey, Betsi, Betsy, Bett, Betta, Bette, Betti, Bettina, Bettine, Betty, Betuska, Boski, Eilis, Elis, Elisa, Elisabet, Elisabeta, Elisabeth, Elisabetta, Elisabette,

Elisaka, Elisauet, Elisaveta, Elise, Eliska, Elissa, Elisueta, Eliza, Elizabetta, Elizabette, Elliza, Elsa, Elsbet, Elsbeth, Elsbietka, Elschen, Else, Elsee, Elsi, Elsie, Elspet, Elspeth, Elyse, Elyssa, Elyza, Elzbieta, Elzunia, Isabel, Isabelita, Liazka, Lib, Libbee, Libbey, Libbi, Libbie, Libby, Libbye, Lieschen, Liese, Liesel, Lis, Lisa, Lisbet, Lisbete, Lisbeth, Lise, Lisenka, Lisettina, Lisveta, Liz, Liza, Lizabeth, Lizanka, Lizbeth, Lizka, Lizzi, Lizzie, Lizzy, Vetta, Yelisaveta, Yelizaueta, Yelizaveta, Ysabel, Zizi, ZsiZsi.

ELK (Hawaiian) Black.

ELKANA (Hebrew) God has created. *Variation:* Elkanah.

ELKE (German) Noble. *Notable:* Actress Elke Sommer. *Variations:* Elka, Elkee, Elki, Elkie.

ELLA (German) Other. *Notable:* Jazz singer Ella Fitzgerald.

ELLE (French) She. *Notable:* Supermodel Elle MacPherson.

ELLEN (English) Light. Variation of Helen. *Notable:* Comedian Ellen DeGeneres. *Variations:* Elan, Elen, Elena, Eleni, Elenyl, Ellan, Ellene, Ellie, Ellon, Ellyn, Elyn, Lene.

ELLIE (English). Short form of Eleanor. *Variations:* Ellee, Eleigh, Elie, Elli, Ellia, Elly.

ELLICE (Greek) Noble. Feminine version of Elias. *Variation:* Elyce.

ELLIS (Hebrew) God is the Lord. *Variation:* Ellys.

ELLISTON (English) Kind and noble.

ELMA (Greek) Helmet; (Turkish) Apple. Feminine version of Elmo.

ELMINA (German) Noble. *Variations:* Elmeena, Elminah, Elmyna.

ELMIRA (English) Princess; (Spanish) True. *Variations:* Elmeira, Elmyra.

ELODIA (Spanish) Wealthy. *Variations:* Elodea, Elodiah.

ELOISE (French) Wise. *Variations:* Eloisa, Eloisia, Eloiza, Elouise.

ELORA (Hindi) God gives the laurel to the winner. *Variation:* Ellora.

ELRICA (German) Great ruler. *Variations:* Elrika, Elryka.

ELSA (German; Scandinavian) Noble. *Notable:* Style maven Elsa Klensch; actress Elsa Lanchester. *Variations:* Ellsa, Elsah.

ELSIE (German) Hard worker. *Variations:* Else, Elsea, Elsi, Elsie, Elsy.

ELSPETH (English) Form of Elizabeth. *Variation:* Elsbeth.

ELSWYTH (Welsh) Willow tree.

ELUNED (Welsh) Image. *Variation:* Eiluned.

ELVA (English) Variation of Olivia. *Variations:* Elvah, Elvia, Elviah.

ELVINA (English) Elf friend. Feminine version of Alvin. *Variations:* Elveena, Elvie, Elvinah, Elvy, Elwina.

ELVIRA (Spanish; Latin) Blond. *Notable:* Elvira, Mistress of the Dark. *Variations:* Elva, Elvera, Elvia, Elvirah, Elvire.

ELYSIA (Latin) Blissful. *Variations:* Eliese, Elise, Elisia, Elyse, Ileesia, Iline, Illsa, Ilyse, Ilysia.

ELYSSA (Greek) Sweet. *Variations:* Elisa, Elissa, Elysa, Elysia, Ilyssa, Lyssa.

EMBER (English) Small glowing fire.

EMBERLYN (American) Combined form of Ember and Lynn. *Variations:*

Emberlin, Emberlina, Emberline, Emberlynn.

EME (Hawaiian) Beloved.

EMELINE (French) Form of Emily. *Variations:* Emelie, Emelina, Emmaline, Emmalynn, Emmeline.

EMERA (English) Swift.

EMERALD (English) A jewel.

EMERSON (English) Son of Emery. *Variation:* Emersyn.

EMET (Hebrew) Truth.

EMIKO (Japanese) Beautiful child.

EMILY (German) Industrious. *Notables:* Writers Emily Brontë and Emily Dickinson. *Variations:* Aimil, Amalea, Amalia, Amalie, Amelia, Amelie, Ameline, Amy, Eimile, Em, Ema, Emalee, Emalia, Emelda, Emele, Emelene, Emelia, Emelina, Emeline, Emelyn, Emelyne, Emera, Emi, Emie, Emila, Emile, Emilea, Emilia, Emilie, Emilka, Emlyn, Emlynne, Emma, Emmalee, Emmali, Emmaline, Emmalynn, Emmeline, Emmiline, Emylin, Emylynn.

EMMA (German) Embracing all. *Notable:* Actress Emma Thompson. *Variations:* Em, Emmi, Emmie, Emmy.

EMMANUELLE (French) God is with us. Feminine version of Emanuel. *Variations:* Em, Emanula, Emmanuela, Emmanuelle, Emmie, Emmy.

EMME (German) Womanly.

EMMY (English) Short form of Emily or Emmanuelle. *Variations:* Emi, Emmi, Emmie.

EMMYLOU (American) Combined form of Emmy and Lou. *Notable:* Singer Emmylou Harris. *Variation:* Emmilou.

EMUNA (Hebrew) Faithful.

ENA (Irish) Bright, shining. Possibly a derivative of Helen. *Variation:* Enah.

ENAKAI (Hawaiian) Fiery sea.

ENCHANTRA (English) Enchanting. *Variation:* Enchantrah.

ENDORA (Hebrew) From the fountain. *Variations:* Endorah, Endorra, Endorrah.

ENFYS (Welsh) Rainbow.

ENGELBERTHA (German) Bright angel. *Variations:* Engelberta, Engelbertina, Engelbertine.

ENGRACIA (Spanish) Graceful.

ENID (Welsh) Life. *Variations:* Eanid, Enidd, Enud, Enudd.

ENNIS (Irish) A town in western Ireland. *Variation:* Inis.

ENOLA (Native American) Magnolia tree.

ENRICA (Italian) Leader of the house. Feminine version of Henry. *Variations:* Enrichetta, Enrieta, Enriqueta.

ENYA (Irish) Fiery. *Notable:* New Age singer Enya. *Variations:* Enia, Enyah.

ENYO (Greek) Goddess of war.

EOS (Greek) Goddess of dawn.

EOGHANIA (Welsh) Youth.

EPIFANIA (Spanish) Revelation. *Variations:* Epifani, Epifaniah, Epifany, Epiphani, Epiphania, Epiphanie, Epiphany.

EPONA (Celtic) Goddess of horses. *Variations:* Eponah, Eponia.

EPONI (African) Black. *Variations:* Eponee, Eponie, Epony.

EPPIE (English) Short form of Euphemia. *Variations:* Epi, Eppi.

ERANTHE (Greek) Delicate flower.

ERASMA (Greek) Desired.

ERATO (Greek) Lovely poet.

ERELA (Hebrew) Angel. *Variations:* Erelah, Erella, Erallah.

ERI (Japanese) Blessed prize.

ERIANTHE (Greek) Lover of flowers. *Variation:* Eriantha.

ERICA (Scandinavian) Leader forever. Feminine version of Eric. *Variations:* Airica, Airika, Ayrika, Enrica, Enricka, Enrika, Ericka, Erika, Errika, Eyrica.

ERIN (Gaelic) Nickname for Ireland. *Notable:* Activist Erin Brockovich. *Variations:* Eireann, Eirinn, Erene, Ereni, Eri, Erina, Erinn, Eryn.

ERINA (Hindi) Speech. *Variation:* Erisha.

ERIS (Greek) Discord.

ERLA (Irish) Young and playful. *Variation:* Erlah.

ERLINA (Spanish) Bearing a shield. *Variations:* Erlinah, Erline, Erlyna.

ERLINDA (Hebrew) Spirit. *Variations:* Erlind, Erlindy.

ERMA (German) Whole. Variation of Irma.

ERMELINDA (German) Wholly gentle.

ERMINE (French) Weasel. *Variations:* Ermina, Erminia, Erminie, Ermy.

ERNA (Scandinavian) Capable.

ERNESTINA (English) Earnest. *Variations:* Erna, Ernaline, Ernesta, Ernestine, Ernestyna.

ERROLYN (English) Area in Britain. Feminine version of Errol. *Variation:* Erroline.

ERSILIA (Italian) Delicate. *Variation:* Ersilla.

ERSKINA (Scottish) From the highest point. *Variation:* Erskena.

ERWINA (English) Boar. Friend. Feminine version of Erwin. *Variations:* Erwena, Erwinna, Erwyna.

ERYL (Welsh) Observer.

ESETERA (Hawaiian) Star. Hawaiian version of Esther. *Variations:* Ekekela, Eseta.

ESHANA (Sanskrit) To wish for.

ESHE (African) Life.

ESI (African) Born on Sunday.

ESME (French) Esteemed. *Variations:* Esma, Esmee, Esmie.

ESMERELDA (Spanish) Emerald. *Variations:* Emerant, Emeraude, Esma, Esmaralda, Esmarelda, Esmiralda, Esmirelda, Ezmeralda.

ESPERANZA (Spanish) Hope. *Variations:* Esperance, Esperantia.

ESTA (Italian) From the east.

ESTEE (English) Bright star. Form of Estelle. *Notable:* Cosmetics icon Estée Lauder. *Variations:* Esti, Estie, Esty.

ESTELLE (French) Star. *Notables:* Actresses Estelle Parsons and Estelle Getty. *Variations:* Essie, Essy, Estee, Estela, Estelita, Estella, Estrelita, Estrella, Estrellita, Stelle.

ESTHER (Hebrew) Star. *Notable:* Aquatic-film star Esther Williams. *Variations:* Essie, Essy, Esta, Ester, Etti, Ettie, Etty.

ESTRELLA (French) Child of the stars. *Variation:* Estrelle.

ETAIN (Irish) Irish sun goddess.

ETANA (Hebrew) Dedication. Feminine version of Ethan.

ETENIA (Native American) Rich.

ETERNITY (French) Everlasting.

ETHANA (Hebrew) Feminine form of Ethan. Strong and steadfast. *Variation:* Ethanna.

ETHEL (English) Noble. *Notable:* Actress/singer Ethel Merman. *Variations:* Ethelda, Etheline, Ethelyn, Ethelynne, Ethille, Ethlin, Ethyl.

ETHELINDA (German) Noble serpent. *Variations:* Etheleen, Ethelena, Ethelende, Ethelina, Ethelind, Ethylinda.

ETHETE (Native American) Upright.

ETHNE (Irish) Fire. *Variations:* Ethna, Ethnea, Ethnee.

ETOILE (French) Star.

ETSUKO (Japanese) Happiness. Joyful child. *Variations:* Etsu, Etsuyo.

ETTA (English) Diminutive. Short form of Henrietta. *Notable:* R&B singer Etta James.

EUDORA (Greek) Altruistic gift. *Variation:* Eudore.

EUDOSIA (Greek) Good gift. *Variations:* Eudocia, Eudokia, Eudoxia.

EUGENIA (Greek) Well born. Feminine version of Eugene. This is the name of the Duke and Duchess of York's second daughter. *Variations:* Eugena, Eugenie, Eugina.

EULALIA (Greek) Well spoken. *Variations:* Eula, Eulala, Eulia, Eulie.

EUN (Korean) Silver.

EUNICE (Greek) Victorious. *Variations:* Eunise, Euniss, Eunys.

EUPHEMIA (Greek) Of good reputation. *Variations:* Eufemia, Eupheme.

EUPHROSYNE (Greek) Joy and mirth.

EURYBIA (Greek) Goddess of the seas.

EURYDICE (Greek) Greek mythological figure; wife of Orpheus. *Variation:* Euridice.

EUSTACIA (Greek) Fruitful. *Variations:* Eustace, Stacey.

EUTERPE (Greek) Giver of pleasure.

EUZEBIA (Polish) Pious. *Variation:* Euzeba.

EVA (Hebrew) Giver of life. *Notable:* Actress Eva Longaria. *Variations:* Ebba, Evaine, Evathia, Evchen, Eve, Evelina, Eveline, Evi, Evicka, Evike, Evita, Evka, Evonne, Evy, Ewa, Yeuka, Yeva.

EVADNE (Greek) Good fortune. *Variations:* Evadney, Evadnie.

EVANGELINE (Greek) Good news. *Variations:* Evangelia, Evangelina, Evangeliste.

EVANIA (Irish) Sprited youth. *Variations:* Evana, Evanna.

EVANTHE (Greek) Flower. *Variation:* Evantha.

EVE (Hebrew) Life. *Notables:* Singer Eve; actress Eve Arden. *Variation:* Evie.

EVELYN (Irish) Young and lively. *Variations:* Aveline, Eoelene, Evaleen, Evaline, Eveleen, Eveline, Evelyne, Evelynn, Evelynne, Evlin, Evline, Evlun, Evlynn.

EVERELDA (English) Boar in battle.

EVETTE (French) Form of Yvette.

EVONNE (French) Form of Yvonne.

EVITA (Spanish) Life. *Notable:* Argentina's First Lady Evita Peron.

EVZENIE (Czech) Well born. *Variations:* Evza, Evzenka, Evzicka.

EWELINA (Polish) Life. *Variations:* Ewa, Ewalina, Ewaline.

EYOTA (Native American) Greatest. *Variation:* Eyotah.

EZRELA (Hebrew) God is my strength. *Variations:* Ezrella, Ezrelle.

FABIA (Latin) One who grows beans. Feminine version of Fabian. *Variations:* Fabiana, Fabiane, Fabianna, Fabienne, Fabiola, Fabiolah, Fabya, Fabyah, Fabyan, Fabyana, Fabyanah, Fabyane, Fabyann, Fabyanna, Fabyannah, Fabyanne.

FABRIZIA (Italian) One who works with her hands. *Variations:* Fabrice, Fabricia, Fabrienne, Fabritzia.

FADILA (Arabic) Virtue. *Variations:* Fadilah, Fadyla.

FADWA (Arabic) Self-sacrificing.

FAHIMA (Arabic) Smart.

FAIDA (Arabic) Abundant. *Variation:* Fayda.

FAINA (English) Joyful. *Variations:* Faine, Fayna, Feana.

FAIRLEE (English) From the golden meadow. *Variations:* Fairlea, Fairleah, Fairlei, Fairleigh, Fairley, Fairli, Fairlia, Fairliah, Fairlie, Fairly.

FAIRUZA (Arabic) Turquoise. *Variations:* Fairoza, Faroza, Farusa, Faruza.

FAITH (English) Faith. *Notables:* Singer Faith Hill; actress Faith Ford. *Variations:* Faithe, Faythe.

FAIVA (Polynesian) Game.

FAIZAH (Arabic) Triumphant. *Variations:* Faiza, Fayza, Fayzah.

FAKHIRA (Arabic) Magnificent woman. *Variations:* Fakheera, Fakira, Fakirah.

FALA (Native American) Crow-like. *Variations:* Fala, Falla, Fallah.

FALDA (Icelandic) Folded wings.

FALINE (Latin) Catlike. *Variations:* Faleen, Falene, Fayleen, Faylene, Falina, Faylina, Fayline.

FALLON (Irish) Related to a leader. *Variations:* Falan, Fallan, Falon, Fallyn, Falyn.

FALZAH (Arabic) Triumphant.

FAMKE (Dutch) Little girl. *Variation:* Femke.

FAN (Chinese) Mortal.

FANCHON (French) Freedom. *Variations:* Fanchona, Fanchonah, Fanchone.

FANCY (French) Engaged. *Variations:* Fancey, Fanci, Fancie.

FANG (Chinese) Fragrant.

FANG HUA (Chinese) Fragrant flower.

FANNY (English) Short form of Frances. *Notable:* Actress/comedian Fanny Brice. *Variations:* Fani, Fannie.

FANTASIA (Greek) Imaginative. *Notable:* Former American Idol Fantasia Barrino. *Variations:* Fantasha, Fantasya, Fantazia.

FANTINE (French) Childlike. *Variation:* Fantina.

FANUA (Polynesian) Land.

FANYA (Greek) Garland. *Variation:* Fania.

FAOILTIARNA (Irish) Lord of the wolves. *Variation:* Faoltiama.

FARDOOS (Arabic) Utopia.

FAREWELL (English) Goodbye. Beautiful spring.

FARFALLA (Italian) Like a butterfly. *Variation:* Farfalle.

FARICA (German) Leader of peace. *Variations:* Faricah, Faricka, Farika.

FARIDA (Arabic) Unique. *Variations:* Faridah, Farideh.

FARIHA (Arabic) Happy. *Variation:* Farihah.

FARLEY (English) From the sheep meadow. *Variations:* Farlea, Farlee, Farleigh, Farli, Farlie.

FARRAH (English) Pleasant; (Arabic) Beautiful. *Notable:* Actress Farrah Fawcett. *Variations:* Fara, Farah, Farra.

FARREN (English) Wandering. *Variations:* Faren, Farin, Faron, Farrin, Farron, Farryn, Faryn, Feran, Ferin, Feron, Ferran, Ferren, Ferrin, Ferron, Ferryn.

FARSIRIS (Persian) Princess.

FARYL (Irish) Courageous. *Variations:* Farryl, Farell.

FATHIYA (Arabic) Victorious.

FATIMA (Arabic) To abstain. *Variations:* Fatimah, Fatma, Fatuma.

FATIN (Arabic) Bewitching. *Variations:* Fatina, Fatinah.

FAUSTINE (Latin) Lucky. The feminine version of Faust. *Variations:* Fausta, Fauste, Faustia, Faustiana, Faustina.

FAVIANNA (French) Hopeful. *Variations:* Faviana, Favianne.

FAVOR (French) Approval.

FAWN (French) Young deer. *Variations:* Faina, Fanya, Fauan, Faun, Fauna, Faunee, Faunia, Fawna, Fawne, Fawnee, Fawnia, Fawnya.

FAXON (German) Long haired. *Variations:* Faxan, Faxana, Faxanah, Faxane, Faxann, Faxanna, Faxanne, Faxen, Faxin, Faxina, Faxinah, Faxine, Faxyn, Faxyna, Faxynah, Faxyne.

FAY (French) Fairy. Diminutive of Faith. *Notables:* Actress Fay Wray; writer Fay Weldon. *Variations:* Fae, Faie, Fayanna, Fayanne, Faye, Fayetta, Fayette, Fayla, Fayleen, Faylene, Fey.

FAYINA (Russian) Free one.

FAYME (French) Famous. *Variations:* Faim, Faima, Faime, Fama, Fame, Faym, Fayma.

FAYOLA (Nigerian) Lucky. *Variations:* Faiola, Faiolah, Fayolah.

FAYRUZ (Arabic) Turquoise.

FAYZA (Arabic) Winner. *Variations:* Faiza, Faizah, Fawzia.

FEBE (Greek) Form of Phoebe. Bright and shining. *Variations:* Febee, Febey, Febie.

FEBRUARY (Latin) Purification.

FEDORA (Greek) Gift from God.

FEIDHLIM (Irish) Hospitable.

FEIGEL (Hebrew) Bird. *Variations:* Faga, Faiga, Faige, Faigel, Feiga, Feygl.

FELA (Latin) Nickname for Felicity.

FELDA (German) From the field. *Variations:* Felde, Feldy.

FELICIA (Latin) Happy. Lucky. Feminine version of Felix. *Variations:* Falecia, Falicia, Falicie, Falisha, Falishia, Felice, Feliciana, Felicidad, Felicienne, Felicita, Felicitas, Felicity, Felise, Felisha, Felita, Feliz, Feliza, Phylicia.

FELICITY (English) Happy.

FELINA (Latin) Catlike. *Variations:* Feleena, Felinah, Felyna.

FELIPA (Spanish) Lover of horses. *Variation:* Felipina.

FELORA (Hawaiian) Flower. *Variations:* Felorena, Folora, Polola, Pololena.

FEMI (African) Seeking love. *Variations:* Femie, Femmi, Femmie, Femmy.

FENFANG (Chinese) Fragrance.

FENIA (Scandinavian) Ancient mythological figure. *Variations:* Fenja, Fenya.

FENNELLA (Irish) White shoulder.

FEODORA (Russian) Gift from God. Feminine version of Theodore. *Variations:* Fedora, Fedoria.

FERLISA (Italian) Happy.

FERN (English) Fern. *Variations:* Fearna, Ferna, Ferne, Ferny.

FERNANDA (German) Brave traveler. Feminine version of Ferdinand. *Variations:* Ferdinanda, Fernande, Fernandette, Fernandina.

FERNLEY (English) Valley of ferns. *Variations:* Fern, Ferne, Fernlee, Fernleigh, Fernly.

FIA (Italian) Flame.

FIALA (Czech) Violet.

FIAMMA (Italian) Fiery. *Variation:* Fiammetta.

FIDDA (Arabic) Silver. *Variation:* Fizza.

FIDELIA (Latin) Faithful. *Variations:* Fidela, Fidele, Fidella, Fidelle.

FIDELITY (Latin) Faithful. *Variations:* Fidelina, Fidelma.

FIFI (French) Nickname of Josephine. *Variations:* FeeFee, Fifine.

FILBERTA (English) Brilliant.

FILIA (Greek) Friendship. *Variations:* Filea, Filiah.

FILIPPA (Italian) Lover of horses. Feminine version of Philip. *Variations:* Felipa, Filipa, Filipina, Filippina, Philippa.

FILOMENA (Italian) Strong friend. *Variations:* Filimena, Filumena, Philomena.

FINA (Italian) Nickname for Serafina. Serpent.

FINCH (English) Bird. *Variation:* Fynch.

FINEEN (Irish) Beautiful daughter. *Variations:* Fineena, Fyneen, Fyneena.

FINESSE (French) Delicate.

FINOLA (Irish) White shoulders. *Variations:* Effie, Ella, Fenella, Finella, Fionnaghuala, Fionneuala, Fionnghuala, Fionnuala, Fionnula, Fionola, Fynella, Nuala.

FIONA (Irish) Fair, white. *Variations:* Fionan, Fionna, Fionne.

FIORALBA (Italian) Dawn flower.

FIORELLA (Italian) Little flower. *Variation:* Fiore.

FIRMINA (French) Firm and strong. *Variations:* Fireena, Firminah, Firmine.

FLAIR (English) With style. *Variations:* Flaire, Flare.

FLAMINIA (Latin) Priest. *Variations:* Flamina, Flamyna.

FLANNA (Irish) Red hair. *Variations:* Flana, Flanagh.

FLANNERY (Irish) Red hair. *Notable:* Writer Flannery O'Connor.

FLAVIA (Latin) Yellow hair. *Variations:* Flaviana, Flavie, Flaviere, Flavyere, Flavyia.

FLEUR (French) Flower. *Variations:* Fleura, Fleuree, Fleuretta, Fleurette.

FLO (American) Short form of Florence.

FLORA (Latin) Flower. *Notable:* Actress Flora Birch. *Variations:* Fiora, Fiore, Fiori, Fleur, Fleurette, Fleurine, Flo, Flor, Florann, Floranne, Flore, Florella, Florelle, Floretta, Florette, Flori, Floria, Floriana, Florianne, Florie, Floriese, Florina, Florine, Floris, Florrie, Florry, Floss, Flossey, Flossie.

FLORENCE (Latin) Flourishing. *Notable:* Actress Florence Henderson. *Variations:* Fiorentina, Fiorenza, Florance, Florence, Florencia, Florentia, Florentina, Florentyna, Florenze.

FLORIDA (Spanish) Flowery. *Variations:* Floridia, Florinda, Florita.

FLORIMEL (Latin) Combination of flower and honey. *Variations:* Florizella, Florizelle.

FLOSSIE (English) Short form of Florence.

FLOWER (English) Flower.

FLYNN (Irish) Red headed. *Variations:* Flinn, Flyn.

FOLA (Nigerian) Honorable.

FOLADE (Nigerian) She brings honor.

FOLAMI (Nigerian) Respect me.

FOLAYAN (Nigerian) Walking proudly.

FOLUKE (Nigerian) God's care.

FONDA (Spanish) Inn.

FONTANNA (French) Fountain. *Variations:* Fontaine, Fontana, Fontane, Fontanne, Fontayne.

FORBA (Scottish) Headstrong.

FORSYTHIA (Latin) Flower name.

FORTUNA (Latin) Lucky. *Variations:* Fortunata, Fortune.

FRAN (Latin) Short form of Frances. *Notable:* Actress Fran Drescher. *Variations:* Frann, Franni, Frannie, Franny.

FRANCES (Latin) One who is from France. Feminine version of Francis. *Notable:* Actress Frances McDormand. *Variations:* Fan, Fancy, Fania, Fannee, Fanney, Fannie, Fanny, Fanya, Fran, Franca, Francee, Franceline, Francena, Francene, Francesca, Francetta, Francette, Francey, Franchesca, Francie, Francina, Francine, Francisca, Françoise, Frank, Frankie, Franni, Frannie, Franzetta, Franziska, Paquita.

FRANCESCA (Italian) Form of Frances. *Variations:* Franchesca, Franzetta.

FRANCHELLE (French) From France. *Variation:* Franchella.

FRANCINE (French) Form of Frances. *Variations:* Francene, Francina, Francyne.

FRANÇOISE (French) From France.

FRANKIE (American) Nickname for Frances or Francine. *Variations:* Franke, Franki, Franky.

FRANTISKA (Czech) Free woman. *Variations:* Frana, Franka.

FRAUKE (German) Little lady.

FRAYDA (Hebrew) Happy. *Variations:* Fradel, Frayde, Freida, Freide, Freyde.

FREDA (German) Peaceful. *Notable:* Artist Frida Kahlo. *Variations:* Freada, Freeda, Freida, Frida, Frieda, Fritzi, Fryda.

FREDDI (English) Nickname for Frederica or Winifred. *Variations:* Freddie, Freddy.

FREDERICA (German) Peaceful ruler. *Notable:* Model Frederique Van Der Wal. *Variations:* Frederika, Frederike, Frederique, Fredrica, Fredrika.

FREESIA (English) Flower name.

FRENCHIE (American) From France. *Variations:* Frenchee, Frenchi, Frenchy.

FREYA (Scandinavian) Noble lady. *Variations:* Fraya, Frayah, Frea, Freja, Freyah, Freydis, Freyja, Froja.

FRIGG (Scandinavian) Beloved. *Variation:* Frigga.

FRITZI (German) Short form of Frederica. *Variations:* Fritze, Fritzie, Fritzy.

FRODINA (German) Smart friend. *Variations:* Frodine, Frodyn, Frodyna.

FRONDA (Latin) Leafy branch.

FRONIA (English) Wise. *Variations:* Frona, Froneah, Froniah, Fronie, Froniya, Froniyah.

FRULA (German) Hard working. *Variation:* Frulla.

FRUMA (Yiddish) Pious one. *Variation:* Frume.

FUAMNACH (Irish) Jealous.

FUJI (Japanese) Wisteria. *Variations:* Fujiko, Fujiyo.

FUKAYNA (Arabic) Knowledgeable.

FULANDE (Hindi) Flower. *Variation:* Fulangi.

FULLA (Scandinavian) Mythological fertility goddess.

FUMIKO (Japanese) Child of treasured beauty.

FUSCHIA (Latin) Purple flower name.

FULVIA (Latin; Italian) Blond. *Variation:* Fulvie.

FUYU (Japanese) Winter. *Variation:* Fuyuko.

GABBATHA (Hebrew) From the temple mound. *Variations:* Gabatha, Gabathia.

GABRIELLE (French) Devotion to God. Feminine version of Gabriel. *Notables:* Volleyball player Gabrielle Reece; tennis star Gabriela Sabatini. *Variations:* Gabrela, Gabriel, Gabriela, Gabrielah, Gabriell, Gabriella, Gabriellah, Gabriellia, Gabriello, Gabrila, Gabrilla, Gabriolett, Gabrioletta, Gabriolette, Gabryel, Gabryela, Gabryiela, Gavra, Gavrielle, Gavrilla, Gavrille, Gavryl, Gavryla, Gavryle, Gavryll, Gavrylla, Gavrylle.

GABLE (French) God is my strength. *Variations:* Gabal, Gabala, Gabalah, Gabale, Gaball, Gaballa, Gaballah, Gaballe, Gabel, Gabela, Gabelah, Gabele, Gabell, Gabella, Gabellah, Gabelle.

GABY (French) Short form of Gabrielle. *Variations:* Gab, Gabb, Gabbea, Gabbee, Gabbey, Gabbi, Gabbie, Gabby, Gabe, Gabea, Gabee, Gabey, Gabi, Gabie.

GADA (Hebrew) Lucky. *Variation:* Gadah.

GADARA (Armenian) Mountain peak. *Variation:* Gadarra.

GADY (English) Little friend. *Variations:* Gadea, Gade, Gadey, Gadi, Gadie.

GAEL (Irish) Form of Gail. Father's joy. *Variation:* Gaela.

GAENOR (Welsh) Fair. Smooth.

GAETANA (Italian) From Gaeta, Italy. *Variations:* Gaetan, Gaetanah, Gaetane, Gaetanna, Gaetanne, Gaitana, Gaitanah, Gaitann, Gaitanna, Gaitanne, Gaytana, Gaytane, Gaytanna, Gaytanne.

GAFNA (Hebrew) Vine.

GAI (French) Lively. *Variations:* Ga, Gae, Gaie, Gaye.

GAIA (Greek) Earth. *Variations:* Gaea, Gaeah, Gaiah, Gaioa, Gaya, Gayah.

GAIL (Hebrew) My father rejoices. *Notable:* Writer Gail Sheehy. *Variations:* Gael, Gaela, Gaelen, Gaell, Gaella, Gaelle, Gaila, Gailah, Gaile, Gailean, Gaileana, Gaileane, Gaileen, Gaileena, Gailina, Gailine, Gailyn, Gailyna, Gailyne, Gale, Galey, Galie, Gayel, Gayell, Gayella, Gayelle, Gayl, Gayla, Gayle, Gayleen, Gayleena, Gaylia, Gayliah, Gaylina, Gayline, Gaylyn, Gaylyna, Gaylynah, Gaylyne.

GAIRA (Scottish) Petite woman. *Variations:* Gaera, Gayra.

GALA (French) Festive. *Variations:* Galah, Galla, Gallah.

GALADRIEL (Sindarin, a literary language) Radiant maiden. Name of elf princess from J. R. R. Tolkien's *Lord of the Rings* trilogy.

GALATEA (Greek) White as milk. *Variations:* Galanth, Galantha, Galanthe, Galatee, Galati, Galatia, Galatiah, Galatie, Galaty, Galatya, Galatyah.

GALAXY (Greek) Vault of stars. *Variations:* Galaxee, Galaxey, Galaxi, Galaxia, Galaxiah.

GALEED (Hebrew) Friendship. *Variations:* Galead, Galida.

GALEN (Irish) Lively. *Variations:* Gaelen, Gaylen, Gaylene.

GALENA (Greek) Healer. *Variations:* Galana, Galanah, Galane, Galean, Galeana, Galeane, Galeena, Galeenah, Galeene, Galeah, Galene, Galina, Galinah, Galine, Gallana, Gallanah, Gallane, Galleena, Galleenah, Galleene, Galen, Galenah, Galene, Gallin, Gallina, Gallinah, Galline, Gallyn, Gallyna, Gallynah, Gallyne, Galyn, Galyna, Galynah, Galyne.

GALI (Hebrew) Hill, mound. *Variations:* Gal, Galee, Galice, Galei, Galeigh, Galie, Gallee, Galley, Galila, Galli, Gallie, Gally, Galy.

GALIA (Hebrew) Wave. *Variations:* Galea, Galeah, Galiah, Gallea, Galleah.

GALIENA (German) High one. *Variations:* Galiana, Galianna.

GALILANI (Native American) Friendly. *Variations:* Galilanee, Galilaney, Galilanie, Galilany.

GALILEE (Hebrew) From the sacred sea.

Goth Baby Names

If you're a heavy-metal fan, like to dress in black, and find the dark-side fun, here's a list of baby names—mostly unisex at that—for your little Goth-in-training! (G=Girl, B=Boy, U=Unisex)

Ankha (G)	Lynx (U)
Aunika (G)	Malificent (U)
Crow (B)	Mysterie (U)
Dickinson (B)	Onyx (U)
Elvira (G)	Ozzie (B)
Emily (G)	Plath (U)
Esperanza (G)	Rasputin(a) (U)
Kat (U)	Raven (U)
Lucifer (B)	Shelley (U)
Lunaria (G)	Voltaire (B)

GALINA (Russian) Bright one or shining one. Variation of Helen. *Variations:* Galaina, Galainah, Galaine, Galayna, Galaynah, Galayne, Galean, Galeana, Galeanah, Galeane, Galeen, Galeena, Galeenah, Galeene, Galena, Galenah, Galene, Galenka, Galia, Galiana, Galianah, Galiane, Galiena, Galinah, Galine, Galinka, Galka, Galkah, Galochka, Galya, Galyag, Galyn, Galyna, Galynah, Galyne.

GALLA (Celtic) Stranger. *Variations:* Galah, Gallah.

GALYA (Hebrew) God has redeemed. *Variations:* Galia, Gallia, Gallya.

GAMBHIRA (Hindi) Noble.

GAMEL (Scandinavian) Elder. *Variations:* Gamala, Gamalah, Gamale, Gamela, Gamelah, Gamele.

GAMILA (Arabic) Beautiful. *Variations:* Gamela, Gamelia, Gamilla, Gemila, Gemilla, Jamila.

GAMMA (Greek) Third letter of the Greek alphabet.

GANESA (Hindi) Goddess of wisdom. *Variations:* Ganesah, Ganessa, Ganessah.

GANYA (Hebrew) Garden of God. *Variations:* Gana, Gania, Ganice, Ganyah.

GARDA (German) Guardian. *Variation:* Gardah.

GARDENIA (English) Flower name. *Variations:* Gardeen, Gardeena, Gardeene, Gardena, Gardene, Gardin, Gardina, Gardine, Gardner, Gardyn, Gardyna, Gardynah, Gardyne.

GARI (German) Spear. Feminine version of Gary.

GARIMA (Hindi) Importance. *Variations:* Garmeena, Garminah.

GARLAND (French) Wreath. *Variations:* Garlan, Garlana, Garlanah, Garlanda, Garlande, Garlandera, Garlane, Garleen, Garleena, Garleenah, Garleene, Garlena, Garlenah, Garlene, Garlind, Garlinda, Garlindah, Garlinde, Garlyn, Garlynd, Garlynda, Garlyndah, Garlynde.

GARNET (English) Dark-red jewel. *Variations:* Garneta, Garnett, Garnetta, Garnette.

GARYN (English) Spear carrier. *Variations:* Garan, Garana, Garane, Garin, Garina, Garine, Garran, Garrana, Garrane, Garrin, Garrina, Garrine, Garron, Garyn, Garyna, Garyne, Garynna, Garynne.

GASHA (Russian) Good. Russian version of Agatha. *Variations:* Gashia, Gashka.

GASPARDA (French) Treasured. *Variation:* Gaspara.

GAVINA (Latin) White falcon. *Variations:* Gaveena, Gavyna.

GAVRILLA (Hebrew) Heroine. *Variations:* Gavrel, Gavrela, Gavrelah, Gavrelia, Gavreliah, Gavrell, Gavrella, Gavrellah, Gavrid, Gavrieela, Gavriela, Gavrielle, Gavrila, Gavrilla, Gavrille, Gavryl, Gavryla, Gavryle, Gavryll, Gavrylla, Gavrylle.

GAY (French) Joyful. *Variations:* Ga, Gae, Gai, Gaie, Gaye.

GAYLE (Hebrew) Rejoicing. Form of Gail. *Variations:* Gayla, Gaylah, Gaylene, Gaylia, Gaylyn.

GAYNA (English) White wave. *Variations:* Gaena, Gaenah, Gaina, Gainah, Gaynah.

GAYORA (Hebrew) Valley of light. *Variation:* Gayoria.

GAZELLE (Latin) Gazelle. Graceful. *Variation:* Gazella.

GAZIT (Hebrew) Smooth stone.

GEBA (Hebrew) From the hill.

GEFEN (Hebrew) Vine. *Variations:* Gafna, Gafnit, Gaphna, Geffen.

GEFJUN (Scandinavian) Giver of wealth. *Variations:* Gefion, Gefjon.

GELASIA (Greek) Inclined to laughter.

GELILAH (Hebrew) Rolling hills. *Variations:* Gelalia, Gelalya, Gelila, Gelilia, Geliliya.

GELSEY (English) Last name. *Variations:* Gelsi, Gelsie, Gelsy.

GELYA (Russian) Messenger.

GEMINI (Greek) Twin. *Variations:* Gemella, Gemelle, Gemina, Geminine.

GEMMA (Italian) Precious stone. *Variations:* Gem, Gema, Gemmie, Jemma.

GEN (Japanese) Spring.

GENA (French) Form of Gena, Geneva, Genevieve. *Variations:* Geena, Genah, Genia.

GENELL (American) Form of Janelle.

GENEROSA (Spanish; Italian) Generous.

GENESEE (Native American) Wonderful valley.

GENESIS (Hebrew) Beginning. *Variations:* Genessa, Genisa, Genisia, Genisis, Jenessa.

GENEVA (French) Juniper. *Variations:* Geneeva, Geneevah, Geneieve, Genevah, Geneve,

Genevera, Genevra, Genevrah, Genevia, Geneviah, Genevra, Genneeva, Genneevah, Ginevra, Ginevrah, Ginneeva, Ginneevah, Ginneva, Ginnevah, Gyniva, Gynivah, Gynniva, Gynnivah, Gynnyva, Gynnyvah, Janeva, Jeneva, Jenevah, Jenevia, Jeneviah.

GENEVIEVE (French) White. *Notable:* Actress Geneviève Bujold. *Variations:* Genavieve, Geneveeve, Genivieve, Gennie, Genny, Genofeva, Genovefa, Genovera, Genoveva, Jenevieve.

GENIE (English) Short form of Eugenia or Eugenie. *Variations:* Geeni, Geenie, Geeney.

GENJI (Japanese) Ruling clan.

GENNA (English) Variation of Jenna. *Variations:* Gena, Genah, Gennae, Gennah, Gennai, Gennay.

GENNIFER (English) Variation of Jennifer. *Variations:* Gen, Genifer, Genny.

GEONA (Hebrew) Glorification. *Variation:* Geonit.

GEORGIA (Latin) Farmer. Feminine version of George. *Notable:* Artist Georgia O'Keeffe. *Variations:* Georgeann, Georgeanne, Georgeina, Georgena, Georgene, Georgetta, Georgette, Georggann, Georgganne, Georgiana, Georgianne, Georgie, Georgienne, Giorgia, Giorgina, Giorgyna, Jorga, Jorgia, Jorgina, Jorja.

GEORGINA (English) Form of Georgia. *Variations:* Georgie, Georgine, Georgy.

GERALDINE (German) One who rules with a spear. Feminine version of Gerald. *Notable:* Politician Geraldine Ferraro. *Variations:*

Ceraldina, Deraldene, Geralda, Geraldeen, Geraldina, Geralyn, Geralynne, Geri, Gerianna, Gerianne, Geroldine, Gerry, Jeraldeen, Jeraldene, Jeraldine, Jeralee, Jere, Jeri, Jerilene, Jerrie, Jerrileen, Jerroldeen.

GERILYN (American) Combination of Geraldine and Lynn. *Variations:* Geralin, Geralina, Geralyn, Geralynn, Gerilynn, Gerilin, Gerilina.

GERANIUM (Latin) Flower name.

GERDA (Scandinavian) Guarded. *Variations:* Gard, Gerd, Gerde.

GERI (American) Nickname for Geraldine. *Variations:* Gerri, Gerry, Jeri, Jerry.

GERIANNE (American) Combined form of first names "Gerry" and "Anne."

GERLINDE (German) Soft spear. *Variations:* Gerlind, Gerlinda.

GERMAINE (French) One from Germany. *Notable:* Writer Germaine Greer. *Variations:* Germain, Geramaina, Germana, Germane, Germayn, Germayne, Jermain, Jermaine, Jermane, Jermayn, Jermayne.

GERSEMI (Scandinavian) Gem.

GERTIE (German) Short form of Gertrude. *Variations:* Gert, Gerti, Gerty.

GERTRUDE (German) With the strength of a spear. *Notable:* Writer Gertrude Stein. *Variations:* Geertrud, Geertruda, Geertrude, Geitruda, Gerti, Gertie, Gertina, Gertraud, Gertrud, Gertruda, Gerty, Girtrud, Gertruda, Girtrude, Truda, Trude, Trudey, Trudi, Trudie, Trudy, Trudye.

GERUSHAH (Hebrew) Banishment. *Variation:* Gerusha.

GERVAISE (French) Spear. *Variations:* Gervaisa, Gervis, Gervayse.

GESSICA (American) Form of Jessica. *Variations:* Gesica, Gesika, Gesikah, Gessica, Gessika, Gessikah, Gessyca, Gessyka, Gesyca, Gesyka.

GEVA (Hebrew) Hill. *Variation:* Gevah.

GEVIRAH (Hebrew) Queen. *Variation:* Gevira.

GHADA (Arabic) Graceful. *Variations:* Ghadah, Ghayda.

GHALIYA (Arabic) Pleasant odor. *Variation:* Ghaliyah.

GHISLAINE (French) Sweet oath. *Variation:* Gislaine.

GHITA (Italian; Greek) Pearl. *Variations:* Ghyta, Ghytah, Gyta, Gytah.

GHUFRAN (Arabic) To forgive.

GIA (Italian) Queen. *Variations:* Giah, Gya, Gyah.

GIACHETTA (Italian) Supplanter.

GIACINTA (Italian) Hyacinth. *Variations:* Giacintah, Giacynta, Giacyntah, Gyacinta, Gyacynta, Gyacyntah.

GIACOBBA (Italian) Replacer. The feminine form of Jacob. *Variations:* Giacoba, Giacobah, Giacobbah, Gyacoba, Gyacobba, Gyacobbah.

GIADA (Italian) Jade. *Notable:* Celebrity chef Giada De Laurentiis.

GIALIA (Italian) Youthful. *Variations:* Giala, Gialiana, Gialietta.

GIANNA (Italian) God is good. Feminine version of John. *Variations:* Geona, Geonna, Gian, Giana, Gianah, Giancinthia, Gianel, Gianela, Gianele, Gianella, Gianelle, Gianet,

Gianeta, Gianete, Gianett, Gianetta, Gianina, Giannina, Giannine, Gianoula, Gyan, Gyana, Gyanah, Gyann, Gyanna, Gyannah.

GIBORAH (Hebrew) Strong. *Variation:* Gibora.

GIDGET (American) Petite girl. *Variations:* Gigette, Gydget.

GIGI (French) Short form of Georgina, Gilberte, or Virginia. *Notable:* Tennis player Gigi Fernandez. *Variations:* Geegi, Geegie, Gigee, Gigie.

GILA (Hebrew) Joy. *Variations:* Gela, Geela, Gilah, Gilla, Gyla, Gylah.

GILADAH (Hebrew) Hill of testimony. *Variations:* Galat, Geela, Gila, Gili, Gilia.

GILANAH (Hebrew) Happy. *Variations:* Gilana, Gilane, Gilania, Gilaine, Gylana.

GILBERTE (French) Shining pledge. Feminine version of Gilbert. *Variations:* Gilberta, Gilbertia, Gilbertina, Gilbertine, Gilbertyna, Gilbertyne, Gilbirt, Gilbirta, Gilbirte, Gilbirtia, Gilbirtina, Gilbirtine, Gilburta, Gilburte, Gilburtia, Gilburtina, Gilburtyna, Gilbyrta, Gilbyrte, Gilbyrtia, Gilbyrtina, Gilbyrtyna, Gylberta, Gylbertah, Gylberte, Gylbertina, Gylbertynan, Gylbirta, Gylbirte, Gylbirtia, Gylbirtina, Gylbirtyna, Gylburta, Gylburte, Gylburtia, Gylburtina, Gylburtyna, Gylbyrta, Gylbyrte, Gylbyrtia, Gylbyrtina, Gylbyrtyna.

GILDA (English) Golden. *Notable:* Comedian Gilda Radner. *Variations:* Gildah, Gylda, Gyldah.

GILEAD (Hebrew) Mountain of testimony.

GILIAH (Hebrew) God's joy. *Variations:* Gilia, Giliya, Giliyah.

GILL (English) Downy. *Variations:* Gilli, Gillie, Gilly.

GILLIAN (English) Youthful. *Variations:* Gillaine, Gilana, Gilena, Gilenia, Gilian, Giliana, Giliane, Gillan, Gillianne, Gillyanne, Gyllian, Gylliana, Gylliane.

GILSEY (English) Jasmine.

GIN (Japanese) Silver.

GINA (Italian) Nickname for names such as Regina and Angelina. *Notables:* Italian actress Gina Lollobrigida; actress Geena Davis. *Variations:* Geena, Gena, Ginat, Ginia.

GINERVA (Celtic) White as foam. *Variation:* Ginevra.

GINGER (English) Like the fragrant spice. *Variations:* Ginga, Ginja, Ginjer, Gynger, Gynjer.

GINIA (Latin) Purity. *Variations:* Giniah, Gynia.

GINNIFER (Welsh) Form of Jennifer. White. *Variations:* Ginifer, Gynnifer.

GINNY (English) Nickname for Virginia. Pure. *Variations:* Ginney, Ginni, Ginnie.

GIOCANDA (Italian) Happy.

GIOFFREDA (Italian) God's peace. *Variation:* Giofreda.

GIOIA (Italian) Happiness.

GIORDANA (Italian) Form of Jordan. *Variations:* Giadana, Giodana, Giordanna.

GIORSAL (Scottish) Graceful. *Variation:* Giorsala.

GIOSETTA (Italian) God's progeny.

GIOVANNA (Italian) God is good. *Variations:* Giavanna, Giovana, Giovannah, Giovanetta.

GIRAIDA (Italian) Farmer.

GIRALDA (German) Spear ruler. *Variations:* Giraldah, Gyralda.

GIRISA (Hindi) Lord of the mountain.

GISA (Hebrew) Hewn stone. *Variations:* Gissa, Gisse, Giza, Gizza.

GISELLE German; French) Oath; pledge. *Notable:* Model Gisele Bundchen. *Variations:* Gelsi, Gelsy, Gisel, Gisela, Gisele, Giselia, Gisella, Gizela, Gizella, Gizelle, Gysela, Gyselle, Gyzela, Gyzelle.

GITA (Sanskrit) Song. *Variations:* Geeta, Gitah, Gitta, Gyta.

GITANA (Spanish) Gypsy. *Variations:* Gitane, Gitanna, Gytana.

GITEL (Hebrew) Good. *Variations:* Gitela, Gitele, Gittel, Gytella, Gytelle.

GITTA (Hungarian) Power. Diminutive of Brigitte. *Variation:* Gitte.

GITUSKA (Czech) Pearl.

GIVOLA (Hebrew) Blossom.

GIUDITTA (Italian) Woman from Judea.

GIULIA (Italian) Form of Julia. *Variations:* Giuliana, Giulietta.

GIUSEPPA (Italian) God's progeny. *Variation:* Giuseppina.

GIUSTINA (Italian) Fair and just.

GLADE (English) From the meadow. *Variations:* Glaid, Glayde.

GLADIOLA (Italian) Flower name.

GLADYS (Welsh) Lame. Form of Claudia. *Notable:* Singer Gladys Knight. *Variations:* Gladis, Gladiz, Gwladus, Gwladys.

GLEDA (Icelandic) Happy. *Variation:* Gledah.

GLENDA (Welsh) Holy and good. *Notable:* Actress Glenda Jackson. *Variations:* Glendah, Glinda, Glynda.

GLENNA (Irish) Narrow valley. *Notable:* Actress Glenn Close. *Variations:* Glen, Glenn, Glennette.

GLENYS (Welsh) Holy. *Variations:* Glenice, Glenis, Glenise, Glennis, Glennys, Glenyse, Glenyss.

GLORIA (Latin) Glory. *Notables:* Feminist Gloria Steinem; actress Gloria Swanson; clothing designer Gloria Vanderbilt; singer Gloria Estefan. *Variations:* Gloree, Glori, Glorianna, Glorianne, Glorie, Glorielle, Glorien, Glorienna, Glorienne, Glorria, Glory, Gloryanna, Gloryanne, Gloryenna, Gloryenne.

GLUCKE (Yiddish) Good luck. *Variations:* Gluckel, Gluke, Glukel.

GLYNIS (Welsh) Small valley. *Notable:* Actress Glynnis O'Connor. *Variations:* Glinice, Glinis, Glinise, Glinnis, Glyness, Glynnis, Glynyss.

GOBNAIT (Celtic) Little smith. *Variations:* Gobinet, Gobnet.

GODELIEVE (Dutch) God love.

GODFREYA (German) Peace of God.

GODIVA (English) Gift from God.

GOLDA (English) Golden. *Notable:* Israeli Prime Minister Golda Meir. *Variations:* Goldarina, Goldarine, Goldia, Goldie, Goldif, Goldina, Goldy.

GOLDIE (English) Golden. *Notable:* Actress Goldie Hawn. *Variations:* Goldee, Goldi, Goldy.

GOMER (Hebrew) To complete.

GORANE (Slavic) From the mountain.

GORAWEN (Welsh) Bringing joy.

GORMLAITH (Gaelic) Splendid lady.

GRACE (Latin) Grace. *Notables:* Singers Grace Slick and Grace Jones; actress Grace Kelly. *Variations:* Engracia, Engracie, Graca, Gracella, Gracelle, Gracey, Graci, Gracia, Graciana, Gracie, Graciela, Gracy, Grasiela, Gratia, Grayce, Grazyna.

GRAINNE (Irish) Goddess of grain. *Variations:* Grainnia, Grania, Granna.

GRAZIELLA (Italian) Form of Grace. *Variations:* Grazia, Grazie, Grazielle, Graziosa.

GREER (Scottish) Observant. *Notable:* Actress Greer Garson. *Variations:* Grear, Grier.

GREGORIA (Latin) Alert. Feminine form of Gregory. *Variations:* Gregoriana, Gregorina.

GRESSA (Scandinavian) Grass.

GRETA (Scandinavian; German) Pearl. Short form of Margaret. *Notables:* Actress Greta Garbo; TV journalist Greta Van Susteren. *Variations:* Grete, Gretie, Gretta, Grette.

GRETCHEN (German) Pearl. Form of Margaret. *Notable:* Actress Gretchen Mol. *Variations:* Grechen, Grechyn, Gretchin, Gretchyn.

GRETEL (German) Short form of Margaret. *Variations:* Gretal, Grettal, Grettel, Gretelle, Gretyl.

GRETNA (Scottish) Scottish village.

GRISCHA (Russian) Watchful. *Variations:* Greesha, Grisha, Gryscha.

GRISELDA (German) Gray fighting maid. *Variations:* Grisilda, Grishilda, Grizelda, Zelda.

GRISWALDA (German) From the grey woods. *Variations:* Griswalde, Grizwalda.

GUADALUPE (Spanish) Valley of wolves. *Variation:* Lupe.

GUANG (Chinese) Light and glory.

GUDA (Scandanavian) Good. *Variations:* Gudah, Gudda.

GUDRUN (Scandinavian) Fight. *Variations:* Gudren, Gudrin, Gudrina, Gudrinne, Gudruna, Guro.

GUIDA (Italian) Guide.

GUIDITTA (Italian) Praised.

GUILLERMA (Spanish) Combination of will and helmet. Feminine version of William.

GUINEVERE (Welsh) Fair. Yielding. *Variations:* Gaenor, Gayna, Gaynah, Gayner, Gaynor, Guenevere, Guinievre, Gwenivere, Gwenora, Gwenore, Gwynifor, Gwynivere.

GULL (Scandinavian) Gold. *Variations:* Gula, Gulah, Gulla, Gullah.

GUNDA (Scandinavian) Warrior. *Variation:* Gundah.

GUNHILDA (Scandinavian) Woman warrior. *Variations:* Gunda, Gunhilde, Gunilda, Gunilla, Gunnhilda.

GUNN (Scandinavian) Battle. *Variation:* Gun.

GUNNBORG (Scandinavian) Fortified battle. *Variation:* Gunborg.

GUNNLOD (Scandinavian) Ancient mythological figure.

GUNNVOR (Scandinavian) Cautious in war. *Variations:* Gunver, Gunvor.

GURICE (Hebrew) Lion cub. *Variations:* Guri, Gurie, Gurit.

GUSSIE (English) Short form of Augusta. *Variations:* Gussi, Gussy.

GUSTA (Latin) Short form of Augusta. *Variations:* Gustee, Gustie, Gusty.

GUSTAVA (Scandinavian) Staff of the gods. Feminine version of Gustav. *Variation:* Gustavah.

GWEN (Welsh) Short form of Gwendolyn or Guinevere. White. *Notable:* Singer Gwen Stefani. *Variations:* Guin, Gwenn, Gwin, Gwinne, Gwyn, Gwynn, Gwynne.

GWENDOLYN (Welsh) White brow. *Notable:* Poet Gwendolyn Brooks. *Variations:* Guendolen, Guenna, Gwenda, Gwendaline, Gwendia, Gwendolen, Gwendolene, Gwendolin, Gwedolina, Gwendoline, Gwendolynn, Gwendolynne, Gwenette, Gwenna, Gwennie, Gwennifer, Gwenny.

GWENEAL (Welsh) Blessed angel.

GWENFREWI (Welsh) Blessed peace.

GWENLUAN (Welsh) Blessed flood.

GWERFUL (Welsh) Shy. *Variations:* Gweirful, Gwerfyl.

GWYNETH (Welsh) Happiness. *Notable:* Actress Gwyneth Paltrow. *Variations:* Gwynedd, Gwenith, Gwennyth, Gwenyth, Gwynith, Gwynn, Gwynna, Gwynne, Gwynneth.

GYANDA (Hindi) Learned.

GYPSY (English) Wanderer. *Variations:* Gipsi, Gipsy, Gypsee, Gypsi, Gypsie.

GYTHA (Scandinavian) Warlike.

HA (Vietnamese) Kissed by the sun.

HABIBA (Arabic) Cherished. *Variations:* Habibah, Haviva.

HACHI (Japanese) Good luck. *Variation:* Hachiko.

HADARA (Hebrew) Beauty. *Variations:* Hadar, Hadarah, Hadaria, Hadariah, Hadarya, Hadaryah.

HADASSAH (Hebrew) Myrtle. *Variations:* Hada, Hadas, Hadasa, Hadassa.

HADEEL (Arabic) Like a dove.

HADEENA (English) Meadow of flowers. *Variations:* Hadina, Hadyna.

HADIYA (African) A gift. *Variation:* Hadiyah.

HADLEY (English) Meadow of heather. *Variations:* Hadlea, Hadleah, Hadlee, Hadleigh, Hadli, Hadlie, Hadly.

HADRIA (Latin) From Hadria. *Variations:* Hadriana, Hadriane, Hadrienne.

HADY (Greek) Soulful. *Variations:* Haddie, Haddy, Hadea, Hadee, Hadi, Hadie.

HADYA (Arabic) Guide. *Variations:* Hadi, Hadia.

HAE-WON (Korean) Grace.

HAFSAH (Arabic) Lioness. *Variations:* Hafsa, Hafza.

HAFWEN (Welsh) Fair summer. *Variations:* Hafwena, Hafwenah, Hafwin, Hafwina, Hafwinah, Hafwine, Hafwyn, Hafwyna, Hafwynah, Hafwyne.

HAGAI (Hebrew) Abandoned. *Variation:* Hagae.

HAGAR (Hebrew) Stranger. *Variations:* Hagara, Hagarah, Hagaria, Hagariah, Haggar.

HAGIA (Hebrew) Joy. *Variations:* Hagice, Hagit.

HAGNE (Greek) Pure.

HAIDEE (Greek) Modest. *Variations:* Haidea, Haideah, Haidey, Haidi, Hadia, Hady, Hadya, Haydee.

HAILEY (English) Hay meadow. Form of Hayley. *Variations:* Haile, Hailea, Haileah, Hailee, Hailei, Haileigh, Haili, Hailie, Haily, Haylea, Hayleah, Haylei, Hayleigh, Hayless, Hayley, Hayli, Haylie, Hayly.

HAIWEE (Native American) Dove. *Variations:* Haiwi, Haiwie.

HAJAR (Arabic) To abandon. *Variation:* Hagir.

HAKANA (Turkish) Empress. *Variation:* Hakanna.

HAKUMELE (Hawaiian) Poet.

HALA (Arabic) Halo. *Variation:* Halah.

HALCYON (Greek) Kingfisher. *Variations:* Halcion, Halcione, Halcyone.

HALDANA (Scandinavian) One who is half Danish. *Variations:* Halda, Haldaine, Haldanah, Haldane, Haldanna, Haldayne, Haldi, Haldie.

HALEAKUA (Hawaiian) God's house.

HALETTA (Greek) Girl from the meadow. *Variation:* Halette.

HALFRIDA (German) Calm heroine. *Variations:* Halfreda, Halfredah, Halfredda, Halfreddah, Halfridah, Halfrieda, Halfryda, Halfrydah.

HALIA (Hawaiian) Remembering a loved one. *Variations:* Haleah, Haleigha, Haliah, Halya.

HALIAKA (Hawaiian) Leader of the house. Hawaiian version of Harriet. *Variations:* Hariaka, Hariata.

HALIMA (Arabic) Gentle. *Variations:* Haleema, Halimah, Halymeda.

HALIMEDA (Greek) Of the sea. *Variations:* Halimedah, Halymeda, Halymedah.

HALINA (Russian) Shining one. Russian version of Helen. *Variations:* Halinah, Haline, Halyn, Halyna, Halynah, Halyne.

HALKU (Hawaiian) Flower.

HALLIE (English) Form of Hayley. *Notable:* Actress Halle Berry. *Variations:* Haleigh, Hali, Halie, Halle, Hallee, Hally.

HALOLANI (Hawaiian) Fly like a bird.

HALONA (Native American) Good luck. *Variation:* Halonna.

HAMA (Japanese) Beach. *Variation:* Hamako.

HAMIDA (Arabic) To praise. *Variations:* Hameedah, Hamidah.

HANA (Japanese) Flower. *Variations:* Hanae, Hanako.

HANALEI (Hawaii) Beautiful flowers.

HANAN (Arabic) Merciful.

HANIA (Hebrew) Resting place. *Variation:* Haniya.

HANIFAH (Arabic) True believer. *Variations:* Hanifa, Hanyfa, Hanyfah.

HANITA (Hindi) Grace.

HANNAH (Hebrew) Grace. *Variations:* Chana, Chanah, Channa, Channah, Hana, Hanah, Hanna, Hanne, Hannele, Hannelore, Hannie, Honna.

HANSA (Hindi) Swan. *Variations:* Hansika, Hansila.

HANSINE (Scandinavian) God is good.

HAPPY (English) Glad. *Variation:* Happi.

HAQIKAH (Arabic) Truthful.

HARA (Hindi) Tawny. *Variations:* Harah, Harrah.

HARALDA (Scandinavian) Powerful army. Feminine version of Harold. *Variations:* Harelda, Harilda, Heralda.

HARITA (Hindi) The wind.

HARLENE (English) From the bare meadow. *Variations:* Harlean, Harleana, Harleanah, Harleane, Harleen, Harleena, Harleenah, Harleene, Harlena, Harlenah, Harlin, Harlinah, Harline, Harlyn, Harlyna, Harlyne.

HARLEQUIN (French) Colorful. *Variation:* Harlequinne.

HARLEY (English) Rabbit pasture. *Variations:* Harlea, Harlee, Harleigh, Harlie, Harly.

HARLOW (English) Army. *Variations:* Harlo, Harlowe.

HARMONY (Latin) Harmony. *Variations:* Harmonee, Harmoni, Harmonia, Harmonie.

HARPER (English) Harp player. *Notable:* Writer Harper Lee.

HARRIET (German) Leader of the house. Feminine version of Harry. *Notable:* Writer Harriet Beecher Stowe. *Variations:* Harrie, Harrietta, Harriette, Harriot, Harriott, Harryetta, Harryette, Hatsie, Hatsy, Hattie, Hatty.

HARSHA (Hindi) Happiness. *Variations:* Harshida, Harshika, Harshina.

HARU (Japanese) Born in spring. *Variations:* Harue, Haruko, Harumi.

HASANATI (Arabic) Good.

HASIA (Hebrew) Protected by the Lord. *Variations:* Hasiah, Hasya.

HASIDA (Hebrew) Righteous.

HASIKA (Hindi) Laughter.

HASINA (African) Lovely and good. *Variations:* Haseena, Hasena, Hasinah, Hassina, Hasyna.

HASNA (Arabic) Strong.

HATEYA (Native American) Push with the foot.

HATHOR (Egyptian) The goddess of love. *Variations:* Hathora, Hathore.

HATHSHIRA (Arabic) Seventh daughter.

HATSU (Japanese) Firstborn.

HATTIE (English) Form of Harriet. *Variations:* Haddie, Haddy, Hatty.

HAUKEA (Hawaiian) Snow. *Variations:* Haukia, Haukiah.

HAULANI (Hawaiian) Royalty.

HAUMA (Hindi) Gentle. *Variations:* Haleema, Halimah.

HAUOLI (Hawaiian) Joyful.

HAVA (Hebrew) Life. *Variation:* Havva.

HAVANA (Spanish) Capital of Cuba.

HAVEN (English) Refuge. *Variation:* Havin.

HAVIVA (Hebrew) Beloved. *Variation:* Havivah.

HAYA (Japanese) Fast.

HAYAT (Arabic) Alive.

HAYDEN (English) Valley of hay. *Notable:* Actress Hayden Panettiere. *Variations:* Hadan, Haden, Hadin, Hadon, Hadun, Hadyn, Haidan, Haiden, Haidin, Haidn, Hadon, Haidun, Haidyn, Haydan, Haydee, Haydin, Haydn, Haydon, Haydun, Haydyn, Heydan, Heyden, Heydin, Heydn, Heydon, Heydun, Heydyn.

HAYFA (Arabic) Dainty.

HAYLEY (English) Meadow of hay. *Notable:* Child-actress Hayley Mills *Variations:* Hailea, Haileah, Hailee, Hailei, Haileigh, Hailey, Haili, Hailia, Hailiah, Hailie, Halea, Haleah, Halee, Halei, Haleigh, Hali, Halia, Haliah, Haley, Halie, Halley, Halli, Hallie, Hally, Haylea, Hayleah, Haylee, Hayleigh, Haylie.

HAZAN (Turkish) Born in autumn. *Variations:* Hazanna, Hazanne, Hazen.

HAZAR (Arabic) Nightingale.

HAZEL (English) From the hazelnut tree. *Variations:* Hayzel, Hazal, Hazeline, Hazell, Hazella, Hazelle, Hazle.

HEATHER (English) Purple flower. *Notables:* Actresses Heather Locklear and Heather Graham. *Variations:* Heatherlee, Hether.

HEAVEN (English) Paradise. *Variations:* Heavan, Heavenly, Heavin.

HEBE (Greek) Youth. *Variations:* Heba, Heebee. Hebi.

HEDDA (English) Warfare. *Notable:* Gossip columnist Hedda Hopper. *Variations:* Heda, Heddi, Heddie, Hetta.

HEDIAH (Hebrew) Echo of God. *Variations:* Hedia, Hedya.

HEDVIKA (Czech) War of strife.

HEDWIG (German) Struggle. *Variations:* Hadvig, Hadwig, Hedvig, Hedviga, Hedvige, Hedwiga, Hedwige.

HEDY (Greek) Wonderful. *Notable:* Actress Hedy Lamarr. *Variations:* Hedi, Hedia, Hedyla.

HEIDI (German) Noble. *Variations:* Heida, Heide, Heidie, Hidee, Hidi, Hydie.

HEILWIG (German) Healthy battle maid.

HELAINE (French) Light. Form of Helen. *Variations:* Helaina, Helayna, Helayne.

HELEN (Greek) Light. *Notables:* Actresses Helen Hayes and Helen Hunt; writer Helen Keller. *Variations:* Hela, Helan, Hele, Helenka, Hellen, Hellin.

HELENA (Scandinavian) Form of Helen. *Notable:* Actress Helena Bonham Carter. *Variations:* Heleena, Helina, Helyna.

HELENE (French) Form of Helen. *Variations:* Heleen, Heline, Helyne.

HELGA (German) Holy.

HELIA (Greek) Sun. *Variation:* Helya.

HELIANTHE (Greek) Bright flower.

HELICE (Greek) Spiral. *Variation:* Helicia.

HELKI (Native American) Touch. *Variations:* Helkee, Helkie.

HELMA (German) Helmet. *Variations:* Helmah, Hillma, Hilma.

HELMINE (German) Constant protector. Feminine version of William.

HELOISE (French) Famous in war. *Notable:* "Household Hints" columnist Heloise. *Variation:* Heloisa.

HELSA (Danish) Glory to God. *Variation:* Helsia.

HEMALI (Hindi) Golden.

HENDA (Yiddish) Favor, grace. *Variations:* Hende, Hendel, Hene, Heneh, Henna.

HENRIETTA (German) Leader of the home. Feminine version of Henry. *Variations:* Heinrike, Hendrika, Hendrinka, Henka, Hennie, Henny, Henrie, Henrieta, Henriette, Henrika, Henrinka, Henriquetta, Henryetta, Hetta, Hettie.

HENYA (Hebrew) Grace of the Lord. *Variation:* Henye.

HEPHZIBAH (Hebrew) Delight. *Variations:* Hephsibah, Hephzabah, Hepzibah.

HERA (Greek) Queen. *Notable:* In mythology, queen of the goddesses and wife of Zeus. *Variations:* Heria, Herra.

HE-RAN (Korean) Graceful orchid.

HERBERTA (German) Brilliant warrior. Feminine form of Herbert. *Variations:* Herbertia, Herburta, Herburtia, Herbyrta.

HERLIA (Greek) Most beautiful.

HERLINDIS (Scandinavian) Gentle army.

HERMIA (Greek) Messenger. Feminine version of Hermes.

HERMINA (German) Soldier. *Variations:* Herma, Hermia, Hermine, Herminia.

HERMIONE (Greek) Earthly. *Notable:* In literature, Harry Potter's friend Hermione Granger. *Variations:* Hermyona, Hermyone.

HERMOSA (Spanish) Beautiful.

HERNANDA (Spanish) Brave traveler. Feminine form of Hernando.

HERODIAS (Greek) To watch over.

HERSCHELLE (Hebrew) A deer. *Variation:* Hershelle.

HERTHA (German) Earth. *Variations:* Heartha, Herthia, Herthya.

HERUTA (Hebrew) Freedom. *Variation:* Herut.

HESPER (Greek) Evening star. *Variations:* Hespera, Hesperia, Hespira.

HESTER (Greek) Star. Variation of Esther. *Notable: The Scarlet Letter* heroine Hester Prynne. *Variations:* Hesther, Hestia.

HETA (Native American) Rabbit hunt.

HEULWEN (Welsh) Sunshine.

HIALEAH (Native American) Beautiful pasture. *Variations:* Hialea, Hialee, Hialei, Hialeigh, Hiali, Hialie, Hialy, Hyalea, Hyaleah, Hyalee, Hyalei, Hyali, Hyalie.

HIAWASSEE (Native American) Meadow.

HIBA (Arabic) Present.

HIBERNIA (Latin) Latin name for Ireland. *Variations:* Hibernea, Hibernina, Hibernine, Hibernya.

HIBISCUS (Latin) Flower name.

HIDE (Japanese) Excellent. *Variations:* Hideko, Hideyo.

HIDEKO (Japanese) Splendid child.

HIERONYMA (Hebrew) God is high.

HIKA (Polynesian) Daughter. *Variations:* Hikah, Hyka.

HIILANI (Hawaiian) Carried by heaven.

HIKARI (Japanese) Radiance. *Variation:* Hikaru.

HIKMAT (Arabic) Wise.

HIKULEO (Polynesian) Echo.

HILARY (Latin) Cheerful. *Notables:* Actresses Hilary Swank and Hilary Duff; Secretary of State Hillary Clinton. *Variations:* Hilaree, Hilaria, Hilarie, Hillaree, Hillarie, Hillary, Hillery, Hilliary, Hylary, Hyllary.

Great Names in Sports

BOYS:
Alex (Rodriquez), Baseball
Andre (Agassi), Tennis
Apolo (Ohno), Speed Skating
Arnold (Palmer), Golf
Dale (Earnhardt), Racecar Driving
David (Beckham), Soccer
Deion (Sanders), Football
Derek (Jeter), Baseball
Drew (Brees), Football
Earvin ("Magic" Johnson), Basketball
Kobe (Bryant), Basketball
Lance (Armstrong), Cycling
LeBron (James), Basketball
Michael (Jordan), Basketball
Muhammad (Ali), Boxing
Oscar (De La Hoya), Boxing
Peyton (Manning), Football
Roger (Federer), Tennis
Shaquille (O'Neal), Basketball
Shawn (White), Snowboarding
Tiger (Woods), Golf
Tiki (Barber), Football
Tom (Brady), Football
Troy (Aikman), Football
Wayne (Gretsky), Hockey

HILAUA (Hawaiian) Loud.

HILDA (German) Battle woman. *Variations:* Hildah, Hilde, Hildee, Hildi, Hildie, Hildy, Hylda, Hyldee, Hyldie.

HILDEGARDE (German) Battle. *Variations:* Hildagarde, Hildegard, Hildeguarda, Hyldegarde.

HILDEMAR (German) Famous in battle. *Variations:* Hildemara, Hildemare, Hyldemar, Hyldemara.

HILDRETH (German) War counselor. *Variation:* Hildred.

HILLEVI (Scandinavian) Safe in battle.

HILMA (German) Nickname for Wilhelmina. *Variations:* Hilmah, Hylma.

HILTRAUD (German) Battle strength. *Variations:* Hildrud, Hiltrude.

HIMANI (Hindi) Snow covered. *Variation:* Heemani.

HINDA (Hindi) Female deer. *Variations:* Hindel, Hindelle, Hynda.

HINE (Polynesian) Girl. *Variations:* Hina, Hyna, Hyne.

HIOLAIR (Irish) Happy.

HIPPOLITA (Greek) Horse freer. *Variations:* Hippolyta, Hippolyte.

HIRAL (Hindi) Brilliant.

HIROKO (Japanese) Benevolent. *Variations:* Hiriko, Hyriko, Hyroko.

HIROMI (Japanese) Generous beauty.

HISA (Japanese) Everlasting. *Variations:* Hisae, Hisako, Hisayo.

HISANO (Japanese) Meadow.

HISOKA (Japanese) Reserved.

HITI (Eskimo) Hyena.

HITOMI (Japanese) Beautiful eyes.

HIVA (Polynesian) Song.

HOA (Vietnamese) Flower.

HOAKA (Hawaiian) Bright.

HOALOHALANI (Hawaiian) Spiritual friend.

HOALOHANANI (Hawaiian) Beautiful friend.

HODA (Arabic) Direction. *Notable:* Talk-show host Hoda Kotb. *Variation:* Huda.

HODEL (Yiddish) Myrtle tree. *Variations:* Hode, Hodeh, Hude, Hudel.

HOKUALOHI (Hawaiian) Shining star.

HOKUAO (Hawaiian) Morning star.

HOKUAONANI (Hawaiian) Beautiful star.

HOKULANI (Hawaiian) Divine star. *Variation:* Hoku.

HOLA (Spanish) Hello. *Variation:* Ola.

HOLDA (German) Hidden. *Variations:* Holde, Holle, Hulda.

HOLLANDER (Dutch) From Holland. *Variations:* Holland, Hollanda, Hollande.

HOLLIS (English) Near the holly. *Variations:* Hollace, Holice, Holissa, Hollisa, Hollise, Hollyse.

HOLLY (English) Plant. *Notable:* Actress Holly Hunter. *Variations:* Hollee, Holleigh, Holley, Holli, Hollie, Hollyann.

HOLOMAKANI (Hawaiian) Wind. *Variations:* Kani, Makani.

HONEKAKALA (Hawaiian) Honeysuckle.

HONESTA (Lating) Honesty. *Variations:* Honest, Honestee, Honestia, Honestie, Honesty.

HONEY (English) Sweetener. Term of affection. *Variations:* Honee, Honi, Honia, Honie, Hunni, Hunnie, Hunny.

HONG (Chinese) Pink. *Variation:* Hoong.

HONOR (English) Honorable. *Variation:* Honour.

HONORA (English) Honorable woman. *Variations:* Honorah, Honorata, Honore, Honoria, Honorina, Honorine.

HOPE (English) Hope.

HORATIA (Latin) Timekeeper. Feminine version of Horatio. *Variation:* Horacia.

HORTENSE (Latin) From the garden. *Variations:* Hortensia, Ortensia.

HOSANNA (Hebrew) Deliver us. *Variations:* Hosana, Hosannah, Hosannie, Hoshana.

HOSHI (Japanese) Star. *Variations:* Hoshiko, Hoshiyo.

HO-SOOK (Korean) Pure lake.

HOTARU (Japanese) Firefly.

HOWARDINA (German) Guardian of home. *Variations:* Howardena, Howardine.

HRISOULA (Greek) Golden.

HUA (Chinese) Flower.

HUALING (Chinese) Flowery tuber.

HUAN (Chinese) Satisfaction.

HUATA (Native American) A basket of seeds.

HUAU (Hawaiian) Bright.

HUBERTA (German) Intelligent. Feminine version of Hubert.

Variations: Huberte, Hubertia, Huette, Hughberta.

HUE (Vietnamese) Old-fashioned.

HUGUETTE (French) Little smart one. *Variation:* Huguetta.

HUIAN (Chinese) Obliging.

HUIFANG (Chinese) Fragrant.

HUILING (Chinese) Wise jade.

HUIQING (Chinese) Good luck.

HULDA (Scandinavian; German) Loved one. *Variations:* Huldah, Hulde, Huldie, Huldy.

HUMILIA (Latin) Humble.

HUNTER (English) Hunter.

HUONG (Vietnamese) Blossom.

HURIYAH (Arabic) Angel.

HUSNI (Arabic) Beauty.

HUSNIYA (Arabic) Excellence. *Variation:* Husniyah.

HUSO (African) A bride's sadness.

HUYANA (Native American) Falling rain.

HUYNH (Vietnamese) Yellow.

HWA-YOUNG (Korean) Beautiful flower.

HYACINTH (Greek) Flower name. *Variations:* Hyacintha, Hyacinthia, Hyacinthe.

HYDERIA (Greek) Of the water.

HYE (Korean) Graceful.

HYGEIA (Greek) Goddess of health.

HYO-SONN (Korean) Tender.

HYPATHIA (Greek) Highest. *Variations:* Hypatia.

HYUN (Korean) Smart and loving.

More Great Names in Sports

GIRLS:
Anna (Kournikova), Tennis
Babe (Didrikson Zaharias), Track and Field
Billie Jean (King), Tennis
Danica (Patrick), Auto Racing
Lindsey (Vonn), Skiing
Maria (Sharapova), Tennis
Martina (Navratilova), Tennis
Mary Lou (Retton), Gymnastics
Mia (Hamm), Soccer
Michelle (Wie), Golf
Nadia (Comaneci), Gymnastics
Oksana (Baiul), Skating
Picabo (Street), Skiing
Rebecca (Lobo), Basketball
Serena (Williams), Tennis
Sheryl (Swoopes), Basketball
Steffi (Graf), Tennis
Tara (Lipinski), Skating
Venus (Williams), Tennis

IA (Celtic) Yew tree. *Variation:* Iah.

IAMAR (Arabic) Of the moon. *Variation:* Iamara.

IANA (Scottish) God is gracious. Feminine form of Ian (John). *Variations:* Ianna, Iyana.

IANEKE (Hawaiian) God is good. *Variations:* Ianete, Iani.

IANIRA (Greek) Enchantress. *Variations:* Ianirah, Ianyra, Ianyrah.

IANNA (English) Feminine form of Ian. God is gracious.

IANTHE (Greek) Flower. *Variations:* Iantha, Ianthia, Ianthina, Ianthine, Ianthya.

IARA (Brazilian) Water queen. *Variation:* Iaria.

IBERIA (Latin) From Iberian peninsula.

IBERNIA (Irish) Woman of Ireland.

IBOLYA (Hungarian) Violet. *Variations:* Ibolia, Iboliya.

IBTESAM (Arabic) Smiles often.

IDA (German) Hard working. *Notable:* Actress Ida Lupino. *Variations:* Idaia, Idalene, Idalia, Idalina, Idaline, Idalya, Idalyne, Idaya, Ide, Idell, Idella, Idelle, Idetta, Idette, Idia, Iduska, Idys, Iida.

IDABELLE (English) Combined form of Ida and Belle. Hard working and beautiful. *Variations:* Idabel, Idabela, Idabell, Idabella.

IDALIA (Greek) Sun. *Variations:* Idahlia, Idalya.

IDE (Irish) Thirst.

IDELLE (Welsh) Form of Ida. *Variations:* Idela, Idele, Idella.

IDINA (English) From Edinburgh, Scotland. Form of Edina. *Notable:* Actress Idina Menzel.

IDOLA (Greek) Idolized one.

IDONY (Scandinavian) Goddess of spring. *Variations:* Idona, Idonea, Idun.

IDRA (Hebrew) Fig tree.

IDRIYA (Hebrew) Duck. *Variation:* Idria.

IDUNA (Scandinavian) Beloved. *Variations:* Idonia, Idun.

IERNE (Latin) From Ireland. *Variation:* Ierna.

IFAMA (African) All is well.

IFE (African) Love.

IGERNE (French) Maiden.

IGNACIA (Latin) On fire. Feminine version of Ignatius. *Variations:* Ignacie, Ignacya, Ignatia, Ignazia, Ignia, Ignya.

IGRAINE (Celtic) Graceful. *Variations:* Igraina, Igrainah, Igrayn, Igrayna, Igraynah, Igrayne.

IHAB (Arabic) To give.

IHSAN (Arabic) Benevolent. *Variations:* Ihsana, Ihsanah.

IKABELA (Hawaiian) Pledged to God. *Variation:* Ikapela.

IKIA (Hebrew) God helps me. *Variations:* Ikea, Ikiah, Ikyah.

IKU (Japanese) Nurturing. *Variation:* Ikuko.

ILA (Hungarian) Form of Helen.

ILANA (Hebrew) Tree. *Variations:* Elana, Elanit, Ilanah, Ilane, Ilani, Ilanit, Illana, Illanna.

ILARIA (Italian) Joyful.

ILENE (English) Variation of Eileen. *Variations:* Ilean, Ileane, Ileen, Ileena, Ilena, Ileni, Ilein, Ilien, Iline, Ilini, Ilyne.

ILESHA (Hindi) God of the earth. *Variation:* Ilecia.

ILIA (English) One who comes from the town of Troy, also known as Ilium. *Variations:* Iliah, Illia, Illiah, Illya, Ilya.

ILIANA (Greek) From Troy. *Variations:* Ileana, Ileane, Ileanna, Illeana, Illeanne, Illiana, Illianna, Illianne, Illyana, Illyanne, Ilyana, Ilyanne.

ILIMA (Hawaiian) Flower.

ILISA (Scottish) Form of Alisa. *Variations:* Ilissa, Ilysa, Ilyssa.

ILKA (Slavic) Admirer.

ILMA (English) Variation of William.

ILONA (Hungarian) Light. Form of Helen.

ILSA (German) Pledge of God. Variation of Elizabeth. *Variations:* Ilse, Ilsie.

ILUMINADA (Spanish) Shines brightly.

IMA (Japanese) Now. *Variations:* Imae, Imako.

IMALA (Native American) Disciplined.

IMAN (Arabic) Faith. *Notable:* Model Iman. *Variations:* Imanee, Imani.

IMANA (African) God of all.

IMANUELA (Spanish) Faithful.

IMARA (African) Firm.

IMBER (Polish) Ginger. *Variation:* Imbera.

IMELDA (German) Embracing the fight. *Notable:* Philippine First Lady and shoe fanatic Imelda Marcos. *Variation:* Imalda.

IMENA (African) Dreamer. *Variation:* Imene.

IMIN (Arabic) Conviction.

IMKE (German) Whole.

IMMA (Hebrew) Mother.

IMMACULADA (Spanish) Innocent. *Variations:* Immacolata, Immaculata.

IMOGEN (Latin) Innocent. *Notable:* Comedian Imogene Coca. *Variations:* Imagen, Imagene, Imagina, Imajean, Imogeen, Imogena, Imogene, Imogenia, Imogine.

IMPERIA (Latin) Imperial.

IMPREZA (Italian) Badge.

INA (Greek) Pure. *Variation:* Ena.

INAM (Arabic) Charitable. *Variation:* Enam.

INANNA (Babylonian) The goddess of war. *Variation:* Inanne.

INARA (Arabic) Illumination.

INARI (Finnish) Lake. *Variations:* Inaree, Inarie, Inary.

INAS (Arabic) Friendly. *Variations:* Inaya, Inayah.

INDIA (English) From India. *Variations:* Indea, Indi, Indiah, Indya.

INDIANA (English) From India. *Variations:* Indeana, Indeanna, Indianna, Indiannah, Indianne, Indyana, Indyanah, Indyann, Indyanna, Indyannah, Indyanne.

INDIGO (Latin) Dark blue.

INDIRA (Hindi) Beauty. *Notable:* Indian Prime Minister Indira Gandhi. *Variations:* Indirah, Indyra.

INDRA (Hindi) Supreme god; god of the sky. *Variations:* Indrah, Indre.

INDRANEE (Hindi) Wife of Indra, the god of the sky. *Variation:* Indrayani.

INDU (Hindi) Moon.

INDUNA (Scandinavian) Lover. *Variations:* Indunah, Indunia.

INÉS (Spanish) Pure. Variation of Agnes. *Variations:* Inesita, Inessa, Inetta, Inez, Ynes, Ynesita, Ynez.

INGA (Scandinavian) Protected by Ing, the Norwegian god of peace. *Variations:* Ingaar, Inge, Ingelisa, Ingelise, Inger, Ingo, Ingvio.

INGEBORG (Scandinavian) Protector of Ing, the Norwegian god of peace. *Variations:* Ingaberg, Ingaborg, Ingabork, Ingeberg, Ingmar.

INGEGERD (Scandinavian) Ing's fortress. *Variations:* Ingegard, Ingjerd.

INGRID (Scandinavian) Beautiful. *Notable:* Actress Ingrid Bergman. *Variation:* Ingred.

INIGA (Latin) Fiery. *Variations:* Inigah, Inyga.

INOA (Hawaiian) Name.

INOCENCIA (Spanish) Innocence. *Variations:* Inocenta, Inocentia, Innocence.

INOLA (Native American) Black fox.

IOLA (Greek) Dawn. *Variation:* Iole.

IOLANA (Hawaiian) To soar. *Variations:* Iolanah, Iolane, Iolani, Iolanna.

IOLANTHE (English) Violet. *Variations:* Iolanda, Iolande, Iolantha.

IONA (Greek) Scottish island. *Variation:* Ionia.

IONANNA (Hebrew) Filled with grace. *Variations:* Ionana, Ionanne.

IONE (Greek) Violet. *Variations:* Ionee, Ioni, Ionie.

IORA (Latin) Gold.

IORWEN (Welsh) Beautiful woman. *Variations:* Iorwenne, Iorwin, Iorwyn.

IOSEPINE (Hawaiian) God adds. *Variations:* Iokepina, Iokepine, Kepina.

IPHIGENIA (Greek) Sacrifice. *Variations:* Iphigena, Iphigeniah, Iphigenie, Iphigenya.

IRELAND (English) From Ireland. *Variation:* Irelyn.

IRENE (Greek) Peace. *Notables:* Actresses Irene Ryan and Irene Cara. *Variations:* Arina, Arinka, Eirena, Eirene, Eirini, Erena, Erene, Ereni, Errena, Irayna, Irean, Ireana, Ireanah, Ireane, Ireen, Ireena, Iren, Irena, Irenea, Irenee, Irenka, Irine, Irini, Irisha, Irka, Irusya, Iryna, Iryne, Orina, Orya, Oryna, Reena, Reenie, Rina, Yarina, Yaryna.

IRETA (Greek) Serene. Varation: Irete.

IRINA (Russian) Form of Irene.

IRIS (Greek) Rainbow. *Notable:* Latina TV personality Iris Chacon. *Variations:* Ires, Irisa, Irisha.

IRMA (German) Complete. *Variation:* Erma.

IRMALINDA (German) Entirely gentle.

IRMGARD (German) Entirely protected. *Variation:* Irmgarde.

IRTA (Greek) Pearl-like.

IRVETTE (English) Friend of the sea. Feminine version of Irving.

ISABEL (Spanish) Pledge to God. Version of Elizabeth. *Notables:* Actresses Isabelle Adjani and Isabella Rossellini. *Variations:* Isa, Isabeau, Isabelita, Isabella, Isabelle, Isobel, Issi, Issie, Issy, Izabel, Izabele, Izabella, Izabelle, Izebela, Ysabel.

ISADORA (Greek) Gift from Isis. Feminine version of Isidore. *Notable:* Dancer Isadora Duncan. *Variation:* Isidora.

ISAMU (Japanese) Energetic.

ISANA (German) Strong willed. *Variations:* Isanna, Isanne.

ISATAS (Native American) Snow. *Variation:* Istas.

ISAURA (Greek) Ancient country in Asia. *Variation:* Isaure.

ISEULT (Irish) Ruler of the ice. *Variations:* Hisolda, Isolda, Isolde, Ysenit, Yseult, Ysolte.

ISHA (Hebrew) Woman; (Hindi) Protector.

ISHANA (Hindi) Desire. *Variation:* Ishani.

ISHI (Japanese) Stone. *Variations:* Ishie, Ishiko, Ishiyo, Shiko, Shiuo.

ISHTAR (Babylonian) Goddess of love, war, and fertility.

ISIS (Egyptian) Goddess of ancient Egypt.

ISLA (Gaelic) From the island. *Variations:* Islai, Isleta.

ISLEEN (Gaelic) Form of Aislinn. Inspiration. *Variations:* Islene, Isline.

ISMAELA (Hebrew) God listens. *Variations:* Isma, Mael, Maella.

ISMAT (Arabic) To protect.

ISMENE (Greek) The daughter of Oedipus and Jocasta.

ISOKA (African) Gift from God. *Variations:* Isoke, Soka.

ISOLDE (Welsh) Fair maiden. *Variations:* Isold, Isolda. Isolt.

ISRA (Arabic) Night trip.

ISTVAN (Hungarian) Crowned with laurels.

ITA (Irish) Thirsty.

ITALIA (Latin) From Italy. *Variations:* Itala, Talia.

ITIAH (Hebrew) God is here. *Variations:* Itia, Itiel, Itil, Itiya.

ITO (Japanese) Fiber.

ITUHA (Native American) Oak tree.

IUANA (Native American) Wind blowing over a bubbling stream.

IUDITA (Hawaiian) God is praised. *Variation:* Iukika.

IUGINIA (Hawaiian) Well bred. *Variations:* Iugina, Iukina, Iukinia.

IUILE (Irish) Form of Julia.

IULAUA (Hawaiian) Good talker. *Variation:* Ulalia.

IULIA (Hawaiian) Form of Julia. *Variations:* Iuliana, Kulia, Kuliana.

IUNIA (Hawaiian) Good victory. *Variations:* Iuana, Iunika.

IUSITINA (Hawaiian) Righteous. Form of Justine. *Variation:* Iukikina.

IVA (Slavic) Short form of Ivana. *Variation:* Ivah.

IVANA (Slavic) God is good. Feminine version of Ivan. *Notable:* Donald Trump's ex-wife Ivana Trump. *Variations:* Ivanah, Ivania, Ivanka, Ivanna, Ivannah, Ivannia.

IVEREM (African) Good luck.

IVETTE (French) Alternate form of Yvette.

IVONETTE (German) Yew tree. *Variation:* Ivonetta.

IVONNE (French) Alternate form of Yvonne.

IVORY (Latin) Ivory. *Variations:* Ivoree, Ivoreen, Ivori, Ivorie, Ivorine.

IVRIA (Hebrew) From the land of Abraham. *Variations:* Ivriah, Ivrit.

IVY (English) Plant. *Variations:* Iva, Ivee, Ivey, Ivi, Ivie.

IWA (Japanese) Rock.

IWALANI (Hawaiian) Sea bird.

IWONA (Polish) Form of Yvonne.

IXCHL (Mayan) Rainbow lady.

IYABO (African) Mother comes back.

IYANA (Hebrew) Form of Iana, the feminine form of John. *Notable:* Writer/motivational speaker Iyanla Vanzant. *Variations:* Iyanla, Iyanna, Iyannia.

IYRIA (Hebrew) In Abraham's land. *Variations:* Ivriah, Ivrit.

IZANAMI (Japanese) Invited woman.

IZDIHAR (Arabic) Blossoming.

IZEGBE (African: Nigerian) Long-awaited child. *Variation:* Izebe.

IZUMI (Japanese) Fountain.

IZUSA (Native American) White stone.

IZZY (American) Short form of Isabel. *Variations:* Issey, Issy, Izi, Izzey, Izzi, Izzie.

JA (Hawaiian) Fiery. *Variation:* Jah.

JAAMINI (Hindi) Night. *Variations:* Jaaminee, Jaaminey, Jaaminie, Jaaminy.

JACARANDA (Latin) Tree of purple flowers. *Variations:* Jackaranda, Jakaranda.

JACEY (American) Short form of Jacinta or Jacqueline. *Variations:* J.C., Jace, Jacee, Jaci, Jacia, Jacie, Jaciela, Jacy, Jaysee.

JACINTA (Spanish) Hyacinth. Feminine version of Jacinto. *Variations:* Glacinda, Glacintha, Jacenta, Jacinda, Jacintha, Jacinthe, Jacinthia, Jacki, Jacky, Jacquetta, Jacqui, Jacquie, Jacynth, Jacyntha, Jacynthe, Jasinda, Jasinta, Jazinta.

JACKIE (English) Nickname for Jacqueline. *Notable:* Writer Jackie Collins. *Variations:* Jacki, Jacky, Jacqui, Jakki.

JACOBINA (Hebrew) Supplanter. Feminine version of Jacob. *Variations:* Jacoba, Jaakobah.

JACQUELINE (French) He who replaces. Feminine version of Jacob. *Notables:* U.S. First Lady Jacqueline Kennedy (Onassis); actress Jacqueline Bisset. *Variations:* Jacaline, Jacalyn, Jackalin, Jackalyn, Jackeline, Jackelyn, Jacketta, Jackette, Jacki, Jackie, Jacklin, Jacklyn, Jacky, Jaclyn, Jaclynn, Jacoba, Jacobette, Jacobina, Jacolyn, Jacqualine, Jacqualyn, Jacqualynn, Jacquelean, Jacquelene, Jacquelin, Jacquelyn, Jacquelyne, Jacquelynn, Jacquelynne, Jacqueta, Jacquetta, Jacquiline, Jacquline, Jacqulynn, Jaculine, Jakelyn, Jaqueline, Jaquelyn, Jaquith.

JADE (Spanish) Jade stone. *Notable:* Actress Jada Pinkett. *Variations:* Jada, Jadda, Jadee, Jaden, Jadena, Jadera, Jadi, Jadira, Jady, Jadyn, Jaid, Jaida, Jaide, Jayd, Jayda, Jayde, Jaydn, Jaydra.

JADWIGE (Polish) Protected in battle. *Variations:* Jadwig, Jadwiga.

JAE (Latin) Jaybird. *Variations:* Jaya, Jaylee, Jayleen, Jaylene, Jaylynn.

JAE-HWA (Korean) Very beautiful.

JAEL (Hebrew) Mountain goat. *Variations:* Jaela, Jaeli, Jaelyn.

JAFFA (Hebrew) Beautiful. Feminine version of Yaffa. *Variations:* Jaffe, Jaffi, Jaffice, Jaffit, Jafit.

JAGODA (Slavic) Strawberry.

JAHA (African) Dignity. *Variation:* Jahara.

JAHZARA (Ethiopian) Beloved princess.

JAIA (Hindi) Victorious. *Variations:* Jaea, Jaiah, Jayah.

JAIRA (Spanish) God teaches. *Variation:* Jairah.

JAKAYLA (American) Combined form of Jacqueline and Kayla. *Variations:* Jakaela, Jackaila.

JALA (Arabic) Clear.

JALAJAA (Hindi) Lotus. *Variation:* Jalitaa.

JALANEELI (Hindi) Moss.

JALEESA (American) Combined form of first names "Jay" and "Lisa." *Variations:* Ja Leesa, Ja Lisa, Jalisa.

JALENA (America) Combined form of first names "Jay" and "Lena." *Variations:* Jalana, Jalani, Jalanie, Jalean, Jaleena, Jalen, Jalene, Jalina, Jaline, Jalyn, Jalynn, Jalynne, Jaylen, Jaylena, Jaylene, Jaylin, Jaylina, Jayline, Jaylynn, Jelena, Jelina, Jelyna.

JALEXA (American) Creative variation of Alexa.

JALILA (Arabic) Great. *Variation:* Jalile.

JALINDA (American) Combination of Jay and Linda. *Variations:* Jalynda, Jelinda, Jelynda.

JALINI (Hindi) One who lives by the water.

JAMAICA (English) The island country. *Notable:* Writer Jamaica Kincaid. *Variations:* Jameika, Jameka, Jamica, Jamika.

JAMALA (African) Friendly.

JAMIE (English) One who replaces. Feminine version of James. *Notable:* Actress Jamie Lee Curtis. *Variations:* Jaima, Jaime, J'aime, Jaimee, J'aimee, Jaimey, Jaimi, Jaimie, Jaimy, Jamea, Jamee, Jamesha, Jamessa, Jameta, Jami, Jamia, Jamiah, Jayma, Jayme, Jaymee, Jaymi, Jaymie.

JAMILA (Arabic) Beautiful. *Variations:* Gamila, Gamilah, Jameela, Jamelia, Jamelle, Jamilah, Jamilla, Jamillah, Jamille, Jamillia.

JAN (Hebrew) God is good. *Variations:* Janaca, Janda, Jandia, Jandie, Jani, Janika, Janina, Janine, Jann, Janni.

JANA (Hebrew) Gracious. *Variations:* Janah, Janalee, Janalina, Janaline, Janalisa, Janalise, Janalyn, Jania, Janiah, Janna, Yana, Yania, Yanna, Yannie.

JANAE (Hebrew) God answers. *Variations:* Janai, Janais, Janay, Janaye, Jannae, Jeanae, Jeanay, Jenae, Jenai, Jenay, Jenaya, Jenee, Jennae, Jennay.

JANAIA (Arabic) Fruit harvest. *Variations:* Janaiah, Janaya, Janaye.

JANAKI (Hindi) Mother. *Variation:* Janika.

JANAN (Arabic) Spirited. *Variations:* Janani, Janany, Jananya.

JANE (English) God's grace. *Notables:* Actress Jane Fonda; writer Jane Austen. *Variations:* Jaen, Jain, Jaine, Jainee, Jainey, Jainy, Janee, Janey, Janica, Janie, Jayne, Sheenagh, Sheenah, Sheina, Shena.

Top Names in Ireland

BOYS:
1. Jack
2. Sean
3. Daniel
4. Conor
5. James
6. Ryan
7. Adam
8. Michael
9. Alex
10. Luke

GIRLS:
1. Sophie
2. Ava
3. Emma
4. Sarah
5. Grace
6. Emily
7. Katie
8. Lucy
9. Aoife
10. Chloe

Top Names in Northern Ireland

BOYS:
1. Jack
2. Daniel
3. James
4. Matthew
5. Ryan
6. Harry
7. Charlie
8. Ethan
9. Conor
10. Adam

GIRLS:
1. Sophie
2. Katie
3. Grace
4. Emily
5. Olivia
6. Lucy
7. Ellie
8. Jessica
9. Emma
10. Chloe

JANELLE (French) God is good. *Variations:* Janel, Janela, Janele, Janelis, Janell, Janella, Janiel, Janiela, Jannel, Jannell, Jannella, Jannelle, Janyll, Jaynell, Jaynella, Jaynelle, Jenelle, Nell.

JANESSA (American) Combination of Jane and Vanessa. *Variations:* Janesse, Janeska, Janiesa, Janiesha, Janissa, Jannessa, Jenessa.

JANET (English) Diminutive of Jane. *Notables:* Singer Janet Jackson; actress Janet Leigh. *Variations:* Janeta, Janeth, Janett, Janetta, Janette, Jannet, Janneth, Jannetta, Janot, Jenet, Jenett, Jenetta, Jenette, Jennetta, Jennette, Joanet, Sinead, Siobahn, Sioban, Siobhan.

JANEVA (American) Combined form of Jan and Eva. *Variations:* Janeeva, Janiva, Jeneva, Jeneeva, Jeniva.

JANICE (English) Form of Jane. *Notables:* Supermodel Janice Dickinson; singer Janis Joplin. *Variations:* Janess, Janessa, Janesse, Janiece, Janis, Jannice, Jannike, Jannis, Janyce, Janys, Janyse.

JANIKA (Slavic) Form of Jane, Janet, or Janice. *Variations:* Janaca, Janeca, Janecka, Janeeka, Janica, Janicka, Jannica.

JANINE (English) God is good. Feminine version of John. *Notable:* Comedian Janeane Garofalo. *Variations:* Janean, Janeane, Janeen, Janina, Jannine, Janyne, Jeneen, Jenina, Jenine, Jenyne.

JANITA (Scandinavian) God is good. *Variations:* Jaantje, Janeata, Janeeta, Janeita, Janitra, Janitza, Jannike, Jans, Jansje, Janyta.

JANNA (Hebrew) Form of Johanna. *Variation:* Jannah.

JANOAH (Hebrew) Quiet. *Variation:* Janowa.

JANUARY (Latin) Born in January. God of the door. *Notable:* Actress January Jones.

JANY (Hindi) Fire.

JAPERA (African) Complete.

JARAH (Hebrew) Honeycomb. *Variations:* Jara, Jarra.

JARDENA (French) Garden. *Variations:* Jardan, Jardana, Jardane, Jardania, Jardee, Jardenia, Jardine, Jardyn.

JARINA (Greek) Working the earth. *Variations:* Jareena, Jarine, Jaryna.

JARITA (Arabic) Water urn. *Variations:* Jara, Jari, Jaria, Jarica, Jarida, Jarietta, Jarika, Jarina, Jaritta, Jaritza, Jarina, Jarrine.

JARKA (Czech) Spring. *Variations:* Jaruse, Jaruska.

JARMILA (Czech) One who loves spring.

JARNSAXA (Scandinavian) Ancient mythological figure. *Variation:* Iarnsaxa.

JAROSLAVA (Czech) Glorious spring.

JASMINE (Persian) Flower name. *Notable:* Actress Jasmine Guy. *Variations:* Jasmeen, Jasmin, Jasmina, Jazmin, Jazmine, Jessamine, Jessamyn, Yasiman, Yasman, Yasmine.

JASWINDER (Hindi) The god of the sky's thunder.

JATARA (Irish) From the rocky hill. *Variations:* Jatarah, Jataria, Jatarra, Jatori, Jatoria, Jatorie.

JATHIBIYYA (Arabic) Attractive. *Variations:* Gathbiyya, Gathbiyyah,

Gathibiyya, Gathibiyyah, Gazbiyya, Gazbiyyah, Jathbiyya, Jathbiyyah, Jathibiyyah.

JAVANA (Malaysian) From Java. *Variations:* Javan, Javanna, Javanne, Javon, Javona, Javonna.

JAVIERA (Spanish) Shining. *Variations:* Javeera, Xaviera.

JAVONA (Hebrew) God is gracious. *Variations:* Javonah, Javone, Javonna, Javonnah, Javonne.

JAWAHIR (Arabic) Gem. *Variation:* Gawahir.

JAXINE (American) Combined form of Jackie and Maxine. *Variations:* Jaxee, Jaxeen, Jaxi, Jaxie, Jaxyne.

JAY (Latin) Happy. *Variations:* Jai, Jaie, Jaye.

JAYA (Hindi) Victory. *Variations:* Ja Wanti, Janatika, Jayamala, Jayanti, Jayashree, Jayna, Jayt.

JAYDRA (Arabic) Goodness. *Variations:* Jadra, Jaidra.

JAYLA (American) Feminine form of Jay. *Variations:* Jaela, Jaila, Jaylah, Jaylan, Jeyla.

JAYLEE (American) Combined form of Jay and Lee. *Variations:* Jaylea, Jayleigh, Jayley, Jaylie.

JAYLENE (English) Blue jay. *Variations:* Jae, Jaelene, Jailene, Jayleen, Jaylena, Jayline, Jaynell.

JAZELLE (American) Combined form of Jasmine and Michelle. *Variations:* Jasel, Jasell, Jasella, Jaselle, Jazel, Jazell, Jazella, Jazzel, Jazzell, Jazzella, Jazzelle.

JAZLYN (American) Combined form of first names "Jasmine" and "Lynn." *Variations:* Jaslean, Jasleen, Jaslyn, Jaslynn, Jazlin, Jazline, Jazlyne, Jazlynn, Jazlynne, Jazzalyn, Jazzlyn.

JAZZ (American) Jazz. Short form of Jasmine. *Variations:* Jas, Jassie, Jaz, Jazi, Jazie, Jazzi, Jazzie, Jazzy.

JEAN (Scottish) God is good. Feminine version of John. *Notables:* Actress Jean Harlow; Weight Watchers' founder Jean Niditch. *Variations:* Jeana, Jeane, Jeanette, Jeanna, Jeanne, Jeannie, Jennette.

JEANNETTE (English) Form of Jean or Jane. *Variations:* Janette, Janetta, Jeannetta, Jenet, Jenett, Jenette.

JEANNINE (French) Form of Jean or Jane. *Variations:* Janine, Janeane, Jeanene, Jeanine, Jenine, Jennine.

JEBONG (Filipino) Funny, petite.

JEDIDA (Hebrew) Friend. *Variation:* Jedidah.

JEHAN (French) God is gracious. *Variation:* Jehanne.

JELENA (Russian; Serbian) Light. *Variations:* Jalaina, Jalaine, Jalana, Jalanna, Jalanne, Jalayna, Jalayne, Jalean, Jaleana, Jaleane, Jaleen, Jaleena, Jaleene, Jalene, Jalina, Jaline, Jalyna, Jelaina, Jelaine, Jelana, Jelane, Jeleen, Jeleena, Jelene, Jilena.

JEMIMA (Hebrew) Dove. *Notable:* Breakfast icon Aunt Jemima. *Variations:* Jamima, Jemimah, Jemmie, Jemmimah, Jemmy, Mima, Mimma.

JEMINA (Hebrew) Right handed. *Variations:* Jem, Jemi, Jemine, Jemma, Jemmi, Jemmie, Jemmy, Mina.

JEMMA (English) Precious stone. *Variations:* Gemma, Jemah, Jemmah, Jemmia.

JENA (Hindi) Patience.

JENDAN (African) Thankful.

JENDAYA (African) To give thanks.

JENELLE (English) Yielding. Version of Guinevere. *Variations:* Jenel, Jenell, Jenella, Jeneel, Jeneil.

JENICA (Romanian) Form of Jane. *Variation:* Jenika.

JENILEE (American) Combination of Jennifer and Lee. *Variations:* Jenalee, Jenaleigh, Jenalie, Jenelea, Jenelee, Jeneleigh, Jenileigh, Jennalea, Jennalee, Jennilee, Jennileigh.

JENILYN (American) Combined form of first names "Jennifer" and "Lynn." *Variations:* Jenalin, Jenalyn, Jenilin, Jenilyn, Jenilynn, Jennalyn, Jennilyn.

JENNA (English) Form of Jennifer. *Notable:* Actress Jenna Elfman. *Variations:* Jannarae, Jena, Jenesi, Jenn, Jennabel, Jennah, Jennalee, Jennalyn, Jennasee.

JENNEKE (Greek) Wise.

JENNICA (English) God is good. *Variations:* Jenica, Jenicka, Jenika, Jennicka, Jennika.

JENNIFER (Welsh) White. Smooth. Soft. Variation of Guinevere. *Notables:* Actress/singer Jennifer Lopez; actress Jennifer Garner. *Variations:* Genn, Gennifer, Genny, Ginnifer, Jen, Jena, Jenalee, Jenalyn, Jenarae, Jenefar, Jenefer, Jenene, Jenetta, Jeni, Jenice, Jeniece, Jenifar, Jenifer, Jeniffer, Jenilee, Jenilynn, Jenise, Jenita, Jenn, Jennafar, Jennessa, Jenni, Jennie, Jennifar, Jennifir, Jennika, Jennilyn, Jenniver, Jennyann, Jennylee, Jeny, Jinny.

JENNY (Welsh) Short form of Jennifer. *Notables:* Actress Jenny McCarthy; diet guru Jenny Craig. *Variations:* Geni, Gennee, Gennie, Genny, Jenee, Jeney, Jeni, Jennee, Jenney, Jenni, Jennie, Jeny.

JERALDINE (German) Alternative form of Geraldine. Spear carrier. *Variations:* Jeraldeen, Jeraldeena, Jeraldeene, Jeraldena, Jeraldene, Jeraldin, Jeraldina, Jeraldinah, Jeraldyna, Jeraldynah, Jeraldyne.

JERALYN (American) Combination of Jeri and Lynn. *Variations:* Jeralin, Jeralina, Jeralinah, Jeraline, Jeralyna, Jeralynah, Jeralyne, Jerelyn, Jerilee, Jerilyn, Jerilyna, Jerilynah, Jerilyne, Jerilynn, Jerralyn, Jerrilyn.

JEREMIA (Hebrew) The Lord is great. Feminine version of Jeremiah. *Variations:* Jeramia, Jeramya, Jeremya.

JERENI (Russian) Peaceful. *Variations:* Jerenee, Jerenia, Jereniah, Jerenie, Jereny, Jerenya, Jerenyah.

JERI (English) Short form of Geraldine or Jeralyn. Feminine form of Gerald or Jerry. *Variations:* Geri, Jeree, Jerey, Jeri, Jerie, Jerree, Jerrey, Jerri, Jerrie, Jerry, Jery.

JERIEL (Hebrew) God has witnessed *Variations:* Jeriela, Jerielle.

JERICA (American) Combination of Jeri and Erica. *Variations:* Jerika, Jeriqua, Jerrica, Jerrika, Jeryka.

JERMAINE (French) Form of Germaine. From Germany. *Variations:* Germain, Germaina, Germainah, Germaine, Germayn, Germayna, Germaynah, Germayne, Jermain, Jermaina, Jermayne.

JEROMA (Latin) Feminine form of Jerome. Holy. *Variations:* Geroma, Geromah, Jeromah, Jerometta, Jeromette.

JERSEY (English) Place name. *Variations:* Jersee, Jersi, Jersie, Jersy, Jerzee, Jerzi, Jerzie.

JERUSHA (Hebrew) Possession; inheritance.

JESSALYN (English) Combined form of first names "Jessica" and "Lynn." *Variations:* Jesalin, Jesaline, Jesalyn, Jesilyn, Jeslyn, Jessalin, Jessalina, Jessalinah, Jessaline, Jessalyn, Jessalyna, Jessalyne.

JESSAMINE (French) Jasmine flower. *Variations:* Jesamina, Jesaminah, Jesamine, Jesamon, Jesamona, Jessamond, Jesamone, Jesamyn, Jesamyna, Jesamynah, Jesamyne, Jessamin, Jessamina, Jessaminah, Jessamon, Jessamona, Jessamonah, Jessamone, Jessamy, Jessamyah, Jessamyn, Jessamyna, Jessamyne, Jessemin, Jessemina, Jesseminae, Jesseminah, Jessmin, Jessmina, Jessminah, Jessmine, Jessmon, Jessmona, Jessmonah, Jessmone, Jesmy, Jessmyn, Jessmyna, Jessmynah, Jessmyne.

JESSENIA (Arabic) Flower. *Variations:* Jesene, Jesenia, Jessene, Jessenya.

JESSICA (Hebrew) He beholds. *Notables:* Singer Jessica Simpson; actress Jessica Alba. *Variations:* Jesica, Jesicah, Jesicka, Jesika, Jessaca, Jessah, Jessalin, Jessalina, Jessaline, Jessalyn, Jessalynn, Jessca, Jesseca, Jessecah, Jesseka, Jessekah, Jessia, Jessiah, Jessicah, Jessieka, Jessika, Jessikah, Jessikia, Jessiqua, Jessiquah, Jessique, Jessiya, Jessyca, Jessycka, Jessyka,

Jessyquah, Jezeca, Jezecah, Jezecka, Jezeka, Jezekah, Jezica, Jezicah, Jezicka, Jezika, Jezikah, Jeziqua, Jeziquah, Jezyca, Jezycah, Jezycka, Jisica, Jisicah, Jisicka, Jisika, Jisikah, Jisiqua, Jisiquah, Jysica, Jysicah, Jysicka, Jyssica, Jyssicah, Jyssicka, Jyssika, Jyssikah, Jyssiqua, Jyssiquah, Jyssyca, Jyssycka, Jyssyka, Jyssykah, Jysyka, Jysykah, Jysyqua, Jysyquah, Jezika.

JESSIE (Hebrew) Nickname for Jessica. *Variations:* Jess, Jessa, Jesse, Jessea, Jessey, Jessi, Jessie.

JESUSA (Spanish) Feminine form of Jesus. God is salvation.

JETHRA (Hebrew) Plenty.

JETTE (Scandinavian) Black. *Variations:* Jeta, Jetah, Jetia, Jetje, Jett, Jetta, Jettah, Jetti, Jettia, Jettiah, Jettie, Jetty, Jettya.

JEUNESSE (French) Youthful.

JEWEL (French) Jewel. *Notable:* Singer Jewel Kilcher. *Variations:* Jewelana, Jewell, Jewella, Jewelle.

JEZEBEL (Hebrew) Unexalted. *Variations:* Jesabel, Jesabelah, Jesabele, Jesabell, Jesabella, Jessabel, Jez, Jezabel, Jezebella, Jezebelle, Jezzie.

JIA (Chinese) Fine.

JIAO (Chinese) Delicate beauty.

JIAYI (Chinese) Auspicious one.

JIAYING (Chinese) Good and clever.

JIE (Chinese) Cleanliness, purity.

JIERA (Lithuanian) Vivacious.

JILL (English) Young. Shortened version of Jillian. *Notables:* Actresses Jill Ireland, Jill Clayburgh, and Jill St. John. *Variations:* Gil, Gill, Gyl, Gyll, Jil, Jilli, Jillie, Jilly, Jyl, Jyll.

JILLIAN (English) Young. *Notable:* TV personality Jillian Barberie. *Variations:* Gilli, Gillian, Gillie, Jilaine, Jilane, Jilian, Jiliana, Jillana, Jilleen, Jilliana, Jillianne, Jilliyanne, Jillyan, Jillyanna.

JIMENA (Spanish) Heard.

JIN (Japanese) Tender.

JINGHUA (Chinese) Leek flower.

JINJING (Chinese) Crystal clear.

JINAN (Arabic) Paradise.

JINDRISKA (Czech) Ruler at home. *Variations:* Jindra, Jindrina, Jindruska.

JING-WEI (Chinese) Small bird.

JIN-KYONG (Korean) Bright jewel.

JINNAT (Hindi) Heaven.

JINX (Latin) Spell. *Variation:* Jynx.

JIRINA (Czech) Farmer. *Variation:* Jiruska.

JISELLE (American) Form of Giselle.

JIVA (Hindi) Immortal essence. *Variation:* Jivah.

JIVANTA (Hindi) To create. *Variation:* Jiyvanta.

JO (English) Short form of Joanna, Josephine, or any name beginning with "Jo." *Variations:* Jo, Joey, Jojo.

JOAKIMA (Hebrew) God will judge. *Variation:* Joachima.

JOAN (Hebrew) God is good. *Notables:* Actresses Joan Crawford, Joan Allen, and Joan Cusack. *Variations:* Joani, Joanie, Joannie, Jone, Jonee, Joni.

JOANNA (English) Form of Joan. *Variations:* Joana, Joannah, Johanna.

JOANNE (English) God is good. *Notable:* Actress Joanne Woodward. *Variations:* JoAnn, JoAnne, Johanna, Johanne.

JOAQUINA (Spanish) Flower; (Hebrew) God will establish. *Variation:* Joaquine.

JOBETH (American) Combination of first names "Jo" and "Beth." *Notable:* Actress JoBeth Williams.

JOBY (Hebrew) Persecuted. Feminine version of Job. *Variations:* Jobee, Jobey, Jobi, Jobie, Jobina.

JOCASTA (Greek) Shining moon.

JOCELYN (Latin) Joyous. *Variations:* Jocelin, Jocelina, Joceline, Jocelyne, Joci, Jocie, Josaline, Joscelin, Josceline, Joscelyn, Joselina, Joseline, Joselyn, Joselyne, Josiline, Josline, Jossalin, Jossalina, Jossaline, Jossalyn.

JOCHEBED (Hebrew) God is glory.

JOCOSA (Latin) Playful.

JODELLE (French). *Variations:* Jo Dell, Jodell.

JODHA (Hindi) Sixteenth-century Hindi woman.

JODY (Hebrew) Praised. *Notable:* Actress Jodie Foster. *Variations:* Joda, Jode, Jodea, Jodee, Jodett, Jodetta, Jodette, Jodey, Jodi, Jodia, Jodie, Jodis, Joedee, Joedey, Joedi, Joedie, Joedy.

JOELLE (French) God is Lord. Feminine version of Joel. *Variations:* Joel, Joell, Joella, Joellen, Joellyn, Joely.

JOHANNA (German) Form of Joanna. *Variations:* Johana, Johnna.

JOHARA (Arabic) Jewel.

JOKLA (African) Robe of adornment.

JOLÁN (Hungarian) Purple flower.

Most Popular African American Names

BOYS:
1. Jayden
2. Joshua
3. Elijah
4. Jaden
5. Justin/Christian
6. Jeremiah
7. Isaiah
8. Jordan
9. Christopher/Michael
10. Barack

GIRLS:
1. Madison
2. Kayla
3. Makayla
4. Michelle
5. Nevaeh
6. Jada
7. Brianna
8. Chloe
9. Alyssa/Destiny
10. Gabrielle/Imani

JOLANDA (Greek) A form of Yolanda.

JOLÁNTA (Czech) Violet. *Variation:* Jolana.

JOLENE (American) Combination of first name "Jo" and the suffix "lene." *Variations:* Jolaina, Jolaine, Jolana, Jolane, Jolanna, Jolanne, Jolanta, Jolante, Jolean, Joleana, Joleane, Joleen, Joleena, Joleene, Jolena, Jolenna, Jolenne, Jolian, Jolin, Jolina, Joline, Jolinn, Jolinne, Jolyn, Jolynn, Jolynne, Jolyon.

JOLIE (French) Pretty. *Variations:* Jolee, Jolei, Joleigh, Joley, Joli, Joline, Jolli, Jollie, Joly.

JOLISA (American) Combination of Jo and Lisa. *Variations:* Jolissa, Jolyssa.

JONA (Hebrew) Dove. *Variations:* Jonah, Jonati.

JONATHA (Hebrew) Gift of God. Feminine form of Jonathan.

JONAVA (Lithuanian) Feminine form of Jonas. Dove.

JONELLA (English) God is good to all. *Variations:* Johnelle, Jonell, Jonelle, Joni, Jonie, Jony.

JONI (American) Familiar form of Joan. *Notable:* Singer Joni Mitchell. *Variations:* Joanee, Joani, Joanie, Jonee, Jonie.

JONINA (Hebrew) Dove. *Variations:* Jona, Jonati, Jonit, Jonita, Yona, Yonit, Yonita.

JONNA (English) God is good. Variation of John. *Variations:* Jahnna, Johnna.

JONQUIL (English) Flower name. *Variations:* Jonquila, Jonquille.

JORA (Hebrew) Autumn rain. *Variations:* Jorah, Joran.

JORDAN (English) To descend. *Notable:* Former American Idol Jordin Sparks. *Variations:* Jordain, Jordaine, Jordana, Jordanna, Jordee, Jordey, Jordi, Jordie, Jordin, Jordon, Jordy, Jordyn, Jourdan.

JORGINA (Spanish) Variation of Georgia. Farmer.

JORI (Hebrew) Form of Jordan. Short form of Marjorie. *Variations:* Joree, Jorie, Jorri, Jory, Joryn.

JORJA (Russian) Form of Georgia. Farmer. *Notable:* Actress Jorja Fox. *Variations:* Jorga, Jorgia, Jorgie, Jorgina, Jorgine, Jorjia, Jorjina.

JOSELYN (Latin) Form of Jocelyn. *Variation:* Josselyn.

JOSEPHINE (Hebrew) God will add. Feminine version of Joseph. *Notable:* Singer Josephine Baker. *Variations:* Josaffina, Josafine, Josaphina, Josaphine, Josefa, Josefena, Josefina, Josefine, Josepha, Josephe, Josephena, Josephene, Josephin, Josephina, Josephiney, Josephyn, Josephyna, Josephyne, Josett, Josetta, Josette, Jozafin, Jozafina, Jozafine, Jozapata, Jozaphin, Jozaphina, Jozaphinah, Jozaphine, Jozaphyna, Jozaphyne, Jozefa, Jozefin, Jozefina, Jozefinah, Jozefine, Jozephin, Jozephina, Jozephinah, Jozephine, Jozephyna, Jozephynah, Jozephyne.

JOSETTE (French) Form of Josephine. *Variations:* Josetta, Jozetta, Jozette.

JOSELLE (American) Form of Josie. *Variations:* Josell, Josella, Jozell, Jozella, Jozelle.

JOSIANE (French) Form of Josephine. *Variations:* Josianna, Josianne.

JOSIE (English) Familiar form of Josephine. *Variations:* Joesee, Joesey, Josea, Josee, Josey, Josi, Joze, Jozee, Jozey, Jozi, Jozy.

JOSS (German) Short form of Jocelyn. *Notable:* Singer Joss Stone.

JOVANA (Latin) Majestic. *Variations:* Jovan, Jovanna, Jovannah, Jovanne, Jovenna, Jovenne.

JOVITA (Latin) Gladden.

JOY (English) Happiness. *Notable:* Comedian Joy Behar. *Variations:* Gioia, Joi, Joia, Joie, Joya, Joye.

JOYANNA (English) Joyful grace. *Variations:* Joianna, Joianne, Joyana, Joyanne.

JOYCE (Latin) Joyous. *Notables:* Columnist/therapist Dr. Joyce Brothers; writer Joyce Carol Oates. *Variations:* Joice, Joycee, Joycia, Joycianna, Joyous, Joyousa, Joyse.

JOYITA (Spanish) Jewel.

JOYLYN (English) Joyful one. *Variations:* Joilene, Joilin, Joilina, Joilyn, Joylin, Joylina.

JU (Chinese) Chrysanthemum.

JUANA (Spanish) God is good. Feminine form of Juan (John). *Variation:* Juanna.

JUANITA (Spanish) God is good. Feminine form of Juan (John). *Variations:* Juanetta, Juanicia.

JUABAI (Hindi) Mother of the founder of the Maratha confederacy in the seventeenth century.

JUBAL (Hebrew) Stream.

JUBILEE (Hebrew) Jubilant. *Variations:* Jubilea, Jubileigh, Jubilia.

JUCOSA (Latin) Playful.

JUDE (Latin) Praised. *Variations:* Judeen, Judeena, Judina, Judine.

JUDITH (Hebrew) Admired, praised. *Variations:* Jitka, Jucika, Judey, Judi, Judie, Judit, Judita, Judite, Juditha, Judithe, Juditt, Juditte, Judy, Judye, Jutka, Yehudit.

JUDY (English) Short form of Judith. *Notable:* Singer Judy Garland. *Variations:* Judee, Judi, Judie.

JUH (Hindi) Flower.

JUHEINA (Arabic) Intelligent. *Variation:* Judaina.

JUICY (American) Luscious. *Variations:* Jucee, Jucey, Jucie, Jucy.

JULA (Polish) Form of Julia.

JULENE (Latin) Youthful. *Variations:* Juleen, Juleena, Juleene, Julenia, Julinca, Juline, Julinka, Juliska, Julleen, Julline, Julyne.

JULES (English) Form of Julia. *Notable:* TV host Jules Asner.

JULIA (Latin) Young. *Notables:* Actress Julia Roberts; TV chef Julia Child. *Variations:* Giulia, Iulia, Jula, Julcia, Julee, Juley, Juli, Juliana, Juliane, Julianna, Julianne, Julica, Julie, Julina, Juline, Julinka, Juliska, Julissa, Julka, Yula, Yulinka, Yuliya, Yulka, Yulya.

JULIANA (Italian) Form of Julia. *Notables:* Actresses Julianna Margulies and Julianne Moore. *Variations:* Julian, Juliane, Juliann, Julianna, Julianne.

JULIE (English) Young. Form of Julia. *Notable:* Actress Julie Andrews. *Variations:* Jule, Julee, Juli.

JULIET (English) Form of Julia. *Variations:* Juletta, Julette, Julieta, Julietta, Juliette, Julita, Julyette.

JULISA (American) Combination of Julia and Lisa. *Variations:* Julessa, Julissa.

JULY (Latin) Youthful. Born in July.

JUMANA (Arabic) Pearl. *Variation:* Jumanah.

JUMAPIU (African) Born on Sunday.

JUMOKE (African) Loved by all.

JUN (Japanese) Obedient. *Variation:* Junko.

JUNE (Latin) The month. *Notable:* Singer June Carter Cash. *Variations:* Junae, Junel, Junella, Junelle, Junette, Juni, Junia, Junie, Junille, Junina, Junine, Junita.

JUNIPER (English) Juniper tree.

JUNO (Latin) Queen of heaven. *Variations:* Juneau, Juneaux.

JURISA (Slavic) Storm. *Variations:* Jurissa, Juryssa.

JUSTINE (French) Just. Feminine version of Justin. *Variations:* Justeen, Justeena, Justena, Justina, Justinna, Justyne, Justyna.

JUTKA (Hungarian) Praise God.

JYOTI (Hindi) Light of the moon. *Variation:* Jyotsana.

KAAMILEE (Hindi) Desirous.

KAANAN (Hindi) Forest.

KAAONA (Hawaiian) Hawaiian summer month.

KAARINA (Scandinavian) Pure.

KAASU (Hindi) Lustrous.

KACEY (English) Vigilant. Variation of Casey. *Variations:* K.C., Kace, Kacee, Kaci, Kacia, Kacie, Kacy, Kasey, Kasie, Kaycee, Kayci, Kaycie, Kaysie.

KACHINA (Native American) Sacred dancer. *Variations:* Kachin, Kachine, Kachinee.

KACIA (Greek) Short form of Acacia. *Variations:* Kasia, Kaycia.

KADENZA (Latin) With rhythm.

KADESHA (American) Combination of Kady and Aisha.

KADIAH (Hebrew) A pitcher. *Variations:* Kadia, Kadya.

KADICE (Slovic) A waterfall in Slovenia.

KADIN (Arabic) Beloved companion. *Variations:* Kadan, Kaden, Kadyn.

KADY (English) Variation of Cady or Katy. *Variations:* Kadee, Kadie.

KAEDE (Japanese) Maple.

KAELIN (Irish) Pure. Form of Cailin. *Variations:* Kaelan, Kaelen, Kaeline, Kaelyn, Kaelynn, Kailin, Kailyn.

KAGAMI (Japanese) Mirror.

KAGISO (African) Peace.

KAHOKO (Hawaiian) Star.

KAI (Hawaiian) Sea. *Variation:* Kae.

KAIKO (Japanese) Forgiveness. *Variation:* Kaiyo.

KAILANI (Hawaiian) Sky. Sea. *Variations:* Kaelana, Kaelanah, Kaelanea, Kaelanee, Kaelaney, Kaelani, Kaelania, Kaelaniah, Kaelanie, Kaelany, Kaelanya, Kailana, Kailanah, Kailanea, Kailanee, Kailaney, Kailania, Kailaniah, Kailnie, Kailany, Kailanya, Kaylana, Kaylanah, Kaylanea, Kaylanee, Kaylaney, Kaylani, Kaylania, Kaylaniah, Kaylanie, Kaylany, Kaylanya.

KAILASH (Hindi) Himalayan mountain. *Variations:* Kailasa, Kailase.

KAIMAUE (Hawaiian) Calm seas.

KAISA (Scandinavian) Pure.

KAITLIN (Irish) Pure. Form of Katherine. *Variations:* Caitlin, Kaitlinn, Kaitlinne, Kaitlynn, Katelin, Katelyn, Katelynne.

KAKALA (Polynesian) Flower.

KAKALINA (Hawaiian) Pure. *Variations:* Kakarina, Katalina.

KAKAULANI (Hawaiian) In the sky.

KAKIELEKEA (Hawaiian) White gardenia.

KAKRA (African) Second born of twins.

KAL (English) Yellow flower.

KALA (Hindi) Black one. *Variation:* Kalah.

KALALA (Hawaiian) Bright. Hawaiian version of Clara. *Variation:* Kalara.

KALAMA (Hawaiian) Flaming torch.

KALAMELA (Hawaiian) Hawaiian version of Carmen. *Variation:* Kalameli.

KALANA (Hawaiian) Flat land.

KALANI (Hawaiian) Of the heavens. *Variations:* Kalana, Kalanah, Kalanea, Kalanee, Kalaney, Kalania, Kalaniah, Kalanie, Kalauni, Kalona, Kalonah, Kalonea, Kalonee, Kaloney, Kaloni, Kalonia, Kaloniah, Kalonie, Kalony.

KALANIT (Hebrew) Flower. *Variations:* Kalanice, Kaleena, Kalena, Kalina.

KALAUDIA (Hawaiian) Lame. Hawaiian version of Claudia. *Variations:* Kalaudina, Kalaukia, Kalaukina, Kelaudia, Kelaukia.

KALAUKA (Hawaiian) Famous. *Variation:* Kalarisa.

KALAYA (Thai) Beautiful lady.

KALEA (Hawaiian) Bright. *Variations:* Kahlea, Kahleah, Kaleah, Kalee, Kalei, Kaleigh, Kaley, Kali, Kalie, Kaly, Karlee, Karlei, Karleigh.

KALEI (Hawaiian) Wreath of flowers.

KALERE (African) Short woman.

KALI (Hindi) The black one *Variations:* Kalee, Kallee. Kalli.

KALIFA (African) Chaste and holy woman.

KALIGENIA (Greek) Beautiful daughter.

KALIKA (Hindi) Flower pod.

KALILA (Arabic) Beloved. *Variations:* Kaila, Kailey, Kaleela, Kaleigh, Kalie, Kalilla, Kaly, Kayle, Kaylee, Kayleen, Kayleigh, Kaylene, Kayley, Kaylie, Kaylil, Kylila.

KALILEA (Polynesian) Pillow talk.

KALILINOE (Hawaiian) Rain.

KALINA (Slavic) Flower. *Variations:* Kaleen, Kaleena, Kalena, Kalene.

KALINDA (Hindi) The sun. *Variations:* Kaleenda, Kalindi.

KALINDI (Hindi) A river. *Variation:* Kaleendi.

KALINI (Hawaiian) Pure. Hawaiian version of Karen.

KALINN (Scandinavian) Stream.

KALINO (Hawaiian) A bright light.

KALIONA (Hawaiian) One lion.

KALISA (American) Combination of Kay and Lisa. *Variations:* Kaleesa, Kalisha, Kallisa, Kaylisa.

KALISKA (Native American) Coyote pursuing a deer.

KALITA (Hindi) Famous.

KALLI (Greek) Singing lark. *Variations:* Cal, Calli, Callie, Colli, Kal, Kallie, Kallu, Kally.

KALLIRROE (Greek) Beautiful stream. *Variations:* Callirhoe, Callirhot, Calliroe, Callirrhoe, Callirroe, Callirrot.

KALLISTA (Greek) Most beautiful. *Variations:* Cala, Calesta, Calista, Callie, Cally, Kala, Kalesta, Kali, Kalie, Kalika, Kalista, Kalli, Kallie, Kally, Kallysta.

KALLOLEE (Hindi) Happy.

KALMA (Scandinavian) Goddess of the dead.

KALOLA (Hawaiian) Woman. Hawaiian version of Carol. *Variation:* Karola.

KALOME (Hawaiian) Peace.

KALONICE (Greek) Beautiful victory.

KALOTE (Hawaiian) Small beauty. Hawaiian version of Charlotte. *Variations:* Halaki, Harati, Kaloka, Kaloke, Kalota.

KALPANA (Hindi) Imagination.

KALTHUM (Arabic) Fat cheeked. *Variation:* Kalsum.

KALUWA (African) Overlooked.

KALUYAN (Cambodian) Supreme.

KALYAN (Hindi) Beautiful.

KALYCA (Greek) Rosebud. *Variations:* Kali, Kalica, Kaly.

KAMA (Sanskrit) Beloved.

KAMALA (Hindi) Lotus. *Variation:* Kamalika.

KAMALI (African) Guardian angel.

KAMANIKA (Hindi) Beautiful. *Variation:* Kamaniya.

KAMARI (African: Swahili) Like the moon. *Variation:* Kamaria.

KAMATA (Native American) Throwing bones.

KAME (Japanese) Tortoise. *Variations:* Kameko, Kameyo.

KAMEA (Hawaiian) Only one.

KAMEKE (African) Blind person.

KAMELI (Hawaiian) Honey.

KAMELIA (Hawaiian) Vineyard. *Variation:* Komela.

KAMI (Polynesian) Love.

KAMILA (Arabic) Perfect. *Variations:* Kamala, Kameela, Kamilah, Kamilia, Kamilla, Kamillah, Kamla.

KAMINARI (Japanese) Thunder.

KAMOANA (Hawaiian) Ocean.

KANA (Hindi) Tiny. *Variation:* Kanika.

KANAN (Indian) From the garden.

KANANI (Hawaiian) Beautiful.

KANARA (Hebrew) Canary. *Variation:* Kanarit.

KANDA (Native American) Magical.

KANE (Japanese) Talented. *Variation:* Kaneko.

KANEESHA (African American) Unknown definition. *Variation:* Kaneisha.

KANENE (African) Sty in the eye.

KANERU (Japanese) To do two things at once. *Variation:* Kane.

KANESTIE (Native American) Guide.

KANI (Hawaiian) Sound.

KANIH (African) Black cloth.

KANIKA (African) Dark and beautiful. *Variations:* Kanikwa, Kaniqua.

KANJANAA (Hindi) God of love.

KANNITHA (Cambodian) Angel.

KANOA (Hawaiian) Free one.

KANTA (Hindi) Desire.

KANTHA (Hindi) Delicate woman.

KANTI (Hindi) Lovely. *Variation:* Kantimati.

KANYA (Hindi) Virginal. *Variation:* Kania.

KAORU (Japanese) Fragrant. *Variation:* Kaori.

KAPIKA (Hawaiian) Gazelle.

KAPONIANANI (Hawaiian) Consecrated beauty.

KAPUA (Hawaiian) Flower.

KAPUAULA (Hawaiian) Red flower.

KAPUKI (African) First-born daughter.

KARA (Greek) Dear. *Variations:* Kaira, Karah, Karalee, Karalyn, Karalynn, Kari, Kariana, Karianna, Karianne, Karie, Karielle, Karrah, Karrie, Kary.

KAREN (Greek) Pure. Form of Katherine. *Notable:* Singer Karen Carpenter. *Variations:* Caren, Carin, Caron, Carren, Carrin, Carron, Caryn, Kareen, Karenna, Karin, Karina, Karon, Karyn, Keren, Kerena, Kerran, Kerrin, Kerron, Keryn.

KARENZA (Scottish) Love. *Variations:* Kerensa, Kerenza.

KARIDA (Arabic) Virginal. *Variation:* Kareeda.

KARIMA (Arabic) Noble. *Variations:* Kareema, Karimah.

Top Names of the 1910s

BOYS:
1. John
2. William
3. James
4. Robert
5. Joseph
6. George
7. Charles
8. Edward
9. Frank
10. Thomas
11. Walter
12. Harold
13. Henry
14. Paul
15. Richard
16. Raymond
17. Albert
18. Arthur
19. Harry
20. Donald

GIRLS:
1. Mary
2. Helen
3. Dorothy
4. Margaret
5. Ruth
6. Mildred
7. Anna
8. Elizabeth
9. Frances
10. Virginia
11. Marie
12. Evelyn
13. Alice
14. Florence
15. Lillian
16. Rose
17. Irene
18. Louise
19. Edna
20. Catherine

KARIS (Greek) Grace.

KARISMA (English) Variation of Charisma. *Variations:* Karizma, Kharisma.

KARISSA (Greek) Dear. *Variations:* Karisa, Karysa.

KARLA (German) Woman. Feminine form of Carl.

KARLENE (Latvian) Woman. Feminine version of Charles. *Variations:* Karleen, Karlen, Karlena, Karlina.

KARMA (Hindi) Fate.

KARMEL (Hebrew) Garden of grapes. *Variations:* Cami, Carmel, Carmia, Karmeli, Karmi, Karmia, Karmiel, Karmielle.

KARMEN (Latin) Song. Variation of Carmen. *Variations:* Karmina, Karmine, Karmita.

KARMIL (Hebrew) Red.

KARMYN (Latin) A form of Carmen. Song.

KARNIA (Hebrew) Horn of God. *Variations:* Carnia, Karni.

KARNIELA (Hebrew) Horn blower. *Variations:* Carniela, Carnielah, Carniele, Carniell, Carniella, Carnielle, Karniel, Karniela, Karnielah, Karniele, Karniella, Karnielle, Karnyel, Karnyela, Karniell, Karnyella, Karnyelle.

KAROL (German) Form of Carol. Courageous. *Variations:* Karola, Karole, Karolle.

KAROLAINA (Hawaiian) Woman. *Variations:* Kalalaina, Kalolaina, Kalolina, Karalaina, Kealalaina.

KAROLINA (Polish) Form of Caroline. *Variations:* Karalina, Karaline, Karoline, Karolyn.

KARPURA (Hindi) Princess from the twelfth century.

KARSTEN (Greek) Anointed one. *Variations:* Karstan, Karstin, Karstyn.

KARUNA (Hindi) Compassion.

KASA (Native American) Dress made of fur. *Variations:* Kahsha, Kasha.

KASARNA (Indonesian) Beautiful melody.

KASEY (Irish) Alternative to Casey. *Variations:* Kacee, Kacey, Kaci, Kacie, Kacy, Kaicee, Kaicey, Kaici, Kaicie, Kaicy, Kasy, Kasey, Kaycee, Kaycey, Kayci, Kaycie, Kaycy.

KASI (Hindi) The holy city.

KASIA (Polish) Purity.

KASINDA (African) Child born after twins.

KASMIRA (Slavic) Bringing peace. Feminine version of Casimir.

KASSANDRA (Greek) Prophet. *Variations:* Kasandra, Kasandrah, Kasondra, Kasondrah, Kassandrah, Kassandria, Kasandriah, Kassondra, Kassondrah, Kasundra, Kasundrah, Kazandra, Kazandrah, Kazandria.

KASSIANA (Greek) Pure.

KASTURBA (Hindi) Musk.

KASUMI (Japanese) Mist.

KAT (Greek) Pure. Short form of Katherine.

KATANIYA (Hebrew) Small. *Variations:* Katania, Ketana.

KATE (Greek) Short form of Katherine and its derivatives. *Notable:* Actress Kate Winslet. *Variations:* Cate, Kait, Kayt.

KATECIA (American) Combined form of Kate and Latisha. Pure and happy. *Variations:* Katechia, Katesha, Kateshia.

KATEKE (African) An overstayed guest.

KATELYN (Celtic) Alternative to Caitlin. Pure beauty. *Variations:* Katelan, Katelen, Katelin, Katelynn, Katelynne, Kaitlan, Kaitlen, Kaitlin, Kaitlyn, Kaitlynn, Kaitlynne, Katlan, Katlen, Katlin, Katlyn, Katlynn, Katlynne.

KATERI (Native American) Purity. *Varitations:* Katerie, Katery.

KATERINA (Russian) Purity. Form of Katherine. *Variation:* Katarina.

KATH (American) Purity. A short form of Katherine. *Variations:* Cath, Catha, Cathe, Katha, Kathe.

KATHERINE (Greek) Pure. *Notable:* Actress Katharine Hepburn. *Variations:* Caitriona, Caren, Caron, Caryn, Caye, Ekaterina, Kaatje, Kaethe, Karrin, Kata, Kataleen, Katalin, Katalina, Katarina, Kateke, Katerina, Katerinka, Katharin, Katharina, Katharine, Katharyn, Kathereen, Katherin, Katherina, Kathren, Kathrine, Kathryn, Kathryne, Katia, Katica, Katina, Katushka, Katya, Kay, Kisan, Kit, Kitti, Kittie, Kitty, Kotinka, Kotryna, Yekaterina.

KATHLEEN (Irish) Form of Katherine. *Notable:* Actress Kathleen Turner. *Variations:* Cathleen, Cathlene, Cathlyn, Kathleena, Kathleenah, Kathleene, Kathlein, Kathleina, Kathleinah, Kathleine, Kathlin, Kathlina, Kathlinah, Kathline, Kathlyn, Kathlyna, Kathlnah, Kathlyne, Kathlynn, Kathlynne.

KATHY (English) Short form of Katherine. Pure. *Notables:* Actress Kathy Bates; comedian Kathy Griffin. *Variations:* Cathy, Kathe, Kathea, Kathee, Kathey, Kathi, Kathia, Kathie, Kathya, Kathye.

KATIA (Russian) Form of Katherine.

KATIE (English) Short form of Katherine. *Notable:* TV news host Katie Couric. *Variations:* Katea, Katee, Katey, Kati, Katy.

KATRIEL (Hebrew) Crowned by God.

KATRINA (Scandinavian) Form of Katherine. *Variations:* Katreena, Katrine, Katriona, Katryna, Kattrina.

KATSU (Japanese) Triumphant. *Variation:* Katsuko.

KATSUMI (Japanese) Victorious beauty.

KATURA (African) Relief.

KATYAYANI (Hindi) Goddess.

KAUILA (Hawaiian) Acclaimed woman.

KAULA (Hawaiian) Clairvoyant.

KAULANA (Hawaiian) Famous one.

KAULUWEHI (Hawaiian) One garden.

KAUSALYA (Hindi) Mother of Rama. *Variations:* Kaushali, Kaushalya.

KAVERI (Hindi) River.

KAVINDRA (Hindi) Poet.

KAWAIMOMONA (Hawaiian) Sweet water.

KAWENA (Hawaiian) Fire.

KAWENAULA (Hawaiian) Red sunset.

KAYA (Native American) Wise child.

KAYDEE (American) Alternative to Kady.

KAYLA (English) Pure. *Variations:* Kaela, Kaelah, Kaelea, Kaeleah, Kaelee, Kaelei, Kaeleigh, Kaeley, Kaeli, Kaelia, Kaelie, Kaely, Kaelyn, Kahla, Kahlea, Kahlee, Kahlei, Kahleigh, Kahley, Kaila, Kailan, Kailea, Kailee, Kailey, Kailin, Kalee, Kaleigh, Kalen, Kaley, Kalie, Kaylea, Kayleen, Kayleigh, Kayley, Kayli, Kaylia, Kaylie, Kayly.

KAYLAN (English) Joyful. *Variations:* Kaelyn, Kailan, Kaylen, Kaylin.

KAYLENE (English) Pure. *Variations:* Kaylean, Kayleane, Kayleen, Kayleene, Kayline, Kaylyne.

KAZIA (Polish) Destroyer of peace.

KAZIMIERA (Polish) Peace is proclaimed. *Variations:* Kasimera, Kasimiera, Kasimira, Kasimirah, Kasmira, Kasmirah, Kasmiria, Kasmiriah, Kasmirya, Kasmyra, Kazmira, Kazmirah, Kazmiria, Kazmiriah, Kazmyra, Kazzmira, Kazzmiria, Kazzmirya, Kazzmyrya.

KAZUE (Japanese) Harmonious. *Variation:* Kazuko.

KAZUMI (Japanese) Harmonious beauty.

KEALA (Hawaiian) Road. *Variations:* Kealah, Keela, Keelah, Keila, Keilah, Keyla, Keylah, Kiala, Kiahla, Kialah.

KEALANI (Hawaiian) White heaven.

KEALOHA (Hawaiian) Cherished friend.

KEALOHI (Hawaiian) Shining friend.

KEARA (Irish) Dark. *Variations:* Keera, Keira, Kera, Kiara, Kiera.

KEATON (English) Kite town. *Variation:* Keeton.

KEDMA (Hebrew) Toward the East. *Variation:* Kedmah.

KEELY (Irish) Brave. Form of Kelly. *Variations:* Kealea, Kealee, Kealei, Kealeigh, Kealey, Keali, Kealia, Kealie, Kealy, Keelea, Keelei, Keeleigh, Keeley, Keeli, Keelie, Keighley, Keilie, Keyley, Kieley, Kiely.

KEENA (Irish) Brave. *Variation:* Kina.

KEESHA (African) Favorite. *Variations:* Keisha, Keshia, Kiesha.

KEEYA (African) Like a flower.

KEFIRA (Hebrew) Young lioness. *Variations:* Kefirah, Kefire, Kefrya.

KEHINDE (African) Second born of twins.

KEI (Japanese) Awe.

KEIJA (Scandinavian) Purity.

KEIKI (Hawaiian) Child. *Variation:* Keikana.

KEIKO (Japanese) Joyful child.

KEILANA (Hawaiian) Glorious calm. *Variations:* Kealaina, Kealainah, Kealaine, Kealana, Kealane, Kealanah, Kealanna, Kealannah, Kealanne, Keelana, Keelanah, Keelaina, Keelainah, Keelane, Keelayn, Keelayna, Keelaynah, Keelayne, Keilanah, Keilane, Keilaina, Keilaine, Keilanah, Keilanna, Keilannah, Keilanne, Keilayn, Keilayna, Keilaynah, Keylana, Keylanah, Keylane, Keylaina, Keylainah, Keylaine, Keylayn, Keylayna.

KEIRA (Irish) Princess. Alternative to Keara. *Notable:* Actress Keira Knightley.

KEISHA (African) Precious. *Variations:* Keasha, Keeshia, Keeshiah, Keeshy, Keeshya, Keishah, Keishia, Keishiah, Keishya, Kesha, Keshah, Keshia, Keshiah, Keshya, Keshyah, Keysha, Keyshah, Keyshia, Keyshiah, Keyshya, Keyshyah.

KEITA (English) Forest. Feminine version of Keith.

KEKE (Hawaiian) Chaste. *Variation:* Kete.

KEKEPANIA (Hawaiian) Crown. *Variation:* Setepania.

KEKILIA (Hawaiian) Poor eyesight. *Variations:* Kekila, Kikilia, Sesilia, Sisilia.

KEKONA (Hawaiian) Second child.

KELA (Hawaiian) Valley. *Variation:* Dela.

KELALANI (Hawaiian) Limitless sky.

KELBY (English) Farm by the river. *Variations:* Kelbi, Kelbie.

KELDA (Scandinavian) Fountain or spring. *Variation:* Kilde.

KELEKA (Hawaiian) To harvest. *Variation:* Kelekia.

KELEKEA (Hawaiian) Gardenia flower.

KELETINA (Hawaiian) Heavenly. *Variation:* Kelekina.

KELILA (Hebrew) Crown. *Variations:* Kaile, Kaille, Kalia, Kayla, Kayle, Keila, Keilah, Kellila, Kellula, Kyle, Kylia.

KELINA (Hawaiian) Moon goddess.

KELLY (Irish) Brave soldier. *Notables:* Singer Kelly Clarkson; talk-show host Kelly Ripa. *Variations:* Kelee, Kellee, Keleigh, Kelie, Kelley, Kellia, Kellie, Kellina, Kelline, Kellisa.

KELSEY (Scottish) Island. *Variations:* Kelcea, Kelcee, Kelcey, Kelci, Kelcie, Kelcy, Kellcea, Kellcee, Kellcey, Kellcia, Kellcie, Kellsea, Kellsee, Kellsey, Kellsi, Kellsie, Kellsy, Kelsa, Kelsea, Kelsee, Kelseigh, Kelsi, Kelsie, Kelsy.

KELULA (Yiddish) Girlfriend.

KEMBA (English) Saxon lord. *Variation:* Kembara.

KENASSA (Gaelic) Beautiful butterfly.

KENDA (Native American) Magic. *Variations:* Kenada, Kenadi, Kendi, Kendie, Kendy, Kennda, Kenndi, Kenndie, Kenndy.

KENDALL (English) Valley of Kent, England. *Variations:* Kendal, Kendala, Kendalla, Kendalle, Kendel, Kendela, Kendell, Kendelle.

KENDELLANA (English) Valley of light. *Variations:* Kendelan, Kendelana, Kendelane, Kendelin, Kendelina, Kendeline, Kendellan, Kendellane, Kendellyn, Kendellyna, Kendellyne, Kendelyn, Kendelyna, Kendelyne.

KENDRA (English) Knowledgeable. *Notable:* Playboy Playmate and reality star Kendra Wilkinson. *Variations:* Kena, Kenadrea, Kendrah, Kendria, Kendrya, Kenna, Kindra, Kinna, Kyndra.

KENISHA (American) Beautiful woman. *Variations:* Keneisha, Keneshia, Kennesha.

KENNA (Scottish) Attractive. Feminine form of Kenneth. *Variations:* Kennae, Kennina.

KENNEDY (Irish) Armored chief.

KENNICE (English) Beautiful. *Variation:* Kennise.

KENTON (English) Place name.

KENYA (English) African country. *Variations:* Kenia, Kenyatta.

KENZIE (Scottish) Attractive. *Variations:* Kensey, Kensie, Kenzi.

KEOHI (Hawaiian) One woman.

KEOKIANA (Hawaiian) Farmer. *Variations:* Geogiana, Geogina, Keokina.

KEOLA (Hawaiian) One life.

KEONA (Hawaiian) Gift of God.

KEOSHA (Sanskrit) Lovely.

KEPILA (Hawaiian) Fortune teller. *Variations:* Kipila, Sebila, Sibila.

KERANI (Hindi) Sacred bells. *Variations:* Kera, Kerie, Kery.

KEREM (Hebrew) Orchard.

KEREN (Hebrew) Horn. *Variation:* Kerrin, Keryn.

KERENSA (Cornish) Love. *Variations:* Karensa, Karenza, Kerenza.

KERRY (Irish) Dark haired. *Notable:* Actress Kerry Washington. *Variations:* Keri, Kerr, Kerra, Kerrey, Kerri, Kerrianne, Kerrie.

KERRYN (Irish) Dark haired. *Variations:* Kerin, Kerrin, Kerryn, Keryn.

KESAVA (Hindi) Lots of hair.

KESHA (African) Favorite child. *Notable:* Singer Ke$ha. *Variations:* Kecia, Keshah.

KESHET (Hebrew) Rainbow. *Variations:* Kesetta, Kesette, Kesheta, Keshette.

KESI (African) Daughter with a difficult father. *Variations:* Kesee, Kesey, Kesie, Kesy.

KESIA (African) Favorite child. *Variations:* Keishia, Keshia, Kesiah, Kessia, Kessiah, Kessya, Kezia, Keziah, Kezzia, Kezziah.

KESSEM (Hebrew) Magic.

KESSIE (African) Fat.

KETI (Polynesian) Pure.

KETIFA (Hebrew) To pick. *Variations:* Ketifah, Ketipha.

KETINA (Hebrew) Girl. *Variations:* Ketinah, Kettina, Ketyna.

KETURAH (Hebrew) Perfume. *Variation:* Ketura.

KETZIA (Hebrew) Tree bark. *Variations:* Kazia, Kesiah, Ketzi, Ketziah, Kezi, Kezia, Keziah, Kissie, Kizzie, Kizzy.

KEVINA (Irish) Handsome. Feminine version of Kevin. *Variations:* Keva, Kevern, Keverna, Keverne, Kevia, Kevine, Kevinne, Kevonna, Kevyn, Kevyna.

KEZIAH (Hebrew) Cassia tree. *Variations:* Kazia, Kesiah, Ketzi, Ketziah, Kezi, Kezia, Keziah, Kissie, Kizzie, Kizzy.

KEWANEE (Native American) Prairie hen. *Variation:* Kewaunee.

KEYANA (Hawaiian) Moon goddess.

KEYNA (Welsh) Jewel.

KEZIA (Hebrew) Cassia tree. *Variations:* Keziah, Kezya.

KHADIJAH (Arabic) First wife of the prophet.

KHALIDA (Arabic) Eternal. *Variations:* Kahlida, Khalyda.

KHALILA (Arabic) Good friend. *Variations:* Kahlia, Khali, Khalia, Khalilah, Khalya.

KHLOE (Greek) Form of Chloe. Flourishing woman.

KIA (African) Start of the season. *Variations:* Kiah, Kya.

KIANA (Hawaiian) Variation of Diana. *Variations:* Kianah, Kianna. Kyana, Kyanna.

Top Names in Argentina

BOYS:
1. Thiago
2. Santiago
3. Benjamin
4. Lautaro
5. Joaquin
6. Santino
7. Valentino
8. Matias
9. Bautista
10. Mateo

GIRLS:
1. Sofia
2. Mia
3. Valentina
4. Martina
5. Camila
6. Morena
7. Catalina
8. Julieta
9. Victoria
10. Delfina

KIARA (American) Form of Ciara. Dark. *Variations:* Keira, Kiarra, Kiera, Kierra.

KIBIBI (African) Little girl.

KICHI (Japanese) Lucky. *Variations:* Kichee, Kichie, Kichy.

KIELE (Hawaiian) Gardenia flower. *Variations:* Kieley, Kieli.

KIEU (Vietnamese) Graceful.

KIFIMBO (African) A twig.

KINGE (German) Brave war.

KIKI (Spanish) Short form of Enriqueta. *Variation:* Kikee.

KIKILIA (Hawaiian) Blind.

KIKU (Japanese) Chrysanthemum. *Variations:* Kikue, Kikuko.

KILEY (Gaelic) Handsome. *Variations:* Kilia, Kilee, Kileigh, Kylee, Kyleigh, Kylie.

KILIA (Hawaiian) Heaven.

KILIWIA (Hawaiian) Forest. *Variation:* Silivia.

KILLARA (Australian) Always there. *Variations:* Kilara, Killarah.

KIM (English) Short form of Kimberly. *Notables:* Actress Kim Basinger; reality-show star Kim Kardashian. *Variations:* Khim, Khym, Kimmie, Kimmy, Kym.

KIMAMA (Native American) Butterfly.

KIMAYA (Hindi) Godlike.

KIMBALL (English) Bold warrior. *Variations:* Kimbal, Kimbel.

KIMBERLY (English) King's meadow. *Variations:* Kim, Kimba, Kimba Lee, Kimball, Kimber, Kimberlea, Kimberlee, Kimberlei, Kimberleigh, Kimberley, Kimberli, Kimberlie, Kimberlyn, Kimbley, Kimmi, Kimmie, Kymberlea, Kymberlee, Kymberleigh, Kymberlia, Kymberlie, Kymberly.

KIMI (Japanese) Superb. *Variations:* Kimee, Kimey, Kimie, Kimiko, Kimiyo, Kimmi, Kimmie, Kimmy.

KIMIKO (Japanese) Noble child.

KIMIMELA (Native American) Butterfly.

KIMORA (American; Japanese) Form of nickname "Kim." *Notable:* Kimora Lee Simmons.

KIN (Japanese) Gold.

KINA (Hawaiian) To judge. *Variations:* Keena, Kinah, Kyna.

KINDILAN (Australian) Happy. *Variations:* Kindilana, Kindilane.

KINETA (Greek) Dynamic. *Variations:* Kinet, Kinett, Kinetta, Kynetta, Kynette.

KINI (Hawaiian) God is good. *Variations:* Kinikia, Kinitia, Sinitia.

KINNERET (Hebrew) Harp.

KINSEY (English) Offspring. *Variations:* Kinsee, Kinsley.

KINSLEY (English) King's meadow. *Variations:* Kinslee, Kinsleigh, Kinslie.

KINSHASHA (African American) The capital of Zaire.

KINTA (Native American) Beaver. *Variations:* Kintah, Kynta.

KINU (Japanese) Silk. *Variations:* Kinuko, Kinuyo.

KIOKO (Japanese) Happy child. *Variations:* Kiyoko, Kyoka, Kyoko.

KIONA (Native American) Brown hills. *Variations:* Kionah, Kiowa, Kyona, Kyowa.

KIRA (Bulgarian) Throne. *Variations:* Kirah, Kirra.

KIRAN (Hindi) Light. *Variations:* Kirana, Kirina.

KIRBY (English) Farm near a church. *Variations:* Kerbee, Kerbi, Kerbie, Kerby, Kirbee, Kirbi, Kirbie.

KIRI (Hindi) Amaranth. *Variations:* Kirsi, Kiry.

KIRIAH (Hebrew) Village. *Variations:* Kiria, Kirya.

KIRIANNE (Australian) Combined form of Kiri and Anne. *Variations:* Kirian, Kiriana, Kiriane, Kiriann, Kirianna, Kirianne, Kyrian, Kyriana, Kyrianah, Kyriane, Kyriann, Kyrianna, Kyrianne, Kyryan, Kyryana, Kyryann, Kyryanna, Kyryanne.

KIRIKA (Japanese) Flower from the Paulonia tree.

KIRILEE (Australian) Combined form of Kiri and Lee. *Variations:* Kiralee, Kiraleigh, Kiraley, Kirilea, Kirileigh, Kiriley, Kirrilee.

KIRIMA (Eskimo) Hill.

KIRITINA (Hawaiian) Christ. *Variations:* Kilikina, Kirikina.

KIRSA (German) Cherry.

KIRSI (Hindi) Amaranth flower.

KIRSTEN (Scandinavian) Christian. *Notable:* Actress Kirsten Dunst. *Variations:* Karsten, Keerstin, Kersten, Kerstin, Kerstyn, Kiersten, Kierstin, Kirsta, Kirstain, Kirstan, Kirstin, Kirstina, Kirstine, Kirstyn, Kirstynn, Kyrstin.

KIRSTIE (Scandinavian) Form of Kirsten. *Notable:* Actress Kirstie Alley. *Variations:* Kerstea, Kerstee, Kersti, Kerstie, Kerstey, Kirstea, Kirstee, Kirstey, Kirsti, Kirsty,

Kurstea, Kurstee, Kurstey, Kursti, Kurstie, Kursty.

KISA (Russian) Kitten. *Variations:* Keesa, Kysa.

KISHANDA (American) Newly created. *Variations:* Keesha, Kisha.

KISHI (Japanese) Beach. *Variation:* Kishiko.

KISHORI (Hindi) Young girl.

KISKA (Russian) Pure.

KISMET (Arabic) Destiny.

KIT (Greek) Short form of Katherine. *Variation:* Kitt.

KITA (Japanese) North.

KITARA (Greek) Musical instrument. *Variation:* Kithara.

KITRA (Hebrew) Wreath.

KITTY (English) Short form of Katherine. *Notable:* Actress Kitty Carlisle. *Variations:* Kiti, Kittee, Kittey, Kitti, Kittie.

KIVA (Hebrew) Protected. *Variation:* Kivah.

KIWA (Japanese) Born on the border. *Variations:* Kiwako, Kiwayo.

KIYOKO (Japanese) Pure child.

KIYOMI (Japanese) Pure beauty.

KIYOSHI (Japanese) Shining.

KIZZY (American) Short form of Keziah. *Variations:* Kissee, Kissie, Kizee, Kizey, Kizi, Kizie, Kizzee, Kizzey, Kizzi, Kizzie, Kyzee, Kyzey, Kyzi, Kyzie, Kyzy, Kyzzee, Kyzzey, Kyzzi, Kyzzie.

KLARA (Hungarian) Bright. Form of Clara. *Variations:* Klari, Klarice, Klarika.

KLARISSA (German) Bright. Form of Clarissa. *Variations:* Klarisa, Klarise.

KLOTHILDA (German) Alternative to Clothilda. Famous battle maid.

KO (Japanese) Daughter's obligation.

KOANA (Hawaiian) God is good. *Variations:* Ioana, Koanna.

KODELIA (Hawaiian) Daughter of the sea. *Variation:* Kokelia.

KOEMI (Japanese) Little smile.

KOFFI (African) Born on Friday. *Variations:* Kofi, Koffe, Koffee.

KOHAKU (Japanese) Amber.

KOHANA (Japanese) Little flower.

KOHIA (Polynesian) Passion flower.

KOHINOOR (Arabic) Light.

KOKO (Japanese) Stork. *Variation:* Coco.

KOKUMO (African) This child will not die.

KOLAB (Cambodian) Rose.

KOLEKA (Hawaiian) Gift from God. *Variation:* Kolekea.

KOLENELIA (Hawaiian) Horn. Hawaiian version of Cornelia. *Variation:* Korenelia.

KOLENYA (Native American) To cough.

KOLEYN (Australian) Winter. *Variations:* Kolein, Kolyne.

KOLFINNIA (Scandinavian) Cool white. *Variations:* Kolfinia, Kolfinna.

KOLIKA (Hawaiian) Hawaiian version of Doris.

KOLINA (Scandinavian) Form of Katherine or Colleen.

KOLOE (Hawaiian) Blooming.

KOLOLIA (Hawaiian) Glory. *Variation:* Goloria.

KOMA (Japanese) Pony. *Variation:* Komako.

KOMAL (Hindi) Dainty. *Variation:* Komala.

KOME (Japanese) Rice. *Variation:* Komeko.

KONA (Hawaiian) Female. *Variations:* Koni, Konia.

KONANE (Hawaiian) Lunar glow.

KONEKO (Japanese) Kitten.

KONIA (Hawaiian) Talent.

KOPEA (Hawaiian) Wise. *Variations:* Kopaea, Sopia.

KORA (Greek) Girl. *Variations:* Cora, Corabel, Corabella, Corabelle, Corabellita, Corake, Coralyn, Corella, Corena, Coretta, Corey, Cori, Corie, Corilla, Corinna, Corinne, Corissa, Corlene, Corri, Corrie, Corrin, Corrissa, Corry, Cory, Coryn, Coryna, Corynn, Korabell, Koree, Koreen, Korella, Korenda, Korette, Korey, Kori, Korie, Korilla, Korissa, Korri, Korrie, Korrina, Korry, Kory, Korynna, Koryssa.

KORINA (English) Maiden. *Variations:* Corinna, Corinne, Korine, Korinna, Korinne.

KOURTNEY (English) Alternative to Courtney. *Variations:* Khourtney, Kortnee, Kortney, Kortnie, Kourteney, Kourtnea, Kourtni, Kourtnie.

KOSOKO (African) Born to die.

KOSTYA (Russian) Faithful.

KOTO (Japanese) Harp. *Variation:* Kotone.

KOU (Japanese) Peace and happiness.

KRESZENTHIA (German) To spring up. *Variation:* Kreszenz.

KRIEMHILD (German) Battle mask. *Variation:* Krimhilde.

KRIS (Scandinavian) Short form of Kristina or Kristin.

KRISTA (Scandinavian) Short form of Kristina. *Variations:* Kristabel, Krysta.

KRISTIN (Scandinavian; German) Form of Christine. *Notables:* Actresses Kristin Davis and Kristin Chenoweth. *Variations:* Kristen, Krysten, Krystin.

KRISTINA (Greek; Scandinavian) Christian. Form of Christina. *Variations:* Kristeen, Kristeena, Kristena, Kristi, Kristie, Kristine, Kristy, Krysti, Krystie, Krystina, Krystine, Krysty.

KRYSTAL (American) Clear and bright. Form of Crystal. *Variations:* Kristal, Kristala, Kristalle, Kristel, Kristell, Kristelle, Kristle, Kristyl, Krystle, Krystyl.

KRISTY (English) Short form of Kristina or Kristin.

KUAI Hua (Chinese) Flower blossom.

KUALII (Hawaiian) Queen.

KUAULI (Hawaiian) Fertile.

KUDIO (African) Born on Monday.

KUKANA (Hawaiian) Hawaiian version of Susannah.

KUKIKO (Japanese) Snow girl.

KUKUA (African) Born on Wednesday.

KULANI (Hawaiian) Reaching heaven.

KULWA (African) First born of twins.

KULYA (Native American) Burnt pine nuts.

KUMA (Japanese) Bear.

KUMARI (Hindi) Daughter.

KUMI (Japanese) Braid. *Variations:* Kumiko, Kumiyo.

KUMUDA (Hindi) Lotus.

KUNANI (Hawaiian) Beautiful.

KUNI (Japanese) Rural baby. *Variation:* Kuniko.

KUNIBERT (German) Bright and brave.

KUNIGONDE (Scandinavian) Brave in battle. *Variations:* Cunegonde, Kunigunde.

KUNTHEA (Cambodian) Aromatic.

KUNTO (African) Third-born child.

KURI (Japanese) Chestnut.

KUSA (Hindi) Grass.

KUSHALI (Hindi) Smart girl.

KUSUM (Hindi) Flower.

KVETA (Czech) Flower. *Variations:* Kvetka, Kvetuse, Kvetuska.

KWABINA (African) Born on Tuesday.

KWANESHA (African American) Unknown definition.

KWANITA (Native American) God is good.

KWASHI (African) Born on Sunday.

KWAU (African) Born on Thursday.

KYANA (Australian) Going back.

KYLA (Hebrew) Crown. *Variation:* Kylah.

KYLE (Scottish) Attractive. *Variations:* Kyla, Kylia.

KYLIE (Irish) Graceful. *Notable:* Singer Kylie Minogue. *Variations:* Kiley, Kye, Kylee, Kyleigh, Kylene.

KYOKO (Japanese) Mirror.

KYRA (Greek) Lady. *Notable:* Actress Kyra Sedgwick. *Variations:* Keera, Keira, Kira, Kyrah, Kyrene, Kyria.

KYRIE (Irish) Dark.

KYUNG-SOON (Korean) Gentle respect.

LABIBA (Arabic) Great intelligence.

LABRENDA (African American) Combined form of La and Brenda.

LACARA (African American) Combined form of La and Cara.

LACEY (Latin) Cheer. *Notable:* Actress Lacey Chabert. *Variations:* Lace, Laci, Lacie, Lacy.

LACHANDRA (American; Sanskrit) The moon. *Variations:* Lachanda, Lachandah, Lachander, Lachandrah, Lachandrica, Lachandrice.

LACHELLE (African American) Combined form of La and Michelle. *Variation:* La Chelle.

LACHLANNA (Scottish) Feminine form of Lachlan. From the land of lakes. *Variations:* Lachlanee, Lachlani, Lachlania, Lachlanie, Lochlan, Lochlana, Locklan.

LACOLE (African American) Combined form of La and Nicole. *Variations:* Lacola, Lacolla, Lacolle, Lakole.

LADA (Russian) Goddess of love and beauty. *Variations:* Ladah, Ladda, Ladia, Ladiah, Ladya.

LADANCIA (Slavic) The morning star. *Variations:* Ladanca, Ladanica, Ladanicka, Ladanika, Ladanyca, Ladanycka, Ladanyka.

LADAWN (African American) Combined form of La and Dawn. *Variations:* La Dawn, Ladawna.

LADEAN (African American) Combined form of La and Dean.

LADELLE (African American) Combined form of La and Della. *Variations:* La Dell, Ladella.

LADAVINA (African American) Divine. *Variations:* Ladivine, Ladivyna.

LADISLAVA (Slavic) Glorious ruler. *Variation:* Ladislavia.

LADONNA (American; Italian) The woman. *Variations:* Ladana, Ladanna, Ladanne, Ladon, Ladona, Ladonne, Ladonya.

LADY (English) Woman. *Variations:* Ladee, Ladey, Laydie.

LAEL (Hebrew) From God. *Variation:* Laelle.

LAELLA (French) Elf. *Variations:* Laela, Laelle, Layelle.

LAHELA (Hawaiian) Lamb.

LAILA (Hebrew; Arabic) Night. *Variations:* Lailah, Laliah, Layla.

LAIMA (Latvian) Fortunate. *Variation:* Layma.

LAINA (English) Road.

LAINE (English) Bright one. Variation of Helen. *Variations:* Lainey, Lane, Layne.

LAJLI (Hindi) Humble. *Variation:* Lajita.

LAJNI (Hindi) Shy.

LAKA (Hawaiian) Docile.

LAKAYLA (African American) Combined form of La and Kayla.

LAKEISHA (American) The favorite or the woman. Combination of La and first names Ayesha or Keisha. *Variations:* Lakecia, Lakeesha, Lakesha, Lakeshia, Laketia, Lakeysha, Lakeyshia, Lakicia, Lakiesha, Lakisha, Lakitia, Laquiesha, Laquisha, Lekeesha, Lekeisha, Lekisha.

LAKENDRA (African American) Combined form of La and Kendra.

LAKSHA (Hindi) White rose.

LAKSHANA (Hindi) Sign. *Variations:* Lakshmi, Laxmi.

LAKSHMI (Hindi) Light and beauty.

LAKYA (Hindi) Born on Thursday.

LALA (Slavic) Tulip. *Variation:* Lalah.

LALAGE (Greek) Talkative. *Variations:* Lallie, Lally.

LALASA (Hindi) Peaceful and dove-like.

LALIA (Italian) Well spoken.

LALIKA (Hindi) Beautiful woman.

LALITA (Hindi) Mischievous.

LALLY (English) Babbler. *Variations:* Lalli, Lallie, Lalley.

LAMARA (Slavic) From the mountains. *Variation:* Lamaara.

LAMBRINI (Greek) Light.

LAMIS (Arabic) Soft.

LAMONICA (African American) Combined form of La and Monica.

L'AMOUR (French) Love.

LAMYA (Arabic) Dark lips. *Variations:* Lama, Lamia.

LAN (Chinese) Orchid. *Variation:* Lang.

LANA (English) Rock. Variation of Alanna. *Notable:* Actress Lana Turner. *Variations:* Lanae, Lanice, Lanna, Lannette.

Begins with "La"

A popular trend in girls' names is to combine the prefix "La" with a favorite name, forming a brand-new name. "La" and "Donna" create "Ladonna" (or "LaDonna"), while "La" and "Yvonne" create "Lavonne." If you find a name you like, see how starting it with "La" sounds. You could be onto something!

Lachandra	Laquita
Lachelle	Lashana
Lachina	Lashawna
Ladawn	Lashay
Lajuana	(or Lashea)
Lakeisha	Lashonda
Lakendra	Latanya
Lakenya	Latavia
Lamonica	Latesha
Laneisha	(or Latisha)
Laportia	Latoya
Laqueena	Latricia
Laquinta	Lavonna
Laquisha	Lawanda

LANAI (Hawaiian) A veranda.

LANAKILA (Hawaiian) Triumph.

LANASSA (Russian) Cheerful and lighthearted.

LANDA (Basque) Wished for. *Variations:* Landea, Landia.

LANDRA (German) Counselor. *Variations:* Landrea, Landria, Landrya.

LANE (English) Road. *Variations:* Laine, Lainey, Lanelle, Laney, Lanie, Layne, Laynie.

LANEESHA (African American) Combined form of La and Neesha. *Variations:* La Neesha, Laneisha, Lanisha.

LANELLE (French) From the little road. *Variations:* Lanel, Lanela, Lanell, Lanella.

LANET (Celtic) Little graceful one. *Variations:* Laneta, Lanete, Lanett, Lanetta, Lanette.

LANGLEY (English) From the long meadow. *Variations:* Langlee, Langleigh.

LANI (Hawaiian) Sky. *Variations:* Lanai, Lanea, Lanee, Lania, Lannia, Lanya, Lenai.

LANIECE (African American) Combined form of La and Denise.

LANTHA (Greek) Purple flower. *Variations:* Lanthe, Lanthia, Lanthina.

LANYA (Hungarian) Girl or maid.

LAPAULA (African American) Combined form of La and Paula.

LAPIS (Egyptian) Dark-blue gem.

LAQUARIUS (African American) Combined form of La and Aquarius.

LAQUEENA (African American) The queen. *Variations:* Laqueen, Laquena.

LAQUELA (African American) Eagle. *Variations:* L'Aquila, Laquilla.

LAQUINDA (African American) Fifth born. *Variation:* Laquinta.

LAQUITA (African American) Little one. *Variation:* Laqueta.

LARA (Greek) Cheerful. *Notables:* Actress Lara Flynn Boyle; Tomb Raider's Lara Croft. *Variations:* Larah, Laralaine, Laramae, Lari, Larina, Larinda, Larita.

LARAMIE (French) Tears of love. *Variations:* Laramee, Larami, Laramy.

LAREINA (Spanish) The queen. *Variations:* LaRayne, Lareine, Larena, Larraine.

LARINDA (African American) Combined form of La and Linda.

LARISSA (Greek) Happy. *Variations:* Laresa, Laressa, Larisa, Laryssa.

LARITA (African American) Combined form of La and Rita.

LARK (English) Bird. *Variation:* Larke.

LARUE (French) The street.

LASHANDA (African American) Combined form of La and Shanda. *Variation:* Lashanta.

LASHANIA (African American) Combined form of La and Shania.

LASHANNA (African American) Combined form of La and Shanna. *Variation:* Lashana.

LASHANNON (African American) Combined form of La and Shannon.

LASHARON (African American) Combined form of La and Sharon.

LASHAUN (African American) Combined form of La and Shaun. *Variations:* Lashauna, Lashaunda, Lashaunia, Lashaunta, Lashawna, Lashawnda.

LASHEA (African American) Combined form of La and Shea. *Variations:* Lashae, Lashay.

LASHEBA (African American) Newly created.

LASHELL (African American) Combined form of La and Michelle. *Variation:* Lashelle.

LASHERRI (African American) Combined form of La and Sherri.

LASHONA (African American) Newly created. *Variations:* Lashonda, Lashunda, Lashundra.

LASONIA (African American) Combined form of La and Sonia. *Variation:* Lasonya.

LASSIE (English) Young girl.

LASTARR (African American) Combined form of La and Starr.

LATA (Hindi) Vine.

LATANIA (African American) Combined form of La and Tania. *Variations:* Latanya, Latonia, Latonya.

LATARA (African American) Combined form of La and Tara. *Variation:* Latarra.

LATASHA (African American) Combined form of La and Natasha. *Variations:* Latashia, Lateisha, Latesha, Latosha, Latoshia.

LATAVIA (Arabic) Pleasant.

LATAVIS (African American) Combined form of La and Tavis.

LATENNA (African American) Combined form of La and Teena.

LATIFAH (Arabic) Kind. *Notable:* Actress/singer Queen Latifah. *Variations:* Lateefa, Lateefah, Latifa.

LATIKA (Hindi) Small vine. *Variations:* Latikah, Latyka.

LATISHA (African American) Combined form of La and Tisha. *Variations:* Laeticia, Laetitia, Laticia.

LATIVIA (Latin) Eighth.

LATONA (Latin) Powerful goddess. *Variation:* Latonna.

LATORA (African American) Combined form of La and Tori. *Variations:* Latoree, Latori, Latoria, Latorie.

LATOYA (Spanish) Victorious. *Notable:* Singer LaToya Jackson. *Variations:* Latoia, Latoyia, Latoyla.

LATRICE (African American) Combined form of La and Patrice. *Variations:* Latricia, Latrisha.

LATRINA (African American) Combined form of La and Trina.

LAUDINE (French) Praiseworthy.

LAUDOMIA (Italian) Praise the house. *Variation:* Laudonia.

LAUFEIA (Scandinavian) Leafy island. *Variation:* Laufey.

LAULANI (Hawaiian) Heavenly branch. *Variations:* Laulanea, Laulanee, Laulaney, Laulania.

LAURA (Latin) Laurel. *Notables:* Media psychologist Dr. Laura Schlessinger; actresses Laura Linney and Laura Dern. *Variations:* Larette, Laure, Laureana, Laurena, Lauret, Laureta, Lauretta, Laurette, Lora, Loret, Loreta, Loretta, Lorette, Lorin, Lorita.

LAUREL (Latin) Laurel tree. *Variations:* Laural, Laurell, Laurelle, Lorel, Lorrell, Lorella, Lorelle.

LAUREN (English) Feminine form of Laurence. *Notables:* Actress Lauren Bacall; model Lauren Hutton. *Variations:* Laurin, Lauryn, Loren, Lorena, Lorrin, Loryn.

LAURENTINE (French) From Laurentum. *Variation:* Laurent.

LAURIE (English) Form of Lauren and Laura. *Notable:* Singer Laurie Anderson. *Variations:* Lauri, Laure, Laury, Lori, Lorie, Lorrie, Lorry, Lory.

LAVANNA (African American) Combined form of La and Vanna. *Variations:* Lavana, Lavann, Lavanna, Lavanne, Lavon, Lavona, Lavonna.

LAVEDA (Latin) Pure. *Variation:* Lavetta.

LAVELLE (French) Purity. *Variations:* Lavel, Lavela, Lavell, Lavella.

LAVENDER (English) Lavender flower. *Variation:* Lavenda.

LAVERNE (French) Springlike. *Notable:* Laverne DeFazio, character on classic TV show *Laverne and Shirley*. *Variations:* La Verne, Lavern, Laverna, Lavyrn, Lavyrne, Verna.

LAVETTA (African American) Combined form of La and Yvette.

LAVI (Hebrew) Lion.

LAVINIA (Latin) Roman woman. *Variations:* Lavena, Lavenia, Lavina, Laviner, Lavinie, Levina, Levinia, Livinia, Lovina.

LAVONNE (African American) Combined form of La and Yvonne. *Variations:* La Vonne, Lavon, Lavonna.

LAWANDA (African American) Combined form of La and Wanda.

LAYLA (Hebrew; Arabic) Night. *Variations:* Laela, Laila, Lala, Leila.

LE (Vietnamese) A pear.

LEAH (Hebrew) Weary. *Notables:* Actress Leah Remini; *Star Wars* Princess Leia. *Variations:* Lea, Leia, Leigha, Lia, Liah.

LEALA (French) Loyal. *Variations:* Lealia, Lealie, Leola.

LEALIKI (Polynesian) Waves.

LEANDRA (English) Lioness. *Variations:* Leanda, Leodora, Leoine, Leoline, Leona, Leonanie, Leonelle, Leonette, Leonice, Leonissa.

LEANNA (English) Flowering vine. *Notable:* Singer LeAnn Rimes. *Variations:* Leana, Leane, Leann, Leanne, Lee Ann, Lee Anne, Leeann, Leeanne, Leianna, Leigh Ann, Leighann, Leighanne, Liana, Liane, Lianna, Lianne, Lyana, Lyane, Lyanna, Lyanne.

LEANORE (Scottish) Light from the meadow. *Variations:* Leanora, Leanorah, Lanore, Lanoree, Lanorey, Lanori, Lanoria, Lanorie, Lanory.

LEBA (Hebrew) Loved. *Variation:* Liba.

LECIA (Latin) Short for Alicia, Felicia, or Letitia. *Variations:* Lecy, Lisha, Lishia.

LECIE (French) Happy. *Variations:* Lece, Lecee, Lecey, Leci, Lecie, Lecy.

LEDA (Greek) Woman. *Variations:* Ledell, Leida, Lida.

LEE (English) Meadow. *Notables:* Actresses Lee Grant and Lee Remick. *Variations:* Lea, Leigh.

LEEBA (Hebrew) Heart. *Variation:* Liba.

LEENA (Hindi) Devoted.

LEFNA (Estonian) Light.

LEHUA (Hawaiian) Sacred.

LEI (Chinese) Openhearted. Upright. Honest.

LEIKO (Japanese) Proud. *Variations:* Leako, Leeko, Leyko.

LEILA (Arabic) Night. *Variations:* Laila, Layla, Leela, Leelah, Leilah, Leilia, Lela, Lelah, Lelia, Leyla, Lila, Lilah.

LEILANI (Hawaiian) Heavenly child. *Variations:* Lealanea, Lealanee, Lealaney, Lealani, Lealania, Lealanie, Lealany, Leelanea, Leelanee, Leelaney, Leelani, Leelania, Leelanie, Leelany, Leilanea, Leilanee, Leilaney, Leilani, Leilania, Leilanie, Leilany, Leighlanea, Leighlanee, Leighlaney, Leighlani, Leighlania, Leighlanie, Leighlany, Lelanea, Lelanee, Lelaney, Lelani, Lelanie, Lelany, Leylanea, Leylanee, Leylaney, Leylani, Leylania, Leylany.

LEILI (Hebrew) Night. *Variations:* Laili, Lailie, Laylie, Leilie.

LEINANI (Hawaiian) Beautiful wreath.

LEIRE (Hebrew) Biter. *Variations:* Leyra, Liera.

LEISI (Polynesian) Lace. *Variations:* Leasi, Leesi, Leysi.

LEKASHA (African) Life. *Variation:* Lekashia.

LELIA (Greek) Well spoken. *Variations:* Leli, Leliah, Lellia.

LEMUELA (Hebrew) Devoted to God. Feminine version of Lemuel. *Variation:* Lemuella.

LENA (English) Bright one. Variation of Helen. *Notables:* Singer Lena Horne; actress Lena Olin. *Variations:* Leena, Lenah, Lene, Leni, Lenia, Lina, Linah, Line.

LENIS (Latin) Smooth, silky. *Variations:* Lenice, Lenise, Lennice. Lennis.

LENKA (Czech) Light.

LENNA (German) The strength of a lion. *Variations:* Lenda, Lennah.

LENORE (Greek) Light. Form of Eleanor. *Variations:* Lenora, Lenoria.

LEOCADIA (Spanish) Bright and clear.

LEODA (German) Of the people. *Variation:* Leota.

LEOLANI (Hawaiian) Tall.

LEONA (Latin) Lion. Feminine version of Leon. *Notable:* Hotel owner Leona Helmsley. *Variations:* Leonia, Leonie, Leonine, Leonissa, Leontyne, Liona.

LEONANI (Hawaiian) Beautiful voice.

LEONARDA (German) Brave lion. *Variations:* Lenda, Leonarde.

LEONIE (French) Lioness. *Variations:* Leona, Leonda, Leondra, Leondrea, Leone, Leonela, Leonne.

LEONORA (English) Bright one. Variation of Helen. *Variations:* Leanor, Leanora, Lenor, Lenora, Lenorah, Lenore, Leonara, Leonore.

LEONTYNE (German) Lioness. *Notable:* Opera singer Leontyne Price. *Variations:* Leonine, Leontine.

LEOPOLDINE (German) Brave people. Feminine version of Leopold. *Variations:* Leopolda, Leopoldina.

LEORA (Greek) Light. *Variations:* Leorah, Leorit, Lior, Liora, Liorah, Liorit.

LEOTIE (Native American) Prairie flower.

LEPEKA (Hawaiian) To bind.

LESLIE (Scottish) Grey castle. *Notables:* Actresses Leslie Caron and Lesley Ann Warren. *Variations:*

Leslea, Leslee, Leslei, Lesleigh, Lesley, Lesli, Lesly, Lezlea, Lezlee, Lezlei, Lezleigh, Lezley, Lezli, Lezlie.

LETA (Latin) Happy. *Variations:* Leata, Leeta, Leita, Leyta, Lida, Lita, Lyta.

LETICIA (Latin; Spanish) Happiness. *Notable:* Social arbiter Letitia Baldrige. *Variations:* Letecia, Leteisha, Letisha, Letita, Letitia, Lettice.

LETTY (English) Short form of Letitia. *Variations:* Letti, Lettie.

LEVANA (Hebrew) White moon. *Variations:* Levanna, Lewana, Livana.

LEVINA (Latin) Streak of lightning. *Variation:* Levinna.

LEVITY (Latin) Lighthearted.

LEVONA (Hebrew) Frankincense. *Variations:* Leavona, Leavonia, Leevona, Levonat.

LEWANA (Hebrew) The moon. *Variations:* Lewanna, Liva.

LEXA (English) Protector of man. Short form of Alexandra or Alexis. *Variations:* Lexi, Lexia, Lexie, Lexina, Lexine, Lexy.

LEYA (Spanish) The law.

LI (Chinese) Pretty.

LIADAN (Gaelic) Grey lady. *Variation:* Liadain.

LIAN (Chinese) Graceful tree.

LIANA (French) Twist like a vine. *Variations:* Li, Lia, Lian, Liane, Liann, Lianna, Lianne.

LIAT (Hebrew) You are mine.

LIBBY (English) Short form of Elizabeth. *Variations:* Libbea, Libbee, Libbey, Libbi, Libbie.

LIBENA (Czech) Love. *Variations:* Liba, Libenka, Libuse, Libuska, Luba.

LIBERTY (English) Freedom.

LIDA (Greek) Woman.

LIDIA (Greek) Form of Lydia. *Variations:* Lidea, Lidiya, Lidya.

LIDDY (English) Nickname for Lydia. *Variations:* Liddi, Liddie.

LIDWINA (Scandinavian) Friend of the people.

LIEN (Chinese) Lotus. *Variation:* Lien Hua.

LIESL (German) Nickname for Elizabeth. *Variations:* Leizl, Liesa, Liese, Liesel, Liezel, Lisel, Lisl, Lisle.

LIGIA (Greek) Musical. *Variations:* Liguria, Lygia.

LIHUA (Chinese) Elegant and beautiful.

LIL (American) Short form of Lily or Lillian.

LILA (Hindi) Dance of God. *Variations:* Lilah, Lilia, Lyla.

LILAC (English) Flower name.

LILIA (Hawaiian) Lily flower.

LILAVATI (Hindi) Free will.

LILIA (Hawaiian) Lilies.

LILIBETH (English) Combined form of Lily and Elizabeth. *Variations:* Lilibet, Lilibeta, Lillibet, Lillibeta, Lillibete, Lillibeth, Lillybet, Lillybeta, Lillybeth, Lillybett, Lillybetta, Lillybette, Lilybet, Lilybeta, Lilybeth, Lilybett, Lilybetta, Lilybette, Lylibet, Lylibeta, Lylibete, Lyllibet, Lyllibetta, Lyllibette, Lyllibeth, Lyllybet, Lyllybeta, Lyllybeth, Lyllybetta, Lyllybette, Lylybeth, Lylybet, Lylybeta, Lylybeth, Lylybett, Lylybetta, Lylybette, Lylybeth.

Backward and Forward

These palindrome names are spelled the same forward and backward.

BOYS:	GIRLS:
Abba	Anna
Aja	Ava
Asa	Aviva
Bob	Emme
Gig	Eve
Iggi	Elle
Laval	Hannah
Pip	Lil
	Nan
	Viv

What Were They Thinking? Offbeat Names

While celebrities are often trend-setters, sometimes they really do push the envelope with news-worthy baby names like Zuma Nesta Rock (son of Gwen Stefani), Ever Imre (son of Alanis Morissette), and Bronx Mowgli (son of Ashlee Simpson and Pete Wentz). These make Pussy Galore seem quite old-fashioned. Even Ellen Degeneres once remarked, "I'm planning on naming my child Formica."

LILIHA (Hawaiian) Loathing.

LILITH (Arabic) Of the night. *Variations:* Lillis, Lillith, Lylyth.

LILLIAN (English) Flower. Combination of Lily and Ann. *Notable:* Writer Lillian Hellman. *Variations:* Lileana, Lilian, Liliana, Liliane, Lilias, Lilika, Lillia, Lilliana, Lillianne, Lillyan, Lillyanna, Lilyan, Lylian, Lyliana, Lyliane, Lyliann, Lylianna, Lylianne.

LILO (Hawaiian) Generous.

LILY (Latin) Flower name. *Variations:* Lilea, Lilee, Lileigh, Liley, Lili, Lilia, Lilie, Lillea, Lillee, Lilleigh, Lilley, Lilli, Lillie, Lilly, Lillye, Lilye, Lylea, Lylee, Lyleigh, Lyli, Lylie, Lyllee, Lyllie.

LIN (Chinese) Jade stone.

LINA (Greek) Light. *Variations:* Lena, Linah.

LINDA (Spanish) Pretty one. *Notables:* Singer Linda Ronstadt; actress Lynda Carter. *Variations:* Lin, Linday, Linde, Lindee, Lindi, Lindie, Lindy, Linn, Lyn, Lynada, Lynadie, Lynda, Lynde, Lyndy, Lynn, Lynnda.

LINDEL (English) Valley pool. *Variations:* Lindal, Lindall, Lyndal, Lyndall, Lyndel.

LINDEN (English) Tree name. *Variations:* Lindan, Lindin, Lindon, Lyndan, Lynden, Lyndin, Lyndon, Lyndyn.

LINDSAY (English) Island of linden trees. *Notables:* Actresses Lindsay Lohan and Lindsay Wagner. *Variations:* Lindsaye, Lindsey, Lindsi, Lindsie, Lindsy, Linsay, Linsey, Linzey, Lyndsay, Lyndsey, Lynsay, Lynsey.

LINDY (English) Linden tree. *Variations:* Lindea, Lindee, Lindi, Lindie, Lyndee, Lyndi, Lyndie, Lyndy.

LINETTE (Welsh) Idol. *Variations:* Lanette, Linet, Lineta, Linetta, Linnet, Linnetta, Linnette, Lynetta, Lynette, Lynnet, Lynnette.

LING (Chinese) Delicate.

LINLEY (English) Pool in the meadow. *Variations:* Linlea, Linlee, Linlei, Linleigh, Linli, Linlia, Linly, Lynlea, Lynlee, Lynlei, Lynleigh, Lynley, Lynli, Lynlia, Lynlie, Lynly.

LINNEA (Scandinavian) Lime tree. *Variations:* Lenae, Linae, Linea, Linia, Linnea, Linnia, Lynea, Lynnea, Lynnia.

LIOLYA (Russian) Shining light. *Variations:* Lenushka, Lenusya, Liolia, Lyolya.

LIONA (Hawaiian) Roaring lion. *Variations:* Lionah, Lione, Lionee, Lioney, Lioni, Lionia, Lionie, Liony, Lyona, Lyone, Lyonee, Lyoney, Lyoni, Lyonia, Lyonie, Lyony, Lona.

LIONETTA (Latin) Little lioness. *Variations:* Lionet, Lioneta, Lionett, Lionette, Lyonet, Lyoneta, Lyonett, Lyonetta, Lyonette.

LIORA (Hebrew) Light. *Variations:* Leora, Lior, Lyora.

LIRIENE (French) Reads aloud. *Variations:* Liriena, Lirienne.

LIRIT (Hebrew) Lyrical.

LIRON (Hebrew) This song is mine. *Variations:* Lirona, Lironah, Lirone, Lyron, Lyrona, Lyronah, Lyrone.

LISA (English) Pledged by oath to God. Version of Elizabeth. *Notable:* Actress Lisa Kudrow. *Variations:* Leesa, Leeza, Leisa, Liesa, Liese, Lisanne, Lise, Liseta, Lisetta, Lisette, Lissa, Lissette, Liza, Lizana, Lizanne, Lizette.

LISANDRA (Greek) Liberator. *Variations:* Lissandra, Lizandra, Lizann, Lizanne, Lysandra.

LISBETH (Hebrew) Form of Elizabeth. *Variations:* Lisbet, Lizbet, Lizbeth.

LISELI (African) Light. *Variation:* Liceli.

LISETTE (French) Short form of Elizabeth. *Variations:* Lisett, Lissette, Lysette.

LISHA (Arabic) Darkness before midnight. *Variations:* Lishe, Lysha.

LISSA (Greek) Bee. Short form of Melissa. *Variation:* Lyssa.

LITA (Spanish) Strong woman. *Variations:* Leata, Leatah, Leeta, Leetah, Leita, Leitah, Leighta, Leta, Letah, Leyta, Leytah, Litah, Lyta, Lytah.

LIU (Chinese) Willow.

LIUBOV (Russian) Love.

LIV (Scandinavian) Life. *Notables:* Actresses Liv Tyler and Liv Ullmann.

LIVIA (Latin) Form of Olivia. *Variations:* Liviya, Livya.

LIVONA (Hebrew) Spice. *Variations:* Livia, Liviya.

LIZ (English) Short form of Elizabeth. *Variations:* Lizz, Lizzi, Lizzie, Lizzy, Lyz, Lyzz, Lyzzi, Lyzzie.

LIZA (English) Short form of Elizabeth. *Notable:* Singer Liza Minnelli. *Variation:* Lyza.

LIZBETH (English) Short form of Elizabeth. *Variations:* Lizabet, Lizabette, Lyzbet, Lyzbeth.

LIZENA (Latvian) Form of Elizabeth. *Variations:* Lixena, Lixyna, Lizine, Lyzina.

LIZETTE (American) Short form of Elizabeth.

LLAWELLA (Welsh) Lioness. *Variation:* Lawella.

LOANA (French) Good light. *Variations:* Loanne, Loanne.

LOCKETTE (French) Necklace. *Variations:* Locket, Locketa, Lockett, Locketta.

LODEMA (English) Guide.

LOGAN (Scottish) Hollow. *Variations:* Logana, Logann, Loghan.

LUIGHSEACH (Irish) Torch bringer.

LOIDA (Spanish) Agreeable.

LOIRE (French) River and valley in France.

LOIS (English) Famous soldier. Feminine version of Louis. *Notable:* Superman's love Lois Lane. *Variations:* Loiss, Loissa, Loisse, Lowis.

LOKALIA (Hawaiian) Garland of roses.

LOKAPELA (Hawaiian) Beautiful rose.

LOKE (Hawaiian) Rose. *Variations:* Loka, Lokelani.

LOKEMELE (Hawaiian) Rose from the sea.

LOLA (Spanish) Sorrow. Nickname for Dolores.

LOLITA (Spanish) Small sorrows. *Variations:* Loleata, Loleeta, Loleta, Loletta, Lolieta, Lolyta.

LOLLY (English) Lollipop. *Variations:* Lolli, Lollie.

LONA (Latin) Alone. *Variation:* Lonia.

LONI (English) Ready for battle. Feminine version of Lonnie. *Notable:* Actress Loni Anderson. *Variations:* Lona, Lonee, Lonie, Lonna, Lonni, Lonnie.

LOPEKA (Hawaiian) Bright fame.

LORA (Latin) Alternative for Laura. Laurel. *Variations:* Lorah, Lorra.

LORDYN (American) Combined form of Lori and Jordyn. *Variations:* Lordin, Lordine, Lordyne.

LOREDANA (Italian) Laurel wood.

LORELEI (German) A rocky cliff on the Rhine River. *Variations:* Loralee, Loralie, Loralyn, Lorilee, Lura, Lurette, Lurleen, Lurlene, Lurline.

LORELLE (American) Form of Laurel. *Variations:* Laurelle, Lorella.

LORENA (English) Form of Lauren. *Variations:* Loreen, Loreena, Lorine, Lorina.

LORENZA (Italian) Feminine form of Lorenzo.

LORETTA (English) Laurel. *Notable:* Country singer Loretta Lynn. *Variations:* Laretta, Lauretta, Loreta, Loreto.

LORI (English) Variation of Laurie. *Notable:* Actress Lori Loughlin. *Variation:* Lorie.

LORINDA (Spanish) Form of Linda. *Variations:* Larinda, Larenda, Lorenda.

LORNA (Scottish) Area in Scotland. *Notables:* Singer Lorna Luft; literary character Lorna Doone. *Variation:* Lorrna.

LORRAINE (French) From Lorraine, an area in France. *Notables:* Actress Lorraine Bracco; comedian Laraine Newman. *Variations:* Laraine, Lauraine, Laurraine, Lorain, Loraine, Lorayne, Lorine, Lorrayne.

LOSA (Polynesian) Rose. *Variations:* Losana, Lose.

LOSAKI (Polynesian) To meet.

LOTTA (Scandinavian) Woman. *Variation:* Lotte.

LOTTIE (German) Short form of Charlotte. *Variations:* Lotie, Lotte, Lottey, Lotti, Lotty.

LOTUS (Greek) Lotus flower.

LOU (English) Short form of Louise.

LOUISE (French) Warrior. Feminine form of Louis. *Notable:* Writer Louise Erdrich. *Variations:* Louisa, Louisette, Louisiane, Luisa, Luise.

LOURDES (French) From Lourdes, France.

LOUVAINE (French) Fierce. *Variations:* Louvain, Louvaina, Luvaina, Luvaine.

LOVE (English) Love. *Variations:* Lovey, Lovi, Lovie.

LUANN (English) Combination of Lou and Ann. *Variations:* Louann, Louanne, Luana, Luanna, Luanne.

LUBA (Russian) Love. *Variations:* Lubna, Lubov, Lyuba.

LUBOMIRA (Slavic) Peace loving.

LUBORNIRA (Czech) Great love. *Variations:* Luba, Lubena, Lubina, Lubinka, Lubka, Luboska.

LUCA (Italian) Feminine version of Lucas.

LUCASTA (Latin) From Lucania, feminine form of Lucas; (English) Name from English poem.

LUCERNE (Latin) Lamp. *Variation:* Lucerna.

LUCETTE (French) Light.

LUCIA (Italian) Form of Lucille. *Variation:* Luciana.

LUCIENNE (French) Light. *Variation:* Lucianne.

LUCILLE (French) Light. *Notable:* Comedy legend Lucille Ball. *Variations:* Loucille, Lucilla.

LUCINDA (Latin) Beautiful light. *Notable:* Singer Lucinda Williams. *Variation:* Loucinda.

LUCITA (Spanish) Light.

LUCKY (English) Fortunate. *Variations:* Luckie, Luckye.

LUCRETIA (Latin) Roman clan name. *Notable:* Lucrezia Borgia, Duchess of Ferrara. *Variations:* Lacrecia, Lacretia, Lucrece, Lucrecia, Lucreecia, Lucrezia.

LUCY (English) Light. Short form of Lucille. Feminine version of Lucius. *Notables:* Actresses Lucy Liu and Lucy Lawless. *Variations:* Lucetta, Lucette, Lucia, Luciana, Lucie, Lucienne, Lucilla, Lucille, Lucina, Lucinda, Lucita.

LUDELLA (English) Renowned. *Variations:* Ludela, Ludelle.

LUDIVINA (Slavic) Greatly loved.

LUDMILA (Czech) Loving people. *Variations:* Lidka, Lidmila, Lidunka, Liduse, Liduska, Ludmilla, Luduna, Lyudmila.

LUDOVICA (Scandinavian) Famous in war.

LUELLA (English) Combined form of first names "Lou" and "Ella." *Variations:* Louelle, Louella, Luelle.

LUIGINA (Italian) Famous warrior.

LUISA (Spanish) Form of Louisa. *Variations:* Luisella, Luisina.

LUITGARD (German) Protector of people. *Variations:* Lutgard, Lutgardis.

LULANI (Hawaiian) Heaven's peak.

LULU (German) Short form of Louise. *Notable:* British singer Lulu. *Variation:* LouLou.

LULUBELLE (American) Combined form of Lulu and Belle.

LUMEN (Latin) Illuminated. *Variation:* Lumina.

LUNA (Latin) Roman moon goddess. *Variations:* Lunetta, Lunette, Lunneta.

LUNED (Welsh) Idol worshipper.

LUPE (Spanish) Short form of Guadalupe. *Variations:* Lupi, Lupita.

LURA (English) Laurel.

LURLEEN (German) Temptress. *Variations:* Lura, Lurette, Lurlene, Lurlie, Lurline.

LUSELA (Native American) Bear foot.

LUTE (Polynesian) Friend.

LUZ (Spanish) Light. *Variation:* Lux.

LYDIA (Greek) Woman from Lydia, a region in ancient Greece. *Variations:* Lidi, Lidia, Lidie, Lidka, Likochka, Lydiah, Lydie.

LYNETTE (French) Form of Linette.

LYNN (English) Pretty. Diminutive of Linda; (Welsh) Lake. *Notable:* Actress Lynn Redgrave. *Variations:* Lin, Lina, Linell, Linelle, Linn, Linne, Lyn, Lyndall, Lyndel, Lyndell, Lyndelle, Lynelie, Lynell, Lynna, Lynne, Lynnelle.

LYNTON (English) Lime tree.

LYRA (Greek) Lyre player. *Variations:* Lyre, Lyrea, Lyria.

LYRIC (Greek) Songlike.

LYRIS (Greek) Lyre, a small harp. *Variation:* Lyra.

LYSANDRA (Greek) Variation of Alexandra. *Variations:* Lysana, Lysanne.

LYSISTRATA (Greek) Loosen the army.

MAATA (Polynesian) Lady.

MAB (Irish) Joy. *Notable:* Queen Mab, the legendary Irish fairy queen.

MABEL (English) Lovable. *Variations:* Mabelle, Mable, Maybel, Maybell, Maybelle.

MABYN (Welsh) Youthful. *Variations:* Maban, Maben.

MACARIA (Spanish) Blessed. *Variations:* Macarea, Macarena, Macarie.

MACHALATH (Hebrew) Stringed instrument.

MACHIKO (Japanese) Truthful child. *Variation:* Machi.

MACIA (Polish) Defiant.

MACKENNA (Irish) Child of the handsome one. *Variations:* Mackena, Mackenah, Makena, Makenah, Makenna, Makennah, Mckenna, Mikena, Mikenah, Mikenna, Mikennah, Mykena, Mykenah, Mykennah.

MACKENZIE (Irish) Child of a handsome leader. *Notable:* Actress Mackenzie Phillips. *Variations:* Mac, MacKenzie, Mackenze, Mackenzi, Makensi, Makenzi, Makenzie, McKenzie, Mckenzie.

MACY (French) Weapon. *Notable:* Singer Macy Gray. *Variations:* Macey, Maci, Macie, Masey.

MADDIE (American; English) Short form of Madeline or Madison. *Variations:* Maddee, Maddey, Maddi, Maddy, Madee, Madi.

MADEIRA (Portuguese) From the island of Madeira. *Variation:* Madeera.

MADELINE (French) From Magdalen. *Notables:* Actress Madeline Kahn; U.S. Secretary of State Madeleine Albright. *Variations:* Mada, Madalaina, Madalena, Madalyn, Maddalena, Madelaine, Madelayne, Madeleine, Madelena, Madelene, Madelina, Madelyn, Madilin, Madileine, Madiline, Madilyn, Madolyn, Madge, Magda.

MADGE (Greek) Short form of Margaret or Madeline. *Variation:* Madgie.

MADHAVI (Hindi) Spring.

MADHU (Hindi) Honey.

MADHUR (Hindi) Gentle and kind.

MADIA (Arabic) To praise. *Variations:* Madiha, Madihah.

MADISON (English) Child of a warrior. *Variations:* Maddison, Madisen, Madisson, Madyson.

MADOKA (Japanese) Circle.

MADONNA (Latin) My lady. *Notable:* Singer Madonna.

MADRA (Spanish) Mother. *Variation:* Madrona.

MAE (English) Variation of May. *Notable:* Actress Mae West.

MAEIKO (Japanese) Honest child. *Variation:* Maeko.

MAEMI (Japanese) Honest smile.

MAEVE (Irish) Intoxicating. *Notable:* Writer Maeve Binchy. *Variations:* Maive, Mave, Mayve.

MAFALDA (Italian) Mighty in battle.

MAGALI (French) Pearl. *Variation:* Magalie.

MAGARA (African) To sit.

MAGDA (Russian; Slavic) Form of Magdalen.

MAGDALEN (Greek) From Magdala, area in the Middle East. *Variations:* Magdala, Magdaleen, Magdalena, Magdalene, Magdaline, Magdalyn, Magdelen.

MAGENA (Native American) New moon.

MAGGIE (English) Short for Magdalen or Margaret. *Notables:* Actresses Maggie Smith and Maggie Gyllenhaal. *Variations:* Magee, Magi, Maggi, Maggy.

MAGNILDA (German) Successful in battle. *Variation:* Magnhilda.

MAGNOLIA (Latin) Flowering tree.

MAHA (Arabic) Big eyes.

MAHALA (Hebrew) Tenderness. *Notable:* Singer Mahalia Jackson. *Variations:* Mahalah, Mahalia, Mahaliah, Mahalla, Mahelia, Mehalia.

MAHASKA (Native American) White cloud.

MAHEESA (Hindi) The Hindi god Siva. *Variations:* Mahesa, Mahisa.

MAHEONA (Native American) Medicine woman.

MAHI (Hindi) Earth. *Variation:* Mahika.

MAHIMA (Hindi) Eminence.

MAHINA (Hawaiian) Moonlight.

MAHIRA (Hebrew) Quick. *Variation:* Mahera.

MAHWAH (Native American) Beautiful.

MAHOGANY (Spanish) Rich. Strong.

MAI (Japanese) Dance.

MAIA (Greek) Mother. *Variations:* Maya, Maiya, Mya.

MAIDA (English) Maiden. *Variations:* Maidie, Mayda.

Top Names in Russia

BOYS:
1. Alexander
2. Maksim
3. Artyom
4. Ivan
5. Dmitry
6. Mikhail
7. Nikita
8. Daniil
9. Yegor
10. Kirill

GIRLS:
1. Mariya
2. Anastasiya
3. Darja
4. Anna
5. Yelizaveta
6. Polina
7. Yekaterina
8. Viktoria
9. Sofja
10. Sofiya

MAIKAI (Hawaiian) Good.

MAIKO (Japanese) Dancing child.

MAILI (Polynesian) Breeze.

MAIMI (Hindi) Gold.

MAIRA (Hawaiian) Myrrh. *Variation:* Maila.

MAIRE (Irish) Form of Mary. *Variations:* Mair, Maira, Mairin, Mare.

MAIREAD (Irish) Pearl.

MAIRIN (Irish) Rebellious. *Variation:* Mairenn.

MAISIE (Scottish) Pearl. Short form of Margaret. *Variations:* Maisee, Maisey, Maisi, Maisy, Maizie, Maysee, Maysey, Maysi, Maysie, Maysy.

MAITLAND (English) From the meadow.

MAIZA (Arabic) Discerning.

MAJ (Scandinavian) Pearl. *Variations:* Mai, Maia, Maja.

MAJESTA (Latin) Majesty.

MAJIDAH (Arabic) Magnificent. *Variation:* Majida.

MAKA (Native American) Earth.

MAKADISA (African) Selfish.

MAKALA (Hawaiian) Myrtle Tree. *Variations:* Makaeli, Makailea, Makaileah, Makailee, Makailei, Makaileigh, Makailey, Makaili, Makalia, Makaliah, Makalie, Makaily, Makalah, Makalea, Makaleah, Makalee, Makalei, Makaleigh, Makaley, Makali, Makalia, Makaliah, Makalie, Makaly, Makaylea, Makayleah, Makaylee, Makaylei, Makayleigh, Makayley, Makayli, Makaylia, Makaylie, Makayly.

MAKALEKA (Hawaiian) Pearl. *Variations:* Makalika, Makelesi.

MAKANA (Hawaiian) Gift.

MAKANI (Hawaiian) The wind.

MAKAWEE (Native American) Abundant. *Variation:* Macawi.

MAKAYLA (American) Form of Michaela.

MAKEDA (Hebrew) Bowl.

MALA (Hawaiian) Garden.

MALAK (Arabic; Hebrew) Angel.

MALALANI (Hawaiian) Holy garden.

MALAMA (Polynesian) Shine.

MALAMHIN (Scottish) Smooth brow.

MALANA (Hawaiian) Cheerful.

MALATI (Hindi) Jasmine.

MALI (Thai) Flower.

MALIA (Hawaiian) Defiance. *Variation:* Mali.

MALIAKA (Hawaiian) Hawaiian version of Marietta. *Variations:* Mariata, Meliaka.

MALIE (Polynesian) Lucky.

MALIKA (Arabic) Destined to be queen. *Variations:* Maleeka, Malieka.

MALINA (Hawaiian) Peaceful.

MALINKA (Russian) Small sweet berry. *Variations:* Maleenka.

MALKAH (Hebrew) Queen. *Variations:* Malcah, Malka, Malkia, Malkiah, Malkie, Malkit, Malkiya.

MALKIN (German) Battle maiden.

MALLORY (French) Unfortunate. *Notable:* Mallory Keaton, character on TV's *Family Ties. Variations:* Malloree, Malloreigh, Mallorey, Mallorie, Malorey, Malori, Malorie, Malory.

MALU (Hawaiian) Peace. *Variations:* Maloo, Malou.

MALUHI (Hawaiian) Peaceful.

MALULANI (Hawaiian) Guarded by angels.

MALVA (English) Form of Melba. *Variations:* Malvah, Melva.

MALVINA (Scottish) Feminine form of Melvin. *Variations:* Malveen, Malveena, Malveenah, Malvi, Malvijnah, Malvinda, Malvindah, Malvine, Malwine.

MALVOLIA (Italian) Ill will.

MAMIE (English) Form of Margaret. *Notables:* U.S. First Lady Mamie Eisenhower; actress Mamie Van Doren. *Variations:* Mame, Mamee, Maymee.

MAMIKO (Japanese) Daughter of the sea.

MAMO (Hawaiian) Yellow bird.

MAMTA (Hindi) Tenderness. *Variation:* Mamata.

MANA (Hawaiian) Supernatural power.

MANAL (Arabic) Accomplished.

MANALANI (Hawaiian) Heavenly power.

MANALI (Hawaiian) Powerful queen.

MANAOLANA (Hawaiian) Confidence.

MANAR (Arabic) Beacon.

MANASA (Hindi) Great strength of mind. *Variation:* Manassa.

MANAWALEA (Hawaiian) Generous.

MANDA (Latin) Short form of Amanda.

MANDANA (Persian) Everlasting beauty. *Variation:* Mandanna.

MANDARA (Hindi) Tree.

MANDISA (African) Sweet woman. *Variation:* Manidisa.

MANDRAYA (Sanskrit) An honorable woman.

MANDY (English) Lovable. Short form of Amanda. *Notable:* Singer Mandy Moore. *Variations:* Mandee, Mandey, Mandi, Mandie.

MANETTE (French) Defiant.

MANGENA (Hebrew) Song. *Variation:* Mangina.

MANI (Chinese) Buddhist prayer.

MANIKA (Hindi) Jewel of a mind.

MANISHA (Sanskrit) Intelligence. *Variation:* Maneesha.

MANJIKA (Hindi) Sweet sounds.

MANJULIKA (Hindi) Sweet. *Variation:* Manjula.

MANOLA (Spanish) God is with us. *Variation:* Manolita.

MANON (French) Bitterness. Form of Marie.

MANOUSH (Persian) Born under the sun.

MANSI (Native American) Picked flower. *Variations:* Mancey, Manci, Mancie, Mancy, Mansey, Mansie, Mansy.

MANTRANA (Sanskrit) Of counsel to others.

MANUELA (Spanish) God is among us. Feminine version of Emanuel. *Variation:* Manuelita.

MANULANI (Hawaiian) Like a bird in heaven.

MANYA (Russian) Wished for.

MAPIYA (Native American) Heaven. *Variation:* Mapiyah.

MARA (Hebrew) Bitter. *Variation:* Marah.

MARABEL (English) Beautiful sea. *Variations:* Marabela, Marabele, Marabell, Marabella, Marabelle, Marable, Marbella, Maribel, Maribela, Maribele, Maribell, Maribella, Maribelle, Marybel, Marybela, Marybelah, Marybele, Marybell, Marybella, Marybelle.

MARAEA (Hawaiian) Sea woman. *Variations:* Malaea, Malia, Mele, Mere.

MARATA (Hawaiian) Woman. *Variations:* Malaka, Maleka, Mareka.

MARATINA (Hawaiian) Warlike. *Variation:* Malakina.

MARCARIA (Greek) Happy. *Variation:* Marcariah.

MARCELLA (Latin) Warlike. *Variations:* Marcela, Marcelle.

MARCENA (Latin) Warrior. A feminine form of Mark. *Variations:* Marceena, Marceene, Marcenah, Marcene, Marciana, Marseena, Marseene.

MARCH (Latin) Born in March. *Variation:* Marche.

MARCIA (Latin) Warlike. Feminine version of Mark. *Notable:* Actress Marcia Cross. *Variations:* Marce, Marcee, Marcela, Marcelia, Marcella, Marcelle, Marcena, Marcene, Marcey, Marci, Marcie, Marcina, Marcy, Marsha.

MARCY (English) Short form of Marcia or Marcella. *Variations:* Marcee, Marcey, Marci, Marcie, Marsea, Marsee, Marsie, Marsey, Marsy.

MARDI (French) Tuesday.

MARELDA (German) Famous battle maid. *Variation:* Marilda.

MARELLA (English) Combination of Mary and Elle. *Variation:* Marelle.

MAREN (Latin) Sea. *Variations:* Marin, Marren, Marrin.

MARETTA (English) Defiant. *Variation:* Marette.

MARGANIT (Hebrew) Flower of Israel. *Variation:* Marganita.

MARGARET (English) Pearl. *Notable:* Former British Prime Minister Margaret Thatcher. *Variations:* Greeta, Greetje, Grere, Gret, Greta, Gretal, Gretchen, Gretel, Grethal, Grethel, Gretje, Gretl, Gretta, Groer, Maggi, Maggie, Maggy, Mair, Maire, Mairi, Mairona, Margara, Margareta, Margarethe, Margarett, Margaretta, Margarette, Margarita, Margarite, Marge, Margeret, Margerey, Margery, Margrett, Marguerette, Marguerite, Marj, Marjorie, Meagan, Meaghan, Meaghen, Meg, Megan, Megen, Meggi, Meggie, Meggy, Meghan, Meghann, Peg, Pegeen, Pegg, Peggey, Peggi, Peggie, Peggy, Reet, Reeta, Reita, Rheeta, Riet, Rieta, Ritta.

MARGARITA (Spanish; Italian) Form of Margaret.

MARGAUX (French) The name of a champagne.

MARGE (English) Short form of Margaret or Marjorie. *Notables:* Actress Marg Helgenberger; TV-cartoon mom Marge Simpson. *Variation:* Marg.

MARGIE (English) Short form of Margaret or Marjorie. *Variations:* Margi, Margy, Marjie, Marjy.

MARGO (French) Form of Margaret. *Notables:* Actresses Margot Kidder and Margaux Hemingway. *Variations:* Margaux, Margot.

MARIA (Latin; Italian; Spanish) Form of Mary. *Notables:* Tennis pro Maria Sharapova; journalist Maria Shriver. *Variations:* Marea, Maree, Marie, Marya.

MARIAH (Hebrew) Star of the sea. *Notable:* Singer Mariah Carey. *Variations:* Mariya, Mariyah, Moriah, Moriya.

MARIAMA (African) Gift from God. *Variations:* Mariame, Mariamma.

MARIAN (French) Combination of first names "Mary" and "Ann." *Notable:* Singer Marian Anderson. *Variations:* Mariana, Mariane, Mariann, Marianna, Marianne, Marion, Marrian, Marrion, Mary Ann, Maryann, Maryanna, Maryon, Maryonn.

MARICARA (Romanian) Bitter. Variation of Miriam. *Variations:* Marice, Marieca, Marise.

MARICELA (Spanish) Sea of heaven. *Variations:* Maricella, Marisela, Marisella.

MARICRUZ (Spanish) Cross of the sea.

MARIE (French) Variation of Mary. *Notables:* Scientist Marie Curie; former queen of France, Marie Antoinette. *Variation:* Maree.

MARIEL (Dutch) Form of Mary. *Notable:* Actress Mariel Hemingway. *Variations:* Mariella, Marielle, Meriel, Meriella, Merielle.

MARIETTA (French) Form of Mary. *Notable:* Actress Mariette Hartley. *Variations:* Marieta, Mariette.

MARIFA (Arabic) Possessing great knowledge. *Variation:* Maripha.

MARIGOLD (English) Flower name. *Variations:* Maragold, Marygold.

MARIKA (Danish) Form of Mary. *Variations:* Marieke, Marike, Maryka.

MARIKO (Japanese) Village child.

MARILLA (German) Shining sea. *Variations:* Marila, Maryla.

MARILYN (English) Combination of first names "Mary" and "Lynn." *Notable:* Actress Marilyn Monroe. *Variations:* Maralin, Maralynn, Marelyn, Marilee, Marilin, Marilynne, Marralynn, Marrilin, Marrilyn, Marylin, Marylyn.

MARINA (Latin) From the sea. *Variations:* Marena, Marinda, Marine, Marinna, Marna.

MARINELLA (Italian) Of the sea. *Variations:* Marenella, Marinela.

MARION (French) Form of Marian, Mary. *Notable:* Actress Marion Ross. *Variations:* Mariyon, Maryon.

MARIPOSA (Spanish) Like a butterfly.

MARIS (Latin) Star of the sea. *Variations:* Marieca, Marisa, Marise, Marish, Marisha, Marissa, Marisse, Meris, Merisa, Merissa.

MARISKA (Slavic) Form of Mary. *Notable:* Actress Mariska Hargitay.

MARISOL (Spanish) Sunny sea.

MARISSA (Latin) Of the sea. *Notable:* Actress Marisa Tomei. *Variations:* Maressa, Marician, Marisa, Marisha, Maryssa, Merissa, Merisse, Meryssa.

MARIT (Scandinavian) Form of Margaret. *Variations:* Marete, Maritte.

MARITA (Spanish) Form of Mary.

MARITZA (Arabic) Blessed.

MARJA (Finnish) Form of Mary. *Variations:* Marjae, Marjah.

MARJANI (African) Coral reef. *Variations:* Marjanee, Marjanie.

MARJOLAINE (French) Marjoram. *Variation:* Marjolaina.

MARJORIE (Greek) Form of Margaret. *Notable:* Literary heroine Marjorie Morningstar. *Variations:* Margeree, Margerie, Margery, Marjery, Marjoree, Marjori, Marjory.

MARKEISHA (American) Warrior child. *Variations:* Markeesha, Markesha, Markeshia, Markesia, Markeysha, Markeyshia, Merkeysia, Markiesha, Markieshia, Markiesia, Markisha, Markishia, Markisia, Markysia.

MARKETA (Czech) Pearl. *Variations:* Markeeta, Markia, Markita.

MARKIE (Latin) Warlike. Feminine form of Mark. *Notable:* Actress Markie Post. *Variations:* Markee, Markey, Marki, Marky.

MARLA (English) Short form of Marlene. *Notables:* Actresses Marla Gibbs and Marla Maples. *Variations:* Marlah, Marlee, Marley, Marlo, Marly.

MARLENE (English) Combined form of first and last names "Mary Magdalene." *Notable:* Actress Marlene Dietrich. *Variations:* Marla, Marlaina, Marlaine, Marlana, Marlane, Marlayne, Marlea, Marlee, Marleen, Marleina, Marlena, Marley, Marlie, Marlina, Marlinda, Marline, Marlyn.

MARLISE (English) Sacred. *Variations:* Marlease, Marlesa, Marlese, Marlis, Marlisa, Marliss, Marlissa, Marlisse, Marlys, Marlysa, Marlyse, Marlyss, Marlyssa, Marlysse.

MARLO (English) Form of Mary or Marlene. *Notable:* Actress Marlo Thomas. *Variations:* Marlow, Marlowe.

MARMARA (Greek) Sparkling sea. *Variations:* Marmarra, Marmee.

MARNI (Hebrew) To rejoice. *Variations:* Marna, Marne, Marney, Marnia, Marnie, Marnina, Merina.

MARONA (Hebrew) Flock of sheep.

MAROULA (Greek) Defiant. *Variations:* Maroulah, Maroulla.

MARQUISE (French) Born to royalty. *Variations:* Marchesa, Marchessa, Markaisa, Markeesa, Marquesa, Marquessa, Marquisa.

MARQUITA (Spanish) Ruler. *Variations:* Markeata, Markeda, Markeeda, Markeeta, Marketa, Marketta, Markette, Markia, Markieta, Markita, Markitha, Marqueda, Marqueeda, Marquedia, Marquee, Marqueita, Marqueite, Marqueta, Marquete, Marquetta, Marquette, Marquia, Marquida, Marquietta, Marquiette, Marquisa, Marquite, Marquitia, Marquitra, Marquitta, Marquta.

MARSALA (Italian) Town in Sicily known for wine. *Variation:* Marsalla.

MARSHA (Latin) Warlike. Form of Marcia. *Notable:* Comedian Marsha Warfield.

MARTA (Spanish; Italian; Portuguese) Form of Martha.

MARTHA (Aramaic) Lady. *Notable:* Domestic diva Martha Stewart. *Variations:* Marcia, Marit, Marite, Marlet, Mart, Marta, Martell, Marth, Marthe, Marthena, Marti, Martie, Martina, Martita, Martus, Martuska, Marty, Martyne, Martynne, Masia, Matti, Mattie.

MARTI (English) Short form of Martha or Martina. *Variations:* Martie, Marty.

Top Names in Greece

BOYS:
1. Georgios
2. Konstantinos
3. Dimitrios
4. Ionnas
5. Nikolaos
6. Panagiotis
7. Christos
8. Vasileios
9. Athanasios
10. Evangelos

GIRLS:
1. Maria
2. Eleni
3. Aikaterini
4. Vasiliki
5. Sophia
6. Angeliki
7. Georgia
8. Dimitra
9. Konstantina
10. Paraskevi

MARTINA (Latin) Warlike. Feminine version of Martin. *Notables:* Tennis pro Martina Navratilova; singer Martina McBride. *Variation:* Martine.

MARTIRIO (Spanish) Martyrdom.

MARTIZA (Arabic) Blessed. *Variations:* Martisa, Martisah, Martizah, Martyza, Martyzah.

MARU (Japanese) Round. *Variation:* Maroo.

MARVA (English) Mariner. Feminine version of Marvin. *Variations:* Marveena, Marvena, Marvina.

MARVEL (French) A marvel. *Variations:* Marvela, Marvele, Marvella, Marvelle.

MARWA (Arabic) Rock.

MARY (Hebrew) Bitterness. *Notables:* Singer Mary J. Blige; actress Mary Tyler Moore. *Variations:* Maree, Mari, Marye, Maryk.

MARYAMT (Arabic) Sadness.

MARYBETH (English) Combined form of Mary and Beth. *Variations:* Mareabeth, Mareebeth, Maribeth, Mariebeth.

MARYELLEN (English) Combined form of Mary and Ellen. *Variations:* Marielen, Mariellen, Maryelen.

MARYJO (English) Combined form of Mary and Jo. *Variations:* Mareajo, Mareejo, Marijo, Marijoe, Marijoh, Maryjoe, Maryjoh.

MARYLOU (English) Combined form of Mary and Lou. *Variations:* Mareelou, Mareelu, Marilou, Marilu, Marylu.

MARZIA (Italian) Defense.

MASA (Japanese) Just.

MASADA (Hebrew) Foundation of strength. *Variations:* Masalda, Massada.

MASAGO (Japanese) Sand.

MASARA (African) Sorceress.

MASELA (Hawaiian) Warlike. *Variation:* Makela.

MASHA (Russian) Form of Mary.

MASHAVU (African) Chubby cheeks.

MASIKA (African) Born during the rainy season. *Variation:* Mashika.

MASSIMA (Italian) Superior.

MASUYO (Japanese) Benefit the world.

MATANA (Hebrew) Present. *Variations:* Matanah, Matania, Matanna, Matannah, Matannia, Matanniah, Matanya, Matanyah, Mathena, Mathenah.

MATANGI (Hindi) Inner thought.

MATELITA (Polynesian) Powerful warrior.

MATILDA (German) Maiden in battle. *Variations:* Maddi, Maddie, Maddy, Mat, Matelda, Mathilda, Mathilde, Matilde, Mattie, Matty, Matusha, Matylda, Maud, Maude, Tila, Tilda, Tildie, Tildy, Tilley, Tilli, Tillie, Tilly, Tylda.

MATRIXA (Hindi) Mother. *Variation:* Matrica, Matricah, Matricka, Matrickah, Matrika, Matryca, Matrycka, Matryka.

MATSU (Japanese) Pine. *Variations:* Matsuko, Matsuyo.

MATTHEA (Hebrew) Gift from God. Feminine version of Matthew. *Variations:* Mathea, Mathia, Mattea, Matthea, Matthia, Mattia.

MAUD (English) Short forms of Madeline or Matilda. *Notable:* Actress/model Maud Adams. *Variation:* Maude.

MAUDISA (African) Sweet.

MAULI (Hindi) Hair.

MAULIDI (African) Born during the Islamic month of Maulidi.

MAURA (Irish) Form of Mary. *Notables:* Actress Maura Tierney. *Variations:* Maure, Mauree, Mauri, Maurie, Mauritia, Maury, Moira, Mouira, Moyra.

MAUREEN (Irish) Variation of Mary. *Notables:* Actresses Maureen O'Sullivan, Maureen O'Hara, and Maureen McCormick. *Variations:* Maireen, Maireena, Maireene, Mairin, Mairina, Mairine, Maurena, Maurene, Maurina, Maurine, Maurisa, Maurise, Maurita, Mauritah, Mauritia, Maurizia, Maurn, Maurya, Morain, Moraina, Morainah, Moraine, Morayn, Morayna, Moraynah, Morayne, Moreen, Moreena, Moreene, Moren, Morena, Morene, Morin, Morina, Morinah, Morine, Morreen, Moureen, Moryn, Moryna, Morynah, Moryne.

MAUVE (French) The mallow plant.

MAVIS (French) Thrush. *Variations:* Mavice, Mavise, Mayvis.

MAVONDE (African) Abundant harvest. *Variations:* Mavonda, Mavondia.

MAXINE (English) Greatest in excellence. Feminine version of Maximilian. *Variations:* Maxeen, Maxene, Maxi, Maxie, Maxima, Maximilienne, Maximina, Maxina.

MAY (English) Calendar month. *Variations:* Mae, Mai, Mayleen, Maylene.

MAYA (Hindi) Illusion. *Notable:* Writer Maya Angelou. *Variations:* Maia, Maiah, Mya.

MAYBELLINE (Latin) Form of Mabel. *Variation:* Maybeline.

MAYIM (Hebrew) Water. *Notable:* Actress Mayim Bialik.

MAYSA (Arabic) Walk proudly. *Variation:* Maisah.

MAYTAL (Hebrew) Dew drops. *Variation:* Maital.

MAYTE (Spanish) Lovable. *Variation:* Maite.

MAZAL (Hebrew) Fate. *Variations:* Mazala, Mazalah, Mazel, Mazela, Mazella, Mazelle.

MAZHIRA (Hebrew) Gleaming.

MEAD (Greek) Wine of honey. *Variations:* Meade, Meede.

MEADHBH (Irish) Intoxicating. *Variations:* Meabh, Medb.

MEADOW (English) Beautiful field.

MEARA (Irish) Jolly. *Variations:* Mearah, Mearia, Meira, Meirah, Meyra.

MECA (Spanish) Gentle.

MECHOLA (Hebrew) To dance. *Variation:* Mahola.

MECISLAVA (Czech) Glorious sword. *Variations:* Mecina, Mecka.

MEDA (Native American) Prophet.

MEDEA (Greek) Ruling. *Variation:* Medee.

MEDINA (Arabic) City in Saudi Arabia. *Variations:* Medeana, Medeena, Medinah, Medyna.

MEDORA (English) Gift from mother.

MEDUSA (Greek) Mythological Gorgon.

MEE-KYONG (Korean) Shining beauty.

MEENA (Hindi) Fish. *Variations:* Meenal, Minal, Minali, Minisha.

MEE-YON (Korean) Beautiful lotus blossom.

MEEZA (Hindi) Quarter moon.

MEG (English) Short form of Margaret or Megan. *Notable:* Actress Meg Ryan.

MEGAN (Irish) Form of Margaret. *Notable:* Actress Megan Mullally. *Variations:* Maegan, Maegen, Maeghan, Maeghen, Maeghin, Maeghon, Maeghyn, Maegin, Maegon, Maegyn, Magan, Magen, Maygen, Meagan, Meagen, Meaghan, Meaghn, Meaghin, Meaghon, Meaghyn, Meegan, Meegen, Meeghan, Meeghen, Meeghin, Meeghon, Meeghyn, Meegin, Meegon, Meegyn, Megane, Megann, Meganne, Megen, Meggen, Meghan, Meghen, Meghon, Meghyn, Megin, Megon, Megyn, Meigan, Meigen, Meigin, Meigon, Meigyn, Meygan, Meygen, Meygin, Meygon, Meygyn.

MEGARA (Hindi) First-born child.

MEGGIE (English) Familiar form of Margaret or Megan. *Variations:* Meggi, Meggy, Meghee.

MEGUMI (Japanese) Blessing.

MEHAL (Hindi) Rain. *Variations:* Megha, Mehalle.

MEHIRA (Hebrew) Quick.

MEHITABEL (Hebrew) Benefited by God. *Variation:* Mehetabel.

MEHLI (Hindi) Rain.

MEI (Hawaiian) Hawaiian version of May. *Variation:* Mahina.

MEI-HWA (Chinese) Beautiful flower.

MEIKO (Japanese) Flower bud.

MEI-LIEN (Chinese) Beautiful lotus.

MEIRA (Hebrew) Light. *Variations:* Meiri, Meirit, Meora, Meorah.

MEIRONA (Hebrew) Lamb.

MEI-XING (Chinese) Beautiful star.

MEIYING (Chinese) Beautiful flower.

MEI-ZHEN (Chinese) Beautiful pearl.

MEL (English) Short form of Melanie or Melody.

MELA (Hindi) Religious congregation. *Variations:* Melah, Mella.

MELANIE (Greek) Dark skinned. *Notable:* Actress Melanie Griffith. *Variations:* Malana, Malanah, Malanee, Maleney, Malani, Malania, Malaniah, Malanie, Malany, Mel, Mela, Melaine, Melana, Melane, Melanee, Melaney, Melani, Melaniya, Melanka, Melany, Melanya, Melashka, Melasya, Melena, Melenee, Meleney, Meleni, Melenia, Melenie, Meleny, Melka, Mellanee, Mellaney, Mellani, Mellanie, Mellany, Mellenee, Melleney, Melleni, Mellenie, Melleny, Mellie, Melloney, Mellony, Melly, Melona, Melonah, Melonee, Meloney, Meloni, Melonia, Meloniah, Melonie, Melony, Melonya, Milena, Milya.

MELANTHA (Greek) Dark-violet flower. *Variations:* Melanthe, Melanthia.

MELBA (English) From Melbourne, city in Australia. *Notable:* Singer Melba Moore. *Variations:* Mellba, Mellva, Melva.

MELCIA (Polish) Ambitious.

MELE (Hawaiian) Poem.

MELEK (Arabic) Angel. *Variation:* Meleka.

MELESSE (Ethiopian) Eternal. *Variation:* Mellesse.

MELIA (Hawaiian) Plumeria flower. *Variations:* Melcia, Melea, Meleah, Meleana, Meleena, Meleia, Meleisha, Meliah, Melida, Melya, Melyah, Milica, Milicah, Milika, Milikah, Miliqua, Milique, Mylia, Myliah, Mylya.

MELIAME (Polynesian) Bitter.

MELIKA (Turkish) Great beauty. *Variations:* Melica, Melicca, Melicka.

MELINA (Greek) Honey. *Notable:* Actress Melina Kanakaredes. *Variations:* Meleana, Meleena, Melena.

MELINDA (Greek) Honey. *Variations:* Malina, Malinda, Malindah, Malinde, Malindea, Malindee, Malindia, Mallie, Mally, Malynda, Melindah, Melinde, Melindee, Melindia, Melindiah, Mellinda, Mellindah, Mellynda, Melynda, Mindi, Mindie, Mindy.

MELIORA (Latin) Better. *Variations:* Meliore, Meliorua, Meliorie, Melora.

MELIS (Turkish) Light.

MELISANDE (French) Form of Melissa or Millicent. *Variations:* Melasandre, Melicent, Melisandra, Melisandre, Melisent, Melissande, Melissandre.

MELISSA (Greek) Honey bee. *Notables:* Singer Melissa Etheridge; actress Melissa Joan Hart. *Variations:* Malissa, Malessa, Melessa, Melessah, Melica, Melice, Melisa, Melisah, Melise, Melisenda, Melisent, Melissah, Melisse, Melissent, Melissia, Melitta, Melittah, Mellisa, Melliss, Mellissa, Mellissah, Mellosa, Mellosah, Melosa, Melosah, Melossa, Melossah, Melysa, Melyssa, Melysse,

Milisa, Milisah, Milissa, Mylisa, Mylissa, Mylysa, Mylysah, Mylyssa.

MELITA (Greek) Honey. *Variations:* Malita, Meleta, Meleata, Meleatta, Meleeta, Meleetah, Meleetta, Melitah, Melitta, Melittah, Melyta, Melytah, Melytta.

MELODY (Greek) Song. *Variations:* Melodee, Melodey, Melodia, Melodice, Melodie.

MELORA (Greek) Golden apple. *Variations:* Melorah, Melori, Melorie, Melory, Melorya, Meloryah.

MELOSA (Spanish) Sweet. *Variations:* Malosah, Malossa, Melosah, Melossa, Melossah.

MELROSE (Greek) Sweet rose. Combined form of Melanie and Rose. *Variation:* Melrosa.

MELVINA (Irish) Great chief. Feminine form of Melvin. *Variations:* Malva, Malvina, Melveen, Melveena, Melveenah, Melveene, Melveenia, Melveeniah, Melvena, Melvinda, Melvindah, Melvine, Melvinia, Melviniah, Melvyna, Melvynah, Melvyne, Melvynia, Melvyniah, Melvynya.

MEMA (Spanish) Hard working.

MENA (Dutch) Strength. *Notable:* Actress Mena Suvari. *Variations:* Meana, Meanah, Meena, Meenah, Meina, Meinah, Menah, Menna, Meyna, Meynah.

MENASHA (Native American) Island.

MENIA (Scandinavian) Ancient mythological figure. *Variation:* Menja.

MENORA (Hebrew) Candelabra. *Variations:* Menorah, Minora, Minorah, Mynora, Mynorah.

MENUSCHA (Hebrew) Tranquility. *Variation:* Menuha.

MEONAH (Hebrew) Home. *Variation:* Meona.

MERAB (Hebrew) Fertile.To increase. *Variations:* Meirab, Meirav, Meraba, Merav.

MERALDA (Latin) Emerald. *Variation:* Maralda.

MERAUD (French) Emerald.

MERCEDES (Spanish) Mercy. *Notable:* Actress Mercedes Ruehl. *Variations:* Merced, Merceda, Mercedees, Mercedez.

MERCIA (English) Ancient British kingdom. *Variations:* Mercea, Mercya.

MERCY (English) Merciful. *Variations:* Mercee, Mercey, Merci, Mercie, Mersea, Mersee, Mersey, Mersy.

MEREDITH (Welsh) Great leader. *Notables:* TV host Meredith Vieira; actress Meredith Baxter Birney. *Variations:* Meredithe, Meredyth, Merideth, Meridith, Meridyth, Merridith.

MEREKI (Aboriginal) Peacemaker. *Variations:* Merekee, Merekie.

MERI (Scandinavian) Ocean. *Variation:* Meriata.

MERIEL (Irish) Brilliant seas. *Variations:* Merial, Meriol.

MERILYN (English) Bright sea. *Variations:* Meralin, Meralina, Meraline, Meralyn, Meralyna, Meralyne, Merelan, Merelen, Merelin, Merelina, Mereline, Merelyn, Merelyna, Merelyne, Merilan, Merilen, Merilin, Merilina, Meriline, Merilyna, Merilyne, Merylan, Merylen, Merylin, Merylina,

Meryline, Merylyn, Merylyna, Merylyne.

MERIMA (Hebrew) To lift up. *Variation:* Meroma.

MERINDA (English) Happy. *Variation:* Merynda.

MERIT (English) Due reward. *Variations:* Merrit, Merritt, Meritte.

MERIWA (Intuit) Thorn.

MERLE (French) Blackbird. *Notable:* Actress Merle Oberon. *Variations:* Merl, Merla, Merlin, Merlina, Merline, Merlyn.

MERONA (Aramaic) Sheep. *Variation:* Meronna.

MERRY (English) Happy. *Variations:* Meri, Merri, Merrie, Merrilee, Merrily.

MERVE (Turkish) Mountain near Mecca.

MERYL (English) Bright as the sea. *Notable:* Actress Meryl Streep. *Variations:* Merill, Merrall, Merrel, Merrell, Merrill, Meryle, Meryll.

MESHA (Hindi) Ram. *Variations:* Meshah, Meshai.

MESI (African) Water.

MESSINA (Latin) Middle. *Variations:* Mesina, Messyna.

METSA (Finnish) Woman of the forest.

METTE (German) Mighty in battle.

METUKA (Hebrew) Sweet.

MEUSA (Hawaiian) Bee. *Variations:* Meli, Melika.

MIA (Italian) Mine. *Notable:* Actress Mia Farrow.

MI-CHA (Korean) Lovely girl.

Names You Might Want to Avoid

Due to certain "reputations" of the famous and infamous who share these names, you might want to think twice about bestowing these on your innocent newborn!

BOYS:
Adolf
Attila
Caligula
Darth
Judas
Lucifer
Moammar
Nero
Osama
Saddam

GIRLS:
Delilah
Imelda
Jezebel
Leona
Lizzie
Lorena
Martha
Omarosa
Salome
Tammy Faye
Zsa Zsa

School Daze: Names from Teachers (Part V)

Here's yet another selection of names from an elementary school in Santa Barbara, California:

Abhay	Keighriynne
Briseida	Keiji
Cian	Keir
Davita	Kiara
Deshaun	Maisy
Gopal	Martinique
Greir	Meleton
Jhon	Milocsz
Jiaya	Nayeli
Kaden	Saliah
Kai	Sequoia
Karime	Shahir
Katya	Soren

MICHAELA (Hebrew) Who is like God. Feminine version of Michael. *Variations:* Macala, Macayla, Machaela, Mackayla, Makaela, Makaila, Makala, Makalah, Makayla, Makaylah, Mckaila, Mckalalah, Mckayla, Mekayla, Micaela, Mical, Micala, Micayla, Michael, Michaella, Michaila, Michal, Michala, Michalla, Michayla, Micheala, Michela, Mickaela, Mickaula, Mickayla, Mikaela, Mikaila, Mikala, Mikalah, Mikayla, Mikaylah, Mikela, Mikella, Mikelle, Mikhaila, Mikhayla, Mychaela, Mykaela, Mykaila, Mykala, Mykayla.

MICHELANGELA (Italian) Who is like God?

MICHELLE (French) Who is like God? *Notables:* First Lady Michelle Obama; actress Michelle Pfeiffer. *Variations:* Machell, Machella, Machelle, Mashell, Mashella, Mashelle, Mechel, Mechell, Mechella, Mechelle, Meshell, Meshella, Meshelle, Michaella, Michaelle, Michal, Michalina, Michaline, Michel, Michele, Michelina, Micheline, Michell, Michella, Michellah, Mishel, Mishela, Mishele, Mishell, Mishella, Mishellah, Mishelle, Mychel, Mychela, Mychelah, Mychele, Mychell, Mychella, Mychelle, Myshel, Myshela, Myshelah, Myshele, Myshell, Myshella, Myshellah, Myshelle.

MICHIKO (Japanese) The righteous way. *Variation:* Michi.

MICINA (Native American) New moon.

MICKI (American) Short form of Michaela or Michelle. *Variations:* Mickee, Mickey, Micky, Miki, Mikki.

MIDGE (English) Form of Margaret.

MIDORI (Japanese) Green.

MIEKE (Dutch) Likeness to God. *Variation:* Meike.

MIEKO (Japanese) Wealthy.

MIETTE (French) Sweet little one. *Variations:* Miet, Mieta, Mietah, Mietta, Miettah, Myeta, Myetah, Myett, Myetta, Myettah.

MIEU (Vietnamese) Salt.

MIGINA (Native American) New moon.

MIGISI (Native American: Chippewa) Eagle.

MIGDANA (Hebrew) Gift. *Variations:* Migdanna, Migdannah, Mygdana.

MIGINA (Native American) New moon. *Variations:* Migeana, Migeanah, Migeena, Migeenah, Miginah, Migyna, Migynah, Mygeana, Mygeanah, Mygeena, Mygeenah, Mygina, Myginah, Mygyna, Mygynah.

MIGNON (French) Petite. *Variations:* Mignona, Mignone, Mignonetta, Mignonette, Minyon, Mygnona, Mygnonah, Mygnone, Mignonetta, Mygnonette.

MIGUELA (Spanish) Feminine form of Miguel. Likeness to God. *Variations:* Miguelita, Miquela, Miquelah, Miquella, Miquelle.

MI-HI (Korean) Lovely joy.

MIKA (Japanese) New moon. *Variations:* Mikah, Myka, Mykah.

MIKALA (Hawaiian) Like God. Form of Michaela.

MIKAZUKI (Japanese) New moon.

MIKI (Japanese) Family tree. *Variations:* Mika, Mikee, Mikey,

Mikia, Mikiala, Mikie, Mikiko, Mikita, Mikiyo, Mikka, Mikki, Mikkia, Mikkie, Mikkiya, Mikko, Mikky, Miko, Miky.

MIKILANA (Hawaiian) Flower. *Variation:* Misilana.

MIKKA (Japanese) Third day.

MILA (Slavic) Loved by the people. *Notables:* Actresses Milla Jovovich and Mila Kunis. *Variations:* Milla, Myla.

MILADA (Czech) My love. *Variations:* Miladah, Miladi, Miladie, Milady, Mylada, Myladi, Myladie, Mylady.

MILAGROS (Spanish) Miracle. *Variations:* Milagro, Milagrosa.

MILANA (Italian) Favor.

MILCAH (Hebrew) Adviser. *Variations:* Milca, Milka, Milkah, Mylca, Mylcah.

MILDRED (English) Tender strength. *Variations:* Milda, Mildrid, Mildryd, Myldred, Myldrid, Myldryd.

MILENA (Czech) Grace. *Variations:* Milada, Miladena, Miladka, Milana, Milanka, Milenka, Milka, Miluse, Miluska, Mlada, Mladena, Mladka, Mladuska.

MILETA (German) Generous. *Variations:* Miletah, Milett, Miletta, Milette, Milica, Milicah, Milika, Milikah, Milita, Militah, Milla, Millya, Myleta, Myletah, Mylita, Mylitah, Mylyta, Mylytah.

MILEY (American) Nickname derived from Smiley. *Notable:* Pop singer Miley Cyrus. *Variations:* Milee, Mylea, Myleah, Mylee, Mylei, Myleigh, Myli, Mylie, Myllea, Mylleah, Myllee, Myllei, Mylleigh, Mylli, Myllie, Mylly, Myly.

MILIANI (Hawaiian) Tender caress. *Variations:* Milana, Miliana.

MILICA (German) Hard working. *Variations:* Milka, Mylica, Mylka.

MILILANI (Hawaiian) Give praise. *Variations:* Mililanee, Mililaney, Mililanie, Mililany, Mylilaey, Mylilanee, Mylilani, Myliliania, Mylilianiah, Mylilanie, Mylilany, Mylylanee, Mylylaney, Mylylania, Mylylaniah.

MILIMILI (Hawaiian) Cherished.

MILISENA (Hawaiian) Strong at work. *Variation:* Milikena.

MILLIA (German) Hard working. *Variations:* Milica, Milika, Milikah, Milla, Millah, Milya, Milyah, Mylia, Myliah, Myllia, Mylliah, Myllya, Myllyah.

MILLICENT (German) Born to power. *Variations:* Melicent, Meliscent, Mellicent, Milicent, Milicenta, Milissent, Millisent, Millisenta, Myllicent, Myllicenta, Myllicente, Myllycent, Myllycenta, Myllycente, Myllysent, Myllysenta, Myllysente, Mylycent, Mylycenta, Mylycente, Mylysent, Mylysenta, Mylysente.

MILLIE (English) Short form of Millicent. *Variations:* Mili, Milie, Mille, Millea, Milleah, Millee, Millei, Milleigh, Milli, Millia, Milliah, Millie, Milly.

MILOSLAVA (Czech) Lover of glory. *Variations:* Miloslavia, Miloslawa.

MIMI (French) Form of Miriam or Marie. *Notable:* Actress Mimi Rogers. *Variations:* Mim, Mimsie.

MIN (Chinese) Sensitive.

MINA (German) Protector. Short form of Wilhelmena. *Variations:* Meena, Meenah, Mena, Minah, Myna, Mynah, Mynna, Mynnah.

MINAKO (Japanese) Beautiful child.

MINAL (Native American) Fruit.

MINAMI (Japanese) South. *Variation:* Miniami.

MINDA (Hindi) Wisdom.

MINDY (English) Short form of Melinda. *Variations:* Mindee, Mindi, Mindie.

MINEKO (Japanese) Peak. *Variation:* Mine.

MINERVA (Latin) Wise. The Roman goddess of wisdom.

MINETTA (French) Faithful defender. *Variation:* Minette.

MING (Chinese) Shiny.

MINKA (German) Great strength. *Notable:* Actress Minka Kelly.

MINNA (German) Short form of Wilhelmina.

MINNIE (English) Short form of Minerva or Wilhelmina. *Notable:* Actress Minnie Driver. *Variations:* Mini, Minnee, Minni, Minny.

MINOWA (Native American) Moving voice.

MIO (Japanese) Cherry blossom.

MIRA (Spanish) To gaze. *Notable:* Actress Mira Sorvino.

MIRABAI (Hindi) Krishna devotee and saint.

MIRABEL (Latin) Wonderful. *Variations:* Mirabell, Mirabella, Mirabelle.

MIRACLE (Latin) Marvel.

MIRANDA (Latin) Admirable. *Notable:* Actress Miranda Richardson. *Variations:* Maranda, Meranda, Mira, Miranda, Myranda, Randa, Randee, Randene, Randey, Randi, Randie, Randy.

MIREILLE (French) To admire. *Variations:* Mireia, Mirela, Mirella, Mirelle.

MIRENA (Hawaiian) Beloved. *Variation:* Milena.

MIRIAM (Hebrew) Bitterness. *Variations:* Mariam, Merian, Miri, Miriama, Miriem, Mirriam, Mirrian, Miryam, Myriam.

MIROSLAVA (Czech) Great and famous. *Variations:* Mirka, Miruska.

MIROSLAWA (Polish) Great glory. *Variation:* Mirka.

MISAE (Native American) White sun.

MISAO (Japanese) Loyal.

MISHA (Russian) Form of Michaela. *Notable:* Actress Mischa Barton. *Variations:* Mischa, Mischka, Mishka.

MISOKA (Japanese) Last day of the month.

MISSY (English) Short form of Melissa. *Notable:* Singer Missy Elliott. *Variations:* Missee, Missey, Missi, Missie.

MISTY (English) In a mist. *Variations:* Mistee, Misti, Mistie, Mysti, Mysty.

MITRA (Persian) Heavenly angel.

MITSU (Japanese) Light. *Variation:* Mitsuko.

MITZI (German) Form of Mary. *Notable:* Actress Mitzi Gaynor. *Variations:* Mitzee, Mitzey, Mitzie, Mitzy, Mytzi.

MIULANA (Hawaiian) Magnolia tree.

MIWA (Japanese) Harmony. *Variation:* Miwako.

MIYA (Japanese) Temple. *Variations:* Miyah, Miyana, Miyanna.

MIYO (Japanese) Beautiful generations. *Variation:* Miyoko.

MIYUKI (Japanese) Snow.

MIZELL (English) Tiny gnat. *Variations:* Marzalie, Masella, Mazala, Mazella, Mazila, Mesella, Messella, Mezillah, Mizella, Mizelle, Mizelli.

MIZUKO (Japanese) Water child.

MO (English) Short form of Maureen.

MOANA (Hawaiian) Ocean. *Variations:* Moanah, Moann, Moanna, Moanne.

MOANI (Hawaiian) Light breeze.

MOCHA (Arabic) Chocolate-flavored coffee. *Variation:* Moka.

MODESTY (Latin) Modesty. *Variations:* Modesta, Modestia, Modestina, Modestine.

MOEMA (Portuguese) Dawn.

MOESHA (African American) Drawn from water. *Variation:* Moeshia.

MOHALA (Hawaiian) Flower petals. *Variation:* Moala.

MOHANA (Hindi) Enchanting. *Variations:* Mohini, Mohonie.

MOIRA (Irish) Pure. *Variations:* Moirae, Moirah, Moire, Moirin, Moyra, Moyrah.

MOLARA (Basque) Wished-for child. *Variation:* Molarra.

MOLLY (English) Form of Mary. *Notable:* Actress Molly Ringwald. *Variations:* Molee, Molei, Moleigh, Moley, Moli, Molie, Mollea, Molleah, Mollee, Mollei, Molleigh, Molley, Molli, Mollie.

MONA (Irish) Noble. *Notables:* Da Vinci subject Mona Lisa. *Variation:* Mony.

MONDAY (English) Day of the week.

MONICA (Latin) Advisor. Nun; (Greek) Solitary. *Notable:* White House intern Monica Lewinsky. *Variations:* Monca, Moneka, Moni, Monia, Moniah, Monic, Monicah, Monice, Monicia, Monicka, Monika, Monikah, Moniqua, Monique, Monisa, Monise, Monnica, Monnicah, Monnicka, Monnika, Monniqua, Monnique, Monnyca, Monnyka.

MONIQUE (French) Form of Monica.

MONISHA (Hindi) Great intelligence.

MONSERRAT (Latin) Jagged mountain.

MONTANA (Spanish) Mountain. *Variation:* Montanna.

MOON (English) Like the moon. *Variations:* Moona, Moonah, Moone, Moonee, Mooney, Mooni, Moonia, Mooniah, Moonie, Moony.

MOR (Scottish) Great.

MORA (Spanish) Blueberry.

MORAG (Gaelic) Embraces the sun.

MORELA (Polish) Apricot.

MORENA (Portuguese) Brunette. *Variations:* Moreen, Morella.

MORGAN (Welsh) Great and bright. *Notable:* Actress Morgan Fairchild. *Variations:* Morgain, Morgaina, Morgainah, Morgana, Morganah, Morgann, Morganna, Morganne, Morgayn, Morgayna, Morgaynah, Morgayne, Morgen, Morgin, Morgon, Morgyn.

MORI (Japanese) Forest. *Variations:* Moriko, Moriyo.

MORIAH (Hebrew) The Lord is my teacher. *Variations:* Moria, Morice, Moriel, Morit.

MORINA (Irish) Mermaid. *Variations:* Morinah, Morinna, Morinnah, Moryna, Morynah, Morynna, Morynnah.

MORISSA (Latin) Dark haired. *Variations:* Morisa, Morisah, Morissah, Moriset, Morisett, Morisetta, Morisette, Morysa, Moryssa, Morysse.

MORNA (Scottish) Tender.

MORRIGAN (Irish) Great queen. *Variation:* Morrighan.

MOROWA (African) Queen.

MORWENNA (Welsh) Maiden. *Variations:* Morwen, Morwynna.

MOSELLE (Hebrew) Drawn from the water. Feminine version of Moses. *Variations:* Mosella, Mozella, Mozelle.

MOSI (African) First born.

MOSWEN (African) White.

MOTO (Japanese) Source. *Variation:* Motoko.

MOUNA (Arabic) Desire. *Variations:* Mounia, Muna.

MOYNE (Irish) Flat land. *Variation:* Moyna.

MU LAN (Chinese) Magnolia blossom.

MU TAN (Chinese) Peony blossom.

MUADHNAIT (Irish) Little noble one. *Variations:* Moina, Monat, Moyna.

MUDIWA (African) Beloved.

MUGAIN (Irish) Slave.

MUHAYYA (Arabic) Welcome.

MUIKA (Japanese) Sixth day of the week.

MUIREANN (Irish) Born of the sea. *Variations:* Muirenn, Muirgen, Muirgheal, Muirin, Muirinn, Murainn, Murinnia.

MULLYA (Native American) Acorns falling off a tree. *Variation:* Mulya.

MUMINAH (Arabic) Believer.

MUNA (Arabic) Desire. *Variations:* Munah, Munna.

MUN-HEE (Korean) Educated.

MUNIRAH (Arabic) Teacher.

MURA (Japanese) Village.

MURASAKI (Japanese) Purple.

MURDAG (Scottish) Sea warrior. *Variations:* Murdann, Murdina.

MURIEL (Irish) Bright as the sea. *Notable:* Writer Muriel Spark. *Variations:* Muirgheal, Murial, Muriell, Murielle.

MURPHY (Irish) Sea warrior.

MUSETTA (French) Little bagpipe. *Variation:* Musette.

MUSIDORA (Greek) Gift from the Muses.

MUSLIMAH (Arabic) One who is religious.

MUTETELI (African) Dainty.

MY (Vietnamese) Pretty.

MYFANAWY (Welsh) Child of the water. *Variations:* Myff, Myvanwy.

MYLA (American) Merciful. *Variations:* Milena, Mylah, Myleen, Mylene.

MYLSHA (Arabic) Woman.

MYRA (Latin) Scented oil. Feminine version of Myron. *Variations:* Murah, Myria, Myriah.

MYRDDIN (Welsh) Fortress by the sea.

MYRNA (Irish) Beloved. *Notable:* Actress Myrna Loy. *Variations:* Merna, Mirna, Muirna.

Notable Names from the Music Industry

BOYS:	GIRLS:
Axl	Alanis
Beck	Aretha
Bono	Avril
Bruce	Beyonce
Elton	Bjork
Elvis	Britney
Eminem	Celine
(Marshall)	Cher
Garth	Fergie
Iggy	Gwen
Kanye	Jewel
Mick	Madonna
Moby	Mariah
Ozzy	Miley
P. Diddy (Sean)	Rihanna
Paul	Shakira
Prince	Shania
Ringo	Sinead
Sting	Taylor
Usher	Whitney

MYRTLE (English) Myrtle tree. *Variations*: Mertal, Mertell, Mertella, Mertl, Mirtal, Mirtel, Mirtil, Mirtyl, Murtal, Murtella, Murtelle, Murtl, Myrta, Myrtia, Myrtice, Myrticia, Myrtilla.

MYSTIQUE (French) Mysterious. *Variations*: Mistique, Misty, Mystica.

MYUNG-HEE (Korean) Smart daughter.

NAAMAH (Hebrew) Lovely. *Variations*: Naama, Naamana, Naami, Naamia, Naamiah, Naamiya.

NAARAH (Hebrew) Girl. *Variations*: Naara, Nara, Narah.

NAAVAH (Hebrew) Delightful.

NABIHA (Arabic) Smart. *Variation*: Nabihah.

NABILA (Arabic) Highborn. *Variations*: Nabeela, Nabilah. Nabyla.

NACHALA (Hebrew) Inheritance. *Variation*: Nahala.

NADA (Arabic) Dew at sunrise. *Variations*: Nadah, Nadan, Nadee, Nadi, Nadie, Nadey.

NADALIA (Aboriginal) Fire. *Variations*: Nadala, Nadalei, Nadaleigh, Nadali, Nadalie, Nadalya.

NADETTE (German) Brave bear; (French) Bernadette.

NADEZDA (Czech) Hope. *Variations*: Nadeja, Nadejda, Nadezhda, Nadzia, Nadzieja.

NADIA (Russian) Hope. *Notable*: Gymnast Nadia Comaneci. *Variations*: Nada, Nadiah, Nadiya, Nadja, Nadya, Natka.

NADIDA (Arabic) Equal. *Variation*: Nadidah.

NADINE (French) Form of Nadia. *Variations*: Nadean, Nadeana, Nadeane, Nadeen, Nadeena, Nadeene, Nadena, Nadene, Nadina, Nadyna, Nadyne.

NADIRA (Arabic) Precious. *Variations*: Nadeera, Nadirah, Nadyra.

NADYAN (Hebrew) Pond. *Variations*: Nadian, Nadianne, Nadien, Nadienne.

NAEVA (French) Life. *Variations*: Naeve, Nahvon.

NAEEMAH (Arabic) Generous.

NAFSHIYA (Hebrew) Friendship.

NAGIDA (Hebrew) Wealthy. *Variations*: Nagia, Nagiah, Nagiya, Najidah, Najiyah, Najiyda, Negida.

NAGISA (Japanese) Beach.

NAHARA (Hebrew) Light. *Variations*: Nehara, Nehora.

NAHIDA (Arabic) Elevated. *Variation*: Nahid.

NAHLA (Arabic) Drink.

NAIA (Hawaiian) Dolphin.

NAIDA (Greek) Water nymph. *Variations*: Naiad, Nayad, Nyad.

NAILAH (Arabic) One who succeeds. *Variations*: Naila, Nayla.

NAIMA (Arabic) Content. *Variations*: Naeemah, Naimah.

NAINA (Hindi) Of the eyes. *Variation*: Nainika.

NAIRI (Armenian) Land of rivers. *Variations*: Nairee, Nairia, Nairiah, Nairie, Nairey, Nairy, Nyree.

NAIRITA (Hindi) From the southwest.

NAIRN (Scottish) River of the alder tree. *Variation*: Nairne.

NAJAT (Arabic) Safe. *Variation*: Nagat.

NAJIBA (Arabic) Well born. *Variations*: Nagiba, Nagibah, Najibah.

NAJLA (Arabic) Pretty eyes. *Variations*: Nagla, Najila, Najlaa, Najlah.

NAJMA (Hindi) Star.

NAJWA (Arabic) Confide. *Variation*: Nagwa.

NALANI (Hawaiian) Heavenly calm.

NALIN (Native American) Young woman.

NALINI (Sanskrit) Like a lotus.

NALUKEA (Hawaiian) White wave.

NAMI (Japanese) Wave. *Variation*: Namiko.

NAMISHA (Hindi) Truthful.

NAMITA (Hindi) Devoted.

NAMRATA (Hindi) Modesty.

NAN (English) Grace. Variation of Ann. Short form of Nancy or Nanette.

NANA (Hawaiian) Spring month. *Variations*: Nanah, Nanna, Nannah.

NANALA (Hawaiian) Sunflower. *Variation*: Nanalah.

NANCY (Hebrew) Grace. *Notables*: U.S. First Lady Nancy Reagan; fictional detective Nancy Drew; Olympic skater Nancy Kerrigan. *Variations*: Nan, Nana, Nance, Nancee, Nancey, Nanci, Nancie, Nancsi, Nanette, Nann, Nanna, Nanncey, Nanncy, Nanni, Nannie, Nanny, Nanscey, Nansee, Nansey.

NANDA (Aboriginal) Lake.

NANDANA (Hindi) Happiness. *Variations:* Nandini, Nandita.

NANEK (Hawaiian) Merciful. *Variations:* Naneka, Naneki, Naneta.

NANETTE (French) Petite and graceful. Form of Nancy. *Notable:* Actress Nanette Fabray. *Variations:* Nanet, Naneta, Nanete, Nanett, Nannet, Nannett, Nannetta, Nannette.

NANI (Hawaiian) Beautiful. *Variations:* Nanee, Naney, Nanie, Nannee, Nanney, Nanni, Nannie, Nanny, Nany.

NANISE (Polynesian) Gracious. *Variations:* Naneece, Naneese, Nanice.

NANON (French) Graceful. *Variations:* Nanona, Nanone, Nanonia.

NAO (Japanese) Truthful.

NAOMH (Irish) Saint.

NAOMI (Hebrew) Pleasant. *Notables:* Country singer Naomi Judd; actress Naomi Watts; supermodel Naomi Campbell. *Variations:* Naoma, Naomia, Naomie, Neoma, Noami, Noemi, Noemie, Nyomi.

NARA (Japanese) Oak tree.

NARBFLAITH (Irish) Noble princess.

NARCISSA (Greek) Daffodil. *Variations:* Narcisa, Narciska, Narcisse, Narkissa.

NARDA (Latin) Scented lotion.

NARELLE (English) Woman from the sea. *Variations:* Narel, Narela, Narell, Narella, Narilla, Narille.

NARESHA (Hindi) Leader.

NARI (Japanese) Thunderclap. *Variation:* Nariko.

NARMANDA (Hindi) Pleasure giver.

NASCHA (Native American) Owl.

NASEEM (Hindi) Morning breeze.

NASHOTA (Native American) Twin.

NASIRA (Arabic) To help.

NASPA (Hebrew) The Lord's miracle. *Variations:* Nasia, Nasya.

NASRIN (Arabic) Rose. *Variation:* Nasreen.

NASTASIA (Russian) Resurrection. Form of Anastasia. *Notable:* Actress Nastassja Kinski. *Variations:* Nastassia, Nastassja, Nastasya, Nastya.

NASYA (Hebrew) Miracle of God. *Variations:* Nasia, Nasiah.

NATA (Native American) Creator. *Variations:* Natah, Natia, Natya.

NATALIE (Latin) Born on Christmas. *Notables:* Singers Natalie Cole and Natalie Merchant; actresses Natalie Portman and Natalie Wood. *Variations:* Natala, Natalee, Natalene, Natalia, Natalina, Nataline, Natalka, Natalya, Natelie, Nathalia, Nathalie.

NATANIAH (Hebrew) Gift of God. Feminine version of Nathan. *Variations:* Natania, Nataniela, Nataniella, Natanielle, Natanya, Nathania, Nathaniella, Nathanielle, Netana, Netanela, Netania, Netaniah, Netaniela, Netaniella, Netanya, Nethania, Nethaniah, Netina.

NATASHA (Russian) Born on Christmas. Form of Natalie. *Notable:* Actress Natasha Richardson. *Variations:* Nastasia, Nastassia, Nastassja, Nastassya, Nastasya, Natashia, Tashi, Tashia, Tasis, Tassa, Tassie.

NATESA (Hindi) Lord of the dance. *Variation:* Natisa.

NATHITFA (Arabic) Pure. *Variations:* Nathifa, Nathifah, Natifa, Natifah.

NATIVIDAD (Spanish) Born on Christmas.

NATKA (Russian) Promise.

NATSUMI (Japanese) Summer. *Variations:* Natsuko, Natsuyo.

NAVA (Hebrew) Beautiful. *Variation:* Navah.

NAVIT (Hebrew) Beautiful. *Variations:* Naavah, Nava, Navice.

NAVLYN (Hindi) True love. *Variations:* Navlin, Navlina, Navline.

NAWAL (Arabic) Gift.

NAYANA (Hindi) Beautiful eyes.

NAYO (African) She is our joy.

NAZEK (Turkish) Elegant.

NAZIHAH (Arabic) Trustworthy.

NAZIRA (Arabic) Equal. *Variation:* Nazirah.

NEALA (Irish) Champion. Feminine version of Neil. *Variations:* Nealie, Nealy, Neeli, Neelie, Neely, Neila, Neile, Neilla, Neille.

NEBRASKA (Native American) Land with flat water.

NEBULA (Latin) Cloud.

NECEDAH (Native American) Yellow.

NECHAMA (Hebrew) Comfort. *Variations:* Nachmi, Necha, Neche, Nehama.

NECHE (Native American) Friend.

NECHONA (Hebrew) Appropriate.

NECI (Latin) On fire. *Variations:* Necee, Necey, Necia, Necie, Necy, Neeci, Neecie, Niecee, Nieci, Niecie, Niecy.

Top Names in Germany

BOYS:
1. Leon
2. Lucas
3. Ben
4. Finn
5. Jonas
6. Paul
7. Luis
8. Maximilian
9. Luca
10. Felix

GIRLS:
1. Mia
2. Hannah
3. Lena
4. Lea
5. Emma
6. Anna
7. Leonie
8. Lilli
9. Lena
10. Laura

NEDA (Czech) Born on Sunday. *Variations:* Nedah, Nedda, Nedeljka, Nedia, Nedya, Neida.

NEDAVIAH (Hebrew) God is charitable. *Variations:* Nedavia, Nedavya, Nediva.

NEDDA (English) Properous family. *Variations:* Neddi, Neddie, Neddy.

NEDRA (English) Underground.

NEELAM (Hindi) Blue sapphire.

NEEMA (African) Born during good times.

NEENAH (Native American) Running water.

NEFERTITI (Egyptian) Coming of the beautiful one. *Notable:* Egyptian queen Nefertiti. *Variation:* Nefertara.

NEGAR (Persian) Sweetheart. *Variations:* Nagar, Negah.

NEHA (Hindi) Loving. *Variations:* Nehali, Nehi.

NEHANDA (African) Strong.

NEHEDA (Arabic) Independent.

NEIGE (French) Snow.

NEIMA (Hebrew) Powerful.

NEITH (Egyptian) The goddess of the home. *Variation:* Neit.

NEKA (Native American) Wild goose.

NEKOMA (Native American) Grandmother.

NELDA (English) Elder tree home. *Variation:* Neldah.

NELIA (English) Horn blower. *Variations:* Nelea, Nelee, Nelei, Neleigh, Neliah, Nellia, Nelya.

NELKA (Polish) Stone or fortress. *Variation:* Nela.

NELL (English) Light. *Notable:* Actress Nell Carter. *Variations:* Nella, Nelley, Nelli, Nellie, Nelly.

NELWYN (Welsh) Friend of the light. *Variations:* Nellwin, Nellwinn, Nellwinna, Nellwyna, Nellwyne, Nellwynn, Nelwin, Nelwina, Nelwine, Nelwinn, Nelwinna, Nelwyna, Nelwyne, Nelwynn, Nelwynne.

NEMERA (Hebrew) Leopard.

NENET (Egyptian) Born by the sea. *Variations:* Neneta, Nenete, Nennetia, Nennett, Nennnetta, Nennette.

NEOLA (Greek) Young girl. *Variation:* Neolah.

NEOMA (Greek) New moon.

NEPA (Arabic) Walking backward.

NERA (Hebrew) Candlelight. *Variations:* Neri, Neria, Neriah, Neriya.

NERIDA (Greek) Sea nymph. *Variations:* Nereida, Nerina, Nerine, Nerisse, Nerita.

NERINA (Italian) Water.

NERISSA (Greek) Sea nymph. *Variations:* Nerice, Nerisa, Nerise, Neryssa.

NEREZA (Italian) Darkness. *Variation:* Nerezza.

NERYS (Welsh) Lord.

NESIAH (Hebrew) Miracle of God. *Variations:* Nesia, Nessia, Nesya, Nisia, Nisiah, Nisva.

NESSA (English) Butterfly. Short form of Vanessa.

NESSIE (English) Form of Agnes or Vanessa. *Variations:* Nessi, Nessy.

NETIA (Hebrew) Plant. *Variations:* Neta, Netta.

NETTIE (English) Form of Nanette, Annette, or Antoinette. *Variations:* Neti, Netti, Netty.

NEVA (Spanish) Snow. *Notable:* Actress Neve Campbell. *Variations:* Neiv, Neive, Nevah, Neve, Nevee, Nieve, Nieves.

NEVADA (Spanish) Snow covered.

NEVIAH (Hebrew) Forecaster. *Variations:* Nevia, Nevya, Nyeva.

NEVINA (Irish) Worshipper. *Variations:* Nevinah, Nevine, Nivena, Nivina, Nivine, Nyvina, Nyvine, Nyvyna.

NEYLAN (Turkish) A wish fulfilled. *Variations:* Neilan, Nelana, Nelane.

NEZA (Slavic) Chaste. Form of Agnes. *Variations:* Neisa, Nesah, Neysa, Nezah, Nezza.

NGU (Vietnamese) Sleep.

NGUYET (Vietnamese) Moon.

NIA (Irish) Bright. Form of Niamh. *Notables:* Actresses Nia Vardalos and Nia Peeples. *Variation:* Nea.

NIABI (Native American) Fawn. *Variations:* Niabee, Niabia, Niabie, Niaby.

NIAMH (Irish) Bright.

NIBAL (Arabic) Arrow.

NICHELLE (American) Combined form of Nicole and Michelle. *Variations:* Nichel, Nichela, Nichele, Nichell, Nishel, Nishela, Nishele, Nishell, Nishella, Nishelle.

NICKI (American) Victorious. Short form of Nicole. *Notable:* Actress Nikki Cox. *Variations:* Nicky, Nikki, Niki.

NICOLE (French) Victorious. Feminine version of Nicholas.

Notables: Actresses Nicole Kidman and Nicole Richie. *Variations:* Nacol, Nacola, Nacole, Necol, Necola, Necolah, Necole, Necoll, Necolla, Necolle, Nichol, Nichola, Nichole, Nicholle, Nicki, Nickola, Nickole, Nicola, Nicoleen, Nicolene, Nicolina, Nicoline, Nicolla, Nicolle, Nikki, Nikola.

NICOLETTE (French) Form of Nicole. *Notable:* Actress Nicolette Sheridan. *Variations:* Nicoletta, Nikoletta, Nikolette.

NIDIA (Latin) Nest. *Variation:* Nydia.

NIGELLA (Irish) Champion. Feminine form of Nigel. *Notables:* TV chef Nigella Lawson. *Variation:* Nigelia.

NIHAL (Arabic) One who drinks.

NIKA (Russian) Short form of Nikita or Veronica. *Variations:* Nica, Nieka.

NIKE (Greek) Victory. *Variation:* Nika.

NIKEESHA (African American) *Variations:* Niceesha, Nickeesha, Nickisha, Nicquisha, Niquisha, Nykesha.

NIKITA (Russian) Victorious. *Variations:* Nickeata, Nickeeta, Nickeetah, Nikeata, Nikeeta, Nikeita, Nikitah, Nikkita, Niquita, Nykeata, Nykeeta, Nykeetah, Nykeita, Nykeyta, Nykeytah.

NILDA (Italian; Spanish) Warrior woman.

NILSINE (Scandinavian) Victory of the people.

NIMA (Hindi) Tree. *Variations:* Neema, Neemah, Nema, Nimah, Nyma, Nymah.

NIMESHA (Hindi) Fast. *Variations:* Naimishi, Nimeesha, Nimmi.

NINA (Spanish) Girl; (Hebrew) Grace of God. *Notable:* Jazz singer Nina Simone. *Variations:* Neana, Neena, Ninah, Ninelle, Ninet, Nineta, Ninete, Ninetta, Ninette, Ninita, Ninnette, Ninotchka, Nyna, Nynette.

NINON (French) Grace. Form of Ann.

NINOVAN (Native American) Home.

NIOBE (Greek) Fern. Ancient mythological figure.

NIPA (East Indian) River.

NIRANJANA (Hindi) Full moon.

NIREL (Hebrew) Cultivated pasture. *Variations:* Nirealle, Nirela, Nirelah, Nirell, Nirella, Nyrel, Nyrela, Nyrell, Nyrella, Nyrelle.

NIRVANA (Sanskrit) Bliss.

NIRVELI (Hindi) Water. *Variations:* Nirevelea, Nirveleah, Nirvelee, Nirvelei, Nirveleigh, Nirveley, Nirvelie, Nirvely, Nyrvelee, Nyrvelei, Nyrveleigh, Nyrveley, Nyrvelie, Nyrvely.

NISHA (Hindi) Night. *Variations:* Neesia, Neesha, Nicia.

NISHI (Japanese) West. *Variations:* Nishee, Nishie, Nishiko, Nishiyo.

NISSA (Hebrew) Sign. *Variations:* Nisa, Nisah, Nissah, Nyssa.

NITA (Spanish) God is giving. Short form of Juanita or Anita. *Variations:* Neeta, Nitah, Nitali.

NITARA (Hindi) Grounded.

NITYA (Sanskrit) Eternal.

NIVA (Hebrew) Talk. *Variation:* Neva.

NIXIE (German) Water nymph. *Variations:* Nixee, Nixi.

NOELANI (Hawaiian) Heavenly. *Variations:* Noelanee, Noelaney, No'elani, Noelania, Noelanie, Noelany, Noelanya.

NOELLE (French) Christmas. *Variations:* Noel, Noela, Noele, Noeleen, Noelene, Noelia, Noeline, Noell, Noella, Noelline, Noleen, Nowell.

NOGA (Hebrew) Morning light.

NOIRIN (Irish) Honorable light.

NOLA (Irish) White shoulder. Form of Fionnula. *Variation:* Nolah.

NOLANA (Irish) Champion of the people. Feminine form of Nolan. *Variations:* Noelana, Noelanna, Noeleen, Noeline, Nolanna.

NOLETA (Latin) Reluctant. *Variations:* Noleeta, Nolita.

NONA (Latin) Ninth. *Variations:* Nonah, Noni, Nonia, Nonie, Nonna, Nonnah.

NOOR (Arabic) Light. *Notable:* Queen Noor of Jordan. *Variation:* Noora.

NORA (Greek) Light. Form of Eleanor or Leonora. *Notables:* Writer/ film director Nora Ephron; singer Norah Jones. *Variation:* Norah.

NORBERTA (German) Renowned northerner. Feminine form of Norbert.

NOREEN (Irish) Light. Form of Nora or Eleanor. *Variations:* Noreena, Norene, Norina, Norine.

NORELL (Scandinavian) From the north. *Variations:* Narelle, Norelle.

NORI (Japanese) Principle. *Variation:* Noriko.

NORMA (Latin) From the North. Feminine form of Norman. *Notable:* Actress Norma Shearer. *Variations:* Normah.

NORMANDY (French) Area of northern France. *Variation:* Normandie.

NORNA (Scandinavian) Fate. Goddess of time.

NORRIS (English) Last name.

NOTAKU (Native American) Growling bear.

NOULA (Greek) Grace. *Variation:* Noulah.

NOURA (Arabic) Light. *Variation:* Nourah.

NOVA (Latin) New. *Variation:* Novah.

NOVELLA (Spanish) New little thing.

NOVIA (Spanish) Girlfriend.

NU (Vietnamese) Girl.

NUALA (Irish) White shoulders. Form of Fionnula.

NUBIA (African) Area in ancient Africa.

NUDAR (Arabic) Golden.

NUHA (Arabic) Smart.

NUMA (Arabic) Beautiful.

NUNA (Native American) Land.

NUNIA (Polynesian) Leader.

NUNZIA (Italian) Messenger. Short form of Annunciata. *Variations:* Nunciata, Nunziatella, Nunziatina.

NUR (Arabic) Illuminate. *Variations:* Nura, Nuri, Nurya.

NURA (Aramaic) Light. *Variations:* Noor, Noora, Noura, Nurah, Nuri, Nuria, Nuriel, Nuru.

NURIA (Hebrew) Fire of the Lord. *Variations:* Nuriah, Nuriel.

NURITA (Hebrew) Flower. *Variation:* Nurit.

NUSI (Hungarian) Grace of God. *Variations:* Nucee, Nuci, Nucie, Nusee, Nusie, Nusey, Nusy.

NUTAN (Hindi) New.

NYALA (African) Antelope. *Variation:* Nyela.

NYDIA (Latin) Nest. *Variation:* Nidia.

NYLA (Irish) Champion. *Variation:* Nila.

NYREE (Maori) Sea. *Variation:* Niree.

NYURA (Russian) Grace.

NYUSHA (Russian) Pure. Form of Agnes. *Variation:* Nyushka.

NYX (Greek) Night. *Variation:* Nix.

OADIRA (African) Powerful. *Variations:* Oadeera, Oadirah, Odira, Odyra.

OAKLEY (English) Oak tree. *Variations:* Oake, Oaklie.

OANNA (Romanian) God is good. *Variation:* Oana.

OBA (African) Goddess of the river.

OBEDIENCE (English) Loyalty. *Variation:* Obey.

OBELIA (Greek) Needle. *Variations:* Obeliah, Obelya.

OBIOMA (African) Kind.

OCEANA (Greek) Ocean. *Variations:* Ocean, Oceane, Oceania, Ocena, Oshin, Oshine.

OCIN (Native American) Rose.

OCTAVIA (Latin) Eighth. *Variations:* Aktavija, Octave, Octavie, Oktavia, Ottavia, Tavia, Tavie.

OCTOBER (Latin) Born during the month of October.

ODA (German) Wealthy. *Variations:* Odah, Odda, Oddah, Oddia, Oddiah, Odo.

ODALIS (Spanish) Wealthy. *Variation:* Odalys.

ODANDA (Spanish) Famous land. *Variations:* Odande, Odandia.

ODDFRID (Norse) Beautiful point.

ODDRUN (Scandinavian) Point. *Variations:* Oda, Odd, Oddr.

ODDVEIG (Scandinavian) Woman with a spear.

ODE (African) Born while traveling. *Variations:* Odee, Odi, Odia, Odiah, Odya.

ODEDA (Hebrew) Powerful.

ODELE (German) Wealthy; (Greek) Melody. *Variations:* Odeela, Odela, Odelah, Odelia, Odelinda, Odell, Odella, Odelle, Odelyn, Odila, Odile, Odilia.

ODELETTE (French) Little song. *Variations:* Odelet, Odeleta, Odeletta, Odette.

ODELIA (Hebrew) Praise God. *Variations:* Odeleya, Odeliah, Odelina, Odeline, Odelyna, Odelyne.

ODELLA (English) Wood hill. *Variations:* Odela, Odelle.

ODERA (Hebrew) Plow.

ODESSA (Greek) Long journey. *Variations:* Adessa, Odesa, Odessia, Odissa, Odyssa.

ODETTE (French) Wealthy. *Variation:* Odetta.

ODHARNAIT (Irish) Pale complexion. *Variations:* Orna, Ornat.

ODILA (German) Wealthy. *Variations:* Odilah, Odilla.

ODILE (French) Success in battle. *Variation:* Odille.

ODINA (Native American) Mountain.

ODIYA (Hebrew) Song of God.

OENONE (Greek) Wine woman.

OFIRA (Hebrew) Fawn. *Variations:* Ofirah, Ofra, Ophra, Ophrah.

OGENYA (Hebrew) God is my helper.

OGIN (Native American) Wild rose. *Variation:* Ogina.

OHANA (Hebrew) God is gracious. *Variations:* Ohanah, Ohanna, Ohannah.

OHELA (Hebrew) Tent.

OHEO (Native American) Beautiful.

OHNICIO (Irish) Honor.

OILBHE (Irish) Olive tree.

OISIN (Irish) Young deer.

OJASVEE (Hindi) Shining. *Variation:* Ojasvita.

OJININTKA (Native American) Rose.

OKALANI (Hawaiian) Of the heavens.

OKI (Japanese) Middle of the ocean.

OKIIANI (Hawaiian) From heaven. *Variation:* Okiilani.

OKLAHOMA (Native American) Red people.

OKSANA (Russian) Praise to God. *Notable:* Olympic gold medalist Oksana Baiul.

OKTAWJA (Polish) Eighth.

OLA (Scandinavian) Ancestor. *Variations:* Olah, Olesia, Olesya.

OLABISI (African) To increase.

OLABUNMI (African) Award.

OLALLA (Spanish; Portuguese) Well spoken.

OLANIYI (African) Wealth.

OLATHE (Native American) Beautiful. *Variations:* Olanth, Olantha.

OLAUG (Scandinavian) Devoted to ancestors.

OLDRISKA (Czech) Prosperous ruler. *Variations:* Olda, Oldra, Oldrina, Olina, Oluse.

OLEANDER (English) Evergreen tree. *Variations:* Oleanda, Oliander.

OLEATHA (Scandinavian) Light. *Variations:* Alethea, Oleta.

OLEDA (Latin) Winged. *Variations:* Oleta, Olethea, Olida, Olita.

OLENA (Russian) Brilliant light. *Variations:* Oleena, Olenka, Olenna, Olenya.

OLESIA (Greek) Protector of humanity. *Variations:* Olecia, Olisha.

OLETHEA (Latin) Truthful. *Variations:* Oleathea, Olethia.

OLGA (Scandinavian; Russian) Holy. *Notable:* Gymnast Olga Korbut. *Variations:* Elga, Ola, Olenka, Olesya, Olia, Olina, Olka, Olli, Olly, Olunka, Oluska, Olva, Olya, Olyusha.

OLIANA (Hawaiian) Oleander. *Variations:* Oleana, Oleanna, Oliane, Olianna, Olianne.

Top Names of the 1900s

BOYS:
1. John
2. William
3. James
4. George
5. Charles
6. Robert
7. Joseph
8. Frank
9. Edward
10. Thomas
11. Henry
12. Walter
13. Harry
14. Willie
15. Arthur
16. Albert
17. Clarence
18. Fred
19. Harold
20. Paul

GIRLS:
1. Mary
2. Helen
3. Margaret
4. Anna
5. Ruth
6. Elizabeth
7. Dorothy
8. Marie
9. Florence
10. Mildred
11. Alice
12. Ethel
13. Lillian
14. Gladys
15. Edna
16. Frances
17. Rose
18. Annie
19. Grace
20. Bertha

OLIENKA (Russian) Holy. *Variations:* Olinka, Olyenka.

OLINA (Hawaiian) Happy. *Variations:* Oleen, Oline, Olyna.

OLINDA (Latin) Perfumed. *Variation:* Olynda.

OLISA (African) God. *Variations:* Olissa, Olysa.

OLIVE (Latin) Olive tree. *Variations:* Olivie, Olyve.

OLIVIA (Latin) Olive tree. *Notables:* Actress Olivia de Havilland; singer Olivia Newton-John. *Variations:* Liv, Olia, Oliva, Olive, Olivet, Olivette, Olivine, Ollie, Olva, Olyvia.

OLWEN (Welsh) White footprint. *Variations:* Olwena, Olwenn, Olwenna, Olwenne, Olwin, Olwina, Olwine, Olwyn, Olwyna, Olwyne, Olwynne.

OLYMPIA (Greek) Mount Olympus, home of the Greek gods. *Notable:* Actress Olympia Dukakis. *Variations:* Olimpia, Olympe, Olympya, Pia.

OMA (Hebrew) Devout. *Variation:* Omah.

OMAIRA (Arabic) Red. *Variations:* Omara, Omarah, Omaria.

OMANA (Hindi) Lady. *Variations:* Omania, Omanie, Omanna.

OMEGA (Greek) Final.

OMEMEE (Native American) Pigeon.

OMOLARA (African) Born at the right time.

OMOROSE (African) Beautiful child.

OMUSA (Native American) Misses with an arrow.

ONA (Lithuanian) Grace.

ONATAH (Native American) Child of the earth.

ONDINE (Latin) Little wave. *Variations:* Ondina, Ondine, Ondyne, Undina, Undine.

ONDREA (Czech) Fierce woman. *Variation:* Ondra.

ONEIDA (Native American) Anticipation. *Variations:* Oneeda, Onida, Onyda.

ONELLA (Greek) Light.

ONGELA (American) Angel. Form of Angela. *Variations:* Ongelia, Ongella, Ongelica, Ongelika, Ongelina, Ongeline.

ONI (African) Desired.

ONIDA (Native American) The one we search for.

ONORA (Latin) Honor. *Variations:* Ona, Onoria, Onorine.

ONTARIO (Native American) Beautiful lake.

ONYX (Latin) Black gem. *Variation:* Onix.

OONA (Irish) Unity. *Variations:* Oonagh, Oonah.

OPA (Native American) Owl.

OPAL (English) Gem. *Variations:* Opala, Opaleen, Opali, Opalia, Opalie, Opalina, Opaline, Opalyna, Opalyne.

OPHELIA (Greek) Help. *Variations:* Ofelia, Ofilia, Ophelie.

OPHIRA (Hebrew) Fawn. *Variation:* Ofira.

OPRAH (Hebrew) A fawn. *Notable:* Talk-show personality Oprah Winfrey. *Variations:* Ofra, Ofrat, Ofrit, Ophra, Ophrah, Ophrat, Ophrit, Orpa, Orpah, Orpha, Orphy.

ORA (Latin) Prayer. *Variations:* Orah, Orra.

ORABELLA (Latin) Prayer. Form of Arabella. *Variations:* Orabel, Orabela, Orabelle.

ORALIE (French) Golden. *Variations:* Oralee, Oralia, Orelie, Oriel, Orielle, Orlena, Orlene.

ORANGE (English) Orange. *Variations:* Orangetta, Orangina.

ORELA (Latin) Revelation. *Variations:* Oralla, Orella, Orelle.

ORENDA (Native American) Magic spell. *Variation:* Orinda.

ORETHA (Greek) Form of Aretha.

ORFHLAITH (Irish) Golden lady. *Variations:* Orflath, Orlaith.

ORIANA (Latin) Sunrise. *Variations:* Oraine, Oralia, Orane, Orania, Orelda, Orelle, Oria, Oriane, Orianna, Orianne.

ORINA (Russian) Form of Irene. *Variation:* Orena.

ORINO (Japanese) Weaver's loom. *Variation:* Ori.

ORIOLE (English) Bird name. *Variations:* Auriel, Orella, Oriel, Oriola.

ORIT (Hebrew) Light.

ORLA (Irish) Golden. *Variations:* Orlagh, Orlann, Orlene.

ORLANDA (German) Famous in the land.

ORLENDA (Russian) Female eagle. *Variation:* Orlinda.

ORLY (Hebrew) Light of mine. *Variations:* Orli, Orlie.

ORMANDA (Latin) Noble.

ORNA (Irish) Pale green.

ORNAT (Hebrew) Light.

ORNELLA (Italian) Flowering tree.

ORNICE (Hebrew) Cedar tree. *Variations:* Orna, Ornit.

ORQUIDEA (Spanish) Orchid.

ORSA (Latin) Female bear. *Variations:* Orsala, Orsaline, Orsel, Orselina, Orseline, Orsola.

ORSINA (Italian) Bear-like.

ORSOLA (Italian) Little she-bear. A form of Ursula.

ORTENSIA (Italian) From the garden. Form of Hortense. *Variation:* Ortense.

ORTHIA (Greek) Straight path.

ORTRUN (German) Secret point.

ORVA (French) Golden.

ORYA (Russian) Peace. *Variation:* Oryna.

OSANA (Latin) Praise the lord. *Variations:* Osanna, Ozanna.

OSANNE (French) Deliver us. *Variations:* Osane, Ozane, Ozanne.

OSEN (Japanese) Thousand.

OSEYE (African) Happy one.

OSITA (Spanish) Divine strength. *Variations:* Oseta, Ositha.

OSMA (English) Divine protector. *Variations:* Osmah, Ozma.

OSWALDA (German) Divine power. Feminine form of Oswald. *Variations:* Osvalda, Osvaldia, Oswaldia, Oswaldina.

OTTHILD (German) Successful in battle. *Variations:* Ottila, Ottilia, Ottilie, Ottiline, Ottoline, Otylia.

OTYLIA (Polish) Wealth. *Variations:* Otilie, Ottella.

OUIDA (French) Famous soldier.

OURANIA (Greek) Heavenly one.

OVIA (Latin) Egg. *Variations:* Ova, Ovah, Oviah.

OWENA (Welsh) Well born. Feminine version of Owen. *Variations:* Owenna, Owina, Owyna.

OZARA (Hebrew) Treasure. *Variations:* Otzara, Ozera, Ozora.

PAAVANA (Hindi) Pure. *Variations:* Paavna, Pavana, Pavna.

PAAVANI (Hindi) The Ganges River.

PABLA (Spanish) Small. Feminine form of Pablo, Paul.

PACA (Spanish) From France. Form of Francisca.

PACIFICA (Spanish) Peaceful.

PADMA (Hindi) Lotus. *Variations:* Padmah, Padmani, Padmar, Padmasundara, Padmavati, Padmina, Padmini.

PADRAIGIN (Irish) Of noble descent.

PAGAN (English) Country villager. *Variations:* Pagen, Pagin, Pagyn.

PAGET (English) Little page. *Variations:* Padget, Padgett, Pagett, Pagette.

PAIGE (English) Young helper. *Variations:* Page, Payge.

PAISLEY (Scottish) Feather-like pattern. *Variations:* Paesley, Paesli, Paislea, Paislee, Paislei, Paislie.

PAIVA (Finnish) Born during the day. *Variation:* Payva.

PAJ (Swedish) Pie.

PAKA (African) Kitten.

PALA (Native American) Water. *Variations:* Palah, Palla, Pallah.

PALAKIKA (Hawaiian) Hawaiian version of Frances. From France. *Variation:* Farakika.

PALILA (Hawaiian) Bird. *Variations:* Palilah, Palyla.

PALLAS (Greek) Goddess of wisdom. *Variations:* Palace, Pallassa.

PALLAVI (Hindi) New leaves. *Variations:* Palavi, Pallavee.

PALMA (Latin) Palm. *Variation:* Palmah.

PALMER (English) Palm tree. *Variations:* Palmar, Palmara, Palmaria.

PALMIRA (Italian) Pilgrim. *Variations:* Palmirar, Palmyra.

PALOMA (Spanish) Dove. *Notable:* Fashion designer Paloma Picasso. *Variations:* Palloma, Palometa, Palomita, Peloma.

PAM (English) Sweet as honey. Short form of Pamela. *Notable:* Actress Pam Dawber. *Variations:* Pami, Pamm, Pammi, Pammie, Pammy.

PAMELA (Greek) Honey. *Notable:* Actress Pamela Anderson. *Variations:* Palmala, Pamala, Pamalia, Pamalla, Pamelia, Pamelina, Pameline, Pamelita, Pamella, Pamelyn, Pamilia, Pamilla, Pammela.

PAMERA (Japanese) Loving and sweet.

PANA (Native American) Partridge.

PANCHA (Spanish) From France. *Variation:* Panchita.

PANCHALI (Sanskrit) Princess. *Variations:* Panchalei, Panchalie.

PANDITA (Hindi) Good wife. Scholar.

PANDORA (Greek) All gifted. *Variations:* Panda, Pandorah, Pandorra, Panndora.

PANGIOTA (Greek) All holy. *Variation:* Panagiota.

PANIZ (Persian) Sweet girl.

PANNA (Hindi) Emerald.

PANOLA (Native American) Cotton. *Variations:* Panolah, Panolla.

PANPHILA (Greek) She loves all. *Variations:* Panfila, Panfyla, Panphyla.

PANSOFIA (Greek) Possessing wisdom. *Variations:* Pansofea, Pansofee, Pansofi, Pansofy, Pansophia, Pansophie.

PANSY (English) Flower name. *Variations:* Pansey, Pansi, Pansie, Panzie, Panzy.

PANTHEA (Greek) All the gods. *Variations:* Panfia, Panthia, Panthya.

PANYA (African) Mouse.

PANYIN (African) First born of twins.

PAOLA (Italian) Form of Paula. *Variation:* Paolina.

PAPINA (Native American) Vine on an oak tree.

PAPRIKA (Hungarian) Peppery spice.

PAQUITA (Spanish) Form of Frances.

PARADISA (Greek) Garden. *Variation:* Paradise.

PARI (Persian) Fairy.

PARIS (Greek) The city. *Notable:* Hotel heiress Paris Hilton. *Variations:* Parisa, Parris, Parrish.

PARKER (English) Park keeper. *Notable:* Actress Parker Posey.

PARMENIA (Spanish) Studious.

PARMIDA (Persian) Born to royalty.

PARMINDER (Hindi) Attractive woman. *Variation:* Parmindar.

PARNELLE (French) Small rock. *Variations:* Parnel, Parnell.

PARTHENIA (Greek) Virginal. *Variations:* Parthania, Parthena, Parthenie, Parthina, Parthine, Pathania, Pathena, Pathenia, Pathina.

PARVANI (Hindi) Full moon. *Variation:* Parvina.

PARVATI (Hindi) Child of the mountain.

PARVIN (Hindi) Stars. *Variation:* Parveen.

PASCALE (French) Child of Easter. Feminine version of Pascal. *Variations:* Pascalette, Pascaline, Pascalle, Pascasia, Paschale.

PASQUALINA (Italian) Easter.

PASHA (Greek) Of the ocean. *Variation:* Palasha.

PASSION (Latin) Passion.

PASTORA (Spanish) Shepherd.

PAT (Latin) Noble. Short form of Patricia. *Notable:* Singer Pat Benatar.

PATIA (Spanish) Leaf. *Variations:* Patiah, Patya.

PATIENCE (English) Patience. *Variations:* Paciencia, Patient.

PATRICE (French) Form of Patricia. *Variations:* Patreece, Patryce.

PATRICIA (Latin) Noble. Feminine version of Patrick. *Notables:* Actresses Patricia Heaton and Patricia Arquette; writer Patricia

Cornwell. *Variations:* Pat, Patreece, Patreice, Patria, Patric, Patrica, Patrice, Patricka, Patriza, Patrizia, Patrycia, Patsy, Patti, Pattie, Patty, Tricia, Trish, Trisha.

PATSY (Irish; English) Form of Patricia. *Notable:* Singer Patsy Cline. *Variations:* Patsee, Patsey, Patsi, Patsie.

PATTY (English) Short form of Patricia. *Notables:* Actress Patty Duke; singer Patty Loveless. *Variations:* Patea, Patee, Patey, Pati, Patie, Paty, Pattea, Pattee, Pattey, Patti, Pattie.

PAULA (Latin) Small. Feminine version of Paul. *Notable:* Singer Paula Abdul. *Variations:* Paola, Paule, Paulie, Paulita, Pauly, Paulyn, Pavla, Pola, Polcia, Pollie, Polly.

PAULETTE (French) Form of Paula. *Variations:* Pauletta, Paulette.

PAULINE (French) Form of Paula. *Notable:* Film critic Pauline Kael. *Variations:* Paolina, Pauleen, Paulene, Paulina, Pavlina, Pavlinka, Pawlina.

PAUSHA (Hindi) Month in the Hindi year.

PAVANA (Hindi) Wind. *Variation:* Pavani.

PAX (Latin) Peace.

PAXTON (Latin) Peaceful town.

PAZ (Spanish) Peace.

PAZIA (Hebrew) Golden. *Variations:* Paza, Pazia, Paziah, Pazice, Pazit, Paziya, Pazya.

PEACE (English) Peace.

PEACHES (American) Peach fruit. Term of endearment. *Variations:* Peachee, Peachie, Peachy.

PEARL (Latin) Pearl. *Notables:* Writer Pearl S. Buck; singer Pearl Bailey. *Variations:* Pearla, Pearle, Pearlea, Pearleen, Pearleigh, Pearlena, Pearlette, Pearley, Pearline, Pearly, Perl, Perla, Perle, Perlette, Perley, Perlie, Perlita, Perly, Purl, Purlia, Purlie.

PEBBLES (English) Small stones. Pet name. *Notable:* Cartoon baby Pebbles Flintstone.

PEG (English) Pearl. Short form of Peggy. *Notable:* TV character Peg Bundy. *Variation:* Pegg.

PEGGY (English) Pearl. Form of Margaret. *Notables:* Singer Peggy Lee; ice-skating champion Peggy Fleming. *Variations:* Pegee, Peggee, Peggey, Peggi, Peggie, Pegi.

PEKE (Hawaiian) Bright.

PELA (Hawaiian) Pretty. *Variation:* Bela.

PELAGIA (Greek) The ocean; (Polish) Sea dweller. *Variations:* Pelage, Pelageia, Pelagie, Pelegia, Pelgia, Pellagia.

PELEKA (Hawaiian) Bright. *Variations:* Beke, Bereta.

PELIAH (Hebrew) God's miracle. *Variation:* Pelia.

PELIKA (Hawaiian) Peaceful. Hawaiian version of Freda. *Variation:* Ferida, Peleka.

PELIPA (Native American) Lover of horses.

PELULIO (Hawaiian) Emerald. *Variation:* Berulo.

PEMBA (African) Meteorological power.

PENDA (African) Beloved.

PENELOPE (Greek) Weaver. *Notables:* Actresses Penelope Ann

Miller and Penelope Cruz. *Variations:* Lopa, Pela, Pelcia, Pen, Penelopa, Penina, Penine, Penna, Pennelope, Penni, Penny, Pinelopi, Piptisa, Popi.

PENINAH (Hebrew) Precious stone. *Variations:* Peni, Penie, Penina, Penini, Peninit, Pennina, Penninah.

PENNY (Greek) Short form of Penelope. *Notable:* Actress/director Penny Marshall. *Variations:* Penni, Pennie.

PEONY (English) Flower name. *Variations:* Peoni, Peonie.

PEPITA (Spanish) God will add. Diminutive feminine form of Pepe (Joseph). *Variations:* Pepa, Peta.

PEPPER (Latin) Pepper plant. *Variations:* Pepa, Peppa.

PERACH (Hebrew) Blossom. *Variations:* Perah, Pericha, Pircha, Pirchia, Pirchit, Pirchiya, Pirha.

PERDITA (Latin) Lost.

PEREGRINA (Latin) Wanderer. *Variation:* Peregrine.

PERFECTA (Spanish) Perfect.

PERNELLA (Greek) Rock. *Variations:* Parnella, Pernelia, Pernella, Pernelle, Pernilla, Pernille.

PEROUZE (Armenian) Turquoise gem.

PERRY (French) Pear tree; (Greek) Nymph of the mountains. *Notable:* Actress Peri Gilpin. *Variations:* Peri, Perrey, Perri, Perrie.

PERSEPHONE (Greek) The goddess of spring and rebirth.

PERSIS (Latin) From Persia. *Variation:* Perssis.

PETA (Greek) Rock. Feminine version of Peter. *Notable:* Actress Peta Wilson. *Variation:* Petti.

Top Korean Names

BOYS:
1. Minjoon
2. Jihoo
3. Jihoon
4. Joonsuh
5. Hyeonwoo
6. Yejoon
7. Geonwoo
8. Hyeonjoon
9. Minjae
10. Woojin

GIRLS:
1. Seoyeon
2. Minsuh
3. Seohyeon
4. Jiwoo
5. Seoyoon
6. Jimin
7. Soobin
8. Haeun
9. Yeeun
10. Yoonsuh

PETRA (Greek) Rock. *Variations:* Petrice, Petrina, Petrona.

PETRONELLA (Latin) Small rock. *Variations:* Pernel, Pernelle, Peronel, Peronelle, Petrina, Petronelle, Petronia, Petronilla, Pier, Pierette.

PETULA (Latin) Seeker. *Notable:* Singer Petula Clark. *Variation:* Petulah.

PETUNIA (English) Flower name. *Variation:* Petunya.

PEYTON (English) Warrior's estate. *Variations:* Paiton, Payton, Peyten.

PHEDRA (Greek) Bright. *Variations:* Faydra, Fedra, Phadra, Phaedra, Phedre.

PHEODORA (Greek) Gift from God. Feminine form of Theodore.

PHILADELPHIA (Greek) Brotherly love. *Variations:* Philli, Phillie.

PHILANA (Greek) Lover of people. *Variations:* Filana, Filane, Phileen, Philina, Philine, Phylana.

PHILANTHA (Greek) Lover of flowers. *Variations:* Philanthe, Phylantha.

PHILBERTA (English) Very bright. *Variations:* Filberta, Filberte, Philberte, Phylberta.

PHILIPPA (Greek) Lover of horses. Feminine version of Philip. *Variations:* Philipa, Philippine, Phillipina, Pippa, Pippy, Phylippa.

PHILOMELA (Greek) Lover of music. *Variation:* Filomela.

PHILOMENA (Greek) Beloved. *Variations:* Filomena, Filomina, Philomene, Philomina.

PHILOTHEA (Greek) Love of God. *Variation:* Filothea.

PHILYRA (Greek) Lime tree. *Variation:* Philira.

PHOEBE (Greek) Brilliant. *Notable:* Actress Phoebe Cates. *Variations:* Pheabe, Phebe, Phebea, Pheby, Phoebee, Phoebie, Phoeby.

PHYLICIA (Latin) Happy. Form of Felicia. *Notable:* Actress Phylicia Rashad. *Variations:* Felicia, Filicia, Phileesha, Philicia.

PHYLLIDA (Greek) Greenery. *Notable:* Actress Phyllida Law. *Variations:* Phileada, Phileeda, Philida, Philleada, Philleeda, Phillida, Phyleada, Phyleeda, Phylida.

PHYLLIS (Greek) Foliage. *Notable:* Comedian Phyllis Diller. *Variations:* Philis, Phillis, Philliss, Phillys, Phylis, Phyllida, Phylliss, Phylys.

PIA (Latin) Pious. *Notable:* Actress Pia Zadora. *Variations:* Piah, Pya.

PICABO (American) Town in Idaho. *Notable:* Skier Picabo Street.

PIEDAD (Spanish) Devotion.

PIERA (Italian) Stone. *Variations:* Pierina, Pietrina, Pietronella.

PIERRETTE (French) Rock. Feminine form of Pierre. *Variations:* Perett, Peretta, Perette, Pier, Pieret, Pierett, Pierette, Pierra.

PIETY (English) Devoutness.

PILAR (Spanish) Pillar. *Variations:* Pilla, Pillar, Pylar.

PILI (African) Second born.

PILIKIKA (Hawaiian) Strong.

PILILANI (Hawaiian) Close to heaven. *Variation:* Pililanee.

PILISI (Greek) Branch.

PILUKI (Hawaiian) Leaf.

PINEKI (Hawaiian) Peanut.

PINGA (Hindi) Bronze.

PINQUANA (Native American) Fragrant. *Variation:* Pinquanna.

PIPER (English) Bagpipe or flute player. *Notables:* Actresses Piper Laurie and Piper Perabo. *Variations:* Pipar, Pyper.

PIPPA (Greek) Short form of Philippa. *Variations:* Pip, Pipa, Pippi, Pippy.

PIROUETTE (French) Spinning top. *Variations:* Pirouet, Pirouetta.

PIXIE (English) Tiny. *Variations:* Pixee, Pixey, Pixi.

PLACIDA (Spanish) Calm. *Variation:* Plasida.

PLEASANCE (English) Pleasure. *Variations:* Pleasant, Pleasants, Pleasence.

POCAHONTAS (Native American) Capricious.

POLETE (Hawaiian) Small. *Variations:* Poleke, Polina.

POLLY (English) Form of Paula or Molly. *Notables:* Actresses Polly Bergen and Polly Walker. *Variations:* Pauleigh, Pollee, Polley, Polli, Pollie, Pollyann, Pollyanna, Pollyanne.

POLYXENA (Greek) Very hospitable.

POMAIKAI (Hawaiian) Fortunate.

POMONA (Latin) Apple.

POOJA (Hindi) Worship. *Variation:* Puja.

POPPY (Latin) Flower name. *Variations:* Popi, Poppi, Poppie.

PORTIA (Latin) Offering. *Notable:* Actress Portia de Rossi. *Variations:* Porcha, Porscha, Porsche, Porschia, Porsha, Portya.

POSALA (Native American) Flower.

POSY (Latin) Flower. *Variations:* Posee, Posey, Posi, Posie.

PRAGYATA (Hindi) Wisdom.

PRARTHANA (Hindi) Prayer.

PRATIBHA (Hindi) Tolerance.

PRECIOUS (Latin) Precious. *Variations:* Precia, Preciosa.

PREMA (Hindi) Love.

PREMILLA (Hindi) Love. *Variations:* Premila, Premyla.

PREMLATA (Hindi) Vine.

PRIBISLAVA (Czech) To help glorify. *Variations:* Pribena, Pribka, Pribuska.

PRIELA (Hebrew) Fruit of God. *Variation:* Priela.

PRIMA (Latin) First. *Variations:* Primalia, Primetta, Primina, Priminia, Primula.

PRIMAVERA (Italian) Spring.

PRIMROSE (English) First rose. *Variations:* Primrosa, Prymrose.

PRINCESS (English) Royal title. *Variations:* Prin, Princesa, Princessa.

PRISCILLA (Latin) Old. *Notable:* Actress Priscilla Presley. *Variations:* Precilla, Prescilla, Pricilla, Pris, Priscila, Priss, Prissie, Prissilla, Prissy, Prysilla.

PRISMA (Greek) Cut glass. *Variations:* Prusma, Prysma.

PRISSY (Latin) Short form of Priscilla.

PRITA (Hindi) Dear one.

PRIYA (Hindi) Beloved. *Variations:* Priyal, Priyam, Priyanka, Priyasha, Priyata, Priyati.

PROMISE (Latin) Pledge.

PROSPERA (Latin) Fortunate. *Variation:* Prosperia.

PRU (Latin) Short form of Prudence. *Variation:* Prue.

PRUDENCE (Latin) Cautiousness. *Variations:* Prudencia, Prudie, Prudu, Prudy.

PRUNELLA (Latin) Small plum.

PSYCHE (Greek) The soul.

PUA (Hawaiian) Flowering tree.

PUAKAI (Hawaiian) Ocean flower. *Variation:* Pua.

PUAKEA (Hawaiian) White flower.

PUALANI (Hawaiian) Flower. *Variation:* Puni.

PUANANI (Hawaiian) Beautiful flower.

PULUPAKI (Polynesian) Flower wreath.

PURITY (English) Pure.

PURNIMA (Hindi) Full moon.

PYRALIS (Greek) Fire.

PYRENA (Greek) Fiery. *Variation:* Pyrina.

PYRRHA (Greek) Red.

QADESH (Syrian) Goddess of love and sensuality. *Variations:* Qadesha, Qadeshia, Quedesh, Quedesha, Quedeshia.

QADIRA (Arabic) Powerful. *Variations:* Kadira, Kadirah, Qadirah, Qadyra.

QAMRA (Arabic) Moon woman. *Variations:* Camra, Kamra, Qamara, Qamrah, Qamria.

QEREN (Hebrew) Horn of an animal.

QETSIYAH (Hebrew) Cassia, a bark similar to cinnamon.

QETURAH (Hebrew) Incense. *Variations:* Keturah, Qetura, Qeturia.

QI (Chinese) Wondrous.

QIANG (Chinese) Red rose.

QIAO (Chinese) High and aspiring.

QIAOLIAN (Chinese) Clever.

QIMAT (Hindi) Valuable woman. *Variation:* Qimata.

QING (Chinese) Sky blue.

QINGGE (Chinese) Love song.

QINGLING (Chinese) Lucky years.

QINGZHAO (Chinese) Clear understanding.

QITARA (Arabic) Fragrant. *Variations:* Qitarah, Qitaria, Qitarra.

QIU (Chinese) Autumn.

QIUYUE (Chinese) Autumn moon.

QUANA (Native American) Sweet smelling. *Variations:* Quanah, Quania, Quanna.

QUANEISHA (African American) Life. *Variations:* Quanecia, Quanesha, Quanesia, Quanisha, Quanishia, Quansha, Quarnisha, Queisha, Quenisha, Quenishia, Quynecia, Quynesha, Quynesia, Quynisha, Quynishia, Quynsha, Qynecia, Qynisha, Qynysha.

QUANIKA (Russian) Dedicated to God. *Variations:* Quanikka, Quanikki, Quanique, Quantenique, Quantenyque, Quanyka, Quanykka, Quanykki, Quanyque, Quaqanica, Quaqanyca, Quawanika.

QUARTILLA (Latin) Fourth. *Variations:* Quartila, Quartilah, Quartile, Quartillah, Quartille, Quartyla, Quartylah, Quartyle, Quartylla, Quartyllah, Quartylle, Quintila, Quintilah, Quintile, Quantilla, Quintillah, Quiantille, Quintyla, Quintylah, Quintylla, Quintyllah, Quyntila, Quyntillah, Quyntille, Quyntyla, Quyntylah, Quyntyle, Quyntylla, Quyntyllah, Quyntylle.

QUBILAH (Arabic) Agreement. *Variations:* Quabila, Quabilah, Quabyla, Quabylah, Qubila, Quibilah, Quybla, Quyblah.

QUEEN (English) Queen. *Variations:* Queana, Queanah, Queanee, Queaney, Queani, Queania, Queaniah, Queanie, Queany, Queanya, Queena, Queenation, Queeneste, Queenee, Queenet, Queenetta, Queenette, Queeni, Queenie, Queeny.

QUELLA (English) To pacify. *Variations:* Quela, Quelle.

QUENNA (English) Queen.

QUERALT (Spanish) High crag or rock.

QUERIDA (Spanish) Beloved. *Variations:* Queridah, Querrida.

QUESTA (French) Hunter.

QUETA (Spanish) Home ruler.

QUIANA (American) Grace. *Variations:* Quianna, Quianne.

QUINBY (Scandinavian) Estate of the queen. *Variation:* Quenby.

QUINCY (English) Fifth. *Variations:* Quincey, Quincie.

QUINEVERE (English) Form of Guinevere. *Variation:* Quineviere.

QUINLAN (Gaelic) Slender and strong.

QUINTANA (Latin) Fifth. *Variations:* Quintanah, Quintanna, Quintara.

QUINTELLA (Latin) Fifth. *Variations:* Quinta, Quinella.

QUINN (Gaelic) Advisor. *Variations:* Quin, Quincy.

QUINTESSA (Latin) Essense. *Variations:* Quintesa, Quintesia.

QUINTINA (English) Fifth. *Variations:* Quin, Quinella, Quinetta, Quinette, Quintana, Quintessa, Quintona, Quintonice.

QUIRINA (Latin) Contentious. *Variations:* Quireena, Quirinah, Quiryna.

QUIRITA (Latin) Citizen. *Variations:* Quiritah, Quirite, Quiritta, Quirittah, Quiritte, Quiryta, Quirytta, Quirytte, Quyryta, Quyrytta, Quyryttah, Quyrytte.

QUITA (Spanish) Little one.

QUITERIE (French) Peaceful. *Variations:* Quita, Quitah, Quiteree, Quiteri, Quiteria, Quiteriah, Quitery.

QUORRA (Italian) Heart. *Variations:* Quora, Quoria.

RABAB (Arabic) Pale cloud. *Variation:* Rababa.

RABIAH (Arabic) Breeze. *Variations:* Rabi, Rabia, Raby, Rabya.

RACHANA (Hindi) Creation. *Variations:* Rachanna, Rashana, Rashanda, Roshan.

RACHAV (Hebrew) Large. *Variations:* Rachab, Rahab, Rachev.

RACHEL (Hebrew) Lamb. *Notables:* Model Rachel Hunter; actress Rachel Griffiths. *Variations:* Rachael, Racheal, Racheale, Rachela, Rachele,

Rachell, Rachelle, Raicheal, Raichel, Raichela, Raichella, Raichelle, Raquel, Raychel, Raychela, Raychele, Raychella, Raychelle.

RADCLYFFE (English) Red cliff. *Notable:* Writer Radclyffe Hall. *Variation:* Radcliffe.

RADELLA (English) Counselor. *Variations:* Radela, Radelia, Radellah, Radelle, Radillia, Radyla.

RADHA (Hindi) Prosperity; success.

RADHIYA (African) Agreeable.

RADINKA (Czech) Lively. *Variation:* Radynka.

RADKA (Czech) Happy.

RADMILLA (Slavic) Industrious for the people. *Variations:* Radmila, Ramille, Radmylla.

RADOMIRA (Czech) Glad and famous.

RADOSLAVA (Czech) Glorious and happy.

RADOSLAWA (Polish) Glad for glory. *Variation:* Rada.

RADWA (Arabic) Mountain.

RAE (Hebrew) Lamb. Short form of Rachel. *Notable:* Actress Rae Dawn Chong. *Variations:* Raeann, Raeanna, Raeanne, Raelene, Raelyn, Rai, Ray, Raye, Rayette.

RAFA (Arabic) Well being. *Variations:* Rafah, Raffa.

RAFAELA (Spanish) God heals. Feminine version of Raphael. *Variations:* Rafa, Rafaelia, Rafaella, Rafela, Rafella, Rafelle, Raffaela, Raffaele, Raphaella, Raphaelle, Refaela, Rephaela.

RAFIKI (African) Beloved friend. *Variation:* Raffiki.

RAFYA (Hebrew) God heals. *Variations:* Rafia, Raphia.

RAGHIDA (Arabic) Happy.

RAGNARA (Scandinavian) Battle counsel. *Variations:* Ragna, Ragnarra, Ragnarrah, Ragnaria, Ragnfrid, Ragnfrida, Ragnia.

RAGNBORG (Scandinavian) Counsel. *Variation:* Ramborg.

RAGNHAILT (Gaelic) Battle counsel.

RAGNILD (German) Power. *Variations:* Ragnel, Ragnela, Ragnilla, Ragnille, Ragnhild, Ragnhilda, Ragnhilde, Ragnilda, Ranillda, Renilda, Renilde.

RAHIMA (Hindi) Loving and compassionate. *Variations:* Raheema, Rahimah.

RAI (Japanese) Next. *Variation:* Raiko.

RAIDAH (Arabic) Guide. *Variations:* Raeda, Raida, Rayda.

RAIMONDA (Italian) Wise protector. *Variations:* Raimunda, Raimunde.

RAIN (English) Rain. *Notable:* Actress Rain Pryor. *Variations:* Raen, Raine, Rayn, Rayne.

RAINA (German) Powerful. *Variations:* Raena, Raenee, Raeni, Raenie, Raine, Rainey, Rayna, Reyna.

RAINBOW (English) Rainbow. *Variations:* Raenbeau, Raenbeaux, Raenbo, Raenbow, Rainbeau, Rainbeaux, Rainbo.

RAISA (Yiddish; Russian) Rose. *Variations:* Raise, Raisel, Raissa, Raisse, Raiza, Raizel, Raizi, Rayzil, Razil.

RAJA (Arabic) Anticipation. *Variations:* Raga, Ragya, Rajya.

RAJANI (Hindi) Night. *Variations:* Rajana, Rajni.

RAJATA (Hindi) King. *Variation:* Raji.

RAJNANDINI (Hindi) Princess.

RAKHSHANDA (Arabic) Lustrous. *Variations:* Rakhshana, Rakhshonda.

RAKU (Japanese) Pleasure.

RALEIGH (English) Meadow of roe dear. *Variations:* Ralei, Ralee, Ralie, Rawlee, Rawleigh, Rawley, Rawlie.

RALPHINA (English) Wolf counselor. Feminine version of Ralph. *Variation:* Ralphine.

RAMAA (Hindi) Lovely. *Variations:* Ramana, Ramani.

RAMIA (African) Fortune-teller.

RAMIRA (Spanish) Wise and famous.

RAMLA (African: Swahili) Predicts the future.

RAMONA (Spanish) Wise protector. Feminine version of Raymond. *Notable:* Children's book character Ramona Quimby.

RAN (Japanese) Water lily.

RANA (Spanish) Frog; (Sanskrit) Royal. *Variations:* Ranah, Ranna, Ranya, Rhana.

RANAIT (Irish) Graceful. *Variation:* Ranaita.

RANANA (Hebrew) Fresh. *Variations:* Raanana, Rananah.

RANDA (English) Admirable. Short form of Miranda.

RANDELLA (English) Wolf shield. Feminine form of Randall. *Variations:* Randala, Randale, Randalea, Randalee, Randaleigh, Randali, Randalie, Randalla, Randalle, Randela, Randelia, Randelle.

RANDI (English) Feminine form of Randy, Short form of Miranda. *Variations:* Rande, Randea, Randee, Randey, Randie.

More Celebrity Baby Names

Billy Ray and Nell (Helena Bonham Carter and Tim Burton)

Brandon Thomas and Dylan Jagger (Pamela Anderson and Tommy Lee)

Brooklyn, Romeo, Cruz, and Harper (David and Victoria Beckham)

Bronwyn Golden and Slater Josiah (Angela Bassett and Courtney B. Vance)

Caspar and Clementine (Claudia Schiffer)

Charles Spencer and Tennyson Spencer (Russell Crowe and Danielle Spencer)

Charlie Tamara Tulip and Dolly Rebecca Rose (Rebecca Romijn and Jerry O'Connell)

Chester and Truman (Tom Hanks and Rita Wilson)

Coco Riley (Courtney Cox and David Arquette)

Dashiell John, Roman Robert, and Ignatius Martin (Cate Blanchett)

Delilah Belle and Amelia Gray (Lisa Rinna and Harry Hamlin)

Diezel and Denim (Toni Braxton)

RANI (Hindi) Queen. *Variations:* Rahnee, Rahni, Rahnie, Ranee, Ranie, Ranique, Ranita.

RANIA (Arabic) To gaze. *Variations:* Rahna, Rahnia, Ranea, Raniah.

RANIELLE (African American) God is my judge. Variation of Danielle. *Variations:* Raniela, Raniele, Raniella.

RANITA (Hebrew) Song of joy. *Variations:* Ranice, Ranit, Ranite, Ranitra, Ranitta.

RANJANA (Hindi) Beloved. *Variation:* Ranjita.

RANVEIG (Scandinavian) Housewife. *Variation:* Ronnaug.

RANYA (Hindi) To gaze.

RAOULA (French) Wolf counselor. Feminine form of Raoul. *Variations:* Raoule, Raoulia, Raula, Raulla, Raulle.

RAQUEL (Spanish) Lamb. Form of Rachel. *Notable:* Actress Raquel Welch. *Variations:* Racquel, Racquela, Racquella, Racquelle, Raquela, Raquella, Raquelle.

RASHA (Arabic) Gazelle. *Variation:* Rashia.

RASHIDA (Turkish) Righteous. Feminine version of Rashid. *Notable:* Actress Rashida Jones. *Variations:* Rasheda, Rasheeda, Rasheedah, Rasheida, Rashidah.

RASHINA (Arabic) Wise counselor. *Variation:* Rasheena.

RASIA (Greek) Rose. *Variations:* Rasine, Rasya.

RATHNAIT (Irish) Grace. Prosperity. *Variations:* Ranait, Rath.

RATI (Hindi) Goddess of love and passion. *Variations:* Ratee, Ratie.

RATRI (Hindi) Night. *Variations:* Ratree, Ratrie.

RAVEN (English) Blackbird. *Variations:* Ravenna, Ravenne, Ravin, Ravinne, Rayven, Rayvin.

RAVVA (Hindi) The sun.

RAWIYA (Arabic) Tell a story. *Variations:* Rawiyah, Rawya.

RAYA (Hebrew) Friend. *Variation:* Rayah.

RAYANNE (English) Combined form of Ray and Anne. *Variations:* Raeann, Raeanna, Raeanne, Raianna, Raianne, Reianna, Reianne, Rayann, Rayanna, Rayanne.

RAYLENE (American) Combination of first name "Ray" and suffix "lene." *Variations:* Raelean, Raeleana, Raeleane, Raeleen, Raeleena, Raileana, Raileane, Raileen, Raileena, Raileene, Realean, Realeana, Realeane, Raleen, Raleena, Raleene, Ralina, Raline, Ralyna, Ralyne, Raylean, Rayleana, Rayleane, Rayleen, Rayleena, Rayleene, Rayline.

RAYMONDE (German) Wise protector. *Variations:* Raymonda, Raymondea, Raymondee, Raymondia, Raymunda.

RAYNA (Hebrew) Song of the Lord. *Variations:* Raina, Rainee, Rainey, Rana, Rane, Rania, Rayne, Raynee, Rayney, Renana, Renanit, Renatia, Renatya, Renina, Rinatia, Rinatya.

RAYYA (Arabic) Quenched thirst.

RAZIAH (Hebrew) Secret of God. *Variations:* Razi, Razia, Raziela, Razilee, Razili, Raziya.

RAZIYA (African) Agreeable.

REANNA (Irish) Queen. *Variations:* Reana, Reann, Reannon, Rhianna, Rhiannon, Rianna, Riannon.

REBA (English) Short form of Rebecca. *Notable:* Singer Reba

McEntire. *Variations:* Reaba, Reabah, Rebah, Reeba, Reebah, Reiba, Reibah, Reyba, Reybah, Rheba, Rhebah, Rheiba, Rheibah, Rheyba, Rheybah.

REBECCA (Hebrew) Joined together. *Notables:* Model/actress Rebecca Romijn; basketball player Rebecca Lobo. *Variations:* Becca, Becky, Rabbecca, Rabbeca, Rabbecah, Rabbecca, Rebbeca, Rebbecca, Rebbie, Rebeca, Rebecah, Rebeccah, Rebecka, Rebeckah, Rebeka, Rebekah, Rebekka, Rebekke, Rebequa, Rebequah, Rebeque, Rebi, Reby, Revecca, Reveccah, Revecka, Reveckah, Reveka, Revekah, Revequa, Reveque.

REENA (Greek) Peaceful. *Variations:* Reana, Reanah, Reen, Reenah, Reene, Reenia, Reeniah, Reenie, Reeny, Reenya, Rena, Renah, Rina, Rinah.

REESE (Welsh) Fiery. *Notable:* Actress Reese Witherspoon. *Variations:* Reece, Rhys.

REGAN (Irish) Descendent of the little king. *Variations:* Reagan, Reagen, Reaghan, Reagin, Reagon, Reagyn, Regana, Regane, Regann, Reganna, Reganne, Regen, Reghan, Regin, Reigan, Reigana, Reiganah, Reigane, Reygan, Regyana.

REGINA (Latin) Queen. *Notable:* Actress Regina King. *Variations:* Regena, Reggi, Reggie, Reggy, Regi, Regia, Regie, Regiena, Reginah, Regine, Reginia, Reginna, Regyna.

REHAN (Armenian) Like a flower. *Variations:* Rehana, Rehane, Rehann, Rehanna, Rehanne.

REHEMA (African) Compassion. *Variations:* Reheema, Rehemah, Rehima, Rehimah.

REI (Japanese) Appreciation.

REICHANA (Hebrew) Aromatic. *Variations:* Rechana, Rehana.

REIKO (Japanese) Very pleasant child. *Variation:* Reyko.

REINHILDE (German) Battle counsel. *Variations:* Reinheld, Reinhelda, Reinhilda, Reinhold, Reinholda.

REKHA (Hindi) Line. *Variations:* Reka, Rehah, Rekia, Rekiya.

REMAZIAH (Hebrew) Sign from God. *Variations:* Remazia, Remazya.

REMEDIOS (Spanish) Remedy.

REMY (French) From Rheims in France. *Variations:* Remee, Remi, Remia, Remie, Remmi, Remmy.

REN (Japanese) Lotus.

RENA (Hebrew) Melody. *Variations:* Reena, Renah.

RENATA (Italian; Spanish; German) Reborn. *Variation:* Renate.

RENEE (French) Reborn. *Notables:* Actresses Renee Zellweger and Rene Russo. *Variations:* Ranae, Ranay, Renae, Renai, Renay, Rene, Renelle, Reney, Reni, Renia, Renie, Rennae, Rennay, Renni, Rennie, Renny, Wrenae, Wrenee.

RENITA (Latin) Defiant. *Variation:* Reneata, Reneeta, Reneita.

RESEDA (Latin) Flower.

RETHA (Greek) Virtue. *Variation:* Reatha.

REUBENA (English) Behold the child. Feminine version of Reuben. *Variations:* Reubina, Rubena, Rubenia, Rubina, Rubine, Rubyna.

REUMA (Hebrew) Lofty. *Variations:* Raomi, Reuman, Ruma.

REVA (Hindi) Sacred river. Form of Rebecca. *Variation:* Reeva.

REVAYA (Hebrew) Satisfied. *Variation:* Revaia.

REXANA (Latin) Royal and of grace. Combination of Rex and Anna. *Variations:* Rexann, Rexanna, Rexanne, Rexina.

REYNALDA (German) Wise advisor. *Variation:* Reinalda.

REZA (Czech; Hungarian) Harvest. Variation of Teresa. *Variations:* Rezi, Rezka.

RHEA (Greek) Flowing stream. *Notable:* Actress Rhea Perlman. *Variations:* Rhia, Ria, Riah, Ryah.

RHEDYN (Welsh) Fern. *Variations:* Readan, Readen, Readin, Readon, Readyn, Reedan, Reeden, Reedin, Reedon, Reedyn, Rheadan, Rheaden, Rheadin, Rheadon, Rheadyn, Rhedan, Rheden, Rhedin, Rhedon, Rheedan, Rheeden, Rheedin, Rheedon, Rheedyn.

RHETA (Greek) Eloquent. *Variations:* Reta, Retah, Retta, Rettah, Reyta, Rheata, Rheatah, Rhetta, Rhettah.

RHIANNON (Welsh) Queen. Mythical goddess. *Variations:* Rheanna, Rheanne, Rhiana, Rhiann, Rhianna, Rhiannan, Rhiannen, Rhianon, Rhuan, Rhyannon, Riana, Riane, Rianna, Rianne, Riannon, Rianon, Riona.

RHIANVYEN (Welsh) Fair maiden. *Variations:* Rhianvian, Rhianwen, Rhianwyn, Rhianwynn.

RHODA (Greek) Rose. From Rhodes. *Notables:* character from TV's *Mary Tyler Moore Show* Rhoda Morgenstern. *Variations:* Rhodanta, Rhodante, Rhodantha, Rhodanthe, Rhodelia, Rhodia, Rhodie, Rhody, Roda.

RHONA (Scottish) Rough island. *Variation:* Rona.

RHONDA (Welsh) Grand. Good spear. Noisy. *Notable:* Actress Rhonda Shear. *Variations:* Rhonnda, Ronda.

RHONWEN (Welsh) Fair haired. *Variations:* Ronwen, Roweena, Roweina, Rowena, Rowina.

RHU (Hindi) Pure.

RIA (Spanish) Mouth of a river.

RIANE (Irish) Feminine version of Ryan. Short form of Briana. *Variations:* Riana, Rianne.

RICARDA (Italian) Powerful ruler. Feminine version of Richard. *Variations:* Rica, Ricca, Richarda, Richenda, Richenza.

RICHAEL (Irish) Saint. *Variations:* Ricael, Rickael, Rikael.

RICHELLE (American) Combined form of Rachel and Michelle. *Variations:* Richel, Richela, Richele, Richella, Rishel, Rishela, Rishele, Rishell, Rishella, Rishelle, Rychelle, Ryshelle.

RICKI (English) Short form of Frederica or feminine form of Ricky or Richard. *Notables:* Actress/TV host Ricki Lake; singer Rickie Lee Jones. *Variations:* Rickee, Rickie, Ricky, Rikee, Riki, Rikki, Rikky, Rycki, Ryckie, Rykee, Ryki, Rykie, Ryky.

RICKMA (Hebrew) Woven. *Variations:* Rickmah, Ricma, Ricmah, Ryckma, Ryckmah, Rycma, Rycmah, Rykma, Rykmah.

RIDA (Arabic) Favored by God. *Variations:* Radeya, Radeyah, Reeda, Reida, Ridah, Rydah.

RIDHI (Sanskrit) Prosperous. *Variation:* Riddhi.

RIE (Japanese) Valued blessing.

RIELLE (English) Rye hill. *Variations:* Rialle, Riele.

RIGBORG (Scandinavian) Strong fortification.

RIGMOR (Scandinavian) Powerful courage.

RIHANA (Arabic) Sweet basil. *Notable:* Singer Rihanna. *Variations:* Rihanah, Rihanna, Rihannah.

RIKA (Japanese) Valued fragrance.

RIKE (German) Peaceful ruler.

RIKU (Japanese) Land. *Variation:* Rikuyo.

RILEY (Irish) Valiant. *Variations:* Rilea, Rileah, Rilee, Rilei, Rileigh, Rili, Rilie, Rylea, Ryleah, Rylee, Rylei, Ryleigh, Ryley, Ryli, Rylie, Ryly.

RILLA (German) Stream. *Variations:* Rila, Rilah, Rillah, Rilletta, Rillette.

RIMA (Arabic) Antelope. *Variations:* Reama, Rema, Reema, Rimah.

RIMONA (Hebrew) Pomegranate. *Variations:* Rhimona, Rimonah.

RIN (Japanese) Park. *Variation:* Ryn.

RINA (Hebrew) Joy. *Variation:* Rinah.

RINDA (Scandinavian) Ancient mythological giant. *Variations:* Rind, Rindea, Rindia.

RIONA (Irish) Queen. *Variations:* Rioghnach, Rionach, Rionagh, Rionna.

RISA (Latin) Laughter. *Variations:* Reesa, Resa, Rise, Risha, Riza, Rysa.

RISHONA (Hebrew) Initial. Firstborn. *Variations:* Rishonah, Rishonna, Rhyshona.

RISSA (Greek) Nickname for Nerissa, a sea nymph.

RITA (Spanish) Pearl. Short form of Margarita. *Notables:* Actresses Rita Hayworth and Rita Moreno; singer Rita Coolidge. *Variations:* Reeta, Reta, Ritah, Ritta, Ryta, Rytta.

RITIKA (Hindi) Active.

RITZPAH (Hebrew) Hot coal. *Variations:* Ritspah, Ritzpa, Rizpah.

RIVA (Hebrew) Joined. Form of Rebecca. *Variations:* Reva, Rivah, Rivana, Rivane, Rivanna, Rivanne, Ryva, Ryvana, Ryvanna, Ryvanne.

RIVKA (Hebrew) Bound to God. *Variations:* Rifka, Rifke, Riki, Rivai, Rivca, Rivcka, Rivi, Rivvy.

ROANNA (American) Form of Rosanna. *Variations:* Roana, Roann, Roanne.

ROBERTA (English) Bright fame. Feminine version of Robert. *Notable:* Singer Roberta Flack. *Variations:* Bobbet, Bobbett, Bobbi, Bobbie, Bobby, Robbi, Robbie, Robby, Robena, Robertena, Robertha, Robertina, Robetta.

ROBIN (English) Robin. *Notables:* Actress Robin Wright; radio personality Robin Quivers. *Variations:* Robbin, Robbyn, Roben, Robina, Robine, Robinetta, Robinette, Robinia, Robyn, Robyna.

ROCHELLE (French) Little rock. *Variations:* Rochel, Rochela, Rochele, Rochell, Rochella, Roshela, Roshele, Roshella, Roshelle, Shelley, Shelly.

RODA (Polish) Rose.

RODERICA (German) Famous ruler. Feminine version of Roderick. *Variations:* Rica, Rodericka, Roderika, Roderiqua, Roderique.

ROHANA (Hindi) Sandalwood. *Variations:* Rohan, Rohanah, Rohanna.

ROISIN (Irish) Little rose. *Variations:* Rois, Roisina, Roisinah, Roisine, Roisyn, Roisyna, Roisynah, Roisyne, Roysin, Roysina, Roysinah, Roysine, Roysyn, Roysyna, Roysyne.

ROKEYA (Persian) Dawn. *Variations:* Rokia, Rokiya.

ROLANDA (German) Famous land. Feminine version of Roland. *Notable:* TV host Rolanda Watts. *Variations:* Rolandah, Rolande, Rolandia, Rolina, Rolinda, Roline, Rollande, Rolonda, Rolonde.

ROMA (Italian) Rome. *Notable:* Actress Roma Downey. *Variations:* Romain, Romaine, Romana, Romella, Romelle, Romina, Romola, Romolla, Romula.

ROMHILDA (Italian) Famous battle. *Variations:* Romhilde, Romilda.

ROMY (German) Short form of Rosemary. *Notable:* Actress Romy Schneider. *Variations:* Romee, Romey, Romi, Romia, Romiah, Romie, Romya.

RONA (Scandinavian) Rough isle. *Notable:* Gossip columnist Rona Barrett. *Variations:* Rhona, Roana, Ronella, Ronelle, Ronna.

RONALDA (English) Powerful advisor. *Variations:* Rhonalda, Rhonaldia, Ronaldah, Ronaldia.

RONIT (Hebrew) Joy.

RONIYA (Hebrew) Joy of God. *Variations:* Ronela, Ronella, Ronia.

RONNELLE (American) Feminine version of Ron. *Variations:* Ronala, Ronel, Ronele, Ronell, Ronella, Ronnel, Ronnela.

RONNI (English) Strong counsel. Feminine version of Ronald. Also short form for Veronica. *Notable:* Singer Ronnie Spector. *Variations:* Roni, Ronnette, Ronney, Ronnica, Ronnie, Ronny.

ROONEY (Irish) Red haired. *Notable:* Actress Rooney Mara. *Variations:* Roone, Rooni, Roonie, Roony.

RORY (Irish) Red queen. *Variations:* Roree, Rori.

ROSA (Spanish) Rose.

ROSABEL (French) Beautiful rose. *Variations:* Rosabela, Rosabelah, Rosabele, Rosabell, Rosabella, Rosabellah, Rosabelle, Rosabellia, Rosabelliah, Rosebel, Rosebela, Rosebelah, Rosebele, Rosebell, Rosebella, Rosebellah, Rosebelle, Rosebellia, Rosebelliah, Rozabel, Rozabela, Rozabelah, Rozabele, Rozabell, Rozabella, Rozabellah, Rozabelle, Rozebel, Rozebela, Rozebelah, Rozebele, Rozebell, Rozebella, Rozebellah, Rozebelle.

ROSALBA (Latin) White rose. *Variation:* Rosalva.

ROSALIE (English) Form of Rosalind. *Variations:* Rosalee, Rosalea, Rosaleah, Rosalei, Rosaleigh, Rosali, Rosalia, Roseli, Roselia, Roseliah, Roselie, Rosely, Rozalea, Rozaleah, Rozalee, Rozalei, Rozaleigh, Rozaley, Rozali, Rozalia, Rozaliah, Rozalie, Rozaly, Rozlea, Rozlee, Rozlei, Rozleigh, Rozley, Rozli, Rozlia, Rozliah, Rozlie, Rozly.

ROSALIND (Spanish) Pretty rose. *Notable:* Actress Rosalind Russell. *Variations:* Rosalina, Rosalinda, Rosalinde, Rosaline, Rosalyn, Rosalynd, Rosalyne, Rosalynn, Roselind, Roselynn, Roslyn, Rozalind, Rozalyn, Rozlind.

Top Names in Spain

BOYS:	GIRLS:
1. Daniel	1. Lucia
2. Alejandro	2. Paula
3. Pablo	3. Maria
4. Hugo	4. Sara
5. Alvaro	5. Daniela
6. Adrian	6. Carla
7. David	7. Claudia
8. Javier	8. Marta
9. Sergio	9. Irene
10. Diego	10. Sofia

ROSAMOND (German) Horse protector; (English) Pure rose. *Variations:* Rosamonda, Rosamondah, Rosamonde, Rosamund, Rosemonda, Rosemondah, Rosemonde, Rosemunda, Rosemundah, Rosiemond, Rosiemund, Rosiemunda, Rozamond, Rozamonda, Rozmond, Rozmonda, Rozmondah, Rozmonde, Rozmund, Rozmunda, Rozmundah, Rozmunde.

ROSANGELA (Italian) Rose angel. Combined form of Rose and Angela. *Variations:* Rosangelina, Rosangeline, Roseangela, Roseangelina, Roseangeline.

ROSANNA (English) Graceful rose. Combination of Rose and Anna. *Notable:* Actress Rosanna Arquette. *Variations:* Rosana, Rosanda, Rosannah, Roseana, Roseanda, Roseanna, Roseannah, Rosehannah, Rozanna.

ROSARIA (Italian) Rosary. *Variations:* Rosariah, Rosario, Rozaria, Rozario.

ROSCHAN (Hindi) Dawn. *Variations:* Rochana, Rochani, Roschana, Roshan, Roshana, Roshanara, Roshni.

ROSCISLAWA (Polish) Glory in conquest.

ROSE (Latin) Rose. *Notable:* Actress Rose McGowan. *Variations:* Rosabel, Rosabell, Rosabella, Rosabelle, Rosalee, Rosaley, Rosalia, Rosalie, Rosalin, Rosetta, Rosette, Rosey, Rosi, Rosie, Rosine, Rosita, Rosy, Ruza, Ruzena, Ruzenka, Ruzsa.

ROSEANNE (English) Combination of Rose and Anne. *Notable:* Comedian Roseanne Barr. *Variations:* Rosan, Rosanah, Rosane, Rosann, Rosanne, Rozanne.

ROSELANI (Hawaiian) Heavenly rose. *Variations:* Roselanee, Roselanie.

ROSELLE (French) Form of Rose. *Variations:* Rosal, Rosale, Rosall, Rosalla, Rosallah, Rosalle, Rosel, Rosele, Rosell, Rosella, Rossella, Rosselle, Rozel, Rozele, Rozell, Rozella, Rozelle.

ROSEMARY (Latin) Dew of the sea. *Notable:* Singer Rosemary Clooney. *Variations:* Rosemaree, Rosemarey, Rosemaria, Rosemarie.

ROSIE (English) Familiar form of Rosalind, Roseanne, or Rose. *Notable:* Comedian Rosie O'Donnell. *Variations:* Rosey, Rosy.

ROSSALYN (Scottish) Cape. Feminine version of Ross. *Variations:* Rossalin, Rossaline, Rossalyne, Rosslyn, Rosslynn.

ROSTISLAVA (Czech) One who seizes glory. *Variations:* Rosta, Rostina, Rostinka, Rostuska.

ROSWITHA (German) Renowned strength.

ROTEM (Hebrew) Juniper.

ROUGE (French) Red.

ROULA (Greek) Defiant. *Variation:* Rula.

ROWAN (Welsh) Tree with red berries. *Variations:* Rowana, Rowanne, Rowen, Rowin, Rowyn, Rowynn, Rowynne.

ROWENA (Welsh) White haired. *Variations:* Roweena, Rowenah, Rowina, Rowyna, Rowynna.

ROXANNE (Persian) Dawn. *Variations:* Roxan, Roxana, Roxane, Roxann, Roxanna, Roxannia, Roxianne.

ROXY (Persian) Dawn. Short form of Roxanne. *Variations:* Roxey, Roxi, Roxie.

ROYALE (French) Royal. *Variations:* Royalene, Royall, Royalle.

ROZ (English) Short form of Rosalind or Rosamund. *Variations:* Ros, Rozzy.

RUANA (Hindi) Indian violin. *Variations:* Ruann, Ruanna, Ruanne.

RUBY (English) Red jewel. *Notable:* Actress Ruby Dee. *Variations:* Reubee, Reubie, Reubey, Reuby, Roobie, Rooby, Rube, Rubey, Rubia, Rubie, Rubina, Rubye.

RUCHI (Hindi) Love.

RUCHIKA (Hindi) Attractive.

RUDELLE (German) Famous. *Variations:* Rudel, Rudela, Rudella.

RUDRA (Hindi) Plant.

RUE (French) Street. *Notable:* Actress Rue McClanahan.

RUFARO (African) Happiness.

RUFFINA (Italian) Red haired. Feminine version of Rufus. *Variation:* Rufina.

RUKAN (Arabic) Confident. *Variations:* Rukana, Rukanne.

RUKIYA (African) To arise.

RUKMINI (Hindi) Golden.

RUMER (Slavic) Gypsy. *Notable:* Actress Rumer Willis. *Variations:* Rumor, Rumour.

RUMINA (Latin) Mythological goddess of babies. *Variations:* Rumeena, Ruminah.

RUNA (Scandinavian) Secret lore. *Variations:* Roona, Rula.

RUNCINA (Latin) God of agriculture.

RUOLAN (Chinese) Orchidlike.

RUPAL (Hindi) Beautiful. *Variations:* Rupala, Rupali, Rupinder.

RUPERTA (German) Bright fame.

RUQAYYA (Arabic) Arise. *Variations:* Ruqayah, Ruqayyah.

RURI (Japanese) Emerald.

RUSALKA (Czech) Wood nymph.

RUSTY (American) Red haired. *Variations:* Rustea, Rustee, Rusti, Rustie, Rustey.

RUT (Czech) Devoted companion.

RUTA (Hawaiian) Friend.

RUTH (Hebrew) Companion. *Notable:* Sex therapist Dr. Ruth Westheimer. *Variations:* Rute, Rutha, Ruthe, Ruthella, Ruthelle, Ruthetta, Ruthi, Ruthie, Ruthina, Ruthine, Ruthy.

RUTHANN (American) Cominbination of Ruth and Ann. *Variations:* Ruthana, Ruthanna, Ruthanne.

RUWAYDAH (Arabic) Graceful walk. *Variation:* Ruwaida.

RUZA (Slavic) Rose. *Variations:* Ruz, Ruze, Ruzena, Ruzka.

RYAN (Irish) Little king. *Variations:* Rian, Riana, Riane, Ryana, Ryann, Ryanna, Ryanne.

RYBA (Czech) Fish. *Variations:* Riba, Rybah.

RYO (Japanese) Bright.

RYOKA (Japanese) Bright child. *Variation:* Ryoko.

SAADA (African) Helper.

SABA (Arabic) Morning. *Variations:* Sabah, Sabbah, Sheba.

SABELLA (Spanish) Form of Isabella. *Variations:* Sabela, Sabell, Sabelle.

SABINA (Latin) Sabine, a tribe in central Italy in ancient Roman era. *Variations:* Sabeena, Sabienne, Sabine, Savina, Sebina.

SABLE (English) Black. *Variations:* Sabelle, Sabille.

SABRA (Hebrew) Thorny cactus fruit. *Variations:* Sabrah, Sabre, Sebra.

SABRINA (Welsh) Severn River in Wales. *Variations:* Sabreen, Sabreena, Sabrena, Sabrinah, Sabrinna, Sabryna.

SABRIYYA (Arabic) Patience. *Variations:* Sabira, Sabirah, Sabriyyah.

SACAGAWEA (Native American) Bird woman. *Variation:* Sacajawea.

SACHA (French) Defender of mankind.

SACHI (Japanese) Blessed. *Variation:* Sachiko.

SADA (Japanese) Virginal.

SADE (African) Honorable. *Notable:* Singer Sade. *Variation:* Sharde.

SADHANA (Hindi) Devotion.

SADHBH (Irish) Goodness. *Variations:* Sabha, Sabia, Sadb, Sadbha, Sadhbh, Sadhbha, Saibh, Saidhbhe, Saidhbhin, Sive.

SADIE (Hebrew) Princess. Form of Sarah. *Notable:* Actress Sadie Frost.

Variations: Sadee, Sadey, Sadi, Sady, Saide, Saidi, Saidie, Sayde, Saydi, Saydia, Saydie, Saydy.

SADIQA (Arabic) Sincere.

SADIRA (Persian) Lotus tree. *Variations:* Sadeera, Sadeira.

SADZI (Native American) Sun heart.

SAFA (Arabic) Pure. *Variations:* Safiyya, Safiyyah.

SAFFRON (English) Flower name. *Notable:* Actress Saffron Burrows. *Variations:* Saffren, Saffronia, Saphron.

SAFI (Hindi) Friend.

SAFIYYA (African) Best friend. *Variations:* Safiya, Safiyeh, Safiyyah.

SAGA (Scandinavian) Ancient mythological figure.

SAGARA (Hindi) Ocean.

SAGE (Latin) Wise. *Variations:* Saige, Sayge.

SAHAR (Arabic) Sunrise.

SAHARA (Arabic) Desert. *Variations:* Saharah, Sahari, Sahira.

SAIDAH (Arabic) Happy. *Variations:* Saida, Sayida.

SAILOR (American) One who sails. *Variations:* Sailer, Saylor.

SAINT (English) Holy.

SAKAE (Japanese) Wealth.

SAKARI (Hindi) Sweet one.

SAKI (Japanese) Cape.

SAKIKO (Japanese) Blossoming child.

SAKTI (Hindi) Energy.

SAKUNA (Hindi) Bird. *Variation:* Sakujna.

Atlantic Hurricane Names

2013

Andrea	Humberto	Olga
Barry	Ingrid	Pablo
Chantal	Jerry	Rebekah
Dorian	Karen	Sebastien
Erin	Lorenzo	Tanya
Ferdand	Melissa	Van
Gabrielle	Nestor	Wendy

2014

Arthur	Hanna	Omar
Bertha	Isaias	Paulette
Cristobal	Josephine	Rene
Dolly	Kyle	Sally
Edouard	Laura	Teddy
Fay	Marco	Vicky
Gonzalo	Nana	Wilfred

2015

Ana	Henri	Odette
Bill	Ida	Peter
Claudette	Joaquin	Rose
Danny	Kate	Sam
Erika	Larry	Teresa
Fred	Mindy	Victor
Grace	Nicholas	Wanda

SAKURA (Japanese) Cherry blossom.

SALA (Hindi) Sacred tree.

SALALI (Native American) Squirrel.

SALAMA (Arabic) Peaceful.

SALE (Hawaiian) Princess. *Variations:* Sarai, Sera.

SALENA (Hindi) The moon.

SALHA (Arabic) Ethical.

SALIDA (Hebrew) Happy. *Variations:* Selda, Selde.

SALIHAH (Arabic) Virtuous.

SALIMA (Arabic) Of good health. *Variations:* Saleema, Salema.

SALINA (French) Solemn. *Variations:* Saleena, Salena, Salene, Salinda, Saline.

SALLY (English) Princess. Form of Sarah. *Notable:* Astronaut Sally Ride. *Variations:* Sal, Sallee, Salley, Salli, Sallie.

SALMA (Hindi) Safe. *Notable:* Actress Salma Hayek. *Variation:* Salima.

SALOME (Hebrew) Peaceful. *Variations:* Saloma, Salomi.

SALONI (Hindi) Beautiful one.

SALOTE (Polynesian) Woman.

SALUD (Spanish) Health.

SALUS (Latin) The goddess of health.

SALVADORA (Spanish) Savior.

SALVATRICE (Italian) Savior.

SALVIA (Latin) Healthy. *Variations:* Salva, Salviana, Salvina.

SALWA (Arabic) Comfort.

SAMAH (Arabic) Generous and forgiving. *Variations:* Sama, Samihah, Samma.

SAMALA (Hebrew) Requested of God. *Variations:* Samale, Sammala.

SAMANTHA (Hebrew) Told by God. *Notable:* Actress Samantha Mathis. *Variations:* Sam, Samana, Samanfa, Samanta, Samanthia, Samatha, Samella, Samentha, Sammantha, Sammee, Sammey, Sammi, Sammie, Sammy, Semanntha, Semantha, Simantha, Symantha.

SAMAR (Arabic) Night talk.

SAMARA (Hebrew) Protected by God. *Variations:* Samaria, Sammara, Samarra.

SAMEH (Arabic) One who forgives.

SAMIA (Arabic) Understanding. *Variations:* Samihah, Samira, Samirah.

SAMINA (Hindi) Happy. *Variations:* Sameena, Sameenah.

SAMIRA (Hebrew) Evening talk.

SAMUELA (Hebrew) God has heard. Feminine version of Samuel. *Variations:* Samelle, Samuella, Samuelle.

SAMYA (Arabic) To rise up. *Variations:* Samiya, Samiyah.

SANA (Arabic) To shine. *Variations:* Saniyya, Saniyyah.

SANANDA (Hindi) Joy.

SANCIA (Latin; Spanish) Holy. *Variations:* Sancha, Sanchia, Santsia, Sanzia.

SANDEEP (Punjabi) Enlightened. *Variation:* Sandip.

SANDHYA (Hindi) Born at twilight.

SANDRA (Greek) Protector of mankind. Short form of Alexandra. *Notable:* Actress Sandra Bullock. *Variations:* Sandee, Sandi, Sandie, Sandrea, Sandria, Sandrica,

Sandrina, Sandrine, Sandy, Saundra, Sondra, Zana, Zandra, Zanna.

SANDRINE (French) Form of Sandra. *Notable:* Actress Sandrine Bonnaire. *Variations:* Sandreen, Sandrene.

SANDY (English) Short form of Sandra. *Notable:* Actress Sandy Duncan. *Variations:* Sandee, Sandi, Sandie, Sandye.

SANDYHA (Hindi) Twilight.

SANGITA (Hindi) Musical. *Variations:* Sangyta, Sanjita.

SANGO (Japanese) Coral.

SANJANA (Hindi) Gentle.

SANNA (Scandinavian; Dutch) Lily. *Variations:* Sana, Sanne.

SANSANA (Hebrew) Leaf of the palm.

SANTA (Italian) Saint.

SANTANA (Spanish) Saint. *Variations:* Santa, Santena, Santina.

SANTAVANA (Hindi) Hope.

SANTUZZA (Italian) Holy.

SANURA (African) Like a kitten.

SANUYE (Native American) Red cloud.

SANYA (Hindi) Born on a Saturday; (Arabic) Radiant.

SANYOGITA (Hindi) Twelfth-century queen.

SAOIRSE (Gaelic) Freedom.

SAPATA (Native American) Dancing bear.

SAPNA (Hindi) Dream come true.

SAPPHIRE (Greek) Blue jewel. *Variations:* Safira, Saphira, Sapir, Sapira, Sapirit, Sapphira, Sephira.

SAPPHO (Greek) Sapphire. *Notable:* Greek poet Sappho.

SARAB (Arabic) Fantasy.

SARAH (Hebrew) Princess. *Notables:* Actresses Sarah Jessica Parker and Sara Gilbert. *Variations:* Sadee, Sadie, Sadye, Saidee, Saleena, Salena, Salina, Sallee, Salley, Sallianne, Sallie, Sally, Sallyann, Sara, Sarai, Sareen, Saretta, Sarette, Sari, Sarina, Sarine, Sarita, Saritia, Sarotte, Sarra, Sarrah.

SARAID (Gaelic) Excellent.

SARALA (Hindi) Straight.

SARASVATI (Hindi) Goddess of the arts.

SARASWATI (Hindi) Lake goddess.

SARAUNLYA (African) Queen.

SARI (Hebrew) Princess. Form of Sarah. *Variations:* Sarai, Saray, Saree, Sariah, Sarit, Sarri.

SARIL (Turkish) Running water.

SARISHA (Hindi) Charming.

SARITA (Hindi) River.

SARIYA (Arabic) Night cloud.

SAROJA (Hindi) Born by a lake. *Variation:* Saroj.

SAROJINI (Hindi) Lotuses.

SARONNA (Norse) Ruler with counsel.

SASHA (Russian) Protector of men. Short form of Alexandra or Alexander. *Variations:* Sacha, Sasa, Sascha.

SASKIA (Dutch) Saxon woman.

SASONA (Hebrew) Joy. *Variations:* Sason, Sasson.

SATI (Hindi) Truth speaker.

SATIN (French) Satin fabric.

SATINKA (Native American) Magic dancer.

SATO (Japanese) Sugar.

SATURDAY (Latin) Born on Saturday.

SATURNINA (Spanish) Gift of Saturn. *Variation:* Saturnia.

SATYARUPA (Hindi) Truth. *Variation:* Satarupa.

SAUDA (African) Dark skinned.

SAURA (Hindi) Sun worshiper.

SAVA (Hebrew) Aged.

SAVANNAH (Spanish) Treeless. *Variations:* Savana, Savanah, Savanna, Savonna, Sevanna.

SAVERIA (Italian) New house.

SAVINA (Italian) Sabine. Form of Sabina. *Variation:* Savinah.

SAVITRI (Hindi) Sun god. *Variation:* Savitari.

SAWA (Japanese) Swamp.

SAWNI (Native American) Echo. *Variation:* Suwanee.

SAWSAN (Arabic) Lily.

SAWYER (English) Woodcutter.

SAXONA (English) Sword people. *Variation:* Saxonia.

SAYO (Japanese) Evening birth.

SAYURI (Japanese) Lily.

SCARLETT (English) Red. *Notables: Gone with the Wind* heroine Scarlett O'Hara; actress Scarlett Johannson. *Variations:* Scarlet, Scarletta, Scarlette, Skarlet, Skarlette.

SCHYLER (Dutch) Sheltered. *Variation:* Schuyler.

SCIROCCO (Arabic) Warm wind.

SCOTIA (Latin) Scotland. *Variations:* Scota, Scotta, Skotia.

SCOUT (English) A scout.

SCYLLA (Greek) Sea monster.

SEANA (Irish) Form of Shawna.

SEAMA (Hebrew) Treasure. *Variations:* Seema, Sima.

SEARLAIT (Irish) Womanly. Form of Charlotte. *Variations:* Searlas, Serlait.

SEASON (Latin) Season. *Variations:* Seazon, Seeson.

SEBASTIANE (Latin) One from an ancient Roman city. Feminine version of Sebastian. *Variations:* Sebastiana, Sebastienne.

SEBILLE (English) Fairy. *Variations:* Sebyl, Sebylle.

SECUNDA (Latin) Second.

SEDA (Armenian) Forest echo.

SEDNA (Intuit) Goddess of food.

SEDONA (American) Name of a town in Arizona. *Variation:* Sedonia.

SEEMA (Hebrew) Treasure. *Variations:* Seemah, Sima, Simah.

SEFARINA (Spanish) Gentle wind. Form of Zephyr.

SEIKO (Japanese) Accomplishment.

SEINI (Polynesian) God is gracious.

SEKELAGA (African) Rejoice.

SEKI (Japanese) Stone.

SELA (Polynesian) Princess. *Notable:* Actress Sela Ward.

SELBY (English) Of the manor. *Variations:* Selbee, Selbey, Selbi, Selbie.

SELDA (Yiddish) Happiness.

SELENA (Spanish) Goddess of the moon. *Notables:* Tejano singer Selena Quintanilla Perez; actress Selena Gomez. *Variations:* Celena, Celina, Celinda, Celine, Celyna, Salena, Salina, Salinah, Sela, Selene, Selina, Selinda, Seline, Sena.

SELIMA (Hebrew) Peace. *Variation:* Selimah.

SELMA (German) God's helmet. *Notable:* Actress Selma Blair. *Variations:* Anselma, Selmah, Zelma.

SELVAGGIA (Italian) Wild.

SEMA (Arabic) Omen. *Variation:* Semah.

SEMADAR (Hebrew) Berry blossom. *Variation:* Smadar.

SEMEICHA (Hebrew) Happy. *Variation:* Semecha.

SEMELE (Latin) Mythological mother of Dionysus. *Variation:* Semelle.

SEMINE (Danish) Goddess of the sun and moon.

SEMIRAMIS (Hebrew) Highest heaven. *Variation:* Semira.

SEN (Vietnamese) Lotus flower.

SENALDA (Spanish) Sign.

SENECA (Native American) Tribal name.

SENGA (Scottish) Slender.

SEONA (Scottish) God is gracious. *Variations:* Seonag, Shona.

SEOSAIMHTHIN (Irish) To increase. *Variation:* Seosaimhin.

SEPHORA (Hebrew) Beautiful bird. *Variations:* Sefora, Seforra, Sephoria.

SEPTEMBER (English) Month.

SEPTIMA (Latin) Seventh.

SEQUOIA (Native American) Redwood tree.

SERACH (Hebrew) Plenty.

SERAPHINA (Hebrew) Fiery one. *Variations:* Sarafina, Serafina, Serafine, Seraphine, Serofina.

SERENA (Latin) Serene. *Notable:* Tennis pro Serena Williams. *Variations:* Sareen, Sarena, Sarene, Sarina, Sarine, Sereena, Serenah, Serenna, Serina.

SERENITY (Latin) Peaceful.

SERILDA (German) Female soldier. *Variations:* Sarilda, Serhilda, Serhilde, Serrilda.

SERPUHI (Armenian) Pious.

SESHETA (Egyptian) The goddess of the stars. *Variation:* Seshat.

SETSU (Japanese) Faithful. *Variation:* Setsuko.

SEVATI (Hindi) White rose.

SEVDA (Turkish) Parents' love.

SEVERA (Italian) Stern. *Variation:* Severia.

SEVERINE (French) Stem.

SEVILLA (Spanish) From Seville, Spain. *Variation:* Seville.

SEZJA (Russian) Protector of mankind.

SHABANA (Arabic) Maiden of the night. *Variations:* Shabanna, Shabanne.

SHABIBA (Arabic) Godmother.

SHABNAM (Persian) Raindrop.

SHACHARIYA (Hebrew) Sunrise. *Variations:* Shachar, Shacharia, Shacharit, Shacharita, Shahar, Shaharit, Shaharita.

SHADA (Native American) Pelican.

SHADHA (Arabic) Aromatic.

SHADYA (Arabic) Singer. *Variations:* Shadiya, Shadiyah.

SHAFIQA (Arabic) Sympathetic. *Variations:* Shafia, Shafiqah.

SHAHAR (Arabic) Moonlight.

SHAHINA (Arabic) Falcon.

SHAHIRA (Arabic) Famous. *Variation:* Shahirah.

SHAHNAZ (Hindi) Proud king.

SHAHRAZAD (Arabic) One who lives in the city. *Variations:* Shahrizad, Sheherazad, Sheherazade.

SHAILA (Hindi) Small mountain.

SHAINA (Yiddish) Beautiful. *Variations:* Shaine, Shanie, Shayna, Shayndel, Shayne, Sheina, Sheine.

SHAJUANA (African American) Combined form of Sha and Juana. *Variations:* Shajuan, Shajuanda, Shajuanita.

SHAKA (Hindi) Divine power. *Variation:* Chaka.

SHAKARA (African American) Combined form of Sha and Kara.

SHAKAYLA (African American) Combined form of Sha and Kayla. *Variations:* Shakaila, Shakala.

SHAKEENA (African American) Combined form of Sha and Keena. *Variations:* Shakina, Shaquina.

SHAKETA (African American) Newly created. *Variations:* Shakeya, Shakia, Shakita, Shaqueta, Shaquita.

SHAKILA (Arabic) Beautiful one. *Variations:* Shakeela, Shakeila, Shakila.

SHAKIRA (Arabic) Thankful. *Notable:* Singer Shakira. *Variations:* Shakera, Shaketa, Shakirah, Shakirra, Shaquera, Shaquira.

SHAKTI (Hindi) Divine power.

SHAKUNTALA (Hindi) Bird.

SHALANA (American) Combined form of Sha and Lana. *Variations:* Shalaina, Shalaine, Shalauna, Shalayna, Shalayne, Shalena, Shalene, Shalina, Shaline, Shalyna.

SHALEISHA (African American) Combination of Sha and Aisha. *Variations:* Shalesha, Shalesia, Shalicia, Shalisha, Shalysha.

SHALIMAR (Pakistani) Of the Shalimar Gardens.

SHALIQA (Arabic) Heavenly.

SHALISA (American) Combined form of Sha and Lisa. *Variations:* Shalissa, Shalisse, Shalyssa, Shalysse.

SHALOM (Hebrew) Peace. *Notable:* Actress/model Shalom Harlow.

SHALONDA (African American) Combination of Sha and Londa. *Variations:* Shalinda, Shalona, Shalonde, Shalynda.

SHALVAH (Hebrew) Peace. *Variation:* Shalviya.

SHAMEENA (Hindi) Beautiful. *Variation:* Shamina.

SHAMICA (African American) Combined form of Sha and Mica. *Variations:* Shameeka, Shameka, Shamika, Shamikah.

SHAMIRA (Hebrew) Guardian.

SHAMMARA (Arabic) Prepare for battle.

SHAN (Chinese) Virtuous.

Zodiac Baby: Names by Astrological Sign (Part III)

SAGITTARIUS

BOYS:	GIRLS:
Dustin	Dahlia
Earl	Iris
James	Olivia

CAPRICORN

BOYS:	GIRLS:
Matthew	Annie
Nick	Ivy
Oliver	Julia

AQUARIUS

BOYS:	GIRLS:
Arnold	Amethyst
Lawrence	Jane
Raymond	Viola

PISCES

BOYS:	GIRLS:
Clement	Faith
Jude	Lavender
Randall	Orchid

SHANA (Hebrew) God is gracious. *Notable:* TV journalist Shana Alexander. *Variations:* Shane, Shanna.

SHANASA (Hindi) Wish.

SHANDRA (American) Moon. *Variations:* Shanda, Shandi, Shandia, Shandria, Shandrika.

SHANEIKA (African American) Combined form of Sha and Nica. *Variations:* Shaneka, Shanekia, Shanequa, Shanika.

SHANELLE (African American) Channel. Form of Chanel. *Variations:* Shanel, Shanell, Shannelle.

SHANETTE (African American) Combined form of Sha and Annette. *Variations:* Shanetha, Shanethia, Shanethis, Shanetta.

SHANI (African) Marvelous.

SHANIA (Native American) On my way. *Notable:* Singer Shania Twain. *Variation:* Shaniya.

SHANICE (African American) Combined form of Sha and Janice. *Variations:* Shaneice, Shanese, Shaniece, Shanise, Shannice, Shanyce.

SHANIKA (African American) Combined form of Sha and Nika. *Variations:* Shaneeka, Shaneeke, Shanica, Shanicka, Shanikah, Shaniqua, Shanique, Shenika.

SHANINGO (Native American) Beautiful one. *Variation:* Shenango.

SHANIQUA (African American) Form of Shaneika. *Variation:* Shanique.

SHANISHA (African American) Combined form of Sha and Nisha. *Variation:* Shaneisha.

SHANITA (African American) Conbined form of Sha and Anita.

Variations: Shanida, Shaneeda, Shaneeta, Shanitha, Shanitra.

SHANLEY (Gaelic) Small woman.

SHANNON (Irish) Ancient. *Notable:* Actress Shannen Dougherty. *Variations:* Shanan, Shann, Shanna, Shannah, Shannan, Shannen, Shannie, Shanon.

SHANTA (Hindi) Calm.

SHANTAINA (African American) Saint. Form of Santana. *Variations:* Shantana, Shantainah, Shantayna.

SHANTE (French) Song. Form of Chantal. *Variation:* Shantal.

SHANTECA (African American) Combined form of Sha and Teca. *Variations:* Shanteka, Shantica, Shantika.

SHANTELLE (American) Song. Form of Chantal. *Variations:* Shantel, Shantille.

SHANTI (Hindi) Tranquil.

SHANTIA (African American) Combined form of Sha and Tia.

SHANTILLY (French) Town in France. Form of Chantilly. *Variation:* Shantilli.

SHANTINA (African American) Combined form of Sha and Tina. *Variation:* Shanteena.

SHANTRICE (African American) Combined form of Sha and Patrice. *Variations:* Shantricia, Shantrisha.

SHAPIRA (Hebrew) Good.

SHAPPA (Native American) Red thunder.

SHAQUANDA (African American) Combined form of Sha and Wanda. *Variations:* Shaquana, Shaquandra, Shaquanna.

SHAQUILA (Arabic) Beautiful one. Form of Shakila. *Variations:* Shaquela, Shaquilla.

SHARADA (Hindi) Mature. *Variation:* Sharda.

SHARAI (Hebrew) Princess. Variation of Sarah. *Variations:* Shara, Sharayah.

SHARANEE (Hindi) Guardian. *Variations:* Sharanya, Sharna.

SHARARA (Arabic) Lightning spark.

SHARDA (English) Runaway. *Variations:* Sade, Shardae, Sharday, Sharde.

SHARI (English) A plain. Form of Sharon. *Notable:* Puppeteer Shari Lewis.

SHARIFA (Arabic) Noble. *Variations:* Sharifah, Sharufa, Sherifa, Sherifah.

SHARIKA (Arabic) Good companions. *Variations:* Shareeka, Shariqa.

SHARISE (English) Grace and kindness. *Variation:* Sharice.

SHARLENE (English) Woman. Feminine version of Charles. *Variations:* Sharleen, Sharleyne, Sharlina, Sharline, Sharlyne.

SHARLON (African American) Variation of Sharon. *Variation:* Sharlona.

SHARMA (Hindi) Protection. *Variations:* Sharama, Sharamah, Shirama.

SHARMAINE (Latin) Song. *Variations:* Sharma, Sharmain, Sharman, Sharmane, Sharmayne, Sharmian, Sharmine, Sharmyn.

SHARMILA (Hindi) Providing comfort and protection. *Variation:* Sharmilla.

SHARON (Hebrew) A plain. *Notable:* Actress Sharon Stone. *Variations:* Sharan, Sharen, Sharin, Sharona, Sharonda, Sharone, Sharran, Sharren, Sharron, Sharronda, Sharronne, Sharown, Sharyn, Sheren, Sheron, Sherryn.

SHASHI (Hindi) Moonbeam.

SHASTA (Native American) Triple-peaked mountain.

SHASTI (Hindi) Goddess of children.

SHATARA (Arabic) Hard working.

SHATHA (Arabic) Perfume.

SHATORIA (African American) Combine form of Sha and Victoria. *Variations:* Shatora, Shatori, Shatoya.

SHAUNA (Hebrew; Irish) God is good. Feminine variation of John. *Variations:* Seana, Shaunda, Shaune, Shauneen, Shaunna, Shawna, Shawnda, Shawnna.

SHAVONNE (Hebrew) God is good; (Irish) Form of Siobhan (feminine for John). *Variations:* Shavon, Shavonda, Shavone, Shevon, Shevonne, Shivonne, Shyvon, Shyvonne.

SHAWN (Hebrew) God is good. Another feminine variation of John. *Notables:* Singer Shawn Colvin; actress Sean Young. *Variations:* Sean, Shawna, Shawnee, Shawni, Shawnie.

SHAYLA (Irish) Fairy castle. Form of Shea. *Variations:* Shaela, Shaylee, Shayleen, Shaylene, Shaylyn, Sheyla.

SHEA (Irish) Fairy castle. *Variations:* Shae, Shay, Shaye, Shayla, Shaylee, Shaylin, Shayline.

SHEBA (Hebrew) Pledged daughter. Short for Bathsheba. *Variations:* Sheeba, Shiba, Shyba.

SHEENA (Irish) Form of Jane. *Notable:* Singer Sheena Easton. *Variation:* Shena.

SHEILA (Latin) Blind. *Notables:* Singer Sheila E.; actress Sheila Kelley. *Variations:* Selia, Sheela, Shelagh, Shelia, Shila.

SHEKEDA (Hebrew) Almond tree. *Variations:* Shekedia, Shekediya.

SHEKINAH (Hebrew) God's holy spirit. *Variations:* Shechina, Shekina.

SHELAVYA (Hebrew) To gather. *Variation:* Shelavia.

SHELBY (English) Estate on a ledge. *Notable:* Singer Shelby Lynne. *Variations:* Shelbee, Shelbey, Shellby.

SHELIYA (Hebrew) My God. *Variations:* Sheli, Shelia, Shelli.

SHELLEY (English) Meadow on a ledge. *Notables:* Actresses Shelley Winters and Shelley Fabares. *Variations:* Shellee, Shelli, Shellie, Shelly.

SHELOMIYTH (Hebrew) Peaceful. *Variation:* Shlomit.

SHENANDOAH (Native American) Beautiful girl from the stars.

SHERA (Aramaic) Light. *Variations:* Sheera, Sherah.

SHERICE (American) A plain. *Variations:* Sharice, Shericia.

SHERIDAN (Irish) Wild. *Variations:* Sherida, Sheriden, Sheridon.

SHERIKA (Arabic) Easterner.

SHERRY (French) Dearest. *Notable:* Film producer Sherry Lansing. *Variations:* Cheri, Cherie, Sheree, Sheri, Sherissa, Sherita, Sherri, Sherrie.

SHERYL (French) Dearest. *Notable:* Singer Sheryl Crow. *Variations:* Cheryl, Cheril, Sherell, Sherelle, Sheril, Sherill, Sherilyn.

SHEVA (Hebrew) Pledge.

SHEVONNE (Irish) God is gracious. Form of Siobhan. *Variation:* Shevon.

SHEYANNE (Native American) Red talker. Form of Cheyenne. *Variations:* Shayanne, Shayenne, Sheyenne, Shian, Shianna, Shianne.

SHIFA (Hebrew) Plenty.

SHIFRA (Hebrew) Beautiful. *Variations:* Shifrah, Shiphrah.

SHIGEKO (Japanese) Luxuriant.

SHIKA (Japanese) Deer.

SHIKHA (Hindi) Brightly burning flame.

SHILOH (Hebrew) God's gift. *Variations:* Shilo, Shylo.

SHILPA (Hindi) Strong as a rock.

SHILRA (Hebrew) Lovely. *Variations:* Schilra, Shilrah.

SHIMA (Native American) Little mother. *Variations:* Shimah, Shimma, Shyma.

SHIMONA (Hebrew) To listen. *Variations:* Simeona, Simona.

SHIMRIAH (Hebrew) God protects. *Variations:* Shimra, Shimria, Shimrit, Shimriya.

SHIN (Korean) Faith and trust.

SHINA (Japanese) Loyal. *Variation:* Shinako.

SHINJU (Japanese) Pearl.

SHINO (Japanese) Bamboo.

SHIORI (Japanese) Poem.

SHIRA (Hebrew) Song. *Variations:* Shirah, Shiri.

SHIRIN (Hindi) Sweet. *Variation:* Shirina.

SHIRLEY (English) Bright meadow. *Notables:* Child star Shirley Temple; actresses Shirley Jones, Shirley Jackson, and Shirley MacLaine. *Variations:* Shirl, Shirlean, Shirlee, Shirleen, Shirlene, Shirly, Shirlynn, Shurly.

SHIVANI (Hindi) Life and death. *Variations:* Shiva, Shivana, Shivanie.

SHIZU (Japanese) Quiet. *Variations:* Shizue, Shizuka, Shizuko, Shizuyo.

SHOBHANA (Hindi) Beautiful. *Variations:* Shobha, Shobhini.

SHOMERA (Hebrew) Protect. *Variations:* Shomria, Shomriah, Shomrit, Shomriya, Shomrona.

SHONA (Scottish) God is good. Feminine variation of John. *Variations:* Shonah, Shonda, Shondi, Shone.

SHOSHANA (Hebrew) Lily. Form of Susan. *Variations:* Shosha, Shoshan, Shoshanah, Shoshanna.

SHPRINTZA (Yiddish) Hope. *Variations:* Shprintze, Shprintzel.

SHRADDHA (Hindi) Trusting. *Variation:* Shradha.

SHRIYA (Hindi) Prosperous.

SHU (Chinese) Tender.

SHUALA (Hebrew) Fox.

SHUANG (Chinese) Lively.

SHUCHUN (Chinese) Pure beauty.

SHUKRIYA (Arabic) Thanks. *Variation:* Shukriyyah.

SHUKURA (African) Grateful. *Variation:* Shukuma.

SHULA (Arabic) Flaming.

SHULAMIT (Hebrew) Peaceful. *Variations:* Shelomit, Shlamit, Shula, Shulamith, Sula, Sulamith.

SHUMANA (Native American) Rattlesnake girl. *Variation:* Shuma, Shuman.

SHURA (Russian) Protector of man.

SHYAMA (Hindi) Dark beauty.

SHYLA (Hindi) The goddess Parvati.

SIAN (Welsh) God is gracious. *Variations:* Sianna, Sianne.

SIANY (Irish) Healthy. *Variations:* Slaine, Slainie, Slania.

SIARA (Arabic) Holy and pure.

SIBEAL (Gaelic) God is my oath.

SIBETA (Native American) Fishing under a rock.

SIBONGILE (African) Appreciation.

SIBYL (Greek) Seer, oracle. *Variations:* Sibbell, Sibel, Sibell, Sibella, Sibelle, Sibilla, Sibyll, Sibylla, Sibylle, Sybel, Sybella, Sybelle, Sybil, Sybill, Sybilla, Sybille, Sybyl.

SIDDHI (Hindi) Possessing spiritual power. *Variation:* Sidhi.

SIDONIE (French) From Sidon, a town in the ancient Middle East. *Variations:* Sidaine, Sidonia, Sidony, Sydonia, Syndonia.

SIDRA (Latin) Stars. *Variations:* Cidra, Cydra, Sidri, Sidria, Sydra.

SIEGHILD (German) Victory battle. *Variations:* Sieglinde, Sigi.

SIENA (Italian) Town of Siena, Italy. *Notable:* Actress Sienna Miller. *Variation:* Sienna.

SIERRA (Spanish) Mountain range. *Variation:* Siera.

SIF (Scandinavian) Relationship. *Variation:* Siv.

SIGAL (Hebrew) Treasure.

SIGELE (African) Left.

SIGFREDA (German) Peaceful victory. Feminine version of Sigfried. *Variations:* Sigfreida, Sigfrida, Sigfrieda, Sigfryda.

SIGNE (Scandinavian) New victory. *Variations:* Signa, Signi, Signild, Signilda, Signilde, Signy, Sigyn.

SIGOURNEY (English) Conquerer. *Notable:* Actress Sigourney Weaver.

SIGRID (Scandinavian) Beautiful victory. *Notable:* Clothing designer Sigrid Olsen. *Variations:* Siegrid, Siegrida, Sigred.

SIGRUN (Scandinavian) Secret victory.

SIHAM (Arabic) Arrow.

SIHU (Native American) Flower.

SILENCE (English) Quiet.

SILJA (Scandinavian) Blind.

SILVA (Latin) Forest. *Variations:* Silvaine, Silvana, Silvania, Silvanna, Silvia, Silviana.

SILVER (English) Silver. *Variations:* Silva, Sylva, Sylver.

SILWA (Arabic) Quail.

SIMCHA (Hebrew) Joyful.

SIMI (Native American) Wind valley.

SIMONE (French) God listens. Feminine version of Simon. *Notables:* Actress Simone Signoret; writer Simone de Beauvoir. *Variations:* Simona, Simonetta, Simonette, Simonia, Simonina, Symona, Symone.

SINA (Irish) God is good. *Variations:* Sinah, Sine.

SINCLAIRE (French) Prayer.

SINEAD (Irish) Form of Janet or Joan. *Notable:* Singer Sinéad O'Connor.

SIOBHAN (Irish) Form of Jane or Joan. *Variations:* Chavonne, Chevonne, Chivon, Shiban, Shibani, Shivahn, Shivaun, Sioban.

SIOFRA (Irish) Elf.

SIOMHA (Irish) Good peace. *Variation:* Sithmaith.

SINOBIA (Greek) Sign or symbol.

SINOPA (Native American) Fox.

SIPETA (Native American) Fishing.

SIPORA (Hebrew) Bird-like woman. *Variations:* Sippora, Sipporah.

SIRAN (Armenian) Alluring and lovely. *Variations:* Siroun, Sirune.

SIRENA (Greek) Enchantress. *Variations:* Siren, Sirene, Syrena.

SIRPUHI (Armenian) Holy and pious.

SIRVAT (Armenian) Beautiful rose.

SISEL (Yiddish) Sweet.

SISIKA (Native American) Swallow, a kind of bird.

SISILIA (Polynesian) Blind.

SISSY (American) Short form of Cecilia. *Notable:* Actress Sissy Spacek. *Variations:* Cissy, Sisi, Sisee, Sissee, Sissey, Sissi, Sissie, Syssi, Syssie, Syssy.

SITA (Hindi) The goddess of agriculture. *Variations:* Seeta, Seetha, Siti.

SITARA (Hindi) Morning star.

SITI (African) Lady.

SITKA (Native American) People on the outside. *Variation:* Sytka.

Begins with "Sha"

Taking a girl's name and adding the prefix "Sha" will create a whole new and interesting name. Here are popular variations to consider:

Shadrika	Shaniqua
Shajuana	Shanisa
Shakayla	Shantana
Shakeia	Shantay
Shakena	Shantel
Shakera	Shantice
Shaleah	Shantina
Shaleisha	Shantora
Shalena	Shantrice
Shalonda	Shaquila
Shalonna	Shaquita
Shamika	Sharissa
Shandrice	Sharonda
Shaneisha	Shatoya
Shaneika	Shavonne
Shanice	Shawanna
Shanida	

Girls' Names from Popular Songs

Here's a list of popular songs that include names of girls in the titles, along with who performed the ditties:

Alison—Elvis Costello
Angie—The Rolling Stones
Barbara Ann—The Beach Boys
Beth—Kiss
Billie Jean—Michael Jackson
Sweet Caroline—Neil Diamond
Carrie Anne—The Hollies
Cecilia—Simon & Garfunkel
Delilah—Tom Jones
Donna—Ritchie Valens
Gloria—Laura Branigan
Iris—The Goo Goo Dolls
Jolene—Dolly Parton
Layla—Derek and the Dominoes
Lola—The Kinks
Lucy in the Sky with Diamonds—The Beatles
Maggie May—Rod Stewart
Mandy—Barry Manilow
Michelle—The Beatles
My Sharona—The Knack
Rhiannon—Fleetwood Mac
Rosanna—Toto
Roxanne—The Police
Sara Smile—Hall and Oates
Sherry—The Four Seasons
Valleri—The Monkees
Veronica—Elvis Costello

SIV (Norse) Beautiful bride.

SIVANA (Hebrew) Ninth month of the Jewish calendar.

SIVESTRA (English) Of the forest.

SIXTEN (Scandinavian) Victory stone.

SJOFN (Scandinavian) Love.

SKYE (Scottish) From the Isle of Skye. *Variation:* Sky.

SKYLER (Dutch) Scholar. *Variations:* Schuyler, Skye, Skylar.

SLAINE (Irish) Good health.

SLOANE (Irish) Warrior. *Variation:* Sloan.

SMASHI (Hindi) Moonbeam. *Variations:* Shashibala, Shashini.

SNANA (Native American) Ringing sounds.

SNOWDROP (English) Flower name.

SOBESLAVA (Czech) To overtake glory. *Variations:* Sobena, Sobeska.

SOCORRO (Spanish) Help.

SOFIA (Italian; Spanish) Wisdom.

SOFRONIA (Greek) Wise.

SOHALIA (Hindi) Moon glow.

SOKANON (Native American) Born during the rain.

SOLANA (Spanish) Sunshine. *Variations:* Sol, Solenne, Solina, Soline, Souline, Soulle, Zelena, Zelene, Zelia, Zelie, Zelina, Zeline.

SOLANGE (French) Dignified. *Variation:* Solance.

SOLARIS (Greek) Of the sun. *Variations:* Solarys, Solstice.

SOLEDAD (Spanish) Solitude. *Notable:* TV newscaster Soledad O'Brien.

SOLEIL (French) Sun. *Notable:* Actress Soleil Moon Frye.

SOLVEIG (Scandinavian) Strong house. *Variation:* Solvag.

SOMA (Hindi) Moon.

SONA (Hindi) Golden. *Variations:* Sonal, Sonala, Sonali, Sonika, Sonita.

SONDRA (Greek) Defender of man. Form of Sandra. *Notable:* Actress Sondra Locke.

SONG (Chinese) Pine tree.

SONIA (Slavic) Wisdom. Variation of Sophia. *Notable:* Brazilian actress Sonia Braga. *Variations:* Sonja, Sonya.

SONOMA (Spanish) Place name in Northern California.

SONORA (Spanish) Place name in Northern Mexico.

SOOK (Korean) Purity.

SOOK-JOO (Korean) Pure gem.

SOON-BOK (Korean) Tender.

SOPHEARY (Cambodian) Lovely.

SOPHIA (Greek) Wisdom. *Notables:* Actress Sophia Loren; singer Sophie B. Hawkins. *Variations:* Sofi, Sofia, Soficita, Sofka, Sofya, Sophey, Sophie, Sophy, Zofe, Zofia, Zofie, Zofka, Zosha, Zosia.

SOPHRONIA (Greek) Sensible, prudent. *Variations:* Soffrona, Sofronia.

SOPORTEVY (Cambodian) Angelic.

SORA (Native American) Songbird.

SORAYA (Persian) Princess. *Variation:* Sorya.

SORCHA (Irish) Bright and intelligent.

SOREKA (Hebrew) Vine.

SORINA (Romanian) Of the sun.

SORREL (French) Herb name. *Variations:* Sorrell, Sorrelle.

SOUBRETTE (French) Coquette. *Variation:* Soubret.

SOVANN (Cambodian) Golden.

SOYALA (Native American) Of the winter solstice.

SPARROW (English) A small songbird.

SPENCER (English) Dispenser. *Variation:* Spenser.

SPERANZA (Italian) Hope.

SPRING (English) Springtime.

SRADDHA (Hindi) Faith. *Variation:* Sradha.

SRI (Hindi) Wealth. *Variations:* Shree, Shri.

STACY (Greek) Resurrection. Diminutive of Anastasia. *Variations:* Stace, Stacee, Stacey, Staci, Stacia, Stacie, Stasee, Stasia.

STANISLAVA (Czech) Glorious government. *Variations:* Stana, Stanuska, Stinicka.

STAR (English) Star. *Notable:* Talk-show host Star Jones. *Variations:* Starla, Starlene, Starr.

STARLING (English) Bird name.

STEFANIE (Greek) Crowned. Form of Stephanie. *Variations:* Stefanee, Stefani, Stefaney.

STELLA (Latin) Star. *Notable:* Fashion designer Stella McCartney. *Variations:* Estelle, Estella, Estrella, Stelle, Stellina.

STEPHANIE (Greek) Crown. Feminine version of Stephen. *Notables:* Princess Stephanie of Monaco; actresses Stephanie Zimbalist and Stefanie

Powers. *Variations:* Stefania, Stefanie, Steffi, Stepana, Stepania, Stepanie, Stephana, Stephanine, Stephannie, Stephena, Stephene, Stepheney, Stephenie, Stephine, Stephne, Stephney, Stevana, Stevena, Stevey, Stevi, Stevie.

STERLING (English) Valuable.

STEVIE (Greek) Short form of Stephanie. *Notable:* Singer Stevie Nicks. *Variations:* Stevee, Stevi, Stevona.

STINA (Danish) Short form of Christina. *Variations:* Steana, Steena.

STOCKARD (English) Stockyard. *Notable:* Actress Stockard Channing.

STORM (English) Storm. *Variations:* Stormi, Stormie, Stormy.

STRUANA (Scottish) From the stream. *Variation:* Struanne.

SUBHADRA (Sanskrit) Half sister of Krishna.

SUBIRA (African) Patience.

SU CHIN (Korean) Beautiful thought.

SUE (Hebrew) Lily. Form of Susan or Susanna. *Notables:* Writer Sue Grafton.

SUELLEN (American) Combination of Sue and Ellen. *Variation:* SueEllen.

SUELO (Spanish) Consolation. Short form of Consuelo.

SUGAR (American) Sugar.

SUGI (Japanese) Cedar tree.

SUHA (Arabic) Star.

SUHAD (Arabic) Insomnia. *Variations:* Suhair, Suhar, Suhayr.

SUHAILA (Hindi) Star. *Variation:* Suhayila.

SUHAILAH (Arabic) Gentle.

SUJATA (Hindi) Noble.

SUKEY (English) Form of Susan. *Variations:* Sokie, Sookie, Sooky, Suki, Sukie, Suky.

SUKOJI (African) First daughter born after a son.

SULA (Icelandic) Large bird.

SULAKHNA (Punjabi) Faith.

SULETU (Native American) Flight.

SULTANA (Arabic) Empress. *Variation:* Sultanna.

SULWEN (Welsh) Bright sun. *Variation:* Sulwyn.

SUMA (Sanskrit) Flower.

SUMANA (Hindi) Cheerful.

SUMATI (Hindi) Unity.

SUMI (Japanese) Clear and refined.

SUMIKO (Japanese) Child pure of thought.

SUMITRA (Hindi) Good friend. *Variation:* Sumithra.

SUMMER (English) The season. *Variations:* Somer, Sommer.

SUNAYANA (Hindi) Beautiful eyes. *Variation:* Sunayani.

SUNDARI (Hindi) Beautiful. *Variation:* Sundara.

SUNDAY (Latin) Day of rest. *Variation:* Sundae.

SUN-HI (Korean) Loyalty.

SUNHILDA (German) Battle under the sun. *Variation:* Sunhilde.

SUNI (Native American) Zuni Indian.

SUNILA (Hindi) Blue. *Variation:* Sunilla.

SUNITA (Hindi) Well behaved. *Variation:* Sunitra.

SUNKI (Native American) Successful hunter.

SUNNIVA (Scandinavian) Gift of the sun. *Variations:* Synnova, Synnove.

SUNNY (English) Sunny and bright. *Variation:* Sunni.

SUNSHINE (English) Sun. *Variations:* Sunnie, Sunni, Sunnita, Sunny.

SURAGANA (Hindi) Divine.

SURATA (Hindi) Joy.

SURI (Hebrew) Princess. Form of Sarah.

SURINA (Hindi) Goddess.

SURYA (Sanskrit) Sun god.

SUSAN (Hebrew) Lily. *Notables:* Actresses Susan Sarandon and Susan Lucci. *Variations:* Susetta, Susette, Susi, Susie, Susy, Suzan, Suzetta, Suzette, Suzi, Suzie, Suzy, Zsa Zsa, Zusa, Zuza.

SUSANNA (Hebrew) Form of Susan. *Notables:* Singer Susanna Hoffs; actress Susannah York. *Variations:* Susana, Susanita, Susann, Susanna, Susannah, Susanne, Suzana, Suzane, Suzanna, Suzannah, Suzanne.

SUSIE (American) Nickname for Susan and Susanna. *Notables:* Financial guru Suze Orman; comedian Susie Essman. *Variations:* Susi, Susy, Suze, Suzey, Suzi, Suzie.

SUSHANTI (Hindi) Tranquillity.

SUYIN (Chinese) Simple.

SUZANNE (French) Form of Susan. *Notables:* Actresses Suzanne Somers and Suzanne Pleshette. *Variation:* Susanne.

SUZETTE (French) Form of Susan.

SUZU (Japanese) Bell.

SUZUKI (Japanese) Little bell tree. *Variations:* Suzue, Suzuko.

SUZUME (Japanese) Sparrow.

SVANHILD (Scandinavian) Battle swan.

SVANNT (Scandinavian) Slender.

SVEA (Scandinavian) Kingdom.

SVENJA (German) Swan.

SVETLANA (Czech) Star. *Variations:* Svetla, Svetlanka, Svetluse, Svetluvska.

SWANHILDA (English) Battle swan. *Variations:* Schwanhild, Swanhild, Swanhilde.

SWOOSIE (American) Half swan, half goose. *Notable:* Actress Swoosie Kurtz. *Variations:* Swoozie, Swoozy.

SYBIL (Greek) Prophet. *Variations:* Sibyl, Sybill, Sybille, Sybyl.

SYDNEY (French) Feminine version of Sidney. *Variations:* Sidnee, Sidney, Sidni, Sidnie, Syd, Sydni, Sydnie, Sydny.

SYDELLE (Hebrew) Born to royalty. *Variations:* Sidel, Sidella, Sidelle, Sydel, Sydell, Sydella.

SYLVAN (Latin) Forest. *Variations:* Silvaine, Silvana, Silvania, Silvanna, Silvia, Silviana.

SYLVIA (Latin) From the forest. *Notables:* Writer Sylvia Plath; psychic Sylvia Browne. *Variations:* Silvana, Silvia, Silvianne, Silvie, Sylva, Sylvana, Sylvanna, Sylvee, Sylvie.

SYMPHONY (Greek) Symphony. *Variation:* Symphanie.

SYONA (Hindi) Happy.

SYREETA (Arabic) Companion. *Variations:* Sireeta, Sirita, Syrita.

TABEA (German) Gazelle.

TABIA (African) Talented. *Variations:* Tabiah, Tabya.

TABINA (Arabic) Follower of Mohammed. *Variations:* Tabeena, Tabinah, Tabyna.

TABITHA (Aramaic) Gazelle. *Notable:* TV reporter Tabitha Soren. *Variations:* Tabatha, Tabbatha, Tabbetha, Tabbitha, Tabby, Tabetha, Tabotha, Tabytha.

TABORA (Spanish) Small drum. *Variation:* Taborra.

TACEY (English) Quiet. *Variations:* Tace, Tacea, Tacee, Taci, Tacia, Tacie, Tacita, Tacy, Taycee.

TACINCALA (Native American) Deerlike.

TACITA (Latin) Silent. *Variations:* Taceeta, Taceta, Tasita.

TADDEA (Hebrew) Brave. *Variations:* Taddeah, Tadea, Tadeah, Tadia, Tadya.

TADEWI (Native American) Wind. *Variations:* Tadi, Tadiwi.

TADITA (Native American) Runner. *Variations:* Tadeta, Taditah, Tadra, Tadyta.

TAESHA (American) Happy. *Variations:* Taheisha, Tahisha, Taiesha, Taisha, Taishae, Tayesha, Teisha, Tesha, Tyeisha, Tyeishia, Tyeshia, Tyeyshia, Tyieshia, Tyishia, Tyishya, Tyshia, Tyshya.

TAFFY (Welsh) Beloved. *Variations:* Taffea, Taffee, Taffey, Taffi, Taffie.

TAFLYN (Welsh) Beloved. *Variations:* Taflina, Tafline, Taflyna, Taflyne.

TAFNE (Egyptian) Goddess of light. *Variations:* Taffnee, Taffney, Taffni, Taffnie, Taffny, Tafna, Tafnee.

TAGHRID (Arabic) Singing bird.

TAHCAWIN (Native American) Doe.

TAHIRA (Arabic) Pure. *Variations:* Tahera, Tahere, Taheria, Tahirah.

TAHITI (Polynesian) Eastern rising sun. *Variations:* Tahite, Tahitia, Tahity.

TAHIYYA (Arabic) Welcome. *Variation:* Tahiyyah.

TAHNEE (English) Little one. *Variations:* Tahne, Tahney, Tahni, Tahnia, Tahny, Tahnya.

TAIMA (Native American) Thunder. *Variations:* Taimah, Taimy, Taiomah, Tayma, Taymi, Taymie.

TAINI (Native American) New moon. *Variations:* Taina, Taine, Tainee, Tayna, Tayne.

TAIPA (Native American) Quail.

TAISA (Greek) Bonded. *Variations:* Tais, Taysa.

TAIWO (African) First born of twins.

TAJA (Hindi) Crown. *Variation:* Tajah.

TAJSA (Polish) Royal. *Variations:* Tajsi, Tajsia.

TAKA (Japanese) Honorable.

TAKALA (Native American) Cornstalk. *Variation:* Takalah.

TAKARA (Japanese) Treasure.

TAKAYREN (Native American) Commotion.

TAKEKO (Japanese) Bamboo.

TAKENYA (Native American) Falcon in flight. *Variations:* Takenia, Takenja.

TAKI (Japanese) Waterfall.

TAKIA (Arabic) Worshiper. *Variations:* Takeiah, Takeiya, Takeya, Takeyah, Takiah, Takija, Takijah, Takiya, Takkia, Takkiah, Takkya, Takya, Taqiya, Taqiyah, Taqiyya, Taquaia, Taquaya, Taquiia, Tekeyia, Tekia, Tekiya, Tykeia, Tykeiah, Tykia, Tykya.

TAKIRA (Persian) Sun. *Variations:* Takeara, Takirah, Takiria, Takyra, Takyrah, Taquera, Taquira, Tekeria, Tekyria, Tekyrya, Tikara, Tikira, Tikirah, Tikiria, Tikirya, Tykira, Tykyra.

TAKOTA (Native American) Friendly. *Variation:* Takoda.

TAKUHI (Armenian) Queen. *Variations:* Takoohi, Takouhi.

TALA (Native American) Stalking wolf.

TALAITH (Welsh) Wearing a crown.

TALAL (Hebrew) Dew. *Variations:* Talala, Talila.

TALASI (Native American) Cornflower. *Variations:* Talasee, Talasia, Talasie.

TALE (African). Green.

TALEISHA (African) Life. *Variations:* Taleasha, Taleashia, Taleesha, Taleeshia, Taleesha, Talesha, Taleshia, Taleysha, Talisha.

TALIA (Hebrew) Dew; (Greek) Blossoming. *Notable:* Actress Talia Shire. *Variations:* Tal, Tahlia, Taliah, Talie, Talley, Tallie, Tally, Talora, Talya, Thalie, Thalya.

TALIBA (Arabic) Seeker of knowledge. *Variation:* Talibah.

TALINA (English) Morning dew. *Variations:* Taleana, Taleena, Talena, Talinda, Talyna.

TALINE (Armenian) Monastery. *Variations:* Taleen, Talin, Taline, Talyn, Talyne.

TALISA (Hebrew) Devoted to God. *Notable:* Actress Talisa Soto. *Variations:* Talisah, Talisha, Talisia, Talisiah, Talissa, Talisse, Tallisa, Tallissa, Tallisse, Tallysa, Talysa, Talysia, Talyssa, Telisa.

TALISE (Native American) Beautiful water. *Variations:* Taleese, Talyce.

TALITHA (Aramaic) Young girl. *Variations:* Taleetha, Taletha, Talicia, Talisha, Talita.

TALLIS (French) Forest. *Variations:* Talice, Talisa, Talise, Tallys.

TALLULAH (Native American) Leaping water. *Notable:* Actress Tallulah Bankhead. *Variations:* Tallula, Talula, Talulah, Talulla.

TALLY (English) Short form of Talia. *Variations:* Tallee, Talley, Talli, Tallie.

TALMA (Hebrew) Hill. *Variations:* Talmah, Talmar, Talmara, Talmaria, Talmarya.

TALMOR (Arabic) Perfume. *Variations:* Talmoor, Talmora.

TALOR (Hebrew) Morning dew. *Variations:* Talora, Talore, Taloria, Talorie.

TALUTAH (Native American) Red. *Variation:* Taluta.

TAM (Vietnamese) Heart.

TAMA (Japanese) Jewel. *Notable:* Writer Tama Janowitz.

TAMAH (Hebrew) Marvel. *Variation:* Tama.

TAMAKA (Japanese) Bracelet. *Variations:* Tamaki, Tamako, Tamayo.

TAMANNA (Hindi) Desire. *Variation:* Tamana.

The Baby-Naming Process Can Make Strange Bedfellows

What happens when you and your partner completely disagree? Or if you each detest the name that the other loves most? One solution is to go through your lists of favorites and choose from only those names that you *both* had on your lists. You can always save the other names for a middle name or try again with your next baby.

TAMARA (Hebrew) Palm tree. *Variations:* Tama, Tamah, Tamar, Tamarah, Tamarra, Tamera, Tami, Tamma, Tammara, Tammee, Tammera, Tammey, Tammie, Tammy, Tamor, Tamour, Tamra, Thamar, Thamara, Thamarra.

TAMAS (Hindi) Night. *Variations:* Tamasa, Tamasi, Tamassa, Tamasvini.

TAMASINE (English) Twin. Feminine version of Thomas. *Variations:* Tamasin, Tamasina, Tamasyn, Tamasyne, Tamazin, Tamazina, Tamazine, Tamsin, Tamsine, Tamsyn, Tamzen, Tamzin, Tamzina, Tamzyn, Tamzyna.

TAMATH (Arabic) At a slow pace. *Variations:* Tamatha, Tamathia.

TAMI (Japanese) People. *Variation:* Tamie.

TAMIKA (Japanese) Child of the people. *Variations:* Tameka, Tameke, Tameko, Tamike, Tamiko, Tamiya, Tamiyo, Tamyka, Tamyko.

TAMILA (Russian) Dear one. *Variations:* Tamilla, Tamyla.

TAMMY (English) Twin (Hebrew) Familiar form of Tamara. *Notable:* Singer Tammy Wynette. *Variations:* Tamee, Tamey, Tami, Tamie, Tammee, Tammi, Tammie.

TAMOHARA (Hindi) The sun.

TAMRA (Hebrew) Palm tree. Short form of Tamara. *Variation:* Tamrah.

TAMRIKA (American) Combined form of Tammy and Rick. *Variations:* Tamreeka, Tamriqua.

TANAKA (Japanese) Swamp dweller.

TANAYA (Hindi) Daughter. *Variations:* Tanae, Tanaia, Tanay, Tanuja, Tanujia.

TANDY (English) Team. *Variations:* Tanda, Tandea, Tandee, Tandi, Tandie, Tandra.

TANESHA (African) Born on Monday. *Variations:* Taneesha, Taneisha, Taneshea, Tanicha, Taniesha, Tanisha, Tanitia, Tannicia, Tannisha, Tenecia, Teneesha, Teneisha, Tenesha, Teniesha, Tenisha, Tinecia, Tiniesha, Tynisha.

TANGERINE (English) From Tangiers (in Morocco). *Variation:* Tangerina.

TANGIA (Greek) Angel. *Variations:* Tangea, Tanjea, Tanjia.

TANI (Japanese) Valley. *Variations:* Tanee, Taney, Tanie, Tanni, Tannie, Tanney.

TANIA (Russian) Fairy queen. *Variations:* Tahnia, Taniah, Taniya, Tanja, Tannia, Tanya, Tonya.

TANIEL (American) God is my judge. *Variations:* Taniele, Taniela, Taniella, Tanielle.

TANIKA (Hindi) Rope. *Variations:* Tanica, Tanicka, Tannika, Taneka.

TANITH (Irish) Estate. *Variations:* Tanita, Tanitha.

TANNER (English) Leather worker.

TANNISHTHA (Hindi) Devoted.

TANSY (Greek) Immortality. *Variations:* Tansea, Tansee, Tansey, Tansi, Tansia, Tansie, Tanzi, Tanzee, Tanzia, Tanzie.

TANVI (Hindi) Young woman. *Variations:* Tanvie, Tanvy.

TANYA (Russian) Fairy queen. *Notables:* Actress Tanya Roberts; singer Tanya Tucker. *Variation:* Tonya.

TAO (Chinese) Peach.

TAPASYA (Hindi) Bitter.

TAPI (Hindi) From the river.

TAPPEN (Welsh) Top of the rock. *Variations:* Tappan, Tappin.

TAQIYYA (Arabic) Devotion. *Variations:* Takiyah, Takiyya, Takiyyah, Taqiyyah.

TARA (Irish) Hill. *Notables:* Actress Tara Reid; ice skater Tara Lipinski. *Variations:* Tarah, Taran, Tareena, Tarena, Tarin, Tarina, Tarra, Tarrah, Tarren, Tarryn, Taryn, Taryna, Teryn.

TARACHAND (Hindi) Star. *Variations:* Tarachanda, Tarachandi.

TARAL (Hindi) Rippling. *Variations:* Tarala, Tarale, Tarral, Tarrala, Tarrel.

TARANA (African) Born in daylight. *Variation:* Taranna.

TARANI (Hindi) Light. *Variation:* Tarini.

TAREE (Japanese) Tree branch. *Variations:* Tarey, Tarie, Tary.

TARIAN (Welsh) Coat of arms. *Variations:* Tariane, Tariann, Tarianne.

TARIKA (Hindi) Star.

TARLAM (Hindi) Flowing.

TARUB (Arabic) Cheerful.

TARUNIKA (Hindi) Girl.

TARYN (Irish) Rocky hill. Form of Tara. *Variations:* Taran, Taren, Tarin, Tarina, Tarine, Tarren, Tarrin, Tarrina, Tarrine, Taron, Tarron, Tarryn, Tarynne.

TASANEE (Thai) Beautiful view.

TASARIA (Gypsy) Born at sunrise. *Variations:* Tasara, Tasariah, Tasarla, Tasarya.

TASHA (Russian) Christmas. Diminutive of Natasha. *Variations:* Tashina, Tashka, Tasia.

TASHANEE (African American) Born at Christmas. *Variations:* Tashana, Tashani, Tashania, Tasheena, Tashinah, Tashyna.

TASHELLE (African American) Combined form of Natasha and Michelle. *Variations:* Tashel, Tashela, Tashele, Tashell, Tashella.

TASIA (Slavic) Resurrection. *Variations:* Tasiah, Tasija, Tasiya, Tasya, Tazia, Tazya.

TASIDA (Native American) Rides a horse.

TASMINE (English) Twin. Feminine version of Thomas. *Variations:* Tasmin, Tazmie.

TASSIE (English) Twin. Short form of Tasmine. *Variations:* Tasee, Tasey, Tasi, Tasie, Tassee, Tassey, Tassi, Tassy, Tasy, Tazee, Tazey, Tazi, Tazy, Tazzey, Tazzi, Tazzie, Tazzy.

TATE (Scandinavian) Bubbly. *Variations:* Taite, Tatum, Tayte.

TATIANA (Russian) Fairy queen. *Notable:* Actress/singer Tatyana Ali. Feminine version of Tatius, the ancient Slavic king. *Variations:* Latonya, Tahnya, Tana, Tania, Tanis, Tanka, Tannia, Tannis, Tarnia, Tarny, Tata, Tatania, Tatianna, Tatienne, Tatjana, Tatyana, Tatyanna, Tonia, Tonya, Tonyah.

TATSU (Japanese) Dragon.

TATUM (English) Cheerful. *Notable:* Actress Tatum O'Neal. *Variations:* Taitum, Tatam, Tatem, Tatim, Tatom, Tatym.

TAULAKI (Polynesian) Waiting.

TAURA (Latin) Bull. *Variations:* Taure, Taury.

TAVIA (Latin) Eighth-born child. Short form of Octavia. *Variations:* Tava, Tavja, Tavya.

TAVIE (Scottish) Twin.

TAWANNA (American) Combination of Ta and Wanda. *Variations:* Tawana, Tawanda, Tawanne.

TAWIA (African) Born after twins.

TAWNY (English) Golden brown. *Notable:* Actress Tawny Kitaen. *Variations:* Tawnee, Tawney, Tawni.

TAYANITA (Native American) Beaver. *Variations:* Taianita, Tayaneeta.

TAYEN (Native American) Born of the new moon.

TAYLOR (English) Tailor. *Notable:* Singer Taylor Swift. *Variations:* Tailer, Tailor, Talor, Tayla, Tayler.

TAZU (Japanese) Stork.

TEA (Greek) Gift of God. Short form of Theodora. *Notable:* Actress Tea Leoni.

TEAGAN (Welsh) Poet. *Variations:* Taegan, Taegen, Taegin, Taegon, Taegun, Taegyn, Teagen, Teaghan, Teaghen, Teague, Teegan, Teegen, Teegin, Teegon, Teegun, Teegyn, Tegan, Teigan, Teige, Teigen, Teigin, Teigon, Teigun, Teigyn, Tigan, Tigen, Tigin, Tigon, Tigun, Tigyn.

TEAL (English) River duck. *Variations:* Teale, Teel, Teil.

TEAMHAIR (Irish) Hill.

TEANNA (English) Free spirit. *Variations:* Teana, Teane, Teanne, Teiana, Teiane, Teiann, Teianna, Teianne, Teyan, Teyana, Teyann, Teyanna, Teyanne, Tiana, Tiane, Tiann, Tianna, Tianne, Tyana, Tyanah, Tyann, Tyanna, Tyanne.

TECLA (Greek) Glory of God. *Variations:* Tekla, Thecla.

TEDDI (Greek) Short form of Theodora. *Variations:* Teddea, Teddee, Teddie, Teddy, Tedee, Tedi, Tedia, Tedie, Tedy.

TEDRA (Greek) Gift of God. *Variation:* Teddra.

TEGVYEN (Welsh) Lovely maiden.

TEHLIA (Hebrew) Song of praise.

TELERI (Welsh) Elf clan.

TELEZA (African) Slippery.

TELLUS (Latin) Mother Earth. *Variations:* Tellas, Tellassa, Telasse, Telus.

TELMA (Greek) Willful.

TELYN (Welsh) Harp.

TEMIRA (Hebrew) Tall. *Variations:* Temora, Timora.

TEMPERANCE (Latin) Moderation.

TEMPEST (French) Storm. *Notable:* Actress Tempestt Bledsoe. *Variation:* Tempestt.

TEMPLE (Latin) Temple; house of worship. *Notable:* Animal behavior expert Temple Grandin. *Variations:* Tempel, Templa.

TENNILLE (Irish; Australian) Champion. Powerful. *Variations:* Teneal, Teneale, Tenneal, Tenielle, Tenille.

TENUVAH (Hebrew) Fruits and vegetables. *Variation:* Tenuva.

TEOFILIA (Italian) God's friend.

TEQUILA (Spanish) Liquor name. *Variations:* Takila, Taquila, Tequela, Tequilla.

TERALYN (American) Combination of Terry and Lynn. *Variations:* Teralin, Teralina, Teraline, Teralyna, Teralyne, Terralin, Terralyn.

TERANIKA (Gaelic) Earth's victory.

TERENA (Latin) Tender. Feminine version of Terence. *Variations:* Tereena, Teren, Terenia, Terin, Terina, Terren, Terrena, Terrin, Terrina, Terryn, Teryna.

TERENTIA (Greek) Tender. *Variation:* Terencia.

TERESA (Greek) Harvest. *Notable:* Humanitarian Mother Teresa. *Variations:* Terasa, Teree, Terese, Teresia, Teresina, Teresita, Teressa, Teri, Terie, Terise, Terrasa, Terresa, Terresia, Terri, Terrie, Terrise, Terry, Terrya, Tersa, Terza, Tess, Tessa, Tessie, Tessy, Theresa, Toireasa, Treasa.

TERLAH (Hebrew) Fresh. *Variations:* Tari, Taria, Teria.

TERRA (Latin) The earth. *Variations:* Tera, Terah, Terrah.

TERRELLE (Greek) Form of Teresa. *Variations:* Tarrell, Terall, Terel, Terell, Terriel, Terrill, Terryl, Teryl, Tyrell.

TERRWYN (Welsh) Brave. *Variations:* Terrwin, Terrwynn, Terrwynne, Terwen, Terwin, Terwyn, Terwynn, Terwynne.

TERRY (English) Short form of Teresa or Theresa. *Notables:* Actresses Teri Hatcher and Teri Garr. *Variations:* Teri, Terie, Terree, Terri, Terrie.

TERTIA (Latin) Third. *Variation:* Tersia.

TERUKO (Japanese) Shining child.

TESHUAH (Hebrew) Reprieve. *Variations:* Teshua, Teshura.

TESS (Greek) Reaper. Short form of Teresa. *Notable:* Actress Tess Harper. *Variations:* Tesia, Tessia, Tessie.

TESSA (Polish) Beloved by God. *Variations:* Tess, Tessia, Tessie.

TETSU (Japanese) Iron.

TEVY (Cambodian) Angel. *Variations:* Tevey, Tevi, Tevie.

THADDEA (Greek) Brave. Feminine version of Thaddeus. *Variations:* Thada, Thadda, Thadia, Thadie, Thadina, Thadine, Thadya, Thadyn, Thadyna, Thadyne.

THALASSA (Greek) Ocean. *Variations:* Talassa, Thalasse.

THALIA (Greek) To bloom. *Notable:* Singer Thalia. *Variations:* Thaleia, Thalya.

THANA (Arabic) Happy occasion. *Variations:* Thaina, Thane, Thayna.

THANDIWE (South African) Affectionate. *Notable:* Actress Thandie Newton. *Variations:* Thandee, Thandi, Thandie, Thandy.

THANH (Vietnamese) Brilliant.

THAO (Vietnamese) Respect.

THE (Vietnamese) Pledged.

THEA (Greek) Goddess. *Variations:* Theia, Theya, Thia.

THEDA (Greek) Short form of Theodosia. *Notable:* Silent-film actress Theda Bara.

THEKIA (Greek) Famous God.

THEKLA (Greek) Divine fame. *Variations:* Tecla, Tekla, Thecla.

THELMA (Greek) Willful. *Notable:* Singer Thelma Houston. *Variation:* Telma.

THEMIS (Greek) Goddess of law and order. *Variation:* Themisse.

THEODORA (Greek) Gift of God. Feminine version of Theodore.

Variations: Teddy, Teodora, Teodosia, Theadora, Theda, Theodosia.

THEONE (Greek) Godly. *Variations:* Theona, Theoni, Theonie.

THEOPHANIA (Greek) God's appearance. *Variations:* Theofania, Theofanie, Theofany, Theophanes, Theophanie.

THEOPHILA (Greek) Beloved by God. *Variations:* Theofila, Theofilia, Theophylla.

THEORA (Greek) Watchful.

THERA (Greek) Untamed.

THERESA (Greek) Harvest. *Notable:* Saint Teresa of Avila. *Variations:* Teresa, Terese, Teresia, Therese, Theressa, Thereza, Thersa, Thersea.

THETA (Greek) Greek letter. *Variation:* Thetis.

THETIS (Greek) Mythological sea nymph and the mother of Achilles.

THI (Vietnamese) Poem.

THIRZA (Hebrew) Pleasant. *Variations:* Therza, Thyrza, Tirza, Tirzah.

THISBE (Greek) Mythological heroine.

THISTLE (English) Purple flower.

THOMASINA (English) Twin. Feminine version of Thomas. *Variations:* Thomasa, Thomasena, Thomasin, Thomasine, Thomasyna, Thomasyne, Toma, Tomasina, Tomasine, Tomasyna, Tomasyne, Tommi.

THORA (Scandinavian) Thor's battle. *Notable:* Actress Thora Birch. *Variations:* Thorberta, Thorbjorg, Thordia, Thordis, Thordisa, Thordise, Thordissa, Thordya, Thorgunna, Thorhilda.

THU (Vietnamese) Autumn. *Variation:* Tu.

THURAYYA (Arabic) Star. *Variations:* Surayya, Surayyah, Thuraia, Thuraypa, Thurayyah.

THUY (Vietnamese) Gentle.

TIA (Spanish) Aunt. *Variations:* Teia, Teya, Tya.

TIANA (English) Free spirit. Form of Teanna.

TIARA (Latin) Crown. *Variation:* Tiera.

TIARET (African) Lioness.

TIBELDA (German) Bold. *Variation:* Tybelda.

TIBERIA (Latin) Tiber River. *Variations:* Tibbie, Tibby, Tyberia.

TIERNEY (Irish) Noble. Lord. *Variations:* Tiernan, Tiernee, Tierni, Tiernie, Tierny, Tyernee, Tyerney, Tyerni, Tyernie, Tyerny.

TIFARA (Hebrew) Festive. *Variations:* Tifarra, Tiferet, Tifhara, Tyfara, Tyfarra.

TIFFANY (Greek) God's appearance. (Latin) Trinity. *Notables:* Pop singer Tiffany; actress Tiffani Amber Thiessen. *Variations:* Tifanee, Tifani, Tifanie, Tiff, Tiffanee, Tiffaney, Tiffani, Tiffanie, Tiffiney, Tiffini, Tiffney, Tiffy, Tiphanee, Tiphaney, Tiphani, Tiphania, Tiphanie, Tiphany, Tyffanee, Tyffaney, Tyffani, Tyffanie, Tyffany.

TIGERLILY (English) An orange flower.

TIGRIS (Greek) Tiger. *Variations:* Tigriss, Tyger, Tygris, Tygriss.

TILDA (German) Battle maiden. Short form of Matilda. *Variations:* Tilde, Tildee, Tildey, Tildie, Tildy, Tylda, Tyldee, Tyldey, Tyldi, Tyldie, Tyldy.

Begins with "Ta"

Adding "Ta" to the beginning of, or combining it with, an existing girl's name creates a whole new name. Here are some popular girls' names that begin with "Ta":

Taheisha	Taneisha
Taisha	Tanielle
Takeisha	Tanissa
Takenya	Tanita
Takira	Tashara
Taleisha	Tashauna
Talena	Tasheena
Talisa	Tashelle
Tamesha	Tashina
Tamila	Tashonda
Tamira	Tawanna

School Daze: Names from Teachers (Part VI)

This final selection comes from elementary schools in New York:

Ashling
Chenoa
Deliatant
Dymond
Female
Genesis
Jett
Krysalis
Kum'stane
Lexus
Nica
Prissy
Remi
Roobee
Sarai
Toy
Tryptch

TILLIE (German) Battle maiden. Short form of Matilda. *Variations:* Tili, Tillee, Tilleigh, Tilley, Tilli, Tilly, Tily.

TIMOTHEA (Greek) Honoring God. Feminine version of Timothy. *Variations:* Timaula, Timi, Timie, Timithea, Timmea, Timmee, Timmi, Timmie.

TINA (Spanish; English) Anointed one. Short form of Christina. *Notables:* Singer Tina Turner; comedian Tina Fey. *Variations:* Teena, Tena, Tenia, Tiena, Tyna.

TING (Chinese) Graceful.

TINKERBELL (English) Fairy. *Notable:* Disney character Tinker Bell, from *Peter Pan*. *Variations:* Tinkabel, Tinkabela, Tinkabell, Tinkabella, Tinkerbella, Tinkerbelle, Tynkabel, Tynkabell, Tynkabelle.

TIPONYA (Native American) Great horned owl. *Variations:* Tiponia, Typonia, Typonya.

TIPPER (Irish) Water bearer. *Notables:* Activist Tipper Gore; actress Tippi Hedren. *Variations:* Tippi, Tippy.

TIQVAH (Hebrew) Hope.

TIRA (Hebrew) Camp. *Variations:* Tirah, Tyra.

TIRION (Welsh) Gentle.

TIRZA (Hebrew) Kind. *Variations:* Thirza, Tirtsah, Tirtza, Tirzah.

TISA (African) Ninth child.

TISH (English) Happiness. Variation of Letitia. *Notable:* Actress Tisha Campbell. *Variations:* Teasha, Teashia, Teashya, Teesha, Teeshia, Teisha, Tiesha, Tieshia, Tisha, Tishah, Tishia, Tishra, Titia, Tysha, Tyshia.

TITANIA (Greek) Giant. *Variations:* Tita, Titanya.

TITILAYO (African) Eternal happiness.

TIVA (Native American) Dance.

TIVONA (Hebrew) Nature lover. *Variations:* Tibona, Tiboni, Tivonah, Tivone, Tivoni, Tivonie, Tivony, Tyvona, Tyvone.

TIZIANA (Italian) Giant. *Variations:* Tizia, Tizianna, Tizianne.

TOBY (Hebrew) God is good. Feminine version of Tobias. *Variations:* Tobe, Tobee, Tobey, Tobi, Tobia, Tobie.

TOCARRA (Irish) Dearest friend. *Variation:* Tocara.

TOHUIA (Polynesian) Flower.

TOIBA (Yiddish) Dove. *Variation:* Toibe.

TOINETTE (French) Priceless. Short form of Antoinette. *Variations:* Toinet, Toineta, Toinete, Toinett, Toinetta, Toynet, Toyneta, Toynett, Toynetta, Toynette.

TOIREASA (Irish) Strength. *Variation:* Treise.

TOKI (Japanese) Chance. Hopeful. *Variations:* Tokee, Tokey, Toko, Tokoya.

TOKIWA (Japanese) Steady.

TOKU (Japanese) Virtue.

TOLA (Polish) Flowering. *Variations:* Tolsia, Tolsya.

TOLIKNA (Native American) Coyote ears.

TOLOISI (Native American) Hawk killing a snake.

TOMAZJA (Polish) Twin.

TOMIKO (Japanese) Content child. *Variation:* Tomika.

TOMO (Japanese) Intelligence.

TONI (Latin) Priceless. Short form of Antoinette. *Notables:* Writer Toni Morrison; singer Toni Braxton. *Variations:* Tona, Tonea, Tonee, Tonia, Tonie.

TONNELI (Swiss) Priceless. *Variations:* Tonela, Tonelee, Tonelei, Toneleigh, Toneley, Toneli, Tonelia, Tonelie, Tonelly, Tonnelea, Tonnelee, Tonnelei, Tonneleigh, Tonneley, Tonnelie, Tonnely.

TOOKA (Japanese) Ten days. *Variation:* Tookayo.

TOPANGA (Native American) A place above. *Variation:* Tapanga.

TOPAZ (Latin) A jewel. *Variations:* Topaza, Topazia, Topazza, Topazzia.

TOPSY (English) The topsail. On top. Crazy. *Variations:* Toppsy, Topsey, Topsi, Topsie.

TORA (Japanese) Tiger; (Scandinavian) Thunder. *Variations:* Torah, Torra.

TORBORG (Scandinavian) Thor's hall. *Variations:* Thorborg, Torbjorg.

TORDIS (Scandinavian) Thor's goddess.

TORI (English) Victory. Short form of Victoria. *Notable:* Actress Tori Spelling. *Variations:* Toree, Torey, Toria, Torri, Torry, Tory.

TORIANA (English) Victory. *Variations:* Torian, Toriane, Toriann, Torianna, Torianne.

TORUNN (Scandinavian) Loved by Thor. *Variation:* Torun.

TOSCA (Italian) Tuscany.

TOSHALA (Hindi) Satisfied. *Variation:* Shala.

TOSHIO (Japanese) Year-old child. *Variations:* Toshi, Toshie, Toshiko, Toshikyo.

TOSKI (Native American) Bug. *Variations:* Toskee, Toskey, Toskie, Tosky.

TOTSI (Native American) Moccasins. *Variations:* Totsee, Totsey, Totsia, Totsie, Totsy.

TOTTIE (English) Gift of God. Short form of Dorothy. *Variations:* Totee, Totey, Toti, Totie, Totti, Totty.

TOURMALINE (Singhalese) Gemstone of mixed colors. *Variation:* Tourmalina.

TOVAH (Hebrew) Good. *Notable:* Actress Tovah Feldshuh. *Variations:* Tova, Tovial.

TOYA (Spanish) Victory. Form of Tory. *Variation:* Toia.

TRACY (English) Fierce. *Notables:* Singer Tracy Chapman; comedian Tracey Ullman; tennis pro Tracy Austin. *Variations:* Trace, Tracea, Tracee, Tracey, Traci, Tracia, Tracie, Trasey, Trasi, Trasia, Trasie, Trasy, Treacy, Treesy.

TRANG (Vietnamese) Smart.

TRAVA (Czech) Grass.

TRAVIATA (Italian) Wanderer.

TREASURE (Latin) Treasure.

TREINELLE (German) Purity. *Variations:* Treinala, Treinel, Treinell, Treinella, Treinelle, Trynell, Trynella, Trynelle.

TRESSA (Greek) Short form of Teresa. *Variations:* Tresa, Trisa.

TREVA (Welsh) Homestead. Feminine form of Trevor. *Variation:* Trevia.

TREVINA (Irish) Prudent. *Variations:* Trevanna, Treveana, Treveen, Treveena, Treveene, Trevine, Trevinia, Trevona, Trevora, Trevyn, Trevyna.

TRIANA (Latin) Third. *Variations:* Triane, Triann, Trianna, Tryana, Tryanah, Tryane, Tryann, Tryanna, Tryanne.

TRICIA (English) Noble. Short for Patricia, feminine version of Patrick. *Notable:* Singer Trisha Yearwood. *Variations:* Treasha, Trichia, Trish, Trisha.

TRIFENE (Greek) Delicate. *Variations:* Trifena, Trifenna, Tryfena, Tryfenna, Tryphena, Tryphene.

TRILBY (English) From Thorolf's farm. Literary name. *Variations:* Trilbee, Trilbi, Trilbie, Trillby.

TRINA (Greek) Pure. Short form of Katrina. *Variations:* Treana, Treanee, Treani, Treena, Treenee, Treeni, Treenie, Trini, Trinia, Triny, Tryna, Trynna.

TRINITY (Latin) Triad. *Variations:* Trinidad, Trinita, Triniti.

TRISHA (English) Noble. Form of Tricia or Patricia. *Variations:* Trysha, Tryshia.

TRISHELLE (American) Combined form of Trisha and Michelle. *Variation:* Trishele.

TRISNA (Hindi) Desired. *Variations:* Trishna, Trisnia.

TRISTA (Latin) Sad. *Variations:* Tresta, Trysta.

TRISTABELLE (Latin) Sad. *Variations:* Tristabel, Tristabela, Tristabele, Tristabell, Tristabella, Trystabel, Trystabela, Trystabell, Trystabella, Trystabelle.

TRISTANA (Latin) Melancholy. *Variations:* Tristan, Tristane, Tristanna, Tristen, Tristiana, Tristiane, Tristianna, Tristin, Tristina, Tristyn, Trystan, Trystana, Trystanna, Trystanne, Trystiana.

TRIVENI (Hindi) Three sacred rivers.

TRIXIE (English) She brings happiness. *Variations:* Trix, Trixee, Trixey, Trixi, Trixy, Tryxee, Tryxi, Tryxie, Tryxy.

TROYA (Irish) Warrior. *Variations:* Troia, Troiana, Troiane, Troiann, Troianna, Troianne, Troyan, Troyana, Troyann, Troyanna, Troyanne.

TRUDA (Polish) Spear warrior. *Variations:* Trudah, Trudia, Trudya.

TRUDEL (German) Spear of strength. *Variations:* Trudela, Trudell, Trudella, Trudelle.

TRUDY (German) Spear of strength. Short form of Gertrude. *Variations:* Trudee, Trudey, Trudi, Trudie.

TRUE (English) Truthful. *Variations:* Trulee, Trulia, Trulie, Truly.

TRYPHENA (Greek) Delicacy. *Variations:* Triphena, Tryphana, Tryphene, Tryphenia, Tryphina.

TSIBYA (Hebrew) Gazelle. *Variation:* Tsibyah.

TSIFIRA (Hebrew) Crown.

TSOLER (Armenian) Sparks of the sun.

TSOMAH (Native American) Yellow hair. *Variation:* Tsoma.

TSUHGI (Japanese) Second daughter.

TSULA (Native American) Fox.

TSURUKO (Japanese) Crane.

TUA (Polynesian) Outdoors.

TUALAU (Polynesian) Talking outdoors.

TUCCIA (Latin) Vestal virgin.

TUESDAY (English) Tuesday. *Notable:* Actress Tuesday Weld. *Variation:* Tuesdae.

TUHINA (Hindi) Snow.

TUKI (Japanese) Moon. *Variations:* Tukiko, Tukiyo.

TULA (Native American) Apex. *Variations:* Tulah, Tulla.

TULIKA (Estonian) Buttercup.

TULIP (English) Tulip flower.

TULLIA (Irish) Peaceful. *Variations:* Tula, Tulia, Tulla, Tulya.

TULSI (Hindi) Basil. *Variations:* Tulsia, Tulsy.

TUMI (African) Courage.

TURQUIOSE (French) Blue-green gem. *Variation:* Turkoise.

TUSA (Native American) Prairie dog.

TUSTI (Hindi) Peace and happiness. *Variations:* Tustee, Tustie, Tustey, Tusty.

TUWA (Native American) Earth.

TUYEN (Vietnamese) Angel.

TUYET (Vietnamese) Snow.

TWYLA (English) Twilight. Woven. *Notable:* Choreographer Twyla Tharp. *Variations:* Twila, Twylla.

TYANA (African American) Free spirit. Form of Teanna. *Variations:* Tyanna, Tyanne.

TYESHA (African American) Prosperous. *Variations:* Tiesha, Tyeisha, Tyeshia, Tyisha.

TYBAL (English) Holy place of sacrifice. *Variations:* Tibal, Tibala, Tybala.

TYLER (English) Tiler. *Variations:* Tyla, Tylor.

TYNE (English) River. *Notable:* Actress Tyne Daly. *Variations:* Tine, Tyna, Tynia.

TYRA (Scandinavian) Thor's battle. *Notable:* Supermodel Tyra Banks. *Variations:* Tyrah, Tyran, Tyree, Tyria.

TZADIKA (Hebrew) Loyal. *Variation:* Zadika.

TZAFRA (Hebrew) Morning. *Variations:* Tzefira, Zafra, Zefira.

TZAHALA (Hebrew) Happy. *Variation:* Zahala.

TZEIRA (Hebrew) Young.

TZEMICHA (Hebrew) In bloom. *Variation:* Zemicha.

TZEITEL (Yiddish) Princess.

TZEVIYA (Hebrew) Gazelle. *Variations:* Civia, Tzevia, Tzivia, Tzivya, Zibiah, Zivia.

TZIGANE (Hungarian) Gypsy. *Variations:* Tsigana, Tsigane.

TZILA (Hebrew) Darkness. *Variations:* Tsila, Tsilla, Tsillah, Tzila, Tzili, Zila, Zili.

TZINA (Hebrew) Shelter. *Variation:* Zina.

TZIPIYA (Hebrew) Hope. *Variations:* Tzipia, Zipia.

TZIPPORAH (Hebrew) Bird. *Variations:* Tzippora, Tzipora, Tzippi, Zippora, Zipporah.

TZIYONA (Hebrew) Hill. *Variations:* Zeona, Ziona.

TZOFI (Hebrew) Scout. *Variations:* Tzofia, Tzofit, Tzofiya, Zofi, Zofia, Zofit.

TZURIYA (Hebrew) God is powerful. *Variations:* Tzuria, Zuria.

U (Korean) Gentle.

UADJIT (Egyptian) Snake goddess. *Variation:* Uajit.

UALANI (Hawaiian) Heavenly rain. *Variations:* Ualana, Ualanah, Ualanea, Ualanee, Ualaney, Ualania, Ualanie, Ualany, Ualanya.

UBERTA (Italian) Bright intellect. Form of Huberta. *Variations:* Uberte, Ubertha, Uberthie, Ubertie.

UCHENNA (African) God's will. *Variations:* Uchechi, Uchena.

UDA (German) Prosperous. *Variation:* Udah.

UDELE (English) Wealthy. *Variations:* Uda, Udella, Udelle.

UDIYA (Hebrew) Fire of God. *Variations:* Udia, Uriela, Uriella.

UFARA (Hebrew) Leader. *Variation:* Uphara.

UGOLINA (German) Intelligent. *Variations:* Ugolin, Ugoline, Ugolyna, Ugolyne.

UINISE (Polynesian) Victory.

UJANA (African) Youthful. *Variations:* Ujanah, Uyana.

UJILA (Hindi) Bright light. *Variations:* Ujala, Ujjala, Ujvala.

ULA (Irish) Jewel from the ocean. *Variations:* Eula, Oola, Uli, Ulah, Ulia, Ulla.

ULALIA (Greek) Speaks sweetly. *Variations:* Ulaliah, Ulalya.

ULANI (Hawaiian) Cheerful. *Variations:* Ulana, Ulanah, Ulane, Ulanee, Ulaney, Ulania, Ulanie, Ulany, Ulanya.

ULIANA (Russian) Form of Juliana. *Variations:* Uliane, Ulianna, Ulianne.

ULIMA (Arabic) Wise. *Variations:* Ulema, Uleama, Uleema, Ulimah, Ullima, Ulyma.

ULLA (Swedish) Willful. *Variations:* Ula, Ulah, Ullah.

ULRICA (German) Wolf ruler; (Scandinavian) Noble ruler. *Variations:* Ulricah, Ulricka, Ulrika, Ulrikah, Ulriqua, Ulrique, Ulryca, Ulrycka, Ulryka, Ulryqua, Ulryque.

ULTIMA (Latin) The end. *Variation:* Ultimah.

ULU (African) Second-born girl.

ULUAKI (Polynesian) First.

ULULANI (Hawaiian) Heavenly inspiration. *Variations:* Ululanee, Ululaney, Ululani, Ululania, Ululanie, Ululany, Ululanya.

ULVA (German) Wolf.

ULYSSA (Greek) Wrathful. Feminine form of Ulysses. *Variations:* Ulyssah, Ulyssi, Ulyssia.

UMA (Sanskrit) Flax. *Notable:* Actress Uma Thurman.

UMALI (Hindi) Generous.

UMARIT (Hebrew) Sheaf.

UMAY (Turkish) Hopeful. *Variation:* Umai.

UMAYMA (Arabic) Little mother. *Variations:* Umaima, Umaymah.

UME (Japanese) Plum blossom. *Variations:* Umeki, Umeko.

UMEEKA (Hindi) Like the goddess Parvati.

UMIKO (Japanese) Child of the sea.

UMM (Arabic) Mother.

Hawaiian Names

GIRLS:	BOYS:
Akela	Aikane
Alani	Ailani
Aloha	Kahoku
Iolana	Kai
Keilana	Kale
Kiana	Kane
Leilani	Keona
Noelani	Makani
Oliana	Meka
Palila	Palani
Roselani	

UMNIYA (Arabic) Desire. *Variation:* Umnia.

UNA (Irish) Lamb.

UNDINE (Latin) Wave. *Variations:* Ondine, Undeen, Undina, Undyn, Undyna, Undyne.

UNICE (English) Victorious. Form of Eunice. *Variations:* Unise, Unyce.

UNIQUE (Latin) One of a kind. *Variation:* Unica.

UNITY (English) Oneness. *Variations:* Unita, Unitea, Unitee.

UNN (Scandinavian) Loved. *Variations:* Un, Una, Unah, Unna, Unnah, Unni.

UNNEA (Scandinavian) Linden tree. *Variations:* Unea, Uneah, Unneah.

UPALA (Hindi) Beach.

URANIA (Greek) Heavenly. *Variations:* Urainah, Urainia, Uranie, Uraniya, Uranya, Uriana, Urianna, Urianne.

URANJA (Polish) Heavenly.

URBANA (Latin) Of the city. *Variation:* Urbanna.

URBI (African) Princess. *Variations:* Urbia, Urbiah, Urby, Urbya.

URIKA (Native American) Useful. *Variations:* Urica, Uricah, Uricka, Urikah, Uriqua, Uryca, Uryka, Uryqua.

URIELA (Hebrew) Light of God. *Variations:* Urilla, Uriel, Uriella, Urielle.

URIT (Hebrew) Brightness. *Variations:* Uranit, Uri, Urice, Urita, Uriti, Urith, Uryt, Uryta.

URITH (German) Deserving. *Variations:* Uritha, Uryth.

URSA (Latin) Short form of Ursula. *Variations:* Ursah, Ursea, Ursey, Ursi, Ursie, Ursy.

USAGI (Japanese) Rabbit.

URSULA (Latin) Little female bear. *Notable:* Actress Ursula Andress. *Variations:* Ursala, Ursel, Ursela, Ursella, Ursina, Ursine, Ursola, Ursule, Ursulina, Ursuline, Ursulyn, Ursulyna, Ursulyne, Urzsula, Urzula.

URTA (Latin) Spiny plant. *Variation:* Urtah.

URVASI (Hindi) Celestial maiden.

USHA (Hindi) Dawn. *Variations:* Ushai, Ushas.

USHARA (Hebrew) Fortunate. *Variations:* Usharit, Usheret.

USHI (Chinese) Ox. *Variations:* Ushee, Ushie, Ushy.

USHMIL (Hindi) Warm. *Variation:* Ushmila.

USHRIYA (Hebrew) God's blessing. *Variation:* Ushria.

UT (Vietnamese) From the east.

UTA (German) Fortunate in battle. *Notable:* Actress Uta Hagen. *Variation:* Ute.

UTAH (Native American) Mountain dweller. *Variation:* Utar.

UTANO (Japanese) Song field. *Variations:* Utan, Utana, Utanah.

UTATCI (Native American) Scratching bear.

UTINA (Native American) Woman of my country. *Variations:* Uteana, Uteena, Uteenah, Utinah, Utyna.

UTTARA (Sanskrit) Royal. *Variations:* Utara, Utari, Utaria.

UZOMA (African) On the right path. *Variations:* Uzomah, Uzomma.

UZZA (Arabic) Mighty. *Variations:* Uza, Uzah, Uzzah.

UZZIA (Hebrew) God is strong. *Variations:* Uzia, Uziah, Uzya, Uzzi, Uzziahm, Uzzya.

VACHYA (Hindi) To speak. *Variations:* Vac, Vach, Vachia.

VACLAVA (Czech) More glory.

VADA (Latin) Brave. *Variation:* Veida.

VAIL (English) Valley. *Variations:* Vael, Vale, Vayle.

VAILEA (Polynesian) Water that talks. *Variations:* Vaileah, Vailee, Vailey, Vailia.

VAL (Latin) Strength. Short for Valentina or Valerie. *Variation:* Vall.

VALA (German) Chosen. *Variations:* Valah, Valla, Vallah.

VALBORGA (Norse) Protector. *Variation:* Valborg.

VALDA (Norse) Ruler. *Variations:* Valida, Velda, Vellda.

VALDIS (Norse) Goddess of the dead. *Variations:* Valdiss, Valdys.

VALENCIA (Spanish) Strong. *Variations:* Valence, Valentia, Valenzia.

VALENE (Latin) Strength. *Variations:* Valaina, Valaine, Valean, Valeana, Valeane, Valeen, Valeena, Valeene, Valena, Valeney, Valina, Valine, Vallan, Vallana, Vallane, Vallen, Vallena, Vallene, Vallina, Vallinah, Valline, Vallyna, Vallyne.

VALENTINA (Latin) Strong. *Variations:* Valenteana, Valenteen, Valenteena, Valenteene, Valentin, Valentina, Valentine, Valentyn, Valentyna, Valentyne.

VALERIE (Latin) Strong. *Notables:* Actresses Valerie Harper and Valerie Bertinelli. *Variations:* Valaree, Valarey, Valaria, Valarie, Vale, Valeree, Valeri, Valeria, Valeriana, Valery, Vallarie, Valleree, Vallerie, Vallery, Valli, Vallie, Vally, Valori, Valorie, Valory, Valorya, Valree, Valri, Valrie, Valry.

VALESKA (Slavic) Glorious ruler.

VALLEY (English) From the valley. *Variations:* Vallea, Vallee, Vallei, Valleigh, Valli, Vallie, Vally.

VALMA (Finnish) Loyal defender. *Variations:* Valmar, Valmara.

VALONIA (Latin) Shallow valley. *Variations:* Valona, Valonya.

VALORA (Latin) Brave. *Variations:* Valoria, Valory, Valorya.

VANA (Polynesian) Sea urchin. *Variation:* Vanah.

VANAJA (Hindi) Daughter from the woods. *Variations:* Vanaia, Vanaiah, Vanya.

VANALIKA (Hindi) Sunflower. *Variations:* Vanalikah, Vanalyka.

VANDA (German) Wanderer. Form of Wanda. *Variation:* Vandah.

VANDANI (Hindi) Honor. *Variations:* Vandana, Vandanee, Vandanie.

VANESSA (Greek) Butterfly. *Notables:* Actresses Vanessa Redgrave and Vanessa L. Williams. *Variations:* Vanassa, Vanesa, Vanesha, Vaneshia, Vanesia, Vanesse, Vanessia, Vanexa, Vaniessa, Vanisa, Vaniss, Vanissa, Vanisse, Vannessa, Vanyssa, Venesa, Venessa.

VANETTA (Greek) Little butterfly. *Variations:* Vaneta, Vanette, Vanita, Vannetta.

VANI (Hindi) Voice. *Variations:* Vanee, Vanie, Vany.

VANIA (Russian) Form of Anna. *Variations:* Vanea, Vaniah, Vannia, Vanya.

VANILLA (Latin) Like the vanilla bean. *Variation:* Vanila.

VANJA (Scandinavian) God is good.

VANNA (Cambodian) Golden; (Greek) Short form of Vanessa. *Notable: Wheel of Fortune* letter-turner Vanna White. *Variation:* Vana.

VANORA (Welsh) White wave. *Variations:* Vanoria, Vannora.

VARANA (Hindi) River.

VARDA (Hebrew) Rose. *Variations:* Vardia, Vardice, Vardina, Vardis, Vardit.

VARSHA (Hindi) Rain shower. *Variations:* Varcia, Varisha.

VARVARA (Greek) Stranger. Form of Barbara.

VARUNA (Hindi) Sea wife. *Variations:* Varunah, Varunna.

VASHTI (Persian) Beautiful. *Variations:* Vashtee, Vashtie.

VASILIA (Greek) Royal. *Variation:* Vasiliki.

VASUNDHARA (Hindi) Earth. *Variations:* Vasuda, Vasudhra.

VAYU (Hindi) Air.

VEATA (Cambodian) Wind.

VEDA (Hindi) Knowledge, wisdom. *Variation:* Veeda.

VEDETTE (Italian) Sentry. *Variation:* Vedetta.

VEERA (Hindi) Strong.

VEGA (Arabic) Falling star; (Scandinavian) Star.

VELDA (German) Famous ruler. A form of Valda.

VELESLAVA (Czech) Great glory. *Variations:* Vela, Velina, Velinka, Velka, Veluska.

VELIA (Italian) Concealed.

VELIKA (Slavic) Great.

VELINDA (American) Gentle. *Variations:* Valenda, Valinda, Velenda.

VELMA (German) Protector. *Notable:* Velma Dinkley from Scooby-Doo. *Variation:* Vellma.

VELVET (English) Velvety.

VENETIA (Italian) Venice; Italian city. *Variations:* Vanecia, Vanetia, Vanicia, Venecia, Veneece, Venetia, Venezia, Venice, Venicia, Venise, Venize.

VENETTA (English) Little butterfly. Form of Vanetta. *Variations:* Veneta, Venette.

VENTANA (Spanish) Window.

VENTURA (Spanish) Fortunate. *Variation:* Venture.

VENUS (Latin) Love. *Notable:* Tennis pro Venus Williams. *Variations:* Venis, Venise, Vennice, Venusa, Venusina, Venys.

VENYA (Hindi) Lovable. *Variation:* Venyaa.

VERA (Latin) True. (Slavic) Faith. *Notable:* Fashion designer Vera Wang. *Variations:* Veera, Veira, Verasha, Viera, Vyra.

VERADIS (Latin) Faithful. *Variation:* Veradisa.

VERBENA (Latin) Holy plants. *Variations:* Verbeena, Verbina, Verbyna.

How Do You Pronounce That?

How often have you seen a name you don't know how to pronounce? Did you know that Siobhan is pronounced "shiv-AWN" and Joaquin is pronounced "wah-KEEN"? Don't risk embarrassment. Two cool websites will take the guesswork out of that task: *www.inogolo.com* and *www.hearnames.com*. Type in any name, and you'll get a clickable audio track to hear that name correctly spoken.

VERDA (Latin) Young. *Variations:* Verdea, Verdee, Verdi.

VERDAD (Spanish) Truth.

VERENA (Latin) True. *Variations:* Varena, Varina, Vereena, Verene, Verina, Verine, Veruchka, Veruschka, Verushka, Veryna.

VERITY (Latin) Truth. *Variations:* Verita, Veriti, Veritie.

VERLENE (Latin) Truth. *Variations:* Verlaine, Verlea, Verlean, Verlee, Verleen, Verleine, Verlie, Verlyne.

VERMONT (French) Green mountain.

VERNA (Latin) Springtime. *Variations:* Vernetta, Vernie, Vernita, Virna.

VERONA (Italian) From Verona, Italy.

VERONICA (Latin) True image. *Notables:* Actress Veronica Lake; *Archie* comic's femme fatale Veronica Lodge. *Variations:* Veranique, Vernice, Veron, Verona, Verone, Veronice, Veronicka, Veronika, Veronike, Veroniqua, Veronique.

VERUCA (Latin) A wart. *Notable:* Veruca Salt, character from the Roald Dahl book, *Charlie and the Chocolate Factory. Variations:* Vereca, Verecka, Vereka, Verica, Verika, Verruca, Verucka, Veryka.

VESNA (Slavic) Spring.

VESPERA (Latin) Evening star. *Variations:* Vespa, Vespira.

VESTA (Latin) Goddess of the home. *Variations:* Vessy, Vest.

VEVILA (Gaelic) Lovely voice. *Variation:* Vevilla.

VEVINA (Irish) Kind woman. *Variations:* Veveena, Vevine.

VI (Latin) Short form of Viola, Violet.

VIANCA (American) Combined form of Vivian and Bianca. *Variations:* Vianka, Vyanca, Vyanka.

VIANNA (American) Combination of first names "Vi" and "Anna." *Variations:* Viana, Vianne.

VIBEKE (Danish) Small in stature.

VIBHUTI (Hindi) Sacred ash. *Variation:* Vibuti.

VICA (Hungarian) Life.

VICKY (Latin) Short form of Victoria. *Notable:* Comedian Vicki Lawrence. *Variations:* Vicki, Vickie, Vikki, Vikky.

VICTORIA (Latin) Victorious. *Notables:* Britain's Queen Victoria; singer and designer Victoria Beckham. *Variations:* Torey, Tori, Toria, Torie, Torrey, Torri, Torrie, Torrye, Tory, Vicki, Vickie, Vicky, Victoriana, Victorina, Victorine, Victory, Vikki, Vikky, Vitoria, Vittoria.

VIDA (Hebrew) Beloved; (Spanish) Life. *Variations:* Veda, Veeda, Veida, Vidette, Vieda, Vita, Vitia.

VIDONIA (Portuguese) Vine branch. *Variations:* Veedonia, Vidonya.

VIDYA (Hindi) Instruction.

VIENNA (Latin) Bright and fair. Place name: capital of Austria. *Variation:* Viena.

VIERA (Slavic) Faith.

VIGDIS (Scandinavian) War goddess. *Variations:* Vigdess, Vigdys.

VIGILIA (Latin) Alert.

VIGNETTE (French) Little vine. *Variations:* Vignet, Vigneta, Vignetta.

VIKA (Polynesian) Victory. *Variation:* Vikaheilala.

VILHELMINA (German) Will helmet. Form of Wilhelmina.

VILLETTE (French) Small town. *Variation:* Villetta.

VILMA (Russian) Variation of Wilma.

VIMALA (Hindi) Lovely.

VINA (Spanish) Vineyard. *Variations:* Veina, Venia, Vinia.

VINAYA (Hindi) Humble. *Variations:* Vinata, Vinay.

VINCENTIA (Latin) To conquer. Feminine version of Vincent. *Variations:* Vincenta, Vincentena, Vincentina, Vincentine, Vincetta, Vinnie.

VINH (Vietnamese) Gulf.

VINKA (Icelandic) Friend. *Variation:* Vynka.

VIOLA (Latin) Violet.

VIOLANTE (Greek; Latin) Purple flower. *Variations:* Violanta, Violanth.

VIOLET (Latin) Violet. *Variations:* Viola, Violetta, Violette.

VIRENDRA (Hindi) Brave and noble.

VIRGILIA (Latin) Bearing a rod.

VIRGINIA (Latin) Virgin. *Notable:* Actress Virginia Madsen. *Variations:* Vergenia, Vergie, Verginia, Virgena, Virgene, Virginai, Virginie, Virgy.

VIRIDIS (Latin) Green. *Variations:* Virdis, Virida, Viridia, Viridiana.

VIRTUE (Latin) Virtue. *Variations:* Vertue, Virtu.

VISOLELA (African) Imagination.

VITA (Latin) Life. *Variations:* Veeta, Vitel, Vitella.

VITALIA (Latin) Lively. *Variations:* Vitaliana, Vitaliane.

VITTORIA (Italian) Victory.

VIV (Latin) Short form of Vivian.

VIVA (Latin) Alive. *Notable:* Writer Vita Sackville-West.

VIVECA (Scandinavian) Form of Vivian. *Notable:* Actress Vivica Fox. *Variations:* Vivecka, Viveka, Vivica.

VIVIAN (Latin) Full of life. *Notable:* Actress Vivien Leigh. *Variations:* Viv, Viva, Vivia, Viviana, Viviane, Vivianna, Vivianne, Vivie, Vivien, Vivienne.

VIXEN (Latin) Female fox. *Variations:* Vixxen, Vyxen.

VJERA (Russian) Faith.

VLADIMIRA (Czech) Great ruler. *Variation:* Vladmira.

VLADISLAVA (Czech) Glorious ruler. *Variations:* Ladislava, Valeska, Vlasta.

VOILA (French) Behold.

VOLANTE (Italian) Flying. *Variation:* Volanta.

VOLETA (Greek) Veiled.

VONDA (English) Wanderer. Form of Wanda.

VONDRA (Czech) A woman's love.

VONNA (French) Archer. Form of Yvonne. *Variations:* Vona, Vonne, Vonni.

VORSILA (Czech) Little she-bear. Form of Ursula.

VOSHKIE (Armenian) Golden.

VYOMA (Hindi) Sky. *Variations:* Vyomika, Vyomini.

WACHIW (Native American) Girl who dances.

WA'D (Arabic) Promise.

WADEAN (African) Kind.

WADHA (Arabic) Bright. *Variation:* Wadhaa.

WADI'AH (Arabic) Calm, peaceful.

WAFA (Arabic) Faithful. *Variations:* Wafah, Wafiyya, Wafiyyah.

WAFIQAH (Arabic) Successful. *Variation:* Wafeeqa.

WAFIYAH (Arabic) Faithful. *Variation:* Wafiya.

WAHALLA (Norse) Immortal. *Variations:* Valhalla, Walhalla.

WAHBIYAH (Arabic) Giving. *Variation:* Wahibah.

WAHEEDA (Arabic) One and only. *Variations:* Wahida, Wahidah.

WAIDA (German) Warrior. *Variations:* Waidah, Wayda.

WAIKIKI (Hawaiian) Water from the stream. *Variation:* Waikikee.

WAINANI (Hawaiian) Beautiful water. *Variation:* Wainanee.

WAJA (Arabic) Noble. *Variations:* Wagiha, Wagihah, Wajiha, Wajihah.

WAJD (Arabic) Passionate.

WAJIHAH (Arabic) Distinguished.

WAKANA (Japanese) Plant.

WAKANDA (Native American) Magical. *Variation:* Wakenda.

WAKEISHA (African) Life. *Variations:* Wakeishia, Wakesha, Wakeshia, Wakesia, Wakeysha, Wakeyshah, Wakeyshia, Wakeyshya.

WAKENDA (Norse) To waken. *Variation:* Wakendah.

WALA (Arabic) Loyalty. *Variation:* Walaa.

WALAD (Arabic) Newborn child. *Variations:* Walada, Walida, Walyda.

WALANIKA (Hawaiian) True image. Hawaiian version of Veronica. *Variations:* Walanyka, Walonika, Welonika.

WALBURGA (German) Strong protection. *Variations:* Walberga, Walborg, Waldeburg, Wallburga.

WALDA (German) Ruler. Feminine version of Waldo. *Variations:* Waldena, Waldina, Waldine, Waldyne, Welda.

WALENTYA (Polish) Healthy.

WALERIA (Polish) Strong. Form of Valerie. *Variations:* Waleriah, Waleri, Walerie, Walerya, Walleria.

WALIDA (Arabic) Newborn. *Variation:* Walidah.

WALKER (English) Cloth walker. *Variation:* Wallker.

WALLADA (Arabic) Prolific. *Variation:* Walladah.

WALLIS (English) One from Wales. Feminine version of Wallace. *Notable:* Wallis Simpson, future Duchess of Windsor. *Variations:* Walice, Walise, Wallice, Wallie, Wallisa, Wallise, Walliss, Wally, Wallys.

WALTRINA (German) Powerful people. Feminine version of Walter. *Variations:* Waltina, Waltraud.

WANAAO (Hawaiian) Sunrise. *Variation:* Wanaaonani.

WANAKA (Hawaiian) Wanderer. Hawaiian version of Wanda.

WANDA (German) Wanderer. *Notable:* Comedian Wanda Sykes. *Variations:* Wandela, Wandi, Wandie, Wandis, Wandisa, Wandy, Wonda, Wonnda.

WANETA (Native American) One who moves forward; (English) Pale skinned. *Variations:* Waneata, Waneeta, Waneita, Wanetah, Wanetta, Wanette, Wanita, Wannetta, Wannette.

WANIKA (Hawaiian) God is good. *Variations:* Waneeka, Wanyka.

WAPEKA (Norse) Protective weapon.

WAPIN (Native American) Sunrise.

WARDA (German) Protector. Feminine version of Ward. *Variations:* Wardia, Wardine.

WARNA (German) Defender. Feminine form of Warner.

WASEME (African) People talking.

WASHI (Japanese) Eagle.

WASHTA (Native American) Good.

WASIMAH (Arabic) Beautiful. *Variation:* Wasima.

WASULA (Native American) Bad hair.

WATSEKA (Native American) Woman.

WATTAN (Arabic) Homeland.

WAUNA (Native American) Snow goose.

WAVA (Slavic) Stranger. *Variation:* Wavia.

WAVERLY (English) Meadow of aspen trees. *Variation:* Waverley.

WAYNETTE (English) Wagon maker. Feminine form of Wayne. *Variations:* Waineta, Wainetta, Wainette, Waynella, Waynelle.

WAYNOKA (Native American) Clean water. *Variation:* Wainoka.

WEAYAYA (Native American) Sunset.

WEDNESDAY (English) Day of week: Wednesday.

WEEKO (Native American) Beautiful girl. *Variations:* Weiko, Weyko.

WEETAMOO (Native American) Lover. *Variations:* Weetamoe, Weetamore, Wetamoo, Wetemoo.

WELENA (Hawaiian) Springtime. Hawaiian version of Verna.

WEN (Chinese) Cultured.

WENDE (German) Wanderer. *Variations:* Wenda, Wendaina, Wendaine, Wendalin, Wendalina, Wandaline, Wendalyn, Wendelina, Wendeline, Wendella, Wendelle, Wendelyn.

WENDY (Welsh) Fair one. *Notables:* Playwright Wendy Wasserstein; radio/TV personality Wendy Williams. *Variations:* Wendea, Wendee, Wendey, Wendi, Wendia, Wendie, Wendye, Windy.

WERA (Polish) Truthful.

WERONIKA (Polish) True image. *Variations:* Weronica, Weronicka, Weronikah, Weronike, Weroniqua, Weronique, Weronyca, Weronyka, Weronyqua.

WESLEA (English) Westerly meadow. *Variations:* Wesla, Weslee, Weslei, Wesleigh, Wesley, Wesli, Weslia, Weslie, Wesly.

WESLEY (English) Western meadow. *Variations:* Weslea, Weslee, Wesleigh.

WHALEY (English) Whale meadow. *Variations:* Whalea, Whalee, Whalei, Whaleigh, Whali, Whalia, Whalie, Whaly.

WHITLEY (English) White field. *Variations:* Whitlea, Whitlee, Whitleigh, Whitly.

WHITNEY (English) White island. *Notable:* Singer Whitney Houston. *Variations:* Whitnee, Whitni, Whitnie, Whitny, Whittney.

WHOOPI (English) Excited. *Notable:* Actress Whoopi Goldberg. *Variations:* Whoopee, Whoopey, Whoopie.

WI'AM (Arabic) Harmony.

WICAHPI (Native American) Star. *Variations:* Wicahpee, Wicapi.

WICTORIA (Polish) Victory. *Variations:* Wicktoria, Wictoria, Wiktoria, Wycktoria, Wyctoria, Wyktoria.

WIDAD (Arabic) Love. *Variations:* Wid, Widaad.

WIEBKE (German) War. *Variation:* Wibeke.

WIFAQ (Arabic) Consent.

WIHAKAYDA (Native American) Youngest daughter.

WIJDAN (Arabic) Sentiment.

WIKOLIA (Hawaiian) Victorious. *Variation:* Wiktoria.

WILA (Hawaiian) Faith. *Variations:* Wilah, Wyla.

WILDA (English) Willow. *Variations:* Wilder, Willda, Wylda.

WILEEN (German) Will helmet. Form of Wilhelmina. *Variations:* Wilean, Wileana, Wileena, Wilene, Wilina, Wiline, Willeen, Wyleen, Wylina, Wyline.

WILFREDA (English) Peaceful will. Feminine version of Wilfred. *Variations:* Wilfrieda, Wilfryda.

WILHELMINA (German) Will helmet. Feminine version of William. *Notable:* Queen Wilhelmina of the Netherlands. *Variations:* Wiletta, Wilette, Wilhelmine, Willa, Willamina, Willetta, Willette, Williamina.

WILIKINIA (Hawaiian) Purity.

WILLA (German) Short form of Wilhelmina. *Notable:* Writer Willa Cather. *Variations:* Wila, Willabel, Willabella, Willee, Willeigh, Willi.

WILLETTE (German) Defender. *Variations:* Wilet, Wilett, Willet, Willett, Willetta.

WILLOW (English) Willow tree. *Notable:* TV newscaster Willow Bay. *Variations:* Willo, Willough.

WILMA (German) Will helmet. Short form of Wilhelmina. *Notables:* Olympic track-and-field champion Wilma Rudolph; prehistoric cartoon wife Wilma Flintstone. *Variations:* Wilmah, Wilmette, Wilmina, Wylma.

WILONA (English) To desire. *Varitation:* Wilone.

WIN (English) Short form of Winifred or Edwina. *Variations:* Wyn, Wynn, Wynne.

WINDA (African) Hunter. *Variation:* Wynda.

WINDY (English) Breezy. *Variations:* Windea, Windee, Windi, Windie, Wyndea, Wyndee, Wyndi, Wyndy.

WINEMA (Native American) Female chief. *Variation:* Wynema.

WINIFRED (Welsh) Holy peace. *Variations:* Win, Winifreda, Winifrede, Winifrid, Winifride, Winifryde, Winne, Winni, Winnie, Winny, Wyn, Wynifred, Wynifryd, Wynn.

WINNA (African) Friend. *Variations:* Wina, Wyna, Wynna.

WINNIE (English) Short form of Edwina, Guinevere, Winifred, and Winona. *Variations:* Winee, Wini, Winnee, Winni, Winny, Wynni, Wynnie.

WINOLA (German) Enchanting friend. *Variation:* Wynola.

WINONA (Native American) First-born daughter. *Notables:* Actress Winona Ryder; singer Wynonna Judd. *Variations:* Wanona, Wenona, Winnona, Winonah, Wynnona, Wynona, Wynonah.

WINTER (English) Winter. *Variations:* Winta, Wynta, Wynter.

WIRA (Polish) Blond. *Variation:* Wyra.

WISAL (Arabic) Reunion. *Variation:* Wisaal.

WISAM (Arabic) Medal of honor. *Variation:* Wisaam.

WISCONSIN (Native American) Long river.

WISDOM (English) Wisdom.

WISIA (Polish) Victorious. *Variations:* Wicia, Wikta, Wysia.

WISTERIA (German) Wisteria flower. *Variations:* Wistaria, Wysteria.

WITASHNAH (Native American) Chaste.

WONDER (English) Awe. *Variation:* Wonda.

WORSOLA (German) Little she-bear. *Variation:* Worsula.

WREN (English) Bird. *Variations:* Wrena, Wrenda, Wrenn, Wrenna.

WURUD (Arabic) Rose.

WYAN (Indonesian) First born.

WYANET (Native American) Beautiful. *Variations:* Wianet, Wianeta, Wianetta, Wianette, Wyanetta, Wyanette.

WYETTA (French) Small fighter. Feminine version of Wyatt. *Variation:* Wyette.

WYNELLE (American) *Variations:* Wynette, Wynstelle.

WYNNE (Welsh) Fair, white. *Variations:* Winne, Wyn.

WYOMING (Native American) Big field. *Variations:* Wy, Wyoma, Wyome, Wyomia.

XABRINA (Latin) Form of Sabrina, a Welsh river. *Variations:* Xabreena, Xabrinah, Xabryna.

XADRIAN (American) Form of Adrian. Dark one. *Variations:* Xadriane, Xadrianna, Xadrianne, Xadrien, Xadriena, Xadrienna, Xadrienne.

XAHLIA (Arabic) Flower. *Variations:* Xahliah, Xalia, Xaliah.

XAHRIA (Arabic) Flower. *Variations:* Xahriah, Xaria.

XALVADORA (Spanish) Savior. *Variations:* Xalbadora, Xalbadoria, Xalvadorah, Xalvadoria.

XANA (Greek) Golden haired. *Variations:* Xanna, Xanne.

XANADU (Mongolian) Place of paradise.

XANDI (Greek) Defender of humankind. A form of Sandy. *Variations:* Xandea, Xandee, Xandey, Xandi, Xandie, Xandy.

XANDRA (Spanish) Protector. Short form of Alexandra. *Variations:* Xan, Xandrah, Xondra, Xondrah.

XANDRIA (Greek) Defender of mankind. *Variations:* Xandrea, Xandriah, Xandrya, Xandryah, Xondrea, Xondria.

XANTARA (English) Protector of the earth. *Variations:* Xantarah, Xantarra, Xantarrah, Xantera, Xanterah, Xanterra.

XANTHE (Greek) Yellow. *Variations:* Xantha, Xanthia, Xanthiah, Xanthus.

XANTHIPPE (Greek) Form of Xanthe. *Notable:* Xanthippe was the wife of Socrates. *Variations:* Xantippe, Xantippi.

XAQUELINE (Spanish) Supplanter. Form of Jacqueline. *Variations:* Xacquelina, Xacqueline, Xaqueleen, Xaqueleena, Xaqueleene, Xaquelina.

XARA (Hebrew) Dawn. *Variations:* Xarah, Xaria, Xariah, Xarra, Xarrah, Zara.

XAVIERA (Basque) New house. Feminine version of Xavier. *Notable:* Writer Xaviera Hollander. *Variations:* Xavia, Xavier, Xavierah, Xaviere, Xavyera, Xavyerah, Xavyere.

XELA (French) From the mountain home. *Variations:* Xelah, Xella, Xellah.

XEN (Japanese) Religious. *Variation:* Zen.

XENA (Greek) Hospitable. *Notable:* Character Xena of TV's *Xena: Warrior Princess. Variations:* Xeena, Xeene, Xene, Xina, Xinah, Xyna, Xynah, Zena.

XENIA (Greek) Hospitable. *Variations:* Xeenia, Xeeniah, Xeniah, Xenya, Xenyah, Zenia.

XENIFLORES (Spanish) Protector of flowers. *Variation:* Xeni.

XENOBIA (Greek) Sign or symbol. *Variations:* Xenoba, Xenobea, Zenobia.

XENOSA (Greek) Stranger. *Variations:* Xenos, Xenosah, Zenosa.

XERENA (Latin) Tranquil. *Variations:* Xeren, Xerenah, Xerene, Zerena.

XI WANG (Chinese) Hopeful.

XIA (Chinese) Halo; (Arabic) Light. *Variations:* Xiah, Xya, Xyah, Zia.

XIANG (Chinese) Fragrant.

XIAO DAN (Chinese) Little dawn.

XIAO FAN (Chinese) Little ordinary.

XIAO HONG (Chinese) Morning rainbow.

XIAO HUI (Chinese) Morning sunlight.

XIAO LI (Chinese) Intellectual.

XIAO LIAN (Chinese) Little compassionate one.

XIAO NIAO (Chinese) Small bird.

XIAO QING (Chinese) Blessed with intelligence.

XIAO XING (Chinese) Morning star.

XIMENA (Spanish) God listens. Feminine form of Simon. *Variations:* Ximenah, Ximenia, Ximona, Ximonah, Ximone, Xymenah, Xymona, Xymonah, Zimena.

XIN (Chinese) Elegant, beautiful.

XIN QUAN (Chinese) Beautiful and joyful woman.

XINA (English; Greek) Little. Welcomed. *Variations:* Xinah, Xinia.

XIOMARA (Spanish) Ready for battle. *Variations:* Xioma, Xiomia.

XIRENA (Greek) Alluring, *Variations:* Xireena, Xireenah, Xirenah, Xirene, Xirina, Xirinah, Xyren, Xyrena, Xyrenah, Xyrene, Xyrina, Xyrinah, Xyryna, Xyrynah, Zirena.

XIU LAN (Chinese) Beautiful orchid.

XIU MEI (Chinese) Beautiful plum.

XIU YING (Chinese) Beautiful flower.

XOANA (Spanish) Variation of Joanna. *Variations:* Xoane, Xoanna, Xoanne.

XOCHITL (Native American) Flower.

XOE (Greek) Life. *Variations:* Xo, Xoey, Xoie, Xooey, Zoe.

XOLA (African) Of peace. *Variations:* Xolah, Xolia, Xolla.

XOLANI (Hawaiian) Peaceful. *Variations:* Xolanee, Xolanei, Xolaney, Xolanie, Xolany.

XUAN (Vietnamese) Spring.

XUE (Chinese) Snow.

XUXA (Portuguese) White lily. Form of Susanna. *Notable:* Brazilian children's TV star Xuxa Meneghel. *Variations:* Xuxah, Xuxia.

XYLEENA (Greek) From the forest. *Variations:* Xilean, Xileana, Xileanah, Xileane, Xileen, Xileena, Xileenah, Xileene, Xilin, Xilina, Xilinah, Xiline, Xilyn, Xilyna, Xilynah, Xilyne, Xylean, Xyleana, Xyleanah, Xyleane, Xyleen, Xyleenah, Xyleene, Xylene, Xylin, Xylina, Xylinah, Xyline, Xylyn, Xylyna, Xylynah, Xylyne.

XYLIA (Greek) Forest dweller. *Variations:* Xilea, Xileah, Xiliah, Xyla, Xylya, Xylyah, Zylia.

XYLONA (Greek) From the forest. *Variations:* Xilon, Xilona, Xilonah, Xilone, Xilonia, Xiloniah, Xylon, Xylonah, Xylone, Xylonia, Xyloniah, Xylonya, Xylonyah.

XYLOPHIA (Greek) Forest lover. *Variations:* Xilophia, Xilophiah, Xylophiah, Xylophila, Xylophilah, Zylophia.

YACHI (Japanese) Good luck. *Variations:* Yachiko, Yachiyo.

YACHNE (Hebrew) God is good. *Variation:* Yachna.

YACQUELINE (Spanish) Supplanter. Form of Jacqueline. *Variations:* Yacalin, Yacalyn, Yackalin, Yackalyn, Yacquelin.

YADIRA (Hebrew) Friend. *Variations:* Yadeera, Yadirah.

YAEL (Hebrew) Mountain goat. *Variations:* Jael, Yaala, Yaalat, Yaela, Yaele, Yaell, Yaella, Yaelle.

YAFFA (Hebrew) Beautiful. *Variations:* Yafa, Yaffah, Yaffit, Yapha.

YAGMUR (Turkish) Rain.

YGRAINE (French) Maiden. *Variation:* Igraine.

YAHIVIKA (Native American) Spring.

YAKIRA (Hebrew) Precious. *Variations:* Yakeara, Yakeera, Yekara, Yekarah.

YALANDA (Greek) Violet flower. Form of Yolanda. *Variations:* Yalande, Yalandah.

YALENA (Russian) Light. Form of Helen. *Variations:* Yalana, Yalanah, Yalane, Yaleana, Yaleanah, Yaleane, Yaleena, Yaleenah, Yaleene, Yalina, Yalinah, Yaline, Yalyna, Yalyne, Yelana.

YALGONATA (Polish) Pearl.

YALIKA (Native American) Spring flowers.

YALISHA (American) Noble. Form of Alisha. *Variations:* Yalishe, Yalishia, Yelisha.

YALUTA (Native American) Women talking. *Variations:* Yalutah, Yalute, Yaluti.

YAMA (Hebrew) Sea. *Variation:* Yamit.

YAMARY (Hebrew) Form of Mary. *Variations:* Yamairee, Yamairey, Yamairi, Yamairie, Yamairy, Yamaree, Yamarey, Yamari, Yamaria, Yamariah, Yamaris, Yamarissa, Yamarisse, Yamarya.

YAMELIA (German) Industrious. Form of Amelia. *Variations:* Yameliah, Yamelya, Yamila, Yamile, Yamilla, Yamille, Yamilya.

YAMILETH (Hebrew) Beautiful. *Variations:* Yamile, Yamilet.

YAMILLA (Slavic) Merchant. *Variations:* Yamil, Yamila, Yamile, Yamill, Yamille, Yamyl, Yamyla, Yamyle, Yamyll, Yamylla, Yamylle.

YAMINA (Arabic) Ethical. *Variations:* Yaminah, Yemina.

YAMINI (Hindi) Night. *Variation:* Yaminia.

YAMKA (Native American) Budding flower.

YAMUNA (Hindi) Sacred river.

YANA (Slavic) Gracious. *Variations:* Yanae, Yanah, Yanet, Yanika, Yanina, Yaninah, Yanis, Yanisha, Yanitza, Yanixia, Yanna, Yannah, Yanni, Yannica, Yannick, Yannicka, Yannika, Yannina, Yanyna.

YANAHA (Native American) Brave and confrontational. *Variation:* Yanaba.

YANESSA (American) Butterfly. Form of Vanessa. *Variations:* Yanesa, Yanisa, Yanissa, Yannesa.

YANG (Chinese) Sun.

YANNIS (Hebrew) Gift of God. *Variations:* Yanis, Yanys.

YARA (Hebrew) Honeycomb. (Arabic) White flower. *Variations:* Yaara, Yaari, Yaarit.

YARDENA (Hebrew) To descend. *Variations:* Jardena, Jardenia, Yardenah, Yardenia, Yardeniya.

YARINA (Russian) Peace. *Variations:* Yarinah, Yarine, Yaryna.

YARKONA (Hebrew) Green. *Variation:* Yarkonah.

YARMILLA (Slavic) Market seller. *Variations:* Yarmila, Yarmilah, Yarmillah, Yarmille, Yarmyla, Yarmylla.

YARON (Hebrew) To sing. *Variation:* Yarona.

YAROSLAVA (Russian) Springtime.

YASHILA (Hindi) Successful.

YASHIRA (Arabic) Wealthy.

YASHNA (Hindi) Prayer. *Variation:* Yashnah.

YASHODHANA (Hindi) Prosperous. *Variation:* Yashwina.

YASHODHARA (Hindi) Renowned.

YASLYN (American) Combined form of Yasmine and Lynn. *Variations:* Yaslin, Yaslina, Yasline, Yaslyna, Yaslynn, Yaslynne, Yazlin, Yazlina, Yazline, Yazlyn, Yazlyna, Yazlynn, Yazlynne.

YASMINE (Arabic) Flower. Form of Jasmine. *Notable:* Actress Yasmine Bleeth. *Variations:* Yasmeen, Yasmeena, Yasmena, Yasmene, Yasmin, Yasmina, Yasmyn, Yasmyna, Yasmyne, Yazmin, Yazmina, Yazmine, Yazmyn, Yazmyna.

YASU (Japanese) Calm. *Variations:* Yasuko, Yasuyo.

YATVA (Hebrew) Good. *Variation:* Yatvah.

YAUVANI (Hindi) Youthful.

YEARDLEY (English) In the meadow. *Variations:* Yardleigh, Yardley, Yeardlee, Yeardly.

YEDDA (English) Singer. *Variations:* Yeda, Yedah, Yeddah.

YEDIDA (Hebrew) Dear friend. *Variations:* Yedidah, Yedyda.

YEHUDIT (Hebrew) Praised. Form of Judith. *Variations:* Yudi, Yudit, Yudita, Yuditta, Yuta, Yutke.

YEI (Japanese) Flourishing.

YEKATERINA (Russian) Pure. Form of Katherine.

YELENA (Russian) Light. Variation of Helen. *Variations:* Yalena, Yelain, Yelaina, Yelaine, Yelana, Yelanah, Yelane, Yellaina, Yellaine, Yellayna, Yellena, Yellenah, Yellene.

YELIZABETA (Russian) Consecrated by God. Form of Elizabeth. *Variations:* Yelisabeta, Yelisaveta, Yelizaveta, Yelizavetam.

YEMINA (Hebrew) Strong. *Variations:* Yemena, Yemyna.

YEN (Chinese) Desired.

YENENE (Native American) Sorceress. *Variations:* Yenena, Yenina.

YENTA (Yiddish) Gossiper. *Variations:* Yente, Yentele.

YENTL (Hebrew) Kind.

YEPA (Native American) Snow maiden.

YERUSHA (Hebrew) Dispossessor. *Variations:* Yerushka, Yeruswska.

YESENIA (Arabic) Flower. *Variations:* Yecenia, Yesnia, Yessenia.

YESHARA (Hebrew) Direct.

YESIMA (Hebrew) Strong right hand. *Variations:* Yessima, Yessyma.

YESSICA (Hebrew) Wealthy. Form of Jessica. *Variations:* Yesica, Yesicah, Yesicka, Yesika, Yesikah, Yessica, Yessicah, Yessicka, Yessika.

YETTA (English) Ruler of the house. Form of Henrietta. *Variations:* Yeta, Yettah, Yette.

YEVA (Russian) Give life. *Variation:* Yevka.

YEVGENIA (Russian) Noble. Form of Eugenia. *Variations:* Yevgena, Yevgeniah, Yevgenya, Yevgina, Yevginah, Yevgyna.

YIESHA (Arabic) Woman.

YIN (Chinese) Silver.

YISKA (Hebrew) One who beholds. *Variations:* Yicah, Yickah, Yiskah.

YNEZ (Spanish) Form of Agnes. *Variations:* Inez, Ynes.

YOANA (Hebrew) God is gracious. Form of Joanna. *Variations:* Yoanna, Yohana, Yohanna, Yona.

YOCANDA (Spanish) Delightful.

YOCHANA (Hebrew) God is gracious. *Variation:* Yochanan.

YOCHEVED (Hebrew) God's glory. *Variation:* Yochebed.

YOI (Japanese) Born in the evening.

YOKI (Native American) Bluebird.

YOKO (Japanese) Good child. *Notable:* Yoko Ono, artist and widow of Beatle John Lennon.

YOLANDA (Greek) Purple flower. *Notable:* Singer Yolanda Adams. *Variations:* Eolanda, Eolande, Iolanda, Iolande, Yalanda, Yalinda, Yalonda, Yola, Yoland, Yolande, Yolane, Yolantha, Yolanthe, Yolee, Yolette, Yoli, Yolie, Yolonda, Yulanda.

YOLOTA (Native American) Farewell to spring.

YOLUTA (Native American) Seed.

YON (Burmese) Rabbit.

YONA (Hebrew) Dove. *Variations:* Yonah, Yoni, Yonit.

YONINA (Hebrew) Dove. *Variations:* Yonena, Yoninah, Yonita.

YORDAN (Hebrew) Descend. Form of Jordan. *Variations:* Yordana, Yordyn.

YORI (Japanese) Honest. *Variations:* Yoriko, Yoriyo.

YOSEPHA (Hebrew) God will increase. *Variations:* Yoseba, Yosefa, Yosephia, Yosephina, Yosephine, Yosifa.

YOSHA (Hindi) Woman.

YOSHE (Japanese) Lovely.

YOSHIKO (Japanese) Quiet. *Variations:* Yoshi, Yoshie, Yoshiyo.

YOSHINO (Japanese) Fertile land.

YOUNG-IL (Korean) Excellence.

YOUNG-SOON (Korean) Tender flower.

YOVELA (Hebrew) Happiness. *Variations:* Yovella, Yovelle.

YOYELA (Hebrew) Rejoicing.

YSABEL (Spanish) Form of Isabel. *Variations:* Ysabela, Ysabelah, Ysabell, Ysabella, Ysabelle, Ysbel, Ysbela, Ysbele, Ysbella, Ysbelle,

Ysobel, Ysobela, Ysobele, Ysobell, Ysobella.

YSEULT (French) Beautiful. *Variations:* Yseulte, Ysolt, Ysolte.

YU (Chinese) Jade.

YUANA (Spanish) God is gracious. Form of Juana. *Variations:* Yuanita, Yuanna.

YUDELLE (English) Prosperous. *Variations:* Yudela, Yudelah, Yudele, Yudelia, Yudella, Yudellah, Yudelya.

YUE (Chinese) Moon.

YUKI (Japanese) Snow. *Variations:* Yukie, Yukika, Yukiko.

YULAN (Chinese) Jade orchid.

YULENE (Latin) Youthful. *Variations:* Yulean, Yuleana, Yuleanah, Yuleane, Yuleen, Yuleena, Yuleene, Yulena, Yulenah.

YULIA (Russian) Young. Variation of Julia. *Variations:* Yula, Yulenka, Yuliana, Yuliet, Yuliya, Yulya.

YUN (Chinese) Cloud.

YURI (Japanese) Lily. *Variations:* Yuriyo.

YURIKO (Japanese) Lily child.

YUSRA (Arabic) Rich. *Variations:* Yusrivva, Yusrivvah.

YUSTINA (Russian) Justice. Form of Justine

YVETTE (French) Form of Yvonne. *Notable:* Actress Yvette Mimieux. *Variations:* Yevetta, Yevette, Yvet.

YVONNE (French) Yew wood. *Notable:* Actress Yvonne De Carlo. *Variations:* Yvana, Yvanna, Yvanne, Yvetta, Yvette, Yvone.

ZABEL (Armenian) Bountiful. *Variations:* Zabela, Zabella, Zabelle, Zabelia.

ZABRINA (American) River in Wales. Form of Sabrina. *Variations:* Zabreana, Zabreane, Zabreena, Zabreenah, Zabreenia, Zabrinah, Zabrinia, Zabrinna, Zabrinnia, Zabryna, Zabrynia, Zabrynya.

ZACHARI (Hebrew) God remembers. *Variations:* Zacara, Zacarah, Zacaree, Zacarey, Zacari, Zacaria, Zacariah, Zaccaree, Zaccari, Zachah, Zacharea, Zacharee, Zacharey, Zacharia, Zacharie, Zachary, Zachola, Zackeisha, Zackery, Zakaria, Zakariah, Zakary, Zakira, Zechari, Zecharie, Zechary.

ZADA (Arabic) Fortunate. *Variations:* Zaida, Zayda.

ZAFARA (Hebrew) Singer. *Variations:* Zafarra, Zaphara.

ZAFINA (Arabic) Triumphant. *Variations:* Zafeena, Zafinah, Zafine, Zafyna, Zaphina, Zaphine.

ZAFIRA (Arabic) Victorious. *Variations:* Zafeera, Zafiera, Zafirah, Zafire, Zafyra.

ZAGIR (Armenian) Flowerlike. *Variations:* Zagira, Zagiri, Zagirie.

ZAHARA (Hebrew) Dawn. *Variations:* Zahar, Zaharah, Zahari, Zaharit.

ZAHAVA (Hebrew) Golden. *Variations:* Zachava, Zahava, Zahavah, Zahavi, Zahavia, Zahavit.

ZAHIRA (Arabic) Bright. *Variations:* Zaheera, Zahirah, Zahiya.

ZAHREH (Persian) Happiness. *Variations:* Zahra.

ZAIDA (Arabic) Fortunate. *Variations:* Zada, Zayda.

ZAIDEE (Arabic) Wealthy. *Variations:* Zadea, Zadee, Zadey, Zadi, Zadie, Zady, Zaidea, Zaidey, Zaidi, Zaidie, Zaidy, Zayde, Zaydea, Zaydee, Zaydey, Zaydi, Zaydie, Zaydy.

ZAINAB (Hindi) Plant. *Variation:* Zaenab.

ZAIRA (Arabic) Blossom. *Variations:* Zahara, Zahirah, Zahra, Zahrah, Zara, Zaria, Zuhra.

ZAKELINA (Russian) God remembers. *Variations:* Zackelina, Zackeline, Zacklyn, Zakeleana, Zakeleane, Zakeleen, Zakeleena, Zakelin, Zakelinah, Zakeline, Zakelyn, Zakelyna, Zakelyne.

ZAKIAH (Hebrew; Arabic) Pure. *Variations:* Zaka, Zakah, Zaki, Zakia, Zakiah, Zakiya, Zakiyya.

ZALIKA (African) Well born. *Variations:* Zaleeka, Zalik, Zalikah, Zalyka.

ZALINA (French) Of the moon. *Variations:* Zaleena, Zalena, Zaline.

ZALTANA (Native American) Tall mountain.

ZAMILLA (Greek) Strength of the ocean. *Variation:* Zamila.

ZAMIRA (Arabic) Conscientious. *Variations:* Zameera, Zamirah, Zamyra.

ZAMORA (Hebrew) Praised. *Variations:* Zamorah, Zamorra.

ZAN (Chinese) Support; favor; praise.

ZANDRA (Greek) Defender of mankind. Form of Sandra or Alexandra. *Notable:* Fashion designer Zandra Rhodes. *Variations:* Zandrah, Zandri, Zandria, Zandriah, Zandrie, Zandira, Zandrya, Zondra.

ZANDY (Greek) Short form of Zandra. *Variations:* Zandea, Zandee, Zandey, Zandi, Zandie.

ZANETA (Polish) God is gracious. *Variations:* Zaneata, Zaneeta, Zanetah, Zanete, Zanett, Zanetta, Zanette, Zanita, Zanitah, Zanyta.

ZANNA (Hebrew) Lily. Short form of Susanna. *Variations:* Zana, Zanella, Zanelle, Zanetta, Zanette, Zannia.

ZANTA (Latvian) Bright.

ZANTHE (Greek) Blond. Form of Xanthe. *Variations:* Zanthippie, Zantippie.

ZARA (Hebrew) Dawn. *Variations:* Zahra, Zahrah, Zarah, Zaria, Zarra, Zarrah.

ZARIEL (American) Combined form of Zara and Ariel. *Variations:* Zarial, Zariella, Zarielle.

ZARIFA (Arabic) Graceful. *Variations:* Zareefa, Zarifah, Zaryfa.

ZARINA (Hindi) Golden. *Variations:* Zareana, Zareena, Zarinah, Zarna, Zaryna.

ZARITA (Spanish) Princess. Form of Sarah. *Variations:* Zareata, Zareeta, Zareete, Zaritah, Zaritta, Zaryta.

ZARLA (Australian) Legend. *Variations:* Zarlene, Zarlina.

ZAROLA (Arabic) Huntress. *Variations:* Zarolah, Zarolia, Zarolla.

ZARZIA (Hebrew) Industrious. *Variations:* Zariza, Zarzya.

ZASHA (Russian) Form of Sasha. *Variations:* Zascha, Zashka.

ZAVIERA (Spanish) New house. Form of Xaviera. *Variations:* Zavera, Zavia, Zavira, Zavyera.

ZAWADI (African) Gift. *Variations:* Zawadia, Zawati.

ZAYIT (Hebrew) Olive. *Variation:* Zayita.

ZAYLIA (Greek) Empowered. *Variations:* Zayla, Zaylee, Zayley, Zayli, Zaylie.

ZAYNA (Arabic) Beautiful tree. *Variations:* Zaina, Zania, Zaynah.

ZAZA (Hebrew) Action. *Notable:* Classic film/TV actress Zasu Pitts. *Variations:* Zasu, Zazu.

ZBYHNEVA (Czech) To get rid of anger. *Variations:* Zbyha, Zbysa.

ZDENKA (Czech) From Sidon. *Variations:* Zdena, Zdenicka, Zdenina, Zdeninka, Zdenuska.

ZDESLAVA (Czech) Glory is here. *Variations:* Zdevsa, Zdevska, Zdisa, Zdiska, Zdislava.

ZEA (Latin) Grain. *Variations:* Zia, Zya.

ZEBORAH (American) Variation of Deborah. *Variation:* Zebora.

ZEFFA (Portuguese) Rose. *Variations:* Zefa, Zeffah.

ZEFIRA (Hebrew) Morning.

ZEFIRYN (Polish) Goddess of the west wind. *Variation:* Zephyrine.

ZEHAVA (Hebrew) Gold. *Variations:* Zahava, Zehavia, Zehavit, Zehuva, Zehuvit.

ZEHARA (Hebrew) Light. *Variations:* Zehari, Zeharit, Zehra, Zehorit.

ZEHIRA (Hebrew) Careful. *Variations:* Zehirah, Zehyra.

ZEITA (Portuguese) Rose.

ZEL (Persian) Cymbal.

ZELDA (German) Woman warrior. *Notable:* Zelda, princess from popular video game.

ZELENIA (Greek) Moon goddess. *Variations:* Zeleen, Zeleena, Zeleenia, Zelena, Zelene, Zelenia, Zelina, Zelyna, Zelyne, Zelynia.

ZELENKA (Czech) Fresh. *Variations:* Zelen, Zeleka.

ZELFA (American) In control.

ZELIA (Greek) Enthusiastic. *Variations:* Zeliah, Zelya.

ZELIZI (Greek) Unseeing. *Variations:* Zelizia, Zelizya.

ZELLA (German) Hostile one. *Variations:* Zela, Zelah, Zella, Zellah.

ZELMA (German) Divine helmet.

ZEMIRA (Hebrew) Song. *Variations:* Zemir, Zemirah, Zemyra, Zimira, Zymira.

ZEMORAH (Hebrew) Tree branch. *Variation:* Zemora.

ZEN (Chinese) Purity. *Variation:* Zhen.

ZENA (Greek) Welcoming. *Variations:* Zeena, Zeenah, Zeenia, Zena, Zenah, Zenia, Zeniah, Zenya, Zina, Zinah, Zyna.

ZENAIDA (Greek) Wild dove. *Variations:* Zenaida, Zenaide, Zenayda.

ZENANA (Hebrew) Woman. *Variation:* Zenanda.

ZENDA (Hebrew) Holy.

ZENOBIA (Greek) Strength of Zeus. *Variations:* Zenobie, Zenovia.

ZENZI (German) Thrive.

ZEPHANIA (Greek) Crown. Form of Stephanie. *Variations:* Zefana, Zefania, Zefanie, Zephanie, Zephany.

ZEPHYRA (Greek) Wind from the west. *Variations:* Zefir, Zefira, Zephira, Zephyr.

ZEPPELINA (German) Airship.

ZERA (Hebrew) Seeds.

ZERALDINA (Polish) Spear ruler. *Variations:* Zerelda, Zeraldeena, Zeraldine.

ZERDALI (Turkish) Wild apricot. *Variations:* Zerdalia, Zerdaly.

ZERELDA (German) Armored woman.

ZERENA (Latin) Serene. Form of Serena. *Variations:* Zereena, Zerina, Zeryna, Zireena, Zirena, Zirina, Ziryna, Zyreena, Zyrena, Zyrina, Zyryna.

ZERLINDA (Hebrew) Beautiful dawn. *Variations:* Zelinda, Zerlena, Zerlene, Zerlina, Zerline, Zerlynda.

ZERREN (Turkish) Golden. *Variations:* Zerran, Zerrin, Zerron, Zerryn.

ZETTA (Hebrew) Olive. *Variations:* Zeta, Zetana, Zita, Zyta, Zytta.

ZEVIDA (Hebrew) Gift. *Variation:* Zevuda.

ZEYNEP (Turkish) Ornament.

ZHANE (African) God's grace.

ZHEN (Chinese) Precious.

ZHILAN (Chinese) Orchid.

ZHO (Chinese) Character.

ZHONG (Chinese) Honest.

ZHUO (Chinese) Smart.

ZIA (Arabic) Light; (Italian) Aunt. *Variations:* Ziah, Zya, Zyah.

ZIADA (African) To increase.

ZIGANA (Hungarian) Gypsy. *Variations:* Ziganah, Zigane, Zygana.

ZILLA (Hebrew) Shadow. *Variations:* Zila, Zilah, Zilia, Ziliah, Zilias, Zilina, Zilinah, Zillah, Zilyam Zyliah, Zylina, Zylla, Zylya, Zylyna.

ZILPAH (Hebrew) Dignity. *Variations:* Zilpa, Zillpha, Zilpha, Zulpha, Zylpa, Zylpha.

ZIMENA (Hebrew) Listening. *Variations:* Zimenah, Zimene, Zimona, Zimone, Zymena, Zymona.

ZIMRIAH (Hebrew) Songs. *Variations:* Zimria, Zimriya, Zimra.

ZINA (English) Hospitable. *Variations:* Zena, Zinah, Zyna.

ZINERVA (Italian) Fair haired. *Variation:* Zynerva.

ZINNIA (English) Flower name. *Variations:* Zinia, Zinniah, Zinnya, Zinya, Zynia.

ZINTKALA (Native American) Like a bird.

ZIONA (Hebrew) Heavenly city.

ZIPPORA (Hebrew) Little bird. *Variations:* Cipora, Cippora, Sipora, Sippora, Tzipeh, Tzipora, Tziporah, Tzippe, Zipeh, Zipora, Ziporah, Zipporah.

ZIRAH (Hebrew) Coliseum. *Variation:* Zira, Zirra.

ZITA (Greek) Seeker; (Italian) Little girl. *Variation:* Zitella.

ZITKALA (Native American) Bird.

ZITKALASA (Native American) Red bird.

ZITOMIRA (Czech) To live famously. *Variations:* Zitka, Zituse.

ZIVA (Hebrew) Brilliant. *Variations:* Zeeva, Ziv, Zivit.

ZIVANKA (Czech) Alive. *Variations:* Zivka, Zivuse, Zivuska.

ZIWA (African) Of the lake.

ZIZI (Hungarian) Pledged to God. Short form of Elizabeth.

ZLATA (Czech) Golden. *Variations:* Zlatina, Zlatinka, Zlatka, Zlatuna, Zlatunka, Zlatuse, Zlatuska.

ZOCHA (Polish) Wisdom.

ZOE (Greek) Life. *Notables:* Actresses Zoe Caldwell and Zooey Deschanel. *Variations:* Zoey, Zoi, Zoia, Zoie, Zooey.

ZOFIA (Polish) Wisdom. Form of Sophia. *Variations:* Zofee, Zofey, Zofi, Zofie, Zophee, Zophi, Zophia, Zophie, Zophy.

ZOHARA (Hebrew) Brillance. *Variations:* Zohar, Zoharet, Zohera, Zoheret.

ZOLA (Italian) Piece of earth. *Variations:* Zolee, Zoli, Zolia.

ZONA (Latin) Belt. *Variations:* Zonah, Zonia, Zonna.

ZONDRA (Greek) Defender of mankind. Form of Sondra. *Variations:* Zondria, Zondrya.

ZONTA (Native American) Honest.

ZORA (Slavic) Dawn. *Variations:* Zohra, Zorah, Zorra, Zorrah.

ZORAIDA (Arabic) Charming woman.

ZORINA (Slavic) Golden. *Variations:* Zorana, Zoreen, Zoreena, Zorna, Zoryna.

ZOSA (Greek) Lily. *Variations:* Zosah, Zoza.

ZOSIMA (Greek) Lively. *Variations:* Zosma, Zosyma, Zozima.

ZOYA (Russian) Life. Form of Zoe. *Variation:* Zoyah.

ZSA ZSA (Hungarian) Lily. Form of Susan. *Notable:* Actress Zsa Zsa Gabor.

ZSUZAN (Hungarian) Lily. Form of Susan. *Variations:* Zsuzsana, Zsuzsanne, Zsuzsette.

ZUBAIDA (Arabic) Marigold. *Variations:* Zubaidah, Zubeda.

ZUDORA (Hindi) Laborer.

ZULEIKA (Arabic) Brilliant and beautiful. *Variations:* Zeleka, Zuleyka.

ZULEMA (Hebrew) Peace. *Variations:* Zulima, Zulma.

ZURAFA (Arabic) Lovely. *Variations:* Zirifa, Zurafa.

ZURI (African) Beautiful.

ZURIEL (Hebrew) The Lord is my rock. *Variation:* Zuriela.

ZUWENA (African) Good. *Variation:* Zwena.

ZUZANA (Czech) Lily. Form of Susanna. *Variations:* Zusa, Zusan, Zusana, Zusanna, Zusanne, Zusette, Zuzan, Zuzann, Zuzanna, Zuzanne, Zuzette, Zuzia, Zuzka, Zuzu.

ZVERDA (Slavic) Star. *Variation:* Zverdana.

ZVETLANA (Russian) Star. *Variation:* Zwetlana.

ZYLIA (Greek) Woodland dweller. *Variations:* Zyliana, Zylianne.

ZYTKA (Polish) Rose. *Variation:* Zyta.

APPENDIX A

Bibliography and Research Sources

Books and Journals

Bolton, Lesley. *The Complete Book of Baby Names*. Naperville, IL: Sourcebooks, 2009.

Levitt, Steven D., and Stephen J. Dubner. *Freakonomics*. New York: Harper Perennial, 2009.

Nelson, Leif D., and Joseph P. Simmons. "Moniker Maladies: When Names Sabotage Success." *Psychological Science* 18 (December 2007): 1106–1112.

Varnum, Michael E.W., and Shinobu Kitayama. "What's in a Name? Popular Names Are Less Common on Frontiers." *Psychological Science* 22 (February 2011): 176–183.

Online Articles

BabyCenter India. "India's Top Baby Names in 2010." *www.babycenter.in/pregnancy/naming/india-top-baby-names-2010*.

BabyNameBox.com. GranMamma. "History of Baby Names." *www.babynamebox.com/articles/baby-name-history.html*.

BBPositive.org. "These Romantic and Brilliant Victorian Baby Names." April 4, 2011. *www.bbpositive.org/these-romantic-and-brilliant-victorian-baby-names*.

Chamary, JV. "The Name Game: How Names Spell Success in Life and Love." BBC *ScienceFocus.com*. January 14, 2010. *http://sciencefocus.com/feature/psychology/names*.

Cox, Jeanine. "Baby Naming Traditions around the World." BabyZone.com. *www.babyzone.com/pregnancy/babynames/article/baby-naming-traditions*.

Delaney, Kevin J. "You're a Nobody Unless Your Name Googles Well." *The Wall Street Journal*. May 8, 2007. *http://online.wsj.com/article/SB117856222924394753.html*.

Doyle, Jack. "Mohammed Is Now the Most Popular Name for Baby Boys ahead of Jack and Harry." *MailOnline*. October 28, 2010. *www.dailymail.co.uk/news/article-1324194/Mohammed-popular-baby-boys-ahead-Jack-Harry.html*.

Em, Laura. "Naming Your Adopted Child." *Nameisms* (blog). May 1, 2009. *http://nameisms.blogspot.com/2009/05/naming-your-adopted-child.html*.

Flora, Carlin. "Hello, My Name Is Unique." *Psychology Today*. March 1, 2004, *www.psychologytoday.com/articles/200403/hello-my-name-is-unique*.

Genealogy Today. "Last Name Origins." *www.genealogytoday.com/names/origins*.

"List of Most Popular Given Names." *Wikipedia*, *http://en.wikipedia.org/wiki/Most_popular_names*.

LiveScience. Bryner, Jeanna. "Good or Bad, Baby Names Have Long-Lasting Effects." June 13, 2010. *www.livescience.com/6569-good-bad-baby-names-long-lasting-effects.html*.

LiveScience. Moskowitz, Clara. "Baby Names Reveal More About Parents Than Ever Before." November 30, 2010. *www.livescience.com/9027-baby-names-reveal-parents.html.*

Mayrand Family Association. Mayrand, Lionel E., ed. "Origins and Meanings of Names." *www.mayrand.org/meaning-e.htm.*

"Popular Korean Names." *Korea Insider,* November 19, 2009, *-http://www.koreainsider.com/korean-news/about-korea/popular-korean-baby-names/.*

Rogati, Monica. "Top CEO Names Across the Globe: Brad, Bland or Brand?" The LinkedIn Blog. April 27, 2011. *http://blog.linkedin.com/2011/04/27/top-ceo-names.*

SheKnows Parenting. Beyer, Monica. "The Worst Baby Names." They Named Him What? Bad Baby Names. April 10, 2010. *www.sheknows.com/parenting/articles/814624/they-named-him-what-bad-baby-names-1.*

Suite101.com. Scott, Anika. "What's in a Name?" July 26, 2001. *www.suite101.com/article.cfm/italian_renaissance/75612.*

The Bachelor Guy. "Survey: Want More Sex? Change Your Name to Chris." February 17, 2011. *www.thebachelorguy.com/skills/survey-want-more-sex-change-your-name-to-chris.html.*

"US Babies Get Global Brand Names." *BBC News.* November 13, 2003. *http://news.bbc.co.uk/2/hi/americas/3268161.stm.*

"Why Are Parents Choosing Ever-Stranger Baby Names?" *TheWeek.* February 25, 2011. *http://theweek.com/article/index/212554/why-are-parents-choosing-ever-stranger-baby-names.*

Websites

Aussie Things (Baby Names)
www.aussiethings.com.au/babynames/index.htm

Behind the Name: the Meaning, Etymology and History of First Names
www.behindthename.com

Meaning-of-Names.com
www.meaning-of-names.com

National Hurricane Center
www.nhc.noaa.gov/aboutnames.shtml

Social Security Administration
www.ssa.gov/OACT/babynames

The Baby Name Wizard
www.babynamewizard.com

20000-Names.com
www.20000-names.com/index.htm

APPENDIX B

Baby Name Worksheet

girls' names

mom's favorite name picks

....

....

....

....

....

....

dad's favorite name picks

....

....

....

....

....

boys' names

mom's favorite name picks

....

....

....

....

....

....

dad's favorite name picks

....

....

....

....

....

semi-final name picks

girls' names

....

....

....

....

....

....

boys' names

....

....

....

....

....

....

final name picks

girls' first names

....

....

girls' middle names

....

....

boys' first names

....

....

boys' middle names

....

....

We Have
EVERYTHING®
on Anything!

With more than 19 million copies sold, the Everything® series has become one of America's favorite resources for solving problems, learning new skills, and organizing lives. Our brand is not only recognizable—it's also welcomed.

The series is a hand-in-hand partner for people who are ready to tackle new subjects—like you!

For more information on the Everything® series, please visit *www.adamsmedia.com*

The Everything® list spans a wide range of subjects, with more than 500 titles covering 25 different categories:

Business	History	Reference
Careers	Home Improvement	Religion
Children's Storybooks	Everything Kids	Self-Help
Computers	Languages	Sports & Fitness
Cooking	Music	Travel
Crafts and Hobbies	New Age	Wedding
Education/Schools	Parenting	Writing
Games and Puzzles	Personal Finance	
Health	Pets	